ALTERNATE

OSCARS

One Critic's
Defiant Choices for
Best Picture, Actor, and Actress
—From 1927 to the Present

DANNY PEARY

Delta

A DELTA BOOK

Published by
Dell Publishing
a division of
Bantam Doubleday Dell Publishing Group, Inc.
1540 Broadway
New York, New York 10036

DESIGN: Stanley S. Drate/Folio Graphics Co., Inc.

Library of Congress Cataloging in Publication Data
Peary, Danny. 1949–
    Alternate Oscars : one critic's defiant choices for the best picture, actor, and
actress from 1927 to the present / Danny Peary.
        p.   cm.
    Includes index.
    ISBN 0-385-30332-7 (pbk.)
    1. Academy Award (Motion Pictures)   2. Motion pictures—History.
I. Title.
PN1993.92.P43   1992
791.43'079—dc20   92-9509   CIP

Manufactured in the United States of America

Published simultaneously in Canada

February 1993

10   9   8   7   6   5   4   3   2

KPP

THIS BOOK IS DEDICATED TO
Barbara and Buster,
Marilyn and Cary,
Natalie and Charlie,
Greta and Boris
. . . and Suzanne.

Acknowledgments

I am indebted to a number of terrific people for their help and encouragement with this book. First of all, I must thank my editor and cheerleader Emily Reichert, Bob Miller, and my agent Chris Tomasino for initiating this project, and Craig Schneider, Anne Lawrence, Betsy Bundschuh, Brian DeFiore, and all the other people at Dell for helping me finish it. I am grateful to Barbara Young for her special assistance. Special thanks to Carol Summers, Zane Udris, Joe Koch, Chick Foxgrover, Anne Kostick, Julie Kuehndorf, Nora Merhar, Howard Green, Donna Villani, Tyra Crane, Jeanie Dooha, Suzanne Maroon, Gerald Peary, Stephen Harvey, Jan Zaletski, Paula Klaw and Ira Kramer of *Movie Star News,* Bari Cohen, and to the various people, studios, stores, museums, and distribution companies that have helped me obtain photographs. Finally, I applaud Laura and Joe Peary, Zoë Weaver, and my personal Oscar fanatic, Suzanne Rafer.

The Academy of Motion Picture Arts and Sciences hold their organizational benefit on May 11, 1927, setting the stage for year after year of controversy.

Introduction

The Academy of Motion Picture Arts and Sciences was conceived in early 1927 by MGM boss Louis B. Mayer, the most powerful figure in Hollywood. He intended it to be both an elitist, self-honoring club, with members chosen by Mayer himself, and a union-busting labor organization that would ostensibly unite actors, directors, and writers with producers before those three groups formed their own guilds. (This ploy worked only temporarily.) There were thirty-six founding members, including Mayer, his two lawyers, actor Conrad Nagel, Douglas Fairbanks, Mary Pickford, and director Frank Lloyd. The decision to hold an annual awards ceremony to honor films and individuals was not made until a banquet was held on May 11, 1927, during which more than three hundred of the Hollywood aristocracy paid a hundred dollars to become pioneer members of the Academy. It took another year before a voting system was in place. All members—actors, directors, producers, technicians, and writers—would cast nominating votes in their particular branches. A five-person board of judges, representing each branch, yet controlled by Mayer, would tabulate the votes to determine the nominees and then choose the winners themselves.

The first Academy Awards were given out in 1929. In my view, they got it wrong then, and with few exceptions they have gotten it wrong ever since. Although it was declared that awards would be bestowed based on merit only, that does not always seem to have been the case. It is hard to imagine that members, now totaling over three thousand, have not sometimes been swayed by other factors, such as politics, sentiment, guilt, spite, and an obsession with "prestige." At times, actors and actresses seem to have won for one role as consolation for having lost for an earlier better performance; or, if they have been old enough, as a tribute to their entire careers. Meanwhile we movie fans have been dissatisfied with the prejudicial choices, particularly when we have had to watch the wrong films and stars winning year after year on television. Tuesday morning following each year's telecast is a time reserved for serious griping. Second-guessing the Academy's Oscar selections has become the national sport of the dissatisfied and disenfranchised.

In *Alternate Oscars* I have second-guessed the Academy in every year, arguing for what I believe are the Best Choices for Best Picture (English language), Best Actor, and Best Actress from 1927–28 to 1991. In some cases I have agreed with the Academy's selections, but for the most part I have given Alternate Oscars to pictures and stars who I think were more deserving. I also have listed my runners-up, other films and individuals who are worthy of Oscars. You may think one of them more appropriate than my choice, and I wouldn't put up much of an argument. (I am upset that I was unable to give Alternate Oscars to Myrna Loy, Burt Lancaster, William Powell, or other personal favorites.) To help explain my enthusiasm, I have discussed themes of individual films and analyzed characters portrayed by my winners. Be advised that some of my essays contain complete synopses, including *endings*! This book isn't so much a vehicle for me to give my own arbitrary Oscar choices as it is a catalyst for living-room wars in which everyone takes an emotional stand for his or her own choices. I won't even mind receiving a lot of angry mail.

1927–28

▶ BEST PRODUCTION

WINNER:
Wings (Paramount; William A. Wellman)
Other Nominees: *The Last Command, The Racket, Seventh Heaven, The Way of All Flesh*

▼

THE BEST CHOICE:
Sunrise (Fox; F. W. Murnau)
Award-Worthy Runners-Up: *The Circus* (Charles Chaplin), *The Crowd* (King Vidor)

The inaugural Academy Awards banquet was held on May 16, 1929, three months after the winners were announced on the back page of the Academy's trade publication, the *Academy Bulletin.* With the exception of *The Jazz Singer,* which was disqualified because it had the advantage of being the first and only sound picture, all films that played in Los Angeles between August 1, 1927, and August 1, 1928, were eligible for "Best Picture" consideration. That year, however, and for one time only, there were actually two "best picture" categories, although there was no valid reason why nominees were slotted in one and not the other.

Paramount's *Wings,* William A. Wellman's large-scale action drama about two American flying buddies during World War I, was presented the "Best Production" Award. The "Artistic Quality of Production" Award went to F. W. Murnau's *Sunrise,* which beat out King Vidor's *The Crowd.* (The silly, wild-animal-laden semidocumentary *Chang* was the odd third nominee in this category.) Because the "Best Production" Award was presented after the "Artistic Quality" Award in the ceremonies, *Wings* received most of the prestige and has, in effect, gone down in history as the "Best Picture" winner of 1927–28, while the other category has been forgotten. This is unfortunate, because *Wings* pales in comparison to *Sunrise* (and to *The Crowd,* and Charles Chaplin's unnominated *The Circus,* as well). With weak performances from Charles "Buddy" Rogers and Richard Arlen, an overly peppy Clara Bow, and long flight sequences in which you can't tell friend from foe, *Wings* has dated badly. *Sunrise, The Circus,* and *The Crowd,* on the other hand, remain examples of great silent films.

Considering that Louis B. Mayer and others in the Academy elite had established the awards to honor American productions, it's surprising that *Sunrise* was chosen over *The Crowd* for the "Artistic Quality" Award. Although filmed in Hollywood (at Fox Studios), *Sunrise* was developed by Murnau and his screenwriter Carl Mayer in Berlin, and though filmed by Americans Karl Struss and

Charles Rosher (who deservedly won the Academy Award for Cinematography), its look is distinctly German. Even though the stars of the film, Janet Gaynor and George O'Brien, are American, their (universal) characters and the movie's setting have a distinctly foreign feel. On the other hand, Vidor's social drama was about a typical

George O'Brien and Janet Gaynor, who won the first Academy Award for Best Actress, played the farmer and his neglected wife in *Sunrise.*

American couple and was filmed on location in the quintessential American city, New York. Moreover, *The Crowd* was an MGM production that had been supervised by Mayer himself. But Mayer, no fan of his downbeat, unprofitable film, had ulterior motives when it came to the award winner. He persuaded the other members of his secret final-selection committee—Sid Grauman, Douglas Fairbanks, Sr., and Mary Pickford—to switch their votes to *Sunrise* (no one wanted *Chang*), lest the Academy be accused of fixing the vote in his studio's favor. And, as he admitted to Vidor, *The Crowd* was being bypassed so MGM's *Broadway Melody* could win the next year. (Vidor also lost out as Best Director to Frank Borzage, who helmed Gaynor's *Seventh Heaven,* and Vidor's wife and star, Eleanor Boardman, wasn't nominated as Best Actress to challenge Gaynor.)

While Vidor's masterpiece is every bit as impressive and "artistic" as Murnau's film, I think *Sunrise* is in fact the better choice, if only because it turned out to be more influential: *Citizen Kane* and numerous other films borrowed its visual ideas. Interestingly both *Sunrise* and *The Crowd,* though so different stylistically, are about how a married couple's enduring love neutralizes the hostile, destructive, corruptive powers of the city. In Murnau's fable–morality play (which is subtitled "A Song of Two Humans"), the "evil" temptress (Margaret Livingston) is a city woman who bewitches farmer O'Brien and convinces him to murder his neglected wife, Gaynor. After O'Brien comes to his senses—just as he is about to kill Gaynor—the married couple renew their love in the city. The dowdy Gaynor and brooding O'Brien are transfigured by the love they rediscover: she becomes pretty, spunky, funny, and sexier, in her wholesome way, than the vampish Livingston; he becomes handsome, tender,

caring, and strong. Moreover, the hostile city becomes friendly and sunny under their influence. They sail back to the country (barely surviving a terrifying storm at sea), their bond permanent, the evil woman exiled to the city. (Unlike in Hermann Sudermann's source novella, *A Trip to Tilsit,* the Man does not drown.)

Murnau gave his simple story tremendous emotional impact through breathtaking camerawork that is alternately expressionistic, impressionistic, and lyrical. The motivations and moods of the characters are revealed through exciting camera movements and positions, lighting (the use of darkness; moonlight reflecting on the lake, light reflecting on glass; mist, blurred exposures), choice of settings, scenic design (the city was comprised of false-front, false-perspective buildings; the interiors had slanted walls, ceilings and floors, and dwarfs were used in the background to give the illusion of depth), superimpositions (that reveal thoughts) and other special effects (including rain and dust storms). The most audacious visuals are found in the startling scene in which the dazed O'Brien walks through the misty swamp and lies with the temptress beneath a gigantic moon. It is one of the most erotic scenes ever filmed (and incredible on a large theater screen). Another striking visual sequence is the tram ride that the fleeing, brokenhearted Gaynor and apologetic O'Brien take into the city. Murnau actually built a mile-long tram system, and suspended his camera on a trolley to follow the ride.

Sunrise cost a great deal to make and was a flop at the box office. Perhaps if it had won the award given to *Wings* it would have gotten a financial boost. This might have been extremely beneficial to Murnau, who was denied full autonomy on his future films because of *Sunrise*'s failure.

▶ BEST ACTOR

WINNER:
Emil Jannings *(The Last Command, The Way of All Flesh)*
Other Nominees: Richard Barthelmess *(The Noose, The Patent Leather Kid),* Charles Chaplin *(The Circus)*

▼

THE BEST CHOICE:
Charles Chaplin *(The Circus)*
Award-Worthy Runners-Up: Lionel Barrymore *(Sadie Thompson),* Lon Chaney *(Laugh, Clown, Laugh; London after Midnight),* Emil Jannings *(The Last Command, The Way of All Flesh)*

One of the most memorable and touching moments in the history of Oscar telecasts was Charlie Chaplin's emotional appearance onstage in 1972. Having returned to America after thirty years in exile to be paid tribute at Lincoln Center in New York and then be presented with an honorary Oscar in Hollywood, the humble Chaplin was moved to tears by the standing ovation he received. The town that had cast him aside in the forties because

of his leftist politics and, he'd assumed, still resented him, now fully embraced him. Moreover, the Academy, which had snubbed him even before his politics were an issue, was, through the honorary award, finally admitting that it had never given him his due.

The Academy never knew what to do about Chaplin, so it did little. His nontalking films bridged the silent and sound eras, yet his contribution to filmmaking was consistently overlooked. Consider that *City Lights, Modern Times,* and *Monsieur Verdoux* received no Academy Award nominations. Chaplin was nominated for Best Comedy Direction for *The Circus,* and for Best Original Screenplay for *The Great Dictator,* but lost both times. He was nominated for Best Actor only for *The Circus* and *The Great Dictator,* but was denied awards. In 1927–28, when few disputed he was the greatest talent in movies (only Buster Keaton rivaled him), Chaplin should have been given the first Best Actor Academy Award. Even voters who didn't want to give the award solely as a tribute to his great career up to that point would have been justified in honoring his work in *The Circus.* But the choices in all major categories revealed the bias against comedic talent and foolish reverence for dramatic work that would characterize future Academy voting. While it was an accomplishment that Chaplin was nominated at all—consider how few comic performances were acknowledged in the early years—he had no chance against Emil Jannings, the stocky, imposing German who was considered the top dramatic movie actor in the world. To avoid giving the appearance that they were slighting the world's most famous and popular actor (and to also make it seem unnecessary that he win in later years), Mayer and his selection committee bestowed a "Special Award" on Chaplin for his "versatility and genius in writing, acting, directing, and producing *The Circus.*"

Jannings was a powerful actor who gave excellent performances in Victor Fleming's *The Way of All Flesh* and Josef von Sternberg's *The Last Command.* But his portrayals of a bank cashier-turned-derelict in Fleming's film and the Russian general who winds up a lowly Hollywood extra in Sternberg's movie were just preparations for the greatest of his humiliated characters: the proud Professor Unrath, who loses position and dignity when he falls for Marlene Dietrich's sexy songstress in Sternberg's *The Blue Angel.* Jannings's performances in *The Way of All Flesh* and *The Last Command* didn't merit Best Actor that year. Besides, it doesn't seem right that the first Academy Award was handed to a future Nazi.

The Circus hasn't the scope or emotion of Chaplin's better-known films, but it is a gem and Chaplin gives a splendid performance. He plays a tramp who takes a job as stagehand in a circus, not realizing that the audience considers his natural bumbling while carrying props to be the highlight of the show. He falls in love with the cruel circus owner's pretty daughter (Merna Kennedy), an equestrienne in the show. When she informs him that he is a star, he demands a raise and gets the owner to treat his daughter more kindly than he has in the past. However, when she falls in love with the new tightrope walker, the tramp can no longer be funny.

But Chaplin is hilarious throughout. Some of his best scenes include fleeing from the police, who think he is a pickpocket, through a hall of mirrors; getting chased by a runaway horse while carrying dishes; swallowing an enormous horse pill; and performing a tightrope act while a loose monkey bites his nose. As usual, Chaplin's

As usual, Charlie Chaplin's Little Tramp is left alone, without friends or family, at the end of *The Circus*—only, this time it's by choice.

tramp is both touching and funny as he maintains his dignity: making coffee, he spoons sugar from his vest pocket; he instructs a hungry girl how to eat slowly so she won't hiccup—but when he hiccups he gives her his food; fleeing police with the real pickpocket at his side, he tips his hat as they race in opposite directions.

Chaplin doesn't play for pity in *The Circus.* His tramp is not an innocent, completely sweet character, but someone who has been bruised and hardened after years on the road. Here's a sad sack who, in a priceless bit, makes gaga expressions at a toddler so he can eat the hot dog right out of the child's hand without causing him to cry and alert his father. In another scene, to elude police, the tramp becomes part of a mechanized machine in which his "part" clubs another "part"—actually the pickpocket—on the head and laughs each time. In another, spotting an unconscious man sitting next to him, the tramp uses his cane handle to pull the man to the ground so he can stand on him and get a better look at the equestrienne. It is his love for the girl that brings out the sweetness he'd long suppressed.

In the final sequence the tramp happily orchestrates the girl's marriage to the tightrope walker. He even throws rice at their wedding. He makes up with the brutish circus owner and accepts his clown job back. We worry that Chaplin the screenwriter-director has rushed to a happy ending and forgotten how hurt the tramp was when he discovered she loved someone else. He doesn't seem the kind to shrug off their marriage. Then, in the final moment, we see that we are right. The tramp is not so happy. He has no intention of staying with the circus—it would be unbearable to see the newlyweds together. He knows he doesn't belong. He lets the circus leave without him. As he rises to walk the other way, we notice a slight expression of sadness and weary resignation that almost breaks our hearts. Here, perhaps more than any other moment in Chaplin's movies, we see how much Chaplin feels for his lonely, forever dispossessed, yet indomitable character. That Chaplin could articulate so much emotion with one expression proves he truly was the genius the Academy "honored" in its inadequate way.

▶ BEST ACTRESS

WINNER:
Janet Gaynor *(Seventh Heaven, Street Angel, Sunrise)*
Other Nominees: Louise Dresser *(A Ship Comes In)*, Gloria Swanson *(Sadie Thompson)*

▼

THE BEST CHOICE:
Mary Pickford *(My Best Girl)*
Award-Worthy Runners-Up: Eleanor Boardman *(The Crowd)*, Gloria Swanson *(Sadie Thompson)*

The first Best Actress winner was the youngest, Janet Gaynor. The queen of Fox studio, she was only twenty-one when she starred in Frank Borzage's *Seventh Heaven* and F. W. Murnau's *Sunrise,* and twenty-two when she made Borzage's *Street Angel.* At the time awards could be based on cumulative work, and Gaynor was nominated for her three portrayals of sweet women who have conflicts in life and love. Those few voters who selected the initial Best Actress reasoned that three *good* performances equaled greatness—and it didn't hurt that Gaynor was popular with the public and within the industry. Mary Pickford, one of those on Louis B. Mayer's secret voting committee, was happy for the pretty, instantly likable star who was once groomed to be the next "Mary Pickford" before becoming a romantic lead (often playing opposite Charles Farrell). In less than a year Pickford would be jealous of Gaynor's victory, but at the time she didn't really care who won Academy Awards. She hadn't even used her influence to get a nomination for her sparkling performance in *My Best Girl.* And she might have won, despite its being a comic role, if she'd really put on the pressure. She would prove this the next year when she invited the voters over for tea and not uncoincidentally was voted Best Actress for *Coquette,* one of her worst films. Looking back, I wish that Pickford had been honored that first year for her final silent picture—if not for her immense contributions to the dying silent film, then for giving what I think was her best performance, in a role that at times seems suited for, oddly enough, Janet Gaynor.

Pickford plays Maggie Johnson, a poor girl who lives with her parents and sister on Goat Hill. Because her weak father is a loafer and her sister is running around, Maggie is all that keeps her family together. She works as a stockroom girl in a department store. She falls in love with Joe Grant (Charles "Buddy" Rogers), the new stockroom boy, not knowing he is the son of the store's owner and that he is engaged to a society girl. His father won't let him marry until he proves himself in business. Maggie shows him the ropes and tries to help him get a promo-

In Mary Pickford's last silent film, *My Best Girl,* her stockroom girl is thrilled by the attention of the handsome new stockroom boy, played by the actress's future husband, Charles "Buddy" Rogers.

tion. Soon he falls for her too. However, when she finds out he is rich, she worries that he'll ruin his career if he marries her. So she poses as a gold-digging hussy to drive him away. She returns to her family, afraid to leave them on their own. But she is miserable. Freeing his daughter from an unnecessary burden, her father decides he'll "be the father of the family!" Joe and Maggie reconcile.

Made at United Artists, which Pickford helped found, and with Pickford serving as producer, *My Best Girl* was actually a semiremake of the recent *It,* starring Clara Bow—an actress whose vivacious, hedonistic image was very different from that of America's Sweetheart. Its credited source, however, was a novel by Kathleen Norris. This gentle comedy—with a couple of dramatic moments—provided Pickford with her best adult role, and cast her, as in *Rosita,* as the sole support of adults who may as well be children (which reflected Pickford's private life). Significantly, it was the first feature in which Pickford kissed her leading man. No wonder that when her then-husband, Douglas Fairbanks, saw her and Buddy Rogers on the set, he told confidants that he wasn't merely jealous but *scared.* Rogers developed a crush on Pickford during shooting—it's pretty obvious on screen—and would marry her ten years later.

As an extremely likable flesh-and-blood character Pickford displays an appealing combination of beauty, physical grace, vulnerability, spunk, cheer, and tenderness. She also shows a surprising degree of sophistication and charm as both a light comedienne and romantic lead. She even has a couple of slapstick bits, which she handles smoothly. In one, at the store, she is loaded down with pots, and when she tries to kick one that is stuck on her foot, her bloomers fall down to her ankles. (Director Sam Taylor worked with Harold Lloyd on similar routines.) But what I like best are the romantic scenes between Maggie and Joe. I like how they look at each other while they eat, and how they cuddle on the back of a truck and inside a large crate. And anyone who remembers falling in love will smile as they walk together down the street, oblivious of the hordes of pedestrians, the streetcars and automobiles that whiz around them, and the pouring rain. They look at each other with love. Then the enraptured couple find themselves standing in front of a furniture store where there is a window display of an idyllic scene of marital bliss—children play in front of the fire, Dad reads a paper, Mother sews. "It must be wonderful to spend an evening like that after supper," says Maggie. It is the character speaking, but perhaps these are the wistful thoughts of Pickford herself, as her marriage to Fairbanks crumbles.

Pickford biographer Scott Eyman considered Maggie the character who came closest to the real Pickford. The mingling of shame, devotion, and impatience that Maggie shows toward her family is, according to Eyman, similar to how she felt about her own family, who relied on her to support them. And Maggie's pairing with the youthfully ardent Joe Grant, played by her handsome future husband, is, writes Eyman, "even without hindsight, far more emotional in nature than the nominal love interests her films usually displayed. It is clear that, in a way that Mary herself might not have understood, *My Best Girl* served as some sort of emotional autobiography."

1928-29

▶ BEST PRODUCTION

WINNER:
Broadway Melody (MGM; Harry Beaumont)
Other Nominees: *Alibi, Hollywood Revue, In Old Arizona, The Patriot*

▼

THE BEST CHOICE:
The Wind (MGM; Victor Seastrom)
Award-Worthy Runner-Up: *The Wedding March* (Erich von Stroheim)

In the second year of the Academy Awards, MGM boss Louis B. Mayer got the big payoff for having sabotaged his own film, *The Crowd,* during the previous year's election process. The five-member Central Board of Judges gave MGM three of the seven statues awarded, including the Best Production award to the studio's prized musical *Broadway Melody.* Because he had been so "unselfish" in the first year, Mayer didn't expect anyone to suspect favoritism this year, but everyone in Hollywood noticed that the big winners were Mayer and other members of the Academy elite. As a result, in future years, the entire Academy membership would select winners.

Most likely *Broadway Melody* would have won even without Mayer's influence. Supervised by MGM's creative chief of production, Irving Thalberg, and greatly hyped by Mayer's publicity department—it was promoted as being "100% All Talking! 100% All Singing! 100% All Dancing!"—the film caught the fancy of fans and critics and broke box-office records. This first backstage musical looks more static each year, but upon release it was excitingly innovative, especially since one number was in Technicolor. Moreover, it starred the talented Bessie Love and Anita Page and featured a fine score (including "You Were Meant for Me") by Nacio Herb Brown and Arthur Freed.

Ironically, the best picture of the year, and a film whose greatness has not diminished, was also made at MGM. However, *The Wind* didn't receive any of the hype given *Broadway Melody,* and America's last silent masterpiece (Chaplin's films had soundtracks) was completely ignored when pictures were nominated.

Looking for a starring vehicle to fulfill her MGM contract, Lillian Gish wrote a four-page treatment of Dorothy Scarborough's book *The Wind,* and got the go-ahead from Thalberg to produce the film herself. She hired scriptwriter Frances Marion (who later admitted it was the last screenplay she put her heart into), Swedish director Victor Seastrom (Sjöström in his native country), and Lars Hanson, Sweden's most popular stage actor, to be her male lead. The four had just worked together on the impressive *The Scarlet Letter.*

The Wind, which was shot in 120-degree temperatures in California's Mojave Desert, is the story of an unmarried, gently bred young woman from Virginia who comes to live on a ranch with her male cousin and his family in the harsh, windswept Texas dustbowl. When her cousin's jealous wife forces her out, and the "gentleman" (Montagu Love) who has courted her turns out to be married, the penniless woman agrees to marry a kindly neighbor, Hanson. But she is unable to give him or the hostile land a chance. She feels completely isolated and the constant, howling winds drive her toward madness. While her husband is away rounding up wild horses, hoping to make enough money to send her back to Virginia, Love rapes her. She kills him and buries him in the sand. As originally filmed, the crazed woman then walks off into the wilderness to die. But when exhibitors refused for several months to show such a depressing picture, MGM had no choice but to reshoot the ending: This time Gish declares her love for Hanson, and tells him she will stay with him because she is no longer afraid of the winds.

The Wind is an ahead-of-its-time feminist drama about a woman without money or opportunities who tries to

The rare unmarried woman in a rugged land, Lillian Gish is courted by Lars Hanson (R) and his friend William Orlamond in Victor Seastrom's *The Wind.*

survive in a man's world. The only chance Gish has for an "easy life" is to become the mistress of Love, but she refuses to demean herself. Most interesting is how Marion deals with the relationships Gish has with the film's other female, her cousin's wife, and with Hanson. We dislike the cousin's wife because of her cold treatment of Gish and for imagining her a rival for his affections. However, though she is a bitter woman she is no villain. She dearly loves her husband and without him, in this harsh world, she has no life, no options, so she holds on to him desperately. But as much as she wants Gish out of her life, she won't abandon her to the lecher Love. Hanson is another interesting character. He falls in love with Gish but doesn't want to dominate her (he won't force himself on her). Instead, he wants equality, whereby he and Gish would work together and love each other. He realizes, and Gish comes to understand at the end, only together can they tame the winds.

The Wind is beautifully acted by Gish and the talented, handsome Hanson. His most touching scene occurs when his new wife is disgusted by his attempt to embrace her and he assures her she need not fear his trying again. The picture is also exquisitely photographed (by John Arnold), with much emphasis on motion. Outside, the wind constantly blows (eight airplane propellers were used) as trains, wagons, and men on horseback force their way across the terrain. Seastrom creates a tremendous sense of claustrophobia with repeated shots of the sand swirling toward windows and penetrating everything within Hanson's cabin, including Gish's clothes and long hair. When the door opens, sand rushes inside, making it impossible for Gish to keep the cabin tidy (Hanson doesn't expect her to), and making her feel further trapped. The increasing disorder in the house represents Gish's deteriorating mind. The eerie scene in which her mind wanders with distorted, mad, hallucinatory images caused by the mobile camera that follows her through the dark, shadowy cabin, and a fantasized image of a white horse charging through the skies outside, reminds one of Seastrom's Swedish horror classic,

The Phantom Carriage. The reshot finale may seem a little hokey (she recovers awfully quickly from her mad spell once Hanson enters the cabin), but Seastrom's last shot is a gem: The couple stands in the open doorway of *their* home, arms wrapped around each other, looking out into the wilderness without fear. Not only have the winds been conquered by love, but the wild (nature) and the domestic (the house), and this woman and this man, are as one.

▶ BEST ACTOR

WINNER:
Warner Baxter *(In Old Arizona)*
Other Nominees: George Bancroft *(Thunderbolt)*, Chester Morris *(Alibi)*, Paul Muni *(The Valiant)*, Lewis Stone *(The Patriot)*

▼

THE BEST CHOICE:
Buster Keaton *(Steamboat Bill, Jr.)*
Award-Worthy Runners-Up: George Bancroft *(Docks of New York)*, George Bancroft *(Thunderbolt)*

Warner Baxter charmed his way to the second Best Actor Academy Award as O. Henry's singing, romancing, mustachioed bandito, the Cisco Kid, in *In Old Arizona,* the screen's first outdoor talkie Western. Once a successful stage actor, Baxter's seven-year career in silent pictures was on the downslide when he was offered the part after Raoul Walsh dropped out following an accident. (Walsh took to wearing an eye patch after being permanently blinded in one eye when a jackrabbit crashed through his windshield.) Audiences were taken by Baxter's handsome features, captivating smile, and masculine voice, and his career was secured in sound films. But today the film, which is rarely screened, seems extremely slow, particularly for a Western, and his star-making performance is no better than ordinary.

It would have been more fitting if, after Charlie Chaplin was given the first Best Actor award for *The Circus* (as I suggest), Buster Keaton, his one equal, had won in the second year, for *Steamboat Bill, Jr.* Although not on par with such Keaton masterpieces as *Our Hospitality, Sherlock Junior, The Navigator,* and *The General* (which I think should have swept the first Academy Awards if it had been released late enough in 1927 to have qualified), *Steamboat Bill, Jr.* is Keaton's best silent film of the sound era. His performance was certainly the best—and most versatile—by an actor in 1928–29.

After graduating from an eastern college, Keaton's character arrives in River Junction to meet his father for the first time. The tall, muscular steamship captain, Ernest Torrence, is disappointed to see that his son is a small, weak young man who carries a ukulele and sports a little mustache, beret, and bow tie. Furthermore, Keaton isn't a good pupil when Dad tries to teach him how to operate

his small steamer. Keaton's more interested in courting his college classmate Marion Byron. Torrence frowns upon this because she's the daughter of Torrence's rich rival. He tries to send Keaton back to his home in the East. But Keaton sticks around when Dad is thrown in jail, and attempts a daring rescue, earning Dad's respect. Then, by shrewdly navigating the steamer, he saves Dad, Marion, and her father during a catastrophic storm, with the result that the fathers shake hands and Keaton and Byron are married.

Although it isn't a pivotal Keaton film, I still think of *Steamboat Bill, Jr.* as one of two features (*Our Hospitality* is the other) that best established his sweet persona. There is much gentle humor: Keaton trying to find his father at the train depot by shyly showing every stranger he passes the identifying carnation in his lapel; or a soaked Keaton walking through the rain with a broken umbrella that is turned inside out and stands directly upward. I love those scenes in which his big father pulls him around town, holding his hand. Another scene has Keaton trying on hats in front of a mirror for his father's approval; the scene's highlight (an in joke for Keaton fans) is when he puts on his trademarked pancake hat and takes it off quickly, before his father can see it and toss it away.

The great comic remains stone faced throughout. But we know how his character feels, because no one is better or more hilarious with subtle expressions, eye movement, and double takes. You'll notice how stiff Keaton's character is when first meeting his intimidating father, but by the end, when he has become a one-man rescue squad, he is incredibly agile. Keaton does some amazing acrobatics in *Steamboat Bill, Jr.,* truly risking life

Met with hostility while attempting a romantic rendezvous in *Steamboat Bill, Jr.*, Buster Keaton moves his foot back and forth between his father's boat and that belonging to Marion Byron's father.

and limb in some stunts. The movie's great climax has Keaton racing around and being blown about during a violent storm, as buildings collapse around him. One building even falls directly upon him, but he is spared in this famous stunt because he stands where an *open* second-story window comes down. By the end of the sequence, when Keaton has miraculously saved everyone (including a preacher so he can marry Byron), one can see why many consider him the most lovable of the silent stars and every bit as sexy as the silent screen's romantic athlete, Douglas Fairbanks.

▶ BEST ACTRESS

WINNER:
Mary Pickford *(Coquette)*
Other Nominees: Ruth Chatterton *(Madame X)*, Betty Compson *(The Barker)*, Jeanne Eagels *(The Letter)*, Bessie Love *(Broadway Melody)*

▼

THE BEST CHOICE:
Lillian Gish *(The Wind)*
Award-Worthy Runners-Up: Betty Compson *(The Docks of New York)*, Marion Davies *(Show People)*, Bessie Love *(Broadway Melody)*

Mary Pickford was happy to vote for Janet Gaynor as Best Actress for 1927–28, and didn't even mind that her own terrific performance in *My Best Girl* went unnominated. But, as the story goes, she began to feel jealous that she didn't have a statue herself. So when she was nominated in the second year of the Academy Awards for her performance in *Coquette,* her *first* talkie and *first* film without her famous curls, she got serious. No longer on the voting committee, she invited the current judges to Pickfair for tea, thereby qualifying as the *first* star to campaign for an Academy Award. And she defeated several respected, veteran actresses, including the late Jeanne Eagels, who had died of a drug overdose after making *The Letter*. It was hard for the Academy to justify her victory because the film was one of the worst received of her career; it was generally recognized that she had been miscast as the Southern flirt who ruins men's lives, a part played by Helen Hayes on Broadway. Surely, Lillian Gish was more deserving for her riveting performance in *The Wind*. And even if, as many contended, the award was given to Pickford as a tribute to a great career, Gish was still the better choice. Pickford may have been the most popular actress of the silent era, but Gish was the most talented. If Academy Awards had been given out in the silent era, Lillian Gish would have won a few, having given beautifully conceived performances in such features as *The Birth of a Nation, Broken Blossoms, True Heart Susie, Way Down East,* and *Orphans of the Storm* for D. W. Griffith, and *The White Sister, La Bohème,* and *The Scarlet Letter*.

Gish made her reputation as an innocent, passive heroine who undergoes much suffering. As critic Arthur Lenning wrote of *Broken Blossoms'* Lucy Barrows, Lillian represented "the innocent waif sacrificed in the moral and emotional slaughterhouse of the world." Her parts were more adult after she left Griffith, but she still sought roles that were consistent with those she played for him. Having played Hester Prynne in *The Scarlet Letter,* Gish again played a heroine who is an outcast in her community in *The Wind*. As in her other films Gish is initially virtuous, but learns the ways of the hard, cruel world. She endures much pain, suffering, and humiliation. Unlike her roles in the Griffith films, however, her character does waver from the path of righteousness; she does not survive with honor intact. But when, in *The Wind,* she is attacked by a scoundrel and ravaged by nature, her part recalls the Griffith films. The scene in which she feels trapped in the small cabin while a storm rages outside reminds one of the harrowing scene in *Broken Blossoms* when the terrified Lucy Barrows is locked in a closet while her brutal father stalks outside. Her hysteria in the Griffith scene was so convincing that during the filming, several people on the set became ill watching her; she is just as believable in *The Wind*.

Gish is dynamic in a role that lets her run the gamut of emotions. At first she is carefree, later apprehensive, finally tormented; she tries to suppress her paranoia, but ultimately allows madness to replace her terrible fears. As Gish was well aware, it is through her incredible eyes that we perceive the changes her character goes through. We sense her paranoia the first time she watches the sand swirling toward the train windows (she realizes she isn't strong); later we see absolute fear in those eyes; finally they are blurred and unfocused and we realize she has lost her senses. As it is with her hands and her body, Gish moves her eyes (usually preceding the movement of her head) only at those moments when she wants to convey a thought. No one was more aware of the camera than this shrewd actress.

Gish said working on *The Wind* was the most difficult experience of her career because of the blowing sand, which cut into her skin and shredded her garments, and the intense heat. It was even harder than doing twenty-two takes on an ice floe with her hand in the freezing water in Griffith's *Way Down East.* So the lack of studio support for the film was a great disappointment. Because it failed at the box office, Louis B. Mayer told Gish that her career needed a boost. He said he was going to invent a scandal to soil her pristine image. When she refused to go along with his scheme, he suspended her. Undaunted, she went to New York to do theater. *The Wind* was Lillian Gish's last silent picture.

No one has ever been better at playing traumatic scenes than Lillian Gish, but she outdid herself as the lonely bride driven crazy by *The Wind.*

1929–30

▶ BEST PRODUCTION

WINNER:
All Quiet on the Western Front (Universal; Lewis Milestone)
Other Nominees: *The Big House, Disraeli, The Divorcée, The Love Parade*

▼

THE BEST CHOICE:
All Quiet on the Western Front (Universal; Lewis Milestone)
Award-Worthy Runners-Up: None

It's unfortunate that antiwar films are never made in the midst of a war, but Universal Studios—specifically production chief Carl Laemmle, Jr.—still deserved praise for spending a then astronomical $1.2 million in 1929 to make a faithful adaptation of Erich Maria Remarque's landmark novel, *All Quiet on the Western Front.* There were several antiwar/pacifist pictures released in the late twenties and early thirties, including two German films, G. W. Pabst's *Westfront 1918* and Viktor Trivas's *Hell on Earth;* two English films, Maurice Elvy's *High Treason,* Anthony Asquith's *Tell England;* and in America, James Whale's *Journey's End* and, in 1937, his *The Road Back,* a semisequel to *All Quiet on the Western Front.* But none had the impact of *All Quiet on the Western Front* upon release. I think it still stands as America's strongest pacifist film and deserved the "Best Production" Academy Award it received in 1929–30.

The picture begins in Germany at the outbreak of World War I, not on a battlefield, but in a classroom, where a jingoistic, elderly professor convinces Lew Ayres and all his other naive young students to join Germany's glorious war effort: "After all, is a little experience such a bad thing for a boy? Is the honor of wearing a uniform something from which we should run?" Expecting the brief war the professor promised, the boys enthusiastically enlist en masse, all hoping to be heroes. Once in uniform, they realize that there is no glamour to war. Instead, there are dictatorial officers, endless marches, hunger, fatigue, nostalgia for home, rats in the trenches, mud and rain, bombings, gassings, injuries. There is no heroism. Instead there is confusion, terror, hysteria, madness, amputations, meaningless deaths. All that matters is survival, and those who survive are either insane, without limbs or sight, or unfit to return to civilization where old men still champion wars. Ayres briefly returns home and, in my favorite scene, tells his professor's new students, whom the old man's coaxing to enlist, that war has nothing to do with honor, duty, or a just cause: "It's dirty and painful to die for your country. It's easier to say 'Go out and die' than it is to do it." Ayres is the last of his unit to die, shot as he is reaching from a trench for a butterfly, the one thing of beauty left on the desolate war-ravaged terrain.

The finale, in which we see Ayres's grasping hand become lifeless after a sniper's shot—actually it was director Lewis Milestone's hand—is one of several deservedly celebrated moments in the film. The battle scene in which Arthur Edeson's camera pans while charging soldiers are mowed down by machine-gun fire is as impressive as it is terrifying. It becomes even scarier

A hardened soldier despite his young age, Lew Ayres tries to survive another day in the trenches in Lewis Milestone's antiwar classic, *All Quiet on the Western Front.*

when soldiers break through and jump into the trenches for hand-to-hand combat. (Significantly, not one shot is heroic or glamorizes war; instead we see how vulnerable all soldiers are and want to close our eyes until the fighting stops.) Also memorable is the ankle-level montage in which various soldiers who wear new boots are gunned down. Though the famous "brotherhood" scene in which Ayres talks to the dying French soldier he stabbed is somewhat hokey, it's still moving. In fact, the young Ayres gives an excellent, thoughtful performance, which has too often been overlooked. He understood that he wasn't playing just one individual, but that his soldier represents countless ill-prepared young men who have been sent to war for no reason. Ayres wasn't too embarrassed to play tender moments, as when he puts his face against that of his dying friend in the hospital; when he holds and kisses the hand of a Frenchwoman as she eats (they later sleep together!); when he speaks with his mother and is unable to fully respond to her warmth; and when he reunites at the front with a friend (top-billed Louis Wolheim), only to experience as well the death of this seemingly "invincible" vet.

The human story is so powerful that we forgive some of the stagy scenes. The dialogue, written by George Abbott and Maxwell Anderson (who, along with Dell Andrews, were nominated for an Academy Award for Writing), is delivered with conviction, so we listen intently to the men lament that there have always been unnecessary wars. Milestone, who won the Best Director award, compensates for the early cinema's immobile camera and rooted players by frequently inserting close-ups of his characters and by using sets that have large windows or broken walls so that we are aware of great activity in the background.

George Cukor also worked on the film, helping the actors eradicate any accents so that they come across less as Germans than universal characters. The French banned the film until 1963 because these Germans were portrayed sympathetically. My feeling is that the film has always been well received in America because it shows Germans—our enemies in World War I—coming to their senses in a losing war effort. (Importantly, none of their victims is identified as an American.) As good as the film is (and it holds up), I doubt if American audiences would have received it so well over the years if, with few script changes, these soldiers who question giving up their lives for uniform, flag, and country were Americans.

▶ BEST ACTOR

WINNER:
George Arliss *(Disraeli)*
Other Nominees: George Arliss *(The Green Goddess)*, Wallace Beery *(The Big House)*, Maurice Chevalier *(The Love Parade)*, Maurice Chevalier *(The Big Pond)*, Ronald Colman *(Bulldog Drummond)*, Ronald Colman *(Condemned)*, Lawrence Tibbett *(The Rogue Song)*

▼

THE BEST CHOICE:
Wallace Beery *(The Big House)*
Award-Worthy Runners-Up: George Arliss *(Disraeli)*, Maurice Chevalier *(The Love Parade)*

George Arliss was one of Hollywood's most unlikely leading men. The London-born stage veteran was over sixty when he became a movie star. He hadn't the virility of, say, Sean Connery at sixty, but instead was small and slim, with a pointy face and the look of a Dickens character. But fans and critics believed that his precise, meticulous, theatrical acting style brought respectability to the cinema. And because he was *theatrically* schooled, they believed the accuracy of his many historical portraits—including Alexander Hamilton, Voltaire, Cardinal Richelieu, and the Duke of Wellington—beginning with his Academy Award–winning portrait of England's liberal nineteenth-century prime minister Benjamin Disraeli.

Arliss gave a typically impressive, forceful performance in *Disraeli.* However, what detracted from his work was that, as he wrote in his autobiography, *Ten Years at the Studios,* he played the part exactly as he'd done onstage for several years. Rather than adapting to the new medium, he had the medium—and director Alfred Green—adapt to his stagy style.

The odds were against Wallace Beery's winning the Best Actor award for 1929–30. Arliss, Ronald Colman, and Maurice Chevalier all had strong international reputations, while Beery had been making movies since 1913, mostly playing heavies, without anyone taking much notice. (He was better known for having been married from 1916 to 1918 to Gloria Swanson, his costar in Sennett comedies, than for any particular role.) In fact, Beery's three major rivals each were nominated for two lead roles, while Beery wasn't even top billed in *The Big House,* the only film for which he was nominated. Beery would lose, but the role shot him to stardom.

George Hill's *The Big House* was the first prison drama of the sound era, and MGM's major picture of 1929–30,

Chester Morris is the only prisoner who can calm down brutal Wallace Beery in *The Big House*.

one characterization that broke from stereotypical portrayals of convicts. Lon Chaney was to have played "Machine-Gun" Butch, but his death gave Beery his break, allowing him to establish the persona he'd use until his death in 1949: His Butch is a dangerous brute, but we pity him, even find him lovable, because he doesn't know any better. Perhaps the doctor dropped him on his head when he was born. "From the neck down," says Morris, "you're a regular guy, Butch."

Beery shaved his head to play the bully of the Big House, so when he smiles he looks almost comical—his features were not those of a leading man to begin with—like a cross between W. C. Fields and one of Disney's seven dwarfs. He looks friendly and when he jokes around or boasts of love conquests (though illiterate, he pretends to read love letters from an imaginary woman he calls Myrtle), he's a good guy, a pal. But he doesn't know when to keep his mouth shut, or how to control his violent nature. Only Morris can calm him down and turn his mean mood into something more cheery; then Butch will say his favorite words, "I was only kidding." Almost everything he says (what great lines Frances Marion wrote!) tells us that he has two opposing sides: he fantasizes about Myrtle loving him, yet admits, "If I even knew a dame named Myrtle, I'd kick her teeth in"; he sentimentalizes about his girlfriend Sadie, saying, "I shouldn't have slipped her that ant poison." He misses his mother and, well-meaning, says he "wants to break out to get the little old lady the swellest funeral she ever had." As Beery plays him, Butch is indeed scary and you don't want him let out on the streets. But you forgive almost anything he does because deep down you believe his sheepish apology, "I was only kidding."

nominated for Best Production and Best Actor, and winning Academy Awards for Frances Marion's script and Douglas Shearer's sound recording. Beery was billed second, after Chester Morris, who played his nobler cellmate, but he stole the picture, providing it with its

---

▶ BEST ACTRESS

WINNER:
Norma Shearer *(The Divorcée)*
Other Nominees: Nancy Carroll *(The Devil's Holiday)*, Ruth Chatterton *(Sarah and Son)*, Greta Garbo *(Anna Christie)*, Greta Garbo *(Romance)*, Norma Shearer *(Their Own Desire)*, Gloria Swanson *(The Trespasser)*

▼

THE BEST CHOICE:
Louise Brooks *(Pandora's Box)*
Award-Worthy Runners-Up: Louise Brooks *(Diary of a Lost Girl)*, Helen Morgan *(Applause)*

This was the year that Garbo talked on screen for the first time. So did Gloria Swanson. Musical comedy star Nancy Carroll played in her first drama. And Ruth Chatterton kept on suffering. But Academy members bypassed these nominees to give the Best Actress award to Norma Shearer, MGM's "First Lady of the Screen" and, significantly, the wife of MGM production chief Irving Thalberg. Shearer, who today is one of the least appreciated of the great actresses of the early sound era, was her

usual smart, stylish self in the convoluted drama *The Divorcée;* she made fooling around seem ladylike. The voters may have wanted Shearer to win for *The Divorcée* because they believed she had reached her potential in it. But over the next few years, in films such as *Private Lives, The Barretts of Wimpole Street, Marie Antoinette,* and *The Women,* she'd give performances that displayed much more range, confidence, flair, and wit. In fact, *The Divorcée* proved to be one of her lesser efforts.

I don't consider *Pandora's Box,* G. W. Pabst's magnificent silent film, a candidate for my Best Picture of 1929–30 because it was a German production, but its American star, Louise Brooks, is the only possible choice for Best Actress. Her spellbinding portrayal of Frank Wedekind's Lulu, an ill-fated, fun-loving seductress, whose very existence causes weak men to self-destruct and then, unfortunately, turn against her, was one of the great portraits in silent films and one of the most erotic in film history. Even if *Pandora's Box* had enjoyed more than a brief run in the United States in 1929 (before disappearing until the 1950s) and even if the film and Brooks's role hadn't been considered so scandalous, Brooks would have been denied a Best Actress nomination. That's because she had left for Germany to work with Pabst instead of sticking around to dub her character's voice for her last film at Paramount, *The Canary Murder Case.* When she returned to Hollywood in 1930, having also made Pabst's equally controversial *Diary of a Lost Girl,* and René Clair's French film *Prix de Beauté,* she was virtually blacklisted.

Adapted from Wedekind's once-controversial plays *The Earth's Spirit* and *Pandora's Box,* Pabst's film begins with Lulu as the mistress of a rich, middle-aged newspaper publisher (Fritz Kortner). Insulted that he plans to dump her and marry a respectable woman, Lulu manipulates him into marrying her. On their wedding night he mistakenly thinks she's having a sexual interlude with an elderly friend, Schigolch (Carl Goetz), and tries to force her to shoot herself. In the struggle he is killed. She is convicted of manslaughter but escapes the courthouse. She seduces her dead husband's adult son, Alwa (Franz Lederer), and they take refuge on a gambling boat, where they continually pay off a blackmailer who threatens to turn her in. When Alwa loses their money gambling, the blackmailer attempts to sell her to an Egyptian cabaret owner. Meanwhile, Alwa is caught cheating at cards. Lulu and Alwa escape the boat with Schigolch, after Lulu's loyal female friend (Alice Roberts's Countess is perhaps the screen's first lesbian, and she's portrayed sympathetically!) causes a diversion. The penniless Lulu, Alwa, and Schigolch move into a freezing London garret. To get food on Christmas she goes out into the streets to sell herself. She brings back a stranger to the garret, not minding that he has no money. As she lies in his arms, Jack the Ripper kills her.

Brooks was an ex–Follies girl who enjoyed a degree of fame because of her beauty, her reputation as free-spirited party-girl, and her short square black bob—J. P. McEvoy based *Dixie Dugan* on her—but she couldn't get major roles in American films. In fact, Pabst discovered his Lulu in a second-string role of a circus high-diver in Howard Hawks's *A Girl in Every Port.* (He turned down

Louise Brooks has a temper tantrum when her elderly lover appears at her review in *Pandora's Box.*

the young Dietrich, who went on to play a similar character, Lola Lola, in *The Blue Angel.*) Pabst realized that Brooks was so beautiful and sexy, no one would question that every man in his picture immediately fell for her. Moreover, in her eyes and subtle expressions we see that Brooks (a very intelligent actress) understands Lulu's sexual drives and needs. This woman who kisses and hugs everyone in reach is, as Wedekind wrote, "the personification of primitive sexuality who inspires evil unaware." Her Lulu doesn't try to control her sexual impulses, because she knows she is injecting excitement into the dreary lives of her lovers. She knows men are weak but doesn't think a relationship with her would destroy them. She expects society, including the men who fall for her, will try to condemn her. She protects herself from accusers through smiles and laughter. But

Brooks subtly reveals Lulu's pain, disappointment in those who let her down, and anger. But never self-pity. Brooks's Lulu is a sad victim of the weak men around her, rather than the traditional vamp who causes their downfall. We see deep into Lulu because Brooks somehow transmits her innermost thoughts and her motivations. Even her most energetic and erotic movements express feelings. Yet when she stops being bubbly and stands half-frozen in the London streets and offers her body, she—the actress and character—is incredibly soulful and captures our hearts. Brooks's Lulu made many mistakes in her relationships with men—and she'll make one more—but Brooks convinces us she is someone too sweet and innocent to dislike and too noble, when confronting death, not to admire.

1930–31

▶ BEST PICTURE

WINNER:
Cimarron (RKO; Wesley Ruggles)
Other Nominees: *East Lynne, The Front Page, Skippy, Trader Horn*

▼

THE BEST CHOICE:
City Lights (United Artists; Charles Chaplin)
Award-Worthy Runners-Up: *The Criminal Code* (Howard Hawks), *Tabu* (F. W. Murnau and Robert Flaherty)

Of the five nominees for the first official "Best Picture," only *The Front Page,* Lewis Milestone's satisfyingly rowdy reworking of the Ben Hecht–Charles MacArthur play, could be justified as a candidate. And the worst of the lot was the winner: *Cimarron,* a dull, overblown adaptation of Edna Ferber's best-seller about a troubled couple who live through the evolution of Oklahoma from wild, open prairie to progressive state, with Richard Dix overacting like the hammiest matinee idol and the soap opera ingredients drowning the epic elements. Considering this weak competition, it's really inexcusable that *City Lights,* which is generally regarded as Charles Chaplin's greatest film, wasn't even nominated. In fact, it was mysteriously ignored in all categories. It's possible that the Academy members were paying back Chaplin for refusing to convert to talking films (although he did

employ a soundtrack) because he believed they were much less artistic.

Chaplin began his masterpiece in 1928. Forecasting with his heart, Chaplin believed sound pictures would die out in three years. He intended his new picture to be a tribute to the art of pantomime and in the vanguard of a new wave of nontalking films. He spent $2 million on his gamble and would have gone bankrupt if it had failed. Since his prediction about the sound film's demise was proven wrong by the time *City Lights* was finished and it turned out to be the only new film without dialogue, he was pessimistic when it was released in 1931. Fortunately, *City Lights* received tremendous critical acclaim and did exceptionally well at the box office, which makes the Academy's response to it seem all that much more like sour grapes.

An intruder in the big city, the Little Tramp falls in love with a beautiful young blind woman (Virginia Cherrill, a recently divorced ex-socialite making her movie debut). She sells flowers on the street to support herself and her grandmother. Not knowing he wears rags, she believes he is a rich gentleman and longs for his visits. He becomes a street cleaner to help her pay her rent. Meanwhile he prevents a drunk, lonely millionaire (Harry Myers) from drowning himself. Grateful, the millionaire befriends him, but each time he sobers up, he doesn't recognize the Little Tramp and has the butler kick him out of his house. Drunk, he gives the Little Tramp money to pay for an operation that will cure the flower girl's blindness. But sober, after being conked on the head by burglars, he tells police that he didn't give him the money, making them think it was the Little Tramp who knocked him out. But the Little Tramp runs off with the money and gives it to the girl. Knowing she will be disappointed to see her poor benefactor, he goes away and is soon arrested. Released months later, he comes upon the girl, who now has sight and runs a successful flower shop. She still longs for the man who helped cure her. When she sees the disheveled tramp pass, she laughs at his loving expression. Feeling pity, she offers the Little Tramp a flower and a coin. When she touches his hand, she knows who he is. "You can see?" he asks. "Yes, I can see," she answers, gently lifting his hand to her heart. He smiles and the film fades out.

"Tomorrow the birds will sing!" the Little Tramp tells the depressed millionaire. "Be brave! Face life!" Clearly this is what the Little Tramp must tell himself each day, for it's a cruel world he faces: bourgeois types revere "Peace and Prosperity" statues by chasing away the penniless tramp who sleeps on them; police are enemies of the disenfranchised; even newsboys and butlers bully him; the only aristocrats who befriend tramps are too drunk to remember their own prejudices; and the only pretty woman who wouldn't laugh at a tramp is blind. It's a confusing, topsy-turvy world, where the most dignified, noble character is a tramp, where the person with the most money wants to kill himself while a man without anything tells him about the joys of life. Identities of both people and props are in question. As for people: the blind girl assumes the generous, gallant tramp is rich and handsome; when she actually sees the tramp she mistakes him for a stranger; when sober, the millionaire doesn't remember befriending the tramp; the tramp is wrongly accused of being a burglar; the tramp consents to box a small guy (who has agreed to a fix) but, in a hilarious, inventively choreographed scene, must fight a big substitute. As for props: horseshoes and rabbit's feet prove to be bad luck charms for a boxer who is soundly defeated; the tramp mistakenly eats the confetti that becomes mixed with his spaghetti *and* almost cuts into a man's bald head that he thinks is a plate of food; the

Charlie Chaplin's chivalrous Little Tramp impresses blind Virginia Cherrill in *City Lights.*

tramp washes his face with cheese instead of the soap that finds its way into a coworker's sandwich; the blind girl unravels the tramp's shirt when she mistakenly thinks she's rolling string. As director, Chaplin adds to the confusion by constantly having characters' arms, hands, and legs interlock, almost as if the characters are hugging, dancing, or wrestling with one another. And he adds props—string, ropes, falling confetti—that increase the entanglements.

All these identity problems and mix-ups provide Chaplin with many moments for slapstick and, as in all Chaplin, for poignant moments as well. I get misty about ten minutes from the end of the film, anticipating the classic reunion of the tramp and the girl, who can now see. It's a perfect scene, full of beauty. There are violins (the Spanish *"La Violetera"*), flowers, the lovely Cherrill. And as the girl realizes when she says, "Yes, now I can see," there stands the very essence of beauty in the world in the person of the Little Tramp. He is the only person who can grasp true beauty in a cruel world, one of the city's few "lights."

▶ BEST ACTOR

WINNER:
Lionel Barrymore *(A Free Soul)*
Other Nominees: Jackie Cooper *(Skippy)*, Richard Dix *(Cimarron)*, Fredric March *(The Royal Family of Broadway)*, Adolphe Menjou *(The Front Page)*

▼

THE BEST CHOICE:
Edward G. Robinson *(Little Caesar)*
Award-Worthy Runners-Up: James Cagney *(The Public Enemy)*, Charles Chaplin *(City Lights)*, Fredric March *(The Royal Family of Broadway)*, Adolphe Menjou *(The Front Page)*

Lionel Barrymore's dramatic courtroom finale, concluding with his exhausted, emotionally drained defense attorney dropping dead—after getting Leslie Howard off the hook for killing Clark Gable, long before *Gone With the Wind*—was what it took for him to walk home with the fourth Best Actor award for the pedestrian Norma Shearer vehicle, *A Free Soul.* Among the other nominees little Jackie Cooper WAS *Skippy,* but Barrymore's stiffest challenge came from Fredric March, who was hilariously hammy as, ironically, Lionel's real brother, John, in *The Royal Family of Broadway.*

Charlie Chaplin wasn't nominated for *City Lights,* although no one gave a *better* performance. But since I would give him the Best Picture and Best Director award for this year, as well as the Best Actor awards in both 1927–28 and 1936, my choices for the 1930–31 award came down to either Edward G. Robinson or James Cagney. These little-known Warners actors matched Chaplin with truly exciting performances in seminal gangster pictures, breaking through to stardom and remarkable careers. It's hard to choose between Edward G. Robinson's portrait of Enrico Bandello in Mervyn LeRoy's adaptation of W. R. Burnett's *Little Caesar* and James Cagney as Tom Powers in William A. Wellman's equally tough *The Public Enemy.* The first brooding, the other cheery; both are terrific. If I pick Robinson here, it's partly because I know I have two Academy Awards waiting for Cagney later. It's also because I like Cagney even better in such later films as *Angels with Dirty Faces, The Roaring Twenties,* and *White Heat,* when there are interesting shadings to the gangster he created in *The Public Enemy.* On the other hand, *Little Caesar* was Robinson's quintessential gangster role, the one he returned to with few refinements in *The Last Gangster, Little Giant, Key Largo,* and others. If this Rumanian-born Jewish scholar and artist (Emmanuel Goldenberg) were to get an Academy Award for a hoodlum role—and I think he should— then this is the one. If he'd received it from the Academy in 1930–31, it immediately would have thwarted a five-decade injustice: Robinson was the greatest movie actor never even to be nominated for an Academy Award.

Unlike Cagney's equally remorseless Tom Powers in *The Public Enemy,* "Rico" doesn't become a gangster because of a terrible upbringing. He is just drawn to crime. Not for the money, he explains to his close friend and partner, Joe (Douglas Fairbanks, Jr.), but to get the chance to "have your own way or nothing—be somebody." Whereas Cagney's character seemed to enjoy the excitement of crime (which is why many protested the film), Robinson's Rico lusts for power. Rico and Joe go east, where Rico hooks on with a gang run by Sam Vettori (Stanley Fields). Rico is hurt that Joe drifts away, falling in love with his nightclub dancing partner (Glenda Farrell). But the trigger-happy Rico consoles himself by becoming a first-rate criminal. He even shoots the crime commissioner. When Sam can't take the heat, Rico takes over. He becomes increasingly powerful. He kills those who turn against him. When Joe turns him down about becoming his partner, he threatens to kill him and his

It is about to be the end of Edward G. Robinson's Rico in *Little Caesar.*

girlfriend. But he can't do it. Joe's girlfriend squeals to the police. Rico goes into hiding and ends up on skid row. Angry at newspaper reports that he is a coward, he calls the police to threaten them. They track his call and gun him down.

Robinson is frightening as the swaggering, power-hungry Rico, not a character anyone would want to emulate. When he's just a henchman, he scowls constantly, looks at everyone with sideways glances under a pulled-down hat, and is always snarling, talking back, or arguing. His creed is to "shoot first and argue afterwards," but sometimes he reverses it. He talks loud and fast, punctuating any argument with an emphatic "See?" He uses his thumb when he talks, intimidatingly pointing it at others or thumping his chest like a dictator. Only when he becomes powerful is he cheerful, admiring himself in the mirror, getting his picture taken, combing his hair, having a banquet thrown in his honor, smoking cigars, wearing the outfit and pinky ring that a gangster he envied once wore. When Rico tumbles back to the gutter, he becomes a grotesque, primitive, slovenly figure, drinking (which before he never did), grunting, babbling.

Interestingly, as tough as Rico is, it is clearly suggested that he is a homosexual, whose suppressed sexual aggression manifests itself in his shooting men. Early on, he tells Joe that "this game ain't for guys that's *soft*." At other times he implies that guys who are "soft" aren't real men. But when Rico—the rare gangster who has no women around him—gets tears in his eyes and can't shoot Joe, his henchman complains, "You've gone *soft* too." Fleeing from police, his career in crime over because he couldn't shoot Joe, Rico knows what caused his downfall: "That's what I get for liking a guy too much."

Soon after, in the classic finale, Rico is mowed down by machine-gun bullets while standing behind a sign for a movie musical, *Tipsy, Topsy, Turvy*. Lying in the gutter, he defiantly tells the cops that he kept his promise that they'd never hang him. Then he says his famous last words, "Mother of mercy, is this the end of Rico?" How could Robinson have been bypassed for an Oscar in favor of Lionel Barrymore? He even has a better death scene.

▶ BEST ACTRESS

WINNER:
Marie Dressler *(Min and Bill)*
Other Nominees: Marlene Dietrich *(Morocco)*, Irene Dunne *(Cimarron)*, Ann Harding *(Holiday)*, Norma Shearer *(A Free Soul)*

▼

THE BEST CHOICE:
Marlene Dietrich *(Morocco)*
Award-Worthy Runners-Up: Joan Crawford *(Dance, Fools, Dance)*, Marie Dressler *(Min and Bill)*, Sylvia Sidney *(An American Tragedy)*

Morocco was the second of the six remarkable collaborations of German actress Marlene Dietrich and her discoverer, American director Josef von Sternberg. It was the first picture they made in America, at Paramount, and it beat their earlier German-made film, *The Blue Angel*, into American theaters. This was fortunate, in that Americans first saw Dietrich in an essentially sympathetic characterization, which allowed her immediately to establish herself as a *heroine* in their eyes. Her amoral Lola-Lola in *The Blue Angel*, the role that had already made her a star in Germany, might have frightened them away, as had Louise Brooks's brazen Lulu in the earlier German *Pandora's Box*. Also, in *Morocco*, American viewers got to see her play opposite young and handsome Gary Cooper, her one romantic equal in the Sternberg series, rather than the older, physically unappealing Emil Jannings—one of her many mismatches in Sternberg films.

Young, slender (without the baby fat she had as Lola-Lola), elusive, exotic, and erotic, the Dietrich of *Morocco* was a sensation. She made sense of the term *star quality*. It's really hard to explain why Dietrich impresses as an actress in the film—in fact, many critics contend she doesn't. But I think she is perfect because she understood the importance of "presence" on the screen—and knew she had it—and because she conveyed the self-knowledge that her audience was watching a unique star. (She must have gotten a special kick stunning audiences by wearing a white tux while singing, and ending her number by kissing a female stranger on the mouth!) She was indeed unique, personifying both glamour (equaling Garbo) and sinful sex without guilt (equaling Harlow and West).

Dietrich played Amy Jolly, a woman with a past who is the new singer at a Moroccan club frequented by the Foreign Legion. When legionnaire Cooper hushes a rowdy crowd, she is touched—as if no one has ever come to her defense before. She and "ladies' man" Cooper fall in love, but both insist that their relationship will never last. She tries to convince herself she isn't hooked on him—and when they break up she even has an affair with rich Adolphe Menjou to prove it. But she can't control her feelings. When she sees Cooper has carved her name on the table, she knows he loves her too. In the classic final sequence, which has been much debated by femi-

In Josef von Sternberg's *Morocco*, Marlene Dietrich—who is dressed to match the director's decor—chooses dashing Foreign Legionnaire Gary Cooper over wealthy Adolphe Menjou.

nist critics because Dietrich sacrifices all (though not that much, really) for the man she loves, she says goodbye to the understanding Menjou (an unconventional relationship) and, taking off her high-heeled shoes, joins the native girls who follow Cooper's troop into the desert.

In her tux or a skimpy outfit that reveals her long, sexy legs, Dietrich—who seems to be followed around by smoke—is part of Sternberg's wild decor. Interestingly, her outfits and hairstyle change greatly during the film, from exotic to simple, as Amy begins to think of herself more and more as a typical woman. Amy is one of Dietrich's most interesting women, one of her few for Sternberg who becomes softer as the film progresses. Like most of the others she is defiantly independent, having long ago lost her faith in men: "Every time a man has helped me," she tells Cooper, "there has been a price. What's yours?" She sees no reason to deny herself sex, loving men and letting them love her. She has no guilt, and makes no attempt to defend her actions. Her ironic wit/nature comes from knowing that she is condemned by the male-dominated society for using sex to manipulate men when even they know she must use her body to survive. She maintains an air of superiority and a

startling indifference. Amy believes she won't fully give herself to any man, but if one will recognize her courage and accept her past—as Cooper does—she will be loyal and loving to him. She will even follow him into the desert.

In this rare instance the Academy should be praised at least for having nominated Dietrich for Best Actress. They recognized there was much going on beneath the mask, low-key delivery, and bored expression—and that this film marked the beginning of what promised to be an exciting career. (Never again would they give her a nomination, despite other fascinating portrayals in Sternberg's *Blonde Venus, Dishonored, The Scarlet Empress,* and *The Devil Is a Woman.*) Understandably, the Award went to sixty-year-old Marie Dressler for her tough but softhearted waterfront saloonkeeper in George Hill's *Min and Bill.* As always, she played her part with great skill and emotion—I particularly like the scene where she jealously beats up her oafish beau, Wallace Berry—but her part was one-dimensional. Who wants to see this great, hilarious character actress play a sourpuss for an entire film?

1931–32

▶ BEST PICTURE

WINNER:
Grand Hotel (MGM; Edmund Goulding)
Other Nominees: *Arrowsmith, Bad Girl, The Champ, Five Star Final, One Hour With You, Shanghai Express, Smiling Lieutenant*

▼

THE BEST CHOICE:
Scarface: The Shame of a Nation (United Artists-Atlantic; Howard Hawks)
Award-Worthy Runner-Up: *Grand Hotel* (Edmund Goulding)

There were seven other nominations for Best Picture of 1931–32, but with the exception of Josef von Sternberg's delirious Dietrich drama, *Shanghai Express,* all were dwarfed by *Grand Hotel.* MGM's first all-star cast film is not on a par with the studio's scintillating 1933 comedy *Dinner at Eight*—whose cast also included John and Lionel Barrymore and Wallace Beery—but was an instant Hollywood classic, the ideal Academy selection for Best Picture. (However, when one considers its stellar cast and lavish production values, it's odd that *Grand Hotel* wasn't even nominated in other categories.) Adapted from Vicki Baum's novel and play, *Grand Hotel* is pretty hokey stuff to be sure, but what movie lover is not captivated by the shining "star" performances of John Barrymore, Greta Garbo, and Joan Crawford? Barrymore's gentlemanly, penniless baron-turned-hotel-thief is the pivotal character who inspires depressed dancer Garbo to rekindle her artistic flame, restores cynical stenographer Crawford's faith in men, becomes the first friend to the lonely, dying Lionel Barrymore, and causes the downfall of Wallace Beery's ruthless businessman; a thief who gives so much of himself can't survive. Lionel's character grates on my nerves and Beery struggles with a German accent, but just watching Garbo, Crawford, and John Barrymore interact on screen is quite exciting.

But for real, reel-to-reel excitement, no film better filled the bill than Howard Hawks's *Scarface: The Shame of a Nation,* the best and most ferocious of the gangster cycle. In previous years Academy voters shied away from gangster films because they thought it inappropriate to honor pictures that were being attacked in the press and by civics groups for glamorizing crime. And since censors had delayed *Scarface*'s release for two years and ordered alterations, the timid Academy safely ignored it, giving no nominations to the best picture of the year.

Certainly civics groups didn't think kindly of the numerous spectacular killings in *Scarface,* including a St. Valentine's Day Massacre scene (cleverly shot by Lee Garmes so that those rubbed out lie dead under giant carved *X*'s); gangster kingpin Boris Karloff being shot while bowling a strike (the final pin spins around before toppling over); and an incredible montage of violence as Paul Muni's Tony Camonte takes over the city's boot-legged liquor trade. In fact, this film could be an effective NRA ad for tommy guns and explosives (though the NRA wouldn't appreciate the film's contention that crime escalates for the simple reason that guns are manufactured, making them accessible to criminals). Nevertheless, it is one of the least glamorous visions of criminals and crime in movie picture history. It anticipates *GoodFellas.* There is no need for the studio-imposed scene in which a newspaper editor talks about the evils of crime to a civics

As the title character in Howard Hawks's *Scarface,* Paul Muni, with gun moll Karen Morley and gunman George Raft at his side, takes control of the mob.

group—shades of *Reefer Madness*!—or even (though I like it) an angry police detective sneering, "When I think what goes on in the minds of these lice, I want to vomit."

The gangster world Hawks presents is unsavory, sordid, and not enticing—although, I admit, males might be drawn to the beautiful, trampy women played by Ann Dvorak and Karen Morley (two of the great unsung actresses of the period). The gangsters themselves are childlike, ignorant brutes who could stand no other company but their own and play dangerously stupid games—either rubbing out each other or being killed by police. We don't want to be like them and we don't want to walk the streets when they're around. They may be shooting at each other, but Hawks's frame is filled with innocent bystanders.

Paul Muni is fabulous as the ruthless, fearless, crude Tony Camonte, who heads the gangster army of Johnny Lovo (Osgood Perkins, Anthony's father). He and his coin-flipping friend Guino (George Raft) do away with Lovo's competition. Tony makes a play for Lovo's sharp-tongued mistress, Poppy (Karen Morley), who is too smart for him but is turned on by his reckless bravura. "I like Johnny," he tells her, "but I like you more." Still, Tony is more attached to his adventurous eighteen-year-old sister, Cesca (Ann Dvorak), whom he forbids to date. Lovo fears Tony is muscling in on his territory, so he tries to eliminate him. Tony foils the plot and has Guino kill Lovo. Now Tony is the boss. When he returns from abroad, he finds Cesca with Guino. He kills Guino, not realizing they were married in his absence. Cesca tearfully orders him away from her. Crushed by her rejection, Tony returns to his barricaded apartment. The police, who have learned of Guino's murder, surround the building. Cesca slips into the apartment to kill Tony. But she acknowledges their special bond—"You're me and I'm you; it's always been that way"—and decides to fight the police with him. They are both joyous, fighting to the death together. But she is mortally wounded and he turns coward when he knows he'll be left alone. She is disappointed in her brother, and dies. Tony begs the cops not to shoot him, but when he tries to escape they mow him down.

Ben Hecht wrote the no-punches-pulled screenplay for the Howard Hughes production. He based his crime family on the Borgias so that he had a model for corruption, cruelty, power lust, and decadence. Instead of giving Tony the brother he had in the Armitage Trail source novel, he gave him a sluttish sister, patterned on Lucretia Borgia, so he could introduce an incest theme. The unique, sexy-eyed Ann Dvorak almost steals the film, just as her kid with "grown-up ideas" reclaims her brother from Poppy. The censors were so interested in gangsters that they didn't take a close enough look at Dvorak's suggestive dancing, listen to her double entendres (approaching Guino, she says, "I suppose you need an organ grinder to work with"), notice how her Cesca and Muni's Tony look at each other, or pay attention to Cesca's references to Tony's unbrotherly love for her.

Hecht and Hawks got material for their film from actual Chicago criminals. In fact, George Raft was working for the mob when Hawks hired him. Al Capone, who was the model for Tony and many other movie gangsters, supposedly loved the film and owned his own print. He was one of the lucky ones who could see it. This amazing film was withdrawn from release and didn't resurface until 1979. It had lost none of its power.

► BEST ACTOR

WINNERS:
Wallace Beery *(The Champ)* and **Fredric March** *(Dr. Jekyll and Mr. Hyde)*
Other Nominee: Alfred Lunt *(The Guardsman)*

▼

THE BEST CHOICE:
Paul Muni *(Scarface: The Shame of a Nation)*
Award-Worthy Runners-Up: Wallace Beery *(The Champ)*, Colin Clive *(Frankenstein)*, Boris Karloff *(Frankenstein)*, Fredric March *(Dr. Jekyll and Mr. Hyde)*, Edward G. Robinson *(Five-Star Final)*

For 1931–32, for the only time in Academy history, there was a tie in the Best Actor race, with Fredric March (who actually received one more vote) sharing the honor with Wallace Beery. Between the two I'd give a slight edge to Beery. He was at his most irresistible in *The Champ,* a well-played, though soppy, comedy-laced drama about a boozy has-been boxer whose one redeeming quality is his love for his little son (Jackie Cooper), who adores him. March had the advantage of playing two personalities, if only one character, in Rouben Mamoulian's innovative adult horror film, *Dr. Jekyll and Mr. Hyde.* He would have been more deserving if he'd spent the entire picture as the sadistic, terrifying, monkeylike Hyde—can anyone explain why the serum results in Hyde's having crooked fangs?—but he had too much time to be bland as the *good* doctor. Alfred Lunt, the other nominee, was amusing as the jealous husband in *The Guardsman,* opposite his wife and theatrical partner, Lynn Fontanne,

His incestuous desires unleashed, Paul Muni slaps sister Ann Dvorak for going out with men in *Scarface*.

but he, Fontanne, and the picture grow wearisome. Oddly, in this year when there were eight nominations for Best Picture, there were only three for Best Actor and Actress. The most unfortunate slight was Paul Muni, who gave the performance of his career in *Scarface*.

A veteran of the Yiddish Theater and Broadway, the former Muni Weisenfreund had made a strong impression in two films of the late twenties (receiving an Oscar nomination for his debut in *The Valiant*) but he disliked the new medium and returned to New York. Hawks coaxed him back to films. An extremely serious actor, Muni must have liked the challenge of using a thick accent to play an Italian immigrant, and though he wouldn't get to don a heavy beard, as he would in several of his Warners bios, he did get to sport a long scar on his left cheek. With sloped shoulders and unflattering slicked-down hair that is parted on the right, he at times resembles Fredric March's Hyde, without the monkey makeup.

But Tony doesn't worry about his looks. In fact, he thinks he's handsome, even more so because of his scar (he says it's a war wound, but he got it from some dame in a bar). Muni plays his character as if he were a cocky punk teenager. Unsophisticated and immature (like all the other gangsters), he's self-impressed, overrates his intelligence (he is proud to use the word *disillusioned*), boasts nonstop, acts tough, doesn't listen to his mother (he even covers her mouth with his hand), and is always looking for a good time, either with the boys (out killing people or attending the play *Rain*), or with some sexy female. Machine guns are toys ("Get out of my way, I'm gonna spit!"), women are meat ("I'm not hungry—except for you," he tells Karen Morley's Poppy). He likes anything that is "hot." He's unsophisticated yet thinks he dresses well (he brags that he has three suits identical to the ugly one he wears and that he has a different shirt

for each day; he wears flashy robes); he has a gaudy apartment, but thinks it's the best: "How do you like this place?" he asks the smarter, unimpressed Poppy. "How do you like the view here? How do you like this place?" Then, touching the bed, he says, not so innocently, "You like it?" Poppy and his incestuous sister, Cesca (Ann Dvorak), are attracted to Tony's energy and fearlessness, which compensate for his childishness.

Tony is usually having a good time, and at those moments we fear his recklessness (being childish, he thinks he's invincible). But when he suddenly shifts from being carefree to being serious, he is downright creepy: when he stops his jovial flirting to make a definite move on Poppy; when he sees Cesca embracing some man and goes berserk; and when he stops smiling and starts contemplating his boss Lovo's impending death (knowing Lovo is lying to him about not having been the one to plot his ambush)—Muni's eyes, face, and tone of voice quickly change and we realize what a frightening, depraved individual Tony is.

Muni saves the best for last, when he and Cesca embrace to confirm their perverse bond and they excitedly make a last stand together against the police outside. He has the furtive look of a wounded but dangerous, trapped animal—he would later use a similar look in *I Am a Fugitive from a Chain Gang* and as a militant miner in *Black Fury*—but he also laughs excitedly because he is with his sister, she loves him as he does her, and he can show off to her by firing his machine gun at the cops. Tony is always at his best when he has an audience. So when Cesca is killed and there's no one left to admire him, the immature adult acts like a baby or spoiled little boy who suddenly finds himself without toys or playmates and realizes he is about to be punished for the first time.

▶ BEST ACTRESS

WINNER:
Helen Hayes *(The Sin of Madelon Claudet)*
Other Nominees: Marie Dressler *(Emma)*, Lynn Fontanne *(The Guardsman)*

▼

THE BEST CHOICE:
Joan Crawford *(Grand Hotel)*
Award-Worthy Runners-Up: Constance Bennett *(What Price Hollywood?)*, Marlene Dietrich *(Shanghai Express)*, Marie Dressler *(Emma)*, Ann Dvorak *(Scarface: The Shame of a Nation)*, Norma Shearer *(Private Lives)*, Barbara Stanwyck *(Miracle Woman)*

In 1931 Helen Hayes made her screen debut in a film scripted by her husband, Charles MacArthur, *The Sin of Madelon Claudet,* and Lynn Fontanne made her sound film debut opposite her husband, Alfred Lunt, in *The Guardsman.* The prestige-conscious Academy gave both these legends of the theater encouraging Best Actress nominations for their respective attempts to break into the movies. Hayes won the Academy Award, probably because she starred in a heavy drama while Fontanne's film was a comedy, a genre the Academy frowned upon. Also, it's likely that the award was an inducement for her to continue making films at Louis B. Mayer's MGM, rather than return to Broadway where she was happier. As in most of her films Hayes gives a fine, emotional, if too theatrical, performance in MacArthur's tearjerker. But there was no way she could have overcome the now dated, soapy plot about a woman who sinks into sin in order to secretly pay for her illegitimate son to attend medical school. My choice for Best Actress is Joan Crawford for *Grand Hotel,* MGM's first all-star-cast drama. Film historians usually write only one or two lines about Crawford when discussing the classic picture, preferring to go into more detail about Greta Garbo, John Barrymore, or Lionel Barrymore (few liked Wallace Beery). But it's Crawford who captures my attention every time. I think this is her most appealing role.

In Vicki Baum's depressing drama third-billed Crawford plays Flaemmchen, a poor, ambitious free-lance stenographer who picks up needed money by sleeping with her employers. She comes to Berlin's luxurious Grand Hotel to type for a rich, ruthless, unattractive industrial magnate, Preysing (Wallace Beery). Although married, he is attracted to the pretty stenographer. She doesn't like being with Preysing, but takes comfort in knowing that another hotel guest is a suave, handsome Baron (John Barrymore) who shows an interest in her. She can tell he is a kind man. The Baron even befriends the lonely Kringelein (Lionel Barrymore), an elderly dying man who is having his last fling. But she doesn't know that the Baron is heavily in debt and is planning to steal from a visiting Russian ballerina, Grusinskaya (Greta Garbo). Grusinskaya discovers him in her room, but he is so honestly charming that she is thrilled with his presence. They immediately fall in love, and he inspires her to dance at a high level that will return her to great

popularity. Unable to steal from her, the Baron takes Kringelein's gambling winnings. But he returns the money. Flaemmchen still thinks the Baron is nice, even after he tells her he loves another. To please the Baron, she dances with Kringelein and makes the sick man happy. But it's her choice to take a room adjoining Preysing's and to accompany him to England. Before they can sleep together, Preysing catches the Baron in his room and beats him to death. Preysing is arrested. Grusinskaya goes to catch her train, expecting the Baron will meet her at the station. Both grieving over the Baron, Kringelein and Flaemmchen find comfort with each other. They decide to travel together on Kringelein's money. He even seems to have regained his health.

Crawford was already a major star when she made

In her most dramatic scene in *Grand Hotel* the horrified Joan Crawford discovers that Wallace Beery has just killed benevolent thief John Barrymore.

Grand Hotel, but this was the picture that proved she could both hold her own with the movie elite and be taken seriously as a dramatic actress. Her working-class young woman is, as Stephen Harvey points out in *Joan Crawford*, "fundamentally not different from the characters she had played in *Paid* [1930] and *Possessed* [1931]; she is an ambitious stenographer who embarks on a series of loveless liaisons with wealthy admirers in order to get what she wants. Buoyed by the expert coaching of her old friend, [director] Edmund Goulding, Crawford's usual knowing chic is tempered by a gawky youthfulness which makes her rather sordid character both understandable and appealing." As with her earlier characters, there is a softness under Flaemmchen's tough, wise-to-the-ways-of-men-and-life exterior. The inspirational Baron, who brings out the best in Grusinskaya and Kringelein, does the same for Flaemmchen. She reveals her goodness when she dances with Kringelein at the Baron's request; she shows her appreciation for the goodness of both men, when it's apparent—from her knowing smile when we first see her—that she hasn't met many nice guys in her line of work.

I like most of Crawford's early film roles, but this is her first performance that isn't erratic. In her movements, her sexy hip-out stance, her line readings, and her expressions, Crawford had never been more natural, more honest, and this is gratifying in a film full of grandstanding actors. Real feelings come through, especially in the horrifying moment she discovers John Barrymore's corpse.

Crawford is extremely sexy, with youthful energy, huge eyes and sensual backward glances, a posed slim and angular body, and a robe that is half open. But there is something much more than sexual magnetism at work. What makes Crawford so memorable in *Grand Hotel* is her star quality. Especially in those close-ups that rival Garbo's, Joan Crawford actually *glows*.

1932–33

▶ BEST PICTURE

WINNER:
Cavalcade (Fox; Frank Lloyd)
Other Nominees: *A Farewell to Arms, 42nd Street, I Am a Fugitive from a Chain Gang, Lady for a Day, Little Women, The Private Life of Henry VIII, She Done Him Wrong, Smilin' Thru, State Fair*

▼

THE BEST CHOICE:
King Kong (RKO; Merian C. Cooper and Ernest B. Schoedsack)
Award-Worthy Runners-Up: *Dinner at Eight* (George Cukor), *Duck Soup* (Leo McCarey), *42nd Street* (Lloyd Bacon), *I Am a Fugitive from a Chain Gang* (Mervyn LeRoy), *Queen Christina* (Rouben Mamoulian), *Trouble in Paradise* (Ernst Lubitsch)

The awards for 1932–33 covered the longest period of time in Academy history—seventeen months—so the record number of ten films nominated for Best Picture was justifiable. The decisive winner was *Cavalcade,* for which Frank Lloyd also won the Best Director award. An episodic Noel Coward adaptation about the changes in the household of a British couple (Diana Wynyard and Clive Brook) between 1899 and 1932, *Cavalcade* has fine performances (by an all-British cast), charm, sophistication, and moments of heartbreak. But other than *Smilin' Thru* and *State Fair* it is probably the most forgotten of the nominees and the least screened of Best Picture winners. In fact, while *Cavalcade* has drifted into obscurity (at least in America), many more-deserving films not nominated that were released between August 1, 1932,

and December 31, 1933, have gone on to become classics and/or cult favorites. These include five great films—*King Kong, Duck Soup, Dinner at Eight, Queen Christina,* and *Trouble in Paradise*—as well as *Gold Diggers of 1933, Footlight Parade, Design for Living* (another Noel Coward adaptation), *The Mummy, Back Street, The Invisible Man, Red Dust, One-Way Passage, The Bitter Tea of General Yen, Christopher Strong,* and *Blood Money.*

The cream of this extraordinary crop—which I think rivals that of 1939—is Merian C. Cooper and Ernest B. Schoedsack's *King Kong,* the greatest, most popular, most entertaining, most influential, and most fascinating horror-fantasy film ever made. Because of its genre it was snubbed by the elitist Academy—a Kong-size blunder.

The familiar plot: Gung-ho documentary filmmaker

The natives of Skull Island experience the wrath of Kong when the giant ape comes after his escaped human bride, Fay Wray, in *King Kong.*

Carl Denham (Robert Armstrong) hires penniless Ann Darrow (Fay Wray) to be his first female star. They travel by boat to the uncharted Skull Island, where Denham wants to shoot his movie. Ann falls in love with first mate Jack Driscoll (Bruce Cabot). Hostile natives kidnap Ann and take her into the jungle beyond their great wall, chaining her as a sacrifice to their god, Kong. A dark, fierce, giant ape, Kong is pleased with his bride and takes the screaming Ann deep into the prehistoric jungle, killing most of the crew who follow. While Kong fights a pterodactyl, Driscoll and Ann escape. Kong angrily gives chase, breaking through the wall and killing many natives. Denham and the surviving crew members knock him out with gas bombs. He brings Kong back to New York, where the shackled gorilla is exhibited as "The Eighth Wonder of the World." The king has become a slave. When photographers take pictures of Ann, Kong breaks free and goes on a rampage through the city. He grabs Ann out of a hotel window and carries her up the Empire State Building. He is mortally wounded by machine gun bullets fired from airplanes. He gently puts Ann down, and Driscoll takes her to safety. The mighty Kong falls to his death. Denham says it wasn't the air-

planes that killed Kong: "It was beauty killed the beast." (The movie is structurally compelling, with every scene that takes place on Skull Island having a corresponding scene in New York. For instance, a giant snake is replaced by a snakelike elevated subway; the pterodactyl by airplanes; the mountain lair by the Empire State Building; and so on. Only, on the island it is Ann who is in chains, while in New York it is Kong.)

King Kong is a brilliantly imaginative, thrilling adventure film, with awesome special effects/stop-motion animation by the legendary Willis O'Brien; a splendid, emotion-manipulating silent-movie-like score by Max Steiner; exciting monsters; amazing scenes of destruction and other classic sequences, including Kong's death; and enjoyable performances by Armstrong, Cabot, and the sexy Fay Wray, the best screamer in Hollywood. It can—and is—enjoyed for being marvelous, escapist entertainment. But to have become such a part of the American psyche, it had to have been much more. It interests us so much because it exists on so many levels. It's a complex film that has been interpreted as being everything from a parable about an uneducated black from the country who is humbled and finally destroyed by the big city to an indictment against "bring 'em back alive" big game hunters to, as Harry Geduld and Ronald Gottesman suggest, "a white man's sick fantasy of the Negro's lust to ravish white women," to a parable about the Great Depression. Such readings do make sense.

I interpret *King Kong* as being, after the "realistic" opening in which Denham meets and propositions Ann, Denham's sexual dream. As soon as he and his first female star begin their voyage the film becomes dream-like—we have entered Denham's subconscious.

Denham is a he-man who travels the world with other men. Although virile, he excludes women from his life because he fears they'll strip him of his masculinity: "Some hard-boiled egg gets a look at a pretty face and he cracks up and goes sappy." He insists that his relationship with Ann will be all business—that's how he'd like it. But he has fallen for Ann at first sight. He takes her to Skull (as in cerebral) Island. It has an expressionistic landscape—watery, overgrown, reptile infested, riddled with caves. It is in this fantasized sexual terrain that Kong appears. Kong is Denham's alter ego, the manifestation of his suppressed "animalistic" lust for Ann. Denham unleashes Kong to physically challenge Driscoll and to perform sexually with Ann.

It is not an oversight on the part of the directors that the only time we see Denham and Kong in the same shot on the island is when he puts the beast to sleep (successfully suppressing his sexual desires); in New York we see them together only when Kong is in shackles and when he is dead. When the two aren't seen together, Kong is on the loose, following the directions of some external force, which is, I believe, Denham's subconscious. Denham was protective of Ann in New York and Kong fills that role of protector on the island, saving her from monsters and other men. However, Kong also has sexual designs on Ann, which Denham feebly controls at first—

for instance, he conjures up a giant snake to attack and strangle Kong. In New York, however, the angry Kong attacks the snakelike elevated subway, indicating Denham has lost control. Then Kong takes Ann up the world's biggest phallic symbol: the Empire State Building. Having no penis (is impotence the reason Denham avoids women?), Kong can only commit symbolic intercourse with Ann. But he has carried out the goal of Denham's subconscious. Denham's final words confirm that it is he and not Kong who loved Ann. Earlier Kong had grabbed the wrong woman from the hotel and only knew it was not Ann by her hair color and by smell—he couldn't recognize her face. Denham, not Kong, realizes Ann is a beauty. Once Kong has served his purpose, Denham can let him die. Denham's sexual self can surface at last and he no longer has to enjoy sex vicariously through a surrogate. (In the hastily made 1933 sequel, *Son of Kong*, when Armstrong's Denham romances Helen Mack, the gorilla need not be and is not a sexual being.) Driscoll gets Ann, but Denham got her first.

▶ BEST ACTOR

WINNER:
Charles Laughton *(The Private Life of Henry VIII)*
Other Nominees: Leslie Howard *(Berkeley Square)*, Paul Muni *(I Am a Fugitive from a Chain Gang)*

▼

THE BEST CHOICE:
Charles Laughton *(The Private Life of Henry VIII)*
Award-Worthy Runners-Up: Charles Laughton *(Island of Lost Souls)*, Groucho Marx *(Duck Soup)*, Paul Muni *(I Am a Fugitive from a Chain Gang)*, William Powell *(One-Way Passage)*, Claude Rains *(The Invisible Man)*, Paul Robeson *(The Emperor Jones)*, Spencer Tracy *(The Power and the Glory)*

Although tempted to give an Alternate Oscar to Groucho Marx for his one-of-a-kind portrayal of the dictator of Freedonia, Rufus T. Firefly, in *Duck Soup,* I instead choose Charles Laughton for his one-of-a-kind portrayal of the sixteenth-century British monarch in *The Private Life of Henry VIII,* thereby agreeing with the Academy's Best Actor selection for the first time. The one performance that rivaled Laughton's Henry VIII that year was Laughton's sadistic scientist (whom he based on his dentist) in the gruesome *Island of Lost Souls.*

The Private Life of Henry VIII was the first British film to receive much distribution or acclaim in America. It was Laughton's tenth film distributed in England and America, but the first that earned him international attention. He became the first British actor to win an Academy Award and was soon in demand in Hollywood. Interestingly, Irving Thalberg cast him as Norma Shearer's cold-hearted father in *The Barretts of Wimpole Street* after admiring his work in this film. I would have cast him in a much more sympathetic role, for Laughton's king, though flawed and at times heartless, is by the film's end quite endearing.

Alexander Korda's delightful film downplays politics and ignores Henry's troubles with the Church, and instead concentrates on Henry's marriages. Henry's search for happiness with a faithful, loving wife becomes a sad, frustrating ordeal. He beheads his unfaithful second wife, Anne Boleyn (Merle Oberon), and fifth wife, Catherine Howard (Binnie Barnes); divorces his first wife, Catherine of Aragon (we never see her because screenwriters Lajos Biro and Arthur Wimperis dismiss her as being too respectable to be of interest) and fourth wife, Anne of Cleves (Elsa Lanchester); loses his third wife, Jane Seymour (Wendy Barrie), during childbirth; and, in his old age, settles down with caring but henpecking Katherine Parr (Everley Gregg), complaining to us in the film's last line that "the best of them is the worst."

From marriage to marriage (with several scenes of courtship thrown in), the tone of the film shifts from sad to serious to ironic to, simply, funny. Korda and Laughton empathize with the human, typical-husband/suitor side of the king, whose wife may be unfaithful or overbearing or beat him at his best game (Anne of Cleves wipes him out at cards, even outcheating him). We can relate to the fat fifty-year-old who breaks into tears upon learning that his beloved Catherine Howard has been sleeping with his handsome young friend (Robert Donat as Thomas Culpepper)—although we are aghast that he can be laughing minutes after learning that the sweet Jane Seymour has died—and we can sympathize with him for trying to impress his young wife by proving he can still outwrestle anyone in his kingdom . . . and almost dying in the process.

Because he didn't have to worry about overacting, Laughton was best at playing bigger-than-life characters who are at the center of activity in their worlds. As the loud and lusty monarch who is the *only* figure of importance in his court, he is a joy to watch. His fat, bearded king looks as if he's stepped from a portrait of Henry VIII—he could serve as the model for kings in card decks. He poses, lewdly sits, and glides about with pudgy legs (in tights) spread wide. Whenever he moves, his subjects also move, so that he is always at the center of the action, dominating the frame. He has more energy than anyone (though he slows down when he's older) and, in his court, is the only person with anything significant or funny to say. He puts fear into everyone, yet it seems that everyone from his barber to his minister (Cromwell) chances to say things that annoy or humble him. He is constantly exasperated. At times Laughton's king is almost a clownish figure, as in the feast scene in which he smashes his capon with his fist (squirting those nearby), rips it apart with his hands, eats with his fingers, keeps his mouth open, burps, tosses the bones behind him, and bellows upon being served even more food, "Am I the king or a breeding bull?" We also laugh at him when he courts pretty Catherine Howard, combing his hair and trying to tiptoe past the guards to her room, like a shy college freshman trying to sneak into a women's dorm. But when he aggressively makes his move on Catherine Howard in her chamber, we see that he is no jester, and no innocent.

Next to the capon-eating scene the movie's most famous sequence is the hilarious card game Henry loses to Anne of Cleves, whom he married for diplomacy ("The things I've done for England"). Wanting an immediate divorce so she can be with the man she loves, Anne (wonderfully played by Laughton's wife, Elsa Lanchester) is deliberately obnoxious and distorts her face so that he thinks her too ugly to make love to. There is terrific interplay between Laughton and Lanchester, equal to that between Judy Holliday and Broderick Crawford during the rummy game in *Born Yesterday*. After the furious, yelling Henry pays her off and agrees to divorce her, they become quick friends. He kisses her forehead but just before he kisses her lips, she distorts her face and he does a revolted double take and backs away.

I also like a second, more serious scene that takes

Charles Laughton's proud king is outsmarted by wife Anne of Cleves, played by the actor's wife, Elsa Lanchester, in the funniest segment of *The Private Life of Henry VIII*.

place on a bed. Henry tucks in Catherine Howard, not realizing she will soon rise and sneak off to Culpepper. He is extremely happy with his marriage and this has caused him to mellow considerably. He speaks of other countries trying to draw him into wars. But he tells Catherine that he wants peace, peace, peace. She clearly has other things on her mind, so he apologizes for boring her with his problems, kisses her, and leaves. We realize that Henry, whom we thought stupid at the film's beginning, is the only person in the world with sense. And we realize—as we would with Charles Foster Kane in *Citizen Kane*—that only when feeling loved can Henry, or anyone else, fulfill his potential for greatness.

▶ BEST ACTRESS

WINNER:
Katharine Hepburn *(Morning Glory)*
Other Nominees: May Robson *(Lady for a Day)*, Diana Wynyard *(Cavalcade)*

▼

THE BEST CHOICE:
Greta Garbo *(Queen Christina)*
Award-Worthy Runners-Up: Joan Blondell *(Gold Diggers of 1933)*, Marlene Dietrich *(Blonde Venus)*, Irene Dunne *(Back Street)*, Kay Francis *(One-Way Passage)*, Kay Francis *(Trouble in Paradise)*, Jean Harlow *(Red Dust)*, Miriam Hopkins *(Trouble in Paradise)*, Barbara Stanwyck *(The Bitter Tea of General Yen)*

Katharine Hepburn burst onto the scene in 1932 and won a Best Actress Academy Award for 1932–33 for her third role, as an aspiring young actress in *Morning Glory*. Today, with numerous remarkable characterizations behind her, Hepburn's performance in *Morning Glory*

seems like one of her worst. She played her part just as her brittle, affected character would have.

While Charles Laughton won the Best Actor Award for *The Private Life of Henry VIII*, Greta Garbo also performed royally playing royalty, the queen of seventeenth-century Sweden. Unfortunately neither the remarkable *Queen Christina* nor the actress received Academy Award consideration. The film was released in late December 1933 and may not have played in Hollywood long enough to qualify for the 1932–33 ballots—which, then, doesn't explain its also going unnominated for 1934, but why quibble? I will give Garbo the Best Actress Award she was always denied, and give it to her not for her more heralded *Camille* and *Ninotchka,* but for her finest performance in her finest film.

Beautifully directed by Rouben Mamoulian, the film tells of events that lead to Christina's abdication. Tired of her male advisers clamoring for war and conquest and urging her into marriage, Christina slips away for a brief holiday. Snowbound in a tavern, she agrees to share a room with a handsome Spanish ambassador, Don Antonio (Garbo insisted that her most famous silent-film lover, John Gilbert, whose career had stalled, replace Laurence Olivier, who was originally slated for the role). Seeing her in pants and carrying a sword, he thinks she is a young man. He finds out differently. They spend days making love, and their romance continues in the palace. Their affair causes an uproar in Sweden and in the palace—her slighted ex-lover (Ian Keith) challenges Don Antonio to a duel—and Christina must choose between Don Antonio and her crown.

Garbo evidently had great affinity for Christina, a part written for her by her friend Salka Viertel. Here is a woman who is smart enough, strong enough, independent enough, and has enough integrity to stand firmly against those male advisers who try to pressure her into making bad decisions. Yet her ability to be a leader doesn't take away from her femininity. An enlightened despot, she reads (laughing at Molière's wit), loves art, desires knowledge from around the world. Although she has been successful at waging wars, she feels compassion for her people and desires peace. A romantic, she believes Don Antonio can love her for eternity. Interestingly, she abdicates not because she is incapable of doing a man's job, but because she's no longer allowed to rule in the best way—as a *woman,* with a distinctly *female* brain, heart, and instincts.

Garbo gives a marvelous performance. Never did she display such wit, intelligence, energy, or passion in a part; never did she invest so much of herself in a character. There are so many moments to be treasured: Christina rising in the morning and washing her face with the snow of her window ledge; Christina, who is posing as a man, standing on a tavern bar and settling an argument among customers about the number of lovers their queen has had—she cheers them by telling them a number higher than anyone expected; Christina silently walking around the chamber which she has shared with Don Antonio, memorizing everything with her fingers, eyes, and body; Christina sitting alone at night on her throne for the last time. Just watching Garbo move across the screen—which she could do better than anyone—is a treat. But there is no better moment in the entire film than the last shot of Christina standing still on the ship heading for Spain. William Daniels's camera slowly zooms in for a lengthy close-up of her face as she looks out to sea. Mamoulian told Garbo to clear her mind of all thoughts. Just looking at Garbo's clear eyes and beautiful face is an overwhelmingly emotional experience that only the cinema and this great star could provide. This might be the greatest last shot in movie history.

While her anxious advisers and soldiers look on, Greta Garbo's Swedish queen confronts her angry subjects in *Queen Christina.*

1934

▶ BEST PICTURE

WINNER:
It Happened One Night (Columbia; Frank Capra)
Other Nominees: *The Barretts of Wimpole Street, Cleopatra, Flirtation Walk, The Gay Divorcée, Here Comes the Navy, The House of Rothschild, Imitation of Life, One Night of Love, The Thin Man, Viva Villa, The White Parade*

▼

THE BEST CHOICE:
The Scarlet Empress (Paramount; Josef von Sternberg)
Award-Worthy Runners-Up: *The Gay Divorcée* (Mark Sandrich), *It Happened One Night* (Frank Capra), *It's a Gift* (Norman Z. McLeod), *Twentieth Century* (Howard Hawks)

At the Academy Awards ceremony honoring pictures from 1934, which was the first time films were chosen from a single year, a single picture swept the major awards. Although it was intended to be a small picture by Harry Cohn's minor Columbia Studios, *It Happened One Night* was voted Best Picture, and Frank Capra won as Best Director, Clark Gable and Claudette Colbert won the Best Acting awards for their portrayals of a hard-boiled reporter and a flighty runaway heiress, and Robert Riskin received the award for Best Adapted Screenplay. Capra's classic is usually called the first screwball comedy but the humor is surprisingly controlled, with the squabbling couple only wild at the beginning. Perhaps Howard Hawks's lunatic *Twentieth Century,* in which John Barrymore's theatrical producer and Carole Lombard's snobby actress never stop their sexual battle, should be regarded as the first screwball comedy. In any case, it's the equal of *It Happened One Night* and as deserving of the Best Picture award. However, the best comedy of the year was W. C. Fields's masterpiece, *It's a Gift,* a unique, surreal work that couldn't possibly pave the way for a new genre. The sequence in which Fields tries to sleep on his porch at 4:30 A.M., despite a series of distractions—including an insurance salesman who wants to sell a policy to Carl LaFong ("capital *L,* small *a,* capital *F,* small *o,* small *n,* small *g.* La Fong, Carl LaFong")—is among the most hilarious scenes in the cinema.

My heart is with the Fields film, but since it's more a great vehicle for a great comic than it is great cinema, I think the better choice for Best Picture of 1934 is *The Scarlet Empress,* Josef von Sternberg's bizarre—some would say berserk—historical drama about the rise of Catherine the Great (Marlene Dietrich), "Russia's most powerful and sinister empress." It was released when moviegoers had tired of Sternberg-Dietrich collaborations and it failed at the box office. Critics didn't like it either. However, over the years its status has improved,

first gaining recognition for its amazing visuals and then for having been the rare early film to have made the correlation between sexual politics and political power.

Dietrich's young, intimidated Princess Sophia of Anhalt-Zerbst arrives in brutal, backward Russia to marry and bear a son to Grand Duke Peter (Sam Jaffe), heir to the throne of his aunt, Empress Elizabeth (Louise Dresser). Elizabeth changes Sophia's name to Catherine, changes her religion, and sends her mother away. Peter is a perverted half-wit, so Catherine is glad that he's preoccupied with his mistress (Ruthelma Stevens) and playing with toy soldiers. They despise each other and

Marlene Dietrich's Catherine is not pleased to be married to Sam Jaffe's demented Grand Duke Peter in Josef von Sternberg's delirious historical drama, *The Scarlet Empress.*

never consummate the marriage. Catherine secretly takes lovers. She gives birth to a son, which infuriates Peter because he knows it's not his. When Peter assumes the throne after Elizabeth's death, he plans on executing Catherine. But Catherine is prepared, stating confidently, "I think I have weapons that are far more powerful than any political machine." She becomes queen as Peter is killed in a coup d'état that would have been impossible if she hadn't won over the members of the court and the military by sexual means.

Between the release of *Sunrise* and *Citizen Kane* no American film had more dazzling visuals. Sternberg worked closely with cinematographer Bert Glennon; Paramount costume designer Travis Banton; and Swiss artist Peter Balbusch, Hans Dreier, and Richard Kollorsz on the amazing Byzantine sets—with giant wooden doors and frightening statues—that were meant to be "re-creations" of the Russian court. Other than when Peter (Jaffe is ideal as the demented ruler) curses and spits at his aunt's corpse, the most memorable sequences have no dialogue, just music and sound effects to heighten the impact of the extraordinary images: the wedding ceremony; the wedding banquet; and the sweeping finale when Catherine and the soldiers ride into the castle, she rings the bell signifying she is queen, and Peter is strangled.

Yet Sternberg's most perverse film is far more than the "relentless excursion in style" he thought it to be. It is about a woman who decides she no longer wants to passively follow the limited life's course set out for her by others and turns to an ambitious pursuit of power. After Catherine provides the male baby that she was ordered to conceive by Elizabeth, Catherine stops being bossed around and becomes the familiar Dietrich movie character. She lives by her own code and logic, using her wits and her body (enjoying the sex that will bring her great rewards), and manipulates those men who once thought they were controlling her. The men realize that she is turning the tables on them, yet they respect her for so shrewdly using sex to save herself and to achieve power—in other Sternberg films men resent Dietrich's women for doing the same thing. Dietrich is perfect as Catherine; she is fearless, sardonic, indifferent, playful, ambitious, and as naughtily flirtatious as Mae West. Her naughty innocent—ripe for seduction—becomes a shrewd libertine, and then, in her triumph, a monster who relishes both her power and the means by which she obtained it. She may be crazed, but we forgive her, if only because she's still preferable to Peter.

Also released in 1934 was Paul Czinner's stilted *Catherine the Great.* How angry Sternberg must have been at its critical and commercial success when the failure of his own film hastened the end of his collaboration with his beloved Dietrich. In *The Devil Is a Woman,* his next and final film with Dietrich, a character states what must have been his own attitude toward his unjustly treated *Scarlet Empress:* "Critics don't value genius." The critics weren't the only ones. The Academy members failed to give *The Scarlet Empress* any nominations.

▶ BEST ACTOR

WINNER:
Clark Gable *(It Happened One Night)*
Other Nominees: Frank Morgan *(Affairs of Cellini),* William Powell *(The Thin Man)*

▼

THE BEST CHOICE:
John Barrymore *(Twentieth Century)*
Award-Worthy Runners-Up: W. C. Fields *(It's a Gift),* W. C. Fields *(The Old-Fashioned Way),* William Powell *(The Thin Man),* Claude Rains *(The Man Who Reclaimed His Head)*

Clark Gable got his big break in movies when MGM grew so tired of his complaining about roles that it punished him by loaning him to the lowly Columbia Studios for its unpromising *It Happened One Night.* When Frank Capra's comedy unexpectedly swept the Academy Awards, Gable wound up with a Best Actor statue and the superstardom he might never have achieved if he'd worked only at MGM. Gable was extremely likable as the tough, masculine reporter who reveals a soft side while taming spoiled runaway heiress Claudette Colbert—teaching her the art of hitchhiking (she realizes her legs are a more powerful weapon than his thumb), how to dunk a doughnut in coffee, and how to give the proper piggyback ride; chasing away an obnoxious suitor, joining others in the bus who sing "Man on the Flying Trapeze," and when she's wary that they must share a motel room, hanging up a blanket ("the Walls of Jericho") so that she not fear him or watch him strip (undershirt sales dropped drastically when he revealed he didn't wear one). If there were an Academy Award for "Actor with the Most Presence" or "Actor Best Suited for a Role," then Gable surely would have deserved to win in 1934. But I don't think the limited Gable should have been considered the cinema's best *actor* in any year, not

John Barrymore and Carole Lombard get down-and-dirty in Howard Hawks's seminal screwball comedy, *Twentieth Century*.

even for his agreeable performances in *It Happened One Night, Red Dust, Mutiny on the Bounty,* and *Gone With the Wind.*

Ironically, Gable gave more acceptable performances in thirties movies than John Barrymore, who was regarded as the best actor of the era. The onetime matinee idol became bored while acting in films as he passed fifty, and only occasionally gave performances that weren't tired or hammy. However, in 1934, he suddenly felt revived and gave an hysterically funny performance opposite Carole Lombard in Howard Hawks's screwball classic, *Twentieth Century.* As Oscar Jaffe, a theatrical producer-director who was as hammy while relating to people in his private life as Barrymore was at his worst on the screen, Barrymore found a role that was fun to play, and for which he didn't have to worry about going overboard. In fact, he agreed to do the picture without reading the script because Hawks told him, "It's the story of the greatest ham in the world, and God knows you fit that."

Adapted by Ben Hecht and Charles MacArthur from their play, *Twentieth Century* begins with Jaffe rehearsing a new cast. He maintains faith in a timid unknown named Mildred Plotka (Lombard) and bullies her into giving a great performance. He changes her name to Lily Garland, casts her in all his productions, and makes her into the theater's biggest star. But his jealousy, possessiveness, and phony acts of self-pity drive her away. She goes to Hollywood and becomes a big movie star, while his theatrical career goes downhill. When they wind up on the same cross-country train, the Twentieth Century, he devises a sneaky plan to get her to sign a contract with him to star in his next play.

Barrymore's Jaffe is a complete ham. Even when alone, his eye movements and gestures are exaggerated and affected. He is the epitome of a pretentious theater director, who tries to inspire his actors with such drivel as "the sorrows of life are the joys of art." This egomaniac believes his actors perform well because it is he who inspired them and because they want to contribute to his artistic vision. He is completely unscrupulous, completely shameless, willing to do anything to get what he wants. He uses the soft, weak voice of a dying man while trying to manipulate others into doing his bidding. Jaffe always pretends that his feelings are hurt, and repeatedly "closes the iron door" on those who have been disloyal. When anyone challenges him, he sort of staggers and his eyes become cloudy, as if he's been punched in the stomach. On his endless quest for control, obedience, pity, and admiration, he never stops acting. What makes Lombard's Lily the perfect match is that she acts, too, even offstage. She can match his hamminess and, by film's end, has become just as pretentious as he, even wearing furs to rehearsals. Interestingly, the two never come to their senses—as do Gable and Colbert in *It Happened One Night*—but remain lunatics until the very end. Their furious verbal battles are brilliantly played, with machine-gun-like precision. When their squabbling becomes physical, with the hysterical Lily using her feet to ward off Jaffe, we recall the knockabout fight between Norma Shearer and Robert Montgomery in *Private Lives*—the one earlier major comedy in which the romantic leads engage in slapstick and insanity, instead of leaving that to the supporting players. Lombard established herself as the screen's top comedienne with her performance in *Twentieth Century*. Barrymore was difficult to impress but Lombard was an original—and it's likely that she, even more than Hawks, stimulated him into giving the most energetic, creative, and memorable performance of his movie career. She helped Barrymore deserve the Academy Award that was won by Clark Gable, her future husband.

▶ BEST ACTRESS

WINNER:
Claudette Colbert *(It Happened One Night)*
Other Nominees: Grace Moore *(One Night of Love)*, Norma Shearer *(The Barretts of Wimpole Street)*

▼

THE BEST CHOICE:
Bette Davis *(Of Human Bondage)*
Award-Worthy Runners-Up: Claudette Colbert *(It Happened One Night)*, Carole Lombard *(Twentieth Century)*, Myrna Loy *(Manhattan Melodrama)*, Norma Shearer *(The Barretts of Wimpole Street)*, Margaret Sullavan *(Little Man, What Now?)*

No major Hollywood actress would consider playing sluttish Cockney waitress Mildred Rogers in John Cromwell's seamy adaptation of Somerset Maugham's autobiographical *Of Human Bondage*. But young Warners contract player Bette Davis wasn't concerned about image because no one really knew who she was after twenty-one pictures. She figured that she had her one shot at stardom—albeit at the risk of aborting a potentially successful career—in playing the coldhearted, vulgar opportunist who becomes the strange obsession and near ruin of the intellectual, clubfooted medical student, Philip Carey (Leslie Howard). So after Cromwell offered her the part, she badgered Jack Warner for six months to loan her to RKO. He finally gave in, hoping she'd fail as the only non-British player in a distinguished cast. But her devastating portrayal quickly became the talk of Hollywood, and *Life* called it the best performance ever given by an American actress. Few disputed that Davis deserved to be "Best Actress" of the year, yet when nominations were announced, her name was mysteriously absent.

By this time Academy membership had dwindled to fewer than one hundred (because of defections to the Screen Actors Guild and other guilds), and studio heads wielded tremendous power in the voting process. Clearly, Jack Warner instructed his studio's voters to bypass Davis, whose great success had been at another studio; meanwhile RKO didn't get behind Davis because she was still Warners' property. There was an angry outcry over Davis's politically influenced snub. Even the nominated Norma Shearer—whose strong, intelligent portrayal of Elizabeth Barrett rivaled Davis's Mildred Rogers—supported Davis. So, for the first and only time, write-in ballots were allowed so that she could be recognized. But Davis still finished fourth, with the Best Actress award going to Claudette Colbert for her delightful, if not dynamic, performance as the runaway heiress in *It Happened One Night*. Because there were accusations that the write-in vote had been tampered with so that Davis would still not win, the Academy was forced to turn over the ballots in future years to the independent firm Price-Waterhouse.

In retrospect, Mildred Rogers wasn't Davis's best performance, but Davis always considered it the role with which she was most identified. I'm not sure that's the case, but surely it was the pivotal role in Davis's early career, the part that did indeed make her a star. I think it made such an impression because it was conceived and played in such an original manner. Until the end when Mildred becomes a prostitute and wears heavy makeup—and could understandably excite any man looking for a sexual thrill—there is, by intention, nothing special about Davis's Mildred. Until then she isn't especially pretty (though *this* Mildred is blessed with "Bette Davis Eyes"), isn't overtly sexual or alluring—even her hip-to-the-side poses are all wrong—isn't effectively flirtatious, has a Cockney accent, wears unattractive clothes, isn't smart or knowledgeable, and unless she is made to feel special by gifts bestowed on her, doesn't respond to Philip with any enthusiasm ("I don't mind" is her indifferent reply to all invitations). In his presence she rarely smiles, never laughs, and promises affection and loyalty only when she's desperate for Philip's help (even after being dumped he'll take her back, give her money, provide her with lodging). I don't see Mildred as evil. If she were, she'd latch on to a man with more money than Philip and make a life for herself that is secure. Instead she and

Bette Davis's manipulative Mildred Rogers knows she has a lifelong hold on Leslie Howard's otherwise respectable Philip Carey in *Of Human Bondage*.

her baby hit the streets, her baby dies, and she becomes a prostitute, later dying of syphilis in a charity ward. Davis's Mildred is not a vamp, she is just cheap, stupid, and shallow. She's not someone a sane, cultured man would love. In his highly recommended *The Films of the Thirties* critic Jerry Vermilye questions "how so well-bred a student-doctor could put up with such a guttersnipe." But that's Maugham's point. Just as Davis's intelligent, married woman falls for a ladies' man who is unworthy of her in Maugham's *The Letter,* Philip is drawn to the one woman in his life who is beneath him. He hates himself for being a cripple, and Mildred is his punishment.

Davis makes sure we see more than Mildred's vile nature. We feel genuine sympathy when the sick and penniless prostitute fears that Philip, the only person who has ever cared about her, is about to walk out the door (of course, he won't). She realizes he resents her and wishes she were dead, and so is afraid to hug him or lie to him about loving him. All she can do is move her

fingers uncertainly up and down his chest, terrified he'll push her away. This is a rare moment when Davis's Mildred shows real emotion. For the first time we see her fears about being a nobody in a scary world.

Davis smartly played Mildred in a reserved manner early in the picture, because when she finally tells off Philip in the movie's most famous scene, we are as shocked as he is by her tirade. Her eyes full of rage, her blond hair wild, she causes him to back up when she starts screaming at him for calling her cheap; she looks in the other direction, walks away, but keeps coming back to tell him how she has always laughed at him and to hurl insults about his being "a gimpy-legged monster! Do you know what you are? A cripple! A cripple! A cripple!" Every man who has ever insulted a woman is thankful it's Philip and not he who must endure the first of Davis's many great movie tantrums. She's terrifying. Yes, as Philip Carey sees, Davis's Mildred has no class and no heart. But as she said earlier—and this is her one redeeming quality—"I've still got me pride."

1935

▶ BEST PICTURE

WINNER:
Mutiny on the Bounty (MGM; Frank Lloyd)
Other Nominees: *Alice Adams, Broadway Melody of 1936, Captain Blood, David Copperfield, The Informer, Les Miserables, Lives of a Bengal Lancer, A Midsummer Night's Dream, Naughty Marietta, Ruggles of Red Gap, Top Hat*

▼

THE BEST CHOICE:
The 39 Steps (Gaumont-British; Alfred Hitchcock)
Award-Worthy Runners-Up: *The Informer* (John Ford), *The Man on the Flying Trapeze* (Clyde Bruckman), *Mutiny on the Bounty* (Frank Lloyd), *A Night at the Opera* (Sam Wood), *Top Hat* (Mark Sandrich)

The two films that vied for Academy Award recognition in 1935 were Frank Lloyd's mammoth, $2 million *Mutiny on the Bounty,* and John Ford's minuscule, $200,000 *The Informer,* pictures that, in very different ways, deal with men who turn traitor. The Best Picture Oscar went to Lloyd's adventure, adapted from the Nordhoff-Hall book about an actual mutiny that took place in 1787, when officer Fletcher Christian (Clark Gable) seized the British ship from the tyrannical Captain Bligh (Charles Laughton), and set him adrift in the high seas. But the other major awards went to Ford's grim, stylized adaptation of Liam O'Flaherty's story about a stupid, drunken Irishman (Victor McLaglen) who, in 1922 Dublin, takes twenty pounds in exchange for telling the British police the

whereabouts of his insurgent best friend, a betrayal that results in his friend's death. Although *Mutiny on the Bounty* is too grouchy a picture—for two hours we see Laughton demean sailors and get away with it (the factual ending doesn't provide us with enough vengeance)— and *The Informer* is too stagy, both pictures hold up quite well. However, they aren't films you want to see every time they turn up at a repertory cinema or on TV, as are several other 1935 releases, like *Top Hat* and the unnominated *The 39 Steps, The Man on the Flying Trapeze,* with W. C. Fields, and the Marx Brothers classic *A Night at the Opera,* which includes a sea voyage that is far merrier than the one in *Mutiny on the Bounty.*

For the Best Picture of 1935 I'll bypass *The Man on the*

Flying Trapeze and *A Night at the Opera,* two near-perfect comedies, because I think they fail to equal Fields's best film, *It's a Gift,* or the Marx Brothers' best, *Duck Soup.* On the other hand, *Top Hat* is the quintessential Fred Astaire and Ginger Rogers musical, enduring escapist entertainment that is also supreme art. Still, even though Astaire and Rogers thrill us with even more complicated steps than in *The 39 Steps,* it has an annoying mistaken-identity story line that is far less interesting than the one in Hitchcock's British suspense classic. Whereas Rogers assumes that bachelor Astaire is married, Madeleine Carroll in *The 39 Steps* assumes Robert Donat is a murderer.

A frightened, exotic woman, a complete stranger to him, accompanies Donat back from the theater—where the feature act was Mr. Memory, memorizer of an amazing assortment of facts. She is murdered by foreign spies. He flees to Scotland, one jump ahead of the police, who think he committed the murder in his flat, and the spies, who realize she revealed some secret information. To clear himself he must track down the leader of a spy ring, who has one missing finger, and discover the secret of "the 39 steps." Fleeing from police, he enters a train compartment and kisses its lovely occupant, Madeleine Carroll, so police will think they're lovers. But she tries to turn him in. He escapes. Later, they are handcuffed together by spies pretending to be police. Again he escapes, still handcuffed to the young woman. At first she thinks him guilty and they constantly squabble, but in time she realizes he is innocent and helps him solve the case. They end up back in the theater, with the police, the spy leader, and Mr. Memory on hand for an exciting climax.

Among the most enjoyable of romantic spy thrillers, Hitchcock's classic was adapted from John Buchan's popular novel. The script by Charles Bennett and Alma Reville is consistently clever, with suspense, intriguing ministories and ingenious plot twists, unusual characters, and a romantic relationship that enticingly mixes sophistication with sex. Perfectly cast, the tall, handsome Donat and cool, blond Carroll create what may be the most sexually stimulating relationship between a *gentleman* and a *lady* there has been on the screen. It's a match that catches fire not because of trust but because of handcuffs.

The 39 Steps is an extremely *erotic* picture. Donat meets three women—the exotic spy who comes to his flat; the unhappy, sexually repressed wife of a stern farmer, who is attracted to him and helps him escape; and Carroll, who is handcuffed to him even when they sleep in a bed. Hitchcock places these three females in sexually compromising positions with Donat and doesn't allow them, or Donat, a sexual release. In this way he injects sexual tension into the picture's already tense plot line, heightening the suspense. He also injects humor,

In one of Alfred Hitchcock's many train sequences over the years, fugitive Robert Donat (L) is about to be betrayed to the police by stranger Madeleine Carroll.

but we are kept on edge because Donat can't relax for one moment. Every character he meets is holding in either secret information or, as with the women, secret desires. And every place he enters has enemies either inside or just outside an unlocked door. He never can find safety.

The 39 Steps was the picture that proved Alfred Hitchcock had made the full transition to sound films—which doesn't mean he didn't wisely include effective silent-movie-like passages. It was his first undisputed masterpiece, the picture that made his international reputation, and the one that served as a model for his later romantic and witty suspense thrillers in which a man-on-the-run must prove his innocence. Consistently entertaining and surprising, it's a film that we can watch over and over. One reason is that most of us forget (with good reason) the meaning of "the 39 Steps" about a minute after the picture ends—just as we always forget who killed Floyd Thursby in *The Maltese Falcon.* It's a good thing we don't have the memory of Mr. Memory.

▶ BEST ACTOR

WINNER:
Victor McLaglen *(The Informer)*
Other Nominees: Clark Gable *(Mutiny on the Bounty)*, Charles Laughton *(Mutiny on the Bounty)*, Franchot Tone *(Mutiny on the Bounty)*

▼

THE BEST CHOICE:
W. C. Fields *(The Man on the Flying Trapeze)*
Award-Worthy Runners-Up: Robert Donat *(The 39 Steps)*, Leslie Howard *(The Scarlet Pimpernel)*, Boris Karloff *(Bride of Frankenstein)*, Charles Laughton *(Mutiny on the Bounty)*, Peter Lorre *(Mad Love)*.

Unique in the cinema, W. C. Fields was never considered for a Best Actor award, not even in 1935 when he received (undue) praise for playing Mr. Micawber in *David Copperfield.* That he was a great comic was taken for granted; that he was more than a comic was ignored. The New York Film Critics chose Charles Laughton as its first Best Actor winner for his portrayal of the tyrannical Captain Bligh in *Mutiny on the Bounty,* although Laughton himself preferred his British manservant who becomes his own man in the American West in the 1935 comedy *Ruggles of Red Gap.* Sneering, slightly hunched over, and relishing every opportunity to demonstrate his belief in the divine right of sea captains, Laughton's Bligh is a villain for the ages, one of the most contemptuous figures in cinema history. Indeed, Laughton is marvelous, but I think the role lets him down because it is without nuance—there is no way we can get into his head, no way to figure out if something in his past was responsible for his cruelty. I actually prefer the much less talented Victor McLaglen, the Academy's Best Actor selection, who played Gypo Nolan in *The Informer.* Anyone who has seen a lot of John Ford films is fond of McLaglen—of his mostly humorous scenes that mix heavy drinking and fisticuffs—but knows his range is limited. As Gypo, a rare lead, he again drinks heavily and intimidates people with his large, muscular body. Only, this time he plays it straight and is quite moving as the impoverished Irishman who turns in his best friend for twenty pounds, and then drinks and gives away the money. McLaglen, surprisingly, does a good job, dominating each scene, barreling through the misty Dublin sets, touching us with his final search for salvation. Gypo was considered a villain, but he's far different from Captain Bligh—in fact, he's a pathetic fellow, almost like a once good, but now dangerous dog that has to be shot. This was by far McLaglen's finest performance, but I think it's the direct result of Ford's keeping him in check and, at those moments when he is quiet and confused, filming him at angles that heighten the emotion.

If Boris Karloff's moving portrayal of the monster in *Bride of Frankenstein* were a bit longer or Peter Lorre's portrayal of the bald, creepy doctor in *Mad Love* weren't so bizarre that I'm unsure if he's great or atrocious, then I'd more seriously consider them as Best Actor of 1935.

Lorre certainly deserved a career award, at the very least. Having eliminated the others, I'll pick W. C. Fields in *The Man on the Flying Trapeze* over Groucho Marx for *A Night at the Opera,* giving it to Fields because he carried his film while Groucho had a lot of support—Harpo and Chico would have had to share the award.

Fields plays Ambrose Woolfinger, an underpaid memory expert at a wool company, henpecked husband of Kathleen Howard (who also played his wife in *It's a Gift*), loving father to his grown daughter, Mary Brian, and sole provider for his ungrateful, critical mother-in-law, Vera Lewis (as Cordelia Neselrode) and sponging brother-in-law, Grady Sutton, who takes naps after breakfast rather than seeking a job. In contrast to his other roles, Fields isn't cantankerous, doesn't bully any imbecilic assistants (like Tammany Young in *It's a Gift* and Grady Sutton in *You Can't Cheat an Honest Man*), try to do away with Baby LeRoy, swindle anyone, or do a whole lot of bragging—though he demonstrates a headlock on a local cop that he says no one can break (only to be sent flying over backward and landing on the pavement headfirst). But

W. C. Fields sings a few off-key bars with the two men who were stealing his homemade liquor (Tammany Young and Walter Brennan) and the policeman who is arresting them in *The Man on the Flying Trapeze.*

don't worry: as his nicest guy, Fields is in peak form. In his own stubborn way he's still a rebel and nonconformist. Fields's wife may henpeck him, but she's the one who gets aggravated, correctly calling him "the most trying man on this earth." He may put up with his in-laws, but when he needs an excuse to go to the wrestling matches, his wicked alibi is that his mother-in-law just died from poison liquor. This after hearing her say, "No man whose lips have touched liquor shall touch mine." ("Ah, yes, a pretty sentiment," he replies insincerely, "very nice.") At the end he revolts: he KO's Sutton, takes a swing at his mother-in-law, walks out on his wife, and when they reunite has his two in-laws ride in the uncovered jump-seat of his car during a pouring rain.

It's a pleasure to watch Fields stumble through life and emerge, impossibly, unscathed. I love the beginning when the hysterical Howard wakes him in the early morning to urge him to attend to the burglars singing in the cellar. Instead of rushing down, he takes forever, putting on his socks (blowing into them first) one over the other, swatting a fly on his pillow, happily discovering missing items in a drawer, and deciding to brush his teeth, before finally going downstairs and joining the intruders in some off-key singing. Another hilarious

scene has Fields on the way to the wrestling matches, getting four consecutive driving and parking tickets and being ordered by one sarcastic policeman to read repeatedly a No Parking sign. Also amusing is memory expert Fields providing minute detail to his boss about an obscure business client, reminding him of his two sons, one a tennis player and the other "a manly" little fellow, and the exact scores of their golf match a year before.

A strong candidate for best moment is when Fields, in bathrobe and pajamas, is thrown into jail for having manufactured homemade applejack, and immediately sees his crazed cellmate come toward him, with twisting fingers aimed at his neck. The loony reveals his crime: "I take my scissors and stick them straight into my wife's throat." This prompts Fields to do one of his classic double takes and look for a guard. When the man adds, "I've had three wives, but this is the first one I've killed in all my life," Fields responds, "Oh, that's in your favor, yes. . . . They have no more a case against you than a sheep has against a butcher." For playing a marvelous character no other comic could conceive, and making us laugh nonstop for sixty-five minutes, Fields deserves the Oscar.

▶ BEST ACTRESS

WINNER:
Bette Davis *(Dangerous)*
Other Nominees: Elisabeth Bergner *(Escape Me Never)*, Claudette Colbert *(Private Worlds)*, Katharine Hepburn *(Alice Adams)*, Miriam Hopkins *(Becky Sharp)*, Merle Oberon *(The Dark Angel)*

THE BEST CHOICE:
Katharine Hepburn *(Alice Adams)*
Award-Worthy Runners-Up: Bette Davis *(Dangerous)*, Miriam Hopkins *(Becky Sharp)*, Margaret Sullavan *(The Good Fairy)*

Bette Davis's Best Actress Oscar for *Dangerous* was always considered, even by her, a consolation prize for having been unfairly overlooked by the Academy for *Of Human Bondage.* But her flamboyant portrayal of an alcoholic, has-been actress, who is considered too much of a jinx to employ, is dynamic, even better at times than her Mildred Rogers. In fact, the relationship Davis has with Franchot Tone obviously was intended to recall the one she had with Leslie Howard in the earlier film—she even flies into similar tantrums. If *Dangerous* were a better film—it has a promising, sharply written first half, then goes in wrong directions—then perhaps Davis would receive due credit.

Davis thought the performance of the year was given by Katharine Hepburn in George Stevens's *Alice Adams,* and I agree. I like it far more than her earlier, acclaimed roles in *Bill of Divorcement, Morning Glory* (for which she won the Academy Award), and *Little Women.* She played the heroine of Booth Tarkington's Pulitzer Prize–

winning story, a sweet, smart small-town girl, who is lonely and miserable because the richer boys and girls in town snub her. Her mother (Ann Shoemaker) always nags her weak father (Fred Stone) to go into business for himself so Alice can get the fine things she deserves, but Alice lies to him that she's content. When Alice goes to a society dance, braving to wear an unfashionable dress and have her brother (Frank Albertson) as a date, she is ignored, until a nice, handsome young man, Arthur (Fred MacMurray), asks her to dance. Arthur courts Alice, who is reluctant to tell him she's not wealthy and in good social standing. She is afraid to invite him into her modest home to meet her parents, whom she loves but knows are common. She finally invites him to dinner and it is a disastrous evening. Alice also realizes that someone has told him all about her. She expects him to leave. But after she straightens out her family's problems, she discovers that he's on her porch. He won't go away because he has fallen in love with her.

Katharine Hepburn is excited to be courted by Fred MacMurray in George Stevens's *Alice Adams*.

blue when it counts, and deserves the rewards she seeks. She has suffered a great deal in this town where social standing is everything, but still her eyes sparkle, and still she smiles, refusing to show hurt or admit to herself that she's been insulted. But sometimes she breaks down completely, as when she cries after feeling shamed at the dance. And, in a great bit of acting by Hepburn, she loses her smile in stages—as tears form in her eyes—when she comes to the wrong conclusion about Arthur: "I have the strangest feeling that I'll see you only five more minutes for the rest of my life." Hepburn has her other *great* moment in the dance scene when the embarrassed Alice sits by herself and, thinking everyone is looking at her (as she always does), self-consciously smiles and laughs to herself as if she is being amused by an invisible companion. I also like Alice's teenage reaction (eyes go upward, head goes to the side slightly, body sags) to her mother's insistence she wear her father's coat in the rain before the dance—was Hepburn the model for Molly Ringwald?

Only in *Woman of the Year,* in an adult role, is Hepburn more ravishing than in *Alice Adams*. Stevens wisely included many stunning close-ups of her smooth, slender, beautiful star's face, with those temptingly wet lips and those intelligent, expressive eyes that reveal Alice's simultaneous feelings of excitement that her life is improving and dread that it may get even worse. Thankful that Arthur, her dream-come-true, is interested in her, Hepburn's Alice says, "I don't know why he likes me." We know why.

Once again Hepburn played one of her smart, gutsy, romantic young girls who is fiercely loyal to her family. Alice acts with such affectation that we might dislike her if we didn't admire her for loving those who always let her down. *Or* if Hepburn herself didn't make us root for this girl the actress cared so much about and who, as her mother says, "always underestimates herself." Alice talks too much, tries too hard, and puts on airs, but she is true

1936

▶ BEST PICTURE

WINNER:
The Great Ziegfeld (MGM; Robert Z. Leonard)
Other Nominees: *Anthony Adverse, Dodsworth, Libeled Lady, Mr. Deeds Goes to Town, Romeo and Juliet, San Francisco, The Story of Louis Pasteur, A Tale of Two Cities, Three Smart Girls*

▼

THE BEST CHOICE:
Modern Times (United Artists; Charles Chaplin)
Award-Worthy Runners-Up: *Libeled Lady* (Jack Conway), *Mr. Deeds Goes to Town* (Frank Capra), *Swing Time* (George Stevens)

MGM's expensive musical biopic *The Great Ziegfeld* was the uninspired choice for Best Picture of 1936. The performances by William Powell as big-spending gimmick-minded, woman-loving producer Florenz Ziegfeld, and newcomer Luise Rainer as Anna Held are still im-

pressive, but this is an endless picture (176 minutes), with some of the most boring musical numbers imaginable—even a number with a hundred chorus girls in their underwear is numbing. (Only Fannie Brice stirs things up.)

Several other period pictures were nominated for Best Picture of 1936, while Academy voters disregarded Charles Chaplin's masterwork *Modern Times*, his harsh and hilarious satire about contemporary America. Warners had stopped making social message films, and apparently Hollywood wasn't thrilled that Chaplin took up the slack.

Chaplin is not a tramp at the beginning of *Modern Times*, but a worker on a steel company's assembly line. After turning too many screws he becomes screwy, ending up in an asylum. Released, he's mistaken by police to be the leader of a group of communist marchers (after he innocently picks up and waves a red flag that fell from a truck) and is thrown in jail. After foiling an escape by other prisoners, he is pardoned with a job recommendation from the sheriff. He tries to take the rap for a pretty gamine (I fall in love with Paulette Goddard every time I see this film) who steals bread, but she is arrested. He's arrested, too, for eating a large meal he can't pay for, and is tossed into the same paddy wagon as the girl. She has fallen in love with the gentlemanly tramp. They escape and set up house in an abandoned shack. He takes several jobs but they don't work out. He usually ends up in jail. She becomes a cabaret dancer and gets him a job as a singing waiter. They are successes and their future looks bright. But juvenile authorities attempt to arrest her. They escape again. He cheers her up and makes her smile. They walk hand in hand toward the sun.

Modern Times was Chaplin's last film without actual dialogue, though it does have sound effects (from machines churning to stomachs grumbling) and music, including Chaplin's glorious "Smile" on the soundtrack and Chaplin (in the singing waiter scene) performing the studio-recorded "Titina," the first time he was ever heard on film. Stylistically, Chaplin remained in the silent era, with several scenes recalling specific scenes in his silent classics. However, this film dealt with, as his title states, modern times. Chaplin presents an increasingly industrialized and dehumanized America, where the unemployed march and riot on the streets, where the impoverished steal, and factory workers are turned into extensions of their machines. Machines literally attack workers (Chaplin is pulverized by a short-circuited eating machine), even swallowing them whole (both Chaplin and mechanic Charles Conklin are pulled into machines). Management (Chaplin's employer spends his time doing puzzles, reading the newspaper, taking pills, spying on workers) cares about stepping up production, not employee health or safety—interestingly, Chaplin isn't the only harried worker on the verge of a breakdown. Ironically, Chaplin finds solace in prison, where life isn't complicated. Outside, on the street, policemen bully him and arrest him without reason, and there's no way he can earn enough money to survive.

Modern Times is consistently funny, but while we laugh at Chaplin's cleverly conceived and brilliantly performed antics, we never forget that the two characters we love are in trouble, and are hungry. The majority of scenes in

Charlie Chaplin's lonely Little Tramp finds the perfect companion, orphan Paulette Goddard, in *Modern Times*.

the picture have something to do with food: Chaplin is strapped into the eating machine (a hilarious bit), Goddard steals bananas, Chaplin eats in the prison mess hall, Chaplin munches on an apple in his cell, Chaplin has tea with the minister's wife, Goddard tries to steal bread, Chaplin orders a big meal in a cafeteria though he can't pay for it and will be sent to jail (his hope), Chaplin and Goddard have cake in the department store where he works as a floorwalker, the men who rob the store say they are committing the crime so they can eat, Chaplin and Goddard eat together in the makeshift shack (and in a nice home in his fantasy), Chaplin eats during his factory lunch break and feeds his boss who is trapped in a shut-down machine, Chaplin the waiter serves duck to a customer. The message is clear: If you don't have a job, you starve. But if you can't find "human" work, it's healthier to be unemployed and it's worth risking jail (where you'll be fed) to steal food. For Chaplin and Goddard, paradise is a restaurant—where they can make a living through their "art" (he sings and does pantomime, she dances), and they are surrounded by food.

But their happiness is brief. They must escape the unfriendly city. Chaplin had done this alone in many of his films, with his humanity and dignity intact. But this time the pretty girl walks with him toward the sun. There is reason for him to "Smile."

► BEST ACTOR

WINNER:
Paul Muni *(The Story of Louis Pasteur)*
Other Nominees: Gary Cooper *(Mr. Deeds Goes to Town)*, Walter Huston *(Dodsworth)*, William Powell *(My Man Godfrey)*, Spencer Tracy *(San Francisco)*

▼

THE BEST CHOICE:
Charles Chaplin *(Modern Times)*
Award-Worthy Runners-Up: Gary Cooper *(Mr. Deeds Goes to Town)*, Paul Muni *(The Story of Louis Pasteur)*, William Powell *(My Man Godfrey)*

Extant footage from Josef von Sternberg's *I, Claudius*, which producer Alexander Korda aborted when lead actress Merle Oberon was hurt in an automobile accident, is enough to indicate that had the film been completed, Charles Laughton would have deserved 1936's (or any other year's!) Best Actor Oscar for his stammering emperor. As it was, the Academy finally got around to honoring Paul Muni, who was superb in the Warners bio, *The Story of Louis Pasteur,* but less interesting than in *Scarface, I Am a Fugitive from a Chain Gang,* or *Black Fury.*

The handsome, dapper William Powell was one of the finest actors of the era and it's unfortunate that he never won an Oscar. To spread the award around I'm tempted to give it to him for his bum-turned-butler in the classic screwball comedy, *My Man Godfrey.* Among the nominees for 1936, he's my choice. But Charlie Chaplin—my first two-time winner—just can't be overlooked for *Modern Times.* His performance as a miserable, dehumanized factory worker who becomes a very human and very optimistic tramp is, quite simply, wonderful.

So many images of Chaplin in *Modern Times* are etched in the movie lover's mind, perhaps more than from any other of his films. We all remember Chaplin turning bolts on an assembly line and then being unable to stop his arms from making the turning motion—he automatically tries to turn the buttons on a female worker's dress and chases down the street a fat woman who wears a blouse with a button over each breast. We remember him being strapped to an out-of-control feeding machine (conceived so workers won't waste time eating) and having, first, a corn on the cob spin wildly against his teeth like an amuck electric toothbrush, and, second, a wiper smack him repeatedly on the mouth, and so on. His nervous breakdown has him dancing fairylike through the factory, indiscriminately pushing levers and turning wheels, then happily squirting oil on his boss and the police.

Another great, memorable scene has the blindfolded Chaplin roller-skating on a high floor in the department store, not realizing that he's close to a ledge—when he takes off the blindfold and sees where he is, he panics and forgets how to skate, spinning his wheels and almost going over. A quick scene recalls Chaplin's great slapstick

moments: he eagerly emerges from sleep for his morning dip and dives into nearby water, only to discover that it is only ankle deep. There is one classic scene that recalls Buster Keaton: when he retrieves a wedge for his foreman at the shipyard at which he has just started working, he accidentally launches an unfinished ship. After stoically watching it nosedive into the deep water, he puts on his jacket and derby hat and goes off to look for a new job. Chaplin has two classic sequences in the cabaret: as a waiter he carries a tray with a duck he wants to serve an impatient customer, but every time he nears the table he is spun to the other side of the restaurant by the many dancers on the floor; debuting as a singer, he forgets the words and proceeds to sing in French gibberish, using expressions and body movements to convey that the lyrics are racy. And the final scene is a gem, with Chaplin (using his inimitable walk) and the lovely twenty-

In *Modern Times* Charlie Chaplin has a nervous breakdown while working on a factory assembly line.

one-year-old Paulette Goddard (soon to be the actor's wife) determinedly leaving the city together, hand in hand, to confront the future.

For once Chaplin the director-screenwriter doesn't make it too hard on Chaplin's character. His worst moments come at the beginning in the factory, but his mind is almost gone already. He is thrown into prison several times, but to him prison, where he gets good treatment and is fed, is a sanctuary. Life is hard on the streets, but for once Chaplin has a companion, Goddard's gamine, who adores him as much as the Little Tramp adores

beautiful, unattainable women in earlier Chaplin films. It's surprising censors didn't question Chaplin's presenting an adult male living with a teenage girl, because even though they are shown sleeping apart, this relationship isn't that of a surrogate father and daughter—certainly, in their mutual fantasy, they are married. No matter, we're happy that Chaplin's character has someone who loves him and will walk with him toward the sun that promises a brighter tomorrow. We take comfort that he's optimistic—because this is the last time the Little Tramp appears on film.

▶ BEST ACTRESS

WINNER:
Luise Rainer (The Great Ziegfeld)
Other Nominees: Irene Dunne (Theodora Goes Wild), Gladys George (Valiant Is the Word for Carrie), Carole Lombard (My Man Godfrey), Norma Shearer (Romeo and Juliet)

▼

THE BEST CHOICE:
Jean Harlow (Libeled Lady)
Award-Worthy Runners-Up: Jean Arthur (Mr. Deeds Goes to Town), Paulette Goddard (Modern Times), Katharine Hepburn (Sylvia Scarlett), Carole Lombard (My Man Godfrey)

Luise Rainer, "The Viennese Teardrop," waltzed away with 1936's Best Actress Oscar for her portrayal of entertainer Anna Held in *The Great Ziegfeld*. MGM believed its Austrian import would be the next Garbo and heavily promoted her, at the expense of the studio's resident queen, Norma Shearer, who was nominated for playing the oldest Juliet in history in *Romeo and Juliet*. Making her first public appearance on Academy Award night since the death of her husband, MGM production chief Irving Thalberg, Shearer was edged in the voting by the newcomer. Rainer made a strong impression on viewers. She had beauty, charm, and talent. But seen today her characterization of Held as a sweet, emotional, indecisive, and insecure outsider wavers from being adorable to being irritating. Ironically, her Held has traces of movie characters played by Billie Burke, Ziegfeld's second wife, who was played in the film without humor by Myrna Loy. The celebrated phone call scene in which Held pretends to be happy when she congratulates Ziegfeld on his marriage probably won the Oscar for Rainer. It's a shameless scene that would have gotten an audience reaction no matter which actress played it.

Of the nominated actresses Carole Lombard was most deserving of the Oscar, for she is charming as the dreamy-eyed rich girl who falls head-over-heels in love with the new butler (William Powell, Lombard's ex-husband) in *My Man Godfrey*. However, influenced by the knowledge that I'll give Lombard an Oscar for 1942, I'll skip over her here and select another funny, ill-fated blonde of the era, Jean Harlow, for her dazzling performance in Jack Conway's often-overlooked comedy classic,

Libeled Lady. That one also featured William Powell—along with Myrna Loy and Spencer Tracy—who by the end of filming was Harlow's fiancé.

Harlow plays the unappreciated fiancée of newspaperman Spencer Tracy. Tracy postpones their marriage because the paper is being sued for slander by the rich Myrna Loy. Tracy devises a plan to put Loy into a compromising position so that she'll drop the suit. He hires unemployed reporter Powell, a ladies' man, to seduce Loy. He also has Powell and Harlow marry—just temporarily, Tracy promises her. He wants Powell to make love to Loy just at the time his bride, Harlow, arrives with newspaper cameramen. Loy falls for Powell, but so does Harlow, who is tired of her treatment by Tracy. Powell makes Harlow think he is interested in her, so that she'll not interfere with his relationship with Loy, for whom he has fallen. When Powell, thinking his marriage to Harlow wasn't legal, marries Loy, Harlow explodes, then proves it was legal. She tells off Powell, Loy, and Tracy. She makes up with Loy after a woman-to-woman talk. When Powell and Tracy have a fight, she realizes she still loves Tracy. He loves her too . . . which doesn't resolve the problem: Powell is married to both Loy and Harlow.

One of the great movie discoveries of the thirties is Jean Harlow, who has never gotten enough praise. Her tragic death at age twenty-six curtailed what already was an impressive career. For the platinum blonde—the first to play blond *bad* girls—was far more than the era's top sex symbol. From her early films as a tough broad (often with a heart of gold) who specialized in delivering sarcastic lines to cops, she turned into a passable dra-

Although she has agreed to marry William Powell, Jean Harlow prefers his best friend, Spencer Tracy, in *Libeled Lady*.

ler. That film led to two amusing comedies, *Bombshell* and *The Girl from Missouri.*

But I've always been partial to her in *Libeled Lady*. I think it's her best showcase, for her character is not only sexy but funny, sometimes tough, sometimes sentimental, sometimes silly (as when she talks to Powell in a baby voice), often infuriated, and always a good sport—the actress herself was a good sport in the beauty parlor scene, allowing herself to resemble Medusa. I love her angry pout, how she huffs and puffs through a room with shoulders and legs working in unison, and how she builds up a head of steam while telling Powell and Tracy what jerks they are. Her long tantrums were filmed without cuts, which allowed her to increase her anger with every word. She's also impressive exchanging wisecracks with Powell and Tracy. Because the male characters have known each other for years, the men have their own rhythm when they speak, but Harlow fits her character's witty lines into their flow.

As in *Dinner at Eight* Harlow makes me laugh out loud a couple of times: when after saying her wedding vows with Powell, she weakly kisses him and then gives Tracy, the best man, a long, sexy smooch that perplexes the minister; and when she pretends sadness (for the benefit of witnesses) while waving goodbye to her new husband as he departs into an elevator but without missing a beat throws her arms around Tracy's neck the second the elevator door closes. By the time Harlow's character tells off the characters played by Loy, Powell, and Tracy at the end of the picture, she has stolen the film from her three talented costars.

matic actress—she was best opposite the physical, heman Clark Gable—and first-rate comedienne. She was super as the tramp who earns Gable's respect in *Red Dust* and hilarious as the sexpot who seeks culture in *Dinner at Eight,* playing opposite Wallace Beery and Marie Dress-

1937

▶ BEST PICTURE

WINNER:
The Life of Emile Zola (Warner Bros.; William Dieterle)
Other Nominees: *The Awful Truth, Captains Courageous, Dead End, The Good Earth, In Old Chicago, Lost Horizon, 100 Men and a Girl, Stage Door, A Star Is Born*

▼

THE BEST CHOICE:
Stage Door (RKO; Gregory La Cava)
Award-Worthy Runners-Up: *The Awful Truth* (Leo McCarey), *A Star Is Born* (William Wellman)

RKO brought the hit Edna Ferber–George S. Kaufman comedy-drama *Stage Door* to the screen in 1937, with Gregory La Cava as director, a script adaptation by Morrie Ryskind and Anthony Veiller, and the best group of actresses that would be assembled for a film prior to 1939's *The Women*—and even that film had no two actresses who compared to Katharine Hepburn and Ginger Rogers. Despite disappointing returns at the box office *Stage Door* received outstanding reviews and four Academy Award nominations—Best Picture, Best Director, Best Screenplay (adaptation), and Best Supporting Actress for Andrea Leeds—but since neither Hepburn nor Rogers was nominated, it was apparent that other pictures had more support in the Academy. Sure enough, in a year of such big-budget prestige films as *The Life of Emile Zola, The Good Earth, Captains Courageous,* and *Lost Horizon,* the best picture of 1937 didn't win any Oscars, while the other two outstanding, equally modest productions won only one: *The Awful Truth* won for Best Director (winner Leo McCarey insisted he should have instead won for the year's fourth best picture, *Make Way for Tomorrow*), and *A Star Is Born* won for Best Original Story (although William A. Wellman and Robert Carson clearly took their story from 1932's *What Price Hollywood?*).

The Best Picture winner was *The Life of Emile Zola.* It reunited Paul Muni with William Dieterle, who directed his Best Actor–winning performance in 1936's *The Story of Louis Pasteur.* Muni was terrific again as another man with the courage of his sometimes foolhardy convictions, but this film I loved so much as a kid is quite tiresome today. Anyway, how could the Academy consider honoring this biography in which there is no *verbal* mention that Alfred Dreyfus was Jewish? I'd much rather give the Oscar to *Stage Door,* a picture that gets better as time passes.

Hepburn played Terry Randall, the bright, brash daughter of a millionaire. Against her father's wishes she decides to take a shot at the theater. She moves into the Footlights Club, a boardinghouse full of rarely working actresses. Rich, educated, and upbeat, she has a hard time making friends with this cynical, penniless group, especially her wisecracking roommate, Jean Maitland (Rogers). The one person who likes her is the young, popular Kay (Leeds), a star last year but already forgotten. Jean catches the eye of a skirt-chasing producer (Adolphe Menjou), but he drops her when she hints at marriage. He then makes a play for Terry, who rejects his advances, though Jean assumes she stole him from her. He still makes Terry the star of his new show because it is secretly being financed by Terry's father, who hopes she will flop and return home. Terry doesn't know that this is the part Kay desperately wanted. On opening night the sickly Kay gives the terrified Terry advice on how to play the part. Before going onstage Terry is told by Jean that Kay has committed suicide. Jean blames Terry for her death and says that she hopes she fails. Terrible during rehearsals, Terry plays the part beautifully and then tells the appreciative audience that Kay was the one who was responsible for her success. Jean and Terry embrace. Although a star, Terry remains at the Footlights Club.

Stage Door is a touching, heartfelt tribute to all the vulnerable actresses in America ("a different race of people") who starve and suffer but don't give up and, as Kay says, "make a lot of noise, but . . . just to keep up their courage and hide their fears. . . . Without that job and those lines to say an actress is just like any ordinary girl trying not to look as scared as she feels." It is also the rare film—the same year's excellent crime melodrama *Marked Woman* is another—that deals with camaraderie among women. There are two reasons there is a bond among the women in the Footlights Club: they encourage one another because they all fear they will never succeed in show business; they seem to take turns having jobs and dating men, so that they have all had similar, even identical, experiences. These women come from all types of backgrounds, but they have the same hopes and dreams and the same fears of failure. We recognize their camaraderie before they do: Jean and two women she bickers with, Terry and Linda (Gail Patrick), all show us their softer, helpful, friendlier sides when they are with Kay. It is only a matter of time before Jean and Terry become friends; Jean and Gail Patrick's hostile Linda Shaw will never become civil, but at least they finally come to tolerate each other, with their insults losing their sting.

The picture has some of the snappiest, insult- and wisecrack-filled dialogue in thirties films, and refreshingly, it's all handled by actresses. Hepburn and Rogers, two actresses you'd never think you'd see in the same film, are wonderful together as two women you'd never think would be roommates. Their back-and-forth verbal battles are brilliantly played, with Rogers getting in the wickedest lines ("I bet you could boil a terrific pan of water"; "We started off on the wrong foot, let's stay that way"). Rogers also is quick with the insult when meeting a lumberman and agreeing with him that he has a sense of humor: "Yes, I can tell by the size of your shoes." And she and Patrick really go at it, with Jean informing Linda that it's safe to enter her room because "the exterminator won't be here till tomorrow."

Either Hepburn or Rogers could justifiably have won the Best Actress Oscar, and (what a cast!) Lucille Ball, Ann Miller, Eve Arden, Gail Patrick, and Constance Collier

Katharine Hepburn, Lucille Ball, and Ginger Rogers are housemates in Gregory La Cava's *Stage Door.*

could have received Supporting Actress nominations along with Leeds. The nominated Leeds gave a strong, sympathetic performance in a role that might have been maudlin, playing a sensitive young woman who is similar to the character she wants to play onstage (the part Terry gets). Leeds's memorable suicide scene, in which Kay climbs stairs and smiles at imaginary applause, anticipated the final shot of Gloria Swanson walking toward the camera in *Sunset Boulevard*. Kay, a hungry, depressed young actress, is the film's one completely serious character. She serves as foil to her funnier colleagues, who use humor to mask their sadness. When Kay dies, her friends stop being funny and the film becomes a tearjerker. Just as Kay is inside Terry when she performs, the other actresses fill the dramatic void left by Leeds. The sharp tone switch could have been completely jarring and ruined the film, but with Hepburn and Rogers at the front, this cast pulls it off.

▶ BEST ACTOR

WINNER:
Spencer Tracy *(Captains Courageous)*
Other Nominees: Charles Boyer *(Conquest)*, Fredric March *(A Star Is Born)*, Robert Montgomery *(Night Must Fall)*, Paul Muni *(The Life of Emile Zola)*

▼

THE BEST CHOICE:
Cary Grant *(The Awful Truth)*
Award-Worthy Runners-Up: Paul Muni *(The Life of Emile Zola)*, Spencer Tracy *(Captains Courageous)*

Cary Grant never won an Oscar, partly because of the Academy's prejudice against comedy performances—he got his only nominations for dramatic roles, in *None But the Lonely Heart* and *Penny Serenade*—and partly because he was, yes, taken for Granted. If he weren't nominated in the current year, the reasoning went, he'd turn in a performance of equal caliber the following year for which he could be nominated. But I'd rather not wait for 1938, and his equally great (unnominated) performance in *Bringing Up Baby*. I'll give it to him in 1937, for his first great movie role, opposite Irene Dunne in Leo McCarey's screwball classic, *The Awful Truth*. The 1937 Oscar winner was Spencer Tracy, who in *Captains Courageous* played a poor Portuguese fisherman who becomes surrogate father to the spoiled rich boy (Freddie Bartholomew) he rescues from the sea. Taking the award away from Spencer Tracy seems almost criminal, but while he is extremely likable as Manuel and not nearly as hammy as an Edward G. Robinson would have been, he never mastered the accent; furthermore, his screen time was only about half that of Bartholomew's, making him a more appropriate candidate for Best Supporting Actor.

At the beginning of *The Awful Truth*, Jerry (Grant) returns home from a supposed holiday. That he brings home California oranges tells his wife Lucy (Dunne) that he didn't vacation in Florida as he claims. When she walks in with her handsome singing teacher, Armand (Alexander D'Arcy), Jerry refuses to believe her story that Armand took her to a junior prom, that his car broke down, and that they spent a platonic night in a motel. Because he doesn't trust her, Lucy initiates divorce proceedings. Meanwhile, the judge grants Jerry visitation rights to their dog, Mr. Smith (Asta of *Thin Man* fame).

When Jerry visits, he tries to subvert the courtship of Lucy's rich neighbor from Oklahoma, Daniel (Ralph Bellamy). Thinking Lucy is also having an affair with Armand, he forces his way into Armand's apartment . . . in the middle of her recital. Lucy invites Armand to her apartment to ask him to explain to Jerry that they aren't lovers. But when Jerry turns up unexpectedly to apologize for having ruined her recital, she hides Armand in the bedroom. When Daniel knocks on the door, Jerry hides in the bedroom, too, where he discovers Armand. After Jerry chases Armand from the bedroom, Daniel and his mother walk out on Lucy. She doesn't care because she realizes she still loves Jerry. But he's given up on her. Now it's her turn to win him back. Which she does.

The Awful Truth was the first and best of three films starring Grant and Dunne, preceding *My Favorite Wife* and the comedy-tearjerker *Penny Serenade*. It also was the film that proved Grant could carry a film as a leading man, which he had hinted at in several actress vehicles: Mae West's *I'm No Angel* and *She Done Him Wrong*, Dietrich's *Blonde Venus*, Sylvia Sidney's *Thirty-Day Princess*, and Katharine Hepburn's *Sylvia Scarlett*. Dunne wrote in *Close-Ups* that "I knew little about him except that he was one of the handsomest men in films. I was instantly impressed with his energy and enthusiasm [but] *The Awful Truth* was his first major comedy role, and I could sense his reticence behind the bright spirits. . . . As I watched Cary working each day, I marveled at the excellence of his timing—the naturalness, the ease, the *charm*. Cary was wonderful in the film. . . ."

Cary Grant was indeed wonderful in *The Awful Truth*, trading quips with Dunne, improvising (as director Leo McCarey always wanted his actors to do), making us laugh with double takes, doing slapstick. In 1937 he also

Irene Dunne found her favorite screen partner in Cary Grant in George Stevens's *The Awful Truth,* the first of three films they made together.

made *Topper,* playing the ghost of George Kirby to Roland Young's Cosmo Topper. The film provides an interesting contrast to *The Awful Truth.* In pestering Topper, Grant's character also annoys the audience. In *The Awful Truth,* however, Grant's Jerry remains likable even when deliberately annoying Lucy or the other men in Lucy's life. Watch Jerry play polite host to Armand after he's spent the night with Lucy: although Jerry wants Armand to leave, he serves him eggnog, with an impatient "A little nutmeg?" As he keeps shaking nutmeg into Armand's drink, one can see he'd rather be punching him; finally Armand takes the hint and leaves. When Daniel pays a visit to Lucy, Jerry arrives as well, purportedly to visit Mr. Smith. He plays noisily with the animal, asking it questions, loudly banging on the piano, and singing a duet with the barking dog. He subtly insults the unsophisticated Daniel (Grant would do the same to Bellamy in 1940's *His Girl Friday*), pretending to be impressed by the locale to which he intends taking Lucy, a New Yorker, once they're married: "Not Oklahoma City itself? . . . And if it should get dull, you can always go to Tulsa for the weekend." He pretends to praise Lucy's fidelity to Daniel, raising doubts in Daniel's subconscious: "Never did I have to ask Lucy, 'Where have you been? What were you doing?' I always *knew.*"

Dunne wrote that Grant was different from her other leading men because "he was much more fun." Appropriately, the reason Lucy wants Jerry back is that he is more "fun" than any other man she knows. Here's a full-grown man who wears a suit, but spends much of the picture on the floor, playing with the dog, being jujitsued to the ground by Armand's servant, or just falling down. Unlike a gentleman, he is shameless in his attempts to get Lucy back and to tease her for the poor choices she has made in men since he left. When Daniel reads Lucy a poem he wrote her from his heart, the hiding Jerry tickles her with a pencil to make her laugh out loud. When he sees that Lucy is having a miserable time fast-dancing with Daniel, Jerry tips the band to play an encore. Finding Armand hiding in Dunne's bedroom, he calmly hands him his hat and then ungallantly knocks it out of his hands. Then he starts fighting with him and chases him through the apartment, ruining Daniel's visit with Lucy. One of my favorite ungentlemanly moments is when Daniel's mother meets Jerry and, having heard gossip about him that day, tells him, "It's funny seeing you. . . ." His great response: "It is? Well . . . it's funny seeing you."

What made Grant so wonderful was that while he always maintained his charm, he was never afraid to be the total fool. For instance, Jerry puts on what he thinks is his brand-new derby, but since it belongs to Armand (who's hiding in the bedroom), it's so big that it covers his ears. And when he ruins Lucy's recital, he doesn't just lean back and fall out of his chair, but knocks over the nearby table as well. This is not the suave Cary Grant of so many films. This is the endearing Grant who was terrific at physical comedy and didn't mind looking silly. It's little wonder that when Lucy sees Jerry topple over and make a fool of himself—she knows a gentleman would never even allow himself the opportunity to make a fool of himself—her defenses break down. She realizes she still loves him.

▶ BEST ACTRESS

WINNER:
Luise Rainer *(The Good Earth)*
Other Nominees: Irene Dunne *(The Awful Truth)*, Greta Garbo *(Camille)*, Janet Gaynor *(A Star Is Born)*, Barbara Stanwyck *(Stella Dallas)*

▼

THE BEST CHOICE:
Irene Dunne *(The Awful Truth)*
Award-Worthy Runners-Up: Jean Arthur *(Easy Living)*, Greta Garbo *(Camille)*, Janet Gaynor *(A Star Is Born)*, Katharine Hepburn *(Stage Door)*, Carole Lombard *(Nothing Sacred)*, Anna Neagle *(Victoria the Great)*, Ginger Rogers *(Stage Door)*

In a year with many extraordinary performances by actresses, Greta Garbo was expected to win the Best Actress Oscar for her excellent, if mannered, *Camille*. However, Luise Rainer surprised everyone by winning her second consecutive Oscar as the only Chinese peasant with an Austrian accent in MGM's *The Good Earth*. To be fair, Rainer did a satisfactory job, even if she spent too much of the picture using a stunned, hurt expression, as if she'd just stubbed her toe and didn't want anyone to know her pain. Former silent movie star Janet Gaynor gave her best performance in the original *A Star Is Born*, Barbara Stanwyck pulled out all stops in the classic soap *Stella Dallas*, and Ginger Rogers was truly brilliant in *Stage Door*, a performance for which she never got due acclaim. But I'll pick Irene Dunne, a marvelous actress who never was given a deserved Oscar.

Dunne was terrific in numerous films in a lengthy career, but when I think of her it is always with Cary Grant (he said she was "the sweetest-smelling actress" he ever worked with) being so charming and funny as their characters fall in and out of love in *The Awful Truth*. I wish she'd won the Oscar, because Rainer's career wasn't helped by her second consecutive Academy Award. Her career had already been irreparably damaged by MGM boss Louis B. Mayer, who forced her to appear in several weak films to cash in on her Oscar for *The Great Ziegfeld*.

Dunne's Lucy initiates divorce proceedings when her husband, Jerry (Grant), refuses to believe she isn't having an affair with her singing teacher (Alexander D'Arcy). She becomes engaged to a dull, neighborly Oklahoma oilman, Daniel (Ralph Bellamy). Jerry sabotages that relationship, but gives up on winning Lucy back and becomes engaged to society girl Barbara Vance (Molly Lamont). Lucy realizes she loves him and tries winning him back in turn. Pretending to be Jerry's ill-bred, heavy-drinking sister, she drops in on her rival and her rich family and horrifies them. Jerry's engagement is off. By wrecking her car Lucy sees to it that she and Jerry are stranded at their old country retreat. They sleep in adjoining rooms, separated only by a door that keeps swinging open. Just before midnight, when their divorce will be final, Jerry and Lucy end up in the same bedroom.

Dunne is delightful in *The Awful Truth*, whether doing physical comedy (I love her dance scene with Ralph

Although they won't admit it to each other, Cary Grant and Irene Dunne hope to sleep together before their divorce becomes finalized at midnight, in the wonderfully funny and sexy last scene in *The Awful Truth*.

Bellamy) or letting fly with one-liners. She is hilarious when she pretends to be the tactless, crude Lola, but equally funny when she is more subtle, ending her recital with a melodic laugh when she sees Jerry tangled up in a chair and table. Dunne was adored by moviegoers for being charming, tastefully witty, and a refined, gracious lady. But Lucy and most of her best characters have spunk.

For the first half of *The Awful Truth* Lucy tries to be a lady, patiently countering Jerry's snappy remarks with equally snappy retorts, acting bemused by his wild antics, even being a good enough sport to let him take pot shots at her honor—but only because she knows she is no more a lady than Jerry is a gentleman. In the second half of the film Jerry calms down, and Lucy goes to work, acting just as shamelessly as he did. And Dunne has a field day showing there's fire under her ladylike facade. When Lucy realizes she'll have to win Jerry back from Barbara Vance, she advises him, "Tell her I'd love to meet her—tell her to wear boxing gloves." Pretending to be his sister in front of Barbara and her stuffy family, she greets Barbara with the line "I've seen your pictures in the paper and I've wondered what you look like," feigns drunkenness, does a gyrating, rear-slapping dance, and says, "Don't anybody leave this room, I've lost my purse."

She continues to act drunk so that Jerry will drive her home and then perhaps seduce her. When he says he only intends to drop her off, she wrecks the car. Riding the rest of the way with a motorcycle cop, she bounces up and down on the horn. Then Jerry and Lucy climb into their respective beds. In the sexy finale, Dunne looks beautiful and Lucy, who takes to looking and acting like a lady again, doesn't let on that she wants Jerry to join her in her bed; but having seen her earlier this night, he isn't fooled. The actress herself was a lady, but her characters weren't so pure. Which is why Jerry knows he's a lucky guy.

1938

▶ BEST PICTURE

WINNER:
You Can't Take It with You (Columbia; Frank Capra)
Other Nominees: *The Adventures of Robin Hood, Alexander's Ragtime Band, Boys Town, The Citadel, Four Daughters, Grand Illusion, Jezebel, Pygmalion, Test Pilot*

▼

THE BEST CHOICE:
The Adventures of Robin Hood (Warner Bros.; Michael Curtiz and William Keighley)
Award-Worthy Runners-Up: *Angels with Dirty Faces* (Michael Curtiz), *Grand Illusion* (Jean Renoir), *Snow White and the Seven Dwarfs* (David Hand)

In 1939 Frank Capra was president of both the Academy and the Directors Guild, and the rare director whose name went above the movie title on the marquee. So it's not surprising that Academy voters showed favoritism by giving him his third Best Director Oscar and choosing his adaptation of the George S. Kaufman–Moss Hart stage success *You Can't Take It with You* as 1938's Best Picture. Unfortunately, his screwball comedy about what happens when the idealistic son (James Stewart) of a rich, cold-hearted businessman (Edward Arnold) becomes engaged to a secretary (Jean Arthur) from a nutty lower-middle-class family is only second-rate Capra. Much of the humor is forced, most of the sociopolitical points made by Arthur's preachy, idealistic grandfather (Lionel Barrymore) are vague or unconvincing, and such themes as "the richest men are those with the most friends" are handled better and more honestly in Capra's later *It's a Wonderful Life*.

I am not giving alternate Oscars to foreign-language films, but since Jean Renoir's antiwar classic, *Grand Illusion,* actually received a Best Picture nomination, I have been baited to break my own rules. I'm also tempted to give the award to a great cartoon: Walt Disney's *Snow White and the Seven Dwarfs* (which was released Christmas 1937), the first American animated sound feature and still, along with *Pinocchio,* the best. But my emphatic choice is *The Adventures of Robin Hood,* with the dashing Errol Flynn and lovely Olivia de Havilland pitted against two of the screen's slyest and most arrogant villains, Claude Rains and Basil Rathbone (with mustache and goatee, his Sir Guy looks like Robin's cruel, humorless brother). I'm surprised that the Academy didn't misjudge it as fluffy, escapist children's fare and bypass it entirely, despite Warners' spending $2 million on production. It did win three Oscars and was even nominated for Best Picture, which it might have won if voters had known it would stand the test of time as the cinema's greatest adventure film. (*Robin Hood,* with Kevin Costner, certainly didn't equal it.)

Directed by Warners' all-purpose director, Michael Curtiz (who replaced William Keighley after he went over budget), *The Adventures of Robin Hood* is based on various Robin Hood legends rather than the popular silent film starring Douglas Fairbanks. The setting is England in the late twelfth century, at a time when King Richard is being held for ransom by King Leopold of Austria. In his absence his sly, power-hungry brother, Prince John (Rains), takes control of England. He over-taxes, overworks, steals from, tortures, and kills those under his rule, especially the Saxons who remain loyal to Richard. Sir Robin Hood of Locksley (Flynn) has given up his wealth and position to organize the oppressed Saxons in Sherwood Forest. They terrorize Prince John's men, stealing money and food from those who pass through the forest. He takes supplies from and delays a caravan transporting the beautiful Maid Marian (Olivia de Havilland), Richard's ward. She thinks Robin is a traitor, but he shows her evidence of Prince John's vicious oppression of the people. They fall in love. Prince John, the dangerous Sir Guy (Rathbone), and the cowardly Sheriff of Nottingham (Melville Cooper) trick Robin into participating in an archery tournament. Robin wins and is captured. Marian helps him escape, but is herself imprisoned by Prince John, who plans to declare himself king and execute her. Free, Richard returns to England and befriends Robin. The Saxon forces sneak into the castle on coronation day. Robin's men vanquish Prince John's men in a violent battle, and Robin slays Sir Guy. Richard retakes the throne, exiles his brother, and orders the delighted Robin and Marian to marry.

I first saw *The Adventures of Robin Hood* on television in the fifties. Many times. I thrilled to the action, loved the spectacle—although I was seeing it in black and white—detested the villains played by Claude Rains and Basil Rathbone, and wanted to be either Robin Hood or Errol Flynn and marry either Maid Marian or Olivia de Havilland. When I see the film today in glorious color, I feel exactly the same. What always surprises me is that adults can appreciate the film more than children, for this is a classy, literate, inspiringly directed and acted picture. Much care went into every aspect of the production, from the impeccable casting to Erich Wolfgang Korngold's monumental, action-enhancing, Oscar-winning score. Shot after beautifully composed shot, the visuals are dazzling, even magical. Sol Polito and Tony Gaudio weren't among the eleven Cinematography Oscar nominees, but they deserved to win. My favorite image is of horses charging through Sherwood Forest, which has sunlight filtering through the trees, and racing across a

The screen couple to make all romantics sigh: Errol Flynn and Olivia de Havilland in Michael Curtiz and William Keighley's glorious adventure film, *The Adventures of Robin Hood.*

stream, with water splashing and spraying high into the air. Working with the still-experimental three-strip Technicolor process, the two cinematographers collaborated closely with Carl Jules Weyl, whose designs of the high-walled and cleverly lit castle chambers deservedly won him an Oscar, and costumer Milo Anderson, who must have gotten a good deal on green panty hose.

The picture has terrific action sequences, including the climactic sword fight between Robin and Sir Guy, which takes place all over the castle and incorporates a lot of toppling furniture, athleticism on Flynn's part, winding stone stairways, and Curtiz's trademarked use of giant black shadows on white walls (in a color film!). Also spectacular are Robin's two escapes, and a scene in which Robin and his men swing from vines and drop from trees to ambush Prince John's soldiers. The action never slows down for humor—Robin in battle (like Douglas Fairbanks) keeps smiling and joking; in fact, the scenes in which he recruits Little John (Alan Hale) and Friar Tuck (Eugene Pallette) are funny *physical* confrontations. The action does stop, but the tension doesn't dissipate, for romance. Dashing Flynn and his most frequent and loveliest screen partner, de Havilland, are as romantic a couple as Romeo and Juliet—fittingly, they have a balcony scene that will make most movie lovers sigh. You can tell Flynn really had a crush on de Havilland (however, when this prankster put a dead snake in her panties, he lost his chance for an offscreen romance).

De Havilland's Marian isn't the typical heroine of old-time adventure films. She is central to the action, devising the plan that frees Robin from the gallows, and defiantly speaking out against Prince John's Court of Execution after being charged with treason: "I'd do it again—even if you killed me!" Then again, the man she falls for isn't typical either. What's most peculiar about Robin Hood and Flynn's swashbuckling heroes in *Captain Blood* and *The Sea Hawk* is that they are Hollywood's only acceptable revolutionaries. Forget that these men are fiercely loyal to the British flag; the public let them get away with their guerrilla warfare, their assassinations, their thievery, because Flynn is so utterly engaging as these men. Though a limited actor, he was *perfect* as these brash, courageous, romantic outlaw heroes. They are leaders. They can convince any man that their cause is just and worth fighting for to the death. Whoever looks into Flynn's eyes is seduced.

So we have Flynn's Robin Hood speaking lines that would have had HUAC (House Un-American Activities Committee) members salivating: "We Saxons aren't going to put up with these repressions much longer"; "I'll organize a revolt, exact a death for a death"; "I can feel for beaten, helpless people." "Why, you speak treason," says a surprised Marian. "Fluently," he responds. Robin tells Marian that he fights for justice, not personal reward and, interestingly, the only time he falters is when he seeks personal gain—he is captured when he wins the archery contest to receive a prize from Marian. At all other times he works in unison with his men, never seeking personal glory, always putting himself on the line for the common cause. If you questioned leftists of the sixties, I wouldn't be surprised if as kids they were fans of Flynn's Robin Hood.

▶ BEST ACTOR

WINNER:
Spencer Tracy *(Boys Town)*
Other Nominees: Charles Boyer *(Algiers)*, James Cagney *(Angels with Dirty Faces)*, Robert Donat *(The Citadel)*, Leslie Howard *(Pygmalion)*

▼

THE BEST CHOICE:
James Cagney *(Angels with Dirty Faces)*
Award-Worthy Runners-Up: Robert Donat *(The Citadel)*, Cary Grant *(Bringing Up Baby)*, Charles Laughton *(The Beachcomber)*, Charles Laughton *(St. Martin's Lane)*, Spencer Tracy *(Boys Town)*

Spencer Tracy had such success playing opposite one boy in *Captains Courageous* that MGM cast him with a hundred boys as the real-life Father Flanagan in *Boys Town*. His earnest portrayal in the overly sentimental film earned him a Best Actor nomination and the chance to become the first actor to win the award two times and twice in a row. The New York Film Critics gave its 1938 Best Actor award to James Cagney for Michael Curtiz's exceptional gangster film *Angels with Dirty Faces,* but would the Academy select an actor who played a gangster over an actor who played a priest? No. I'm going to take the award away from Tracy for the second straight year—he plays second fiddle to Mickey Rooney in the second half of *Boys Town*—and give it to Cagney. He deserved at least one Oscar for his peerless gangster portrayals and I think his William "Rocky" Sullivan was his definitive thirties tough guy.

As teenage troublemakers in the tenements Rocky (Frankie Burke, who looks and talks just like Cagney) and Jerry (William Tracy) are loyal friends. Running from cops after having been caught breaking into a boxcar, Jerry falls and escapes being run over by a train only because Rocky comes back to pull him off the tracks. Because of the gesture Rocky is caught. He tells Jerry to run off and not to turn himself in. Rocky goes to reform school. When an adult, he spends much time in prison,

the result of being a headline-making gangster. He takes a three-and-a-half-year rap, expecting his lawyer partner, Frazier (Humphrey Bogart), to have his money waiting when he gets out. Frazier and the powerful Keefer (George Bancroft) try to double-cross him, but the shrewd Rocky steals their account books so that they'll give him the money and let him in on their action. Meanwhile Rocky looks up Jerry, who has become a priest. They resume their friendship. But Jerry worries that Rocky is idolized by the local teens (the Dead End Kids) and, with Rocky's permission (he doesn't believe Jerry has enough clout), launches a campaign to rid the city of criminals. When Rocky overhears Frazier and Keefer planning to rub out Jerry, he kills them both. He is convicted and sentenced to die in the electric chair. He is unafraid. Jerry asks him to pretend to be a coward so that the boys who idolize him will see that gangsters aren't good role models. Rocky says no to his good friend. But just before he is strapped in the chair, he pretends to cry for mercy. Jerry looks thankfully toward heaven. The boys are disappointed when they read of Rocky's cowardice and follow Jerry to the church to pray for him.

In his book *Cagney: The Actor as Auteur,* Patrick McGilligan aptly describes the actor's performance in *Angels with Dirty Faces* as "galvanic, volcanic." Cagney

The Dead End Kids finally respect an adult: unfortunately, it's gangster James Cagney in Michael Curtiz's *Angels with Dirty Faces.*

was the most energetic of actors—and the most intense—but in no film was he more charged up, more potently animated. His mouth works nonstop, grinning, laughing, shooting tough talk ("I know you're a smart lawyer, *very* smart—but don't get smart with me") and street slang as fast as machine gun bullets; he races back and forth across the screen, lifting his shoulders and bringing his arms to his sides before doing any rough stuff; his arms, hands, and dancer's legs are constantly in motion—he kicks, slaps with open palm or with anything in his hand at the time, feigns or throws punches, fires pistols with both hands. McGilligan quotes a *Saturday Evening Post* article Cagney wrote in 1956:

> There was one guy . . . who had a trick way of handling his body while he was engaged in a sidewalk debate. He held his elbows against his sides and argued, and he made his points by poking his finger at you. When he met you, he never said, "Hello, how are you?" He'd ask, "What do you hear?" or "What do you say?" In 1938, when I made *Angels with Dirty Faces,* I dredged this character out of my past and used him.

Gangster movies were often criticized for glorifying their crime-breaking protagonists, and in this case the criticism may have had validity. Mostly because of Cagney, Rocky Sullivan (like Cagney's Tom Powers in *The Public Enemy*) is truly appealing. He may not like himself but we share Jerry's admiration for him: he goes back to rescue the teenage Jerry from an oncoming train although it means getting caught by police and being sent to reform school; he secretly gives Jerry money to help with his recreation center; rather than threatening Jerry when the priest says he'll launch an anticrime campaign that may land Rocky in prison, Rocky shakes his hand and

says, "If I'm in your way, keep stepping just as hard"; he kills Frazier and Keefer rather than allow them to kill Jerry, although he knows this will end his criminal career; and this proud man who doesn't even blink in a hail of police bullets debases his own memory by pretending to be a coward before being executed ("to crawl on my belly") so that Jerry's kids will take a better direction in life than he did. We admire his loyalty to Jerry (and Ann Sheridan's Laury). We know he is touched by Jerry's sincere friendship and fearless honesty (their scenes together are quite moving).

He's a tough guy but we are taken by his infectious grin, even in the face of danger, his sense of humor, his touch of conceit (notice his proud expression when he realizes that the teenagers in his old neighborhood keep track of his exploits), and his humility (his donation to Jerry is sent anonymously). And we like it that he flips a lit cigarette at a mean prison guard and punches him in the jaw, and that he "feels like a million" just before going to the chair.

Cagney is great in the final scene, strongly and defiantly walking toward the electric chair, shaking hands again with his best friend Jerry and, seen only in one of Michael Curtiz's famous shadows, pretending to break down, crying "Don't kill me, please!" It's a powerful moment that makes us admire Rocky even more. Which I suppose is the problem. The Dead End Kids may think Rocky a coward and reform so they don't become like him, but kids seeing the film will idolize Rocky even more. Moreover, they will then witness Jerry, a priest, *lying* to the boys about Rocky's conduct, confirming he was a coward although he knows the opposite to be true. In James Cagney movies crime does pay and criminals are the ones with the most honor.

▶ BEST ACTRESS

WINNER:
Bette Davis (Jezebel)
Other Nominees: Fay Bainter (White Banners), Wendy Hiller (Pygmalion), Norma Shearer (Marie Antoinette), Margaret Sullavan (Three Comrades)

▼

THE BEST CHOICE:
Margaret Sullavan (Three Comrades)
Award-Worthy Runners-Up: Katharine Hepburn (Bringing Up Baby), Katharine Hepburn (Holiday), Norma Shearer (Marie Antoinette)

Bette Davis didn't get the coveted role of Scarlett O'Hara in the upcoming Gone With the Wind, so Warner Bros. tried to console its top female star by giving her the lead in William Wyler's lavish Jezebel. In her first costume picture Davis beat Vivien Leigh into theaters with her version of a willful, self-interested, flirtatious Southern belle of the Civil War era. Here is a young woman, Julie Marston, who is so audacious that she wears a red dress to a ball, and so irresponsible that she costs a man his life in a duel fought over her, and yet is so brave that she risks her life to nurse another woman's seriously ill husband. It's fun to watch Davis in one of her most ostentatious roles, but the more one sees this hokey film, the less interesting is Davis's character. Davis puts so much show into a woman who, unlike Scarlett, is empty at the core. The part could have used *some* subtlety, some indication that much is going on inside Julie that we can't immediately grasp. Bypassing Davis, my choice for Best Actress of 1938 is Margaret Sullavan, for Three Comrades. This was the film for which she received her only Oscar nomination, was voted Best Actress by the New York Film Critics, and which firmly made her as big a screen star as she was a theatrical star.

F. Scott Fitzgerald received his only screenwriting credit as cowriter of Three Comrades, adapting the grim postwar novel by Erich Maria Remarque. After the Armistice concludes World War I, friends Erich (Robert Taylor), Otto (Franchot Tone), and Gottfried (Robert Young) leave the defeated German army and set up an auto repair and taxi business. They barely get by, as the times are hard and Germany is full of despair. They spend much time drinking. Their gloomy world is cheered when they meet Sullavan's indigent Pat Hollman, a fallen aristocrat. Pat is under doctor's care for tuberculosis, but the disease is in remission and she is trying to get the most out of life. All three men fall for Pat, but when it's obvious that her heart belongs to Erich, Otto and Gottfried step aside. In fact, Otto, who feels responsible for his comrades, urges Erich to marry Pat despite her sickness. She chooses Erich over a rich man (Lionel Atwill), who could have taken care of her. On their honeymoon Pat's illness gets worse. The men worry about her and take care of her. Gottfried is killed at a political gathering. Otto gets revenge on the killer. Not wanting to burden Erich and Otto any longer, Pat disobeys her doctor's orders and subjects herself to the chilly air, knowing she will die, which she does. Erich and Otto decide to go to South America to start a new life. The spirits of Pat and Gottfried are beside them.

After a two-year absence, during which she starred in Stage Door on Broadway and married producer Leland Hayward, Sullavan returned to the movies, although it was well known that she had much more respect for theater. Now at MGM, she chose Three Comrades as her comeback vehicle. It was the seventh of only sixteen

Margaret Sullavan returned to the screen in Three Comrades, one of her greatest triumphs.

movies she would make in a career that pretty much ended in 1943, although she'd return in 1950 to star in her final film, *No Sad Songs for Me* (a fitting final title, and epitaph, for this actress who would commit suicide in 1960). For her director she agreed on Frank Borzage, who had directed her in the fine, rarely screened social drama *Little Man, What Now!*, also set in postwar Germany. Borzage's films usually featured characters who are guided by their hearts, so he was the ideal director for this tragic romance. Sullavan tried to teach Fitzgerald how to write *movie* dialogue, but when neither he nor MGM's rewrite men cut enough of what she considered Fitzgerald's "unspeakable" literary dialogue, she and Borzage trimmed words as they went along. Nonetheless, as Pauline Kael writes, *Three Comrades* retains Fitzgerald's spirit: "Bits of the dialogue are elegantly romantic, and the atmosphere has his distinctive chivalrous quality." And Margaret Sullavan, "slender and special, and with her ravishing huskiness, is an ideal Fitzgerald heroine—a perfect Daisy—and she brings her elusive, gallant sexiness to this First World War romance. . . ."

Sullavan was a marvelous, unique, too-often-forgotten actress, who was charming in comedies *(The Good Fairy, The Shop Around the Corner)*, forceful in dramas *(Little Man, What Now?, The Mortal Storm)*, and touching in tearjerkers *(The Shopworn Angel, Three Comrades, Back Street)*. Although I'm partial to Ernst Lubitsch's *The Shop Around the Corner,* in which she played opposite her best leading man, James Stewart, I think she was at her

peak in the underrated *Three Comrades*. She makes us sigh with her romantic words and glances (her characters always have different perspectives on life than those around her), delights us with her gentle humor, and makes our eyes fill with tears. She gives a luminous performance, making us understand why our three heroes (and Atwill) forget their despair while in Pat's presence, and why each falls in love with her. Because of Sullavan, we overlook the three average performances of her costars. (That she could coax an average performance out of Taylor was an accomplishment in itself.) As Frank Nugent wrote in *The New York Times:* "Her performance is almost unendurably lovely." Her every expression moves us; her graceful and thoughtful delivery makes Fitzgerald's most romantic lines seem like poetry. Sullavan is wistful, haunted: as one listens to her distinct, throaty voice one immediately gets the uneasy feeling that Pat already has one foot in heaven. Her suicide by the open window—she inhales the cold air that will destroy her lungs—only hastens what we have always expected. The quiet, noble way Pat dies is fitting for her and, from an acting standpoint, is as effectively restrained as the rest of Sullavan's performance. Most actresses would have overplayed the role, but Sullavan keeps Pat dignified and tender until the end. Pat's death concludes a stunning performance by Sullavan that, as critic Archer Winsten wrote in 1938, "will be remembered long after you have brushed away your tears."

1939

▶ BEST PICTURE

WINNER:
Gone With the Wind (MGM; Victor Fleming)
Other Nominees: *Dark Victory; Goodbye, Mr. Chips; Love Affair; Mr. Smith Goes to Washington; Ninotchka; Of Mice and Men; Stagecoach; The Wizard of Oz; Wuthering Heights*

▼

THE BEST CHOICE:
The Wizard of Oz (MGM; Victor Fleming)
Award-Worthy Runners-Up: *Destry Rides Again* (George Marshall), *Gone With the Wind* (Victor Fleming), *Gunga Din* (George Stevens), *The Lady Vanishes* (Alfred Hitchcock), *Mr. Smith Goes to Washington* (Frank Capra), *Stagecoach* (John Ford), *The Women* (George Cukor)

In what is regarded as the best year ever for Hollywood movies, the Best Picture Oscar went to Hollywood's most publicized, anticipated, and financially successful film,

Gone With the Wind, David O. Selznick's grand-scale adaptation of Margaret Mitchell's Civil War novel. It won ten Oscars in all, including two *special* awards. If not for

Robert Donat's victory over Clark Gable in the Best Actor category, it would have been the first film since *It Happened One Night* to have swept the four major awards. In addition to the Best Picture Oscar, Vivien Leigh deservedly won the Best Actress award for her Scarlett O'Hara, and Victor Fleming was voted Best Director, although George Cukor began the film and Sam Wood finished it.

Indeed, *Gone With the Wind* suffers because too many directorial styles are evident (also too many writers were employed), especially in the second half when interesting conflict (between the states and between Scarlett and Rhett) gives way to turgid soap opera. Nonetheless, *Gone With the Wind* is such a popular film that it defies criticism. And though I am not a fan myself, I wouldn't argue with its Best Picture designation if there weren't another film that is equally popular (and is part of even more movie lovers' psyches), equally spectacular cinematically, even more influential on current filmmakers, and even more impressively directed by the ubiquitous Victor Fleming (although he didn't finish this film either). *The Wizard of Oz* is not faultless—for one thing, the "There's No Place like Home" theme is more credible in *Gone With the Wind*—but I'm one of many who think it's the best film of 1939.

Both films have enormous popularity with mainstream audiences and have fanatical cult followings. But many more movie fans dislike *Gone With the Wind. The Wizard of Oz* has almost universal appeal. Children and adults love the fairy-tale elements: the journey through a strange land, very scary scenes involving Margaret Hamilton's Wicked Witch of the West, and the weird assortment of characters, including a wizard, witches, Munchkins, winged monkeys, talking apple trees, and Dorothy's three companions. Everyone responds to the special effects, the many impressive sets, the brightly colored scenery, the wild array of costumes—as in *Gone With the Wind,* MGM showed off its production capabilities—and the animals, catchy tunes, and, of course, Dorothy. Subconsciously, they may think that what Dorothy's companions desire—a brain, a heart, and courage—is what they hope they have as they grow up.

Teenage girls respond the strongest to *The Wizard of Oz.* To those who have grown up in small, isolated towns and dream of running away for excitement, Dorothy is their surrogate. Oz is their dreamworld, where everything is different, everything is colorful, everything is possible. I believe that in the film (made long after publication of L. Frank Baum's book), Oz represents Hollywood, the Emerald City represents MGM (here, Dorothy and her group are subjected to a beauty treatment, as newcomers to a studio would be), and Frank Morgan's imposing, miracle-working (but really a regular guy) Wizard was meant to be MGM studio chief Louis B. Mayer. The film's strange intention seems to have been to tell all young females who want to run off to Hollywood to stay home.

I interpret *The Wizard of Oz* as a coming-of-age picture, in which a young girl has her last childhood expe-

Four characters who are part of every movie fan's psyche: Judy Garland's Dorothy, Ray Bolger's Scarecrow, Bert Lahr's Cowardly Lion, and Jack Haley's Tin Woodsman in *The Wizard of Oz.*

rience. At the end of the film Dorothy inexplicably realizes, "There's no place like home," and decides to return to Kansas, although *we* saw what a bleak, unfriendly place it is compared to Oz, especially after the Wicked Witch is dead. According to the movie's propaganda the wayward girl has made a mature, practical decision, which signals that she has grown up. It's almost surprising that MGM didn't have the sixteen-year-old Garland, whose well-developed breasts were concealed in a straitjacket-like cloth so she could play the eleven-year-old Dorothy, burst out of her straps to underline Dorothy's passage into "womanhood." If Shirley Temple had played Dorothy, as had been intended, then there would have been no coming-of-age theme.

If Temple had played Dorothy, she would have been terrific, but she would have dominated her costars and the film would have been inferior. Still an insecure minor star, Garland was happy to let her brilliant costars shine and take some of the pressure off her. She is just wonderful. Young, innocent, pretty, funny, and so talented. Ironically, for Garland, this film turned out to be her rite of passage into too-early womanhood. Dorothy is the role that launched her toward a remarkable career, and toward the superstardom she was never able to handle. It is Garland, sixteen and afraid, as much as Dorothy, who beautifully sings "Over the Rainbow" from the heart, hoping that peace and happiness await her. We know Garland didn't find enough in her future, so maybe we watch *The Wizard of Oz* over and over again so we can rewind this film and take Garland back in time to when she was happy, when the camera had just started rolling at the beginning of the yellow brick road, on the safer side of the rainbow.

▶ BEST ACTOR

WINNER:
Robert Donat *(Goodbye, Mr. Chips)*
Other Nominees: Clark Gable *(Gone With the Wind)*, Laurence Olivier *(Wuthering Heights)*, Mickey Rooney *(Babes in Arms)*, James Stewart *(Mr. Smith Goes to Washington)*

THE BEST CHOICE:
Robert Donat *(Goodbye, Mr. Chips)*
Award-Worthy Runners-Up: Henry Fonda *(Young Mr. Lincoln)*, Cary Grant *(In Name Only)*, James Stewart *(Destry Rides Again)*, James Stewart *(Mr. Smith Goes to Washington)*

Robert Donat had been the second male lead in 1933's *The Private Life of Henry VIII,* for which Charles Laughton won the Best Actor Academy Award. Six years later Donat became the second British actor to be so honored, winning for his performance as a Latin teacher at a British boys' school in *Goodbye, Mr. Chips,* from James Hilton's novel. Donat's victory over Clark Gable prevented *Gone With the Wind* from sweeping the four major awards. Actually Donat's chief competition was James Stewart, who really came into his own with an unforgettably energetic, witty, emotional performance as a naive young senator whose idealism is tested in Capra's *Mr. Smith Goes to Washington.* Stewart is great—I also love him as the storytelling, pacifist lawman in the same year's *Destry Rides Again*—but I think Donat is just a bit better. He had made his reputation playing suave, brave men, but now as a ruffled, odd-looking, sweet older man, he had his greatest triumph.

Directed by Sam Wood, with a dedication to the late Irving Thalberg, this popular MGM picture covers sixty-three years in the life of the gentle, scholarly Mr. Chips (actually his name is Chipping)—whom James Hilton based on one of his own schoolmasters—from his first shaky day at Brookfield, through his small triumphs and great tragedies, to his last moments on his deathbed, when he is still integral to the school. Smartly, the script first has us see Chips as an eighty-three-year-old, full of charm and with a quirky personality, looking much like Mark Twain with his bushy white mustache and wild hair, half walking, half running, his body at crooked angles like a combination of Groucho Marx and a Washington Irving character. I say "smartly" because for much of the flashback that soon begins, covering Chips's first years at Brookfield and his early adulthood, Donat is so reserved that he doesn't seem to be acting at all. This was by intention, since the bachelor Chips is a timid, dull stick-in-the-mud, but it didn't allow Donat to showcase his talent. Then Chips meets (in a wonderfully romantic scene on a fog-covered mountain), falls in love with (she gets him to dance the waltz), marries, and lives blissfully with the glorious Katherine (Greer Garson). She helps him conquer his shyness and break down barriers with his pupils; and, before dying in childbirth, inspires him: "My darling, you're a very sweet person, and a very human person, and a very modest person. You have all sorts of unexpected gifts and qualities. . . . Never be afraid, Chips. . . ."

It is through Katherine that the bashful Chips comes alive, and it is then (beginning with the courtship, waltz, and proposal) that Donat breaks off his shackles, expands his characterization (Chips finally dares tell jokes to his students and is so proud when they laugh!) and wins us over as surely as Chips wins the hearts of his many, many students. Sometimes just an expression or blink of a watery eye moves us deeply; at other times his emphatic words give us cheer. His speech to the students on graduation day ("In my mind you remain boys—I shall always remember you") is softly delivered but is as powerful as Stewart's classic sore-throat filibuster in *Mr. Smith Goes to Washington.*

As a kid I was a sucker for movies with nice school-teachers, like *Good Morning, Miss Dove,* with Jennifer Jones, and *Cheers for Miss Bishop,* with Martha Scott. I particularly liked Donat's Chips. He didn't pull rank on students. Moreover, he cared about their welfare and stuck up for them. I loved the scene in which he coura-

Robert Donat finds romantic bliss with Greer Garson in *Goodbye, Mr. Chips.*

geously tells off the new headmaster who insists that Chips—who hasn't changed while the world has worsened around him—either retire or modernize his teaching methods. Chips wants his boys—the only children he has ever had or needed—to continue to leave Brookfield with "grace, dignity, and feeling for the past." Before storming out he tells the headmaster that all the boys really need is "a sense of humor and a sense of purpose." When a little boy hears that the headmaster is harassing his favorite teacher, he says the great line of the film: "If he says another word to Chips, I'll kill him." Earlier in

the film Chips apologizes to his students (how many teachers have done that?) for mistakenly disciplining them at an inopportune time (resulting in the school's losing an important sports event), sincerely saying, "If I've lost your friendship, there's nothing else that I value." The boy's line about killing the headmaster shows that during Chips's many years at Brookfield he earned a whole lot more than the boys' friendship. And Donat, a great actor, makes us see why these kids would feel such love for this special individual. It's nice that he dies with a smile on his face, still talking about his children.

▶ BEST ACTRESS

WINNER:
Vivien Leigh *(Gone With the Wind)*
Other Nominees: Bette Davis *(Dark Victory)*, Irene Dunne *(Love Affair)*, Greta Garbo *(Ninotchka)*, Greer Garson *(Goodbye, Mr. Chips)*

▼

THE BEST CHOICE:
Vivien Leigh *(Gone With the Wind)*
Award-Worthy Runners-Up: Jean Arthur *(Mr. Smith Goes to Washington)*, Bette Davis *(Dark Victory)*, Greta Garbo *(Ninotchka)*, Judy Garland *(The Wizard of Oz)*, Norma Shearer *(The Women)*

For the last time the Oscar winners of 1939 were leaked before the presentation ceremony, but even if word hadn't gotten out, it was no secret that Vivien Leigh would be selected Best Actress for her perfect performance as Scarlett O'Hara in *Gone With the Wind*. I have only limited fondness for the film itself but I fully agree with the Academy's choice of Leigh. (Although I think Judy Garland deserved a Best Actress nomination for her Dorothy in *The Wizard of Oz,* rather than a special "juvenile" actress award.) The casting of this little-known British stage and screen actress, Laurence Olivier's paramour, as the heroine of Margaret Mitchell's best-seller was worth the legendary two-year star search, and justified the rejection of some 1,400 actresses, including Bette Davis, Katharine Hepburn, and finalists Joan Bennett and Paulette Goddard. That Scarlett O'Hara stands as perhaps the greatest, most vivid female character in movie history is the direct result of Leigh's performance.

The New York Times said, "Vivien Leigh's Scarlett is so beautiful she hardly need be talented, and so talented she need not be beautiful. . . ." But it was more than Leigh's stunning beauty and impressive thespian skills that made her portrayal so mesmerizing. It was also her sound judgment, when interpreting a complex character who has terrible judgment. In her best-selling bio, *Vivien Leigh,* Anne Edwards noted that when doing the Scarlett screen tests, the film's initial director George Cukor was excited by Leigh's passionate delivery in scenes for which competitor Joan Bennett tried a sentimental, tearful approach. "There was an indescribable wildness about her," Cukor believed. Edwards astutely points out that in

the scenes with Leslie Howard's Ashley Wilkes, Leigh's Scarlett "was never coy, never a young girl with a crush; she was instead a young girl with a fully matured sensuality, direct in her desire, and dangerously—threateningly—impatient. She was Scarlett as Margaret Mitchell conceived her. . . ."

Leigh is radiant as the slim-waisted, high-spirited, emotional, manipulative, spoiled Southern belle. What may be her greatest achievement is to make us feel compassion for Scarlett even when she acts disgracefully, because we realize she is hurting herself most of all. I think

Vivien Leigh's Scarlett O'Hara and Hattie McDaniel's "Mammy" in *Gone With the Wind.*

her Scarlett is so popular with female viewers because they realize she has good qualities—including her passion, her indomitability, and her intelligence (of course, they also like her beauty)—understand her flaws (primarily that she thinks her worst traits are her best), and sympathize when she repeatedly blows it. Here's a woman with beauty, wit, charm, and numerous suitors, including her perfect match, Rhett Butler (Clark Gable), yet she loves the one man who doesn't love her. It's hard to understand why this dynamic woman would love Ashley Wilkes, who's even wimpier than Leslie Howard's effeminate Percy in *The Scarlet Pimpernel.* And she marries men for whom she has no feeling (when one dies, she's annoyed she must wear black), and winds up rejected by Rhett, at the precise moment she finally

realizes she loves him. She ends up alone on a staircase in empty Tara. She could almost be thought of as a pathetic figure. But Leigh makes female viewers—and all the rest of us too—admire her for being strong and resilient, for being a survivor and for saving her home, Tara. We know what she has been through—if Ashley had seen what we have, he would have loved her. She may be babbling (like a punch-drunk boxer who doesn't recognize defeat) that "Tomorrow is another day," but we take heart that she isn't wallowing in self-pity, and in fact, immediately gets back on her feet—just as the South (which she embodies) will rise again. We think that tomorrow if *she* gives a damn, Scarlett will go after Rhett and bring him home.

▶ BEST PICTURE

WINNER:
Rebecca (United Artists; Alfred Hitchcock)
Other Nominees: *All This, and Heaven Too, Foreign Correspondent, The Grapes of Wrath, The Great Dictator, Kitty Foyle, The Letter, The Long Voyage Home, Our Town, The Philadelphia Story*

▼

THE BEST CHOICE:
The Grapes of Wrath (20th Century–Fox; John Ford)
Award-Worthy Runners-Up: *His Girl Friday* (Howard Hawks), *The Long Voyage Home* (John Ford), *The Philadelphia Story* (George Cukor), *Pinocchio* (Ben Sharpsteen and Hamilton Luske), *The Sea Hawk* (Michael Curtiz), *The Shop Around the Corner* (Ernst Lubitsch)

David O. Selznick produced his second consecutive Best Picture winner in 1940, a year that saw the release of almost as many classics and near classics as 1939. He followed Margaret Mitchell's *Gone With the Wind,* about a strong woman who fights to hold on to her lifelong home, Tara, with Daphne Du Maurier's *Rebecca,* about a frightened woman (Joan Fontaine) who feels like an intruder in her new home, Mandalay (husband Laurence Olivier's dead wife's former home). It was strongly acted by Fontaine, Olivier, and Judith Anderson (giving a chilling portrayal of Mrs. Danvers), and atmospherically directed by Alfred Hitchcock. However, it loses its power once Olivier reveals his *secret* about Rebecca and he rather than his young bride feels frightened. Making his American debut, Hitchcock was nominated for Best Director; but though his picture prevailed, he lost the award to John Ford, who helmed *The Grapes of Wrath,* based on John Steinbeck's controversial best-seller. Strangely, a third film, *The Philadelphia Story,* won the Best Adapted

Screenplay Oscar, as Donald Ogden Stewart defeated *Rebecca*'s Robert E. Sherwood and Joan Harrison and *The Grapes of Wrath*'s Nunnally Johnson. I think *The Grapes of Wrath,* which was produced by Darryl F. Zanuck at 20th Century–Fox, should have won all three awards.

After spending four years in prison on a manslaughter charge, Tom Joad (Henry Fonda) returns to the family farm, only to discover that the bank has foreclosed on the land. Like many poor Oklahoma sharecroppers who have been kicked off their land, the Joads decide to drive to California, where, according to handbills that flood the area, there is supposed to be much work in the fields. Tom joins Ma (Jane Darwell), Pa (Russell Simpson), the rest of the Joads, and the former Preacher Casy (John Carradine) on the arduous drive west. Grandpa (Charley Grapewin) and Grandma (Zeffie Tilbury) die along the way. But California doesn't turn out to be the promised land. It is overrun by starving travelers looking for work. Because so many are desperate to care for their children,

The Joads have difficulty eating while those outside their tent scrounge for food in John Ford's *The Grapes of Wrath*.

growers are able to get away with paying minuscule wages insufficient to buy food. They are at the mercy of deputies and hired thugs who make sure there is no organizing to protest working and living conditions. Just learning himself, Casy tries to explain to Tom that people must stick together so the growers will be forced to pay adequate wages. Because he helps organize a labor strike, Preacher Casy is singled out by deputies. One hits him on the head with a club, killing him. Tom kills the deputy. The Joads flee, ending up in a decent government-run camp. But the police track down Tom. He says goodbye to Ma and escapes into the night, saying he'll follow Casy's lead. The rest of the Joads drive to where there is supposed to be work. Ma tells Pa that she's no longer afraid, because "We keep a-comin'. We're the people that live. They can't wipe us out. They can't lick us. We'll go on forever, Pa, 'cause we're the people."

Left-wing hardliners have complained that *The Grapes of Wrath* isn't radical enough. I don't think it is a radical film, but it is certainly one of the most progressive, politically enlightening pictures ever made in Hollywood. Yes, it seems to whitewash the U.S. government of any blame for the country's social ills: the written foreword tells of "economic changes beyond anyone's control"; the Joads find their one haven in a sanitary, communal goverment-run camp, headed by a guy who resembles Franklin Roosevelt. But the film makes it clear that the law of the land doesn't protect the poor, that cops are enemies, and that the best hope is a communal society. Some leftist critics complain that instead of dealing with the masses, the film puts all its emphasis on one family, which experiences and confronts the ills of society. Actually the film does something quite extraordinary. Initially, it makes us hope the Joads stick together; but then it makes us change our minds, as we come to understand that a mass movement is more important than either individuals or families. At first we sympathize with the Joads' fierce determination to cling to one

another, for even their neighbors and other poor people have turned against them in order to feed *their* families. Their sticking together seems like a noble quality. But eventually we see that they are going in the wrong direction, that they are irresponsibly neglecting what's best for the common good. Tom (influenced by Casy) and Ma (influenced by Tom) come to realize that it's best that the family *not* consolidate but instead join a bigger family. Tom learns from Casy that a man doesn't have a soul of his own but "just a little piece of a big soul, the one big soul that belongs to everybody." The Joads become part of the *family of man*. Once rooted to their Oklahoma home, they now realize that all of America is their home (before they felt like aliens in their own country) and they need not live together to be together. Once the symbol of the family, Ma becomes—when she delivers her inspiring final speech—a symbol of the *people*.

John Ford was attacted to this project because the Joads reminded him of farmers in his native Ireland who were dislocated during a potato famine. Ford was a political conservative, but by not pulling any punches he made a film that has almost shockingly leftist sympathies, which inspires viewers to develop a sociopolitical conscious-ness. It shows that the more politically involved people become (Casy, Tom, Ma), the more energized, the hap-pier, they are. Ford's film is, oddly, about the politicali-zation of Tom and Ma, two well-meaning, ignorant people who always kept to themselves. Ma: "I don't understand it, Tom." Tom: "Me, neither, Ma." But they do understand right from wrong, and that is the first step in their education.

Ford directs the film with respect for Steinbeck's story and affection for his downtrodden but resilient charac-ters. Usually one of the most blatantly sentimental of directors, Ford refrained this time from manipulating us into crying, even during the funeral scenes, because the Joads don't cry then, either, and instead get strength from adversity. But he makes us feel the great loss the Joads and their neighbor Muley (John Qualen) feel when they lose their homes. And he touches us when he shows Ma throwing out mementos, keeping only those—she quickly models an aged pair of earrings and stares at her reflection—for which she has special fondness. And he isn't too shy to have his film be sweet, as when Tom dances with and serenades the giggling Ma, and when a kindly waitress sells Pa a five-cent candy for his two youngest kids, assuring the proud man that they sell two for a penny. Ford worked closely with cinematographer Gregg Toland, whose images are beautiful, although, as Ford said, "he had nothing beautiful to photograph." There are magnificent shots of Tom moving across the landscape, of beautifully lit faces, of characters in close-up speaking powerful words. (This is not a picture you want to see colorized.)

The film succeeds on all levels. Alfred Newman com-posed the fine, simple score, which incorporates Ameri-can standards like "Red River Valley" and "Comin' Around the Mountain," songs familiar to people like the

Joads. Nunnally Johnson wrote a terrific script, taking into consideration that the Okies don't talk too much or too articulately. He gave their few, simple words power by having them delivered from the heart, and inspired by common sense. When his characters give little speeches that include great truths, we believe that these common folks are capable of these profound thoughts, and are not merely serving as mouthpieces for an intellectual screenwriter.

But it all comes down to the people: the characters and the wonderful actors who played them. Henry Fonda as Tom, John Carradine as Casy, John Qualen as Muley, and Charley Grapewin as Grandpa are unforgettable. Heavy-set Jane Darwell, an Irish actress, was an odd choice to play Ma, but she made the part her own. She has that terrific wordless scene in which she throws out mementos, and several monologues, all done without cuts, that are wonderfully moving. Darwell beat out *Rebecca*'s Judith Anderson for Best Supporting Actress, and if their respective roles were an influence on voters, it was, appropriately, good defeating evil. Since Darwell's Ma is separated from Fonda's Tom at the end of the film, it would have been great if Fonda had deservedly won a Best Actor Oscar so he and Darwell could have been reunited on the victory stand.

▶ BEST ACTOR

WINNER:
James Stewart *(The Philadelphia Story)*
Other Nominees: Charles Chaplin *(The Great Dictator)*, Henry Fonda *(The Grapes of Wrath)*, Raymond Massey *(Abe Lincoln in Illinois)*, Laurence Olivier *(Rebecca)*

▼

THE BEST CHOICE:
Henry Fonda *(The Grapes of Wrath)*
Award-Worthy Runners-Up: James Cagney *(City for Conquest)*, Charles Chaplin *(The Great Dictator)*, W. C. Fields *(The Bank Dick)*, Cary Grant *(His Girl Friday)*, James Stewart *(The Shop Around the Corner)*

Having lost to Robert Donat the previous year despite an Oscar-caliber performance in *Mr. Smith Goes to Washington,* James Stewart was now the sentimental choice of Academy voters. I preferred his unnominated performance as a clerk, opposite Margaret Sullavan, in Ernst Lubitsch's *The Shop Around the Corner,* but he won for George Cukor's sparkling comedy *The Philadelphia Story,* from Philip Barry's stage success. Stewart was fine as a newspaper reporter who romances society girl Katharine Hepburn (Cary Grant's ex-wife), all the while unaware that fellow reporter Ruth Hussey loves him; but both Hepburn and Hussey are superior. Stewart himself thought his good friend Henry Fonda deserved the Oscar for his haunting portrait of Tom Joad in *The Grapes of Wrath.* I agree.

Fonda wanted to play the hero of Steinbeck's novel so badly that when Darryl F. Zanuck hinted he'd offer the part to Don Ameche or Tyrone Power, Fonda reluctantly agreed to a long-term contract at 20th Century–Fox to get the part. In retrospect it was the proper decision for him. For, along with his Wyatt Earp in John Ford's *My Darling Clementine* and Abe Lincoln in Ford's *Young Mr. Lincoln,* this is the role with which Fonda is most identified.

The Tom Joad whom Fonda plays so well is tight lipped, tough, but (as he assures Jane Darwell's Ma) not mean, warm but not tender, edgy but not about to erupt in violence, quick to rile but not someone who loses his senses. He is neither emotional nor sentimental. He speaks only the truth and expects the same in return. He minds his own business; as he puts it, "I'm just trying to get along without shoving anybody. That's all." As he walks calmly across the landscape, patiently and silently (not humming, whistling, singing, or talking to himself), we sense that he is comfortable being alone (we're not surprised to learn he's been in prison), yet, as we discover, he is devoted to his family, which is made up of others who have been hardened by an arduous life. His face seems to be chiseled from granite, his eyes are those of someone who doesn't have many happy memories, his voice is without feeling and dry, as if he needs a drink of water. He punctuates his stronger words by slamming a trucker's door (after saying, "You're about to bust a gut to know what I done, ain't ye? Well, I ain't a guy to let you down—homicide"), breaking bottles (after saying, "I killed a guy in a dance hall"), spitting (after saying, "Nobody ever told me I'd be hiding out at my own place").

I think the film is mostly about the political enlightenment of Tom, who begins the film apolitical and ignorant, and ends it by going off perhaps to be an organizer, perhaps a subversive. What's interesting is that the more political he becomes, the more Tom comes alive. Fonda becomes more expressive, and speaks with more conviction. By film's end Tom has completely changed from the character I earlier described. He even dances with and sings to Ma; later he kisses his parents. After watching his family suffer extreme hardships, seeing starving children, witnessing a bully cop shoot a poor woman, and seeing Casy arrested for kicking the cop (Tom actually kicked him but since he is out on parole Casy took the rap), Tom begins to see the light on his own. He tells Ma, "There comes a time when a man gets mad. They're working away at our spirits, they're trying to make us cringe and crawl, working on our decency." The family settles down in a camp and finally has enough money to buy a little food, but Tom is not content. He sneaks out of the camp to learn why other workers have been gathering outside the fences. He learns from Casy (who has been set free) that these workers are on strike for decent wages, while the growers are employing ignorant people, like the Joads, to be strikebreakers. Casy is killed by deputies who want to silence him, and just as Casy predicted, the grower lowers the wages of everyone inside the camp because a strike is no longer in the offing and there is an oversupply of workers. "That Casy, he might have been a preacher, but he saw things clear," says Tom. "He was like a lantern—he helped me to see things too."

Fonda's great moment comes at the end, following more strife. As Fonda is shown in beautiful close-up by Ford, Tom tells his Ma, "I've been thinking about Casy. I've been thinking about us too. About our people living like pigs; good rich land laying fallow. Or maybe one guy with a million acres and a hundred thousand farmers starving. And I've been wonderin' if all our folks stuck together and yelled . . . Maybe it's like Casy said—a fellah ain't got a soul of his own, just a little piece of a big soul, the one big soul that belongs to everybody. . . ."

He speaks calmly but there is excitement in his eyes, as if he has finally found the purpose to his life. He tells Ma that he will flee the police, but he isn't going to disappear. He has a mission: "I'll be around in the dark, I'll be everywhere you look . . . wherever there's a cop beating a guy, I'll be in the way guys yell when they're mad, I'll be in the way kids laugh when they're hungry

During *The Grapes of Wrath* Henry Fonda's Tom Joad and Jane Darwell's Ma Joad become politicized, learning that "the people" are even more important than family.

and they know supper's ready, and when the people are eating the stuff they raised, living in the houses they build, I'll be there too." He admits he doesn't yet understand what's going on, but he intends to "find out what's wrong" so "I can fix it."

Never affectionate when he was apolitical, Tom kisses his sleeping father on the forehead, accepts Ma's kiss on the cheek and gives her one in return, and slips off into the darkness. We last see him walking alone (no one walks like Fonda), but it's not like the dreary shot at the beginning. Now he walks up a not very steep incline under bright, friendly skies. There's finally sun in the life of this man from the Dust Bowl.

▶ BEST ACTRESS

WINNER:
Ginger Rogers *(Kitty Foyle)*
Other Nominees: Bette Davis *(The Letter)*, Joan Fontaine *(Rebecca)*, Katharine Hepburn *(The Philadelphia Story)*, Martha Scott *(Our Town)*

▼

THE BEST CHOICE:
Rosalind Russell *(His Girl Friday)*
Award-Worthy Runners-Up: Bette Davis *(The Letter)*, Joan Fontaine *(Rebecca)*, Greer Garson *(Pride and Prejudice)*, Katharine Hepburn *(The Philadelphia Story)*, Margaret Sullavan *(The Shop Around the Corner)*

Ginger Rogers changed her image, darkening her hair and playing a secretary rather than a chorine in *Kitty Foyle,* from Christopher Morley's popular novel. She won the Best Actress Oscar, besting Katharine Hepburn, her

former RKO studiomate. Hepburn put her career back on track as rich socialite Tracy Lord in MGM's *The Philadelphia Story,* from the stage play Philip Barry wrote especially for her. It has been speculated that Academy voters bypassed Hepburn to counter her election as Best Actress by the New York Film Critics. (Hepburn's selection in New York may have come about only because of a threatened filibuster by some voters.) So Rogers's victory is somewhat tainted, though it's good that she got an Oscar sometime during her career. But *Kitty Foyle* and her performance (and her hairstyles) don't really hold up, especially when compared to her best work with Fred Astaire, or with *Gold Diggers of 1933, Stage Door, Vivacious Lady, Bachelor Mother, Lucky Partners, Roxie Hart, The Major and the Minor, Monkey Business,* and others. My choice for Best Actress of 1940 is Rosalind Russell, who was sensational as a reporter in Howard Hawks's hilarious screwball comedy, *His Girl Friday,* an adaptation of *The Front Page* in which Hildy Johnson is female.

The former star reporter for the *Morning Star,* Hildy Johnson (Russell), tells her ex-husband, conniving editor Walter Burns (Cary Grant), that she is not returning to him or her job. Instead she is marrying Bruce Baldwin (Ralph Bellamy), a stuffy Albany insurance salesman who will definitely give her the home Walter merely promised her. Walter realizes that to win her back before the train for Albany departs, he'll have to remind her that she's a *reporter* and isn't cut out to be a housewife. He manipulates her into interviewing Earl Williams (John Qualen), who is to be executed tomorrow for killing a black cop. While Walter uses a succession of dirty tricks to get Bruce repeatedly arrested, Hildy interviews Earl and then gets an exclusive story about Earl's subsequent escape. She and Walter hide Earl in a desk while reporters, crooked politicians, and police try to track him down. Covering the story, Hildy forgets about Bruce. She realizes she still loves her job, and loves Walter. She agrees to remarry him.

Hildy was part of the tradition of crack, wisecracking reporters that were played by the likes of Glenda Farrell (she was Torchy Blane in a series of movies), Joan Blondell, and Joan Bennett in the thirties. It has been suggested that Hildy was based on Adela Rogers St. John, who also wore tailored suits, but she was inspired equally by the reporter whom Russell played in the 1938 comedy *Four's a Crowd.* Hildy is one of many female characters in Howard Hawks's films who fit snugly into the Hawksian male world without losing their femininity. Hildy thinks she should be a woman instead of an "inhuman" reporter, but she comes to realize that being a reporter doesn't mean she has to stop being a woman and give up some human qualities. This is not a typical screwball comedy about the battle of the sexes, but is instead about sexual differentiation—we see that men have traditionally "female" attributes (i.e., the tough male reporters gossip, Walter is manipulative) while women have traditionally "male" attributes. Russell's Hildy can drink, smoke, wisecrack, think on her feet, run, physically tackle sources, and lift heavy typewriters as well as any male reporter; Walter doesn't send her to safety in a crisis, but pleads for her help: "This is war—you can't desert me now." Yet, as the male reporters agree, Hildy writes better than

In Howard Hawks's *His Girl Friday* reporter Rosalind Russell concedes she is bound for life to editor Cary Grant, who reveals he has the goods on mayor Clarence Kolb and sheriff Gene Lockhart as wide-eyed Billy Gilbert looks on.

any of them and this is because only she exhibits tenderness for her subjects (that's why she's called a "sob sister").

Russell is dynamic. Not only does she keep up the fast-paced dialogue with Grant but, throughout the film, has to carry on several conversations at once (sometimes having one person next to her and one on the phone, at one time having Walter on one line and Bruce on the other). Hildy always does more than one thing at once. Only when she calmly and skillfully interviews Earl Williams does she relax. That's why she's thoroughly convincing as a reporter. I like it that she easily slips into the reporter's rhythm of speech (she talks while others talk—Hawks's trademarked overlapping dialogue); I like her dexterity with phones and typewriters, her look of excitement as a story unfolds around her (Hildy literally chases down a source after Earl's escape, *without* Walter's urging), the way she smiles—revealing her love of her profession—when she tells Walter (whom she's obviously back in love with), "That's the worst jam we've been in in a long time."

Russell/Hildy is a great match and great combatant for the comically ruthless Grant/Walter. Her best moment is when Hildy tells off Walter over the phone, while the awed, spineless male reporters encircle her. In this quick scene she rips up her story for Walter to hear, puts on her hat, slips into the wrong arm of her coat, yanks the phone from its connection (eventually), races back and forth from her desk to her table, and assumes numerous postures as she tells Walter, "Now, you get this, you double-crossing chimpanzee. There ain't going to be an interview, and there ain't going to be a story. . . . I wouldn't cover the burning of Rome for you if they were just lighting it up. And if I ever lay my two eyes on you again, I'm going to walk right up to you and hammer on that monkey skull till it rings like a Chinese gong." Her words are unladylike, but they further convince the men that she's a remarkable *woman.*

1941

▶ BEST PICTURE

WINNER:
How Green Was My Valley (20th Century–Fox; John Ford)

Other Nominees: *Blossoms in the Dust, Citizen Kane, Hold Back the Dawn, The Little Foxes, The Maltese Falcon, One Foot in Heaven, Sergeant York, Suspicion*

▼

THE BEST CHOICE:
Citizen Kane (RKO; Orson Welles)

Award-Worthy Runners-Up: *Ball of Fire* (Howard Hawks), *The Maltese Falcon* (John Huston), *That Hamilton Woman* (Alexander Korda)

Darryl F. Zanuck's disappointment that *The Grapes of Wrath* had not been voted Best Picture of 1940, despite John Ford's selection as Best Director, was lessened when his *How Green Was My Valley* won the Best Picture award for 1941. Ford won his second consecutive Oscar for directing Richard Llewellyn's sensitive memory piece about his proud Welsh mining family. Chief among the Best Picture losers was Orson Welles's groundbreaking *Citizen Kane,* which received nine nominations but won only for the Original Screenplay by Herman J. Mankiewicz and Welles. It has been suggested that the picture's grim tone contributed to its defeat, but it's not as bleak as *How Green Was My Valley,* in which several family members die and the romantic leads (Maureen O'Hara and Walter Pidgeon) end up miserable because she married someone else. More likely it was the Academy's strange prejudice against a film about upper-class characters—voters preferred the poor Welsh miners in Ford's film, and the country-boy Quaker played by Gary Cooper in Howard Hawks's *Sergeant York*—and against an upstart twenty-six-year-old radio-theater director-writer-actor from the East who came to Hollywood and in one fell swoop turned the industry on its ear. Also, it was probable that the Academy didn't want to offend William Randolph Hearst by voting for a picture whose flawed protagonist was supposedly inspired by the controversial newspaper magnate.

Stunningly directed, magnificently acted, and brilliantly written, *Citizen Kane* is usually regarded as the greatest film ever made. I wouldn't argue with that assessment. At very least it is the most influential film of the sound era, the picture that best illustrates the potential of film as a storytelling medium and as an outlet for personal and artistic expression. Everyone who sees it for the first time is astonished; and repeated viewings only increase the impact.

Welles's debut film is about a reporter's (William Al-

land as Thompson) investigation into the life of Charles Foster Kane (Welles), former publisher of the *New York Inquirer* and other papers, onetime gubernatorial candidate in New York, and one of the richest and most powerful men of the twentieth century. Upon his recent death Kane had uttered the word *Rosebud.* Thompson thinks the word's meaning may be the key to Kane's life.

Journalistic in nature, the film takes us along as Thompson researches Kane's life and interviews those closest to him, including Leland (Joseph Cotten), former drama critic of the *Inquirer* and at one time Kane's best friend, Bernstein (Everett Sloane), chairman of the board of the *Inquirer* and Kane's manager since the 1890s, and

At his peak, before his fall, Orson Welles's Charles Foster Kane runs for governor in *Citizen Kane.*

the Marion Davies–influenced Susan Alexander (Dorothy Comingore), Kane's second wife and second-rate entertainer. They tell fascinating stories about Kane, mostly with a negative slant. But when director Welles and cinematographer Gregg Toland interpret their words, we see the contradictions between what Welles manipulates us into accepting as the truth and how Kane is remembered by those who know him. Ironically, Welles creates "realism" (the "true" picture of Kane) through illusion and expressionism. We learn about Kane and the other characters not only through dialogue but also through Welles's creative use of props, screen space, music (by Bernard Herrmann), editing, lighting, sound, costumes, makeup, camera lenses, camera placement, camera movement, and camera angles. Because Welles preferred showing his characters in relation to their settings, Toland (who deserved an Oscar) rarely used close-ups and employed deep-focus photography and expressionistic lighting. As the film progresses, each set loses its human element and becomes forbidding, reflecting the mind-set of the brooding Kane or the people dominated by his will. Welles had a background in radio and was particularly innovative with sound. Much about his characters is revealed through speech patterns. Bernard Herrmann's dramatic score also serves as a storytelling device. The music soars as Kane triumphs, and is wobbly and ominous as Kane experiences a free-fall from grace.

So it is that Welles turns us into investigators more skillful than Thompson, who doesn't have the benefit of Welles's storytelling devices. The disclosure of the meaning of "Rosebud"—it was the name on his childhood sled—is Welles's visual gift to us, and is not granted Thompson. It does help us understand Kane. We decide that Kane was a badly flawed but sympathetic man, who needed love so badly that he tried to buy it, and who was deserted by all he loved and tried to control. Contrary to what most critics contend, the dying Kane doesn't long for his Edenic childhood, because his youth with no friends and a brutal father was miserable. But when he says "Rosebud," he thinks back to his only cherished possession before he became wealthy and could buy anything he wanted, including people. As he reflected years earlier, before he gave up his principles to pursue power (a common Welles theme) and hadn't yet experienced his personal and political slide, "If I hadn't been really rich, I might have been a really great man." At least he was the worthy subject of a really great film.

▶ BEST ACTOR

WINNER:

Gary Cooper *(Sergeant York)*
Other Nominees: Cary Grant *(Penny Serenade)*, Walter Huston *(All That Money Can Buy)*, Robert Montgomery *(Here Comes Mr. Jordan)*, Orson Welles *(Citizen Kane)*

▼

THE BEST CHOICE:

Gary Cooper *(Ball of Fire)*
Award-Worthy Runners-Up: Humphrey Bogart *(The Maltese Falcon)*, Humphrey Bogart *(High Sierra)*, Charles Boyer *(Hold Back the Dawn)*, Cary Grant *(Penny Serenade)*, Robert Montgomery *(Here Comes Mr. Jordan)*, Orson Welles *(Citizen Kane)*

Humphrey Bogart parlayed a double dose of toughness into full-fledged stardom in 1941, when he played detective Sam Spade in John Huston's *The Maltese Falcon* and gangster Roy "Mad Dog" Earle in Raoul Walsh's *High Sierra*. Both parts should have earned him Oscar nominations, maybe awards. The force of Bogart's personality colors our views of both characters, making us like them despite their actions: As was Walsh's intention, Bogart makes us see the decency in "Mad Dog"; but I don't think Huston wanted us to be so taken by Bogart's heroic posture that we fail to recognize that Spade is a true louse. So essential is Bogart's Sam Spade to all us movie fanatics, and so exciting is his performance, that I'd give him the Alternate Oscar for *The Maltese Falcon* if (1) I weren't going to award him two years later for *Casablanca;* and (2) if 1941 weren't such a big year for another superstar, Gary Cooper.

Although I'm not nearly as fond of Cooper as I am of Bogart, I acknowledge that this "invisible-acting actor" made a significant contribution to the cinema. For instance, in 1941 he starred in three major pictures: *Sergeant York* and *Ball of Fire,* for Howard Hawks; and Frank Capra's failure *Meet John Doe.* Cooper even won his first Oscar for playing Alvin York, a pacifist who became America's greatest hero in World War I. However, I think he gave a much better performance—my favorite of his entire career—in Hawks's screwball classic, *Ball of Fire.*

Billy Wilder and Charles Brackett wrote this congenial variation of *Snow White and the Seven Dwarfs.* Cooper is Professor Bertram Potts, a genius bachelor who lives in a large house in New York with seven elderly male scholars (played by seven marvelous character actors). For years they have been holed up with each other while assembling an encyclopedia. Potts, whose specialty is English, decides to venture into the city to gather material for his entry on current American slang. He invites a sexy night-

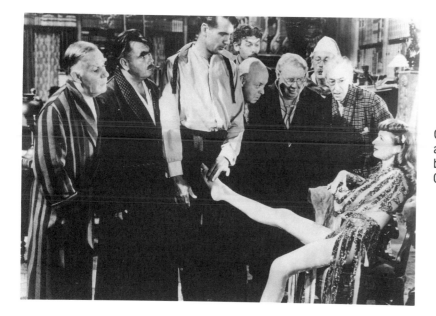

Gary Cooper's bachelor Professor Bertram Potts and his seven elderly male friends are bewitched by Barbara Stanwyck's exotic dancer, Sugarpuss O'Shea, in Howard Hawks's *Ball of Fire.*

club singer, Sugarpuss O'Shea (Barbara Stanwyck), to come to the house to help on his project. Sugarpuss has to go on the lam while her gangster boyfriend, Joe Lilac (Dana Andrews), is being hounded by police about a murder charge. So she moves in with the eight men. She wins over the old men, putting a spark in their lives. "Potsy," as she calls Cooper, quickly falls in love with her. Not wanting to be kicked out, she plays along with him. She accepts his marriage proposal, planning to run away with Lilac when the coast is clear. They all drive to New Jersey for the wedding, but Lilac turns up and whisks Sugarpuss away as planned. Potsy is depressed that he was dumped, not realizing that Sugarpuss has come to love him. Two of Lilac's henchmen keep the encyclopedists at bay with guns until Sugarpuss will agree to marry Lilac. Potsy realizes that Sugarpuss is in trouble. He and his friends overcome the henchmen and rush to stop the wedding. They arrive just in time. Potsy beats up Lilac. He and Sugarpuss will marry.

As "Potsy," Cooper is extremely likable, genuinely funny, and much more aggressive and chatty than some of his most annoying innocents. I have always had trouble believing the level of naiveté of many Cooper heroes. Grown men, they are tongue-tied knuckleheads around women. That is true of Cooper's Alvin York, for instance. But Bertram Potts, naive and old-fashioned as he is, is different. "I'm a perfectly normal man with perfectly normal instincts," he assures Sugarpuss. When his neck becomes hot and sweaty in her presence and needs to be cooled off, he knows what the problem is. He admits that he noticed her with sunlight in her hair and likes the way she breathed on his ear while correcting his spelling of *boogie-woogie*. He tries to send Sugarpuss away because of his sexual attraction to her: "Make no mistake. I shall regret the absence of your keen mind. Unfortunately, it is inseparable from an extremely disturbing body." And how he loves kissing her ("Yum yum!"). Sure, this Cooper is awkward and goofy (he

forgets his tenses!) and has a jerky side, but he is never less than sexually aggressive (in a positive, exciting way) toward Sugarpuss. It's likely that he has never been with another woman, but he knows what he's doing. The way he kisses Sugarpuss (she has to cool her neck with water) shows that he'll match her in the sack. He's no prude.

"Potsy" is Cooper's sweetest character (even Mr. Deeds kept slugging people). Here's a man who has had so few perks in his life that he gets excited just hearing Sugarpuss deliver slang, such as "Shove in your clutch" and "Scrow, scram, scraw!" He thinks it's only the phrases that thrill him, but of course she has a lot to do with it. She excites him. Her energy energizes him. His entire body comes alive. Here's a man who has lived such an isolated existence that he considers the time he spent before he met Sugarpuss to have been "preface" to his life. Dust just piled up on his heart, he tells her, "and it took you to blow it away." How could Sugarpuss not be touched by this good, honest man who is so open with his romantic thoughts? He is the first man to see *her* goodness and is excited rather than turned off by her outright sexiness. Her eyes fill with tears as she listens to him say that he thinks of her every waking hour, and that he wants to take her in his arms. . . . He holds nothing back from her.

He'll risk making a fool of himself by proposing. He'll risk getting killed by Lilac's henchmen to stop her from marrying that brute. He'll read a how-to boxing book just so he can stand up to Lilac for her; and, all arms and legs, he'll teach Lilac a lesson for treating *her* badly. She just makes him so happy and he isn't too shy to show that. He even gets "the itch to yodel." Sugarpuss thinks he resembles a giraffe and would get drunk on buttermilk, but she comes to love him for just those things. Such characteristics start to seem surprisingly sexy to her. By film's end, when she knows *everything* about him, she would even be turned on by his yodeling.

▶ BEST ACTRESS

WINNER:
Joan Fontaine *(Suspicion)*
Other Nominees: Bette Davis *(The Little Foxes)*, Greer Garson *(Blossoms in the Dust)*, Olivia de Havilland *(Hold Back the Dawn)*, Barbara Stanwyck *(Ball of Fire)*

▼

THE BEST CHOICE:
Barbara Stanwyck *(Ball of Fire)*
Award-Worthy Runners-Up: Bette Davis *(The Little Foxes)*, Olivia de Havilland *(Hold Back the Dawn)*, Irene Dunne *(Penny Serenade)*, Geraldine Fitzgerald *(Shining Victory)*, Joan Fontaine *(Suspicion)*, Vivien Leigh *(That Hamilton Woman)*, Barbara Stanwyck *(The Lady Eve)*

For the second consecutive year Joan Fontaine was nominated for Best Actress for playing a distressed young bride who doesn't trust her husband in an Alfred Hitchcock mystery. She lost in 1940, although *Rebecca* was voted Best Picture, but in 1941 she got her Oscar, although the nominated *Suspicion* lost as Best Picture. Among the nominated actresses Fontaine defeated was her more established older sister, Olivia de Havilland, who played a spinster charmed by gigolo Charles Boyer in *Hold Back the Dawn*. The rift between the rivalrous siblings had widened; de Havilland was already smarting at Fontaine's leap to stardom in *Rebecca,* a role Hitchcock had wanted de Havilland to fill (Jack Warner wouldn't loan her to producer David O. Selznick). But, as good as Fontaine and de Havilland were, others deserved the 1941 Oscar more. As Emma Hamilton, opposite Laurence Olivier's Horatio Nelson, in Alexander Korda's superb *That Hamilton Woman,* Vivien Leigh gave a performance that was perhaps better (though its impact was much smaller) than her Oscar-winning Scarlett O'Hara. And Bette Davis was at her soulless best as Regina Giddens in *The Little Foxes.*

But I think 1941 belonged to Barbara Stanwyck, who gave three outstanding performances. She might justly have been given the Oscar for her cocky, fast-talking newspaper reporter who uses unemployed Gary Cooper to make headlines and then falls for him in Frank Capra's depressing misfire *Meet John Doe.* She should have won for either her cocky, fast-talking gangster's moll who uses underpaid professor Gary Cooper and then falls in love with him in Howard Hawks's *Ball of Fire,* or her cocky, fast-talking con artist who uses millionaire Henry Fonda and then falls in love with him in Preston Sturges's *The Lady Eve.* I think Stanwyck is flawless in both comedies, but since I like her character better in the Hawks film, that's the role for which I'll award her an Alternate Oscar.

Stanwyck was a versatile actress who played in all kinds of films, in all types of roles, including dance hall girls, nurses, fallen women, loose women, an American who falls in love with a Chinese warlord (in Frank Capra's *The Bitter Tea of General Yen*), an evangelist (in *Miracle Woman*), crack reporters, petty thieves, bitches and femme fatales (beginning in the mid-forties), and Annie

Oakley. But until she hardened her screen image after 1944's *Double Indemnity,* she most often played young, cynical, independent women from lower-working-class backgrounds. They are cocky about their smarts, wit, toughness, and ability to survive in a man's world, but dislike themselves because they think they have no class and no integrity. They are hard-bitten women. However, their hearts melt once they get to know sweet, honest, and decent men. These unwary men don't realize that initially Stanwyck's women are manipulating them and intend to betray them. They see special qualities in these women that all other men on earth have missed. The Stanwyck woman typically makes amends, discovering that, just as he's insisted, she was worthy of her man after all. Such is the case with Sugarpuss O'Shea.

Sugarpuss is a sassy, sexy nightclub entertainer, whose ambition is to marry rich gangster Joe Lilac (Dana Andrews). When she gets his engagement ring, she beams: "A Third Avenue girl in the major leagues at last." When Gary Cooper's low-paid English professor Bertram Potts proposes, she brushes him aside, explaining "I'm mink coat, I'm no bungalow apron." After all, as Lilac tells Potts, "She sulks if she has to wear last year's ermine." But against her own wishes she falls for "Potsy" because "he's the kind of guy who gets drunk on a glass of buttermilk." Even though she thinks Potsy will no longer have anything to do with her after she goes off with Lilac, she loves him so much that she stubbornly refuses to marry Lilac. She tells Lilac that she won't marry him even if he kills her. She no longer desires money. All she needed was to see that there are good people in the world—in her circle she had never met the likes of Potsy and his seven elderly friends (who are helping him write an encyclopedia). And she needed one opportunity to be decent—Sugarpuss comes through with flying colors.

Stanwyck was never sexier, more vivacious, or more energetic. Sugarpuss O'Shea *is* the title character, who sets a fire in the boring, secluded lives of Potsy and his equally sweet collaborators and housemates (she is their Snow White). She provides a new language to them—the slang Potsy is researching—dances with them, flirts with them, and excites them. Stanwyck zips around the frame with unbridled energy and quick, nonstop talk, as the

Two of the major stars of the era, Barbara Stanwyck and Gary Cooper, were a charming and sexy couple in *Ball of Fire*.

uninhibited Sugarpuss offers opinions, information, slang, wisecracks. She sings, she dances. She is fetching in both glittery bare-midriff costumes and casual dress, and while standing next to the window so the sunlight is in her hair. And she is funny: when her zipper gets stuck, Sugarpuss says casually, "I had this happen one night in the middle of my act. I couldn't get a thing off. Was I embarrassed!" But Stanwyck is also wonderful in those rare moments when Sugarpuss is quiet, with her eyes filling with tears as she listens to Potsy's sincere, romantic words to her. She really makes you see her character's sweetness and goodness, which even Sugarpuss doesn't recognize.

In 1981, at the age of seventy-four, Barbara Stanwyck received an Honorary Oscar and that Academy Award ceremony's only standing ovation. Under any circumstances she deserved the award for a remarkable four-decade career in which she made many classic films, gave many marvelous performances, and never made an enemy. But it's unfortunate that it was meant to atone for her having never been named Best Actress, despite four nominations. She should have gotten recognition as Best Actress exactly forty years before, when she made *Meet John Doe, The Lady Eve,* and, my favorite, *Ball of Fire,* erasing all doubts that she was one of the greatest actresses in that remarkable era of actresses.

1942

► BEST PICTURE

WINNER:
Mrs. Miniver (MGM; William Wyler)
Other Nominees: *The Invaders, Kings Row, The Magnificent Ambersons, The Pied Piper, The Pride of the Yankees, Random Harvest, The Talk of the Town, Wake Island, Yankee Doodle Dandy*

▼

THE BEST CHOICE:
Sullivan's Travels (Paramount; Preston Sturges)
Award-Worthy Runners-Up: *The Magnificent Ambersons* (Orson Welles), *The Palm Beach Story* (Preston Sturges), *To Be or Not to Be* (Ernst Lubitsch)

Hollywood got firmly behind the war effort, so it's not surprising that Warners' flag-waving *Yankee Doodle Dandy,* Paramount's *Wake Island,* and 20th's *The Pied Piper* were heavily promoted and, along with Michael Powell's patriotic, British-made war film, *The Invaders,* received Best Picture nominations. Nor is it a surprise that MGM's *Mrs. Miniver,* unabashed propaganda about a middle-class British family coping with the war, won six major Oscars: 1942's Best Picture, Best Actress (Greer Garson), Best Supporting Actress (Teresa Wright), Best Director (William Wyler), Best Screenplay (George Froeschel, James Hilton, Claudine West, Arthur Wimperis), and Best Cinematography (Joseph Ruttenberg). Wanting Americans to favor his sending our boys overseas in the early stages of our involvement in World War II, President Roosevelt even asked that MGM release its picture earlier than intended. He made no such request of United Artists in regard to *To Be or Not To Be,* Ernst Lubitsch's great comedy, probably figuring Americans were more likely to rally behind brave Brits than beleaguered Poles. In its day *Mrs. Miniver* served its purpose, but today it comes across as being self-conscious, even phony, as this "British" family was written as a typical American family, so American viewers would identify with them and want to help. Today film fanatics respond more enthusiastically to Preston Sturges's comedies *Sullivan's Travels* and *The Palm Beach Story,* Lubitsch's *To Be or Not to Be,* and Orson Welles's flawed (because of studio editing) tour de force *The Magnificent Ambersons,* the only one of these four classics that wasn't a comedy and the only one even nominated for Best Picture.

If there ever had been a tie in the Best Picture category (as there have been in the Actor and Actress categories), I'd allow myself one tie, too, and pick both *Sullivan's Travels* and *To Be or Not to Be* as the co–Best Pictures of 1942. Neither film was adequately appreciated upon release—Lubitsch's film was lambasted by many critics for being a comedy that dealt with unfunny topics like Hitler, the Nazis, the Gestapo, and death—but each gradually became recognized as a masterpiece, among the wittiest and sharpest satires ever filmed. Since *Sullivan's Travels* even makes reference to Lubitsch, it doesn't seem right that these two films should compete for my Alternate Oscar. So if I give it to *Sullivan's Travels* it isn't because of overall quality but because with its images of the destitute, lost, and forgotten people, it is the more timely of the two pictures.

In most of writer-director Sturges's forties comedies, characters' fortunes change overnight, usually for the better. Often they get what they want simply by pretending to be who they want to be. In *Sullivan's Travels* the handsome, much underrated Joel McCrea—who in *The Palm Beach Story* meets a millionaire who immediately gives him money—is a millionaire movie director who dons ragged clothes and pretends to be a hobo, getting more than he bargained for. Known for his escapist musicals and comedies, the well-intentioned Sullivan is so upset by the lack of food and work in America that he wants to experience poverty firsthand so he can qualify to make a serious social document called *Oh, Brother, Where Art Thou?* While the studio executives (Robert Warwick, Porter Hall) and his butler (Robert Grieg) and valet (Eric Blore) worry, he hits the road and the tracks, taking along The Girl he's just met (Veronica Lake), a sweet, aspiring actress who passes as his waif. They endure much misery. When their journey is over, he goes alone to pass out money to the poor. He is knocked out by a hobo who steals his money and shoes and throws him into a boxcar traveling south. The hobo is run over by a train and so badly mutilated that everyone believes the body is Sullivan's. Dizzy from the blow to his head, Sullivan strikes a vicious southern railroad guard and is sentenced to six years on a prison farm. No one believes he is John L. Sullivan. He is beaten, thrown into a hot

Servants Robert Grieg (standing) and Eric Blore are worried when Joel McCrea and Veronica Lake embark on their journey as hoboes in Preston Sturges's *Sullivan's Travels*.

box, and badly mistreated on the farm. His only comfort comes from seeing a Mickey Mouse cartoon at a nearby black church. He joins the other prisoners in laughing madly. Wanting front-page publicity, Sullivan claims he is Sullivan's murderer. When people in Hollywood see his picture, he is freed. His wife, who has remarried, now must give him a divorce. He can marry The Girl. But he doesn't want to make *Oh, Brother, Where Art Thou?* He wants to make more comedies because laughter is all some people have.

Sullivan may conclude that even the most socially conscious filmmakers have an obligation to make comedies, but Sturges shows us that a good Hollywood film can mix the most outrageous comedy with a social message. Sturges, the escapist filmmaker, makes us laugh with hysterical dialogue, satirical barbs directed at irrelevant targets (most notably Hollywood), farcical situations (W. C. Fields could have played the scenes with the on-the-make widow), and outright slapstick: dedicated to "the motley mountebanks, the clowns, the buffoons," and the silent-movie comedians he adored, his film includes wild chases, pratfalls (Sullivan and The Girl trip repeatedly), characters falling in barrels full of water, ripping their pants, getting food spilled on them, getting lamps broken on their heads, madly scratching insect bites. As an acknowledgment to the Hollywood escapist formula, he also injects "a little sex": having McCrea bare chested at times, and Lake, although eight months pregnant, striking a leggy, cheesecake pose by a pool and then taking *two* showers. But Sturges, the social documentarian, makes us pay attention to the parade of poverty's victims that crosses his frame. In Sullivan's Swiftian journey we experience the suffering, the desperation, the hopelessness, the injustice, the lack of dignity. It's just as Sullivan's butler says: Only the rich want to romanticize poverty.

Sullivan's Travels harks back to old silent comedies, throws in some wicked satire and social commentary, and then mixes in elements from several other genres, including prison movies, road movies, and romances. It is brilliantly scripted, with Sturges democratically giving his marvelous supporting cast (including Warwick, Hall, Blore, Grieg, William Demarest, Franklin Pangborn, and Jimmy Conlin) as many good lines and important things to say as the two leads. In fact, the butler's speech about how the morbid rich glamorize poverty and the destitute want to be left alone is the most significant in the film. Everyone in Sturges's cockeyed caravan has a voice, which is why there are few gaps between words. As soon as one character finishes a sentence, another begins, as if words were batons in a relay race. The dialogues are of the rapid-fire variety and the pacing becomes frenetic. In several scenes Sturges builds pacing further by not cutting away from master scenes for close-ups or shots from different angles: for instance, the brilliant early conversation featuring McCrea, Warwick, and Hall runs for 390 feet without a cutaway; and the boxcar scene with McCrea and Lake runs seven script pages without a break. Sturges loves his actors and his characters, and lets them shine.

What finally makes *Sullivan's Travels* so special is the warmth of the characters, from the studio chieftains who care so much about Sullivan and The Girl, to Sullivan's butler and valet, who also care deeply about them, to the kindly people they meet out in the country (the diner owner who gives our hungry twosome free coffee and doughnuts, the blacks who share their church and entertainment with the prisoners, Sullivan's prison friend Trusty who gives him water in the hot box). And Sullivan and The Girl couldn't be nicer, especially to each other. They take care of each other throughout the film, never partaking in the obligatory bickering that most screwball comedy couples do. She's spunky and funny, he's enthusiastic and humble. Both are generous, sentimental, protective. The very tall McCrea and tiny Lake are wonderful together, just like their characters. *Sullivan's Travels* is rarely spoken of as a love story, but what movie fan can't help smiling and sighing while watching this unmarried boy and girl on the road, as they hold hands, hug, worry about each other, laugh together, and, though it may only be in a boxcar and flophouse, sleep in each other's arms.

▶ BEST ACTOR

WINNER:
James Cagney *(Yankee Doodle Dandy)*
Other Nominees: Ronald Colman *(Random Harvest)*, Gary Cooper *(The Pride of the Yankees)*, Walter Pidgeon *(Mrs. Miniver)*, Monty Woolley *(The Pied Piper)*

▼

THE BEST CHOICE:
James Cagney *(Yankee Doodle Dandy)*
Award-Worthy Runners-Up: Jack Benny *(To Be or Not to Be)*, Joseph Cotten *(The Magnificent Ambersons)*, Joel McCrea *(Sullivan's Travels)*, Spencer Tracy *(Woman of the Year)*, Monty Woolley *(The Pied Piper)*

There were several terrific performances by actors in 1942, most notably Joel McCrea's as a humble movie director who tries to do his bit for humanity in *Sullivan's Travels* and Jack Benny's conceited actor who does his bit to sabotage the Nazis in *To Be or Not to Be*. But there was no real competition for Best Actor of 1942, because in Warner's top-grossing musical bio, *Yankee Doodle Dandy,* James Cagney ran or, rather, sang and danced away with the Oscar. His role was the partly humble, partly conceited, superpatriotic showman George M. Cohan, the first entertainer to win the Congressional Medal of Honor.

Because of Cagney's dynamic performance and Michael Curtiz's smooth direction, *Yankee Doodle Dandy* manages to be one of the cinema's most enjoyable musicals—and certainly one of the best star vehicles, despite having almost no conflict. Cohan's life, as told in a chronological, Cohan-narrated flashback to an annoying-voiced President Roosevelt, is ridiculously happy and carefree. It includes lines like "One success followed another"; and when there is a hint of despair, it quickly vanishes: "Eighteen ninety-one found our fortunes flat as a pancake—then came a bolt from the blue. . . ." It's not that things aren't occasionally tough for George, his father (Walter Huston), his mother (Rosemary DeCamp), and sister (Jeanne Cagney), but the Four Cohans (their stage name) are such a tight-knit family that nothing seems to faze them. They always land on their dancing feet. Even when George has trouble striking out on his own, he remains optimistic, knowing that in America hard work pays off. When a play fails, he shrugs it off. George has no problems with his personal or business acquaintances. He gets along swimmingly with his family and his girlfriend and later wife (likable Joan Leslie)—she doesn't even get jealous when he gives her song, "Mary," to another performer ("Fay has the song, but I have the author"). And he has a long, loyal relationship with his producing partner, Sam Harris (Richard Whorf). Other than his father's death (mother and sister are dispatched with only a few words), the worst ordeal George goes through is boredom when he temporarily retires.

It's impossible to imagine anyone else but Cagney as Cohan, another brash Irish-American, who, like the actor,

is devoted to his wife, his family (they share *all* his success), and his country; who has performing in his blood; who is cocksure about his ability to get things done but is modest about his tremendous talent and appeal ("I'm an ordinary guy who knows what ordinary guys want to see"). Cagney played Cohan with the same vitality, swagger, intensity, wit, charm, and creativity he displayed in his best gangster roles. Only, this time he added a genuine affection (rather than mere empathy) for his character that he never showed when playing even his most appealing hoods. Cagney, a nice guy, simply responded to another nice guy.

Plus the ex-hoofer took out his tap shoes. He does

James Cagney and Joan Leslie in Michael Curtiz's star-spangled musical *Yankee Doodle Dandy*.

some great songs (in Cohan's half-talking manner) and dance routines in the picture. He dances in his own inimitable style, which mixes elastic-legged tap with fast, across-the-frame balletlike toe-walking, his legs straight, his rear out, his shoulders moving as if he were a gangster about to strike a blow, his upper torso angled forward, his head raised proudly. He has some great dance moments onstage; and backstage when, disguised as an old man, he shocks Mary (whom he has just met) with some furious footwork; and at the White House, when he taps down the staircase. But what I think impresses me most about Cagney in this film is how he plays scenes equally well with all types of characters, of both sexes and of all ages. I can't think of an actor who was better or more secure playing intimate scenes with other actors.

There are many memorable moments of Cagney in *Yankee Doodle Dandy.* There's his performance of the title song; his exciting dance numbers; his amusing chat with Eddie Foy, Jr. (playing Cohan's dear friend, Eddie Foy); his quirky scenes with Leslie (George and Mary are a peculiar couple); his sweet scene with his sister Jeanne, in which Josie tells her brother that she's getting married, and instead of being angry at her for breaking up the act, he says he'll write a wedding march for her; Cohan amusingly manipulating a producer (S. Z. "Cuddles" Sakall) into financing his first show; Cohan singing a rousing "Over There!" with excited soldiers (a scene that must have been particularly effective because Americans were just being sent to Europe at the time of this picture's release). But the moments I remember most are those when Cagney-Cohan sincerely tells his audience, "My father thanks you, my mother thanks you, my sister thanks you, and I thank you." Cagney and Cohan are the ones who deserve thanks. And they got it: Cohan received this tribute, and Cagney deservedly won his only Oscar.

▶ BEST ACTRESS

WINNER:

Greer Garson *(Mrs. Miniver)*
Other Nominees: Bette Davis *(Now, Voyager)*, Katharine Hepburn *(Woman of the Year)*, Rosalind Russell *(My Sister Eileen)*, Teresa Wright *(The Pride of the Yankees)*

▼

THE BEST CHOICE:

Carole Lombard *(To Be or Not to Be)* and Ginger Rogers *(The Major and the Minor)*
Award-Worthy Runners-Up: Bette Davis *(Now, Voyager)*, Katharine Hepburn *(Woman of the Year)*, Veronica Lake *(Sullivan's Travels)*, Ida Lupino *(The Hard Way)*

Greer Garson was the expected Oscar winner for her portrayal of the gallant British middle-class mother in *Mrs. Miniver,* and celebrated her victory with a legendary interminable acceptance speech. I usually like Garson's performances in the early parts of her pictures, only to tire eventually of her characters' graciousness and perfection. But in *Mrs. Miniver* I dislike Garson's early scenes—mostly unconvincing prewar conversations with Walter Pidgeon—and grow fond of her as the film progresses. Still, I prefer two of the nominated actresses in 1943: Bette Davis, who, because of her fights with her restrictive studio, obviously identified with her lonely, repressed, mother-dominated character, Charlotte Vale, fighting for independence in the supersoap *Now, Voyager;* and Katharine Hepburn, who is sleek and unabashedly sexual in *Woman of the Year,* her first teaming with Spencer Tracy.

But my three favorite actresses of 1942 were not nominated for an Oscar. The more I see Preston Sturges's *Sullivan's Travels,* the more impressed I am with Veronica Lake's performance as The Girl who accompanies a film director (Joel McCrea) on a journey to experience what it is like to be poor. But taking into account my lifelong crush on the blonde with the peekaboo hairstyle, I will,

for now, rate her performance a shade below that of Carole Lombard in *To Be or Not to Be* and Ginger Rogers in *The Major and the Minor.* It's impossible to choose between Lombard and Rogers, great actresses of the thirties whose range expanded in the early forties, so I'll take into account that the Academy split the Best Actress vote once, in 1968, and give them my one shared Best Actress Oscar.

In Lubitsch's hilarious satire Lombard played Maria Tura, Poland's greatest actress and the wife of the egocentric actor Joseph Tura (Jack Benny). When the Nazis invade Poland and the underground is threatened, Maria, Joseph, their hammy acting company, and the flyer with whom she is infatuated (Robert Stack) bravely and patriotically join forces to assassinate a devious spy (Stanley Ridges) before he reveals names of underground members to the foolish Gestapo chief (Sig Ruman).

Lombard considered her performance in *To Be or Not to Be* the best of her career, and I agree. She has many moments in which she reveals why she was the thirties' most celebrated comedienne. Her verbal battles with her even more conceited husband recall the hilarious infighting between Lombard's actress and John Barrymore's egocentric stage director in *Twentieth Century.* I particu-

Carole Lombard, husband Jack Benny, and the rest of their acting troupe find shelter when Warsaw is bombed by Germans in Ernst Lubitsch's controversial comedy, *To Be or Not to Be.*

begin to suspect that "SuSu" is not as young as she pretends to be.

Rogers was at her most appealing as the tough woman who pretends to be a babe in the woods. "You're a peculiar child," she is told. "You bet I am," she responds. What's funny is that her attempts to be a kid aren't particularly convincing because she can't resist saying things with double meanings or under her breath. Her wisecracks are those of Rogers's thirties chorines. She employs an amusing kid's voice, keeps her eyes wide and goofy, walks awkwardly and gracelessly, and displays a vivid imagination, yet she can't really act or talk like a kid: "Goldfishes—look at the one with the flopsy-wopsy ears!" She certainly wasn't this innocent when she was young: "I was a very straightforward child—I used to spit." We always detect the strong, independent, sexy woman waiting to burst free, especially when "Uncle Philip" awkwardly explains to her the facts of life, saying how moths (meaning boys) are attracted to a light bulb. "I'll try and be a well-behaved light bulb," she promises.

For much of the early part of the film SuSu is on the defensive, even enduring (in some amusing scenes) the

larly like her affected mannerisms and voice when she tells Benny that it's of no consequence that he finally asked the director to bill her above him in a play, and her look when he says that he knew she'd feel that way so the billing will stay the same. Also memorable is her sexual-innuendo-filled flirting with Stack's young bomber pilot. Her eyes reveal she is lost in fantasies when he tells her, "I can drop three tons of dynamite in two minutes." But Lombard's Maria switches from being dazzlingly comical to deadly serious, and Lombard reveals how much she had grown as a dramatic actress in the last few years. She is half in a daze, almost whispering her lines, when meeting the cruel, flirtatious Siletzky; moves into an icy calm when she can't get out of the Nazi-controlled hotel; and shows amazing intensity as her role in the actors' conspiracy becomes more dangerous. At times she appropriately seems almost ethereal . . . in this picture that was released two months after her tragic death in a plane crash during a war-bonds selling tour.

In Billy Wilder's risqué comedy *The Major and the Minor,* Ginger Rogers is New York scalp massager Susan Applegate, a tough thirty-year-old who passes herself off as a sweet, pigtailed eleven-year-old in order to get a low-priced train fare from New York to her Indiana hometown. Fleeing from conductors who catch her smoking, she hides in the compartment of a major (Ray Milland), who thinks she is a child. He teaches at a boys' military school but wants to be called to active service. He doesn't know that his supposedly supportive fiancée, Pam (Rita Johnson), keeps foiling his attempts at a transfer. Susan immediately is attracted to "Uncle Philip." She spends a few days in the academy, where she is forced to date the young cadets, and plots with Pam's shrewd younger sister (Diana Lynn) to get Philip his transfer. In time both Philip (who finds himself oddly attracted to Susan) and Pam

Ginger Rogers disguises herself as a little girl in Billy Wilder's *The Major and the Minor.*

amorous advances of several brazen young military students. But it's also fun when she goes on the counterattack, seductively tap-dancing for a naughty cadet so he'll go get his radio and she can use an off-limits switchboard. By pretending to be Pam on the phone, she gets Philip

his transfer. She knows that if Philip goes off to be a soldier, Pam will drop him. Susan Applegate may be Rogers's most dangerous female. She pretends to be a kid, but she has the smarts and motives of a woman in love.

▶ BEST PICTURE

WINNER:
Casablanca (Warner Bros.; Michael Curtiz)
Other Nominees: *For Whom the Bell Tolls, Heaven Can Wait, The Human Comedy, In Which We Serve, Madame Curie, The More the Merrier, The Ox-Bow Incident, The Song of Bernadette, Watch on the Rhine*

▼

THE BEST CHOICE:
Casablanca (Warner Bros.; Michael Curtiz)
Award-Worthy Runners-Up: *Heaven Can Wait* (Ernst Lubitsch), *The Human Comedy* (Clarence Brown), *The More the Merrier* (George Stevens), *Shadow of a Doubt* (Alfred Hitchcock)

With few exceptions the nominees for Best Picture of 1943—at a time when the war effort was intensifying—dealt with characters who staunchly stick to their guns against terrible odds, who preserve their integrity at high prices, who do the right thing. Two such films, *Madame Curie* and *The Song of Bernadette,* had nothing to do with the current war, but placed brave females in conflict with the male establishment—they emerge victorious because they have the courage of their convictions. *For Whom the Bell Tolls* and Noel Coward's *In Which We Serve* took us directly into battle. Warners' two Academy Award competitors, *Casablanca* and *Watch on the Rhine,* placed us on the frightening fringes, where characters have to make quick and decisive political choices.

Casablanca actually premiered in New York in November of 1942. But it didn't qualify for 1942 Oscar consideration because it didn't play in Los Angeles until 1943, when it was reissued to capitalize on the headline-making Roosevelt-Churchill summit in Casablanca, which Eisenhower had secured during his North African campaign. This time it was a hit. Today, it seems hard to believe that *Casablanca,* clearly the class of the nominated films, was a surprise Best Picture winner. Unlike its competitors it wasn't considered a "prestige" picture and it hadn't received critical raves. No one predicted that it eventually would become an all-time classic. If a Warners film were to be elected Best Picture, more likely it would be the studio's adaptation of Lillian Hellman's famous antifascist play, *Watch on the Rhine,* starring Bette Davis

and Paul Lukas (who won the Best Actor Oscar), not the one based on the unproduced obscurity *Everybody Goes to Rick's* by Murray Burnett and Joan Alison. For once the Academy was daring—the New York Film Critics selected *Watch on the Rhine*—and prescient.

Humphrey Bogart is Rick Blaine, a former political activist whom his lover, Ilsa (Ingrid Bergman), left without explanation in Paris on the day of the Occupation. He is a brooding man who has come to Casablanca, where he runs the successful Café Americain. His friend Louis Renault (Claude Rains), a corrupt French Vichy officer, mocks him for having become apolitical. Though Rick claims to care only about himself now, Louis senses that he is still a sentimentalist. Casablanca is a neutral site, although the Vichy control it and the Germans' presence and power in the North African city is increasing. People come from all over, hoping to obtain passports and escape the Nazi onslaught by getting passage to Lisbon. Rick comes into possession of two stolen letters of transit, which will allow anyone who has them to leave without trouble. Ilsa reappears, with her husband, freedom fighter Viktor Laszlo (Paul Henreid). Rick is still furious with her for having deserted him, but she breaks through his defenses and explains that she left him only because she'd learned on that day that Viktor, whom she had thought dead, had escaped a concentration camp. She tells Rick that she still loves him and will stay with him if he helps Viktor escape. Meanwhile, Viktor asks him to help Ilsa flee. Rick loves Ilsa but knows that for Viktor to

Humphrey Bogart has a complex, intriguing relationship with the other three major figures in Michael Curtiz's *Casablanca:* Claude Rains, Paul Henreid, and Ingrid Bergman.

continue his work, Viktor will need Ilsa at his side. He helps them both escape, killing the commanding Nazi officer, Major Strasser (Conrad Veidt). Instead of having Rick arrested, Louis goes off with him to join the French underground.

Casablanca is pretty much a perfect film. All the elements work. For beginners it has a location that is both familiar and exotic, where there is extreme tension from the outset because people from all countries are crowded together. Since it is a port, all those who pass through have "a past," a prerequisite for interesting characters, and since it is still a "free territory" (despite Vichy-German dominance), it is one of the few remaining places where individuals can choose their own destinies (e.g., which side to support in the war).

The picture has a peerless cast, headed by Bogart, Bergman, and Henreid (in roles originally intended for Ronald Reagan, Ann Sheridan, and Dennis Morgan!), Claude Rains, and that great villain Conrad Veidt, and supporting players, including Peter Lorre, Sydney Greenstreet, S. Z. Sakall, John Qualen, Leonid Kinskey, Marcel Dalio, and Dooley Wilson, whose Sam sings and plays on his piano the classic theme "As Time Goes By." That not much actually happens in the film—there is more talk than anything else—is disguised by the emotional intensity of the actors in *every* scene. They play a wonderful array of lead and secondary characters, all in trouble, all plotting something, all making major moral decisions.

Certainly to be commended is the ubiquitous Michael Curtiz, the studio's finest contract director. He made the somewhat overloaded, confusing story move along at a brisk pace. And his wise employment of noirish cinematography (Arthur Edeson also filmed *The Maltese Falcon*) properly conveys the bleakness in Rick's personal life and the total "darkness" that threatens the free world if the Nazis aren't stopped. Curtiz won an Oscar for Best

Director. Another deserved Oscar went to the screenwriters, Julius J. Epstein, Philip G. Epstein, and Howard Koch. The Burnett and Alison play contains a surprising amount of the material that is in the film—including the great "Marseillaise" scene in which Viktor, Rick's orchestra, and loyal French drown out some singing German soldiers—but the three authors sharpened the dialogue, intensified the relationships, made Sam a more dignified character, further politicized the piece, and gave the characters a stronger emotional investment in each other and their causes. They were also responsible for most of the film's classic lines, including "Here's looking at you, kid," "But we'll always have Paris," "You played it for her, you can play it for me," and "Louis, I think this is the beginning of a beautiful friendship."

Casablanca is a strange film because while it contains all the essential plot ingredients for an entertaining film, it doesn't really fit into any genre. It's not really a war film, a spy film, an action film, a suspense film, a romance, or a straight drama. Then again, it's all of these, but in unconventional ways. For instance, it's a romance, but the two leads love each other so much that they don't stay together or even kiss goodbye. It's a suspense film, yet neither the heroine nor, until the very end, the hero is in grave danger—instead, we really only have to worry about Viktor, whose death (which conveniently would come about in a conventional film) would free our lovers to be together. Remarkably, we are made to admire Viktor so much that we want him to survive even if this means crushing Rick and Ilsa's love affair. We agree that Rick and Ilsa should sacrifice their great love (they still have Paris, of course) so that Viktor—the most important of the three—will be able to continue his work.

I guess that above all *Casablanca* is a propaganda piece in which a man who is sitting out the war and ignoring the Cause because of personal problems, comes to realize that he, like all individuals, has an important part to play—and that his part in a monumental event is more important than anything in his personal life. The film is also about loyalty, faith, bravery, and personal sacrifice on both romantic and patriotic levels. Indeed, almost every scene establishes relationships and bonds between two individuals. Those personal relationships will determine the characters' political choices. So it is that if a character proves loyal to a decent person, then that character also will have the correct political stance. For instance, Rick claims that he is apolitical, yet his attachments to those good people who work for him and to some of his sympathetic customers indicate that he is secretly on the right side in the war. At the end their fight will be his.

Interestingly, while the various major characters form strong bonds—Rick and Ilsa, Ilsa and Viktor, Rick and Viktor, Rick and Louis—in which faith in one another is of paramount importance, they, with the exception of Viktor, constantly lie or tell each other half-truths during the last part of the picture. Rick tells Ilsa he'll send Viktor away by himself; Rick tells Louis that he's going to let him trap Viktor; Louis tells Rick he's calling the airport when actually he's phoning Major Strasser; Rick tells Viktor he made a play for Ilsa but she rejected him and Ilsa goes along with this. To cap all the lying, Louis orders his men to round up all the usual suspects even though he knows Rick killed Strasser. These fibbing characters keep surprising each other—though Louis expected Rick to be a "sentimentalist"—and keep surprising us. The final scenes are so exciting and so memorable precisely because they are so unpredictable. Most pleasantly surprised was Claude Rains, who, because the script was being written during filming, didn't anticipate his char-acter's changing suddenly from villain and traitor to France to hero and patriot. It had seemed that Louis used harsh words against Rick in order to get Rick to affirm he was a traitor to his once-strong political integrity so that Louis wouldn't feel guilty about being corrupt himself. But we now surmise that his digs were actually meant to coax Rick back into the fight. If Louis's idol took up the cause, then so would he. (And, thought Warners, so would everyone else.) Rick doesn't have Ilsa at the end, but when he walks off with Louis, we know there couldn't have been a more romantic or satisfying ending.

▶ BEST ACTOR

WINNER:
Paul Lukas *(Watch on the Rhine)*
Other Nominees: Humphrey Bogart *(Casablanca)*, Gary Cooper *(For Whom the Bell Tolls)*, Walter Pidgeon *(Madame Curie)*, Mickey Rooney *(The Human Comedy)*

▼

THE BEST CHOICE:
Humphrey Bogart *(Casablanca)*
Award-Worthy Runners-Up: John Carradine *(Hitler's Madman)*, Joseph Cotten *(Shadow of a Doubt)*, Roger Livesey *(The Life and Death of Colonel Blimp,)* Mickey Rooney *(The Human Comedy)*

In *Casablanca* Humphrey Bogart created one of the screen's greatest heroes, Rick Blaine, a former freedom fighter who needs a good, stiff kiss on the lips (from Ingrid Bergman's Ilsa) to knock sense into his inebriated brain and get him to join the war effort. But the Academy preferred Paul Lukas, as a thoroughly dedicated, professional German freedom fighter in *Watch on the Rhine,* a role he'd played in the theater. Perhaps they voted less for the actor than for Lukas's brave, noble character whose jarring self-definition is "I fight fascists"—certainly a much more laudatory sentiment than Rick's "I stick my neck out for nobody." But the Hungarian Lukas was much better playing foreign villains in *The Lady Vanishes* and *Confessions of a Nazi Spy* than he was as leading men. His performance in *Watch on the Rhine* is as shaky as the alcoholic Rick's hand—at times he sounds like Bela Lugosi.

Bogart became the definitive cool "tough guy" in 1941, when he played Roy "Mad Dog" Earle, a vicious gangster with a good heart; in Raoul Walsh's *High Sierra*; and detective Sam Spade, a hero who's really a cad, in *The Maltese Falcon.* In *Casablanca* he got to play a hero with a good heart. Only, Rick doesn't think of himself in such flattering terms. For much of the picture he wallows in self-pity because Ilsa (Ingrid Bergman) left him. He considers himself a loser, with no heart anymore, no feelings. But his friend Louis (Claude Rains), a genial but corrupt French Vichy officer, realizes Rick is still a "sentimentalist." And, even before Rick wises up and joins the Cause, we watch him take care of those worthy people who need his assistance.

Rick is the cinema's definitive existential hero, a man who must awaken from the dead and make a choice about the direction of his life. When we first see him he's playing chess, an indication of his inactivity in the face of spreading Nazi aggression. He is cynical, callous, and embittered, seeing the world only in terms of his own shattered ego. "One woman has hurt you, you take your revenge on the rest of the world," says Ilsa. "You're a coward and a weakling." He feigns indifference to politi-

Dooley Wilson's Sam tries to console Humphrey Bogart's brooding Rick in *Casablanca.*

cal matters and remains in a limbo state. He will not choose sides. But when he gives his orchestra the go-ahead to play "The Marseillaise" for Viktor to drown out some rowdy Nazi singers, we sense that he is thawing out. At the end of the film Rick, like most Bogart heroes, sacrifices what is dearest to him (Ilsa) for the greater good. When he rejoins the fight, Ilsa looks at him with the same admiration she has always displayed when looking at her resistance fighter husband, Viktor (Paul Henreid).

In their only film together Bogart (in platform shoes) and Bergman are an exciting couple, whether being romantic, arguing, or just looking at each other. Their characters love each other so much that a long-term relationship would consume them both. His face is hard, dark, stubbly even after a shave, ugly; hers is soft, glowing, warm, beautiful. His eyes are cold, narrow, suspicious, introspective; her eyes sparkle with trust, generosity, caring. He is demanding, critical, secretive; she is comforting, loving, open armed. He excites her—later she will respect him as much as she does Viktor—and she brings out the best in him. The film is not saying "opposites attract" but that as the free world becomes endangered, all good people connect through romance or friendship.

Just as Bogart is the film's pivotal figure, interacting with all the others in the cast, Rick is the pivotal figure in the lives of all the other characters. His Café Americain is where everyone gathers and he is the person everyone comes to for business, for help. Those who work for him, Louis, the corrupt owner of the rival "Blue Parrot" (Sydney Greenstreet), black-marketeer Ugarte (Peter Lorre), Ilsa (who gets over her doubts), and even Viktor have faith in him. They believe he has integrity, even if he won't fight Nazis.

What is extraordinary about Bogart's performance is that his personality is so strong that we don't mind that through most of the film his character is not the man of action we expect our movie heroes to be. Instead he broods, drinks, and tells everyone who will listen that he cares only for himself—which is disproved when Ilsa points a gun at him and he tells her, "Go ahead and shoot, you'll be doing me a favor." Rick merely *talks* in the early part of the film. Yet Bogart has so much charisma, so much wit, so much intelligence, so much toughness—despite Rick's letting his sentimentalism show itself repeatedly—that his character is at all times the hero. We *know* Rick is fearless and is not in over his head mixing with all the dangerous and wicked people he does. And that he is as "cool" as Sam Spade ever was, is made evident when the intimidating Major Strasser (Conrad Veidt) shows him the Nazis' dossier on him, which includes his leftist activities. Is Rick shaken by what he reads, knowing he is under Nazi surveillance? His response is the rarely quoted, and ever so cool, "Are my eyes really brown?"

▶ BEST ACTRESS

WINNER:
Jennifer Jones *(The Song of Bernadette)*
Other Nominees: Jean Arthur *(The More the Merrier)*, Ingrid Bergman *(For Whom the Bell Tolls)*, Joan Fontaine *(The Constant Nymph)*, Greer Garson *(Madame Curie)*

THE BEST CHOICE:
Jean Arthur *(The More the Merrier)*
Award-Worthy Runners-Up: Ingrid Bergman *(Casablanca)*, Ingrid Bergman *(For Whom the Bell Tolls)*, Ida Lupino *(The Hard Way)*, Teresa Wright *(Shadow of a Doubt)*

In 1943 the Best Actress Oscar went to newcomer Jennifer Jones for playing a saintly girl who would have rejected such an award, in *The Song of Bernadette*. As was surely the case with Best Actor winner Paul Lukas, the Academy probably voted as much for her noble character as they did for her. The "discovery" of David O. Selznick, who would marry her after her divorce from Robert Walker, Jones supposedly was making her screen debut as the young nineteenth-century peasant who has a vision of the Virgin Mary at Lourdes. But it was soon revealed that in 1939 she'd been in a B western and *Dick Tracy* serial as Phyllis Isley, her real name. Jones, now twenty-five, was properly sweet and innocent as Bernadette ("The last one over the bridge is a goose!") in Henry King's religious drama, but wasn't really given a chance to act. She had to play every scene identically, with a kind, simple smile but little emotion. The scenes themselves are repetitive, with her character refusing to alter her story despite interrogations by one stern person after another. I much prefer her later, hot-blooded temptresses.

My choice for Best Actress is Jean Arthur for George Stevens's comedy gem, *The More the Merrier*. The former Gladys Greene had been a star since 1935 and, until Rita Hayworth shot to stardom in 1941, Columbia Studio's leading lady. She made such classics as *The Whole Town's Talking, Mr. Deeds Goes to Town, The Plainsman, History Is Made at Night, Easy Living, You Can't Take It with You,*

Only Angels Have Wings, Mr. Smith Goes to Washington, The Devil and Miss Jones, and *The Talk of the Town.* Unpretentious, wide eyed, feisty, and optimistic, with a distinctive, lovable voice that critic Stephen Harvey described as "a sandy chirp," Arthur was recognized as one of Hollywood's best and most popular actresses and comediennes. Yet, oddly, it wasn't until she made *The More the Merrier,* her last outstanding picture (with the exception of her final film, 1953's *Shane,* for Stevens) that she received an Oscar nomination. Possibly the Academy repeatedly snubbed her because of her ongoing feud with Columbia kingpin Harry Cohn, or because she was uncooperative with the Hollywood press corps and, according to them, had the reputation for being difficult to work with (though she was a favorite of both Stevens and Frank Capra). In any case, she deserved several nominations and, at least, this one Oscar.

During a housing crunch in Washington, Benjamin Dingle (Charles Coburn deservedly won a Best Supporting Actor award), a government consultant and retired millionaire, rents a room in the apartment of Connie Milligan (Jean Arthur), a much younger, single working woman. He wishes he could find a nice, handsome, clean-cut man to marry her and end her obvious loneliness. When Joe Carter (Joel McCrea), a nice, handsome, clean-cut army sergeant who is on special duty for the government, inquires about the room that Dingle has already taken, Dingle agrees to let Joe share it with him, without informing Connie. She is shocked to discover a new apartment mate, but agrees to let him stay too. As Dingle expected, Connie and Joe are attracted. That Connie is engaged to Pendergaste (Richard Gaines), a dull bureaucrat, doesn't deter Dingle's matchmaking. It takes only one hectic night for his impossible scheming to work and for Connie and Joe to be married.

Arthur is thoroughly charming as a kind, unaggressive—she fights for herself, but doesn't have the heart for it—underdog who is trapped in a dull life until two men magically appear. While the older one manipulates her boring fiancé out of her life, the handsome, younger, not so devious one steps in, seduces her, marries her, and makes her happy. Among Arthur's great comic moments: She explains to the confounded Dingle the intricate, impossibly rigid morning schedule they must keep so they won't bump into each other; she and Dingle constantly bump into each other as their schedule goes awry; while brushing her teeth she does a delayed double take and utters a foamy-mouthed scream on discovering Dingle (whom she has accidentally locked outside) banging on the bathroom window; after whizzing past Joe in her hallway, before she has been told he has moved in, she brakes with both feet and does a delayed, wide-mouthed double take; she hides her head behind Dingle's back while her fiancé learns from Joe—in front of government officials!—that Joe has been sharing her apartment.

Funny as she is, what is most memorable about Arthur's characterization is how sexual it is. We get to know Connie far more intimately than we do the typical movie heroines of the era. We wake up with her in the morning,

Lonely Jean Arthur writes in her diary in George Stevens's classic wartime comedy, *The More the Merrier.*

see her in pajamas, see her change a couple of times, follow her in and out of her bathroom, watch her brush her teeth, see her wearing face cream, see her lying in bed. Connie is lonely, of course, but she's also sexually repressed, as indicated when she quickly hides her journal under her blanket although Dingle is only in the next room. When the very handsome Joe comes along she gives in to her sexual feelings. Even before they meet, and though they are in different rooms of the apartment, Connie and Joe do a hip-moving rumba *together* to a record, as if they had picked up each other's scent.

Their "date"—after Dingle waylays Pendergaste—ends with one of the most exciting sexual sequences in the forties cinema. It's so titillating because it's obvious—from Arthur's eyes, the nervous edge to her voice, and her confused but happy manner—that she is becoming more excited with each step she takes. They are quite physical as they stroll and spin down the street. Then they fall into each other's arms on the front steps. Joe runs his fingers on the bare skin above her chest and then up her neck, before holding her face and kissing her. Then she grabs his face and kisses him back! Next, they go upstairs and into their respective beds. They talk romantically while lying there and missing each other, with a thin wall between them. We see them both in the frame that is split in two by the wall, going one step beyond the sexy "Walls of Jericho" bit in *It Happened One Night.* "I love you," he says. And turning to the wall, her eyes tearing, and looking beautiful, she replies, "I love you more than anything in the world." Arthur wasn't really considered beautiful or sexy, but during this entire sequence she takes one's breath away. One doesn't question why Joe left a bevy of beauties behind in a restaurant to take Connie home.

1944

▶ BEST PICTURE

WINNER:
Going My Way (Paramount; Leo McCarey)
Other Nominees: *Double Indemnity, Gaslight, Since You Went Away, Wilson*

▼

THE BEST CHOICE:
Double Indemnity (Paramount; Billy Wilder)
Award-Worthy Runners-Up: *Gaslight* (George Cukor), *Going My Way* (Leo McCarey), *Laura* (Otto Preminger), *Meet Me in St. Louis* (Vincente Minnelli), *Murder, My Sweet* (Edward Dmytryk)

"**S**chmaltz isn't selling this season," Bing Crosby's Father O'Malley is sad to learn in the middle of *Going My Way*. The discussion in the movie is about songs, but it might have been about movies as well, for 1944 was a year full of creepy melodramas, noir mysteries, and straight dramas. Preston Sturges and Frank Capra still made comedies, but only *Going My Way* itself and *Meet Me in St. Louis* could be classified as schmaltz, in the *best* sense of the word. And they performed exceptionally at the box office. *Going My Way,* a light comedy-drama (with music) about the increasingly affectionate relationship between Crosby's progressive young priest and Barry Fitzgerald's stubborn elderly priest, was the only nondrama nominated for Best Picture. And it won. I think *Going My Way* is flawed, with subplots better suited for the reject basket than the screen, but the interaction between Crosby and Fitzgerald is wonderful and the scene in which Fitzgerald is unexpectedly reunited with his shaking, ninety-year-old mother after forty-five years is one of the cinema's great tearjerking moments, deserving of an honorary Oscar all by itself. I am glad that this charming film won the Best Picture Oscar (and Crosby was voted Best Actor) because that is probably the major reason it is still shown often on television and in repertory theaters, and that people seek it out. However, I think Billy Wilder's *Double Indemnity* was more deserving of the Best Picture Oscar if only because it has been much more influential. *Going My Way* is a "schmaltzy" film from Hollywood's Golden Age that, unfortunately, filmmakers will never try to duplicate. Every couple of years, someone will try, without success, to duplicate *Double Indemnity*.

Fred MacMurray is L.A. insurance salesman Walter Neff. He quickly falls in love with icy blond Phyllis Dietrichson (Barbara Stanwyck) while trying to sell her skinflint husband (Tom Powers) a policy. She tells him that her husband treats her badly and is leaving all his money to her grown stepdaughter (Jean Heather). They plot to murder Dietrichson and run off with the money from

the life insurance policy Neff got him to sign without telling him what it was. One night, Neff kills him, then (hiding his own face) impersonates him on a train. He jumps off the train and places the body on the tracks so it appears that Dietrichson, whose leg was broken, fell off and was killed. Everything goes as planned, but Neff's shrewd friend, Keyes (Edward G. Robinson), the su-

Barbara Stanwyck and Fred MacMurray place her murdered husband on the railroad tracks in Billy Wilder's film noir classic, *Double Indemnity*.

preme insurance agent, suspects murder and puts together the clues. Meanwhile, Neff realizes that Phyllis didn't love him—she's having an affair with her stepdaughter's former boyfriend—but used him to kill her husband and get rich. He kills her, but only after she fatally shoots him.

Superbly acted by MacMurray, Stanwyck, and Robinson (who has *great* scenes talking about the excitement of being an insurance agent and, later, about suicide), moodily scored by Miklos Rosza, and coolly directed by Billy Wilder, this near-perfect adaptation of James M. Cain's bitter pulp masterpiece was scripted by Wilder and Raymond Chandler. Chandler's own *Farewell, My Lovely* was the basis for the year's other film noir classic, *Murder, My Sweet,* with Dick Powell surprisingly effective as Philip Marlowe. *Double Indemnity* is quintessential film noir, characterized by the interacting traits of greed, lust, murder, and double cross; the presence of a cocky, not-smart-enough hero who allows himself be seduced into crime by a femme fatale; and a pervading, oppressive darkness (John F. Seitz did the outstanding cinematography) that threatens to swallow anyone who strays from the moral path. There is the expected male narrator examining from a chastened vantage point, through flashbacks, the process by which he got in over his head. "[I] killed for money and a woman," says the dying Neff. "I didn't get the money and I didn't get the . . . woman. Pretty, isn't it?" Impending doom/fate, an essential ingredient in film noir, is at work: "How did I know that murder could sometimes smell like honeysuckle?"; "I couldn't hear my own footsteps," recalls Neff, about the night of the murder. "It was the walk of the dead man." The script is loaded with the snappy, hard-boiled dialogue that is found in noir thrillers. For instance, when

Phyllis first meets Neff, she explains why she is garbed in a towel: "I've just been taking a sunbath." His immediate response: "I hope no pigeons were out." When he tells her that he knows she wants to kill her husband, she says, "You're rotten." His immediate response: "I think you're swell. As long as I'm not your husband."

The great fun in watching this humorless (except for the ironic dialogue) film is in seeing Neff, who thinks he's so clever, being outmatched by both Phyllis and Keyes. Like many ill-fated heroes in film noir, he allows a woman to ruin his life. He is so *secure* (remember, he sells insurance) that he chances falling into Phyllis's spiderweb, believing he can always escape. But he isn't up to the challenge. She uses sex to keep him confused, so he can never reflect clearly enough ("I've been thinking of you every minute," he says) to realize she is playing him for a fool. She appeals to his vanity, stroking his masculine ego, letting him think he is devising the entire murder plan, when in fact *her* scheming is much more sophisticated. By the time he's figured her out, it is too late. Like the typical film noir hero, he plays out his dead man's hand.

Wilder and Chandler stayed away from Cain's bizarre finale because it would have shocked viewers and incensed critics, but they came up with a suitable alternative that comes close to Cain's ritualistic double suicide. As a nice gesture, however, they allow Neff to die in the presence of his friend Keyes, who has loved him all along, rather than with Phyllis. After all, Neff wasn't a bad guy. It's just that under Phyllis's spell his brain went on vacation, as any man's would. As Keyes detected when comparing him to the other, less successful, men at the office: "You're not smarter, Walter, you're just a little taller."

▶ BEST ACTOR

WINNER:
Bing Crosby *(Going My Way)*
Other Nominees: Charles Boyer *(Gaslight)*, Barry Fitzgerald *(Going My Way)*, Cary Grant *(None But the Lonely Heart)*, Alexander Knox *(Wilson)*

▼

THE BEST CHOICE:
Charles Boyer *(Gaslight)*
Award-Worthy Runners-Up: Humphrey Bogart *(To Have and Have Not)*, John Carradine *(Bluebeard)*, Laird Cregar *(The Lodger)*, Bing Crosby *(Going My Way)*, Fred MacMurray *(Double Indemnity)*

For the second time in seven years an actor playing a priest won the Best Actor Oscar. I would have given the award to Barry Fitzgerald, who sparkled as the older priest in *Going My Way,* rather than to top-billed Bing Crosby, but Fitzgerald's role was really a supporting one (he was nominated in both categories and won for Best Supporting Actor). Crosby was definitely charming as the genial, wise, humble, unpretentious, quietly authoritative

Father O'Malley. It's impossible to imagine anyone else in the role. But if one equates O'Malley with Crosby, it's because the role was shaped for the actor-singer who was the cinema's top box-office attraction at the time. We rightly praise Crosby for seeming so "natural" in the part, yet at the same time recognize that he didn't stretch as an actor any more than he did in the "Road" pictures with Bob Hope. In 1944 the best *performance* by an actor was turned in not by the one who played the year's most likable character, but the one who was the most despicable: Charles Boyer, in MGM's *Gaslight*.

George Cukor directed this creepy psychological thriller, an adaptation of Patrick Hamilton's play *Angel Street*. Thorold Dickinson had filmed it in England in 1939, starring Anton Walbrook and Diana Wynyard, but MGM had successfully forced it out of circulation to pave the way for its new production. Boyer is pianist-composer-teacher Gregory Anton. Years before, under his real name, he got into the good graces of a famous opera singer. He murdered her for her priceless jewels but fled empty-handed when her young niece, Paula, happened upon the scene. Now, Paula (Ingrid Bergman) has grown up and, not recognizing Anton, marries him. He manipulates her into agreeing to move into her aunt's home. He moves all the aunt's belongings to the attic, where he surreptitiously goes each night to search for the jewels. Wanting more freedom in his search, he plots to drive Paula insane and have her committed to an institution. He convinces her that she forgets minor things, that she imagines minor things, and that she steals minor things without realizing it. He also gets her to believe that she is imagining both noises in the attic and the dimming of the gas lights (as if someone were turning up lights elsewhere in the house) soon after he leaves each night. Thinking Anton loves her, Paula believes she is going crazy. Anton's plot would have worked if not for a neighbor (Joseph Cotten), a Scotland Yard detective. He realizes that something peculiar is happening in the Anton house, and that Paula is in trouble.

Today, I fully appreciate the gifted Charles Boyer's versatility and accept this actor with the French accent, gentlemanly manners, and piercing eyes as one of the top romantic leads of the thirties and forties, the last of the "Great Lovers" in the Valentino-Novarro tradition. As a kid, however, I couldn't understand why women played by such beauties as Greta Garbo, Hedy Lamarr, and Ingrid Bergman would fall madly in love with someone who was only slightly more handsome and sophisticated than Peter Lorre. But I responded to him as the villain of *Gaslight*, doing things that might make even Lorre's villains squeamish. His villain in *Gaslight* is unique in the cinema and one of the most dastardly men ever portrayed—worse than the monster who terrorizes Ingrid Bergman in *Dr. Jekyll and Mr. Hyde*—yet he is one monster that no one will dispute exists in the real world.

Gaslight continues to pack a wallop because it is the definitive film study of how a man can dominate a woman through manipulative words and actions as easily and as brutally as he can with his fists. Anton never lays a hand on Paula, yet he constantly humiliates her (often in front of the female servants), accuses her of thievery and forgetfulness, makes her doubt everything about herself. He dominates her, yet makes her think he wants her to have free will. He allows her freedom to go out by herself, but he makes her so paranoid and unsure of herself that she's afraid to leave the house. He won't allow her to have visitors so he can further control her, but

Ingrid Bergman won an Oscar for her dominated wife in George Cukor's *Gaslight,* but Charles Boyer was more deserving as the cad who tries to drive her crazy.

says he's doing her a favor by not forcing her to entertain guests—since, he contends, she doesn't want or is too ill to see them. Also, he tells her, he wants to be alone with his young bride for the time being. And she is too weak to argue.

Boyer is marvelous as this sick fiend who drives Paula to the edge with his accusing eyes and manner, but quickly and nervously pulls back each time he goes so far that she might see through him. Repeatedly his facial muscles contort, showing us he is repressing his fury. Anton occasionally can't control his temper—Boyer's blind rages are as scary as Lorre's—but then Anton's face immediately softens, his eyes twinkle with concern, and he apologizes, claiming he misunderstood her. He feigns tenderness, yet never lets her see his weakness—she doesn't see his stern face become panicky and look foolish when she unexpectedly says she'll go to a recital without him. And he never lets up on her, always acting smug and patronizing, using her name as if it were an icepick: "You are inclined to lose things, Paula . . ."; "Oh, nothing . . . only I've been noticing, Paula . . ."; "Are you becoming suspicious as well as absentminded, Paula?"; "Paula, I hope you're not starting to imagine things again"; "Paula, Paula . . . my watch is gone"; "Answer me, Paula." There is one moment, when she swears that she has been telling him the truth about not stealing things, when he almost forgets himself and acts kindly, saying, "I know you've never lied to me. You're not lying." But he catches himself: "It's worse than lying—you've forgotten." When she asks him to be gentler, he turns away. No wonder that halfway through the picture, Paula looks beaten up, even punch-drunk.

Boyer is properly intense as this cad who can never stop his performance, who can't let down his guard for a moment lest he be unmasked. Yet there is one moment when Anton doesn't hide his mania. Anton willingly takes

Paula outside the house only once, escorting her to the Tower of London to look at the crown jewels. His eyes glow as, hypnotized, he gazes at the largest diamond in the world. His voice is menacing and deathly as he speaks about it. Critic Charles Higham noted, "Boyer's soft, obsessed voice, his increasing pallor, the rigidity of his hands, amount to a case study of grand-manner acting." We realize that, as he confesses to Paula later, his attraction to jewels is "like a fire, a fire on my brain." Maybe as a kid I would have believed the power Boyer's characters have over women if just once they looked at their screen lovers in the way Anton looks at those jewels.

▶ BEST ACTRESS

WINNER:
Ingrid Bergman *(Gaslight)*
Other Nominees: Claudette Colbert *(Since You Went Away)*, Bette Davis *(Mr. Skeffington)*, Greer Garson *(Mrs. Parkington)*, Barbara Stanwyck *(Double Indemnity)*

▼

THE BEST CHOICE:
Barbara Stanwyck *(Double Indemnity)*
Award-Worthy Runner-Up: Ingrid Bergman *(Gaslight)*

Hollywood's most prolific actress, Sweden's Ingrid Bergman won 1944's Best Actress Oscar for *Gaslight* by portraying a woman who is being systematically driven insane by her husband. But an Oscar was deserved more by the star who played the tormentor, Charles Boyer, than by the one whose character he tormented. Bergman was a marvelous actress, but her performance in *Gaslight* doesn't hold a candle to some of her others. Director George Cukor was known for his skilled handling of actresses, but for most of the picture Bergman merely acts docile and dazed. Only at the end, when Bergman's heroine learns the truth about her husband and turns the tables on him, pretending she can't find a knife to set him free from the police, and then telling him off— Bergman never before or after got to display such anger on screen!—does the character switch from being infuriatingly ignorant to interesting. Another candidate for Best Actress, Tallulah Bankhead, the New York Film Critics' choice, was interesting to watch throughout Alfred Hitchcock's *Lifeboat*, but to me her performance seems erratic.

In a weak year for lead actresses Barbara Stanwyck stood above the rest with her chilling portrait of a scheming murderer in Billy Wilder's *Double Indemnity*. Considering her laughable blond hairstyle, one can't say her performance was without flaws, but it was the next thing to it.

Stanwyck plays Phyllis Dietrichson, a former nurse who poisoned her patient and married the dead woman's

unsuspecting husband (Tom Powers). He bought her the house she wanted, but now she's bored with him and unhappy that he plans to leave all his money to his grown daughter, whom she despises. She makes a play for cocky insurance agent Walter Neff (Fred MacMurray), claiming to have fallen for him. She manipulates him into agreeing to murder her husband and devising the murder plot. Walter also shows off by getting her husband to sign an insurance policy that will award Phyllis a small fortune in case of his "accidental" death. They pull off the murder, but Walter's shrewd boss (Edward G. Robinson) suspects a crime. Walter tells Phyllis not to put in a claim for the insurance money or they'll be found out. But she's too greedy. Walter realizes he has been a sap and goes to her house to kill her. He does so, but not before she shoots him.

Phyllis Dietrichson is the prototypical femme fatale of forties film noir. She set the ugly standard for many other greedy, heartless women who ruin the lives of basically decent men in order to get rich. Phyllis was a change of pace for Stanwyck and led to many more unsympathetic characterizations. She had always played tough, manipulative women, but in their early incarnations they showed they had good hearts when the chips were down. Phyllis, however, is a tough, manipulative woman who knows that "I'm rotten to the heart." Stanwyck's earlier women gradually let down their defenses as they get to know lovable, decent, unpretentious men. Phyllis falls in love for all of fifteen seconds with a man who proves to be as

In a role that paved the way for her to play other dangerously disturbed villainesses, Barbara Stanwyck retrieves the gun with which she'll shoot Fred MacMurray in *Double Indemnity*.

much of a louse as she is. And she gives him the one sincere kiss of her life before feeling cold steel against her ribs and pulling back with an expression of confusion, terror, and betrayal just before he kills her.

That *she* should fall in love and be the one who is betrayed are Phyllis's great surprises. She is someone who always gets her way, who can turn on the charm and have any man do her bidding—including Walter, who wrongly believes he is in control. She never stops acting, never stops playing with Walter's mind. She dresses for success, using towels, sunglasses, an ankle bracelet, and that strange blond hair as sexy props. "Oh, I forgot: today's the maid's day off," she says in an intentionally unconvincing manner when Walter comes to sell her a policy. This is her come-on. To encourage him further she plays hard to get, acting offended (but not convincingly so) by his suggestive lines. Then, to reel him in, she plays easy to get. "I want you to be nice to me," she says. Going to his apartment, she kisses him with (fake) passion and gives herself to him, saying repeatedly, "It's straight down the line for both of us." She shrewdly strokes his ego by pretending to be madly in love with

him, and by agreeing to every element in his murder plot. She makes the murder an extension of their love-making, feigning excitement when she tells Walter that her husband is on crutches: "It makes it much better, doesn't it!"

Phyllis feigns everything because she is without emotion, without a soul, without any trace of humanity. When Walter kills her husband, she doesn't blink an eye; she doesn't even bother to look. She has no remorse. Phyllis knows it is her curse to have no feelings, but she also knows that this is what makes her so strong. When she discovers she loves Walter and can't shoot him a second time, she is completely unnerved. In her last few seconds of life, when she pulls back from kissing Walter because she realizes he is about to kill her, all kinds of emotions are evident on her face. It's like the end of a werewolf movie, where at death the monster's face disappears and the human face returns. We see Phyllis immediately before death when her face is in midtransformation, with her newly emerged human side and her monster side in frightening conflict. Judging from her grotesque final expression, I assume her monster side won out.

1945

▶ BEST PICTURE

WINNER:
The Lost Weekend (Paramount; Billy Wilder)
Other Nominees: *Anchors Aweigh, The Bells of St. Mary's, Mildred Pierce, Spellbound*

▼

THE BEST CHOICE:
They Were Expendable (MGM; John Ford)
Award-Worthy Runners-Up: *Scarlet Street* (Fritz Lang), *The Suspect* (Robert Siodmak), *A Tree Grows in Brooklyn* (Elia Kazan)

Billy Wilder's *The Lost Weekend*, 1945's Best Picture winner, was a several-punches-pulled adaptation of Charles Jackson's best-seller about an alcoholic writer (Ray Milland was voted Best Actor). Today, the freshest thing about it is Jane Wyman's makeup (when Wilder wants us to think Milland looks worse, he has girlfriend Wyman look rosier), but it was the first picture to deal with alcoholism and was quite controversial upon release. Its critical and financial success made possible scores of future "problem" pictures about alcoholics, junkies, and mentally ill people. I'm glad somebody's making such films, but I'm not particularly enthralled watching all those troubled characters being mean to their loved ones, having hallucinations, getting sick, feeling sorry for themselves, and contemplating suicide. It's hard to react properly. For instance, *The Lost Weekend* is a strong, well-made picture, with solid acting and impressive location footage on New York streets, but Milland's writer is so unpleasant from the beginning of the picture that it's hard to care about him. I get suspicious Wilder didn't like him, either, and got perverse pleasure from forcing him to sweat and squirm trying to figure out how to get his next drink. I know I feel less sympathy for Milland than guilty pleasure in watching him try to leap over the impossible barriers Wilder puts before him. I suspect that any viewer's "enjoyment" depends on how much he likes seeing Milland suffer.

In a weak year John Ford's *They Were Expendable* is my candidate for Best Picture. Adapted from W. L. White's book by flying ace–screenwriter Frank "Spig" Wead (the protagonist in Ford's *The Wings of Eagles*), this unique World War II film is Ford's affectionate, respectful tribute to his war buddy Lieutenant John Bulkeley (Buckley in the film), and the sailors who manned the PT boats in the Philippines, risking their lives to buy time for an eventual American counterattack.

The picture begins in 1941 in Manila Bay. John Buckley (Robert Montgomery) showcases the four PT boats of his Motor Torpedo Boat Squadron to top navy brass. They are impressed by the boats' maneuverability but think only battleships will be of value if war comes. Because of the brass's indifference, Rusty (John Wayne), Buckley's second-in-command, requests a transfer. Buckley tells him that soldiers have to be team players, but Rusty wants glory, not a seat on the sidelines. However, when Pearl Harbor is attacked and the armed forces are mobilized, Rusty forgets about his transfer. Both he and Buckley are disappointed that the commanding officers limit the PT boats to patrolling and delivering messages. But the war goes badly in the Pacific, and eventually the PT boats are pressed into battle. The PT boats prove extremely capable, even destroying enemy battleships. The men know that they are respected when the PT boats are used to transport Douglas MacArthur. The war takes its toll on the squadron, however. Men are killed or disappear; others are recruited for infantry work and march off into the jungles. Rusty loses contact with Sandy (Donna Reed), a navy nurse he had romanced, when she is trapped on Bataan. One by one the boats are destroyed. Buckley and Rusty receive orders to fly to Australia to put together a new squadron of PT boats, because the navy now realizes their value. They hate leaving their men behind in a

Robert Montgomery and John Wayne survey the dangerous Pacific in John Ford's *They Were Expendable.*

hopeless situation—and Rusty hates leaving Sandy—but they realize that they are going away with the intention of returning in force.

They Were Expendable is one of the most sobering, somber (though there is humor and romance), and sincerely tender World War II films. It is a picture that moves forward on an even keel, without highs and lows, without climaxes, for though the PT squadron has several impressive victories in sea skirmishes, we are well aware that each win costs the lives of men and the damage to or loss of a boat, and that overall, Americans are losing the war in the Pacific. So there is little to cheer about, not even the destruction of enemy ships and planes (we never actually see enemy soldiers), except that some of the men have survived and can continue to *delay* (not stop) the total conquest of the Philippines by the Japanese.

In the opening sequence Ford paid homage to the boats themselves, filming them with the same excitement with which he had shown the cavalry riding through majestic Monument Valley in his westerns. They speed proudly and gallantly across the ocean in formation, skipping across white water, their flags blowing against a clear sky. We immediately understand why Buckley has such confidence in them. They will prove to be the ocean equivalents of "The Little Engine That Could." Interestingly, the men who staff these boats, including Buckley, are never filmed so heroically by Ford. Yes, they do heroic things, but Ford is not interested in our seeing them as heroes. Instead, he presents them as professionals, wisely scared of battle but prepared to do their duty nevertheless, confident in their decisions (there are many strategy sessions in the film) and their skills as soldiers, but cognizant of the dangers involved, and willing to follow all orders even if it means taking on humbling assignments. And paramount is teamwork, not just among the men in the Torpedo Boat Squadron, but with all soldiers in the Pacific. There is tremendous camaraderie, there is a sense of community. The older, veteran soldiers watch over the baby-faced recruits (a familiar Ford theme), and Buckley treats the men in his command as equals: "You're a swell bunch—I'm glad to have been able to serve with you." The men don't even pay attention when they learn they were awarded Silver Stars for individual gallantry. They're more satisfied that MacArthur hitches a ride over perilous waters in their boats!

As the title hints, *They Were Expendable* is, most of all, about sacrifice, not victory. In fact, at film's end it's doubtful that the people we have grown fond of in the Philippines (surviving members of the squadron, Sandy, Russell Simpson's boat repairer, "Pop," who stubbornly protects his pier and home with just a rifle) will be alive when the Americans return. But they are the reason, the film tells us, that we must go back. The great final sacrifice is made by Buckley and Rusty, who fly off to safety to help in the war effort, when Buckley would prefer staying with his men and Rusty wants to look for Sandy. But the people left behind understand why Buckley and Rusty must leave and why they, the expendable ones, must stay behind and fight. It's a strange open ending, one that is about defeat yet is not defeatist.

Ford's picture has great visual beauty (especially of night scenes, including sea battles), a truly wonderful, understated performance by Montgomery, humor ("Holy smoke, Cookie, do you call this soup?" "No, sir, that's dishwater"), propaganda value, and many poignant moments: the men talk with a brave, dying soldier; Sandy (Donna Reed is breathtakingly beautiful) sits alone in a hammock at the dance, left out while Buckley and Rusty talk shop; Sandy dines with Rusty, Buckley, and four other soldiers, giving the lonely men great pleasure. It's a truly moving, disarming film. It has become increasingly popular because of television, but don't see it there for the first time (especially in its colorized version) because it has amazing power on the big screen.

▶ BEST ACTOR

WINNER:
Ray Milland *(The Lost Weekend)*
Other Nominees: Bing Crosby *(The Bells of St. Mary's)*, Gene Kelly *(Anchors Aweigh)*, Gregory Peck *(The Keys of the Kingdom)*, Cornel Wilde *(A Song to Remember)*

▼

THE BEST CHOICE:
Boris Karloff *(The Body Snatcher)*
Award-Worthy Runners-Up: Humphrey Bogart *(To Have and Have Not)*, Henry Daniell *(The Body Snatcher)*, Edward G. Robinson *(Scarlet Street)*, Edward G. Robinson *(The Woman in the Window)*, Charles Laughton *(The Suspect)*, Robert Montgomery *(They Were Expendable)*

For taking on the then-controversial part of an alcoholic, Ray Milland was awarded 1945's Best Actor Oscar. Milland's performance was solid, the best by any of the nominees and maybe the best of his decent career. But he doesn't make you feel enough empathy for his sick, troubled character—instead I kind of enjoy watching him suffer as he tries to figure out ways to secure drinks. At least Milland dared play an unsympathetic character for a change.

My choice for Best Actor of 1945 is Boris Karloff, who made a living playing unsympathetic characters, though with the kindly British bogeyman in such roles, we usually feel some sympathy just the same. Such was the case with Karloff's grave-robber in *The Body Snatcher.* While at RKO in the forties producer Val Lewton specialized in psychological horror films in which villains commit heinous crimes for reasons that make us commiserate with them. We understand their pain. In Lewton there is no pure good and no pure evil, no black and white in regard to heroes and villains, just a *gray* area. So it's appropriate that Karloff played an almost but not entirely diabolical character named Mr. Gray.

This classy, literate Robert Louis Stevenson adaptation was directed by Robert Wise and scripted by Lewton under his pulp-novel pseudonym, Carlos Keith. It is set in 1831 Edinburgh, where Dr. McFarlane (Henry Daniell) is a rich, respected surgeon and medical teacher. He employs coachman Gray to procure recently buried cadavers. Eventually Gray commits murder to obtain bodies quickly. McFarlane despises Gray but needs his services; also Gray holds a deep, dark secret that would ruin him. Years before in England, McFarlane was an assistant to Dr. Knox, when the infamous Burke and Hare were robbing graves for him. Gray supplied bodies to McFarlane and went to prison rather than reveal McFarlane's name. Now Gray laughs that McFarlane will never be rid of him. In a struggle McFarlane kills him. He robs a grave himself, but while transporting the body imagines it's Gray. The horse and buggy go out of control and he is killed.

In Lewton's other horror films (e.g., *Cat People*) the good-versus-evil battle rages within individuals, but in this Jekyll-and-Hyde variation the war is between two men, McFarlane, who in the eyes of the world is "good," and Gray, who is seen as "evil." The irony is that McFarlane (Daniell usually played villains), who won't acknowledge his sins, has an evil side that he denies; and Gray, who goads the reluctant doctor into performing necessary surgery on a crippled little girl, has a good side that he denies. They aren't really two people but, as Gray contends, "closer than if we were in the same skin—for I saved that skin of yours once and you'll not forget it."

Never considered for an Oscar because of the genre he worked in, Karloff is best remembered for his monsters and villains in thirties horror movies. But this marvelous actor was at his best in the Lewton films: *Isle of the Dead,* as a sinister general, *The Body Snatcher,* and *Bedlam,* as the cruel head of an insane asylum. His Mr. Gray is one of the most fascinating of all movie villains (Joel E. Siegel described him as "Uriah Heep [but] more vicious and more pathetic"). Whereas McFarlane is a hypocrite, Gray is a walking contradiction. He dresses in a slovenly manner, drinks too much, is in need of a shave, and doesn't sit like a gentleman, yet he tries to be

Boris Karloff gave a memorably creepy performance as the title character in the Val Lewton–produced *The Body Snatcher.*

dignified, wearing a top hat, being overly polite, and treating with honor those guests who come to his stable dwelling. He's uneducated, yet is able to converse on equal terms with McFarlane, and even outthink him, since the doctor has "knowledge but no understanding." He kills two humans in the film but takes care of his horse and even pets his nervous cat while straddling a murder victim. (He does kill a dog, however.) Also, he is sincerely kind to the lonely crippled girl, who trusts him but not McFarlane. When Karloff scowls and his voice becomes menacing, Gray is truly frightening and you know he's capable of doing anything. But most often Karloff's villain is cheery, smiling, laughing and joking (snidely, I admit). He even sings a snappy street ballad about Burke and Hare, before—in a terrifying moment—he kills McFarlane's blackmailing servant (Bela Lugosi).

We feel we should detest this man that McFarlane considers "a malignant, evil cancer that is rotting my mind," but Karloff won't let us. Gray is just too complicated. He doesn't commit crimes because he enjoys doing so or because it will bring him riches, but as a source of pride. By being a partner in crime of the "great Dr. McFarlane," he keeps McFarlane from thinking he is superior. We can relate to his deep resentment of this doctor who basks in wealth and glory while Gray lives in poverty, and is so condescending toward him. We admire that he turns down McFarlane's offer of wealth if he'll only go away. He explains, "That wouldn't be half so much for me as to have you come here and beg. . . . That is my pleasure. . . . You're a pleasure to me . . . a pride to know that I can force you to my will."

In Karloff's finest moment he stands above and leans over the seated McFarlane and lectures him, revealing himself clearly: "I am a small man, a humble man, and being poor I have had to do much that I didn't want to do. But as long as the great Dr. McFarlane jumps to my will, that long I am a man—and if I have not that, I have

nothing. Then I am only a cabman and a grave robber." At this moment Karloff makes us understand Gray, and suddenly we feel a stronger emotional attachment for him than for McFarlane, who had infinitely more opportunity than Gray to do good in the world. It's upsetting that McFarlane then kills Gray in a struggle because Gray could have killed McFarlane if he'd wanted. But Gray really believed McFarlane was "an old friend." When McFarlane robs a grave after Gray's death, he proves what Gray wanted him to admit: that the "good" doctor was no better than the bad Gray; that, in fact, he had become Gray.

▶ BEST ACTRESS

WINNER:
Joan Crawford *(Mildred Pierce)*
Other Nominees: Ingrid Bergman *(The Bells of St. Mary's)*, Greer Garson *(The Valley of Decision)*, Jennifer Jones *(Love Letters)*, Gene Tierney *(Leave Her to Heaven)*

▼

THE BEST CHOICE:
Joan Bennett *(Scarlet Street)*
Award-Worthy Runners-Up: Lauren Bacall *(To Have and Have Not)*, Ingrid Bergman *(The Bells of St. Mary's)*

The Best Actress Oscar for 1945 went to Joan Crawford for playing a single working woman with daughter problems in Michael Curtiz's *Mildred Pierce*. This James M. Cain adaptation mixed "mother love" soap opera with moody film noir—only, this time it is a woman, Crawford's title character, who is led down a wayward path by the ambitious, immoral femme fatale, specifically Mildred's daughter, played by Ann Blyth. I'm glad Crawford's career was revived by her Oscar—she was one actress who knew how to milk success—but in truth she was better in subsequent films (I particularly like her in *Flamingo Road*) than in what is considered her quintessential role. Crawford has presence of her own, of course, but mistakenly played every scene in an understated manner, when Mildred could have used some fire. She's really not a very interesting character despite her strength and businesswoman status.

Much more impressive among the nominees is Ingrid Bergman, who with smile, eyes, and heart gave the cinema's definitive portrait of *goodness* as a nun in the *Going My Way* sequel, *The Bells of St. Mary's*. Even Father O'Malley describes her as "perfect." Bergman deserved some kind of award for the great sequence (which critic James Agee hated) in which she teaches a little boy to box (in her habit she bounces about, bobbing, weaving, and jabbing) and then guiltily watches him defeat a bully; and for the tearjerking finale when she smiles joyously upon learning that Father O'Malley has transferred her to Arizona not because he dislikes her teaching methods but because she has TB: "You have made me very happy!"

Lauren Bacall certainly deserved Oscar consideration

for her debut in Howard Hawks's *To Have and Have Not*, shooting one-liners and sparks aplenty opposite off-screen lover Humphrey Bogart. She was an electrifying new presence who made nonchalance seem sexy, who made wit seem sexier, who (the actress and the character) flirted with Bogart but made it clear that she didn't want to waste time playing games ("I'm hard to get, all you have to do is ask"), and who turned every line she delivered into a *line*. If her role had been bigger and more integral to the political-action story, which could have used her, then she would have been the best choice for the Oscar.

The sleeper of the year was Joan Bennett, a much taken-for-granted actress, who gave a terrific, overlooked performance as an atypical femme fatale in *Scarlet Street*, Fritz Lang's "noirization" of Jean Renoir's 1931 French film, *La Chienne*. In this fatalistic semicomical melodrama Edward G. Robinson starred as Christopher Cross, a mild-mannered, middle-aged, masochistic bank employee. So dominated by his wife that he must paint in the bathroom, he fantasizes about being loved by a young woman. In Greenwich Village he meets sexy young Kitty March (Bennett), who claims she is an actress. He falls in love with her and she pretends interest in him because she thinks him rich. Her boyfriend, Johnny (Dan Duryea), coaxes her into playing Chris for a sucker to see how much money they can get from him. Chris steals money from his wife and the bank to give to Kitty. She tells Chris she'd marry him if he weren't married. Kitty and Johnny secretly sell Chris's unsigned paintings, which are acclaimed by a powerful critic. Kitty pretends to be the

Trashy Joan Bennett toys with weak Edward G. Robinson in Fritz Lang's fatalistic *Scarlet Street*.

artist. When Chris finds out what she has done, she simply weeps that she needed the money, and he doesn't object. He continues to paint, and she continues to collect the money. He cleverly wriggles out of his marriage but then discovers that Kitty loves Johnny and doesn't want to marry him. He stabs her with an ice pick. Johnny is executed for the crime. Fired from his job for embezzlement, Chris becomes a crazed bum, who wanders the streets and is constantly tormented by Kitty's words: "I love you, Johnny."

Scarlet Street was a companion piece to *The Woman in the Window,* which Lang had filmed with Robinson, Bennett, and Duryea earlier in the year. In that film Duryea blackmails the married Robinson and the younger Bennett, after Robinson kills a man in self-defense in her apartment. Bennett isn't in cahoots with Duryea and doesn't double-cross Robinson—for a femme fatale she is quite sympathetic. The unusual thing about Bennett's femme fatale in *Scarlet Street* is that she isn't particularly smart or shrewd. Yes, Kitty's clever enough to fool both Chris, who knows nothing about women (he's never seen one naked, he assures his wife) and the famous art critic (is Lang insulting his own critics here?). But Johnny, who isn't smart, either, is the brains behind the operation. And it's strictly a clumsy, low-budget operation at that. Chris is hoodwinked by a couple of real losers. It shows what kind of taste he has to fall in love with a woman who is head-over-heels in love with a rotter who slaps her, insults her, stays with her only because she can get money from Chris, and finally wants to kill her. "If I had any sense I'd walk out on you," she tells Johnny. But as he reminds her between slaps: "You don't have any sense."

Bennett did her best work in the four forties melodra-

mas (including *Man Hunt* and *The Secret Beyond the Door*) she made with Lang. She had a long, varied career (starting out as a blonde), but she never had another part like Kitty March. She really let loose playing this "working girl" who is too lazy to work. Kitty has no class whatsoever. Everything about her is cheap, which is why, I suppose, a respectable masochist like Chris would become obsessed with her. She spends all her time lounging around her apartment waiting for sex with Johnny. The sink is filled with dirty dishes and the floor must be disgusting, because Kitty sticks gum into her mouth and lets the wrapper slip through her fingers, spits grape seeds across the room, and even tosses lit cigarettes every which way. She's pretty enough to get any guy she wants, but she's attracted to a lowlife. She lets Johnny knock her about and still jumps into his arms, saying "Oh, jeepers, I love you Johnny!"

Chris pretends she is a lady; his refusal to see the obvious makes his descent into hell complete. He enjoys being wrapped around her dirty little finger, and when she tells him to paint her, he contentedly drops to his knees with her toe polish. Chris will enjoy every humiliation from Kitty, but not the ultimate one: the acknowledgment from her that she is humiliating him. In Bennett's finest moment—a scene that VCR owners will want to replay several times—Kitty sits upright in bed (like Linda Blair in *The Exorcist*) and rips into Chris: "Oh, you idiot, how can a man be so dumb? I wanted to laugh in your face ever since I first met you. You're old and ugly. And I'm sick of you. Sick! Sick! Sick! . . . You kill Johnny? Why, I'd like to see you try. He'd break every bone in your body. *He*'s a man!" These aren't the right words to say to an unhappy man who is within arm's reach of an ice pick.

1946

▶ BEST PICTURE

WINNER:
The Best Years of Our Lives (Goldwyn/RKO; William Wyler)
Other Nominees: *Henry V, It's a Wonderful Life, The Razor's Edge, The Yearling*

▼

THE BEST CHOICE:
It's a Wonderful Life (Liberty Films/RKO; Frank Capra)
Award-Worthy Runners-Up: *The Best Years of Our Lives* (William Wyler), *Henry V* (Laurence Olivier), *My Darling Clementine* (John Ford), *Notorious* (Alfred Hitchcock)

I first saw *It's a Wonderful Life* at a film society screening at the University of Wisconsin in 1967. It's hard to believe that it was then an unknown quantity to even knowledgeable moviegoers, although it starred James Stewart and was directed by Frank Capra, whose other classics were well known. It even had been nominated for a Best Picture Oscar. Since then it has become a rival to *Gone With the Wind, The Wizard of Oz,* and *Casablanca* as our most beloved movie, and a Christmas institution. In 1946 William Wyler's stirring bit of Americana, *The Best Years of Our Lives,* about the homecoming of three soldiers (Fredric March, Dana Andrews, and Harold Russell) at the end of World War II, won seven Academy Awards, including one for Best Picture. It was so timely and so well executed—my only complaint is that the resolutions to the individual stories are too pat, too safe—that it would have been almost unthinkable to have given the award to any other film. But today, it would be unthinkable not to award the Best Picture Oscar to *It's a Wonderful Life.*

George Bailey (Stewart) has spent his entire life giving of himself to the people of Bedford Falls. He has always wanted to travel but has never left because all that keeps rich skinflint Mr. Potter (Lionel Barrymore) from owning the entire town is George's building and loan company, which was founded by his generous father. But on Christmas Eve, Potter steals the business's money that George's uncle Billy (Thomas Mitchell) intended to deposit in the bank. When the bank examiner discovers the shortage later that night, George realizes that he will be sent to jail and the company will collapse. Thinking that his wife, Mary (Donna Reed will impress you with her acting and steal your heart), their young children, and others he loves will be better off with him dead, he contemplates suicide. But the prayers of his loved ones result in a gentle angel named Clarence (according to Capra, Henry Travers was sent to him "by heaven itself") coming to earth to help George, and thereby to earn his wings. He

shows George what things would have been like if he had never been born. It is a nightmarish vision in which the Potter-controlled town is sunk in vice and sin, and those George loves are either dead, ruined, or miserable. He realizes that he touched many people in a positive way and that his life was wonderful. He returns to the real world and runs joyfully through the streets shouting, "Merry Christmas!" He is thrilled to see Mary and his children, not caring that he might have to go to jail. But everyone in town brings money to rescue the man who has bailed them out many times over the years. George realizes he is the richest man on earth because he has the most friends. Clarence gets his wings.

It's a Wonderful Life was daringly and innovatively directed by Capra, who chanced both frightening us and making us cry to get us to agree with his *cheery* vision. And it was brilliantly performed by Stewart, Reed, Travers, and a supporting cast that cared so much about the film's every-person-has-value theme that they didn't worry they were likely going overboard on corniness. As strange as it is wonderful, *It's a Wonderful Life* ranges from riotous comedy to ugly nightmare. Its most admirable hero, George Bailey, spends a great deal of screen time feeling sorry for himself; he's resentful, mean (he even slaps Uncle Billy), tantrum-throwing, even suicidal. In fact, almost all the characters (for example, Ward Bond's Bert and Frank Faylen's Ernie) whom we come to love in the "real" scenes, become terrifyingly cold in the alternate-world, *Twilight Zone*–like sequence. Even George's own mother (Beulah Bondi) denies his existence. From witnessing his disturbing meetings with loved ones and old friends, we come to share George's terror and are quite relieved when he returns to the real world. Capra makes viewers understand the elation George feels as he runs through the streets. We don't even mind that, in another unusual decision, Capra has chosen not to have Potter arrested for his crime. As long as one doesn't shake hands with the devil—what an expression of disgust

Donna Reed and James Stewart are Mary and George Bailey, whose passion for one another doesn't diminish over the years in Frank Capra's *It's a Wonderful Life.*
(Photo courtesy of Barbara Young)

warmth that George feels for everyone in town and the warmth they express in return. We love hearing the unsolicited compliments that fill the script: "I think you're a great guy"; "You look wonderful"; "I'd say you were the prettiest girl in town"; "I like George Bailey"; "I'm glad I know you, George Bailey." We love the romance, as when George first courts Mary: "I'll give you the moon," says George; "I'll take it," replies Mary; and when, in the midst of a squabble, George angrily proposes marriage to the crying Mary (as they stand close and talk into the same telephone to a man who is her suitor and his best friend).

Most of all we love the affection. In a scene that makes me teary long *before* I see it for the millionth time, troubled pharmacist Mr. Gower slaps the young George for not having made a delivery, but then lovingly hugs the boy for refusing to deliver the package because he saw Gower accidentally fill it with poison instead of medicine. Two other scenes are also guaranteed to bring on tears and laughs: Getting his second chance at life, the excited George runs all over the house kissing his children; in the finale the entire town rallies to George's aid, and there is a great deal of hugging, kissing, smiling, and tears of joy.

It's a Wonderful Life is the most comforting of films. It offers confirmation that life is indeed worth living ("I want to live!" George discovers), that each individual is important because he affects countless lives, that everyone benefits if one person doesn't shirk responsibility, and that one's good works do not go unrewarded. Here's a film in which everyone whom George ever helped comes to his side, without his asking—because they love him. When this disillusioned idealist has his moral crisis and thinks his life of generosity was wasted, he has his faith restored by those very people he's spent a lifetime teaching through words and example. It's nice to know that they were paying attention and learned his great lesson: People's most important investments are in each other. It's a terrific theme. And one worth being reminded of every Christmas.

George has when he shakes Potter's slimy hand—then there is nothing to worry about.

Released by RKO, *It's a Wonderful Life* was the first picture produced by Liberty Films, an independent company founded by Capra, George Stevens, William Wyler, and Sam Briskin. It was Capra's first narrative film since 1941, and he chanced that moviegoers still were willing to accept "Capra-corn" after the experience of a devastating war. Scripted by Frances Goodrich, Albert Hackett, and Capra, with an assist from Jo Swerling, it originated as a short story called "The Greatest Gift," which writer Philip van Doren Stern sent to friends as a Christmas card. That explains its unabashed sentimentality, which did turn off cynical viewers in 1946, but gives the picture such tremendous impact.

The best of all sentimental films, it makes us cry not by showing us tragedy, but by depicting characters' kindness and generosity toward one another. We see the

▶ BEST ACTOR

WINNER:
Fredric March *(The Best Years of Our Lives)*
Other Nominees: Laurence Olivier *(Henry V)*, Larry Parks *(The Jolson Story)*, Gregory Peck *(The Yearling)*, James Stewart *(It's a Wonderful Life)*

▼

THE BEST CHOICE:
James Stewart *(It's a Wonderful Life)*
Award-Worthy Runners-Up: Henry Fonda *(My Darling Clementine)*, Rex Harrison *(Anna and the King of Siam)*, Fredric March *(The Best Years of Our Lives)*, Laurence Olivier *(Henry V)*

As part of the near sweep of Oscars by William Wyler's *The Best Years of Our Lives,* Fredric March won his second Best Actor statue for his thoughtful portrait of a returning

soldier who has trouble readjusting to his family and civilian life after World War II. As usual March was a strong, commanding presence but he also displayed tenderness and revealed insecurities rarely evident in his earlier films. He was particularly moving in those scenes when his bank executive defends his decision to his boss to give loans to those returning veterans who are financially strapped and have no collateral. In any other year I would go along with March's Oscar victory. But in 1946 James Stewart played George Bailey in *It's a Wonderful Life*.

George Bailey is one of director Frank Capra's idealist heroes with a tendency toward demagoguery, who have both their faith in themselves and their conservative values tested severely. Having devoted his entire life to the welfare of others, he now feels that his life was wasted. It takes an angel, Clarence (Henry Travers), to show him what a tragedy it would have been to his loved ones and the town itself had George never been born. George learns his lesson—that the richest man is the one who has friends—and because we relate to George, we learn the lesson as well.

The first time we see the adult George Bailey, director Frank Capra freezes the frame so George's guardian angel "can take a look at that face," the face of James Stewart. Clarence's immediate response: "I like George Bailey." It's hard not to like Stewart in any role, but from just that first frame viewers take to George as to few characters in movie history. It's obvious that the actor loves George too—Stewart would later acknowledge that George was his favorite character—because he puts so much of himself into the part, making us share his feelings.

Stewart was, along with James Cagney, the most energetic of actors, but never was he more *alive* than as George Bailey. George never relaxes, never closes his eyes—perhaps because he must be vigilant since he (as owner of the benevolent building and loan company) is all that keeps Lionel Barrymore's villainous Mr. Potter from taking over the town. Restless because he can't leave Bedford Falls, he does everything to expend energy, especially moving his hands and arms when talking. It's delightful when he finds Mary (Donna Reed) waiting at the house on their wedding night, amid a romantic setting, and is so stunned that he can't move his arms and must remain speechless. But at other times his arms swing wildly and he talks up a storm, makes speeches, argues with Potter, yells, screams, paces back and forth in front of Mary's house, runs through the streets, races up and down his stairwell, dances a wild Charleston with Mary, fights, jumps, dives into water, and on and on. He's like Dagwood Bumstead rushing to work each morning. George also is sexually aggressive. He could be in training for a triathlon. His vitality is infectious.

George Bailey was Stewart's first role since returning from active service in the air force. George blended Stewart's prewar image with what would be his harder-edged postwar persona. For much of the picture he is

While talking on the phone to Mary's suitor and George's best friend, Mary and George decide to spend the rest of their lives together in a simultaneously amusing and highly emotional scene in *It's a Wonderful Life*.

the familiar, innocent, small-town boy-next-door, optimistic in an increasingly cynical, chaotic world; a hick philosopher, talking slowly and making sense or talking so fast and exuberantly that his voice changes several octaves and you're sure he's getting a sore throat, as does his earlier idealist in Capra's *Mr. Smith Goes to Washington*. Mary doesn't change at all in the film, rolling with the punches, but George evolves into the pessimistic, tearful, violent, and neurotic character Stewart would play in the fifties in Anthony Mann's westerns and Alfred Hitchcock's *Vertigo*. It must have been shocking for audiences in 1946 to see Stewart's character, who in the early part of the film is a stabilizing influence on everyone he knows, degenerate before their eyes. It was brave of Stewart to show a mean, unsavory, embarrassing side of such a nice guy. But he knew that if he showed George's flaws and weaknesses, George would come across as *human*—not as an angel like Clarence. It also gave him the freedom to show off an incredible range of emotions. Stewart was certainly a great *movie* actor, but only as George Bailey in *It's a Wonderful Life* can we see exactly how great.

► BEST ACTRESS

WINNER:
Olivia de Havilland *(To Each His Own)*
Other Nominees: Celia Johnson *(Brief Encounter)*, Jennifer Jones *(Duel in the Sun)*, Rosalind Russell *(Sister Kenny)*, Jane Wyman *(The Yearling)*

▼

THE BEST CHOICE:
Ingrid Bergman *(Notorious)*
Award-Worthy Runners-Up: Irene Dunne *(Anna and the King of Siam)*, Olivia de Havilland *(To Each His Own)*, Celia Johnson *(Brief Encounter)*, Myrna Loy *(The Best Years of Our Lives)*, Donna Reed *(It's a Wonderful Life)*

Olivia de Havilland spent many years playing parts she didn't want, fighting with Warner Bros. to get out of her contract (she succeeded where Bette Davis had failed), and competing with sister Joan Fontaine for the favor of critics, fans, and Academy voters before she got what she was seeking, a Best Actress Oscar. But I'll quickly take it away from her. I've always had a soft spot for de Havilland—as a kid I loved her opposite Errol Flynn in eight films. And I think she was extremely good in Mitchell Leisen's five-hankie soap, *To Each His Own,* as a long-suffering unmarried woman whose son doesn't know she's his mother. But she gave equal or better performances in roles that were more novel. Although the film was built around her, an ego boost she never enjoyed at her old studio, it's hard to believe that she went to war with Jack Warner to get such ordinary roles.

If Myrna Loy's part in *The Best Years of Our Lives* were a bit more substantial (she considered it her best performance) and if Donna Reed didn't have such little screen time during the second half of *It's a Wonderful Life,* I would consider giving my Alternate Oscar to either of them. Instead, I'll award it to Ingrid Bergman for her spy who goes beyond the call of duty in Alfred Hitchcock's suspense classic *Notorious.* I bypassed Bergman's award-caliber performances in *Casablanca* and *For Whom the Bell Tolls* in 1943, *Gaslight,* for which she won the Academy's 1944 Best Actress Oscar, and Hitchcock's *Spellbound* and *The Bells of St. Mary's* in 1945. But since *Notorious* marked the end of the brief period when this Swedish import was Hollywood's busiest and most respected star—and because she would never make another *great* film—it's fitting that it be the film for which she is honored.

Bergman played Alicia Huberman, a sexually promiscuous, heavy-drinking, self-loathing daughter of a convicted Nazi spy. Because she is a loyal American, FBI agent Devlin (Cary Grant) recruits her to serve as a spy in Rio de Janeiro, where the Nazis are up to something. She and Devlin fall in love, but she is convinced he thinks she's still amoral. Devlin is upset when she is assigned to have an affair with and get information from a powerful Nazi, Alexander Sebastian (Claude Rains), a friend of her late father who has loved her for several years. Alicia wants Devlin to tell her not to accept the job, but he

stubbornly insists it's her choice. Feeling rejected, she agrees to do it. Devlin acts coldly toward her. She becomes Sebastian's lover and, when Devlin doesn't protest, agrees to marry him. Devlin comes to a big party thrown by Sebastian and with Alicia's help finds uranium hidden in wine bottles in the cellar. Sebastian discovers that the bottles have been tampered with and realizes his wife and Devlin are agents. Not wanting his dangerous Nazi friends to realize that he was foolish enough to marry a spy, Sebastian and his mother systematically poison Alicia. Devlin had wanted to leave Rio and forget Alicia but he worries when she misses their final rendezvous. He goes to Sebastian's house and finds her ill. He takes her out the front door, while Sebastian can do nothing without raising the suspicions of his Nazi cohorts. They leave Sebastian behind to face a terrifying end.

Everyone who discussed Bergman's image before she made *Notorious* used such words as *virginal* (though she'd play only one nun), *good, pure,* and *wholesome* (though there had been erotic interplay with Humphrey Bogart in *Casablanca*). But now she went against type and played a woman who was somewhat alcoholic, had slept around, and takes a sleazy job that requires that she give her body to a man she doesn't love. In *Casablanca* she felt guilty and in *Gaslight* she felt that she had no strength, no mind, no identity; and in *Notorious* she's a woman who has a hard time not despising herself. She was the offspring of a deviant, she led a life of easy virtue, and now the man she loves allows her to give her body to someone else, reasoning that such an act is consistent with her past amorality. Devlin, whose name is very close to Devil, is, in effect, her pimp. It does not raise Alicia's self-esteem to find Nazi Sebastian to be more trusting, loving, and devoted to her than Devlin, who represents the American flag.

But Alicia has strength, resilience, and courage. She refuses to hate herself or lose self-respect, despite Devlin's casting her to the wolves and his subsequent spite and condescension. If he doesn't understand her actions, then it's his problem. Like Marlene Dietrich's heroines Bergman's Alicia sees no reason to defend herself. She just carries on, doing what's right and expecting nothing in return. Eventually, Devlin wakes up, defends her

Ingrid Bergman and Cary Grant are embittered lovers who lose their one opportunity to sleep together, in Alfred Hitchcock's suspense classic *Notorious*.

against higher-ups when they are disrespectful, stops thinking she chose just any job over him, and comes to the rescue.

The early scenes are the most jarring to those who identify Bergman with Sister Benedict in *The Bells of St. Mary's*. She's surprisingly effective as a drunk, and sexy as she shows Devlin she's a loose woman. She's also quite amusing delivering lines that seem written for a tough detective in a film noir thriller. When Devlin comments on her tipsy condition, she insists, "The important drinking hasn't started yet." Brushing most of the hair out of her eyes, she pushes the car accelerator to the floor for Devlin's benefit: "I want to make it eighty and wipe that grin off your face." When a cop pulls her over, she says, "People like you oughta be in bed." My favorite line is one she speaks to Devlin—"You're quite a boy"—which was unlike anything any actress had said to Cary Grant since he'd costarred with Mae West in the early thirties.

Bergman is a woman fighting for survival, who has no foundation, and no support other than backbone. Everything is up front, every expression and every line she says is the direct result of the ongoing battle in her head. In his line of work Devlin isn't used to such honesty. He doesn't trust her advances, assuming, "You enjoy making fun of me, don't you?" Bergman has a great reaction, putting her hand to her face as if thinking, *Why should he believe I'm sincere?* and smiling warmly, replying, "No, Dev, I'm making fun of myself. I'm pretending I'm a nice, unspoiled child whose heart is full of daisies and buttercups. . . ." She wants so much for him to believe her that she defiantly admits she has just slept with

Sebastian for the first time, knowing that for once Devlin will not question her veracity. Sometimes Bergman smiles when she says it, but we feel sorry for Alicia nevertheless: "Why don't you believe me, Dev, just a little. . . . Why won't you?"

Bergman is rarely listed among the great screen lovers, but there weren't many more sensual actresses when given the opportunity. She and Bogart were incredibly romantic in *Casablanca,* but I think there are moments in *Notorious* when Bergman's Alicia is even more alluring than Ilsa. You will be mesmerized by those eyes, lips, subtle expressions, and movements. Sex is a major theme in *Notorious* and it is embodied by Alicia. Devlin wants her, despite the many men who have already had her. How it must drive him crazy every time he thinks of the night Alicia was given her assignment; the idea that the unappealing Sebastian has rights to her that he, Devlin, does not. Hitchcock filmed their earlier kissing sequence in one take, in close-up, and it's quite memorable. He placed Bergman and Grant on a balcony, locked in an embrace, holding each other tightly and talking (about such odd things as her cooking him a chicken) between sensual kisses; then he had them walk into the hotel room while still intertwined so Devlin could speak on the phone and she could kiss him some more; and then—still without a cut—have him go to the door and exit, after more kisses. Grant's Devlin definitely missed out on a lot by spitefully not returning to the arms of Bergman's Alicia when later he came back into the room. In movie history few heroines (as opposed to "other women") were more eager for sex and romance.

1947

▶ BEST PICTURE

WINNER:
Gentleman's Agreement (20th Century–Fox; Elia Kazan)
Other Nominees: *The Bishop's Wife, Crossfire, Great Expectations, Miracle on 34th Street*

▼

THE BEST CHOICE:
Monsieur Verdoux (Classic Entertainment, Inc./United Artists; Charles Chaplin)
Award-Worthy Runners-Up: *Black Narcissus* (Michael Powell and Emeric Pressburger), *Great Expectations* (David Lean), *Miracle on 34th Street* (George Seaton), *Nightmare Alley* (Edmund Goulding), *Out of the Past* (Jacques Tourneur)

Darryl F. Zanuck, chief of production at 20th Century–Fox, was never regarded as a great humanitarian but, recognizing powerful story material, occasionally made films *(The Grapes of Wrath, The Ox-Bow Incident, Pinky)* that both called attention to and railed against prejudice against minorities, outsiders, the poor. In his production of *Gentleman's Agreement* he dared tackle the subject of anti-Semitism: Gregory Peck poses as a Jew and learns of discrimination firsthand for a magazine series he's writing. Adapted by Moss Hart from Laura Z. Hobson's bestseller and directed by Elia Kazan, Zanuck's film was considered one of the most significant of the many postwar social-issue films. Of course, its theme is still relevant, but the picture comes across today as dated and weak kneed, with the major issue in the story being nothing more important than whether Peck's fiancée, Dorothy McGuire, can acknowledge her own anti-Semitism and change. At least 1947's other anti-Semitism picture, *Crossfire,* about the murder of a Jew (in the book by Richard Brooks a homosexual was killed), recognized that unchecked bigotry can lead to much worse than denial of country club membership.

A startling number of cynical pictures were produced in 1947. A priest was killed in *Boomerang,* a cackling Richard Widmark kicked an invalid down a flight of stairs in *Kiss of Death,* Susan Hayward became an alcoholic in *Smash-Up—The Story of a Woman,* phony fortune-teller Tyrone Power hit the bottle and almost became a geek in *Nightmare Alley,* ghetto boxer John Garfield sold out his integrity in *Body and Soul,* Joan Crawford flirted with insanity in *Possessed,* actor Ronald Colman lost his mind and became a murderer in *A Double Life,* and Santa Claus was locked up in a mental hospital in *A Miracle on 34th Street;* and that doesn't even take into account what Rosalind Russell went through in *Mourning Becomes Electra.* Moreover, the protagonists were killed in such films as *A Double Life, Odd Man Out, Out of the Past,* and *Monsieur Verdoux.*

It's odd that in this year overflowing with bleak films critics (James Agee was an exception) should so indict Charles Chaplin's *Monsieur Verdoux,* in which he played a Landru-like bluebeard. Chaplin regarded his intelligent, provocative, and often hilarious "comedy of murders" as his best film, but it came out when his image in America had been tarnished by a dismissed paternity suit and the declaration by government officials, the American Legion, and the Hearst Press that he was a communist or, at best, a "fellow traveler." Because of negative press reaction and threatened theater boycotts by the American Legion and religious groups—who were aware that the Breen Office had considered banning it on moral grounds—the picture floundered so badly (one Broadway theater actually lowered ticket prices) that Chaplin withdrew it from distribution in America. It wouldn't return for seventeen years!

Verdoux narrates the story from his grave. For thirty-five years he was a hardworking bank teller in Paris. When the Depression hit in 1930, he was fired. Needing to support his invalid wife (Mady Correl) and small boy in their country home, Verdoux secretly took on a series of identities and married middle-aged and elderly women all over France, eventually disposing of them and investing their money in the stock market. After the disappearance of one woman, Thelma Couvais, the police suspected a bluebeard and tried to track him down. Meanwhile, he murdered another woman, Lydia Floray, because he needed money in a hurry to avoid ruin. He also plotted the murder of a loudmouthed "wife," Annabella Bonheur (Martha Raye, at her best), but she—the symbol of indestructible vulgarity—always slipped away unharmed. One night he picked up a hungry, penniless, desperate young woman, The Girl (Marilyn Nash), planning to test a poison on her. But upon her revelation that she'd once obsessively cared for her invalid husband, and still had optimism even after his death, Verdoux changed his mind, gave her money, and sent her away.

Charles Chaplin's title character in *Monsieur Verdoux* tries to prevent Martha Raye from giving her money to this shady pair so he can kill her and take it for himself.

He used the poison on a snooping detective. Verdoux seduced Madame Grosnay (Isobel Elsom), but when Annabella turned up as a guest at their wedding, he fled. Verdoux lost his home and all his money when the market crashed. His wife and child then died. He stopped his murderous enterprise and awakened from a nightmare. Years later The Girl, rich because a munitions manufacturer fell for her, offered to take care of Verdoux. But weary and lonely, he instead allowed his capture by police. In court he questioned why people should allow themselves to become so incensed by the murderer of fourteen people when they support governments that go to war and kill many thousands of people. He was executed.

In 1989 those who raved about *Crimes and Misdemeanors* claimed Woody Allen had "done what couldn't be done"—mixed outrageous comedy with murder, cynical observations on both the world and personal relationships, and thoughtful discourse about the role of religion and personal morality in a world where sinners are the ones who profit. But Chaplin had done the same thing more than forty years before.

Despite its morbid plot line *Monsieur Verdoux* is full of wit, ranging from Verdoux's sardonic lines to wild Chaplinesque slapstick. Verdoux's scenes with Martha Raye's loudmouthed, nasty Annabella are some of the funniest in all of Chaplin's work. The sequence in which he tries to poison her is his most complex comedy routine. It takes place all over Annabella's house and involves the maid's mistakenly switching a bottle containing peroxide with Verdoux's bottle containing poison, the maid's putting that poison on her hair, Verdoux putting the peroxide in Annabella's wineglass, the glasses being switched, the horrified Verdoux accidentally drinking from Annabella's glass and assuming he is about to die (he'll get his stomach pumped). Also hilariously complicated is Verdoux's discovery of Annabella at his wedding to Madame Grosnay—stunned, he spits his cocktail on the heads of two gentlemen—and his attempt to hide from her behind other guests and under tables.

In addition to the humor, the picture has charm (Verdoux, the gentleman, has enough to make any romantic woman fall under his spell), poignancy (we feel Verdoux's pain), and tenderness. I always have an emotional response when Verdoux is so touched by The Girl's love of life—romantic music is on the soundtrack—that he takes from her the wine he laced with poison, changing his mind about killing her, and instead gives her money and sends her home. Ironically, his action causes her to cry about how kind people can be. Yet we never forget that the Chaplin who wrote and directed this film is quite cynical, quite serious. No one would think that Charlie Chaplin could give us the creeps, but that's our reaction just before he kills Lydia.

Chaplin doesn't want us to hate his character, but he does make us keep our distance—in just the same way he pushes The Girl away the second time they meet. He doesn't justify Verdoux's murders, but he makes it clear that they are the acts of a society-created madman ("Despair is a narcotic—it blows life into indifference"). He allows Verdoux time to expound his philosophy, but doesn't necessarily agree with his character's opinions. Indeed, everything Verdoux says during those years in which he commits murders are the words of a wise but insane man. So that we won't necessarily agree with Verdoux at those times, Chaplin wrote rational words for The Girl that counter Verdoux's pessimism. For instance, when Verdoux emphatically states that "it's a ruthless world, and one must be ruthless to cope with it," she silences him with "It's a blundering world, and a very sad one, yet a little kindness can make it beautiful." When Verdoux then gives her enough money to get by, he proves her point.

Verdoux does reflect Chaplin's view, however, when he speaks in court. His is a plea for world peace and disarmament and a scathing attack on capitalism. Whether it's a matter of individuals or of countries conducting *business* ("wars, conflicts—it's all business"), money equates with human death. Chaplin blames us for condoning the warfare of states that kill countless people for economic reasons while condemning individuals like himself who kill a few people to make ends meet: "Numbers sanctify." And he blames capitalist governments for pursuing a path toward war while their starving people walk the streets and capable workers like Verdoux are sent out to pasture. The condemned Verdoux implies that all those present in court are as *guilty* or as *innocent* as he is and that with war on the horizon they will join him soon, in heaven or hell, or just six feet under. Because Chaplin wants viewers to decide for themselves where Verdoux is bound, he doesn't make Verdoux so sympathetic or likable that we automatically forgive his crimes. Instead he makes us decide for ouselves Verdoux's degree of guilt and, even more disturbing, whether we should share the responsibility for his crimes. Though Verdoux regrets having committed the murders, he himself isn't sure if he was a sinner or a victim. Chaplin's own uncertainty about how Verdoux should be judged is evident in his final shot: as Verdoux marches across an open courtyard toward the gallows, he walks the line between sunlight and shadows.

▶ BEST ACTOR

WINNER:

Ronald Colman *(A Double Life)*

Other Nominees: John Garfield *(Body and Soul)*, Gregory Peck *(Gentleman's Agreement)*, William Powell *(Life with Father)*, Michael Redgrave *(Mourning Becomes Electra)*

▼

THE BEST CHOICE:

Charles Chaplin *(Monsieur Verdoux)*

Award-Worthy Runners-Up: John Garfield *(Body and Soul)*, Edmund Gwenn *(Miracle on 34th Street)*, Robert Mitchum *(Out of the Past)*

At the age of fifty-seven, after thirty years in the cinema, Ronald Colman took home his only Best Actor Oscar for *A Double Life,* pleasing many in Hollywood who thought the award was long overdue. I remember being impressed the first few times I saw Colman in the George Cukor–directed, Garson Kanin–scripted melodrama, playing a snooty theater actor who so inhabits his Othello role that he strangles a waitress (Shelley Winters) and nearly does the same to his leading lady (Signe Hasso) onstage. Then again, I was impressed by Colman in almost all his films, dating back to the silent era, perhaps because of his fine reputation and, in sound films, that deep, melodious, refined voice. But with time comes the sad realization that this handsome and dignified screen presence wasn't a particularly good actor. In *A Double Life* he's not convincing as the actor or as the crazed killer the actor becomes. Moreover, his award-guaranteeing scenes as Othello, which critics of the day loved almost as much as did the audiences in the movie, reveal his limitations as an actor. He looks impressive but is dull in the stage scenes. Of nominated actors the best leading man in 1947 was Edmund Gwenn, who was perfect as Kris Kringle in *Miracle on 34th Street.* But Gwenn was unfairly nominated for and won as Best *Supporting* Actor—meaning Richard Widmark, who supported Victor Mature in *Kiss of Death,* kicked that invalid down the stairs for nothing.

The best performance in 1947 was without question by Charles Chaplin. In *Monsieur Verdoux,* which he also directed, wrote, scored, and produced, Chaplin played a fired Parisian bank teller who marries and murders women for their money to support his real, invalid wife and boy during the Depression. James Agee wrote, "Chaplin's performance is the best piece of playing I have ever seen."

Chaplin took a chance in 1940 by playing a loony Hitler in *The Great Dictator.* But he didn't worry about losing his loyal audience because he also portrayed a lovable Jewish barber in the film. However, in *Monsieur Verdoux* he hadn't anything to fall back on. Though his Verdoux had several identities and sides to his personality, Chaplin played just one character, a serial killer—not someone Chaplin fans would readily embrace.

In fact, Chaplin had to strategize how to make audiences neither hate his murderer nor automatically forgive him because they loved the actor playing him. Instead, he wanted them to feel ambivalent toward Verdoux, detesting his crimes but understanding the sad circumstances and crazed mental state that motivate him. Because Chaplin plays him, and because he is a tortured, driven man who only kills for his family's sake, we want so much to like him. Yet, when he murders Lydia Floray (Margaret Hoffman), we recognize what a ruthless monster Verdoux is. His voice changes, his humor disappears, he gives us chills. Our only solace comes from the fact that the murder takes place offscreen and that Lydia was a lifeless, cold-blooded sort. However, when he picks up a young, beautiful, penniless stranger, The Girl (Marilyn Nash), so he can test a deadly poison on her, we know that if he kills her, we won't forgive him. Fortunately, he changes his mind, when she tells him her sad story—about how she also obsessively took care of an invalid—and conveys her sense of optimism about life. After taking the poisoned wine from her, he smiles to himself and it's moving because we realize (just as he does) that she's managed to touch the small part of his heart that still has feeling. So we never turn totally against Verdoux. It helps that he fails to carry out his plots to murder his obnoxious "wife" Annabella (Martha Raye) and likable fiancée Marie Grosnay (Isobel Elsom), because both these women are full of life.

Of course, we respond warmly to Verdoux when Chaplin makes us laugh. At forty-eight he was still a masterful physical comedian, as exhibited when he backflips out a

Charles Chaplin's flattering words to an elderly prospective victim in *Monsieur Verdoux* are inspired by beautiful florist Barbara Slater, who is overwhelmed upon hearing them.

he quickly sits down, legs crossed, with the hilariously innocent expression of a naughty five-year-old. When she catches him approaching her with a noose, he explains he wants to lasso a fish. He's prevented from killing her by the arrival of some yodelers. He himself plunges into the water and nearly drowns.

It's most interesting watching Chaplin play a dapper, gentlemanly Lothario, capable of seducing any woman he speaks to, including The Girl, if he had wanted her. In his conquests he's as aggressive as Groucho Marx (who could almost play this part) but uses words like Charles Boyer. When he calls Madame Grosnay from a flower shop, his romantic words (her eyes are "beautiful, like the loneliness of distant stars—I often wonder who you are in the dark") and passionate delivery completely overwhelm the young female florist who inspires them. (At other times he'll smell roses before voicing beautiful sentiments to not-so-beautiful women.) The florist realizes that this Verdoux fellow is probably the world's most romantic man and greatest lover.

I see Verdoux as the flip side of Chaplin's Little Tramp. Though Verdoux still acts in a gentlemanly manner, he has long given up the dignity and self-respect that is key to the Little Tramp's resilience and survival. While as much a lover of beauty as the Little Tramp, he responds more strongly to the uglier side of life. The Little Tramp remains the eternal optimist while Verdoux is the ultimate cynic. Though beaten by the world, Verdoux still wants to be part of it. Committing murders is his way of conducting business; it permits him to stay in the mainstream. The Little Tramp, on the other hand, sticks to the fringes, an affront to the heartless, rich people who run the world. He doesn't want to be governed by society's mad, unfair rules. He'd rather leave town. So he walks toward the sun at the end of his films, while Verdoux winds up walking toward the gallows.

window and when, without stopping his conversation or spilling his tea, he tumbles off a couch and onto his knees while proposing to Madame Grosnay. All of Chaplin's scenes with Martha Raye—Annabella is loud and vulgar, has fits of anger, and laughs like a horse—are hilarious, mixing slapstick with verbal wit. Particularly funny is Verdoux's attempt to drown her *American Tragedy*-style in a lake. When she suspects something is fishy,

---

▶ BEST ACTRESS

WINNER:
Loretta Young *(The Farmer's Daughter)*
Other Nominees: Joan Crawford *(Possessed)*, Susan Hayward *(Smash-Up—The Story of a Woman)*, Dorothy McGuire *(Gentleman's Agreement)*, Rosalind Russell *(Mourning Becomes Electra)*

▼

THE BEST CHOICE:
Deborah Kerr *(Black Narcissus)*
Award-Worthy Runners-Up: Joan Bennett *(The Macomber Affair)*, Betty Grable *(Mother Wore Tights)*, Jane Greer *(Out of the Past)*, Susan Hayward *(Smash-Up—The Story of a Woman)*

Loretta Young was given about as much chance of besting her four formidable competitors in the Best Actress race as her stubborn Swedish housekeeper in *The Farmer's Daughter* had of outpolling her employer (Joseph Cotten) in a race for a congressional seat. But she won both times. In 1947 Young's upset victory was considered

quite exciting, but today it seems like the most boring choice ever in the Best Actress category. Young may have deserved an Emmy for years of twirling through a door without once ripping her dress as the hostess of the television anthology series *The Loretta Young Show,* but an Oscar is wasted on her. Despite being a lovely and warm presence in the cinema for twenty-six years (1927–53), she made only a half-dozen noteworthy movies, and wasn't all that impressive in any of them.

The New York Film Critics made the wiser choice, selecting an actress ignored by the Academy: Deborah Kerr. The beautiful, little-known Scottish actress was superb as a troubled young nun who must choose between the sacred and profane in *Black Narcissus*, an erotic masterpiece (about nuns!) made by Britain's heralded director-writing team, Michael Powell and Emeric Pressburger. Kerr's vast talent and star quality were so evident from this one performance—which was superior to anything Young did in her long career—MGM immediately brought her to Hollywood . . . where she fulfilled her promise.

Photographed by Jack Cardiff and designed by Alfred Junge, this stunningly beautiful color film was adapted from the novel by Rumer Godden. Kerr is Sister Clodagh, a young Irish-born nun in Calcutta, who is given authority for the first time. She and four nuns under her charge are assigned to set up a hospital and school for females in a great palace on a high, barely accessible mountain ledge in a remote section of the Himalayas. The palace was previously the residence of a potentate's harem and its dark chambers seem haunted by its sinful past. The eerie wind that howls through the empty corridors, the pounding native drums, the disturbing presence of a handsome and virile British agent named Dean (David Farrar), and the budding romance that develops between a sensual native girl (Jean Simmons) and a young native general (Sabu as the only male student), who wears the intoxicating Black Narcissus perfume, creates an erotic setting in which the nuns find their commitment to the order severely tested. All feel ill. All have doubts about their ability to persevere. They make mistakes in dealing with the people and their customs, and eventually drive them away. An older nun (Flora Robson) wants to be transferred because her faith has diminished and thoughts of her past life have returned. Sister Clodagh remembers the one love affair of her life—when he went away, she became a nun. Sister Clodagh and the other young nun, Sister Ruth (Kathleen Byron), find they must come to terms with their feelings toward Mr. Dean. Sister Ruth becomes jealous of Sister Clodagh because of Dean's obvious attraction toward her and challenges all of her orders. Unable to sleep, she gradually loses her mind. She refuses to renew her vows and puts on a dress and, defiantly in front of Clodagh, bright red lipstick. When Dean rejects her advances, Sister Ruth tries to knock Sister Clodagh over the cliff, but in the act falls to her own death. Dean is upset when Sister Clodagh leaves. She has been reassigned and will no longer be given authority.

Michael Powell and Deborah Kerr had broken off their engagement a couple of years before he and Pressburger asked her to play Sister Clodagh, who was originally intended to be ten years older than the twenty-six-year-old actress. Powell described Sister Clodagh as "the Admirable Crichton among missionary nuns. She is cer-

tain of her vocation and proud to be tested in her first command." It's a very difficult role because Kerr must convey Sister Clodagh's strength although during her "test" she softens (becoming friendlier and more tolerant) and feels herself weaken. Ultimately she leaves in what could be construed as defeat (indeed, she has been demoted). But Kerr understood that the only reason Sister Clodagh survives at all in this haunted palace on a seemingly godforsaken mountain is because she has tremendous strength of character and a true faith in God. In fact, Sister Clodagh's counterpart, Sister Ruth—with her slender face, cheekbones, and long nose, Byron could be Kerr's sister—dies because she is weak and has lost her faith.

When she undertakes her assignment, Sister Clodagh assumes a superior, humorless stance (alienating Dean) because she fears that she'll be vulnerable to him. She later realizes that allowing her *human* side to come through does not mean that she'll yield to the temptations of the flesh and forsake God. Indeed, it is as a human being, scared and needing help, that she further commits herself to God. She survives Sister Ruth's ambush on the side of the mountain specifically because she is praying at the time of Ruth's attack, and even in this remote part of the world her prayers are answered.

When Kerr accepted her part she realized that just as the "good" Sister Clodagh is challenged by the "bad" fallen angel, Sister Ruth, she herself would be hard pressed not to let Kathleen Byron overwhelm her in a much showier part. Byron is splendid as this woman who goes crazy on screen (she deserved a Best Supporting Actress award), but Kerr more than holds her own, although her character doesn't allow her the opportunity for emotional excess. She rarely smiles and only comes near tears once. Sister Clodagh is not a stoic. She is very

Nun Deborah Kerr examines native girl Jean Simmons as David Farrar looks on in *Black Narcissus,* directed by Michael Powell and Emeric Pressburger.

much *human*. But as she is strong of character, her changes don't take place as quickly as do those of Sister Ruth or the other nuns. Kerr, with help from Cardiff's penetrating close-ups, conveys Sister Clodagh's metamorphosis, patiently and subtly. At first it is only through Kerr's eyes that we can tell what is going on in Sister Clodagh's head, then her voice begins to convey telling inflections, her face and body relax, and finally she is freer with her smiles and words. By the end you know exactly who Sister Clodagh is—which is also what she has been trying to find out the entire story.

Ingrid Bergman is a beautiful nun in 1945's *The Bells of St. Mary's*. Kerr is beautiful and she is, most definitely,

sexy too. Except for the flashbacks that were excised for American release (presumably so we wouldn't get the wrong idea about women who become nuns), Kerr's figure and flaming red hair (which, Powell said, shone "in the sun like burnished copper") are covered. But Dean is understandably turned on by her lovely, liquid eyes; those high cheekbones; her soft, tempting lips that seem red even when she's not wearing lipstick; her sure, thoughtful voice; and a face that is sensitive, intelligent, and prideful. As usual, Kerr plays a *lady*. And as usual her lady is erotic—only more so than usual. If she hadn't become a nun, one could imagine her rolling around in the heavy Hawaiian surf with Burt Lancaster.

1948

▶ BEST PICTURE

WINNER:

Hamlet (Rank–Two Cities; Laurence Olivier)
Other Nominees: *Johnny Belinda, The Red Shoes, The Snake Pit, The Treasure of the Sierra Madre*

▼

THE BEST CHOICE:

The Treasure of the Sierra Madre (Warner Bros.; John Huston)

Award-Worthy Runners-Up: *Fort Apache* (John Ford), *Letter from an Unknown Woman* (Max Ophüls), *Red River* (Howard Hawks)

What true *movie* fan wouldn't prefer watching John Huston's *The Treasure of the Sierra Madre* for the hundredth time to squirming through Laurence Olivier's screen adaptation of *Hamlet*? But prestige-minded Academy members were blinded by the imposing specter of Shakespeare, Olivier, and a British cast that dressed in royal garb and didn't trip over difficult lines. They did give Oscars to Huston for his direction and screenplay but didn't go along with the New York Film Critics, who had selected *Treasure* as Best Picture. To congratulate themselves on their highbrow tastes they made *Hamlet* the first British production to receive the Best Picture Oscar. This angered studio heads who financially supported the Academy. *Hamlet* isn't without merits, of course—not with Olivier himself in the lead. But Olivier's direction isn't imaginative, he pretty much ignores the other actors, his visuals have little thematic relevance (it isn't enough just to move the camera), and much of the production looks no better than a kinescope of some fifties American television drama. And until Hamlet's swordfight with Laertes, the picture drags; Olivier deleted almost two hours from the play, yet it still seems too

long. Olivier's *Hamlet* doesn't equal either his earlier *Henry V* or his later *Richard III,* a splendid movie adaptation. And it doesn't equal *The Treasure of the Sierra Madre,* one of the greatest American pictures.

Humphrey Bogart played Fred C. Dobbs, a down-and-out American reduced to begging for handouts in Tampico, Mexico. Stiffed by a construction boss (Barton MacLane), Dobbs and Curtin (Tim Holt), a fellow American, beat up the boss to get their pay. With that money and small winnings Dobbs gets in the lottery, they go mining for gold with a third American they meet in a flophouse: Howard (Walter Huston), an aged, slightly balmy, but experienced prospector. After much traveling and climbing Howard finds a rich deposit in a mountain. He teaches the other two how to mine gold and warns them that gold has an adverse effect on men. Soon Dobbs and Curtin are hiding their shares from each other. When Dobbs is knocked unconscious during a cave-in, Curtin considers leaving him there, but is moved to rescue him anyway. Dobbs becomes increasingly paranoid about his partners, talks to himself incessantly, and keeps his gun handy. Another American, Cody (Bruce Bennett), follows

Tim Holt and Humphrey Bogart try to digest the words of wisdom of veteran prospector Walter Huston in John Huston's epic adventure *The Treasure of the Sierra Madre.*

Curtin back from town and insists that the men make him their partner. Dobbs and Curtin decide to kill him and Howard goes along with the decision. But bandits, led by Gold Hat (Alfonso Bedoya), attack the camp, hoping to take their guns and money. They kill Cody but flee upon the arrival of *federales.* The three partners close up the mountain and head back with $105,000 of gold dust among them. On the trail Howard saves the life of a little native boy who almost drowned. The boy's people insist that Howard stay with them to be honored. Dobbs and Curtin go on ahead, planning to meet up with Howard later. Dobbs decides they should steal Howard's gold. Curtin keeps a gun pointed at him to protect the gold. When Curtin falls asleep, the delirious Dobbs takes the gun and shoots him. But Curtin crawls away and finds help. Just before reaching town Dobbs is waylaid by Gold Hat and two of his men. They kill him and steal his burros and pelts. Thinking the gold is sand, they let it blow away. They are arrested and executed for trying to sell the stolen burros. Arriving in town, Howard and Curtin laugh at their bad luck. Howard returns to the tribe to be its medicine man; Curtin will go back to America and look up Cody's widow. The gold blows back to the mountain from which it came.

John Huston adapted his exciting, witty script from a novel by B. Traven, a mysterious recluse whose identity was known only to his secretary. (Huston dealt with Traven's representative, who many people suspected was Traven.) Many of the best lines and most of the scenes come from the book. To achieve authenticity, as well as a dirty, gritty, dangerous feel to his picture, Huston insisted on shooting on location in Mexico—it was the first narrative American movie filmed entirely out of the States. He hired Mexican character actors and amateurs

and wisely chanced including long bits of dialogue that were delivered in Spanish and had no subtitles, prompting Jack Warner, upon seeing rushes, to believe Huston was simultaneously making a Spanish version of the film. I think Huston's major contribution to the film was making Gold Hat a continuing character—in the book Dobbs is killed by a stranger named Miguel. As played by Alfonso Bedoya the vile, smiling, almost comical bandito chief could have been conceived by Luis Buñuel. He is one of the screen's great punk-bully villains. His great moment comes when he tries to pass himself and his men off as *federales* and Dobbs asks to see their badges. His oft-quoted response: "Badges? We ain't got no badges. We don't need no badges. I don't have to show you any stinkin' badges!" Bogart is terrific as the unkempt, undesirable, and untrustworthy Fred C. Dobbs, but that's often forgotten because of Walter Huston's marvelous Best Supporting Actor portrayal of the grizzled, toothless, slightly loco but wise and philosophical Howard *and* the scene-stealing antics of Alfonso Bedoya—Gold Hat even delays the firing squad that executes him long enough to put his hat back on.

At first glance *The Treasure of the Sierra Madre* seems to be an action-adventure film geared for young boys, with its treasure hunt in unknown territory, gunplay, fisticuffs (the scene in which Dobbs and Curtin fight with their boss, McCormick, in a bar is a classic), tension and squabbling among partners, brutal villains, no women. But it is also a complex character study about what the discovery of gold can do to individuals ("changing a man's soul"). It's easy to condemn Dobbs for his betrayal of his partners, but Howard isn't so judgmental, reasoning, "He's not a real killer as killers go—I think he's as honest as the next feller, or almost." Howard admits to Curtin that if he were younger, he also might have turned on Curtin and stolen the gold. Curtin can't be too self-righteous about Dobbs, either, because he almost let Dobbs die in the cave-in; would have killed Dobbs if he tried to steal his share of the gold; and cast the deciding vote to kill Cody so they wouldn't have to share their gold with him. He just happens to be a little more decent than Dobbs.

Dobbs isn't totally bad either. When he takes money from his unconscious, swindling boss, he takes only what is due him. He splits his lottery winnings with Curtin and Howard, financing their expedition. When Curtin offers to pay him back with interest, Dobbs refuses. Before the expedition begins, Dobbs truly believes he has enough character not to become as greedy as most men who find gold: "It wouldn't happen that way with me. I'd swear it wouldn't. I'd take only what I set out to get." So his greatest betrayal is of himself. He just doesn't understand the power of gold, how it can intrude on his mind.

Most of the tension in the picture is caused by *intrusion;* the lure of gold intruding on minds of and relationships among the three men, and different characters intruding on space "belonging" to others. In Tampico, Dobbs annoys a successful American (John Huston) by repeatedly asking him for handouts. A little boy bugs Dobbs so much that he buys a lottery ticket. Dobbs annoys Howard by interrupting his rapid-fire flophouse monologue about gold mining. Dobbs and Curtin interrupt McCormick's date to demand their earnings. The three Americans travel through Mexico. Bandits interrupt the train journey. The Americans walk through the Mexican wilderness. They rape a mountain for its gold. Cody enters their camp and tries to force himself into the partnership. Gold Hat's bandits attack the camp. Gold Hat and two men ambush Dobbs. And the bandits' sale of Dobbs's burros is interrupted by the *federales,* who arrest them.

In another classic scene Howard and Curtin, after laughing uproariously about the joke nature has played on them—the gold returning to the mountain—decide they will be intruders no longer: Howard will retire as the welcomed medicine man of a native tribe, and Curtin will go back to the States, look up Cody's wife, and perhaps fulfill his dream of working on a fruit farm. Strangely, by the time Howard and Curtin are discussing their futures, Dobbs, played by the movie's star, has been dead for about fifteen minutes of screen time. And they waste little time conversing about him. This underlines one of the film's most important themes: In a country where there is instant justice, *life is cheap.* Bandits are killed without a trial and dropped into unmarked graves; after Gold Hat's attack on the train is foiled, the relieved conductor says, "Not many passengers were killed"; Cody is killed, needlessly fighting beside the three men who were about to execute him; at Cody's death Dobbs laments, "One less gun," and soon suggests, "Well, I guess we'd better dig a hole for him." Gold Hat kills Dobbs for a few pelts and burros, and while his corpse is still warm, Gold Hat's men fight over his shoes.

Dobbs tries to give his life undeserved value. Throughout the film he talks of himself in the third person, as if he were an athlete being interviewed. He says, "Fred C. Dobbs doesn't say nothing he doesn't mean"; "If you know what's good for you, you don't monkey around with Fred C. Dobbs"; "Fred C. Dobbs ain't the kind of guy who likes being taken advantage of." What's amusing about the gloating of this insecure, inconsequential man is that he won't even rate a grave and tombstone, much less an epitaph.

▶ BEST ACTOR

WINNER:
Laurence Olivier *(Hamlet)*
Other Nominees: Lew Ayres *(Johnny Belinda),* Montgomery Clift *(The Search),* Dan Dailey *(When My Baby Smiles at Me),* Clifton Webb *(Sitting Pretty)*

▼

THE BEST CHOICE:
Anton Walbrook *(The Red Shoes)*
Award-Worthy Runners-Up: Humphrey Bogart *(The Treasure of the Sierra Madre),* Montgomery Clift *(The Search),* John Garfield *(Force of Evil),* Laurence Olivier *(Hamlet),* James Stewart *(Call Northside 777),* John Wayne *(Red River),* Clifton Webb *(Sitting Pretty)*

The Academy's choice of Laurence Olivier for 1948's Best Actor is quite understandable. Even with a blond haircut that makes him look like Dwayne Hickman in TV's *The Many Loves of Dobie Gillis,* you just assume that Olivier is *perfect* as Hamlet and that if you find something lacking in his performance, then there's something lacking in your own understanding of both Shakespeare and acting. Nevertheless, I believe that his portrayal of the troubled Danish prince isn't as compelling as it should have been. That Olivier, the actor, keeps "center stage" for the entire lengthy production has less to do with his part or his interpretation than with Olivier, the director, keeping his supporting players in check so that they don't outshine him (their performances are instantly forgettable). While Olivier displays awesome talent, what is more impressive is the physicality he exhibits, particularly during Hamlet's deadly swordfight with Laertes. One can understand why Olivier was considered a sex symbol.

My choice for Best Actor of 1948 is Anton Walbrook for *The Red Shoes,* the ballet classic directed by Michael Powell and Emeric Pressburger. This handsome, mustachioed Austrian came from a family of clowns, but he projected refined European elegance, grace, charm, and wry wit in German, English, and American pictures, from the early thirties to the late fifties. He made indelible impressions in the title role of *Michael Strogoff,* as the villain who tries to drive his wife insane in the original *Gaslight* (released in England in 1940), the "master of ceremonies" in Max Ophüls's *La Ronde,* the King of Bavaria in Ophüls's *Lola Montes,* and in Powell and Pressburger's *49th Parallel/The Invaders,* and *The Life and Death of Colonel Blimp.* But he's best remembered for his ballet impresario, Boris Lermontov.

Impressed that beautiful young ballerina Vicky Page (Moira Shearer) prefers dance to life itself, the unfriendly, dictatorial Boris Lermontov offers her a minor position with his National Ballet Company, the most prestigious in England. He also hires Julian Craster (Marius Goring), a brash music student, to be his orchestra coach. When his star ballerina (Ludmilla Tcherina) quits the company to get married, Boris is furious because he thinks a dancer can't be in love and perform with full dedication. He decides to make Vicky his star and has Julian compose a ballet for her from a story by Hans Christian Andersen, "The Ballet of the Red Shoes," in which a girl dies because she can't remove her ceaseless dancing shoes. The ballet is a sensation and Vicky goes on to star in more Lermontov productions. But when Vicky and Julian fall in love, Boris turns against them. He fires Julian, prompting Vicky to quit and go away with him. After much time Lermontov swallows his pride and offers Vicky the opportunity to dance *The Red Shoes* again—on the night Julian is to conduct his new opera. But Julian comes to the theater to convince Vicky to not dance, and to go away with him. Lermontov argues that she must dance and forget her marriage. The tearful Vicky walks toward the stage, but her red shoes pull her elsewhere. She jumps in front of a train. Dying, she asks Julian to remove her shoes. The crying Lermontov announces that the ballet will go on as planned, with a spotlight glowing where Vicky would have danced.

In the most beloved and influential of all ballet films, Walbrook gives a sad, disturbing portrait of a complex, frustrated man who is so dedicated to his art—he calls ballet his religion—that he suppresses his human qualities. As insecure as he is pompous, he hides behind a defense comprised of a stone face, an authoritative position that allows for no dissenters, and smart, smug remarks and answers to everything. He wears dark glasses and watches his ballets from behind a curtain, in the shadows. An artist without talent of his own, he seeks personal satisfaction by finding others with budding talent and nurturing them to greatness: "I want to create something big out of something little," he confides to Vicky. "To make a great dancer out of you." So devoted is he to ballet that he feels betrayed when anyone fails to share his vision and would compromise their talents for something as trivial as love and marriage. He chooses to "ignore" human nature, thinking Vicky will do the same and concentrate solely on their joint mission: "You shall dance, and the world shall follow. Shhh! Not a word. I will do the talking, you will do the *dancing*!" When she goes off with Julian, Boris tries to block out all his feelings, but this time it is he who can't ignore human nature. He feels anger, jealousy, and spite; he even misses her. Completely cold in the beginning, Boris hints that he isn't entirely without emotion when he excitedly tells Vicky that he wants to make her into a great dancer (and star) and when he joins his dance company ("my family") at a party. He sheds all shackles in the final sequence

Anton Walbrook's Boris Lermontov casts a possessive eye at Moira Shearer's Vicky Page in *The Red Shoes,* while Leonide Massine's Ljobov prepares for the performance.

when, his hair wild, he frantically argues with Vicky and Julian about her need to dance and give up marriage. It's Walbrook's finest moment: he throws both arms into the air in triumph, then drops them to his sides as if he's just scored the winning touchdown. Soon after, openly weeping, he haltingly tells the ballet audience that Vicky will never dance again, but the ballet will go on as planned.

Boris is presented by the directors as if he were a sinister villain in this modern-day fairy tale, so it is with reluctance that we recognize his finer qualities. He gives both Julian and Vicky their big breaks, instinctively believing in them and putting himself on the line on their behalf. The ballet company members are intimidated by him, yet it is he who calms them with a cheery demeanor and encouragement before performances—tellingly, he assures Vicky that he believes in her but, lest he become too revealing of his emotions, brusquely turns and walks away while wishing her luck. In this film about a woman who must choose between her work and her man, Boris comes across as the bad guy because he insists Vicky sacrifice Julian for dance. We expect that what he asks is unfair because he seems too obsessed, wild, crazed. But what Boris wants for Vicky is what is best for her, what she truly wants for herself. If he had only shown his sensitive side *before* she ran to her death, then we might have seen he was right about her. Vicky wouldn't have asked Julian to give up composing, so why should Julian ask her to give up dance? The selfish Julian is the piece's villain—Boris would never have removed the shoes from Vicky's feet at the end.

▶ BEST ACTRESS

WINNER:
Jane Wyman *(Johnny Belinda)*
Other Nominees: Ingrid Bergman *(Joan of Arc)*, Irene Dunne *(I Remember Mama)*, Olivia de Havilland *(The Snake Pit)*, Barbara Stanwyck *(Sorry, Wrong Number)*

▼

THE BEST CHOICE:
Joan Fontaine *(Letter from an Unknown Woman)*
Award-Worthy Runner-Up: Olivia de Havilland *(The Snake Pit)*

After years in lightweight roles Jane Wyman got her big break in *Johnny Belinda*. She played Belinda, a courageous, deaf-mute farm girl who learns sign language, falls in love with a kindly doctor (Lew Ayres), is raped and becomes pregnant by a brutish fisherman (Stephen McNally), gives birth to a boy she names Johnny, and kills the fisherman to protect her child. The part was so strong already that Wyman really wasn't required to act. Indeed, director Jean Negulesco had her give a remarkably restrained performance (she rarely changes expressions), so it wouldn't be so evident that they were milking the audience for sympathy. In plain clothes, without makeup or styled hair, Wyman just smiled prettily and kept her eyes wide open—sometimes you can detect a light mysteriously directed at her eyes so that they seem to sparkle with goodness. Belinda, who loves her child, hasn't a mean thought in her head, and nobly suffers in silence, comes across as extremely huggable and lovable. Academy members were even more inclined to select Wyman 1948's Best Actress because she had just lost her premature baby and separated from husband Ronald Reagan (who hadn't been thrilled that she devoted so much time and energy to her role in this film).

I think that the two best performances of the year were given by the feuding sisters Olivia de Havilland and Joan Fontaine. De Havilland was excellent in a showy role, as a mental patient who goes through hell before recovering in *The Snake Pit*. But I prefer Fontaine's exquisite, disarmingly subtle, unnominated performance in Max Ophüls's *Letter from an Unknown Woman*, as a woman whose entire life is determined by her obsessive love for a musician who doesn't even know her name.

Ophüls's finest American film, scripted by Howard Koch, is set in nineteenth-century Vienna. Cynical, self-loathing Stefan Brand (Louis Jourdan), a middle-aged pianist who never fulfilled his youthful potential, plans to sneak out of the city before morning rather than fight a duel he has no chance of winning. But he spends the night reading a letter sent to him by a dying woman. As a teenager Lisa Berndle (Fontaine) fell in love with the handsome pianist when he moved into her apartment complex. Her mother remarried and they moved away, but her love for Stefan didn't diminish. She rejected a suitor because "I wasn't free." As a young lady she moved back to Vienna and worked as a model. Each night she stood watching Stefan's building, just to see him pass, often with a woman on his arm. One night he stopped and they met. They had a romantic evening, culminating in their making love. He went on tour and though he promised to return to her in two weeks, immediately forgot her. Lisa gave birth to Stefan's son and eventually married the rich, understanding Johann Stauffer (Marcel Journet). When the boy was nine, Lisa went to the opera and Stefan came up to her, asking where he knew her from and saying he must see her again because he needed her inspiration. Lisa told her husband that she had to leave him for Stefan, because he needed her. She went to Stefan's apartment and discovered that he had no idea who she was, that the words he had said to her were the ones he used on every woman he wanted to seduce. Wanting love rather than sex, she walked out. Their son died of typhoid. She died, too, before she signed her letter. Stefan's manservant tells Stefan her name was Lisa. Stefan realizes that Lisa and their son were his lost chance for a happy life. He goes to fight the duel.

Max Ophüls often made dreamy, romantic films about women whose hearts dictate the course of their lives. Joan Fontaine was the ideal choice to be an Ophüls heroine because she was at her best playing such women.

Joan Fontaine thrills to her only evening with Louis Jourdan in Max Ophüls's *Letter from an Unknown Woman*.

In *Rebecca,* opposite Laurence Olivier, and *Suspicion,* opposite Cary Grant, her women were overwhelmed by handsome men and, without really knowing them, married them, trusting the pounding beat of their hearts. In *Letter from an Unknown Woman* she again falls in love at first sight and again throws caution to the wind, giving herself to a man without hesitation. Fontaine evolves from an awkward, lovesick schoolgirl to a shy, sweet young woman of charm and beauty, to a lovely, educated, gracious, extremely refined lady, but her love does not change through the years. In the earlier two films the men were annoyingly unresponsive; here, the man, Louis Jourdan's egocentric pianist Stefan Brand, doesn't even know her name. He doesn't realize that of all the women he has met in his meaningless life, she was the one he needed. Her love is indestructible, whether he is (momentarily) responsive or completely indifferent.

At first glance Lisa seems so weak and so controlled by a man (though he doesn't realize it) that many actresses would feel uncomfortable playing her—probably many modern actresses would argue with their male directors and screenwriters to demand script changes. After all, here is a woman who admits, "I have had no will but his, ever"; who tells him, "Please talk about yourself"; and who concludes, "My life can be measured by the moments I've had with you . . . and our child." But we shouldn't judge her so harshly. Lisa is always sweet, polite, humble, and selfless (like Fontaine's best characters), but Fontaine projects her underlying strength, determination, and confidence, which in fact come from her great love. She has no need to feel debased. Unlike many love-obsessed male and female characters in movies, she doesn't resort to trickery or deadly games, force herself on him, or make his life miserable so that he'll come to her. Instead, she calmly and graciously keeps her distance, never feeling sorry for herself, never interfering in his life. She leads an independent existence, much of it as a single, unwed mother of a son (who tells her, "You're wonderful"). She will willingly return to that status, because she has enough strength to leave her secure life with her husband. She already showed such fortitude when she refused to tell Stefan she was pregnant with his child because "I wanted to be the one woman you had known who asked for nothing."

Her great love is not a sign of weakness or stupidity. She, like Ophüls, understands that such an unequivocal love mustn't be undervalued. She cherishes her great love for Stefan—it is enough for both of them. She realizes that it is not *her* mistake to love him as much as she does, but his for not reciprocating. She knows that this unhappy, lonely man "needs me as much as I've always needed him." She knows he should love her. She understands him better than he does himself. She even understands his problem with his music, shyly telling him on their one glorious date—proof to us that they'd be a great couple—that "sometimes I felt when you were playing that you haven't quite found . . . what you're looking for." She is what he is looking for, but he doesn't see the light until he reads her letter, after her death. His final, gallant act, which will unite them in death, proves that he was capable of giving her as much love as she did him. She hadn't misjudged him.

1949

▶ BEST PICTURE

WINNER:
All the King's Men (Columbia; Robert Rossen)
Other Nominees: *Battleground, The Heiress, A Letter to Three Wives, 12 O'Clock High*

▼

THE BEST CHOICE:
Gun Crazy (United Artists; Joseph H. Lewis)
Award-Worthy Runners-Up: *The Heiress* (William Wyler), *On the Town* (Stanley Donen and Gene Kelly), *They Live by Night* (Nicholas Ray), *White Heat* (Raoul Walsh)

Cynical movies about the simultaneous moral corruption of individuals and society—with the sheeplike masses just waiting to be manipulated by false prophets—flourished in the postwar years. In the fifties Billy Wilder's *The Big Carnival/Ace in the Hole* and Elia Kazan's *A Face in the Crowd* were but two of many films that made viewers ashamed of themselves. But in 1949 there was already Mark Robson's *Champion,* about a cad boxer who is considered a hero, and *All the King's Men,* about Willie Stark (Broderick Crawford), a once-honest dirt farmer who becomes a corrupt, dictatorial, power-mad governor of a Southern state by conning the common folks into believing he's still one of them. Director-screenwriter Robert Rossen's adaptation of Robert Penn Warren's best seller, which was inspired by the career of Louisiana's Huey Long, won numerous awards worldwide, including the Best Picture Oscar. Today the scenes that work best are those that illustrate how our political system "works"—essentially, for Stark to get elected and to get any worthwhile program across, he must be corrupt ("shake hands with the devil") and all-powerful. Also impressive are the many authentic crowd scenes (Rossen hired thousands of extras), and the quirky performance by Mercedes McCambridge, who copped a Best Supporting Actress Oscar in her debut as Stark's campaign strategist–mistress. But the politics get lost because of some romantic subplots and a conventional secondary story involving Stark's relationship with his disrespectful son (John Derek).

My choice for Best Picture of 1949 is Joseph H. Lewis's B-budgeted couple-on-the-run picture, *Gun Crazy.* It's just as cynical as *All the King's Men,* features two characters who are as dispossessed as Willie Stark is initially (Stark will find security in power, they find it in love), but, unlike Rossen's film, it continues to look better with time.

Although nonviolent, Bart Tare (John Dall) has had a lifelong passion for guns and is a crack shot. He goes to a carnival and immediately falls for a sexy, amoral trick-shot artist, Annie Laurie Starr (Peggy Cummins). She is turned on by him when he bests her in a shooting contest. He joins her act. After a run-in with the owner, they leave the carnival. They marry and she promises to try to be good. But when their money runs out, she threatens to leave unless they pull off a few robberies. Bart is upset by their crime spree, but comforted by her words of love. Annie suggests robbing a meat plant and then splitting up for a few months. She kills two people but tells Bart that she didn't harm anyone. Trying to please her, he lies by telling her he killed a driver. Annie is surprised to discover that she loves Bart too much to leave him. She admits to the murders and offers to go away, but he won't hear of it. They are tracked down by the police in the mountains. Having no chance to escape, they embrace. Annie gets ready to shoot at the police, but Bart kills her first. The police kill him.

Gun Crazy was not considered an Oscar contender in 1949. In fact, few people even knew it existed until 1967, when it was hailed as an influence on *Bonnie and Clyde.* There have been many couple-on-the-run films—including the same year's *They Live by Night,* Nicholas Ray's exciting debut—but I don't think any is as exciting or fascinating. While set against a backdrop of a poor, insensitive small-town America of the forties, and reflecting a postwar malaise ("Everything in these forty-eight states *hurts* me!" sneers Annie), *Gun Crazy* remains remarkably contemporary. It paints an ugly portrait of a

Frightened cabbie Shimin Ruskin doesn't realize he's safe as long as John Dall and not Peggy Cummins is the one holding the gun in Joseph H. Lewis's B masterpiece *Gun Crazy.*

country that is turned on by speed, sex, violence, and crime; and in fact, draws a disturbing correlation among those four traits.

The picture was adapted by MacKinlay Kantor and Millard Kaufman from Kantor's story in *The Saturday Evening Post.* However, director Lewis is responsible for the picture's technical daring, energy, excitement, emotion, and emphasis on sex. Lewis chanced filming the extraordinary on-location bank robbery sequence in one take. His running camera was set up in the back of a car and real pedestrians were not informed a film was being shot (one yells that the bank has been robbed!). He also decided that Annie and Bart wouldn't split up after the meat-plant robbery but would run to each other and embrace in the middle of the street, even with the cops closing in. The scene is pivotal because it marks the point when Annie realizes she loves Bart as much as he does her.

Lewis's greatest contribution was the offbeat casting of relative unknowns John Dall and English actress Peggy Cummins, who are both outstanding. They were willing to try anything, including blatant sexuality, from Annie and Bart's steamy meeting at the carnival until their death scene. To Annie guns equate with sex, money, and excitement, and the firing of guns while committing crimes is how the pair of them fuel their sexual flame—just as Warren Beatty and Faye Dunaway do in *Bonnie and Clyde.* (Guns to the orphaned Bart have always been his source of identity—"I've just got to have a gun. [It makes me] feel good inside, like I'm somebody.")

Lewis continuously films Annie and Bart in two-shots, keeping out the horrible world that offers them no chance at a happy life. As the film builds to a climax, he has Cummins and Dall constantly hugging, touching, and kissing. Even when the deaths of the lovers are imminent, and they are tired, battered, and terrified, Bart still calls Annie "honey" and they still express their love for each other. Annie apologizes for having dragged the decent Bart to his death alongside her, but he says truthfully, "I wouldn't have it any other way." So it is that the violent *Gun Crazy* is one of the most passionate, romantic movies in memory.

▶ BEST ACTOR

WINNER:
Broderick Crawford *(All the King's Men)*
Other Nominees: Kirk Douglas *(Champion)*, Gregory Peck *(12 O'Clock High)*, Richard Todd *(The Hasty Heart)*, John Wayne *(Sands of Iwo Jima)*

▼

THE BEST CHOICE:
Kirk Douglas *(Champion)*
Award-Worthy Runners-Up: James Cagney *(White Heat)*, John Dall *(Gun Crazy)*, Cary Grant *(I Was a Male War Bride)*, Gene Kelly *(On the Town)*, Ralph Richardson *(The Fallen Idol)*, Robert Ryan *(The Set-up)*, John Wayne *(She Wore a Yellow Ribbon)*

In 1949 Broderick Crawford became arguably the worst actor ever to win a Best Actor Academy Award. After a dozen undistinguished years of performances that failed to prove he deserved anything better than to be in films nobody saw, the burly Crawford was perfectly cast as Willie Stark, a two-fisted corrupt politician, in *All the King's Men,* who shouts almost every line and runs roughshod over everyone he deals with. After he received similar critical plaudits for *Born Yesterday* and *The Mob,* someone noticed that Crawford was incapable of playing a character any differently. Willie Stark just happened to be a good fit.

Among those actors who gave stronger performances in 1949 were John Wayne, as an aged cavalry officer in *She Wore a Yellow Ribbon;* James Cagney as an insane, mother-fixated gangster in *White Heat;* and Kirk Douglas as a gutsy but greedy boxer in *Champion.* Taking into account that I've already designated Cagney the Best Actor in 1938 and 1942, and will do the same for Wayne in 1952, I am giving Douglas the Alternate Oscar for 1949. He would give even better performances in *The Big Carnival/Ace in the Hole, The Bad and the Beautiful, Lust for Life,* and a few other films, but in those years other actors deserved the Oscar even more. Anyway, *Champion* should be singled out because it was the pivotal role of Douglas's career, making him an immediate star and establishing him as the screen's quintessential "heel."

Midge Kelly (Douglas) and his lame brother, Connie (Arthur Kennedy), work at a California diner. The owner forces Midge to marry his daughter, Emma (Ruth Roman), after he discovers they have been lovers. Not wanting to be tied down, Midge deserts her as soon as the vows are said. Midge grew up in poverty, so he looks for a way to make money. He decides to box. He convinces a retired boxing coach, Haley (Paul Stewart), to come out of retirement and train him. For a couple of years he fights across the United States. One more win,

against Johnny Dunne (John Day), will earn him a title shot, but mobsters tell him to throw the fight or he'll never get a crack at the championship. He defies the order and wins. Gangsters beat up Midge, Connie, and Haley. Midge is considered a hero across America for not backing down to gamblers. Midge dumps Haley and signs a contract with a big-time promoter, Harris (Luis Van Rooten), who promises him a title shot. Perhaps ridding himself of a conscience, Midge chases his brother Connie away. He becomes champion and is now rich. He has an affair with Harris's wife, Palmer (Lola Albright), but dumps her when Harris promises him the entire purse of his upcoming title defense against Dunne. Feeling edgy about the big fight, Midge rehires Haley and gets Connie to come back to his corner. Connie has plans to

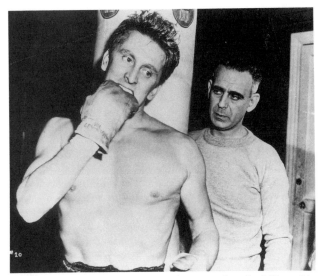

Hateful boxer Kirk Douglas and his nice-guy trainer Paul Stewart in *Champion.*

marry Emma, who has divorced Midge. Midge seduces Emma. Before his bout with Dunne, Midge knocks the infuriated Connie to the dressing room floor. In the ring Dunne tears him apart, but Midge refuses to quit. He finally knocks out Dunne. Midge talks nonsense and then has a brain hemorrhage in his dressing room and drops dead.

In most boxing films heroes find they are not strong enough to avoid corruption, but Midge is one fighter who wants to be corrupted. "The fight business stinks," says Haley, and that's why it's the ideal line of work for Midge. He nobly refuses to throw the first fight to Dunne, but when money, fame, and fine women beckon, he signs a contract with "the devil," Harris. Raised in poverty, it's his belief that "nice guys don't make money," so his course is intentionally ruthless. He dumps everyone who loves him and rubs shoulders or sleeps with only those who'll help him get ahead. The naive public thinks him a champion in more ways than one, but he's a scoundrel. He wins a sportsman's award in a scene that directly follows one in which he threatens a woman who loves him (Marilyn Maxwell), in a most unkind manner: "You're going to be a good little girl or I'm going to put you in the hospital for a long, long time."

Midge's motivation isn't so bad: "I'm going to get somewhere, make money, take care of the old lady. I'm not going to be a 'Hey, you,' all my life. I want to hear people call me mister. I'm going to make something of myself." However, he rises to the top by stepping on people. Midge ("I'm tired of being pushed around!") wants to pay back everyone who did him wrong throughout his life. As Connie points out after watching him fight, "You were hitting a lot of guys . . . all the guys who ever hurt you."

Some of the heels Douglas portrayed (such as his reporter in *The Big Carnival/Ace in the Hole*) start listening to their conscience by the end of the films, and feel guilty before they die. But Midge is worse. We like Midge at times because he is protective of his brother, smothers his mother with kisses, and has guts enough always to get in the last punch, even when defeated. And before his big fight he feels so insecure and isolated that he brings back Haley and Connie to help him train. So we hope he will reform. But Midge disappoints us by seducing Emma and decking his lame brother Connie.

Midge is an ideal role for Douglas. He was born to play characters who are ambitious, cocky, insensitive, and manipulative. The role also let Douglas be more physical than in other parts—he is like a young Cagney in the training and boxing scenes. The women who are attracted to him are quite obviously turned on by his body. But Douglas is at his best when he talks . . . loudly. Every word he spits out is full of anger, disgust, and conceit. He thinks he has something to say, but others detect a sickness in his diatribes. Midge admits to Emma that he doesn't really know how to smile because his life has been so unhappy, but once Midge hears the crowd ("the first time in my life people are cheering for me!"), collects big money, and wins the title, Douglas quite often exhibits his familiar I've-now-got-the-upper-hand-and-you-can-do-nothing-about-it grin. Johnny Dunne knocks it off Midge's face. Then, in a scene that will give viewers chills, Douglas's fighter has a breakdown, forgetting time and place and slamming his fist into his locker before collapsing. This may well be the most memorable moment in Douglas's exceptional acting career.

► BEST ACTRESS

WINNER:
Olivia de Havilland *(The Heiress)*
Other Nominees: Jeanne Crain *(Pinky)*, Susan Hayward *(My Foolish Heart)*, Deborah Kerr *(Edward My Son)*, Loretta Young *(Come to the Stable)*

THE BEST CHOICE:
Olivia de Havilland *(The Heiress)*
Award-Worthy Runners-Up: Joan Crawford *(Flamingo Road)*, Peggy Cummins *(Gun Crazy)*, Susan Hayward *(My Foolish Heart)*

Olivia de Havilland capped a tremendous decade for herself (*Hold Back the Dawn, They Died with Their Boots On, To Each His Own, The Dark Mirror, The Snake Pit,* among others) with William Wyler's *The Heiress,* from a 1949 play by Ruth and Augustus Goetz that was "suggested" by Henry James's novel *Washington Square.* She won numerous awards for playing the shy spinster, Catherine Sloper, including her second Best Actress Oscar. This time, I agree with her selection by the Academy.

The story is set one hundred years ago. Catherine lives on Washington Square in a large house with her widowed father, Dr. Austin Sloper (Ralph Richardson), and flighty widow aunt, Lavinia (Miriam Hopkins). In her thirties, she has never had a suitor, and rarely leaves the house. Although sweet and not unattractive, she is painfully shy, not particularly clever, and has no social skills. Her lack of self-esteem is heightened by her polite but cold, superior father, who always compares her unfavorably to her late mother. Catherine meets handsome, clever Morris Townsend (Montgomery Clift) at a dance and he becomes her suitor. He proposes and she accepts. Catherine's father insists this young idler is only interested in her because her mother has left her money and she stands to inherit much more when he dies. He tries to discourage Catherine, even taking her to Europe. She realizes her father despises her and tells Morris she will elope with him. She also tells Morris that her father has disinherited her. Morris does not keep the rendezvous, but goes away. Catherine remains in the house but is no longer friendly with her father, insisting that she would have married Morris even if he did want her only for her money. When Dr. Sloper is about to die, she refuses to come to his bedside. Catherine inherits her father's fortune. Morris returns. He insists he loves her. Catherine tells him to return that night and they will elope. Morris returns, but Catherine has ordered the door bolted. He bangs and bangs on the door but she leaves him there and goes upstairs in the final shot of the movie.

Even without makeup and wearing an unflattering coiffure, de Havilland is too pretty to play a woman who has *never* been courted. So she has the unfortunate task of presenting someone whose manner, lack of talent, and lack of personality make her such a bad catch that men avoid her despite her decent looks, $10,000-a-year inheritance from her mother, and the promise of great wealth when her father dies. Her Catherine smiles, and has a pleasant and agreeable manner—and even tells Lavinia a joke—but de Havilland conveys through walk, voice, and manner that Catherine is unformed. It's obvious that she has been deprived of love and affection her whole life by her father and other men, that she is extremely withdrawn and, in her father's house, isolated. Catherine endures her father's subtle insults—reminders why he considers her "unmarriageable"—with just momentary sadness, indicating that she has been his target for so long that she accepts them as part of the daily routine. Catherine is so candid and direct with her father when they sit and talk—de Havilland speaks clearly and with expert diction to him—that it's obvious that years before he instructed her as to how she was supposed to speak to him. However, he didn't take time to teach her how to speak to anyone else.

As her father intended, Catherine is a social cripple. She can't dance, play piano, or engage in polite conversation. As her father points out, she has no grace, charm, or subtle wit. She doesn't know how to flirt, tease, or make love; when Morris leans toward her, she bends backward. "I've known you all your life and I've yet to see you learn anything," her father tells her coldly. "With one exception—you embroider neatly."

Catherine is overwhelmed by Morris's attention, which comes when her chance for happiness seems remote. De Havilland has wonderful expressions as Catherine dances with this handsome young man at a well-attended party. She is attracted to his beauty, but she is won over by his constant flattery. Also, she gets to express feelings of love to Morris that she has always suppressed. How startled

Olivia de Havilland deservedly won a Best Actress Oscar as a spinster who is charmed by cunning Montgomery Clift in William Wyler's *The Heiress.*

and prideful she is when Morris confesses his love for *her.* She tells her father "that he should have everything, everything a man could want—and he wants *me.*" How de Havilland's face glows when Morris speaks well of Catherine in front of her father, when she never had the nerve to speak up for herself. How openly passionate she is when Catherine kisses Morris. How flattered her Catherine seems when Morris asks if she has been true to him, since she would be loyal to her dying breath even if—and she knows this would never happen—any other man should flirt with her. This fortune hunter lies to her, saying, "You're everything I've ever yearned for in a woman," but in fact, we realize, since Catherine is so grateful to him for having freed her from her father's unkind grasp, that she indeed would be the perfect wife-lover to him after all. As vulnerable as Catherine is, she jeopardizes herself for him, without worrying about the consequences should she have misjudged him. De Havilland yanks hard on our heartstrings when the eloping Catherine, waiting for the tardy Morris, tells Lavinia, clearly and with perfect diction, "He *must* come, he *must* take me away, he *must* love me, he *must.* Morris *will* love me—for all those who didn't."

Deserted and heartbroken, she climbs the stairs of her father's house, knowing that she is forever trapped there with an insensitive man whose criticisms of her have just been validated by Morris. But she has gained terrifying strength from this devastating experience. Before, she never contradicted her formidable father. Now, she stands up to him with proud defiance. She tries to force him to disinherit her. She withdraws her love from him when he finally wants it, rejecting his call to his deathbed. De Havilland experimented with vocal intonations in the forties, and in *The Heiress* the evolution of Catherine from timid victim to a hard woman who gives back as much as she takes is evident in her voice. In the beginning Catherine speaks in hushed tones and it doesn't seem physically possible for her to raise her voice. But late in the film Catherine's voice is husky, strong, and fearless. Now she has confidence and power. Now she can defend, even avenge, herself. "Yes, I can be very cruel," she tells a surprised Lavinia. "I've been taught by masters."

Now Catherine leans back from Morris, not out of fear but because she loathes his embraces. She relishes turning the tables on him, and rejecting his love. She pretends she'll elope with him but has no intention of going through with it. Her humiliation won't be forgotten. With venom in her voice and cold eyes de Havilland's Cathe-

rine tells Lavinia, "He came back with the same lies, the same silly phrases. He has grown greedier with the years. The first time he only wanted my money, and now he wants my love too. Well, he came to the wrong house. And he came twice. I shall see that he never comes a third time."

By rejecting Morris, Catherine condemns herself to permanent spinsterhood. But as she comfortably climbs the stairs in *her* house, her father dead in his grave and Morris banging on the bolted front door, she knows that she has, at least in some hollow way, triumphed.

1950

▶ BEST PICTURE

WINNER:
All About Eve (20th Century–Fox; Joseph L. Mankiewicz)
Other Nominees: *Born Yesterday, Father of the Bride, King Solomon's Mines, Sunset Boulevard*

▼

THE BEST CHOICE:
Sunset Boulevard (Paramount; Billy Wilder)
Award-Worthy Runners-Up: *All About Eve* (Joseph L. Mankiewicz), *The Asphalt Jungle* (John Huston), *In a Lonely Place* (Nicholas Ray), *The Third Man* (Carol Reed), *Winchester '73* (Anthony Mann)

The favorite for 1950's Best Picture Oscar was writer-director Joseph L. Mankiewicz's *All About Eve,* about a great forty-year-old stage actress (Bette Davis as Margo Channing) who wrongly believes age will cause her to lose both her theatrical throne and the love of a younger man (Gary Merrill). Its chief competitor was *Sunset Boulevard,* scripted by director Billy Wilder, producer Charles Brackett, and D. M. Marshman, Jr., about a great fifty-year-old movie actress (Gloria Swanson as Norma Desmond) who refuses to believe age will result in her losing both her star status and the love of a younger man (William Holden). Both had savagely witty scripts about ambitious young people (Anne Baxter's actress Eve, Holden's writer Joe Gillis) who get into the good graces of the neurotic actresses in order to further their own careers. Both featured comebacks by actresses who had once been at the top of their profession, with Davis playing an actress trying not to fade away and Swanson playing a faded actress hoping for a comeback. In each case the director turned his star loose, realizing she would understand the character, and the results were stunning.

The Academy had to choose between two instant clas-

sics, but *All About Eve* was the clear-cut choice, even though Charles Brackett was the president of the Academy. After all, Mankiewicz's victorious film attacked a safe target as far as the Academy was concerned—the people of the New York theater. Meanwhile Wilder and Brackett offended a lot of Hollywood bigwigs by assailing the studios, directors, and producers (members of the Academy included) for turning their backs on Hollywood tradition by intentionally making junk (with *All About Eve* being the rare exception). If that weren't enough reason to give my Best Picture vote to *Sunset Boulevard,* then it deserves the award because it's one of the most sincere tributes ever paid to the great films, filmmakers, and stars of the past—a necessary tribute, because few in 1950 Hollywood seemed to remember.

Sunset Boulevard is narrated with great cynicism by a dead man, Joe Gillis (Holden), once a struggling Hollywood writer. He was penniless when he pulled into a driveway on Sunset Boulevard to avoid the repo men. He thought the crumbling mansion was deserted, but the vain, wealthy Norma Desmond, a queen of the silent screen, lived inside with her devoted servant, Max (Erich von Stroheim), who, Joe later discovered, was her first director and first husband. She wanted to make a comeback for all her fans—not realizing that Max was the author of all her fan mail—and had written a script of *Salome* to star in. She despised the current cinema, which emphasized talk rather than faces, and wanted to work again with Cecil B. DeMille to restore the cinema to its earlier greatness. Needing money, Joe lied that her script was fascinating and just needed doctoring. She hired him to rework it. At first he lived over the garage and then moved into the house. She became increasingly possessive, and he allowed it. Joe walked out once but returned when Norma attempted suicide. DeMille hated Joe's script, but Norma believed otherwise and began an extensive health regimen to prepare for her comeback. When Joe fell in love with Betty (Nancy Olson), a young script reader, Norma called her up to scare her away, telling her about Joe's not-so-innocent life. Joe broke off with Betty and packed to go home to Ohio. In anger, Norma shot him. Having lost her mind, she believes that the newsreel cameras that appear in her house after the murder belong to DeMille, and that she is filming *Salome*.

Uncompromisingly bitter, gloomy, and morbid, *Sunset Boulevard* combines the horror film with film noir. Its plot, oddly, is a revamp(ir)ing of *Dracula's Daughter*. That 1936 sleeper was about another ageless, cultured woman who lives in a secluded castle in the hills with her creepy manservant (also played by a director), attempts to reenter the world with the help of a young doctor (in *Sunset Boulevard* Joe is Norma's "script doctor") and then tries to "possess" him, despite his love for a young woman. Horror-movie images abound: the decaying mansion with artifacts of a bygone age; rats scurrying in Norma's swimming pool; Norma, lying on her bed, pulling Joe's head down toward her with curled hands and fingers, as if she were a vampire about to sup on his blood; Norma and Max conducting a solemn funeral for her dead chimpanzee; during her beauty treatment, Norma's face recalling the bride of Frankenstein. There are references to *King Kong* and to *Waxworks;* Norma is referred to as a sleepwalker, a vampire-zombie image; and Joe is called a "ghostwriter." What better setting for a "ghost" story than cruel Hollywood, a town built on illusions and delusions, where people like Norma grow old but remain young on film, where the great stars of the past have vital talent but, rejected and now forgotten, take their places among the walking dead. (Norma loves the attention she receives from the old-timers at the studio, but she'd be aghast if she had to deal with the classless agents, producers, and partygoers with whom Wilder has Joe rub shoulders.)

Andrew Sarris suggested that *All About Eve* won the Best Picture Oscar because *Sunset Boulevard* was made in the already outmoded noir style of the forties. In making his elegy to old-style Hollywood films, Wilder intentionally used the noir style to lament its passing and to call attention to the fact that the new product in Hollywood (including *All About Eve*) hadn't much visual style. His picture also takes thematic and plot elements

Gloria Swanson and her young, disenchanted lover William Holden party alone in Billy Wilder's *Sunset Boulevard.*

from the film noir: its cynical, hyperbolic first-person narration; its fatalism; its Los Angeles backdrop and the importance of the automobile; its weak, flawed, doomed hero, who allows himself to be swayed and tarnished by money and a powerful, manipulative woman.

We shouldn't pity Joe for being unfortunate enough to fall into the clutches of a pathetic, deranged woman, because a wholesome young woman is his for the asking. He has many opportunities to leave Norma but doesn't, because he has no confidence he can make it on his own. He knows what he's getting into by the time he commits himself to her and becomes her lover. He allows himself to become financially dependent on her, losing all self-respect. (At first he thinks he's shrewd enough to exploit her, but soon realizes that she's in firm control.) In his narration Joe is constantly critical of Norma, trying to arouse our pity at his predicament when what we ought to feel is disgust. When he is with Norma, he is rarely complimentary, although her old movies and private acting performances (she does a great Chaplin impersonation) prove what a remarkable talent she is. All he can say is "You used to be big." He laughs at her writing deficiencies, but he's the writer and it's his final draft of her story that DeMille detests. Throughout the film Joe thinks the has-been actress is getting a bargain by having him as her lover, but he's really not worthy of her. She once danced with the world's greatest lover, Valentino—now she dances with a nobody. Who is Joe to be critical of the great Norma Desmond, just because she has delusions about her own current fame? Joe is just one more Hollywood male in the sound era who refuses to give Norma her due, who knifes her in the back. Norma in turn has no respect for him, though she loves Joe and needs him to nurse her fragile ego. He says nothing nice to her, but his presence is quite reassuring. Norma understands Joe's intentions toward her but doesn't worry. After all, it's not he who's exploiting her, but the reverse.

In *Sunset Boulevard* Norma Desmond criticizes the current cinema for forgetting about faces and pure acting, and for emphasizing dialogue. Wilder deliberately set out to make a film that had a lot of great dialogue (as well as the narration) but also was extremely visual. Despite Wilder's standout direction, John F. Seitz's moody photography, the outstanding, no-holds-barred script, the authentic Hollywood milieu, the fine star-making per-formance by Holden, and much else that deserved praise, the film achieved greatness on the strength of Gloria Swanson's brilliant, intense, devilishly funny performance. The silent actress spoke indeed but made use as well of all the best eye-grabbing ploys of her movie prime. I believe Wilder thought Norma Desmond had what it took to still be a star and play the lead in a box-office success. Gloria Swanson, who came out of retirement to play this lead, proved his point.

► BEST ACTOR

WINNER:

José Ferrer *(Cyrano de Bergerac)*

Other Nominees: Louis Calhern *(The Magnificent Yankee)*, William Holden *(Sunset Boulevard)*, James Stewart *(Harvey)*, Spencer Tracy *(Father of the Bride)*

▼

THE BEST CHOICE:

Spencer Tracy *(Father of the Bride)*

Award-Worthy Runners-Up: Humphrey Bogart *(In a Lonely Place)*, Marlon Brando *(The Men)*, John Garfield *(The Breaking Point)*, Sterling Hayden *(The Asphalt Jungle)*, Robert Newton *(Treasure Island)*, James Stewart *(Harvey)*, James Stewart *(Winchester '73)*

In 1950, José Ferrer re-created his most famous stage role for the screen in Stanley Kramer's production of *Cyrano de Bergerac* and became the first Puerto Rican–born Best Actor winner. I recently saw the picture for the first time in years and was surprised how subdued Ferrer was as Rostand's poetic swordsman with the long nose, the big heart for Roxanne (Mala Powers), and the right words for tongue-tied Christian (William Prince). In other familiar roles he ripped into his dialogue, spitting it out with a clear, deep voice and a superior, often insolent manner. He could get as hammy as Vincent Price. Ironically, *Cyrano de Bergerac* could have used the typically flamboyant Ferrer in this potentially showy role—Steve Martin had the right idea in the *Cyrano*-inspired *Roxanne*—for today the picture reminds me of, perhaps because it *looks* like them, the most stilted, sleep-inducing historical dramas of the early thirties. I'll take away Ferrer's Oscar and give it to Spencer Tracy, who not only turned in *two* better performances than Ferrer in 1950, but whose movie career was far worthier of an Academy Award selection. I didn't go along with Tracy winning back-to-back Oscars in 1937 and 1938 for *Captains Courageous* and *Boys Town,* and I didn't award him in years he gave better performances but still had other actors outshine him. So it's past time to give tribute to one of the truly great actors. It would be appropriate to award him for *Adam's Rib,* one of the best of his films with Katharine Hepburn, but surprisingly, he is far more interesting in the much more conventional *Father of the Bride,* in the role Steve Martin would play in the 1991 remake. Of his later films it is an even better showcase than John Ford's 1958 comedy-drama *The Last Hurrah.*

Vincente Minnelli's film is a comedy, scripted by Frances Goodrich and Albert Hackett, but the versatile veteran actor used *all* his old tricks . . . because being father of a bride isn't always funny.

Spencer Tracy's acting isn't easy to describe, of course, because he was so effortless and natural, so relaxed, and so soft spoken (bad directors would tell him to speak louder). The joy one has while watching Tracy comes when his even-keeled characters have surprising reactions (emotional responses, sarcastic outbursts, temper tantrums) when something or someone gets a "rise" out of them. Throughout *Father of the Bride* Tracy's Stanley Banks finds his tranquil middle-class existence in turmoil. Just about everything gets a "rise" out of him.

The picture begins with the shocked, worn-out Stanley rubbing his toes, putting on a fallen shoe, and telling us (actually warning us), "I would like to say a few things about weddings. . . ." With Stanley as narrator we flash back three months, to the day Stanley's only daughter, twenty-year-old Kay (Elizabeth Taylor in a surprisingly effective performance), announces to Stanley and his wife, Ellie (Joan Bennett), that she's marrying someone named Buckley. He pretends calm, eating his ice cream as if it were lumpy fertilizer, but his suspicious look and questions upset Kay. At last his patience gives out: "Who is this Buckley anyway? And what's his last name? I hope it's better than his first one." He can't remember Buckley from among the others in his daughter's date parade: "It couldn't be that genius who said he'd fix my radio—she couldn't do that to me." He thinks her too young to make such a commitment and doesn't take her seriously. He acts like a spiteful child himself. He hates that Kay now listens to Buckley's advice while ignoring her own father's: "From here on her love would be doled out like a farmer's wife tossing scraps to a family rooster." He's very polite to Buckley when he takes Kay on a date, desiring to give the impression that he is an adult, a father who is always in control. But the minute they are out the door, Stanley says, "I don't like him."

That night, while the couple is out, Stanley can't sleep. Tracy's eyes are wide as his best scene begins. Acting just as unreasonably as Tracy's characters acted toward Hepburn's when they were losing arguments, Stanley repeatedly sits up and lies down (there are no cuts during his big speech), while conjecturing nonsense about Buckley to the unworried Ellie: "[I bet he] figures on moving in with us. And then when the food gets a little bad, why he'll dump the kids on us and skip. Probably done it before. Probably got a wife somewhere else. . . . How do we know—maybe he's got a criminal record. . . . Those soft-spoken fellows who look you right in the eye and would put a bullet in back of our necks and never turn a hair. Mark my words—this is going to end in tragedy." That said, he falls asleep and Ellie stays up worrying.

Tracy has amusing scenes when Stanley talks to Buckley about the young man's finances and ends up boringly discussing only his own, and when Stanley and Ellie visit Buckley's parents and he has trouble with small talk ("Not too sweet . . . and not too dry," he rates his drink) and then talks ad nauseam about Kay, only to fall asleep the moment the subject switches to Buckley. As the wedding preparations progress, the king of the castle becomes increasingly obsolete ("Stanley, from now on don't answer the phone"). Mr. Banks is only as important as his checkbook. He puts up resistance (finding out it will cost $3.75 a head at the reception, he states, "The 151st person who comes into this house is going to be thrown out on his neck"), tells the pricey caterer that he doesn't want a wedding cake because "every Tom, Dick, and Harry has one," and even suggests to Kay that she elope. But Tracy's characters always have hearts of gold, and Stanley is no exception: everything Kay and Ellie want, they get. Still, Stanley isn't happy when all the $3.75 guests accept their invitations: "What crust coming all the way from Pittsburgh." And he isn't eager to buy a new tux, as long as he can squeeze into his old one ("If that button gives way," Ellie points out, "it's going to put out somebody's eye").

We feel for Stanley as he tries to reestablish his importance with Kay. He is happy to comfort her when she wants to call off the wedding, but ends up feeling foolish when it turns out Kay isn't angry at Buckley for being untrue but for wanting to fish on their honeymoon. They don't need his help when they reconcile. The wedding back on, Stanley goes to the rehearsal, where he finds out that Kay won't even be there *and* the stand-in by his side can't stop sneezing. But Stanley is not forgotten. On the night before the wedding, with neither he nor Kay able to sleep, they have a father-to-daughter talk over milk and midnight snacks. It's Tracy at his best, com-

pletely calm and in charge, warmly reassuring a nervous person that all will be fine: "Look, kitten, get this into your head. There's not a thing to worry about. Not a— Not a thing. Whenever you've been bothered, I've always been around, haven't I? Well, I'll be around when that wedding march starts too. All you have to do is take my arm, lean on me, and relax. I'll do the rest." It's such a sweet moment, when the affection between the characters (which we haven't really seen before) and that between the actors is evident. "Oh, you *are* wonderful," Kay says, feeling relaxed now. "Nothing ever fazes you, does it?" He's proud, even smug, until he remembers the absurdity of what she's just said. But he won't tell her.

Tracy has two more nice scenes before the wedding. One has Stanley seeing Ellie all dressed up for the occasion, looking at her with such an awed, loving expression that he doesn't even have to tell her what he's thinking—she hugs him appreciatively. In the other scene the father sees his beautiful young daughter in her wedding gown, all grown up and looking like "a princess in a fairy tale."

The wedding ceremony has no hitches (although Stanley admits to us his pain over losing Kay). But there is such pandemonium at the reception that Stanley has to run up the stairs, in and out doors, and through crowds of people to try to get to Kay, and still he never gets to kiss her before she and Buckley drive away to their honeymoon. He's sad, he's lonely. But he gets a phone call from Kay at the train depot. She couldn't get away without telling her father that she loves him. Tracy's touched, relieved, happy, loved-and-needed expression is the one all prospective fathers of brides take comfort in.

Spencer Tracy proudly walks Elizabeth Taylor down the aisle in Vincente Minnelli's *Father of the Bride*.

▶ BEST ACTRESS

WINNER:
Judy Holliday *(Born Yesterday)*
Other Nominees: Anne Baxter *(All About Eve)*, Bette Davis *(All About Eve)*, Eleanor Parker *(Caged)*, Gloria Swanson *(Sunset Boulevard)*

▼

THE BEST CHOICE:
Gloria Swanson *(Sunset Boulevard)*
Award-Worthy Runners-Up: Bette Davis *(All About Eve)*, Katharine Hepburn *(Adam's Rib)*, Judy Holliday *(Born Yesterday)*, Betty Hutton *(Annie Get Your Gun)*, Maureen O'Hara *(Rio Grande)*

Perhaps the most lovable of stars, Judy Holliday won a Best Actress Oscar for her first lead in a movie, reprising the Broadway role that won her a Hollywood contract. In George Cukor's comedy *Born Yesterday,* I think she was a bit too stagy and mannered as Billie Dawn, a dumb blonde who wises up and dumps her thug boyfriend (Broderick Crawford) for a nice writer (William Holden). But that's not the reason I wouldn't give her the Oscar: in 1950 there were two even more dazzling performances.

Bette Davis never was better than as Margo Channing in *All About Eve.* Yet in *Sunset Boulevard* Gloria Swanson gave a performance for the ages as a silent movie queen who plans her return and ends up, in a classic denouement, giving her final close-up to newsreel cameramen covering the crazed woman's arrest for murder. Not only was she more dynamic than Davis (which seems impossible), but she proved that she was the one actress capable of a characterization that was even more egocentric and neurotic. Indeed, Swanson's loony, past-obsessed Norma Desmond, herself a relic among the many relics that fill her decaying mansion, has less in common with Davis's Margo than with Davis's warped ex-star in *What Ever Happened to Baby Jane?,* a 1962 Grand Guignol that *Sunset Boulevard* anticipated. Like Baby Jane, Norma deceives herself into thinking she'll be welcomed back to pictures despite a long absence. But unlike Baby Jane, Norma actually has the talent to succeed onscreen if she gets the opportunity.

Swanson was never enraptured with Hollywood and didn't stick around long after her star had faded. But like Norma she understood what it was to have enormous fame and power and then, because of the advent of sound, be deemed obsolete. Playing a part originally offered to Mary Pickford and Pola Negri, Swanson seems to be trying to do much more than showcase her own long-neglected talents. She is striking a blow for all the other discarded silent movie stars who, she proves, *could* act, with or without dialogue. Speaking Norma's lines, Swanson must have gotten tremendous pleasure championing silent movies and ripping apart the 1950 Hollywood product. "Still wonderful, isn't it?" Norma asks rhetorically while showing Joe one of her old films (actually it's *Queen Kelly,* which Swanson made with Erich von Stroheim). "And *no* dialogue. We didn't need

dialogue. We had faces. There just aren't faces like that anymore."

Swanson makes her point that films without dialogue could be great, but at the same time helps director-screenwriter Wilder remind us of the power of strongly written dialogue. Swanson doesn't alternate between silent passages and ones with dialogue. Norma Desmond may have been a peerless silent movie actress and may pose like an old-style glamour queen behind too much makeup, veils, feathers, and smoke escaping from a cigarette in a long holder, but she is too vain to be silent for even a second. She must talk about herself. So Swanson's Norma delivers lines with the import of a Shakespearean tragedienne, simultaneously using all the exaggerated gestures and glances of a silent-movie leading lady. Swanson acts with her large eyes, her hands, her fingers, her mouth, her teeth, her nostrils, and head, tilting it for effect. A tough, tough broad, her Norma doesn't mince words, but chews them and spits them out with tremendous force. Swanson has a great moment when Norma is showing Joe her old films and becomes infuriated that no one is banging down her door for her

In the famous final shot in *Sunset Boulevard,* Gloria Swanson's faded actress Norma Desmond walks toward the newsreel camera, while Erich von Stroheim's Max directs her as if she were once again performing for the movie camera.

services. She stares at the screen, saying, "Those imbeciles! Haven't they got any eyes? Have they forgotten what a star looks like?" Then she jumps up and, taking a horror-movie pose that would frighten Margaret Hamilton or Gale Sondergaard, gloats triumphantly: "I'll show them! I'll be up there again, so help me!" She is a bitter, embattled woman who must come to her own defense because in all of Hollywood, only her manservant Max (von Stroheim), her first husband and first director, hasn't abandoned her. So Swanson bares her teeth, flares her nostrils, and widens her eyes, putting all her strength and pity, too, into her words. I love Norma's reaction when she realizes Joe wants to delete a scene from her script: "Cut away from me! . . . Put it back. . . . They want to see me. Me—Norma Desmond!" And when she responds to his comment that she used to be big: "I *am* big. It's the pictures that got small."

Swanson doesn't relax throughout the entire picture. Holden's Joe is the lazy one, the deadbeat. Norma has energy to spare, and unlike Joe, she at least attempts to fulfill her ambition. Everything she does and says is dramatic, even overwhelming. She tosses her script across the room to Joe (she was a star, no lady); dancing with him, she rips the feathered hat from her head and sails it across the room rather than simply putting it down; and when Joe complains of her possessiveness, she doesn't act demurely, but slaps him and screams, "What you're trying to say is you don't love me! Say it! Say it!" This leads to a suicide attempt. When Joe next attempts to leave, she shoots him in the back, killing him. She holds nothing back. She is an extraordinary woman. Yes, she's crazy now, but because of Swanson we like her better than we do Joe, and can see traces of the onetime star DeMille still speaks fondly of: a lovely little girl of seventeen with more courage and wit and heart than ever came together in one youngster. (Of course, he is actually speaking about Swanson.) Norma has been so badly hurt that, as strong as she is, she is terribly insecure about being rejected (it's disarming to see her cry when old-timers on the Paramount lot remember her). Joe's attempt to leave her is the final straw. Her turning on him, rather than once again on herself in a suicide attempt, is actually a positive step. For it she is rewarded with instant fame and one more close-up. We are comforted by the words of the dead narrator, Joe: "The dream that she clung to so desperately had enfolded her."

1951

▶ BEST PICTURE

WINNER:
An American in Paris (MGM; Vincente Minnelli)
Other Nominees: *Decision Before Dawn, A Place in the Sun, Quo Vadis, A Streetcar Named Desire*

▼

THE BEST CHOICE:
Strangers on a Train (Warner Bros.; Alfred Hitchcock)
Award-Worthy Runners-Up: *The African Queen* (John Huston), *The Big Carnival/Ace in the Hole* (Billy Wilder), *A Streetcar Named Desire* (Elia Kazan), *The Thing* (Christian Nyby)

Vincente Minnelli's *An American in Paris,* with struggling American artist Gene Kelly romancing French shopgirl Leslie Caron to a wonderful George Gershwin score, became the rare musical to be selected Best Picture by the Academy. Voters seeking "prestige" and "class" were undoubtedly swayed by the marvelous twenty-minute musical finale, consisting of several imaginatively choreographed and designed ballet interludes. But it is by far the best production number in the picture, as Kelly's athleticism didn't always mesh with Minnelli's elegant balletic style. Moreover, Alan Jay Lerner's script failed to exploit potentially interesting relationships between Kelly and his patron Nina Foch, and Caron and Georges Guétary, the older man who takes care of her. The story is too proper, the romance between Kelly and Caron too predictable.

Nineteen fifty-one's most popular film is undoubtedly John Huston's *The African Queen,* certainly one of the best romantic adventure films. Once slovenly, alcoholic river rat Humphrey Bogart and prim Katharine Hepburn fall in love, there is no picture that is more entertaining. But it's slow going and surprisingly conventional until

Hepburn feels exaltation steering Bogie's boat through the rapids and they experience their first kiss.

Billy Wilder's bitter *The Big Carnival/Ace in the Hole,* in which reporter Kirk Douglas makes sure a man remains trapped in a cave so that he can have an exclusive story, and the Howard Hawks–produced science fiction classic *The Thing,* in which a handful of soldiers battle a vegetable from outer space, are, I think, almost flawless. However, I still pick Alfred Hitchcock's *Strangers on a Train* as the Best Picture of 1951.

While on a train, wealthy amateur tennis star Guy Haines (Farley Granger) meets Bruno Anthony (Robert Walker), a brilliant but obviously crazy man. He knows that Guy is in love with Ann (Ruth Roman), a senator's daughter, but can't get a divorce from his philandering wife, Miriam (Laura Elliott). Bruno suggests that he murder Miriam and Guy murder Bruno's critical father. The police wouldn't suspect them of murdering people they don't know. Guy doesn't take Bruno seriously. But Bruno strangles Miriam at an amusement park, and then expects Guy to kill his father. When he realizes Guy has no intention of complying, Bruno decides to incriminate Guy in Miriam's death. Guy must try to win a tennis match quickly, elude police who suspect he killed Miriam, and beat Bruno to the amusement park before he plants Guy's cigarette lighter at the scene of the murder.

Scripted by Raymond Chandler and Czenzi Ormonde, Hitchcock's suspense classic was adapted from a novel by Patricia Highsmith, who also wrote about a strange, deadly male "partnership" in *Ripley's Game* (which became the movie *The American Friend*). The relationship between Guy and Bruno, two rich young men who don't work for a living, is quite intriguing. As mad as Bruno is, he is just the person "nice guy" Guy secretly wants to meet, to do his dirty work for him. For Guy would like Miriam out of his life, even dead if that's the only way to do it. He wants to enter politics eventually, and marriage to a senator's daughter will be much more beneficial than marriage to his wife, who works in a record store and is pregnant by someone else. However, Guy is too dull and too "normal" to commit the crime or even consider he wants it done. It takes someone like Bruno, who'll do anything. But with Miriam dead Guy no longer needs Bruno, his alter ego. Bruno suddenly reminds him of his own guilt. Also, Bruno, hurt at Guy's rejection, is dangerous—especially to Guy's career. To compete with Bruno, Guy must change. As the tennis announcer says of his play, Guy has always been a "quiet, methodical player, almost lackadaisical—as a rule he plays slowly between points, well within himself." Now on and off the court Guy starts "taking chances." That's why he can eliminate Bruno, the chance-taking side of his personality. He clears his name, can wed Ann, and gets a senator for a father-in-law. Meanwhile his godsend Bruno gets nothing—in fact, he gets killed for helping Guy.

Hitchcock was in a mild slump when he directed *Strangers on a Train,* having had no critical successes since *Notorious* in 1946. His new film received mixed reactions. Since then it has come to be recognized as

Farley Granger is amused by stranger Robert Walker's loony idea that they perform murders for one another, not realizing he is deadly serious in Alfred Hitchcock's *Strangers on a Train.*

one of his masterpieces, the film that launched an amazing decade of offbeat, craftily directed suspense classics. Highsmith provided an ingenious, half-comical premise, Robert Walker gave the performance of his career as the creepy, childish lunatic, and Hitchcock came up with many clever devices for building suspense. Hitchcock's plotting of Miriam's murder is particularly devious. He throws us off guard by having Miriam scream while going through the Tunnel of Love. Her murder occurs a short time later, after we thought she was killed and before we expect it the second time. Bruno simply walks up to her, asks her confirmation that she is Miriam, and strangles her. We witness the murder through her fallen, broken glasses, so everything is weirdly distorted, as if we've entered Bruno's mind. Another great sequence has Hitchcock cutting back and forth between Guy playing tennis and Bruno trying to retrieve Guy's lighter from under a street grating, building tension by having both men perform in front of crowds. The exciting finale has Guy and Bruno wrestling on an out-of-control merry-go-round while a park attendant crawls underneath to reach the levers. Instead of using an athlete to accomplish this feat, Hitchcock had an old man do the crawling—and he takes forever. Surprisingly, when he pulls the levers, the merry-go-round doesn't slow down but spins wildly and crashes (a miniature was used), probably killing several of the children on the ride.

Two other visuals are memorable. One has Guy and Bruno, on the night of Miriam's death, guiltily watching a police car from behind the prisonlike bars of a gate. More famous: at a tennis match everyone in the stands moves his head back and forth to follow the movement of the ball. Except for Bruno, who stares straight ahead at Guy. He's the type who always stands out in a crowd, even when seated.

▶ BEST ACTOR

Humphrey Bogart *(The African Queen)*
Other Nominees: Marlon Brando *(A Streetcar Named Desire)*, Montgomery Clift *(A Place in the Sun)*, Arthur Kennedy *(Bright Victory)*, Fredric March *(Death of a Salesman)*

▼

THE BEST CHOICE:

Alastair Sim *(A Christmas Carol)* and **Robert Walker** *(Strangers on a Train)*
Award-Worthy Runners-Up: Humphrey Bogart *(The African Queen)*, Marlon Brando *(A Streetcar Named Desire)*, Kirk Douglas *(The Big Carnival/Ace in the Hole)*

The Academy finally got around to giving a Best Actor Oscar to Humphrey Bogart in 1951, choosing to honor a member of the old guard rather than those upstarts from the New York stage, Montgomery Clift and Marlon Brando. Bogart gave a fine performance as an alcoholic but admirable and surprisingly romantic small-boat captain in John Huston's *The African Queen*. He and Katharine Hepburn are among the most mutually supportive lovebirds in cinema history. But I prefer Bogart playing morally ambivalent characters.

In 1932 Fredric March and Wallace Beery shared the Academy Award for Best Actor. I've save my shared Best Actor Oscar for 1951, when there were two truly outstanding performances.

My first pick is the wonderful British character actor Alastair Sim, who was a marvelous choice to play Scrooge in the best movie version of Dickens's *A Christmas Carol*. He is initially heartless and friendless, as stingy with kindness as he is with money. He curses Christmas, shoves aside young carolers, and refuses to accept Christmas cheer or give money to help the unfortunate through the holidays. His selfishness has taken its toll: he has a stone face and breathes like a dying asthmatic. But as he takes his journeys with the ghosts of Christmas past, present, and future, Scrooge "chills out" and repents. Sim will make you feel both Scrooge's heartache and his shame—especially when Cratchit (Mervyn Johns), his grossly underpaid assistant, generously asks his family to give Scrooge a Christmas toast. And you'll get misty eyed.

Scrooge wakes up Christmas morning a new man. And suddenly Sim is the warmest, most delightful screen presence imaginable. He can't stop laughing. He excitedly dances and hops about, thrilled that he hasn't missed Christmas. He says, "I don't know what to do," and sings, "I don't know anything." By the time he announces, "I must stand on my head," viewers are likely to have happy tears flowing down their cheeks. My favorite bit has him calling from his window to a boy outside, asking the lad to run an errand for him. Before Scrooge hated kids, but now anything this common boy does greatly impresses him: "What an enchanting boy." Sim's Scrooge keeps smiling and giggling as he makes amends and does good deeds. After he surprises Cratchit by not firing him for his tardiness, instead giving him a raise and promising to

help him support Tiny Tim and the rest of his family, Scrooge says, "I don't deserve to be so happy. I can't help it. I just can't help it." And he throws away his pen because work and making money have no meaning around Christmastime. It's wonderful to watch Scrooge in such good humor, but those moments that have even more impact are those when he is briefly serious, but humble and repentant, with his loyal housekeeper, with his nephew and his wife, and with Cratchit. What's heartwarming is that he doesn't even think that his actions deserve praise. As this man, who wasted many good years being mean and selfish, says humbly, "I've just come to my senses."

My second Best Actor selection is Robert Walker, who surprised everyone with a cleverly conceived portrait of psychopath Bruno Anthony, in Alfred Hitchcock's *Strangers on a Train*. Walker had always played lightweight roles, but Hitchcock sensed there was a darker side to this actor who came from a broken home, had two unsuccessful marriages in the forties, had been an alcoholic, and had recently been institutionalized for a year following a nervous breakdown. He was a terrific choice to play the total stranger who offers to kill the unfaithful

Alastair Sim's Ebenezer Scrooge begins to see strange, ominous visions in *A Christmas Carol*.

wife of tennis player Guy Haines (Farley Granger)—freeing him to marry a senator's daughter—if Guy will do away with his critical father.

Raised by an unsupportive father and daffy mother, Bruno is a loner (Hitchcock often has him stand or sit by himself) who desperately wants a friend. Since there are hints that he's homosexual, Bruno desires a Guy. To Bruno, a friend is someone "who would do anything for you." So it's not such a big thing to ask Guy to kill his father, or to kill Miriam—Guy's wife—for his friend. It's a great blow when Guy doesn't come through for him and wants to institutionalize him. He spitefully tries to incriminate Guy for Miriam's murder. There is no other motive than revenge, for there is no chance that the police will connect Bruno, a stranger, with the crime. When Guy doesn't come through for him, Bruno acts as hurt and deserted as the spoiled, mother-pampered child he is. Even when dying, he steadfastly refuses to tell police that Guy didn't kill Miriam. Walker is an intimidating villain but his character is so interesting because he is weak at the core. He faints, he has anxiety attacks, he becomes upset when Guy says he's sick, he lapses into immaturity. His immaturity is apparent in his choice of robe, tie, and shoes. It is also evident when he shows off his strength to Miriam at the amusement park, pops the balloon of a young boy he passes at the park, and has a semihysterical outburst upon dropping Guy's lighter down a sewer shaft. And in how he responds to Guy's "betrayal": "You're spoiling everything. . . ."

Bruno is far and away the cleverest, most idealistic, most surprising and productive ("I certainly admire people who do things") character in the film. He and not Guy mocks a conservative judge for condemning men to death, shows disgust that business picks up near murder

Robert Walker, as insane Bruno Anthony, perplexes Senator Leo G. Carroll and daughter Ruth Roman in *Strangers on a Train.*

scenes, has a "silly" plan to blow up the White House. His helping a blind man across the street overshadows Guy's rescue of a boy on the runaway merry-go-round, because the ride crashes and the boy is probably killed anyway. We also must appreciate Bruno for killing Miriam, freeing Guy to pursue marriage with a woman he loves and a career in politics. Maybe Guy should have done away with Bruno's father, for that old man is the one responsible for turning a potentially great person, "a very clever fellow," into a lunatic.

▶ **BEST ACTRESS**

WINNER:
Vivien Leigh *(A Streetcar Named Desire)*
Other Nominees: Katharine Hepburn *(The African Queen)*, Eleanor Parker *(Detective Story)*, Shelley Winters *(A Place in the Sun)*, Jane Wyman *(The Blue Veil)*

▼

THE BEST CHOICE:
Vivien Leigh *(A Streetcar Named Desire)*
Award-Worthy Runner-Up: Katharine Hepburn *(The African Queen)*

It was the challenge of playing another queenly, vibrant—if even more badly bruised—Southern belle in *A Streetcar Named Desire* that induced Vivien Leigh to return to Hollywood for the first time since her Oscar-winning performance as Scarlett O'Hara in 1939's *Gone With the Wind*. She had played Blanche Dubois, Tennessee Williams's most tragic heroine, for seven months on the stage when her husband, Laurence Olivier, directed

Streetcar in London, to capacity houses and mixed reviews. That was in 1949, two years after Elia Kazan directed the Broadway production. When Kazan cast his Warner Bros. film, he used three of his four stage stars: Marlon Brando as Stanley Kowalski, Blanche's brutish brother-in-law; Kim Hunter as Blanche's pregnant younger sister, Stella; and Karl Malden as Blanche's wishy-washy suitor, Mitch. But for Blanche he replaced

Vivien Leigh's despairing Blanche Dubois is grateful for the attention of Karl Malden's Mitch in Elia Kazan's *A Streetcar Named Desire.*

Jessica Tandy with Leigh, who had more box-office clout. She rewarded him with an emotionally devastating portrayal that won her a much-deserved second Oscar.

Blanche Dubois has been seen as Scarlett O'Hara all twisted and torn. But she is something more. Those of us who see the optimistic twenty-six-year-old Leigh in Scarlett surely see in Blanche the older Leigh who suffered from depression and experienced mental breakdowns. No doubt her own condition helped her understand and sympathize with Blanche—at times it seems like she is exorcising her own demons. Leigh was attracted to Blanche's spirit, which certainly rivaled that of Scarlett O'Hara. But her Blanche hasn't the resilience of her Scarlett. Her spirit is almost broken and her confidence is shattered even before she arrives in New Orleans to stay with her kind sister and aggressive, unsympathetic brother-in-law. Her past was unbearably sorrowful (the young man she loved—a homosexual in the play—killed himself) and humiliating (she was kicked out of a hotel because of her indiscriminate sexual habits, she lost her teaching job because of an affair with a seventeen-year-old). She has lost her youth, she has no prospects. Although she smiles, brags, fishes for compliments, and flirts shamelessly, she is on her last legs. She is in the midst of a breakdown, she is on the edge of insanity. She wants to stop the hemorrhaging, but can't find solace in Stanley's home. Because his life is built around bolstering his own ego, he can't tolerate Blanche's tone of superiority, her bragging about her past, and her moral pretensions, especially since he thinks she's failed to live up to her own standards in that regard (barring her claim that she has "never been deliberately cruel" to anyone). In Williams's plays the very men who have the chance to help helpless women usually choose to destroy them instead. Mitch rejects her when he learns that she isn't "clean," and Stanley rapes her and commits her to an asylum.

Blanche is too delicate to survive tragedies, and to be trapped in around-the-clock turbulence. "I don't want realism," she says revealingly, "I want music." Battered and broken, she feebly tries to save herself, but her look is that of someone who feels impending doom. She acknowledges, "I'm fading now." Leigh plays Blanche as if someone were turning on and off her currents; she fades in and out. Leigh searches for her momentary lapses into sanity, when Blanche stops performing and her talking makes sense; when she is truthful and insightful, and reveals tremendous depth of feeling, even at the expense of scraping all her nerve endings. The part is difficult because Blanche has no foundation, no key that can be turned to put her back into the correct mode of motion and speech. Not anymore. Everything solid has been clawed out of her. She's all artifice because only scattered moments of her past aren't too painful to remember. Leigh just tries to latch on to the few remnants of the lovely, youthful Blanche that Stella remembers: "Nobody was as tender and trusting as she was." As there are no flashbacks, we never see the tender, touching young Blanche, just this flighty flirt doing a high-wire act—yet Leigh gives us glimpses of her. If we didn't know how special Blanche once was from watching Leigh, we wouldn't understand the magnitude of her tragedy, that she has fallen so far and been hurt so much.

Leigh is powerful in those excitingly intimate and tense scenes with Marlon Brando (their different acting styles actually help the friction between the characters), in which Blanche tries desperately to hold her own against the "common," muscular, sweaty, T-shirt-clad Stanley. But in those scenes Blanche must put up a strong front—and act—or be devoured. So it is that Leigh puts so much care and feeling into a brief, seemingly minor scene in which Blanche flirts with a young man who is collecting for the newspaper. Away from the accusatory glances and condescending remarks, Blanche regains her power. She shines. She is wistful, poetic, haunting, alluring, and both amoral (she kisses the entranced young man) and moral (she hurries him off before she gets carried away). It is Blanche at her best, revealing her true self and still sweeping a male off his feet. She still has what she had as a young woman. Only Scarlett could compare to her.

1952

▶ BEST PICTURE

WINNER:
The Greatest Show on Earth (Paramount; Cecil B. DeMille)
Other Nominees: *High Noon, Ivanhoe, Moulin Rouge, The Quiet Man*

▼

THE BEST CHOICE:
Singin' in the Rain (MGM; Gene Kelly and Stanley Donen)
Award-Worthy Runner-Up: *The Quiet Man* (John Ford)

In 1952 Cecil B. DeMille's *The Greatest Show on Earth,* entertaining junk about the circus, was voted Best Picture for no discernible reason, other than that more voters probably knew somebody in the all-star cast or huge production crew. Having selected *An American in Paris* the previous year's Best Picture, the Academy wasn't inclined even to nominate Gene Kelly's superior *Singin' in the Rain,* 1952's best picture, the ultimate musical for *movie* lovers and, I believe, the best musical of all time.

Singin' in the Rain is set in Hollywood in 1927. Don Lockwood (Kelly) and Lina Lamont (Jean Hagen) are the silent cinema's most popular romantic duo. Offscreen, Don detests his costar because when he and his vaudeville partner, Cosmo (Donald O'Connor), broke into film as stuntmen on her pictures, she was snobby to him. Fleeing fans, Don jumps into the car of pretty Kathy Selden (twenty-year-old Debbie Reynolds), a contract player at the studio. They quarrel because each thinks the other stuck up. She doesn't admit she is a fan of his and claims to be a serious actress, but Don next sees her at a party jumping out of a cake and singing with other chorus girls. She throws cake at Don but it hits Lina, who has Kathy fired from the studio. Don and Kathy fall in love. When the studio converts to sound and *The Dueling Cavalier* becomes *The Dancing Cavalier,* Don and studio exec R.F. (Millard Mitchell) worry that audiences will laugh at Lina's high-pitched voice. So Don gets Kathy a job dubbing dialogue and singing for Lina. Lina becomes an even bigger star. Jealous that Don loves Kathy and wants her to be his new costar, Lina has it written into Kathy's contract that Kathy can never be anything more than her ghost voice. But in front of a live audience Lina embarrasses herself with her talking voice. She then lip synchs while Kathy sings behind a curtain. But Cosmo and R.F. pull up the curtain to show the audience that it's Kathy's voice they love. Lina's star days are over. Don and Kathy will costar in a new musical called *Singin' in the Rain.*

Produced by Arthur Freed, scripted by Adolph Green and Betty Comden, and directed by Kelly and Stanley Donen, *Singin' in the Rain* is one of the great joys of the cinema. It has originality, spirit, wit, terrific performances, wonderful musical numbers, innovative choreography, talent galore, and true love for the film medium. Not only did Kelly and Donen use film innovatively to enhance the production numbers, but Comden and Green wrote one of the most perceptive, informative, and interesting movies about movies. Making use of stories told by old-timers at MGM who remembered when the advent of sound turned Hollywood upside down, ending some careers and giving birth to others, Green and Comden spoof Hollywood types: suicidal stuntmen like Don and Cosmo who tackle any assignment to make money and break into pictures; starlets like Kathy who claim to be serious thespians but will

Gene Kelly, Debbie Reynolds, and Donald O'Connor exhibit infectious spirit and joy while they are dancin' and *Singin' in the Rain,* directed by Kelly and Stanley Donen.

jump out of cakes for a taste of show business; brainless gossip columnists who believe anything stars tell them and brainless stars who then take stock in what the gossip columnists write; tough directors who act like generals in the midst of a war; producers who go by initials instead of names; cocky actors like Don who know the importance of an attractive, if false, image ("Dignity— always dignity"). Of course, a film that mocked Hollywood had little chance of receiving support from Academy members. So *Singin' in the Rain* (like *The Bad and the Beautiful,* in which Kirk Douglas plays a ruthless producer) wasn't even nominated.

Singin' in the Rain doesn't let down between production numbers. Everything is a delight, even the romance between Don and Kathy. I love Don's hilarious movie stunts, which no one could possibly survive; Don's knife-in-the-back squabbling with Lina (Jean Hagen is brilliant); Lina's futile diction lessons, where she can't properly pronounce the letter *a* in the phrase "I can't stand it"; the scene in which stunned partygoers watch a film with a weird host who explains the new "sound film"; the many humorous incidents involving microphones on the set; and the finale in which it is revealed that Kathy is singing for Lina.

But *Singin' in the Rain* really shines during the spectacular songs and dances. Kelly generously shared his spotlight, and O'Connor and Reynolds joined him in some of the most jubilant athletic dancing in cinema history. Highlights include Kelly and O'Connor playing each other's fiddles and climbing on each other during "Fit as a Fiddle and Ready for Love"; Kelly and O'Connor bewildering their stuffy diction coach with tongue twisters and flying feet in the "Moses" number; Kelly, Reynolds, and O'Connor dancing on furniture in perfect step and singing the infectious "Good Mornin'"; O'Connor stopping the show by dancing up walls and doing somersaults in his amazing "Make 'Em Laugh" solo (the one newly written Arthur Freed–Nacio Herb Brown song). Almost everything in the extravagant "Broadway Rhythm" number is memorable, especially Kelly dancing a dreamlike ballet with long-legged Cyd Charisse, and Kelly singing out several times, "Gotta dance!"

And we always look forward to Kelly dancing happily through puddles in a driving rain and singing the title song—a classic sequence that has inspired almost everyone to imitate Kelly while walking home in the rain. As he sings, "I'm laughing at clouds so dark up above, / There's a song in my heart and I'm ready for love," you can't help feeling better yourself. My favorite moment is when the camera glides directly over Kelly's beaming face for a close-up just as he sings, "There's a smile on my face." This is the key moment in what is certainly the most uplifting musical ever made.

▶ BEST ACTOR

WINNER:

Gary Cooper *(High Noon)*
Other Nominees: Marlon Brando *(Viva Zapata!),* Kirk Douglas *(The Bad and the Beautiful),* José Ferrer *(Moulin Rouge),* Alec Guinness *(The Lavender Hill Mob)*

▼

THE BEST CHOICE:

John Wayne *(The Quiet Man)*
Award-Worthy Runners-Up: Charles Chaplin *(Limelight),* Kirk Douglas *(The Bad and the Beautiful),* Cary Grant *(Monkey Business),* Alec Guinness *(The Lavender Hill Mob),* Gene Kelly *(Singin' in the Rain)*

Gary Cooper became the first actor since Warner Baxter in 1928–29 to be voted Best Actor for appearing in a Western, when he was honored for *High Noon.* Cooper had won an Oscar in 1941, but it seemed more appropriate that he win for a genre that he'd been so vital to since the early thirties. However, Cooper's victory for *High Noon* can be attributed less to acting than to the actor's strong presence and the memorable character he played—a lawman who must face, despite being scared, four outlaws by himself when the frightened townspeople refuse to help him. Cooper seems weary in the role. I much prefer him in *The Westerner* and *Man of the West,* among other Westerns. My choice for Best Actor is an even greater Western movie icon, John Wayne. Wayne gave Oscar-worthy performances in several Westerns—

including *Red River, She Wore a Yellow Ribbon, The Searchers,* and *The Man Who Shot Liberty Valance*—and in 1969 for *True Grit* became the fourth and last actor to win a Best Actor Oscar for a Western. However, I want to give him an Alternate Oscar for 1952 for a non-Western, John Ford's boisterous Irish comedy (with serious underlying themes), *The Quiet Man,* both Ford and Wayne's most popular film.

Wayne plays Sean Thornton, who grew up in America but now returns to his birthplace, Inisfree, in Ireland. He buys his late mother's cottage and land from the Widow Tillane (Mildred Natwick), angering his brawny neighbor, Red Will Danaher (Victor McLaglen), who wanted the land himself. Sean and Will's gorgeous, temperamental sister, Mary Kate (Maureen O'Hara), immediately fall in

John Wayne is content to have Maureen O'Hara's furniture as her dowry but she insists he also get her money from her brother in John Ford's *The Quiet Man.*

love but Will won't let Sean court her. Several of the townspeople—including our narrator, Father Peter Lonergan (Ward Bond), Reverend Cyril Playfair (Arthur Shields), and Michaeleen Oge Flynn (Barry Fitzgerald)—conspire to get Sean and Mary Kate married. They convince Will that the Widow Tillane will marry him if there is no other woman in his house. So Will allows Sean to court and marry Mary Kate. However, when the Widow Tillane refuses to marry Will—she doesn't like his taking for granted that she'll have him—he spitefully refuses to give Mary Kate the money for her dowry. Sean doesn't care about the money, but Mary Kate refuses to sleep with him until he demands what is hers from Will. Without her dowry she feels that she is still a servant. She assumes Sean is scared to fight Will, but the fact is he's worried he'll kill him. Sean was formerly a boxer and had vowed to stop fighting after he killed an opponent. Playfair tells him that he should fight for love. Mary Kate does make love with Sean, but the next morning tries to leave him—she loves him too much to see him embarrassed because he won't fight for her rights. Sean yanks her from the train and drags her the five miles to Inisfree. Everyone from miles around gathers to see him confront Will. He gives her back to Will. Embarrassed, Will gives Sean her dowry. She opens a furnace door and allows

Sean to throw the money into the fire, showing it was receiving the dowry, not the money itself, that mattered to her. After the fight between Sean and Will begins, she proudly goes home to prepare dinner for her husband. Sean can't wait to get home to her but he and Will fight for hours, becoming friends. Will courts the Widow Tillane. Sean and Mary Kate settle down, and will start a family.

Sean is one of several Wayne characters—including ones in Ford's *Three Godfathers* and *The Searchers*—who had led violent lives but now seek salvation and/or paradise. This is Wayne's gentlest character since his young sailor in Ford's *The Long Voyage Home,* and it is his most relaxed performance. The movie's title is appropriate, because Sean has a quiet strength. He is formidable, without Will's need to be a bully or braggart. He has such confidence in his masculinity that he doesn't mind showing anybody that he is polite, emotional, sentimental, and sweet enough to plant roses. He never hides his love from Mary Kate, never assumes a paternal or authoritarian stance with her—he wants them to be equals—never tries to change her, because he knows she's the best. He's full of passion, as we see when he sweeps Mary Kate into his arms and kisses her (a great, classic scene) after finding her in his house, and again when he kisses her in the rain (what a sexy moment). But he's also so unabashedly romantic that his words to Mary Kate are like poetry: "Some things a man doesn't get over so easily. Like the sight of a girl coming through the fields with the sun in her hair. Kneeling in church with a face like a saint. . . ." When he holds Mary Kate it is with tenderness, when he is kissed by her his face shows that he feels her love and sexual passion throughout his entire body and in his head, and when he looks at her it is with awe and appreciation. He's not afraid to thank her, a stranger, for cleaning his house, which she insists was just a good Christian act: "I know it was, Mary Kate Danaher, and it was nice of you." (I love Wayne's considerate, sincere delivery of these words.) And when, after they are married, he reminds her that her unwillingness to have sex with him means they won't have children, he quickly apologizes. He even lets her drive the horse and buggy into town.

All of Wayne's scenes with O'Hara, his best leading lady, are terrific, whether comedic or romantic or highly sexual. When they look at each other, or when one of them makes a suggestive remark, it is genuinely risqué. (Ford's sexiest film is narrated by a celibate.) There is always electricity between them—their kisses even result in an electrical storm. Wayne also works well with the male actors. He is at ease in all his dealings with Inisfree's Irish eccentrics. And he is funny in all his meetings with Victor McLaglen's Will Danaher. Their lengthy brawl is a classic, full of whimsy and well-choreographed fisticuffs (in actuality they never touched one another and the only person injured during the making of the film was O'Hara). It's okay that Sean expend his excess energy in this way just once, because from now on he and Mary Kate will be sharing their bedroom.

▶ BEST ACTRESS

WINNER:
Shirley Booth *(Come Back, Little Sheba)*
Other Nominees: Joan Crawford *(Sudden Fear)*, Bette Davis *(The Star)*, Julie Harris *(The Member of the Wedding)*, Susan Hayward *(With a Song in My Heart)*

▼

THE BEST CHOICE:
Judy Holliday *(The Marrying Kind)*
Award-Worthy Runners-Up: Julie Harris *(The Member of the Wedding)*, Jennifer Jones *(Ruby Gentry)*, Maureen O'Hara *(The Quiet Man)*, Debbie Reynolds *(Singin' in the Rain)*, Ginger Rogers *(Monkey Business)*

Forty-five-year-old Shirley Booth had been acting professionally for twenty-nine years before she made her first movie, Hal Wallis's production of her greatest Broadway success, *Come Back, Little Sheba*. For her thousandth (or more) portrayal of blowsy Lola Delaney, who listens to radio soaps, eats fattening chocolates, pines for her lost dog, Sheba, and aggravates her husband (Burt Lancaster) to such a degree that he has become an alcoholic, Booth was a runaway Oscar winner. She was initially thrilled by the honor but then realized that by winning for her first film, she wouldn't be given a chance to grow as a movie actress. And she was right. Already typecast, she was unable to get roles worthy of a Best Actress winner—she would have done better had she been considered a supporting actress. So in 1961 she turned to television, starring as a maid who essentially runs the house in which she is employed in the long-running *Hazel*. Today, an Oscar seems wasted on Booth, so meager was her contribution to the cinema (though this wasn't her fault). Besides, in 1952, Judy Holliday gave her best performance in George Cukor's seriocomedy *The Marrying Kind*. And there were few better than Holliday at her best. Not surprisingly the Academy, which had given her the Best Actress award two years earlier for *Born Yesterday*, didn't even bother to give her a nomination, underestimating her subtler portrayal.

Holliday's Florence Keefer and her husband Chet (Aldo Ray) want a divorce. They go to the Domestic Relations Court and tell Judge Carroll (Madge Kennedy) what went wrong with their marriage. Although they have entirely different perspectives on what happened, the sequence of events is clear. They met in Central Park, quickly fell in love, and married. They moved into a Manhattan housing project, Stuyvesant Town. They had a baby boy, and then a girl. He worked as a postman, and wouldn't let her work. So they had no extra money. Chet felt uneasy because Florence's sister (Sheila Bond) had married a man with money (John Alexander). He resented their interference in his marriage. Florence and Chet bickered. One night he was late for a party; she was furious with him and in response he got drunk. All his money-making schemes fell through. They almost won money on a radio game show, but instead of giving her own correct answer to the title of a song, she gave Chet's

choice and lost. Resentment increased. Then tragedy struck: their son drowned. Time passed. Chet was hit by a truck and hospitalized, forcing Florence to go to work. When he got a promotion at work, he thought that might impress Florence; but she inherited money from her ex-boss and Chet's salary increase seemed insignificant. Chet was jealous and suspicious as to the reasons why her late boss should have left her money. Friction turned to hostility and they decided to split. Because both Florence and Chet hear the other speak of the marriage in such a way that each knows there has always been a great deal of love and caring between the two, they decide to stay together.

A true sleeper, *The Marrying Kind* was Holliday's follow-up to the Cukor-directed *Born Yesterday*, the role with which she knew she would always be most identified. Also scripted by Garson Kanin (with an assist from wife, Ruth Gordon), it was designed as a showcase for her, to prove that she had enough versatility to play in all kinds of films and that she could play a *real* character.

Despite their love for one another Judy Holliday and Aldo Ray have difficulty dealing with their problems in George Cukor's sleeper *The Marrying Kind*.

Not a play adaptation, it allowed Holliday to build a character from scratch. Florence would have none of Billie Dawn's idiosyncrasies, and Holliday wouldn't seem so self-conscious playing her. Like other Holliday characters Florence is funny and endearing, and has a singular logic about life, which completely befuddles everyone else, including Chet. Like other Holliday characters she seeks happiness along a rocky road, stubbornly refusing to compromise her way of doing things. What is different is that Florence is a flawed Holliday character, rather than one who is instinctively correct all the time. This is an honest portrayal. Chet may be more responsible for the near breakup of the marriage, but Florence isn't an innocent bystander. She can be extremely aggravating, insensitive, unsupportive, unforgiving, even selfish. She pushes Chet in the wrong direction by making it impossible for him to find solace in her arms. He may be wrong for not letting her work, but she doesn't understand his humiliation that he can't properly support her.

Holliday is delightful during the film's comic moments—she had impeccable timing and a unique delivery (it's a wonderful scene when she sings "Dolores" while accompanying herself on the ukulele). But she is equally effective during serious moments. It's devastating when Florence, not wanting to hurt Chet's pride, gives his *wrong* answer to the "Stop the Music" radio quizmaster instead of her *correct* answer, and they fail to win $2,600. This is a nightmarish, relationship-crushing moment we can all relate to. It is her own fault for not trusting herself, though she blames him for it. Also memorable is Holliday sitting on the beach and learning that her young son has just drowned. Her reactions in this scene alone should convince everyone of her dramatic range.

At the time Holliday was making *The Marrying Kind,* she was being hounded by HUAC. Moreover, she so disliked her boozing, chauvinistic costar (whom Columbia studio head Harry Cohn was promoting for stardom) that she would bristle if his name came up years later. Nonetheless, she gave a performance that not only is considered her best by many of her devotees but which also convinced Holliday herself that she was genuinely a good actress—something her earlier roles hadn't done. Oddly, until she impressed herself as Florence Keefer, she had plans to quit acting and become a writer. What a loss that would have been.

1953

▶ BEST PICTURE

WINNER:
From Here to Eternity (Columbia; Fred Zinnemann)
Other Nominees: *Julius Caesar, The Robe, Roman Holiday, Shane*

▼

THE BEST CHOICE:
Shane (Paramount; George Stevens)
Award-Worthy Runners-Up: *The Big Heat* (Fritz Lang), *Stalag 17* (Billy Wilder)

Spurred on by the success of Fred Zinnemann's *High Noon* in 1952, Hollywood studios continued to make adult Westerns as a viable alternative to the kiddie cowboy shows that dominated early television. Zinnemann's picture had given the genre credibility in the eyes of the Academy (which John Ford's great Westerns never really did), but it still chose the inferior *The Greatest Show on Earth* over his Western as Best Picture. No Western had won the award since *Cimarron* in 1930–31. Ironically, in 1953, the first year the Oscar ceremony was telecast, Zinnemann benefited from the Academy members' unwillingness to cast their final votes for a Western. His adaptation of James Jones's *From Here to Eternity,* with Montgomery Clift, Burt Lancaster, Deborah Kerr, Frank Sinatra, and Donna Reed heating up things on and around a Honolulu army post prior to Pearl Harbor, won eight Oscars (tying *Gone With the Wind*'s record), including Best Picture and Best Director. (Sinatra and Reed won Supporting Actor and Actress awards.) Its chief competition, *Shane,* George Stevens's stirring Western from Jack Schaefer's fine novel, managed only a Best Color Cinematography Oscar out of six nominations, and it's likely it won that only because Zinnemann's film was made in black and white. Buoyed by strong acting and a number of "rule-breaking" heroes and heroines, *From Here to Eternity* is a quality picture in spite of its soap elements and the unsatisfying resolutions for most of its characters. But I prefer *Shane,* and remaining loyal to a movie that had such impact on me as a kid, I choose it as the first Western to win an Alternate Oscar for Best Picture.

Joe Starrett (Van Heflin), his wife, Marion (Jean Arthur), and boy Joey (ten-year-old Brandon de Wilde was nominated for Best Supporting Actor) live on a Wyoming ranch in what was once an open range. He is the leader of the few homesteaders who have put up stakes in the verdant valley and have withstood the threats of the two Ryker brothers, tough cattlemen who want the range open again. Joe hires Shane (Alan Ladd), a passing stranger, to help work the farm. He doesn't ask Shane about his past, but it's clear that he was a gunfighter who has deaths on his conscience. Joe becomes Shane's close friend, Marion is attracted to him, and Joey idolizes him. Shane recognizes them as the family he never had. Joe and Shane win a fistfight with several of the Rykers' men. So the Rykers hire gunman Jack Wilson (Jack Palance also was nominated for Best Supporting Actor) to frighten the settlers. Wilson bullies one settler (Elisha Cook, Jr.) into drawing on him, and kills him. Joe wants to go to town to fight Wilson and the Rykers. But Shane knows Joe is unprepared for an old-style gunfight. He knocks Joe out. He tells Marion that he's tried to fit into the community and avoid violence but realizes that's not his fate. He rides into town. Joey gives chase. Shane kills Wilson and one of the Rykers. Joey warns him of an ambush by the other. Shane twirls and kills him, but is shot himself. He tells Joey goodbye and rides off, bleeding. The boy calls, "Shane! Come back!"

I've always had a special fondness for *Shane.* As a kid I wanted to be Brandon de Wilde's wide-eyed boy because he had the fearless, quick-drawing, two-fisted Shane as a friend, and also the surprisingly humble Shane himself, as played with quiet dignity and intelligence by handsome Alan Ladd. In fact when I'd act out the final shootout, I'd yell Joey's "Shane! Look out!" and then immediately become Shane, twirling and firing upward at the (imaginary) villain on the second floor who is shooting at my back. Those were the days. . . . Western historian William K. Everson wrote that *Shane* has lost its luster over the years, especially in comparison to John Ford's seminal Westerns. But I still get a warm feeling when watching it. I think it's a terrific picture, one that pretty much defines the "Western" and, like Ford's great classics, shows such films could be much more than shoot-'em-ups.

There is much in *Shane* to appreciate. There are exceptional performances by actors who rarely appeared in Westerns—Ladd revived his career playing Shane, and Arthur (who hadn't been in a movie since 1948) ended her career in style. *Shane* has a great hero of the mythic variety, an unforgettably loathsome villain in Jack Palance's Jack Wilson, and intriguing relationships among *all* the characters, not just between Shane and each of the Starretts. It also has gorgeous photography by Loyal Griggs; a nifty, authentic precivilization "town" with only

Alan Ladd and Van Heflin solidify their friendship in George Stevens's *Shane.*

a few buildings; and a stunning Grand Tetons location, which immediately explains why the homesteaders and Rykers fight over this land. Looking at the sky and mountains, one also senses that God—who just may have sent Shane—is watching over the settlers who intend to raise their families and build churches here. I like the way Stevens repeatedly photographs the animals (horses, cattle, dogs) that share the environment. And I like his emphasis on work, and on rituals like dinner, picnics, dances, funerals, meetings, shopping, and even fistfights and gunfights, which are usually preceded by obligatory threats and insults. (Shane even anticipates Robert De Niro in *Taxi Driver:* "You speakin' to me?" . . . "I don't see nobody else standing there.") In this primitive, lawless world, all the men risk their lives, foolishly it seems, because they fear backing down to threats in front of their wives, children, and friends. Their pride and stubbornness will either get them through their harsh lives or get them killed for no good reason.

There are several excitingly choreographed fight sequences, as well as the classic scene in which Palance's smirking villain bullies and then guns down (in the mud) an overmatched homesteader, played by Elisha Cook, Jr. (Cook made a career of playing men who boast to cover up their weaknesses.) But *Shane* is special because of all its wonderful *small* moments: Shane and Starrett cement their friendship by spending hours digging out a stubborn tree trunk (also a highlight of the book); Shane and Starrett, fighting back-to-back in a saloon against Ryker's men, smile when they realize they're winning; throughout the film Joey's eyes grow wide as he watches Shane do heroic things; loner Shane watches Starrett kiss Marion, and his slight change of expression reveals he knows what he's missing most in life; Starrett—who isn't jealous of Shane—tells Marion that if he's killed she'll be taken care of, implying he knows that Shane and his wife could be a loving couple too; Shane goes to his room, too uncomfortable to see Marion after overhearing Joey tell her, "I just love Shane—I love him almost as much as Pa"; Shane and Wilson, who has accompanied the Rykers to Starrett's ranch, wordlessly size each other up and try to show each other that they aren't frightened of their inevitable confrontation; the outsider, unmarried Shane tells the homesteaders that they must stay in the valley for the sake of their families. There's no dialogue in many of the film's best moments—just slight eye movements and changes of expression that reveal so much about how the characters feel about one another. For instance, we'd know Joey loves Shane even if he didn't say it; his parents never state their love for Shane, but we know it just the same.

Shane is the classic "Westerner." This ex-gunslinger emerges through a graveyard from the dying prehistoric, precivilized mythic West. He wants to hang up his gun and be part of the new, civilized West. But civilization has no place for violent men like him, or Wilson, or the Rykers. He can't escape his past and must pick up his gun again, eliminating the barbarians from his time and dying himself, just so civilization can emerge. When he kills again, to prevent Starrett, the symbol of the new, nonviolent era, from having to do it, Shane seals his fate: "A man has to be what he is, Joey. . . . There's no living with a killing. There's no going back." So after taming the land that now has no place for him, the bleeding and dying (at least metaphorically) Shane rides stoically toward the sunset and his place in Western mythology. The boy's not so innocent words "And mother wants you!" remind Shane once more of what he was never meant to have: a wife, a son, a home, and peace. He paved the way for civilization but leaves it prematurely without a protector. A hundred years since Shane rode away and forty years since this film was made, most of us still feel vulnerable, and when we see this film again, we want to join Joey in his famous final, forever unanswered, plea: "Shane! Come back!"

▶ BEST ACTOR

WINNER:
William Holden *(Stalag 17)*
Other Nominees: Marlon Brando *(Julius Caesar)*, Richard Burton *(The Robe)*, Montgomery Clift *(From Here to Eternity)*, Burt Lancaster *(From Here to Eternity)*

▼

THE BEST CHOICE:
Montgomery Clift *(From Here to Eternity)*
Award-Worthy Runners-Up: Alan Ladd *(Shane)*, Burt Lancaster *(From Here to Eternity)*, John Wayne *(Hondo)*, Charles Winninger *(The Sun Shines Bright)*

When William Holden won a Best Actor Oscar for his portrayal of a bitter, rugged, opportunistic POW in Billy Wilder's *Stalag 17,* he at last shook off his lightweight image. Even his cynical, doomed writer in Wilder's *Sunset Boulevard* hadn't accomplished this. Portraying a heel, he is wrongly suspected by his fellow prisoners of being in league with the Germans. Looking back over Holden's career, *Stalag 17* remains one of his best films—he didn't appear in that many first-rate pictures—but his performance is, disappointingly, weaker than in numerous later roles, including one as a similar character in *The Bridge on the River Kwai.* He was well cast as the character played by John Ericson on Broadway, but I don't think he really added anything special to the part. Much more impressive, and more exciting, is Montgomery Clift's portrait of another soldier with big problems in Fred Zinnemann's Best Picture winner, *From Here to Eternity.*

From James Jones's best-seller, the picture is set in Hawaii in 1941. Clift is Robert E. Lee Prewitt, a new arrival at the army base. He has transferred from the bugle corps to this infantry division because he refused to be part of a boxing team at the other base. He had blinded a friend while sparring, and had lost his heart for boxing. However, Captain Holmes (Philip Ober) is proud of his company's boxing team and instructs the other boxers—most of them officers—to give Prewitt the treatment to coerce him into changing his mind. He is constantly harassed and forced to do a tremendous amount of work, but he endures it all. His only friend higher than a corporal is Holmes's chief aide, Sergeant Milt Warden (Burt Lancaster), who is having an affair with Holmes's unhappy wife, Karen (Deborah Kerr). Warden gets Prewitt weekend passes. Prewitt goes with his best friend, Angelo Maggio (Frank Sinatra), to a social club. Prewitt falls for one of the young women who work there, Lorene (Donna Reed). She falls for him, too, but doesn't want to marry a soldier. Maggio has a feud with "Fatso" (Ernest Borgnine), who runs the stockade. When he is arrested for leaving his guard post, getting drunk, and fighting MP's, Maggio is sent to the stockade. Meanwhile, Prewitt is still getting the treatment. He finally is bullied into fighting one of the officers out in the yard. He is victorious. Holmes's superiors see that Holmes doesn't attempt to stop the fight and won't discipline the officer who started it. He is forced to resign from the army. Prewitt won't have to box. Maggio, fed up with the

Burt Lancaster gets his first look at the newly transferred Montgomery Clift in Fred Zinnemann's *From Here to Eternity*.

punishment he has been receiving from "Fatso," dies while trying to escape the stockade. Prewitt has a knife fight with "Fatso" in an alley. He kills "Fatso" but is wounded himself. He goes AWOL while recuperating at Lorene's. Warden and Karen break up. When Pearl Harbor is attacked, Prewitt attempts to return to camp. Lorene begs him to stay, saying she will marry him. He is shot and killed by American soldiers when he won't identify himself. Karen and Lorene take the same ship to the mainland, grieving for their lost loves.

I think the most appealing aspect of *From Here to Eternity* is that the five major characters, played by top-billed Lancaster, Clift, Kerr, Reed, and Sinatra, are rule-breakers. It's indicative of his personality that Prewitt is named after Robert E. Lee, the number-one Rebel. You look into Clift's sensitive yet determined eyes and you know his character is an idealist—Warden calls him a hardhead—unwilling to compromise his values even if it means suffering. He tells the intimidating boxers assigned to bully him: "Look, I told Holmes and I'm telling you, I ain't fighting. I quit fighting. You guys want to put the screws on, go ahead. I can take anything you can dish

out." Like other Clift characters Prewitt knows that he must make correct choices or he won't be able to live with himself. If he boxes, he knows that his conscience will cause him more suffering than the men giving him the treatment. So he sticks to his guns. "I know where I stand—a man don't go his own way, he's nothing."

Clift was such a cerebral, introspective actor that it is exciting just to watch him think. He lies motionless in his cot with his eyes open, or silently smokes a cigarette, or broods over a beer in a bar, and that is enough for us, even if we don't know what Prewitt's problems are. His handsome face doesn't show much emotion. Even when he cries while playing taps after Maggio's death, his pained expression is subtle. If Clift's eyes should move ever so slightly—as when he is given unfair orders—then we know exactly what Prewitt is thinking. Clift does a lot of wordless acting in *From Here to Eternity,* and when he has lines, he delivers them with an offbeat rhythm that makes us listen and arouses our curiosity about his character. But what is different about this Clift performance is that it is extremely physical. We see Prewitt box, have a knife fight, shoot a little pool, fall down some stairs, run, march, dig a hole, get down on his knees to do chores, stumble about when drunk. All this physical activity means that he sweats a lot during the picture, which I'm sure contributed to his sex-symbol image. (Also: this character is really attracted to women.)

The only thing that doesn't ring true is Prewitt's devotion to the army. As Lorene says, the army has always done badly by him, treated him unfairly. At the end men in *our* army shoot him to death. It's as if Prewitt picked the wrong country's army to be in. Prewitt says he wants to be a career soldier, that the army has made him, an orphan, feel like he belongs, and that being in the service provided him the opportunity to become a bugler. Prewitt may say "ain't," but the actor playing him seems too smart to think that a nonconformist like Prewitt would be happy to lose himself in the service for the rest of his life. As Warden says, Prewitt is a hardhead. The last place Clift's hardhead should be is in the army.

▶ BEST ACTRESS

WINNER:
Audrey Hepburn *(Roman Holiday)*
Other Nominees: Leslie Caron *(Lili)*, Ava Gardner *(Mogambo)*, Deborah Kerr *(From Here to Eternity)*, Maggie McNamara *(The Moon Is Blue)*

▼

THE BEST CHOICE:
Gloria Grahame *(The Big Heat)*
Award-Worthy Runners-Up: Doris Day *(Calamity Jane)*, Audrey Hepburn *(Roman Holiday)*, Marilyn Monroe *(Gentlemen Prefer Blondes)*, Geraldine Page *(Hondo)*, Jane Russell *(Gentlemen Prefer Blondes)*

Audrey Hepburn began her still-ongoing love affair with moviegoers by playing a princess who finds fleeting

romance with Gregory Peck in *Roman Holiday.* She was enchanting in her debut role and one can't really quarrel with the Academy's decision to select her as Best Actress. But I think she became more deserving of the award a few years later, when she stopped relying so heavily on charm and looks and made breakthroughs as an actress. For 1953 I'd prefer giving the Oscar to a great, underrated actress who was at her peak: Gloria Grahame. After making a moderate impression in two melodramas directed by former husband Nicholas Ray, *A Woman's Secret* in 1949 and *In a Lonely Place* (opposite Humphrey Bogart) in 1950, she had a banner year in 1952, appearing in four films and winning a Best Supporting Actress Oscar playing Dick Powell's trampy Southern wife in *The Bad and the Beautiful*. This led to four leading-lady roles in 1953, the best of which was her brave gangster's moll in Fritz Lang's *The Big Heat*.

In Lang's violent classic melodrama, which wedded forties film noir with those fifties exposé films that were inspired by the televised Kefauver crime hearings of 1951, Grahame played Debby Marsh, the girlfriend of sadistic gangster Vince Stone (Lee Marvin). Stone is the right-hand man for the rich crime lord Mike Lagana (Alexander Scourby), who runs the town. The picture's main character is the rare honest cop, Dave Bannion (Glenn Ford), investigating the suicide of a policeman whose corrupt wife Bertha (Jeanette Nolan) claims he killed himself because of ill health. But the dead cop's barfly girlfriend suggests he did it out of guilt about being on Lagana's payroll. She is rubbed out before she can talk to Bannion, so he realizes that she told the truth. He intensifies the investigation of Lagana and Stone, even after being ordered off the case. When he threatens Lagana, Lagana's men plant a bomb in his car. His wife, Katie (Jocelyn Brando), is killed in the explosion. He resigns from the force and has his friends look after his daughter. He blindly seeks revenge. After Debby talks to Bannion, Stone throws hot coffee in her face, disfiguring her. She goes to Bannion for help. At first he is condescending—she is hurt that he refuses to speak of his wife to her—but eventually he recognizes her goodness. Bertha has her husband's letter of confession implicating Lagana, but it will be mailed to authorities only upon her death. Afraid Bannion will kill Bertha to make sure that letter is delivered, and go to jail for this crime, Debby kills Bertha first. She then throws hot coffee in Stone's face, making his capture by Bannion possible. She is shot. Before she dies, Bannion—who no longer feels the need to kill—respectfully tells her about Katie. She says, "I like her . . . I like her a lot."

Grahame was an underrated, one-of-a-kind actress with kittenish good looks and a somewhat dazed expression. She gave special meaning to such terms as *fallen woman, tarnished lady,* and *femme fatale,* which she definitely is not in *The Big Heat*. Debby is one of her many sensuous, flirtatious women who are unhappy with their lives, and feel they are unworthy of the men they fall for. She was in the same situation with James Stewart in *It's a Wonderful Life* and Robert Mitchum in *Macao*. Grateful that men

Gloria Grahame cozies up to detective Glenn Ford in Fritz Lang's *The Big Heat*.

even consider them their friends, they will make great sacrifices for them. Debby is shot while helping Bannion fight ex-boyfriend Vince Stone.

In her sorry circle Debby never is recognized for being special. She leads a useless life, sleeping, shopping, and gabbing nonstop. She seems to be searching for someone with whom she can engage in polite conversation or who can be her straight man. She's too good to be stuck with the brutal Vince, but until she meets Bannion she believes that he is typical of all men. When Vince disfigures her with hot coffee (Grahame plays much of the film with blistered-face makeup), she finally realizes she deserves better; ironically, at the same time, her disfigurement forces her to stop being vain. Now she fights for self-esteem. And Grahame makes sure Debby emerges as someone we can truly admire. Debby envies Katie, who chose good, poor Bannion instead of a bad man with money. She believes that having been with Stone, she can never be Katie's equal. But Bannion's increasing support and affection make her realize that she is special after all. And when she's dying, and Bannion tells her about his late wife, she realizes that he has come to regard her as being in Katie's class. She is touched. And we're touched because she was willing to give up her life—and save Bannion a lifetime in prison—just for this small reward. Debby's last words are that she likes Katie. Our last thoughts are that we like Debby—just as much as Grahame obviously does.

1954

▶ BEST PICTURE

WINNER:
On the Waterfront (Columbia; Elia Kazan)
Other Nominees: *The Caine Mutiny, The Country Girl, Seven Brides for Seven Brothers, Three Coins in the Fountain*

▼

THE BEST CHOICE:
Salt of the Earth (Independent Productions Corporation and the International Union of Mine, Mill, and Smelter Workers; Herbert Biberman)
Award-Worthy Runners-Up: *Johnny Guitar* (Nicholas Ray), *Rear Window* (Alfred Hitchcock), *Seven Brides for Seven Brothers* (Stanley Donen), *A Star Is Born* (George Cukor)

Elia Kazan's moderately budgeted Best Picture winner, *On the Waterfront,* which Budd Schulberg based on newspaper articles by Malcolm Johnson about corruption in the longshoremen's union, won eight Oscars in 1954, tying the record set by *Gone With the Wind* and *From Here to Eternity* (proving it makes sense to choose titles that answer the popular question, "Where?"). It's still a powerful film, with strong dialogue, Hoboken locales that contribute to its authenticity, and riveting performances by Best Actor winner Marlon Brando, as an exploited dockworker who turns informer against the criminal union, and Best Supporting Actress Eva Marie Saint (her movie debut). But Karl Malden grates on one's nerves as a crusading priest, and it's hard not to resent the attempts of Kazan and Schulberg, two HUAC informers, to manipulate us into admiring Brando's Terry Malloy for testifying before a government commission. Also, some critics think the picture is antiunion.

If there was a labor film in 1954 that deserved acclaim it was Herbert Biberman's legendary 16mm independent production, *Salt of the Earth,* the greatest political narrative ever made in the United States. Alfred Hitchcock's *Rear Window* and George Cukor's uncut version of *A Star Is Born* were certainly worthy of the Oscar. But it gives me special payback pleasure to give my Alternate Oscar to a picture that was made by people blacklisted in Hollywood (director Biberman, producer Paul Jarrico, writer Michael Wilson, cinematographers Leonard Stark and Stanley Meredith, composer Sol Kaplan, actor Will Geer, among them), television workers, and blacks not allowed in Roy Brewer's segregated International Alliance of Theatrical and State Employees; was cast mostly with the working people the film is about; was condemned in the Hollywood press, *The New York Times,* and by RKO boss Howard Hughes and members of HUAC; was processed surreptitiously because Hollywood labs refused to handle it; was edited secretly; and was booked into only thirteen theaters nationally (and those theaters were picketed) because Brewer's IATSE projectionists refused to show it. One doubts that it even played in Hollywood long enough to qualify for Oscar consideration. All the better.

Salt of the Earth tells the true story of a thirteen-month strike at a zinc mine in New Mexico that was won because the wives of the miners took over the picket line after a Taft-Hartley injunction enjoined the men from picketing. The men swallowed their pride and took over the women's work at home. The film focuses on a Mexican-American couple, Ramon Quintero (Juan Chacon, the president of the local that went on strike) and his pregnant wife, Esperanza (Rosaura Revueltas, a respected professional Mexican actress who never got to be in another film because of her participation in this picture). With two children, and living in a home that has no indoor plumbing or hot water, they are not getting along at the time the men go on strike after a worker is injured. She becomes angry when the all-male union drops its demand for better sanitation in the houses, deciding to ask only for safer working conditions. When the women replace the men on the picket line, Ramon won't allow Esperanza to join in. But she disobeys. He is forced to take over the housework and learns that Esperanza was right about the need for sanitation. He also gains respect for her and the other women as the picket line holds fast. When she is arrested, he takes care of their new baby. Political action excites Esperanza, but Ramon is uncomfortable with her having as much importance as he in the home. She tells him that all she wants is for both of their lives to improve. Dispirited, Ramon goes hunting on the day he is supposed to watch the women picketers, in case of trouble. But his wife's words sink in and he rushes back home. There he finds that the sheriff (Geer) is evicting his family. Suddenly friends, fellow workers, union men, organizers, women, and children arrive and

The wives of the striking miners "man" the picket lines in Herbert Biberman's *Salt of the Earth.*

put all their belongings back. Frightened, the sheriff and his men back off. In the face of such solidarity the mineowners realize they must give in to the workers' demands. Ramon thanks his brothers and sisters. With their victory they now have hope for their children, the salt of the earth.

This remarkable film was labeled subversive before its release, but in fact it's prohuman rather than anti-American. It doesn't call for revolution, just solidarity among workers—and their families—against the power elite, to obtain fair wages and decent living conditions. The film shows how white bosses discriminate against Mexican-American workers and try to turn the Anglo workers against them, too, by creating an unequal salary structure. It makes a plea for racial brotherhood and sexual equality, which are the weapons with which to combat discrimination and exploitation. Also noteworthy, this picture

broke ground by giving women proper recognition as a force in the labor movement. It also anticipated with startling accuracy the concerns of the women's movement of the seventies, making an issue of equality in jobs, equality in the home, and sexual equality. For the first time in a narrative set in America, women stand next to their men in the face of the oppressor. Significantly, their liberation is achieved, as it must be, by the women themselves. This in turn liberates their men, who were just as trapped and depressed as they by sex-role conventions. Esperanza tells Ramon, "I want to rise. And push everything up with me as I go." She is true to her word. Ramon benefits from her liberation through political action and their shaky relationship becomes solid.

Salt of the Earth is filled with moments that are simple yet stirring. It's hard not to be moved when an old woman joins the picket line; when the unhappy Esperanza returns from the picket line with her face aglow; when Esperanza's son brags about *her;* and when Ramon takes the baby from his imprisoned wife and accepts child-rearing responsibilities. The film's most famous moment has Esperanza and the other women prisoners annoying the sheriff by constantly demanding "The formula! The formula!" for her baby. We see the power of women united. We respond to all these characters because they aren't epic figures, just common workingmen and -women. But we realize that when they stand together, they take on heroic proportions.

Salt of the Earth is still difficult to see in America, though it turns up on PBS occasionally, is screened at leftist gatherings (often on campuses), and is available on video. Of course, it's a shame that it never received adequate distribution here, but that in itself will always be a reminder of how bad the McCarthy era was. Interestingly, it found a mass audience in the Soviet Union and China and has played on television in Western countries. Even though it didn't become the first independent picture to win the Best Picture Oscar (that would have been a joke!), producer Paul Jarrico tells me that "it has been seen, probably, by more people than any film in history."

▶ BEST ACTOR

WINNER:
Marlon Brando *(On the Waterfront)*
Other Nominees: Humphrey Bogart *(The Caine Mutiny,)* Bing Crosby *(The Country Girl),* James Mason *(A Star Is Born),* Dan O'Herlihy *(Adventures of Robinson Crusoe)*

▼

THE BEST CHOICE:
Marlon Brando *(On the Waterfront)*
Award-Worthy Runners-Up: Charles Laughton *(Hobson's Choice),* James Mason *(A Star Is Born)*

By 1954 it was generally conceded that Marlon Brando was the greatest, most electrifying actor in movies. Despite his condescending attitude toward motion pictures, the Academy now considered Hollywood's rudest "bad boy" one of its own—he had permanently abandoned the New York theater—so it was willing to give him a Best Actor Oscar for playing a troubled dockworker in Elia Kazan's *On the Waterfront,* the Best Picture winner. Brando professed disdain for awards but was so carried away by his victory that he reportedly almost kissed gossipmonger Louella Parsons backstage. He later came to his senses and gave the statue to a friend, with the recommendation to turn it into a lamp. Statue or lamp, Brando deserved to win it.

Brando is Terry Malloy, a not-so-bright ex-boxer who now has a job on the docks in return for favors he does for crooked longshoreman union boss Johnny Friendly (Lee J. Cobb). His smarter brother, Charley (Rod Steiger's movie debut), also works for Friendly. Terry gets the dockworker who has been testifying to a government committee against Friendly to come out of hiding so Friendly's men can lean on him. But they murder him instead, which upsets Terry. He becomes romantically involved with the dead man's sister, Edie (Saint), who wants to get to the bottom of the murder. Terry tells a crusading priest, Father Barry (Karl Malden), about his involvement. The Father persuades Terry to consider testifying. When another dockworker is murdered, Terry tells his brother that he doesn't know what he'll do. When Charley is killed for failing to silence Terry, Terry testifies against Friendly. He isn't allowed to work on the docks. None of the other longshoremen will speak to him for having ratted. He tries to beat up Friendly but Friendly's men beat him up instead. The rest of the longshoremen respect him now and refuse to work unless Terry is allowed to lead them onto the docks. Although badly beaten he leads the men back to work in defiance of Friendly, who has lost his hold on the men.

Marlon Brando reveals his sensitive side to Eva Marie Saint in Elia Kazan's *On the Waterfront,* for which he was voted Best Actor and she won as Best Supporting Actress.

Brando is neither as frighteningly explosive as he was as the T-shirt clad Stanley Kowalski in Kazan's *A Streetcar Named Desire* nor as much fun as he was as the overaged, leather-jacketed motorcycle gang leader in *The Wild One.* Yet even as the punch-drunk, slow-witted Terry, Brando is just as powerful and charismatic a screen presence and just as sexy as he had been in his two other signature roles of the early fifties. And playing a character without conceit or cockiness for a change, he's less strained and not at all affected. Yes, he gets teary a few times too many and does a little "method" mugging—looking every which way for the right words or help or an explanation he can understand—but this is one of Brando's most straightforward characterizations. His performance is satisfying because unlike Stanley or his rebel, Terry isn't just a part but someone Brando obviously cares about.

Without striving for too much sympathy for his sad, lonely character, Brando is quite touching. His intimate scenes with screen newcomer Eva Marie Saint (who won a Best Supporting Actress award) are particularly affecting. Both actors are extremely patient in their deliveries, hesitating momentarily before speaking. Trying to fight through each other's shyness and inexpertise at romance and trying to get clues as to what the other is thinking, Terry and Edie listen carefully to what the other says and weigh their own words. Because they know honesty is essential to making their relationship work, they both are daring enough not to hold back their own feelings. While having a beer date with her, Terry's "Don't go, I've got my whole life to drink" reveals so much! As in *The Wild One* Brando's character is so affected by a good woman's love and concern that he reveals his tender side. Edie looks closely at him, when others have turned away, and she discovers his sweet and decent side (Edie knows it's an indication of something good that he takes care of pigeons). When Edie touches Terry's cheek for the first time, his whole body feels it and tears well up in his eyes. Terry has *never* known gentleness before—even when the men he knows joke around they slap and jab this ex-boxer's cheek. Now she touches him softly. Later she'll kiss and hold him. Terry doesn't take her affection casually: "She's the first nice thing that's ever happened to me."

Terry realizes that Edie is the only one who cares about him as a person (Father Barry just sees him as a means to bring Johnny Friendly down). He now knows that Johnny Friendly isn't his friend and acknowledges that his brother, who pretends to protect him, actually sold him out. In the classic Brando-Steiger conversation in the back of a cab, Terry tells Charley that he shouldn't have ordered him to take a dive in his big fight: "I coulda had class. I coulda been a contender. I could have been somebody. Instead of a bum—which is what I am." But through Edie, Terry begins to think for himself and his self-esteem improves: "They always said I was a bum—well, I ain't a bum, Edie."

Unfortunately, Kazan and screenwriter Schulberg have Terry make up for his deceit in the ring by coming clean in front of the government commission investigating waterfront corruption, testifying against Johnny Friendly although everyone but Edie and Father Barry will turn against him. The young man who tended pigeons becomes a stool pigeon with their blessing. His defiant act is meant to be his triumph over all the bad people who have run and ruined his life. (In Schulberg's novelization of his script Terry is murdered for ratting.) Kazan and Schulberg, perhaps defending themselves for having been friendly witnesses before HUAC, make Terry a hero for squealing (rather than have him undermine Friendly's operation without going to authorities). So we won't have a chance to reflect on what he has done, they cover their

tracks by having Terry physically attacking Friendly and then getting badly beaten by Friendly's henchmen, somehow regaining the respect of the other longshoremen who were angry at his testimony. In a scene that makes no sense, the bleeding Terry—whom Friendly wouldn't allow to work—leads all the men to work, while Friendly tries to stop them. Terry becomes a symbol, even a Christian martyr in Father Barry's eyes, but I preferred him when he was just a simple guy trying to be no more than a somebody. That Brando is so compelling is the only reason we don't immediately realize that the film is manipulating us into supporting squealers.

▶ BEST ACTRESS

WINNER:
Grace Kelly *(The Country Girl)*
Other Nominees: Dorothy Dandridge *(Carmen Jones)*, Judy Garland *(A Star Is Born)*, Audrey Hepburn *(Sabrina)*, Jane Wyman *(Magnificent Obsession)*

▼

THE BEST CHOICE:
Judy Garland *(A Star Is Born)*
Award-Worthy Runners-Up: Dorothy Dandridge *(Carmen Jones)*, Judy Holliday *(It Should Happen to You)*, Jennifer Jones *(Beat the Devil)*, Grace Kelly *(Rear Window)*, Eva Marie Saint *(On the Waterfront)*

When Judy Garland's movie career came to a temporary halt in 1951, it wasn't under the best conditions. MGM, her studio since 1936, suspended her indefinitely because, claiming physical and emotional problems, she hadn't been able to complete either *Annie Get Your Gun* or *Royal Wedding*. Her suspension and marital breakup with Vincente Minnelli prompted a nervous breakdown and supposed suicide attempt, and soon she found herself without a studio. After singing successes in London and New York, Hollywood beckoned again. She formed her own production company, Transcona Enterprises, and her new husband-manager, Sid Luft, persuaded Warner Bros. to underwrite her new film, give them studio facilities, and allow Garland to choose a mutually acceptable project for her comeback.

Garland decided to do a remake of the venerable 1937 Janet Gaynor–Fredric March classic, *A Star Is Born*. She had starred in a radio version during her MGM days. George Cukor would direct in Technicolor and CinemaScope (a first for a musical), and Moss Hart would write the caustic yet compassionate you-and-me-against-the-world (Hollywood) script. Judy would play actress-singer Esther Blodgett/Vicki Lester, who becomes a great star just when the once-great career of her new husband, actor Norman Maine, hits the skids and he becomes an alcoholic. James Mason would play the loving but increasingly depressed man who helps her career but can do nothing to save his own. Garland's shrewd decision to remake *A Star Is Born* was intended to improve her image. Significantly, she would be able to present herself

to the public as a strong, mature, responsible woman who could take care of a person, Norman Maine, whose grave problems were similar to those the public knew Garland had in real life.

When Cukor's glorious 181-minute version of *A Star Is Born* was released in September 1954, it had tremendous emotional impact on critics and moviegoers, including future archivist Ron Haver, who would later restore his favorite film. In *The New York Times* Bosley Crowther raved that the "performances from Miss Garland and Mr. Mason make the heart flutter and bleed." Garland immediately became the favorite to win the Best Actress Oscar, and not only for sentimental reasons. But she lost—while anxious reporters filled her hospital room, a day after she gave birth to Lorna—to another actress who played the suffering wife of an alcoholic: Grace Kelly in *The Country Girl*. Perhaps some viewers felt that Garland's role, which includes a scene in which Vicki wins an Oscar, was more calculated to win its star an Oscar than was Kelly's, which had the beautiful actress wearing plain clothes, glasses, and no makeup (we today recognize that as the perfect Oscar formula!). But a sounder reason for Garland's defeat is that voters didn't realize the scope of her performance: after its initial release Warner Bros. cut twenty-seven minutes from the picture, including two Garland numbers and important moments that reveal much about Esther-Vicki. Moreover, they didn't know whether to vote for her performance in the uncut film or the cut one in general release. When the damaged shortened version proved to be a box-office dud, the spiteful

Judy Garland's Vicki Lester brings the only joy to the life of James Mason's Norman Maine in George Cukor's *A Star Is Born*.

Jack Warner, still smarting from the picture's expense, decided not to buy ads to promote his Oscar nominees, including Garland. That didn't help either.

The 181-minute version, which Ron Haver miraculously restored, shows that Esther-Vicki was the finest performance in Garland's career. This woman has amazing depth, wit, resilience, graciousness. Garland always played nice girls, but this is the first time the character's goodness comes directly from the soul. Esther-Vicki is Garland's most mature character and the one who has the most passion. Her relationship with Norman is, despite his increasing alcoholism and depression, quite wonderful. They are one of the most supportive couples in screen history, always giving each other love and understanding at those times no one offers a word of kindness. He gives her the encouragement and confidence she needs to pursue a career, and he never resents her success even when out of work and in the throes of self-pity. And she never forgets the part he played in her success: "I'm just giving back the gifts he gave me." When the famous Vicki Lester emerges from solitude after her no-longer-famous husband's suicide, she introduces herself on the radio to an international audience as "Mrs. Norman Maine." This classic moment has so much impact for the simple reason that it shows the purity of their love. Esther-Vicki may have stopped crying when she introduces herself, but Garland's deeply felt words get us going.

Significantly, playing Esther-Vicki let Garland demonstrate her remarkable musical versatility, allowing her to belt out a soulful torch song, offer us a jazz or pop tune, and perform a song and dance that would be appropriate for vaudeville ("Born in a Trunk" deserves its legendary reputation). Whereas we are *told* Janet Gaynor's Esther-Vicki has talent in the 1937 film, Garland proves her star has talent. We understand why Norman is so moved by her when he watches from the shadows as she sings "The Man That Got Away." We, too, see the spark of greatness. Through Esther-Vicki, Garland was able to express fully what singing and performing meant to her. She comes alive. Dressed in clown makeup, Esther-Vicki brushes away the tears to sing "Lose the Long Face," and we see the essence of Garland, who spent many years singing away her tears.

It was somewhat tragic that Garland didn't win her deserved Oscar. It might have made up for *A Star Is Born*'s disappointing box-office returns. As it was, she emerged from a flop with nothing to show for it. She was no longer in demand in Hollywood and wouldn't make another movie for seven years. Everyone's loss.

1955

▶ BEST PICTURE

WINNER:
Marty (Hecht-Lancaster/United Artists; Delbert Mann)
Other Nominees: *Love Is a Many-Splendored Thing, Mister Roberts, Picnic, The Rose Tattoo*

THE BEST CHOICE:
The Night of the Hunter (United Artists; Charles Laughton)
Award-Worthy Runners-Up: *The Blackboard Jungle* (Richard Brooks), *East of Eden* (Elia Kazan), *Kiss Me Deadly* (Robert Aldrich), *Mister Roberts* (John Ford and Mervyn LeRoy), *Rebel Without a Cause* (Nicholas Ray)

In 1955 Hollywood was still trying to lure viewers away from their television sets with big-budgeted, wide-screen color productions, yet the Academy selected a black-and-white film as its Best Picture for the third straight year and chose a modestly budgeted film for the second straight year. Moreover, *Marty* was the first film to be based on a television drama. Paddy Chayefsky's screen adaptation of his teleplay, directed by TV vet Delbert Mann and with Ernest Borgnine replacing Rod Steiger as the plump, lonely Italian butcher from Brooklyn who blows his one shot at romance, appealed to viewers who wanted films about common, unglamorous people. Today, the picture is disappointingly static and uninvolving, a relic of its time, though there are some effective moments. When Marty's loser friend Angie asks his oft-repeated "What do you feel like doing tonight?" not many of us would answer that we want to watch *Marty*. But you might want to watch some of the other pictures made in 1955. I'm tempted to give my Alternate Oscar to Nicholas Ray's seminal troubled-youth film, *Rebel Without a Cause,* which has had tremendous emotional impact on me and millions of others worldwide. However, I'll pick the equally great but not as widely seen *The Night of the Hunter,* which could have used an Oscar boost to get due recognition.

Robert Mitchum gave perhaps his finest and, with the possible exception of his sadist in *Cape Fear,* his creepiest portrayal as a phony preacher. Harry Powell marries and murders widows for their money, believing he is helping God do away with women who arouse men's carnal instincts. Arrested for auto theft, he shares a cell with condemned killer Ben Harper (Peter Graves) and tries to get him to reveal the whereabouts of the $10,000 he stole. Only Ben's nine-year-old son, John (Billy Chapin), and four-year-old daughter, Pearl (Sally Jane Bruce), know the money is in Pearl's doll and they have sworn to their father to keep this secret. After Ben is executed, Preacher goes to Cresap's Landing to court

Ben's widow, Willa (Shelley Winters). He overwhelms her with his Scripture quoting, sermons, and hymns, and she agrees to marry him. On their wedding night he tells her they will never have sex because it is sinful. When the depressed, confused, guilty woman catches him trying to force John to reveal the whereabouts of the money, she is resigned to her fate and lets Preacher stab her to

Robert Mitchum gets some nasty ideas while watching a movie in Charles Laughton's frightening "fairy tale," *The Night of the Hunter.*

death. He almost stabs the children but they escape downriver. The Preacher follows. After a long, arduous journey John and Pearl are taken in by a Bible-quoting widow, Rachel Cooper (Lillian Gish), who cares for other orphans as well. She knows the children are troubled but doesn't know why. Preacher turns up and demands his stepchildren. Rachel sees John is terrified and that Preacher is a phony. She chases him away. When he breaks into the house, she shoots him in the rear. The coward runs into the barn, where he is arrested. John swings the doll at him and the money pours out—he no longer has to keep the secret that has burdened him. Preacher is convicted of murder. John and Pearl settle in with Rachel, who marvels at how children abide and endure.

Adapted by Charles Laughton and James Agee (who got full screen credit) from Davis Grubb's exciting Depression-era novel, Laughton's single directorial effort is one of the great "discovery" films. Laughton supposedly didn't care about the plight of John and Pearl Harper— he probably was attracted to Grubb's story because it called for an unorthodox visual style and because of its malevolent, obsessed villain—and so detested child actors Billy Chapin and Sally Jane Bruce that he had Mitchum direct them. So it's amazing that *The Night of the Hunter* conveys such heartfelt empathy toward helpless little children, and that it has such insight into the cruel, dangerous, frightening world of children, particularly orphans.

The story is part children's nightmare, part gothic horror film (at one point Preacher chases the kids as if he were the Frankenstein monster), part religious parable (as told to a child), part Grimm fairy tale, and part animated-cartoon fairy tale. It is full of the sort of imagery, props, locations, and animals that a child like John might see in a dream. As this film stresses, for unprotected children who exist in a wilderness of fear and confusion, nightmares continue even when they are awake. John and Pearl are much like Hansel and Gretel lost in the wilderness, who find refuge not with a witch who cooks children but a Mother Goose figure who cares for orphans. Rachel tells the children to be aware of false prophets (a Bible-story image), of wolves in sheep's clothing (a fairy-tale image). Preacher, a human wolf in sheep's clothing, is the classic deceitful fairy-tale villain who is ready to pounce on innocents. Like the wolves and other sneaky villains in cartoons, he also supplies the slapstick humor that provides the film's necessary moments of levity: while chasing the kids, he is always tripping, getting his fingers smashed, or getting conked on the head, and finally he gets shot in the behind, which causes him to howl as he runs at supersonic speed into the barn. His howling, his mock crying, even his creepy L-O-V-E vs. H-A-T-E (the letters tattooed on his fingers),

hand wrestling, and deep-voiced sermonizing have elements of absurd humor. Which doesn't mean he isn't terrifying. The two orphans, who, before they meet Rachel, have no friends and no adults to turn to, would turn to God were they not convinced that God is on the side of this evil man who quotes the Bible and claims to be a preacher. How lonely and afraid the children feel, and how guilty John feels for keeping his father's secret from this man of God. It is the religious Rachel who shows them that God is on their side and that the Preacher is the sinner.

As Rachel, Lillian Gish triumphantly returned to the screen. She matches Mitchum with a powerful performance. And exhibiting goodness, solemnity, and determination that characterized Gish's silent movie heroines, tiny Rachel perfectly counters Mitchum's massive, intimidating, hammy Preacher. In my favorite scene Preacher starts singing the hymn "Leaning on the Everlasting Arms," while hiding in the darkness and planning his attack on Rachel's home. Surprisingly, Rachel, gun in hand, starts singing her version—which includes references to Jesus—to soften the effect of the blasphemer's rendition. For a moment they harmonize and you know that she can't be intimidated. Like John and Pearl—who didn't trust anyone—we fall in love with Rachel and feel secure that she will protect these otherwise helpless children. Forget all those movie superheroes—Rachel is the answer to every scared child's prayers.

Laughton spent a great amount of time studying the techniques of D. W. Griffith and the German expressionists before undertaking his first directorial assignment. His picture looks different from any other film of the period. He and cinematographer Stanley Cortez came up with a remarkable number of amazing shots, many taken from unusual angles and employing innovative lighting. In the day the frame is either hazy or so bright that everything is washed out; at night there are dust, smoke, fog, and spooky shadows—the scariest shadow is the Preacher's, which forms on the wall of the children's room. At one point Laughton puts his camera in a helicopter; at other times he puts it directly behind a character's face, or covers the character with shadows; even indoors the camera is kept at a distance so we see characters in relation to the floor, walls, ceilings, and props. It's all quite exciting. My favorite shot is of John and Pearl floating downriver on their skiff, with the near bank and its animals in the foreground and the starry sky and fertile far bank in the background—it's a magical multiplane image straight out of a Disney cartoon. Laughton made an auspicious debut as a director, but because his film failed he aborted his effort to bring *The Naked and the Dead* to the screen, and never directed again, which is a real shame. Surely a Best Picture Oscar would have changed his mind.

▶ BEST ACTOR

WINNER:
Ernest Borgnine *(Marty)*
Other Nominees: James Cagney *(Love Me or Leave Me)*, James Dean *(East of Eden)*, Frank Sinatra *(The Man With the Golden Arm)*, Spencer Tracy *(Bad Day at Black Rock)*

▼

THE BEST CHOICE:
James Dean *(Rebel Without a Cause)*
Award-Worthy Runners-Up: James Cagney *(Mister Roberts)*, James Dean *(East of Eden)*, Henry Fonda *(Mister Roberts)*, Robert Mitchum *(The Night of the Hunter)*

As an Italian-born butcher living in Brooklyn, Ernest Borgnine surprised viewers by showing he could play someone with a tender side instead of another of his outright villains. His performance in *Marty* won him the Oscar and offers to play non-Italian butchers. Borgnine did a commendable job, but did he deserve the Oscar? Forget it. Nineteen fifty-five was the year of James Dean, who excited young viewers even more than Hollywood misfits Marlon Brando and Montgomery Clift and became an instant cult hero. In his first starring role he was mesmerizing as Cal Trask in Elia Kazan's *East of Eden*. But he was more natural, less mannered, in his follow-up, as Jim Stark in Nicholas Ray's contemporary juvenile-delinquent film *Rebel Without a Cause*. This time his conception of a misunderstood youth who can't articulate his anxieties no longer seemed calculated, but real. In *East of Eden* he fitted his personality into a part created by Steinbeck; this time, we believed that his part and his personality merged. We believed that his sensitive, lonely, brooding, angry misfit allowed us to see the real James Dean. Those of us who saw *Rebel* during its initial release, which came right after Dean's shocking and fatal car crash, were further convinced that there was a bond between Jim Stark and James Dean when we watched the scene in which Jim participates in a deadly car race.

Before Jim's first day in his new high school he is arrested for being drunk and disorderly. Also arrested that night is Judy (Natalie Wood), who was wandering around late at night, and Plato (Sal Mineo), who killed some puppies. Like Jim they are having problems dealing with their parents. Jim can never get a moment's peace at home with his loving but ranting mother (Ann Doran) and weak father (Jim Backus), who'll never listen to his problems. Judy gets no affection from her father. The disturbed Plato's parents spend their time abroad. On a school trip to the planetarium the next day, Jim befriends Plato. But Jim's taunted by a gang led by Buzz (Corey Allen), Judy's boyfriend. They fight with knives. That night the two race toward a cliff in stolen cars while all the other teens watch. Whoever jumps out first is the loser. Buzz plunges over the cliff in his car and is killed. Upset, Jim and Judy go off together. They fall in love. They go with Plato to a deserted mansion, where they find tem-

porary peace. Buzz's friends track Jim there, wanting to discourage him from squealing to the police. They chase Plato, who shoots one. Plato runs into the planetarium. The police trap him inside. Jim goes inside and removes the bullets from Plato's gun. But Plato panics while surrendering and holds up the gun. The police shoot him. Jim's father promises Jim that they will face everything together from now on. Jim and Judy embrace.

Whereas Cal Trask could probably use a few years of analysis, Jim Stark seems to need only parental support ("You're tearing me apart") and friendship. Cal isn't someone you'd want to seek out as a friend, but Jim is someone who appeals to everyone. The picture is so emotional because Dean creates a character (remember, we equate him with this character) whom everybody on- and offscreen is attracted to. He may be lonely, but in one day Plato takes him as his only friend and father figure; Buzz, his rival, thinks he's cool enough to be his friend; and Judy falls in love with him. We respond to Jim

It's hard not getting emotional watching the romance develop between lonely James Dean and Natalie Wood in Nicholas Ray's *Rebel Without a Cause*, which was released soon after Dean's death.

in the same way, either wanting him as friend or boy-friend, or identifying with him. All teenage boys who consider themselves misunderstood can identify with Jim Stark. They relate to his inability to communicate with adults, his self-destructive streak, and his rebel image. Teenage girls respond to his shyness, protectiveness, bravery, willingness to cry, good looks, and tender way of kissing; as Judy says, "A girl wants a man who's gentle and sweet and who doesn't run away." Jim is the rare juvenile without pretense, who speaks only when he has something to say, who won't let you down. Because he's not judgmental or cocky, he readily adapts to whichever person he's with, which is why he's the only person around who could be friends with both Plato and Buzz. He represents *all* troubled youths who need a chance, a direction, a cause (significantly Nicholas Ray's picture is on the side of the young). But rather than being a neutral, wishy-washy, middle-of-the-road figure, merely a calming influence on the others, he is in just as much turmoil as they are, living on the edge, smashing his hands into a policeman's desk because he doesn't know what to do with his anger, putting his life on the line. We get the urge to comfort him, listen to him—he usually mumbles unless he is sure someone cares what he has to say—and give him the support he needs to tame his violent streak.

As Jim Stark, Dean acted less with his eyes than with his (usually soft) voice and body. He had the most realistic body movements of anyone on screen. He didn't worry about posture or facing the person he speaks to; often he slouches or just slumps to the ground. He's on his back in several scenes, including ones with Natalie Wood; and on a couple of occasions the athletic Dean actually rolls over—other actors didn't do such things onscreen. I like the way he shuffles when he walks, to show uncertainty; and how he drops into a half crouch, like a boxer about to come out punching. Everything he does or says seems "cool." Among my favorite moments are: when the initially unfriendly Judy rebuffs his offer of a ride to school and runs to her friends, he softly says, "I love you too"; when he tells her he kissed her because "I felt like it"; when Plato asks him if he can keep his red jacket and (obviously not thinking how valuable it will become to movie-memorabilia collectors) he responds, "Well, what do you think?"; when he signifies to Buzz that he's listening to his "chickie run" instructions simply by taking his lit cigarette from his mouth; and when, after Buzz's death, he extends his hand to the shocked Judy. All Dean fans have such moments ingrained in their memories, perhaps since 1955. That's the incredible impact Dean had on us in *Rebel Without a Cause*.

▶ BEST ACTRESS

WINNER:
Anna Magnani *(The Rose Tattoo)*
Other Nominees: Susan Hayward *(I'll Cry Tomorrow)*, Katharine Hepburn *(Summertime)*, Jennifer Jones *(Love Is a Many-Splendored Thing)*, Eleanor Parker *(Interrupted Melody)*

▼

THE BEST CHOICE:
Anna Magnani *(The Rose Tattoo)*
Award-Worthy Runners-Up: Bette Davis *(The Virgin Queen)*, Julie Harris *(East of Eden)*, Susan Hayward *(I'll Cry Tomorrow)*

The Academy went against the Hollywood grain when it selected unglamorous character actor Ernest Borgnine as 1955's Best Actor for playing an unglamorous character, a plump, lonely Italian butcher, in Delbert Mann's *Marty*. It showed surprising consistency—and better judgment—by choosing forty-six-year-old Anna Magnani as Best Actress for playing a plump, lonely Italian seamstress in Daniel Mann's *The Rose Tattoo*, adapted by Tennessee Williams from his play. At least Borgnine was familiar to American moviegoers, but Magnani, though a big star in Europe, was essentially an unknown.

This highly emotional Italian actress had raven-black hair, expressive eyes, and was "pleasantly plump" (as Burt Lancaster's character describes her character in *The Rose Tattoo*). She had been successful in the Italian theater since the twenties, but didn't become a major film star until she starred as the pregnant mother in Roberto Rossellini's anti-Nazi *Open City,* which began her

country's "neorealism" film movement. She previously had been considered a comic actress, but her warm, passionate, heartfelt performances—and her unforgettable death scene, when she is shot in the back on the Rome streets—made viewers recognize she could do anything. For the next few years she'd play in comedies and dramas depicting postwar problems in Italy, usually as earthy, exuberant, temperamental women with hard lives, hungry children, and lethargic husbands. One of her best roles was as an amorous actress in Jean Renoir's *The Golden Coach*. Renoir described her as "an animal" and called her the world's greatest actress, a view held by other directors and critics. Tennessee Williams was such a big fan that he wrote his play *The Rose Tattoo* specifically for her. She turned it down because her English was bad (Maureen Stapleton took the part), but she worked on her speech, improved dramatically, and came to America when Paramount decided to produce

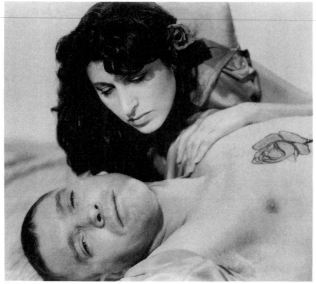

Anna Magnani falls for Burt Lancaster, who has the same tattoo that adorned her late husband, in *The Rose Tattoo*.

the film five years later. Daniel Mann, who also directed Susan Hayward to an Oscar nomination in *I'll Cry Tomorrow,* got the directorial assignment. He had directed the stage play, as well as directing stage actress Shirley Booth to an Oscar in 1952, also opposite Burt Lancaster, in 1952's *Come Back, Little Sheba.* He was the support Paramount figured she needed.

The story takes place on America's Gulf Coast. Magnani is a Sicilian-born seamstress, who is mother to lovely fifteen-year-old Marisa Pavan, and devoted wife to a virile trucker with a rose tattoo on his chest. He is killed while smuggling. Magnani is so heartbroken that she spends the next three years sitting in the house in various states of undress. She comes out of her funk when her daughter falls in love with a young sailor, Ben Cooper. She makes him swear not to take away Pavan's innocence. Magnani is so devoted to the memory of her dead husband that she refuses to believe he was unfaithful with blond blackjack dealer Virginia Grey. She allows herself to be courted by Burt Lancaster's extremely aggressive, not-too-bright trucker. He makes her laugh, except when she sees he has had a rose tattooed on his chest to please her. At first she resists Lancaster, but her defenses break down. Eventually she learns the sad truth about her unfaithful husband. She even lets her daughter run off with the sailor.

The Rose Tattoo doesn't really hold up today, but Magnani is still amazing to watch. There was no one else like her on the American screen. She holds nothing back; her performance is vibrant, lusty, witty. Several pounds overweight and her youth gone, she is still sexy, as when she passionately kisses her husband's back as he sleeps. She has several jarring dramatic scenes when she is extremely emotional and feels the pain of her character. Her finest moment comes when she sees the priest and her neighbors entering her home and realizes that something dreadful has happened to her husband. In a black slip, she warily walks toward them, holding her throat. She asks them to speak but realizing what they'll say, backs up and orders, "Don't speak!" several times before collapsing. Magnani is also at her best when she confronts the priest later and insists he tell her if her husband confessed to cheating on her. She grabs him and violently turns him around and around. When Magnani's women are throwing temper tantrums, they aren't the type anyone wants to argue with. Later she almost beats up Lancaster.

This film was ideal as Magnani's introduction to American audiences because she had the chance to display all kinds of emotions, from crying to playing the martyr to having fits to laughing heartily ("from the heart") with Lancaster. She constantly throws the viewer off guard with her humor. I like what she makes the sailor go through to win her approval, while she locks Pavan outside the house. Soon Pavan tells her beau to kiss Magnani's cheek. She pulls away—"Kiss me?"—but playing the queen, consents: "Kiss my hand." Also amusing is her deadpan look when she gives the crying Lancaster her hanky to dry his eyes and instead he blows his nose before handing it back to her. A minute later her eyes widen with excitement and she gets dizzy upon seeing Lancaster's muscular body: "My husband's body on . . . a man who smells like a goat." She has great dignity, but she will allow herself to be courted by this happy fellow she refers to as a "clown." It's a treat to see Magnani's character finally let herself laugh and be happy with him because this actress had the uncanny ability to make us feel whatever emotions her women feel.

Anna Magnani made only three more English-language films: *Wild Is the Wind* in 1957, *The Fugitive Kind* (Williams also wrote the source play, *Orpheus Descending,* for her) in 1960, and Stanley Kramer's *The Secret of Santa Vittoria* in 1969. Some would say she didn't deserve a Best Actress Oscar because of her relatively minor contributions to the Hollywood cinema. But I'm glad she got it, as a tribute to her remarkable overall career and reminder that for a brief time this great one-of-a-kind Italian actress showed every starlet in Hollywood how it should be done.

1956

▶ BEST PICTURE

WINNER:
Around the World in 80 Days (United Artists; Michael Anderson)
Other Nominees: *Friendly Persuasion, Giant, The King and I, The Ten Commandments*

▼

THE BEST CHOICE:
The Searchers (Warner Bros.; John Ford)
Award-Worthy Runners-Up: *Invasion of the Body Snatchers* (Don Siegel), *The Killing* (Stanley Kubrick), *Richard III* (Laurence Olivier)

The year 1956 was dominated by lengthy, wide-screen, super-budget extravaganzas with bigger-than-life characters and exotic locales. Even King Vidor's *War and Peace* seemed dwarfed by *Around the World in 80 Days,* Cecil B. DeMille's *The Ten Commandments,* and *Giant,* with Rock Hudson, Elizabeth Taylor, and James Dean down Texas way. Taylor's husband, Mike Todd, produced an expensive, three-hour adaptation of Jules Verne's novel, starring David Niven as Phileas Fogg. The most hyped picture of the year, it was strategically released as a theatrical "event," with higher prices and limited screenings. For his only film before his death in a plane crash, Todd wisely offered cameos to almost every actor in the universe. How could the Academy members vote against their friends? *Around the World in 80 Days,* escapist entertainment at best, won the Best Picture Oscar. Lost among the epics was John Ford's unnominated, unnoticed *The Searchers,* the year's best picture, my choice as best movie Western, and an influence on such diverse pictures as *Dirty Harry, Once Upon a Time in the West, Hardcore,* and *Taxi Driver.*

Frank Nugent liberally adapted Alan Le May's fine novel (in which the lead character is killed). Not long after Ethan Edwards (John Wayne) returns to Texas—it's rumored he has turned outlaw—nomadic Comanches under a chief named Scar (Henry Brandon) massacre his brother Aaron, his sister-in-law Martha, and nephew Ben, and abduct his nieces, Lucy and young Debbie (Lana Wood). Ethan gives chase, along with Lucy's fiancé Brad Jorgenson (Harry Carey, Jr.) and Martin Pawley (Jeffrey Hunter), Aaron's adopted son. Because Martin is part Cherokee the racist Ethan won't consider him a relative, even though it was Ethan who saved him from the Indians who massacred his parents. When Ethan discovers that Lucy has been raped and murdered, the crazed Brad rides into the Indian camp and is killed. Ethan and Martin spend years tracking down Scar, during which time Ethan grows fond of Martin. Martin would rather be courting

Brad's sister Laurie (Vera Miles), but he knows that if Ethan finds Debbie now that she has been defiled by Indians, Ethan will kill her. A Mexican trader takes them into Scar's camp, where Ethan and Scar insult each other. Also present is the teenage Debbie (Natalie Wood), now one of Scar's brides. Later, she comes to the spot where Ethan and Martin are camped to tell them to go away. Ethan would shoot her if Martin didn't get in the way. Scar and several Indians attack but Ethan and Martin escape. They return home, just in time for Martin to stop Laurie's wedding to a rival suitor. That night it's reported that Scar is camped nearby. Martin sneaks into the camp prior to the cavalry attack and kills Scar. Ethan rides after Debbie. She runs away and falls, thinking he'll kill her. But he picks her up securely in his arms, having had a

After years of looking, John Wayne and Jeffrey Hunter find out what happened to abducted Natalie Wood in John Ford's cult Western *The Searchers.*

change of heart. Ethan, still holding Debbie, and Martin return to the Jorgensons', where Martin and Debbie will now live. Ethan walks away as the door to the Jorgenson cabin shuts behind him.

What the late Stuart Byron termed "The Super-Cult Movie of the New Hollywood" in 1979, was my favorite film as a kid in the fifties, before it disappeared from circulation in the sixties. Today I see flaws, but I still think it is a *great* movie, with breathtaking visual beauty (for the ninth time Ford shot footage in red-clayed Monument Valley), a fascinating epic story, and John Wayne's finest performance and most interesting character. It's a splendidly directed film full of action, humor, intriguing relationships, and, to build tension, interrupted rituals (funerals, weddings, dinners, and so on). Images of settlers, Indians, and the landscape evoke emotional responses.

Some moments have extraordinary impact: Ward Bond's Captain Clayton drinks his coffee and pretends not to notice that Martha folds Ethan's coat in a manner that betrays her love for him; as Ethan rubs down the back of his tired horse, his face reveals the anguish he feels because he is too far away to prevent Indians from massacring his family; the imposing Scar stands over the frightened Debbie as she hides by a grave; Debbie runs toward Martin for their first embrace in five years; and, in a scene that always affects me emotionally, Ethan, instead of killing Debbie, lifts the scared girl into his arms and says tenderly, "Let's go home, Debbie."

A most peculiar aspect of the film is that the long search by Ethan and Martin for Debbie is a waste of time: Scar eventually brings her back to the area from which he took her. Even then, it's old Mose Harper (Hank Warden) who discovers her whereabouts, not Ethan or

Martin. The search, then, is not the search for a kidnapped girl, but Ethan's search for himself, his way of finding inner peace. He must purge himself of the racism and savagery that is embodied by Scar, his alter ego. The cleansing of Ethan's soul is central to a picture obsessed with the concepts of *pure* and *impure*. To Ethan, Scar's name signifies that he continuously defiles the once-pure Debbie, thereby putting a blemish (a "scar") on the name of the pure-blooded Edwards family. Ethan feels that if he kills Debbie, not Scar, he can end what he feels is the family's, and particularly Martha's disgrace (it's obvious that he loved Martha too). His feelings toward a mixing of the bloods—symbolically conveyed when he almost dies from an Indian's poison arrow—dominates his life.

It is proper that Martin, rather than Ethan, kills Scar because he does so for the right, "moral" reasons and not just because Scar is an Indian. Significantly, once the savage Scar is dead, Ethan no longer feels the urge to kill Debbie. His own "savage" instincts have been purged from body and mind. His racism hasn't vanished but he has come to realize that it is wrong, and that anyone with such feelings doesn't belong in the emerging civilization, where the white settlers *must* mix in all ways with the red-skinned Native Americans and everyone *must* live in harmony. So it is, in the film's classic last shot, that he doesn't enter the Jorgenson home with Martin and Debbie, where people from several different heritages will form a new family. Instead he walks toward the wilderness (the past) from which he came, a myth figure with his divine mission completed and his soul purified. And the closing door of civilization (the present and future) shuts him out. He is instantly obsolete.

▶ BEST ACTOR

WINNER:
Yul Brynner *(The King and I)*
Other Nominees: James Dean *(Giant)*, Kirk Douglas *(Lust for Life)*, Rock Hudson *(Giant)*, Laurence Olivier *(Richard III)*

▼

THE BEST CHOICE:
Laurence Olivier *(Richard III)*
Award-Worthy Runners-Up: Yul Brynner *(The King and I)*, Kirk Douglas *(Lust for Life)*, Sterling Hayden *(The Killing)*, Burt Lancaster *(The Rainmaker)*, James Mason *(Bigger Than Life)*, John Wayne *(The Searchers)*

Yul Brynner was drafted from Broadway to re-create his stubborn Siam despot in 20th Century–Fox's excellent musical version of *The King and I.* Just as Deborah Kerr found the king, audiences thought this bald, handsome, slightly scary newcomer to be magnetic, amusing, powerful, sexy, et cetera, et cetera, et cetera. Kirk Douglas won the New York Film Critics' Best Actor award for his strong performance as Vincent Van Gogh in *Lust for Life,* but the Academy went with the popular choice, picking

Brynner. In truth, there should have been a battle *royal,* with Laurence Olivier as King *Richard III* toppling Brynner's king. If Olivier hadn't already won in 1948 for his melancholy Dane in *Hamlet,* he might have been given proper consideration for his riveting portrayal of the wicked Richard. It was his best screen performance—*Richard III* is superior screen Shakespeare—and one of the finest performances of the decade.

To play the fifteenth-century English monarch with the

bad back and worse reputation, Olivier wore a pageboy haircut, dark brows, and a long, sharp false nose that makes his Richard look like a cross between an overaged Prince Valiant wannabe and Albert Dieudonné as the title character in Abel Gance's *Napoleon.* Whatever noble bearing he might have had is undermined by his twisted, deformed back and arm and a silly hat and costume that gives him a freakish-clownish appearance. No one could look at the Duke of Gloucester and consider him a threat to the throne of Edward IV (Cedric Hardwicke), although that's exactly what he is. In his early deception he doesn't pretend to be court jester, but instead is as sickeningly, if more convincingly, ingratiating and 'umble as Uriah Heep, offering double doses of flattery and assurances of loyalty to those he plans to eliminate; putting extra emphasis on the title "Lord" when addressing noblemen; and amusingly assuring all those in court that he'd "rather be a peddler" than king.

But we know better. For Olivier the director wisely had Olivier the actor deliver Richard's soliloquies to us, in a direct manner to suggest it gives him pleasure to reveal his diabolical nature, confess heinous past crimes, and plot aloud his future atrocities to an audience who can do nothing about it. As Pauline Kael contends, Olivier "makes Shakespeare's 'son of hell' such a magnetic, chilling, amusing monster that the villainy arouses an almost immoral delight." He clearly, emphatically, pridefully states that "I am subtle, false, and treacherous," and that his single purpose is to "torment myself to catch the English throne." He admits having murdered Edward, the Prince of Wales; his desire to marry and then do away with Edward's widow, the Lady Anne (Claire Bloom); and his scheme to move closer to the ultimate prize. As Kael points out, "Olivier succeeds with the soliloquies as neither he nor anyone else on film before." She notes that "they're intimate but brazen." He is as straightforward with us as he is duplicitous with those in the English court. As he strides into a long shot so we can get a good look at his gnarled form or moves to within an inch of the camera, he reveals a sly wit, a frightening ferocity and egocentricity, and a snide superiority and vengeful anger toward the nondeformed world he wants "to bustle in." What is jolting as he speaks to us is that he isn't the typical madman lusting for power, but a clear-headed, ambitious schemer extraordinaire.

Olivier's Richard expresses the same amusement and amazement as we do that his bold plot works so smoothly, that he can eliminate his opposition one by one without anyone being the wiser, and that, in a creepy scene, he can seduce the virtuous Lady Anne and have her kiss him lewdly although she wants him dead and is not physically attracted to him. No one can resist him, no one even tries. At first we are his only confidants; then he plots with his wicked cousin Buckingham (Ralph Richardson). Eventually, he is quite open about his desires; for

Laurence Olivier's treacherous Richard seduces Claire Bloom's Lady Anne, although she despises him, in *Richard III.*

instance, when he wants to get rid of his two young nephews, he simply says, "Shall I be plain—I wish the bastards dead." He is actually fond of some of those he kills along the way ("I do love thee so," he says of his cousin Clarence, played by John Gielgud, "but I will shortly send thy soul to heaven") and is warmed by their love for him. But he is of single purpose. What becomes clear is that of all the wimps, moral men, and children who might have ruled, none was more fitting to be king than this ruthless monster. He is the only one who can accomplish *anything,* whose vision isn't clouded by guilt, sentiment, or superstition.

However, Olivier's Richard doesn't prove to be a strong leader. His dream comes true when he *becomes* king: how he eases into his throne, how he loves having men who once disrespected him bow and kiss his hand, how he relishes being able openly to give orders of execution. But though he gloats, his sense of purpose has vanished. He doesn't have the pleasure of ruling the people who had been above him, because he has rid the world of the last of them, and now he has time to sleep—which I sense Olivier's ever-calculating Richard never did while in pursuit of the throne. Suddenly, in deep, agonizing dreams, he recalls his crimes and is stabbed by the accusatory looks and words ("Despair and die!") of his victims. He had coveted the crown with every fiber of his wretched being, but alone on Bosworth Field, when knocked to the ground in the heat of battle, his crown rolling away, he is willing to trade, even up, "my kingdom for a horse!" Too late are his priorities in good order.

▶ BEST ACTRESS

WINNER:
Ingrid Bergman *(Anastasia)*
Other Nominees: Carroll Baker *(Baby Doll)*, Katharine Hepburn *(The Rainmaker)*, Nancy Kelly *(The Bad Seed)*, Deborah Kerr *(The King and I)*

▼

THE BEST CHOICE:
Katharine Hepburn *(The Rainmaker)*
Award-Worthy Runners-Up: Carroll Baker *(Baby Doll)*, Ingrid Bergman *(Anastasia)*, Judy Holliday *(The Solid Gold Cadillac)*, Marilyn Monroe *(Bus Stop)*

Twentieth Century–Fox gave Ingrid Bergman her first part in an American film in six years, the lead in *Anastasia*. In doing so it broke the unofficial Hollywood blacklisting of Bergman for having had an affair with Italian director Roberto Rossellini while she was still married and having had his baby three months before they were legally free to marry. In Anatole Litvak's turgid drama, in a role played by Viveca Lindfors on Broadway, Bergman portrayed a derelict amnesiac who is hired to pose as the long-missing daughter of the deposed Czar Nicholas II of Russia—and may in fact be her. Hollywood and all Americans suddenly got collective amnesia and forgot the scandal, welcoming Bergman back with open arms. Her friendly reception freed the Academy members to vote her Best Actress without fear of negative feedback. Bergman gave a strong, highly emotional performance, but today it seems like she wasted it in a dull, uninterestingly directed picture. I much prefer watching Katharine Hepburn in *The Rainmaker,* in the role Geraldine Page played on the stage.

As in the theater, Joseph Anthony directed; N. Richard Nash adapted his own play. Kansas is in the midst of a terrible drought. Spinster Lizzie Curry returns from visiting relatives to the family ranch where she lives with her kindly father, H.C. (Cameron Prud'Homme), her dominating brother Noah (Lloyd Bridges), and loving, high-strung younger brother Jim (Earl Holliman). She is smart and funny, but believes she is plain-looking. She is extremely lonely and wants so much to get married, but no men are interested in her. She has a crush on the sheriff, File (Wendell Corey), but he shows no interest in her or any other woman. The men try to manipulate File into courting Lizzie, but he resists. When he visits, Lizzie makes a fool of herself trying to act less smart than she really is so he won't be intimidated. Tired of watching Lizzie's heart being broken, Noah coldly informs Lizzie that she'll be an old maid and she might as well get used to the idea. But then her life changes when a fast-talking con man, Starbuck (a splendid performance by Burt Lancaster), rides up to the ranch and convinces H.C. to pay him to bring rain to the land. Lizzie is annoyed by Starbuck for tricking her father, but when the persuasive, enthusiastic dreamer admonishes her for not having faith in him or in herself, she is taken with him. He is

downright inspiring. They have a few hours of romance, during which time he convinces her that she is beautiful, and that she is entitled to her dreams of happiness. He almost convinces her to ride away with him, but when File shows up to arrest Starbuck for swindles elsewhere and shows deep interest in Lizzie and jealousy toward Starbuck, she decides to stay behind. She will marry File. Starbuck is thrilled because for the first time in his career, the rain he promised pours down.

I selected Hepburn as the Best Actress of 1935 for *Alice Adams,* and now I am giving her a second Alternate Oscar for again playing someone with much love to give, but without confidence and without a suitor. Hepburn reveals the same warmth and sympathy for Lizzie as she did for Alice. Like Alice she tries too hard and dreams for—we wrongly assume—too much. Her Lizzie almost breaks the hearts of her father and brothers: "Pride—I ran out of that a long time ago. I just want to be a woman: . . . I want—I want to make somebody happy. I want somebody to be glad he found me the way I'll be glad I

Katharine Hepburn's happiness will be short-lived after being welcomed home by her brothers, Lloyd Bridges and Earl Holliman, and father, Cameron Prud'Homme, in *The Rainmaker.*

found him. I want him to be able to tell me who he is and to tell me who I am too . . . because heaven knows I have no idea who I am. And I want to be able to do things for him . . . all kinds of things, and he never has to say 'thank you' because 'thank you' is our whole life together." Of course, Hepburn delivers this speech in a way to tug at your heart. But to be honest, in the early part of the picture I'm not all that fond of her characterization. Even if the point is that Lizzie doesn't have much life in her—the arid land symbolizes her—there still should be some spark for File and Starbuck to respond to. However, Hepburn loosens up soon after and completely wins me over—I think this is one of her best post–*African Queen* roles. She just had to wait for her character to be stimulated—by File's visit, Noah's cruelty toward her, and Starbuck's convincing compliments. She makes us feel Lizzie's needless desperation around dull

File (Hepburn herself is hilarious), when she nervously flirts with him (he tells her to stop and be herself); her great hurt when Noah insults her; and her elation when Starbuck takes her in his arms out in the barn.

The romantic scene between Lizzie and Starbuck is among the most memorable in Hepburn's career. Every kiss brings her Lizzie further to life. Her time with Starbuck is a wonderful experience of the sort she had worried would always be denied her. She looks into his appreciative eyes: "I can't believe what I see. Is it me? Is it really me?" It is really she whom she sees reflected. "Are you plain, Lizzie?" he asks. "No, I'm beautiful," she says, firmly believing him. And we agree. As they kiss, Hepburn's Lizzie truly looks ravishing. "The world's turned clear around," she says happily. Because of Starbuck the rain falls heavily on Kansas and Lizzie is "fertile," ready for File's love, marriage, and children.

1957

▶ BEST PICTURE

WINNER:
The Bridge on the River Kwai (Columbia; David Lean)
Other Nominees: *Peyton Place, Sayonara, 12 Angry Men, Witness for the Prosecution*

▼

THE BEST CHOICE:
Paths of Glory (United Artists; Stanley Kubrick)
Award-Worthy Runners-Up: *A Face in the Crowd* (Elia Kazan), *Sweet Smell of Success* (Alexander Mackendrick), *12 Angry Men* (Sidney Lumet)

For the second consecutive year the Academy's choice for Best Picture was an epic. David Lean's 161-minute *The Bridge on the River Kwai* combined the talents of the English, American, and Japanese to the tune of seven Oscars overall. The year's other critically acclaimed antiwar film, Stanley Kubrick's low-budget black-and-white *Paths of Glory,* won no Oscars, received no nominations. Adapted from Pierre Boulle's novel by Boulle and, uncredited, the blacklisted Michael Wilson and Carl Foreman, Lean's World War II picture is set in a Japanese POW camp located between Burma and Siam and is about a stubborn, by-the-books British colonel (Best Actor winner Alec Guinness), who foolishly accepts the challenge of the camp commander (Sessue Hayakawa) to have his troops build a railroad bridge for their captors. Meanwhile an American who escaped the camp (William Holden) and a staunch British officer (Jack Hawkins) are dispatched to blow up the bridge. The acting and visuals are still impressive, but the film's weak structure (we

leave behind the Guinness-Hayakawa story line just when we'd be forced to decide to root for or against the British soldiers who race against time to build the bridge) and a wild, confusing, thematically ambiguous ending betrays the film's fascinating premise. Its reputation has diminished while Kubrick's film has come to be regarded as a masterpiece.

Adapted from Humphrey Cobb's 1935 novel by Kubrick, Calder Willingham, and Jim Thompson, *Paths of Glory* is set in France (although it was filmed in Germany) during World War I. The head of the French command (Adolphe Menjou) appoints a glory-seeking general (George Macready) to supervise an attack on an enemy position called "the anthill." Macready orders a sympathetic colonel (Kirk Douglas, who convinced United Artists to make the picture) to order the suicidal attack, although he assumes half of the men will be killed. When almost all the men who leave their trenches are mowed down, Macready tries to force advancement by having the survivors fired upon—but he can't get that order obeyed. With his mission a failure, Macready terms the men cowards and wants them punished. Menjou agrees to have each of the three platoons randomly select one man to stand trial for treason. Douglas, a lawyer before the war, defends the three soldiers (Ralph Meeker, Joseph Turkel, Timothy Carey) but isn't allowed to build a case in the army's kangaroo court. Although Douglas tells Menjou about Macready's order to fire on his men, Menjou allows the execution to be carried out. Only then does Menjou order an inquiry into Macready's action. He asks Douglas to take over Macready's position. He refuses. The rest of the men are called back to the trenches.

Like *The Bridge on the River Kwai, Paths of Glory* is about the madness of war and is an attack on the military mind. While the film sidestepped controversy in America because it is about the French army in World War I (which explains why it was banned in France until 1970), Kubrick meant his film to apply to self-serving officers in all armies who, traditionally, have sacrificed their own men, their pawns, rather than look weak. While it doesn't actually state that wars shouldn't be fought, it *is* an antiwar film because it makes it clear that *all* armies are led by narrow-minded career officers like Macready and Menjou ("troops are like children in that they . . . crave discipline—and one way to maintain discipline is to shoot a man now and then"), men who are obsessed with flag, country, and image and have no regard for the obedient soldiers in the trenches. As Douglas reminds the crazed Macready, "Patriotism is the last refuge of a scoundrel."

In his autobiography Douglas claimed Kubrick rewrote Willingham's original script to make it more commercial and in his revised script had Menjou commute the death sentences to thirty days and made him and Douglas friends at the end—sort of like Bogart and Rains at the end of *Casablanca*. But Douglas refused to do that weaker picture and Kubrick went back to the mercilessly uncompromising first script. There is nothing commercial in this picture. Even the trial is without clever twists or histrionics. Scene by scene the story just gets bleaker and bleaker. We end up with the disillusioned, condemned Turkel attacking a priest; Turkel and Meeker fighting and Turkel being knocked out; the tough, mean-looking Timothy Carey weeping inconsolably, and the three men being executed without fanfare—Turkel is even revived from unconsciousness just in time to see the firing squad take aim.

If the film has a weakness, it's that it is just too easy to agree with the director's point of view (as it is with the same year's liberal courtroom drama *12 Angry Men,* my favorite nominated film of 1957). At least in *The Bridge on the River Kwai,* Guinness's officer is given the opportunity to express a "sensible" personal philosophy about why he is ordering his men to build the Japanese bridge. We then can reject it. It might have been a good idea to allow Menjou the opportunity to express his personal philosophy—I'm sure we would have rejected it as well. The deck is just too stacked. I also don't like Douglas's last line to Menjou—"I pity you." It sounds false and

In Stanley Kubrick's antimilitaristic *Paths of Glory,* George Macready stands between Kirk Douglas and Richard Anderson, who are the opposing attorneys in the court-martial trial he has demanded.

weak, a cliché: that's also the last line the moral Susan Harrison delivers to her corrupt brother Burt Lancaster before walking out on him at the end of the same year's *Sweet Smell of Success.*

But everything else rings true and has impact. The acting is first rate (especially by the breathlessly maniacal Macready)—the characters are essentially "types" but they all come across as distinct people. The dialogue is sharp and original, especially in the many confrontation scenes involving two or three characters. There are bits of dialogue and numerous scenes atypical of war movies, as well as moments that recall films like *The Red Badge of Courage* (in an impressive tracking shot Macready moves along through the trenches, giving similar pep talks to individual soldiers before battle), *Attack!* (cowardly officer Wayne Morris reminds one of Eddie Albert), and *Patton* (Macready slaps a soldier). And Kubrick's direction of both dialogue and action scenes is exceptional. I like in particular how he uses light in night sequences to build tension. I also appreciate that he took time to figure out how much of his characters' bodies should be in the frame during each scene. He's most effective when he places two or three characters in a poorly lit, enclosed space, shoots them so only their shoulders and heads are in frame, and has them argue with each other. There are so many of these tight shots that when Kubrick pulls back to shoot Douglas sitting/lying on his bed while giving orders to the standing Wayne Morris—informing the cowardly officer that he must lead the firing squad—we can feel the queasy Morris's disorientation.

The lack of attention received by *Paths of Glory* kept the twenty-eight-year-old Kubrick from achieving the notoriety he aspired to at the time. He'd make *Spartacus* in 1960 and *Lolita* in 1962, but he really wouldn't become famous until 1964, when he directed another much-debated film about the insanity of war, *Dr. Strangelove.* What's frightening is that the mad generals in that comedy aren't all that different from the realistic generals in *Paths of Glory.*

▶ BEST ACTOR

WINNER:

Alec Guinness *(The Bridge on the River Kwai)*

Other Nominees: Marlon Brando *(Sayonara)*, Anthony Franciosa *(A Hatful of Rain)*, Charles Laughton *(Witness for the Prosecution)*, Anthony Quinn *(Wild Is the Wind)*

▼

THE BEST CHOICE:

Andy Griffith *(A Face in the Crowd)*

Award-Worthy Runners-Up: Tony Curtis *(Sweet Smell of Success)*, William Holden *(The Bridge on the River Kwai)*, Charles Laughton *(Witness for the Prosecution)*

After years of great performances in black-and-white British films, Alec Guinness finally received international attention and a Best Actor Oscar by costarring with American superstar William Holden in David Lean's big-budget blockbuster *The Bridge on the River Kwai.* It was ostensibly a British film, but it had American financing, distribution, and promotion. In this "madness-of-war" film, set in a Japanese prisoner-of-war camp located between Burma and Siam in 1943, Guinness played Colonel Nicholson, an obsessively resolute British officer who is determined to keep the command and respect of his men even in this hostile setting. To keep them disciplined ("Without law there is no civilization") and to give them renewed pride in being British soldiers, he *motivates* them—he isn't a martinet—to hurriedly build an impressive railroad bridge for their Japanese captors, who have failed at this endeavor. He doesn't take into account that he is collaborating with the enemy, and that the bridge is not a testament to British ingenuity but to the foolishness of its officers. Guinness gave a fine characterization, but I don't think that after he figured out his voice and walk in preproduction, the role was much of a challenge. Nicholson's such a one-note character that he is nearly a John Cleese–like send-up of staunch British officers.

Strong, wrongheaded individuals with the power to manipulate the troops/masses into doing their bidding had been turning up on the screen with increasing frequency since *All the King's Men* and *The Big Carnival/Ace in the Hole,* and in 1957 General Nicholson had company: Burt Lancaster's vicious gossip columnist in *Sweet Smell of Success,* George Macready's glory-hungry general in *Paths of Glory,* and, best of all, Andy Griffith's ambitious, folksy philosopher in Elia Kazan's *A Face in the Crowd.* Some critics found Griffith loud and overbearing as "Lonesome" Rhodes, but I think Rhodes sticks in our memory just for that reason. Surely, the unnominated Griffith didn't rival Guinness as an actor, but he's my choice for 1957's Best Actor.

In Pickett, Arkansas, Marsha (Patricia Neal), a roving radio reporter, does a live interview with "Lonesome" Rhodes, a transient she discovers in jail. Playing guitar and offering homespun humor, Lonesome is a natural near a microphone. After his release he gets his own radio program, where his pointed stories about relatives and philosophizing about what's troubling the poor people in America earn him great popularity. He then becomes a national television star, spokesman for an ineffective vitamin (that thrives because of his endorsement), and champion of the common people. He is thrilled by his ability to sway the American public. Marsha knows that he is a fake, but loves him too much to leave him. He needs Marsha, but—after buying off his ex-wife—marries a seventeen-year-old baton twirler (Lee Remick). He helps change the image of a dull senator whom the ultraconservatives are running for president. With the senator in the White House he'll be appointed secretary of national morale and could become the most powerful man in the country. Only Marsha can stop him. She does so by sabotaging his live television broadcast and letting the national audience hear what he says about them when he thinks the microphone is off. Lonesome insults his audience and his popularity takes an immediate nosedive.

A Face in the Crowd was the debut film for Griffith, who had made a splash on Broadway as the naive, harmless country boy who joins the army in the comedy

An adoring public is taken in by Andy Griffith's Lonesome Rhodes in Elia Kazan's cynical *A Face in the Crowd.*

No Time for Sergeants. For Griffith fans who saw that play or the film adaptation (which Griffith made after *A Face in the Crowd*), or who got used to his easygoing country sheriff in the long-running *Andy Griffith Show*, Lonesome Rhodes is quite a shock, a perversion of the other two characters (and of the naive Griffith of comedy albums). Lonesome is abrasive, ambitious, shrewd, and manipulative, making a mockery of the people who trust him. He never lets up: he sings loudly, he grins from ear to ear. He talks so ostentatiously, so incessantly, so enthusiastically, and with so many inflections and sound effects, that it's amazing he doesn't go hoarse or those around him don't lose their hearing. The North Carolina–born Griffith studied to be a preacher, and that's evident in this volcanic performance, where Lonesome continually takes center stage and, with unbridled energy and the right mix of superiority and humility, attempts to convince everyone around him that he is right.

Only, this "preacher" is a fraud, a sinner. As his fame and power mount, Lonesome is in ecstasy. He seems to be having rapid-fire orgasms as he lies in bed and moves his head from side to side as he names each type of person who agrees with his every word. When under-aged majorettes run toward this national folk hero, he doesn't duck for cover but runs into their arms, happily accepting their hugs and kisses and saying, "Oh, it's wonderful!" At first he is frightened by his own power, but soon he can't stop bragging about it, usually repeating himself: "Just put yourself in my hands—I'll have them loving him—I mean loving him!"; "I'm not just an entertainer, I'm an influence . . . A force! A force!" Griffith

makes his character more and more monstrous—he sings about being a "Free Man" but he should be shackled. Telling Marsha about his new name for a grassroots group to back the senator, he asks rhetorically, "How do you like that name? Huh? Huh? Huh? Huh?" Here Griffith, with sweaty body and fists clinched, gives one chills. On the TV shows, when Lonesome expounds his conservative philosophy to redneck sycophants (in scenes staged like those on *Hee Haw*), he is merely creepy. When Lonesome has made a fool of himself on national television and no one shows up for his lavish dinner and he hugs the servants in an effort to get them to say they love him, Griffith's character is pathetic. But we aren't meant to feel pity for *him*—but shame that *we*, the media-influenced public, would make such a man into a hero.

At the end he stands alone in his penthouse, rejected by his fans and screaming to Marsha below to return to him, trying to manipulate her once more. But she leaves (just as Susan Harrison leaves brother Burt Lancaster high above in his apartment at the end of *Sweet Smell of Success*). Lonesome learns that it really is lonely at the top.

The monster out of his system, Griffith would never play such a high-strung, explosive character again. In fact, he made only a handful of comedies before finding his niche on television, first in his comedy series and later in *Matlock*, playing a lawyer. It's almost too bad, because he was capable of playing a villain different from all others who appeared in the cinema. I say "almost," because I don't think anyone could stand to see *or hear* another Lonesome Rhodes.

▶ BEST ACTRESS

WINNER:
Joanne Woodward *(The Three Faces of Eve)*
Other Nominees: Deborah Kerr *(Heaven Knows, Mr. Allison)*, Anna Magnani *(Wild Is the Wind)*, Elizabeth Taylor *(Raintree County)*, Lana Turner *(Peyton Place)*

▼

THE BEST CHOICE:
Joanne Woodward *(The Three Faces of Eve)*
Award-Worthy Runners-Up: Deborah Kerr *(Heaven Knows, Mr. Allison)*, Patricia Neal *(A Face in the Crowd)*

After being pushed off a roof in her second film, the original *A Kiss Before Dying*, Joanne Woodward reached new heights in her third film. She won a much-deserved Oscar for *The Three Faces of Eve*, director-writer-producer Nunnally Johnson's biographical case study about a woman with a multiple-personality disorder. It helped that Woodward was a relative unknown without a specific screen image, because it allowed her to take her unusual character in any direction she wanted and to play three distinct personalities without viewers' being forced to suspend disbelief. It would be difficult enough for them to accept the truth-based story.

Eve White, a dull, drab Georgia housewife and mother, suffers from blackouts and headaches, so her family doctor sends her to psychiatrist Dr. Luthor (Lee J. Cobb). She seems to be getting better when her angry husband, Ralph (David Wayne), brings her into Luthor's office, telling Luthor that Eve tried to strangle their daughter. Eve doesn't remember this happening. Luthor is surprised when a second personality emerges, Eve Black. Eve Black is mischievous, sexy, and irresponsible. She likes to have a good time and doesn't see what's wrong with that, since she insists she's not married and not a mother. She says she wanted only to scare Eve White's daughter. Eve Black doesn't like Eve White and since childhood has let Eve White take punishment for her troublemaking. Ralph is too simple to understand the complicated nature of his wife's problem. Impatient, he takes a job in Florida. Luthor treats Eve, calling on both parts of her personality during each session. He fears that Eve Black is taking control. Eve goes to Ralph in Florida; during her stay there, her alter ego emerges and makes a spectacle of herself, going out on the town and carousing. When Eve White returns from the evening out, remembering nothing, the furious Ralph slaps her. Eve decides to divorce him. At one point she almost commits suicide. Therapy continues. Eve Black herself now suffers blackouts. A third personality emerges, Jane, who is strong, smart, and well balanced. Jane falls in love but postpones marriage until she feels she is cured, and can remember Eve White's past. Eve White feels she is fading away. Luthor compels Eve-Jane to remember a traumatic incident from her youth: she was forced to kiss her dead grandmother. The shock of this event was the origin of her disorder. Jane now remembers everything. Eve White and Eve Black are gone and Jane has taken over. She will marry because she is cured.

Interestingly, the real Eve, Christine Sizemore, wasn't yet cured, despite what her therapist, Dr. Corbett Thigpen (with Dr. Harvey M. Cleckley) wrote in the book on which the film was based. She would see four more therapists, and attempt suicide, before she found the psychiatrist who cured her at age sixty, seventeen years after this movie was made. Twenty-two personalities emerged during those years, three at a time. But in 1957, long before *Sybil*, the three-pronged Eve was about all viewers could handle (the movie's premise genuinely *shocked* us); and to think that the lovely, sensitive Woodward's character had not been cured would have been too much for them to stand.

While the film has lost much of its initial power (a great deal of the script is foolish), Woodward is still compelling, whether she is quiet, hysterical, naughty, flirtatious, creepy, sweet, weak, or strong. Although she wasn't fond of her own performance because she felt she couldn't devote enough time to any of Eve's three personalities, it is one of her best. At the time it was an ideal showcase for this versatile actress, whose talents were still a secret. Many major actresses wanted the multicharacter, every-emotion-on-display part, which was ready made for critical accolade ("a tour de force performance") *if* the actress were capable of doing a great job as three distinct people. Woodward was capable of this difficult task and was thoroughly convincing as the mousy, boring, gentle Eve White; the cheap, crude, playful Eve Black; and the dignified, responsible, calm Jane— although Woodward drops her Southern accent as Jane, seemingly to emphasize the character's intelligence (despite having been born in Georgia herself). She has many

Lee J. Cobb's psychiatrist is disturbed when the vulgar Eve Black emerges in *The Three Faces of Eve,* for which young Joanne Woodward deservedly won a Best Actress Oscar.

exceptional scenes, including her emotional sessions with the psychiatrist as the confused, pained Eve White and her nights on the prowl as the sexy, hedonistic Eve Black. My favorite scene is extremely moving: Eve White, realizing that she's fading away, speaks to her daughter for the last time as herself—she knows that the next time, another woman (Jane) will be in her body, mother to her child.

There is, quite properly, always a sense of sadness to Woodward's performance, in all three incarnations of Eve. I think it's significant that she even makes us feel sorry for Eve Black when she starts to fade away. Because whatever her faults, Eve Black was essentially a real person, with fears and worries of her own, and her death is somewhat tragic (since she didn't actually try to kill the child). In fact, the most interesting aspect of the film is that when Eve Black wasn't destroying Eve White's life, she was actually helping her. She is presented as a manifestation of timid Eve White's rebellion against her sexually repressive husband. Eve White should thank those actions of Eve Black (chasing men, buying sexy clothes) which prompted Ralph's hostile reactions that, in turn, motivated Eve White to leave him and her unhealthy marriage. In fact, she sacrificed herself for Eve White's happiness. Once Ralph is gone, Eve White can break free and reveal those once-repressed sides of her personality and become a full woman: Jane. Woodward's Eve Black, who shared so much with Woodward's Eve White, is now obsolete with the exile of Ralph and the simultaneous, gradual emergence of Jane. But I think that her subsequent disappearance is as painful to watch as the dismantling of the "sick" HAL computer in *2001: A Space Odyssey.* If you look back, Eve Black provided this film with almost all of its life.

1958

▶ BEST PICTURE

WINNER:
Gigi (MGM; Vincente Minnelli)
Other Nominees: *Auntie Mame, Cat on a Hot Tin Roof, The Defiant Ones, Separate Tables*

▼

THE BEST CHOICE:
Touch of Evil (Universal; Orson Welles)
Award-Worthy Runners-Up: None

Gigi was a successful attempt by MGM to make the movie equivalent of the popular 1956 Broadway musical *My Fair Lady*. Its source was Colette's novelette (which had been turned into a French play, a 1950 French movie, and a Broadway play with Audrey Hepburn) about a teenage girl in turn-of-the-century Paris who is trained by a wealthy aunt to be a courtesan. *My Fair Lady* composers Lerner and Loewe cleansed the story so that it's about a happy-go-lucky adolescent (Leslie Caron) who takes daily lessons on being a *lady*, causing a longtime family friend (Louis Jourdan) to see her in a new light. Meanwhile, her grandmother (Hermione Gingold) is courted by a long-ago suitor (Maurice Chevalier). Directed by Vincente Minnelli and produced by Arthur Freed, *Gigi* is a lavish, uplifting film with charming performances and a fine score. It didn't deserve to win a record nine Oscars, but the Academy voters figured that a film liked by most everyone was a safe choice. Today, many moviegoers and critics would champion Alfred Hitchcock's disturbing *Vertigo* as 1958's Best Picture, but while I acknowledge it has a brilliant premise and many fascinating elements, I think that it eventually takes the wrong turn, switching from being a bizarre mystery to an unpleasant character study of a love-obsessed man. My choice for Best Picture is Orson Welles's B melodrama, *Touch of Evil,* one of the most excitingly directed pictures of the decade.

The film is set in a wild Mexican border town, where someone plants a bomb in the car of prominent American Rudy Linneker. He and his mistress are killed while driving through customs. The crime is investigated by heralded American detective cop Hank Quinlan (Welles), aided by his idolizing partner Pete Menzies (Joseph Calleia). Quinlan resents that his investigation is being observed by a respected young Mexican narcotics officer, Mike Vargas (Charlton Heston), who postpones his honeymoon with his American bride, Susie (Janet Leigh). While Vargas is away, Susie is threatened by Papa Grandi (Akim Tamiroff), head of the town's vice now that Vargas

has thrown his brother in jail. Grandi tells her that Vargas had better not build a case against his brother. When one of Grandi's young thugs tries to throw acid in Vargas's face, Vargas sends Susie to a "safe" American motel, not realizing that it's owned by Grandi. Meanwhile, the Mexican-hating Quinlan arrests a murder suspect, Sanchez (Victor Millan), a young Mexican whom Linneker didn't want for a son-in-law. But Vargas realizes that Quinlan set up Sanchez, planting dynamite in the boy's apartment so that Menzies could find the "evidence." Investigating Quinlan's past, Vargas discovers this has been his modus operandi for getting arrests and convictions. He threatens to expose Quinlan to authorities. Quinlan decides to discredit Vargas. Susie is drugged by Grandi's youth gang and placed unclothed in a cheap hotel. Quinlan strangles Grandi and leaves his body next to Susie so she'll be arrested. But Menzies discovers Quinlan's cane there and realizes his partner has tried to frame her. Disillusioned, he wears a wire so Vargas can get evidence on his friend. Quinlan discovers the ploy and, hurt at the betrayal, shoots Menzies. Before he can kill Vargas, the dying Menzies kills his idol.

Orson Welles had long been unable to get financing to direct an American, major-studio film. But in 1957 he had the good fortune to act for producer Albert Zugsmith in Universal's low-budget *Man in the Shadow.* Zugsmith became so fond of Welles that when Universal assigned him a script adapted from Whit Masterson's *Badge of Evil,* he convinced the studio to let Welles direct, rewrite the script, and play the villain of the piece. Given free rein, Welles had the most fun he'd had since he first came to Hollywood and made 1941's *Citizen Kane,* when he compared filmmaking to playing with an electric train. *Touch of Evil* was something new: a trashy work of art. Everything on the screen was down and dirty: the locations were sleazy, the characters were seedy or downright perverse, and the story involved sex, drugs, corruption, abduction, murder, betrayal, and racism. While the characters wallow in a hellhole, the film exists on a much

Orson Welles's corrupt American detective produces false evidence for Charlton Heston's honest Mexican officer in the Welles-directed *Touch of Evil.*

higher plane. (Watching the aged, smiling Chevalier sing "Thank Heaven for Little Girls" is a much more uncomfortable experience.) It is a sharply written, complex character study of three men—Vargas, Quinlan, and Menzies—and an intriguing exploration of the unusual relationships between Mexican Vargas and American racist Quinlan; Mexican Vargas and American Susie; Quinlan and Menzies; and Quinlan and Marlene Dietrich's Tanya, a prostitute who has known him for many years.

Moreover, it is among the most technically audacious and awe-inspring films in Welles's career. Even casual viewers will realize that everything in this film is the result of a director's constantly making choices in regard to the placement of actors within the frame, scene lighting, and camera movement in relation to his interacting performers, props, and sets. He experimented with sound, music (composed by Henry Mancini), space (cinematographer Russell Metty used deep-focus photography), editing, and unusual camera angles. The astonishing, lengthy one-take opening, which begins a few blocks on the Mexican side of the border and ends up on the American side, is deservedly legendary. Metty panned, lifted, boomed, and lowered his camera to follow the action, which involved the placement of dynamite in Linneker's car trunk, the car being driven across the border, the introduction of Vargas and Susie, and an explosion at the exact moment the newlyweds kiss. Almost as impressive is the intricate one-take scene in Sanchez's small apartment, in which Quinlan grills Sanchez, Vargas knocks over an empty shoebox, and action takes place all over the tiny space as Metty's camera moves every which way—we understand just how trapped Sanchez feels.

Welles shoots his story as if it were a nightmare. The isolated-motel sequence prefigures *Psycho:* Janet Leigh's sexy Susie (Welles, as Alfred Hitchcock would, emphasized Leigh's large chest) meets a skinny "night man"

(Dennis Weaver) who is an infantile sex degenerate; and, while scantily clad, is tormented and drugged by a youth gang headed by a forty-year-old, leather-jacketed lesbian (Mercedes McCambridge at her most bizarre). Welles's Tijuana-like Mexican border town (Masterson's major setting was an unspecified California city) is a creepy night world of bars, strip joints, and run-down hotels, where main drags that are crowded with strippers, sailors, and juvenile delinquents run perpendicular to empty, spooky film-noirish side streets and alleys. All of the police are on the take, vice laws are being broken behind every door. Welles uses his border town thematically, to call attention to the divisions between Mexicans and Americans; past, present, future; wild frontier towns and civilization; law and anarchy; and the reality and the reputation of both the corrupt Quinlan and Vargas's Mexico. It is the proper setting for conflict between the young, just-married Mexican Vargas (in the book, the character is American and has been married for years) and the American Quinlan, an aging thirty-year widower. Vargas is nowhere near the detective Quinlan is, but with his strong morality and sense of justice (not to mention better grooming habits), he's the better role model. That the Mexican is the hero and the American the villain is one way in which *Touch of Evil* breaks the rules.

Welles wore a putty nose, makeup that aged him twenty years, a sloppy outfit, and additional padding to play Quinlan, a character who dominates the frame and the picture itself. At a time when Welles's reputation kept him from getting assignments, he must have felt great satisfaction playing a character whose good reputation gives him freedom to do anything he wants. Quinlan is one of his many fragile tragic heroes, potentially great men who have sold out their integrity and morality to smooth the path to their particular thrones. And having achieved power, they now abuse it. We sympathize with Quinlan because his crimes against criminals are acts of revenge: his wife's murderer had got off scot-free because of lack of evidence. It does not escape us that the by-the-book Vargas himself resorts to two-fisted hooliganism when his wife is in trouble. We also realize that Quinlan (unlike the villain in the book) never frames anyone who is not guilty, including Sanchez. His motives are pure, if not his actions. "He *was* some kind of a man," states Tanya. But not anymore. When he reluctantly goes into cahoots with the vile Grandi to set up Susie and ruin Vargas, we realize he has stooped so low that he must be stopped. Like most of Welles's movies, from *Citizen Kane* to *Chimes at Midnight, Touch of Evil* deals with loyalty and betrayal between friends. When Menzies rejects Quinlan for Vargas, Quinlan correctly feels betrayed by the one man he loves and trusts, and whose adoration he thrives on. Asked if she loved Quinlan, Tanya says with Dietrich's characteristic irony, "The cop did. The one who killed him. He loved him." As in *The Third Man,* where writer Joseph Cotten's Holly Martins begrudgingly helps the police trap his longtime friend, Welles's drug-dealing Harry Lime, the strange theme of *Touch of Evil* is: *Betrayal can be more moral than loyalty.*

► BEST ACTOR

WINNER:
David Niven *(Separate Tables)*
Other Nominees: Tony Curtis *(The Defiant Ones)*, Paul Newman *(Cat on a Hot Tin Roof)*, Sidney Poitier *(The Defiant Ones)*, Spencer Tracy *(The Old Man and the Sea)*

▼

THE BEST CHOICE:
Alec Guinness *(The Horse's Mouth)*
Award-Worthy Runners-Up: Rock Hudson *(The Tarnished Angels)*, Spencer Tracy *(The Last Hurrah)*

In 1958 the Academy agreed with the New York Film Critics and named David Niven the year's Best Actor. Niven gave what was probably his most respectable performance in the screen adaptation of Terence Rattigan's *Separate Tables,* playing what was probably his least respectable character: a boastful but untruthful "major," who turns out to be a child molester. As usual, Niven gave a solid, professional performance. Only, this time he was more serious than he had been in the many thankless roles he'd had in his career. Evidently, that was enough to convince the Academy that he deserved an Oscar. A handshake, maybe, not an Oscar. Perhaps the Academy was trying to make up for having ignored his Phileas Fogg two years before while giving numerous nominations to *Around the World in 80 Days?* Or maybe it just wanted to acknowledge a long career in which Niven began as a stuntman and worked his way up through the ranks. No matter that his career was as undistinguished as Douglas Fairbanks, Jr.'s, with light-weight continental roles in lots of films that could be described by the adjective *frothy.* Certainly, Niven's popularity in the Hollywood community—he was a nice, witty, gracious gentleman—was a contributing factor to his victory. Although part of the Hollywood community, Niven was the second Brit in a row to take home the Best Actor Oscar. Having won the award in 1957 for *The Bridge on the River Kwai,* Alec Guinness wasn't even nominated for his marvelous performance in 1958's *The Horse's Mouth,* though it surpassed both his own performance in David Lean's film and that of Niven in *Separate Tables.*

Guinness himself wrote the script adaptation of Joyce Cary's 1944 novel, long a staple of American college-literature courses. It was the third part of Cary's trilogy, following 1941's *Herself Surprised* and 1942's *To Be a Pilgrim,* which with compassion and wild passion, and wry and rowdy humor, presented individuals coping with an England that was changing socially and politically. Guinness played Cary's greatest creation, stubbornly iconoclastic painter Gulley Jimson, whose models included William Blake and Cary's friend Dylan Thomas.

Down and out, undisciplined, often drunk, Gulley lives on a decrepit boat, where he paints Adam, Eve, and the serpent on the walls in the near dark. His desire is to find large surfaces on which to paint his epic visions. He would have money if he could sell his old paintings, but his clever ex-wife (Renée Houston) sold all but one to the rich Hickson (Ernest Thesiger), who keeps them in his mansion and won't let Gulley near them. His bartender "girlfriend," Coker (Kay Walsh), goes with him to his ex-wife, in hopes of getting the one painting she owns. Gulley even flirts with her, but she won't give up the painting. When an unsuspecting bourgeois couple goes on vacation, Gulley takes over their apartment so he can paint *The Raising of Lazarus* on their wall. Hickson dies and Gulley's art is exhibited at the National Gallery. At last he is famous, but he's still broke. Again he tries to sweet-talk the painting away from his wife, but she outsmarts him. Depressed by his continuous bad luck, he is suddenly inspired when he sees a large bare wall in a church intended for demolition. He recruits many amateur artists to paint his gargantuan vision of *The Last Judgment.* They are happy to pay teacher fees to Gulley, now that he is famous. The painting is completed, but the demolition is not called off to preserve the masterwork. Gulley bulldozes the wall himself. He jumps on his boat and takes it downriver, enthusiastically looking for new horizons.

Coming between his authoritarian soldiers in *The Bridge on the River Kwai* and *Tunes of Glory,* Guinness's incorrigible anarchist artist was pretty much neglected by British moviegoers, who I suppose would have had a better response if this very funny picture were *funny* in the clear way Guinness's Ealing comedies had been funny. American critics have always had mixed reaction to Guinness in the film, usually taking a negative stance if they have uncommon affection for the Gulley in the novel. For instance, Pauline Kael contends that "Guinness's portrait of Gulley isn't all that one might hope (it lacks passion and innocence and the real fire of insolence)"—although it should be pointed out that while she found the entire film lacking, she admitted "how marvelously enjoyable it is." I'm inclined to agree with Harlan Jacobson, who wrote in *American Film* in 1983 that Guinness's Gulley "remains perhaps the best sketch of artist-as-bohemian in all cinema: neither Titan (Charlton Heston as Michelangelo) nor martyr (Kirk Douglas as Van Gogh) but a human bag of bones on comic-visionary overdrive." I'd go one step farther and state that Guinness gives one of the best, if not the best, sketches of an artist (the suffering, the creative process) of any kind in all of cinema.

Guinness has given some superb performances in his

In a "borrowed" apartment, eccentric artist Alec Guinness loses his temper with sculptor Michael Gough in Ronald Neame's adaptation of Joyce Cary's *The Horse's Mouth*.

career, but if he can be criticized for anything it is that once he devises a voice and a delivery, a walk, a posture, and an attitude for a particular character, he won't deviate at all from that characterization throughout the film. This applies to his Fagin in *Oliver Twist,* eight victims in *Kind Hearts and Coronets,* comic criminals in *The Ladykillers* and *The Lavender Hill Mob,* inventor in *The Man in the White Suit,* noble cardinal in *The Prisoner,* Colonel Nicholson in *The Bridge on the River Kwai,* red-haired martinet in *Tunes of Glory,* Obi Wan Kenobi in the *Star Wars* movies, and many other memorable characters. But while Gulley Jimson has a distinctly dry, unpleasant voice, coughs incessantly and annoyingly, has a stubbly beard, walks with quick, insecure steps on straight legs, has arms that are stiff against his sides, bad posture, and is always in need of a shave, a wash, and a change of clothes, his actions and even his moods are unpredictable. He's self-destructive and self-pitying ("Brick and broken glass and an old garbage can—that's the story of my life"), and probably sickly (he's had the cough for thirty years), but he constantly revives himself through his art. His art is what cheers him, keeps him alive, and motivates him to attempt absurd endeavors. He is usually grouchy, but at least the art makes him tolerable (of course, he accepts only self-criticism of his work). His most noble characteristic is that he'll try anything to keep painting (this is when Guinness is at his most hilarious): lying, flirting, flattering amateurs about their artistic gifts, audaciously confiscating the rich vacationers' apartment, charging art students to paint his artistic vision on a wall, pretending to be the high-voiced "Duchess of Blackpool" over the phone. In his personal relationship with Coker

he's passive, obedient, and shy (he won't even let her see him naked). But when it comes to his art, he is aggressive. We admire him for having so few scruples that one of his victims admits, "I want to cut off his head with a meat cleaver." Many people would send him to jail, but the prison guards have had enough of this uncivil, rambunctious rebel.

We'd almost think Gulley insane if it weren't for several moments when he talks about art and what it means to him. Guinness's character is suddenly clearheaded, wise, inspired and inspiring. It turns out that this man who runs his life in such a haphazard fashion has an intellectual approach to his art: "You have to know when you succeed, and when you fail, and why. Know thyself, in fact. In short, you have to think." We get into the mind of this artist when he recalls how he worked in an office until he saw a Matisse, which "skinned my eyes for me, and I became a different man. I had a conversion. I saw a new world—a world of color." He wants Coker to share a bit of that world with him, by trying to teach her "to feel the picture with your eyes . . . the lights and the shades, the cool and the warm." He wants her to feel the props and the people. He wants to teach her "a great happiness." He wants her to share his only happiness . . . but though she realizes he has talent, she can't understand what excites him and pushes him to create. No one but another great artist could grasp how he feels, what he sees, or what he paints. So it is that like all struggling, dedicated artists, he must remain alone and isolated, an irritant to society, an idol to aspiring young artists, an outsider, a visionary with a great new, but probably impossible, idea in his head.

▶ BEST ACTRESS

WINNER:
Susan Hayward *(I Want to Live!)*
Other Nominees: Deborah Kerr *(Separate Tables)*, Shirley MacLaine *(Some Came Running)*, Rosalind Russell *(Auntie Mame)*, Elizabeth Taylor *(Cat on a Hot Tin Roof)*

▼

THE BEST CHOICE:
Susan Hayward *(I Want to Live!)*
Award-Worthy Runners-Up: Ingrid Bergman *(The Inn of the Sixth Happiness)*, Kim Stanley *(The Goddess)*

Susan Hayward has pretty much been neglected since the sixties, when we film fanatics started ignoring those pictures that hadn't been directed by bona fide "auteurs." We weren't interested in Hayward's "star" vehicles of the forties and fifties because they were directed by craftsmen and studio pros rather than stylists. Consequently, we missed several powerhouse performances by a remarkable actress. I think she's the actress of that era who most needs rediscovery, and the best film to start with is *I Want to Live!,* which won her a Best Actress Oscar on her fifth and final nomination. Hayward played B-girl Barbara Graham, who'd gained coast-to-coast notoriety in 1955 when she was executed along with two male acquaintances in San Quentin for having allegedly participated in a disabled woman's murder. Robert Wise's picture, which takes a strong stance against capital punishment, supports Graham's innocence, contending that she was convicted in the press before her trial began. A major source for the strong Oscar-nominated script by Nelson Gidding and Don Mankiewicz were articles written in the *San Francisco Examiner* by Ed Montgomery (played in the film by Simon Oakland), who first thought her guilty and then became her chief advocate.

Hayward took the role without having read the script because she had been moved by the Graham case. Wise said that Hayward related to Graham. She'd had misfortunes herself. She'd had a difficult childhood in a Brooklyn tenement, furious battles with the press, and family problems throughout her life. In the fifties, after a divorce and a bitter custody battle for her twin sons, she attempted suicide—only to discover later that she wanted to live. Like Graham, who had a difficult childhood, was a target of the press, separated from her husband, and lost her child when she went to prison, Hayward was a tough woman who fought for her own survival, mostly against men (her husband, reporters, agents, judges, studio executives). "Barbara Graham had no way to fight back," wrote Wise in *Close-Ups,* "and this is what I think attracted Susan. She thought she understood what Graham had to contend with."

Hayward displays volcanic energy as this party girl who won't sit still even in the dentist's chair (yet won't allow herself to move when seated in the gas chamber before the unfriendly eyes of reporters). From the first time we see her, sitting up in the hotel-room bed and stretching in near ecstasy while her satisfied john lies beside her, she is always moving about, dancing (she loves jazz), hugging and kissing men, mingling with her wild crowd. Until she has a baby, life is to her the roll of the dice, as she often indicates with a wave of a clutched, then open hand. She takes her lumps, willingly making sacrifices and taking raps for irresponsible men, even going to jail on their behalf. She's so strong that she kicks out her husband, deals with crooks and cops, talks tough to everyone, and doesn't think she needs anyone to protect her. But she learns differently when she is arrested and

Still expressing independence despite being jailed, Susan Hayward's convicted murderer Barbara Graham wears a sexy nightgown in Robert Wise's *I Want to Live!*

the wolves try to devour her. Because she is a woman on death row, she is big news, and is exploited unmercifully. "I'm the little ball bouncing around the roulette wheel, everyone begging me to land where it's going to do *them* the most good. Circulation for the newspapers, promotion for the cops." But this tough cookie doesn't crack. She has her soft moments, even cries on occasion (mostly about losing her young son), but she's still defiant. On death row she throws her nightgown in the matron's face, and she refuses to be searched by a nurse: "Get this straight, Miss Bedpan, nobody's going to go pawing all over me. I'm through with all that stuff!" When the nurse introduces herself with "Hello, Barbara. My name's Barbara too," she replies, "I'm Mrs. Graham to you."

Hayward is convincing showing the gutsy, rough side of Graham, but some of her finest moments come when Graham calms down and speaks forthrightly to someone she is fond of. She reveals her integrity (her Graham is to be respected) when she demands that her lawyer not ask the governor for a reprieve: "Don't beg for my life."

Until late in the film all the men in the picture seem to have conspired against her (cops, the other men who were arrested for the murder and know the truth, her husband, Montgomery, the judge, the DA). However, she has some well-played, tender scenes with women: first with her friend (Virginia Vincent) who visits her in jail and touches Graham deeply by saying she knows she's innocent; and then with the nurse, who proves to be her caring friend-sister (she, too, was separated from her unworthy husband). Considering all the "important" things going on, it's surprisingly moving when Graham makes up with the nurse by telling her, "Barbara, my name's Barbara too." She even gives the nurse a toy tiger for her children. Only when Barbara knows that she isn't about to be attacked can she reveal her kind side.

We believe Hayward's Barbara Graham when she says, "I'm not afraid to die." The words are reassuring, but Hayward's heartfelt performance in the last few scenes makes us see the cruelty and criminality of the death penalty, as well as the lack of dignity accorded to those who are about to lose their lives. It is sickening to watch her death march and execution. We take consolation that Barbara was looking forward to coming "face to face" with the only one who knows of her innocence. Not God, she tells her priest, but the murder victim.

1959

▶ BEST PICTURE

WINNER:
Ben-Hur (MGM; William Wyler)
Other Nominees: *Anatomy of a Murder, The Diary of Anne Frank, The Nun's Story, Room at the Top*

▼

THE BEST CHOICE:
Some Like It Hot (Ashton-Mirisch/United Artists; Billy Wilder)
Award-Worthy Runners-Up: *North by Northwest* (Alfred Hitchcock), *Rio Bravo* (Howard Hawks)

In 1959 the Academy continued its trend of honoring big-budget productions when MGM's studio-saving biblical drama *Ben-Hur,* a mammoth remake of its 1925 silent classic, won an unprecedented eleven Oscars. These included Best Picture, for producer Sam Zimbalist; Best Director, for William Wyler; and Best Actor, for Charlton Heston, who played a suffering Jew who literally finds Christ. Significantly, it lost only in the writing category. Today, the great sea battle and spectacular climactic chariot race are still impressive, but they are no longer so overwhelming that we can ignore the banal script, which reworks too many elements found in Hes-

ton's *The Ten Commandments;* hasn't enough action sequences; and drags after the chariot-race death of Ben-Hur's nemesis, Messala (Stephen Boyd).

Ben-Hur must have seemed refreshingly simple-minded in a year that was dominated by sobering dramas—remember, this was the year of *The Diary of Anne Frank* and *On the Beach!* The other nominated films were a particularly downbeat group, with the only humor coming in Otto Preminger's *Anatomy of a Murder* when flustered lawyer James Stewart must question uninhibited Lee Remick about her wearing a girdle and panties. The year's most entertaining films evidently weren't con-

Jack Lemmon's "Daphne" and Marilyn Monroe's Sugar exchange girl talk in Billy Wilder's *Some Like It Hot*.

sidered serious enough to warrant Best Picture consideration, which is a shame because they were also the year's best films: Alfred Hitchcock's witty Cary Grant suspense thriller, *North by Northwest;* Howard Hawks's witty John Wayne western, *Rio Bravo;* and Billy Wilder's *Some Like It Hot,* one of the year's few outright comedies (and probably more shocking than any of the dramas) and my choice for the Oscar.

The setting is Chicago in 1929. Broke bass player Jerry (Jack Lemmon) and sax player Joe (Tony Curtis) witness Spats Columbo (George Raft) and his henchman murder several gangsters. They flee, but Spats gets a look at them. To get out of town they dress up as women—Jerry takes the name "Daphne," Joe becomes "Josephine"—and join Sweet Sue and her Society Syncopaters, an all-girl band headed for a Miami hotel. In their female guises they befriend lovely singer Sugar Kane (Marilyn Monroe), who confesses that she always falls in love with men who play the sax. But she wants to forget musicians and marry a shy millionaire with glasses. In Miami, Joe slips out of his female garb and pretends to be the spectacled millionaire Sugar wanted. She is impressed. Meanwhile, a real millionaire, Osgood Fielding (Joe E. Brown) falls for "Daphne." They go dancing, while Joe sneaks Sugar aboard Osgood's yacht, pretending it's his. They all fall in love. Jerry forgets he's a man and accepts Osgood's marriage proposal. But both relationships are placed in jeopardy when Spats and other gangsters arrive at the hotel. Spats spots Jerry and Joe. They try to flee and while in hiding see Spats and his gang massacred by rival gangsters. Again they flee, but not before Joe confesses to Sugar. She gives chase and joins Joe in the back of Osgood's motorboat. She says it doesn't matter that he's no millionaire and plays the sax. Jerry admits to Osgood that he's not a female. To Jerry's surprise Osgood doesn't seem to care.

Inspired by a German silent film, *Fanfares of Love,* *Some Like It Hot* is one of Hollywood's truly great come-

dies. It features sparkling, high-energy comic performances by Marilyn Monroe, Jack Lemmon, Tony Curtis, and Joe E. Brown; a dazzling array of lead and secondary characters, all with quirky, aggressive personalities; hilarious, furious, and often sexy interplay among those characters; an enlightened ahead-of-its-time sexual-identity theme; frenetic pacing; and a script by Wilder and I.A.L. Diamond that is consistently clever, daring, and provocative, straddling the boundaries of bad taste: there are many double entendres and references to homosexuality, lesbianism, oral sex (Sugar's sick of getting the "fuzzy end of the lollipop"), transvestism, impotence, and sex change.

Like most farces *Some Like It Hot* deals with disguise and deception. Everyone lies about something, everyone pretends to be who he isn't. They even confuse themselves. Tony Curtis's Joe becomes "Josephine" (an Eve Arden without humor) and Jack Lemmon's Jerry becomes the lively "Daphne." Ostensibly, it's to get away from gangsters, but subconsciously it's to escape the harsh male world—where men must act like men—that has left them penniless bachelors. Ironically, Joe and Jerry virtually become the parts they play or, more accurately, free the female sides of their personalities, as would Dustin Hoffman years later in *Tootsie*. *Some Like It Hot* is on the surface a silly comedy, but it was the first picture to subvert traditional sexual stereotyping since 1935's *Sylvia Scarlett,* in which Katharine Hepburn poses as a young boy so she can have opportunities in a male-dominated world. Its theme is that when a person lives as the other sex, he/she has the opportunity to explore previously latent aspects of his/her personality. "Josephine" and "Daphne" are not the alter egos of Joe and Jerry, but their female sides, positive extensions of these men who needed improvement.

At first Joe and Jerry take advantage of their female attire to spy on the scantily clad women musicians. But their emerging female consciences keep them from taking further advantage. They develop a "female perspective," referring to men negatively as "they" and treating women with increasing respect and concern. Jerry even forgets he's not female, accepting Osgood's marriage proposal. Significantly, when Joe and Jerry become women, they don't become silly movie-women but tough, smart, fun-to-be-with broads, who take guff from no man and are loyal, protective friends to Sugar. When Joe does try to dupe Sugar, he dresses as a *male* millionaire. When he dresses as a male he falls into the trap of acting like the stereotypical male he's always been, using women. But as "Josephine" he develops a sisterly affection for Sugar, and wouldn't dupe her or dump on her. Sugar trusts "Josephine" (and "Daphne") and opens up to "her" as she wouldn't to any man. So only as "Josephine" can Joe behold the real, wonderful Sugar, and learn how she deserves to be treated by men. It is significant that when he gives her a sincerely loving goodbye kiss (not knowing she'll follow him) he is in full drag (a startling scene!). This shows that even if they become a heterosexual couple, he wants them to retain their special *female* bond, which is characterized by friendship and trust. At the beginning of the film males and females are identified by what they wear or carry—spats, toothpicks, badges, guns, hats, musical instruments, high heels—but at the end they are identified by who they are. They have been liberated from their traps and trappings.

Some Like It Hot contains many wonderful moments and such classic scenes as Monroe's Sugar sexily wiggling up the train compartment aisle and singing "Running Wild"; Sugar sharing secrets and a train berth with the increasingly titillated "Daphne"; Sugar confiding to "Josephine" her desire to avoid sax players and marry a shy, spectacled millionaire; Sugar kissing Joe's spectacled

false-millionaire in an attempt to cure him of the impotency he pretends; "Daphne" dancing into the night with Osgood, a flower moving from mouth to mouth on their deadpan faces; "Josephine" reminding "Daphne" of the reasons why s/he can't marry Osgood. But as good as this picture is, it all might have amounted to nothing if the ending were a cop-out. Wilder and Diamond came through, boldly. When "Daphne" can't convince Osgood that they shouldn't marry, Jerry pulls off his wig and confesses he's a man. Without blinking Osgood silences his fiancée with: "Nobody's perfect." The *perfect* punch line.

▶ BEST ACTOR

WINNER:
Charlton Heston *(Ben-Hur)*
Other Nominees: Laurence Harvey *(Room at the Top)*, Jack Lemmon *(Some Like It Hot)*, Paul Muni *(The Last Angry Man)*, James Stewart *(Anatomy of a Murder)*

▼

THE BEST CHOICE:
Jack Lemmon *(Some Like It Hot)*
Award-Worthy Runners-Up: Tony Curtis *(Some Like It Hot)*, Cary Grant *(North by Northwest)*, Dean Martin *(Rio Bravo)*, Paul Muni *(The Last Angry Man)*, John Wayne *(Rio Bravo)*

I think it would have been fun to have seen Steve "Hercules" Reeves as the lead in William Wyler's *Ben-Hur*. Understandably, the part went to the king of the *American* epic, Charlton Heston (but only after another unlikely choice, Rock Hudson, backed out). Heston gave no more than a credible performance as a toga-clad Jewish patrician, Judah Ben-Hur, who is exiled from Rome (for not informing on Jewish rebels) and spends years as a galley slave, defeats the former friend (Stephen Boyd) responsible for his captivity in a deadly chariot race, and witnesses Christ cure his mother and sister of leprosy. Nevertheless Heston should be commended for having been a figure sturdy enough for Wyler to hang his colossal film on—and for not taking himself quite as seriously as he had when he *was* Moses in 1956's *The Ten Commandments*. However, he didn't really deserve the 1959 Best Actor Oscar (would Steve Reeves also have ridden the eleven-Oscar *Ben-Hur* wave?). I could see giving my Alternate Oscar to Cary Grant, who was funny and dashing in Alfred Hitchcock's *North by Northwest;* or John Wayne, who was funny and formidable as an outmanned sheriff in *Rio Bravo;* or costar Dean Martin, who was surprisingly effective as his recovering-alcoholic deputy. But my choice is Jack Lemmon, who gave one of the cinema's great comic performances in *Some Like It Hot.*

Four years after winning the Best Supporting Actor Oscar for his sneakily resourceful Ensign Pulver in *Mister Roberts,* Lemmon earned his first Best Actor nomination and should have won the award. In *Some Like It Hot* he

is howlingly funny as a broke bass player, Jerry, who flees gangsters with his best friend, Joe (Tony Curtis), a sax player. They dress as women and join an all-female band, in which beautiful Sugar Kane (Marilyn Monroe) is the lead singer. Jerry takes the name "Daphne" and Joe settles for "Josephine." While Joe/Josephine takes a third identity, that of a male millionaire, in order to court the benignly gold-digging Sugar, "Daphne" somehow ends up engaged to a real male millionaire, Osgood Fielding (Joe E. Brown).

Once again, Lemmon is a character who is excitable, frantic, flustered, argumentative, cynical, sarcastic, curious, horny, and slightly mischievous, and who finds himself in an insane predicament. After early resistance, much anxiety, and many double takes, this Lemmon character also gives in to, actually jumps into, the zaniness and allows himself to become screwy and happy. As in all of his most successful comedies, he's appealing here because, in addition to his immense talent, he seems to be enjoying himself so much, especially when his character goes wild. Here he seems to be having a great time playing a man who at first enjoys "playing" a woman— how aroused Jerry is (and funny Lemmon is) when the unsuspecting Sugar cuddles with "Daphne" in a train berth—and then enjoys "being" a woman.

In his relationship with Joe, Jerry (player of a curvaceous bass instrument that gangsters have shot holes in) is the "female" who is always taken advantage of by his irresponsible pal (player of a phallic saxophone). He is

Millionaire Joe E. Brown is Jack Lemmon's date for the evening in *Some Like It Hot.*

tical swimsuits, wiggle, wear makeup, and chase millionaires. "Daphne" protectively gives Sugar advice: "If I were a girl—and I am . . ." Initially, he wishes he were dead instead of having to pretend he's a woman, but later wishes he were dead when he remembers he's a man. When he goes off dancing with Osgood (to allow Joe time to seduce Sugar on Osgood's yacht), he smiles at his date, wearing a slightly sick (and very funny) expression as they leave arm in arm. But as they dance (the film's comic highlight), Osgood insists that he lead "Daphne," and once in the female role, "she" succumbs to his charms. In a great bit in the hotel room "Daphne" can't stop dancing, even when lying down. "She" tells Joe that she's engaged. Joe asks, "Who's the lucky girl?" "I am," "Daphne" responds. Joe tries to reason with his friend, asking desperately, "Why would you want to marry a guy?" "Security," is Daphne's reply. As Brandon French suggests, Jerry's feminization is "the expression of a 'normal' male longing for passivity and dependence."

Jerry becomes much happier as a woman. He has liberated the female side of himself and improved as a human being. Lemmon gives us the impression that Jerry would like an excuse not to go back to being a male and dressing like a male (you can hear the disappointment in his voice as he reminds himself, "I'm a boy. I'm a boy. I'm a boy. Oh, boy, am I a boy. . . ."). Joe does this when he portrays the fake millionaire, but Lemmon remains in drag from the time Jerry first dons a blond wig, dress, and heels early in the picture. We've gotten so used to Daphne—she has become a real person—that it's jarring when he removes his wig at film's end to show Osgood the primary reason they shouldn't marry. I get the feeling that when Osgood indicates to Jerry/Daphne that his/her sex doesn't matter—"Nobody's perfect"—his flustered fiancée won't try to come up with other excuses and will go ahead with the ceremony. Jerry wants security, doesn't he? Yes, he can get it by marrying Osgood, but he'll get more of it by continuing to be "Daphne."

also Joe's feminine conscience, who tells him to treat women with respect. So it's not surprising that Jerry takes to being a "female" quite easily, assuming the fancy name "Daphne" instead of the "Geraldine" that Joe suggested. He also dumps "her" luggage on the first man he sees, Osgood (symbolically, Brandon French points out, "divesting himself of all male burdens"). Sugar becomes "Daphne's" role model: they have blond hair, wear iden-

---

▶ BEST ACTRESS

WINNER:
Simone Signoret *(Room at the Top)*
Other Nominees: Doris Day *(Pillow Talk)*, Audrey Hepburn *(The Nun's Story)*, Katharine Hepburn *(Suddenly, Last Summer)*, Elizabeth Taylor *(Suddenly, Last Summer)*

▼

THE BEST CHOICE:
Marilyn Monroe *(Some Like It Hot)*
Award-Worthy Runners-Up: Angie Dickinson *(Rio Bravo)*, Audrey Hepburn *(The Nun's Story)*, Lee Remick *(Anatomy of a Murder)*, Eva Marie Saint *(North by Northwest)*, Simone Signoret *(Room at the Top)*

It now seems almost inconceivable that Marilyn Monroe was never nominated for an Oscar. But the conservative Academy shrugged off the fact that on the screen she was

Hollywood personified and refused to honor either the sex symbol or the malcontent and troublemaker. Her fights over scripts and salaries with Twentieth's chief of production, Darryl F. Zanuck, which resulted in her walking out on her contract and spending two years in New York, and loyalty to husband Arthur Miller despite his determination not to name names to HUAC, infuriated Academy members even more than her long-ago nude calendar shot and *Playboy* layout. She deserved the Oscar for a delightful comic portrayal in Billy Wilder's *Some Like It Hot,* but the Academy refused to warmly welcome the prodigal daughter back after two years. Instead it welcomed a blond foreigner to its collective bosom. (Ironically, the Academy was unaware that her politics were far to the left of Monroe's.)

Simone Signoret, a French actress in a British film, became the first actress in a non-American film to win the Best Actress Oscar. In Jack Clayton's depressing *Room at the Top* she played an unhappily married middle-aged woman who has an affair with an angry young social climber (Laurence Harvey). After he abandons her, she gets drunk and has a (deliberately?) fatal car accident. As had been the case in her European films, Signoret was impeccable, giving one of her typically strong, moving, honest portrayals. Significantly, American viewers were taken with a rare movie female who is forty and slightly overweight yet is extremely sexual (though I don't know why anyone would waste time with Laurence Harvey). Signoret's part wasn't really substantial but she was impressive enough to have warranted the Best Actress Oscar . . . had it not been for Marilyn Monroe in *Some Like It Hot.*

As in 1953's *Gentlemen Prefer Blondes* Monroe seems extremely happy on the screen as Sugar Kane, a wide-eyed singer–ukulele player with a fixation on sax players. But it wasn't a happy experience. She was so unnerved by Wilder that she needed forty takes on some scenes. At times her confidence was so shattered that she locked herself in her dressing room for hours with personal acting coach Paula Strasberg, or Miller. Wilder decided to print any take in which she was good, even if costars Jack Lemmon and Tony Curtis weren't also at their peak. You'll notice that Monroe is alone in the frame, in close-up, in several shots in the train scene when she talks to Curtis's "Josephine," indication that she was less inclined to blow lines when talking directly to Wilder than to Curtis. Lemmon got along with Monroe, but Curtis was angered by her costly delays, especially when he had to spend hours in drag. (He later compared kissing her to kissing Hitler.) Monroe was so unpopular that she wasn't even invited to the wrap party. Only when the film became the top-grossing comedy of all time was her contribution fully appreciated. As Wilder would say years after his antagonism toward her had subsided, "Anyone can remember lines, but it takes a real artist to come on the set and not know her lines and give the performance she did."

From the first time we see Monroe, wiggling along a train platform "like Jell-O on springs," as Lemmon's Jerry/Daphne says, Wilder emphasizes her sexuality. He has her sing "Running Wild" while shaking her way up and down a train aisle. He places her in Oscar-winning diaph-

anous gowns and uses lighting effects that direct our eyes toward her barely concealed breasts. Her character, Sugar, is without question a sex object. She talks in a sexy, hushed voice, and is easy prey for any wolf—she admits that she can't resist saxophone players. She falls for any line, even those of Tony Curtis's fake millionaire. He even manipulates her into kissing away his fake impotency. She doesn't know how to protect her honor, or even that she should protect it: "Just imagine: me, Sugar Kovalchick from Sandusky, Ohio, on a millionaire's yacht—if my mother could only see me now." Sugar has a healthy attitude toward sex, but she leaves herself open to being used and hurt.

However, like most Monroe characters, Sugar isn't a tramp. She isn't even as dumb as she thinks, but naive and, as Curtis's "Josephine" says, "just careless." And though she's accessible to any interested male, her sexuality is not her only asset. Janice Welch wrote of the typical Monroe heroine, "Men are attracted to them erotically at first, but soon recognize other qualities: sensitivity, vulnerability, generosity, openness, and honesty." This applies to Sugar. Lemmon's Jerry and Curtis's Joe want only Sugar's body at first. They later cherish her friendship. Jerry will use her as his role model when he tries to pass as a female. Joe will want her for his wife.

One of the reasons I like Monroe so much in *Some Like It Hot* is that she plays a character who has been pushed around in life ("I'm tired of getting the fuzzy end of the lollipop") but doesn't try to win audience sympathy or pass herself off as lovable, as she does in other films. Instead, Monroe concentrated on comedy. She is truly funny in this film, whether sharing a train berth and innocently (on *her* part) cuddling with Lemmon's aroused "Daphne," or telling Curtis's "Josephine" that she wants to marry a millionaire with glasses because they are "gentle and sweet and helpless. . . . They get

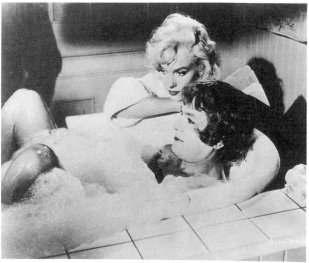

In *Some Like It Hot* Marilyn Monroe pines for the man she loves, not realizing that her female friend in the tub, Tony Curtis's "Josephine," *is* that man.

those weak eyes from reading—you know, those long, tiny little columns in *The Wall Street Journal.*" It's not surprising that she works well with Lemmon, but her scenes with Curtis are equally amusing. I like it when Curtis's millionaire pretends not to be aroused by her kisses, saying that "it's like smoking without inhaling," and she has a Judy Holliday–like response: "So inhale!"

When he tells her a ridiculous story about how the love of his life walked off a cliff as they attempted an embrace without glasses, what can she say but "Talk about sad." But she steams up his glasses and cures his "impotency" with sensuous kisses, explaining she learned this skill getting donations for the Milk Fund. This is Monroe at her best: sexy and funny at the same time.

▶ BEST PICTURE

WINNER:
The Apartment (Mirisch/United Artists; Billy Wilder)
Other Nominees: *The Alamo, Elmer Gantry, Sons and Lovers, The Sundowners*

▼

THE BEST CHOICE:
Psycho (Paramount; Alfred Hitchcock)
Award-Worthy Runners-Up: *The Apartment* (Billy Wilder), *Elmer Gantry* (Richard Brooks), *Spartacus* (Stanley Kubrick)

Some Like It Hot broke box-office records in 1959 but was pretty much shut out in the Oscar Derby. The Academy had continued its long-standing tradition of shortchanging out-and-out comedies. To satisfy Academy members a picture couldn't just be funny but had to have either music (as did 1958's Best Picture, *Gigi*) or a serious side. Billy Wilder might have realized this when he followed *Some Like It Hot* with *The Apartment,* the best cynical comedy-drama since 1950's Best Picture, *All About Eve.* Not unexpectedly, the Academy voted it 1960's Best Picture and gave Oscars to Wilder for Directing, Wilder and I.A.L. Diamond for Original Screenplay, Daniel Mandell for Editing, and Alexander Trauner and Edward G. Boyle for Art Direction–Scenic Design. *The Apartment* was daring in its day because of the amorality of its characters and because it mixed humor with such serious elements as a suicide attempt. Today, it's somewhat dated and it still has a dubious premise—a young insurance clerk gets promoted by letting married executives (who have enough money for hotel rooms!) use his apartment for illicit affairs. However, the performances still hold up: Jack Lemmon as the ambitious but harried schnook; the short-haired Shirley MacLaine as the unhappy elevator operator Lemmon loves; and Fred MacMurray as Lemmon's unscrupulous married boss and MacLaine's inconsiderate lover.

But what happens in Lemmon's apartment is far less compelling than what happens in Janet Leigh's motel room in *Psycho.* In 1960 the list of nominees for Best Picture was weak, yet the Academy couldn't find a spot for this Alfred Hitchcock masterpiece. Always conscious of prestige, the Academy didn't think it appropriate that its Best Picture be an adaptation of a pulp novel (by Robert Bloch); a tawdry tale of madness, sex, and violence; a (gasp) *horror* movie. No one knew how seriously to take Hitchcock's pitch-black comedy. Few doubted that it was the most terrifying film ever made. (Most of us who saw it back then still think so and remain wary of taking showers in motels to this day.) But there were many who wondered if it was tasteless. After all, there had never been a Best Picture winner, even a nominee, about a sexual psychopath who dresses up as, and believes he is, his mother, whom he murdered, dug up from the grave, and keeps preserved.

Perhaps indignant because Hitchcock denied them special advance screenings lest they reveal the surprise ending, critics initially denounced the director for going overboard on the sex and violence in an extremely tame movie era. But when *Psycho* became a huge commercial success, they were less wary about treating it respectfully. There was much to appreciate: Anthony Perkins's astonishing portrait of Norman Bates/"Mrs. Bates," a fascinating villain who has become a cultural icon; Janet Leigh's intelligent, controlled, and daringly sexy performance as Marion Crane (and her willingness to be killed off early in the picture); Joseph Stefano's chilling yet witty script; Bernard Herrmann's classic violin-and-cello-dominated score that helps build suspense and punctuates shocks;

"Mother" keeps a watchful eye from the window in Alfred Hitchcock's *Psycho.*

George Tomasini's standout editing, which is particularly effective in the forty-five-second shower sequence; the art and scenic direction of Joseph Hurley, Robert Clatworthy, and George Milo, who gave every set a seedy look (and found an odd array of pictures for the various walls); the sliced-by-a-knife titles of Saul Bass; and John Russell's versatile camerawork, which was equally effective on intricate mobile and strikingly composed static shots. Of course, every aspect of the film was supervised by Hitchcock, who with *Psycho* perfected the blueprint for nerve-racking thrillers.

Hitchcock lets us know with the opening shot that he is manipulating us when he forces us to be a Peeping Tom on a hotel meeting between the bra-clad Marion Crane (Leigh) and bare-chested boyfriend, Sam (John Gavin). But we don't object. We let him take us on a wild roller-coaster ride, jolting our nerves and emotions. He amuses himself, keeping us off balance by playing with the time element. Most things happen *before* we expect them to; Marion stealing money from her firm, Marion being killed so early in the picture, private eye Arbogast (Martin Balsam) being killed. Since "Mrs. Bates" is an old lady, we expect her to wait for her victims, but she walks directly toward the shower to stab Marion, and, in what

is an equally unnerving scene, races out of her room with knife held high to stab Arbogast, whom we fully expected to walk into her room before being attacked. When Arbogast falls backward to the base of the stairs, we expect the old lady to take a few seconds before reaching him and finishing him off. But she pounces on him immediately. Hitchcock and Tomasini really play with time in the shower sequence, where everything happens quickly yet time seems to stand still and Marion's brutal death seems to go on forever.

Between the shock sequences Hitchcock frays our nerves by forcing us to share the various characters' guilt, paranoia, and dementia. Listen to the script and you'll be surprised by how many unfriendly *questions* are asked. At one time or another everyone is suspected of something, is suspicious of someone else, is on the defensive, and/or is being interrogated. Everyone lies or has something to hide. Everyone has some form of guilt. Different characters do what they shouldn't do, wander where they shouldn't go. And Hitchcock makes us identify with them, be it Marion stealing the money, Norman spying through a hole in the wall on the disrobing Marion, Marion's sister Lila (Vera Miles) sneaking through the Bates house in search of Mrs. Bates. Those of us who were boys in 1960, when other family movies didn't show what Hitchcock did, had extra guilt because we followed Leigh's nude Marion into the bathroom (!) and into the shower. Our excitement didn't have only to do with fear for her safety, but the knowledge we were getting away with something. To see her killed was devastating because it seemed to us that she was punished for a sexual moment we were both experiencing, she as an exhibitionist and we as underaged voyeurs. After Marion's death we were completely traumatized as we sat in our movie seats, hoping Mrs. Bates wasn't aware there were witnesses to the murder, or that our mothers wouldn't drag us from the theater.

I think what I find most intriguing about *Psycho* is how we learn all about the course that led to Norman's insanity before we meet him. In Bloch's novel Norman appears at the beginning, but in Stefano's script he doesn't appear until Marion arrives at the motel. We learn about Norman's irrational behavior from watching Marion, a ten-year secretary who impulsively steals money so she can marry debt-ridden Sam. As with many Hitchcock films, we see, in her actions, how easy it is for a "normal" person to break the daily routine and "go a little mad." And we see how one impulsive act can lead to other senseless acts, lying, escalating guilt and paranoia, and submersion of one's real identity. Marion commits a felony, just as Norman did ten years before. She has just as difficult a time answering the questions of a highway cop and car dealer as Norman will have when interrogated by Arbogast and Sam. She, too, can't cover her guilt. Growing increasingly paranoid as she drives toward Sam's hometown (only to end up at the Bates Motel), she even begins to fabricate conversations and hear voices of people she knows. This isn't very different from what Norman does, only she isn't so crazy *yet* that she takes part in those conversations. Marion and Norman are destined to meet because they are linked. They face each other, two friendly people who are, to varying degrees, still controlled by their dead mothers, and who have secrets, false identities, guilt and paranoia, crimes in their pasts. As they converse about "personal traps," they understand each other. Marion realizes that she could become like Norman: "I stepped into a private trap back there and I'd like to go back and try to pull myself out of it, before it's too late for me *too*." But she can't go back. This woman named Crane is destined to be executed by the young man whose hobby is *bird* taxidermy.

▶ BEST ACTOR

WINNER:
Burt Lancaster *(Elmer Gantry)*
Other Nominees: Trevor Howard *(Sons and Lovers)*, Jack Lemmon *(The Apartment)*, Laurence Olivier *(The Entertainer)*, Spencer Tracy *(Inherit the Wind)*

▼

THE BEST CHOICE:
Anthony Perkins *(Psycho)*
Award-Worthy Runners-Up: Montgomery Clift *(Wild River)*, Alec Guinness *(Tunes of Glory)*, Trevor Howard *(Sons and Lovers)*, Burt Lancaster *(Elmer Gantry)*, Jack Lemmon *(The Apartment)*, Laurence Olivier *(The Entertainer)*

Dating back to his debut in 1946's *The Killers,* Burt Lancaster was one of Hollywood's most appealing, screen-dominating leading men. But the jury was still out on the former trapeze artist's (constantly improving) acting abilities until he played Sinclair Lewis's charlatan revivalist in Richard Brooks's adaptation of *Elmer Gantry.* With booming voice, toothy grin, boundless energy, dauntless spirit, exaggerated gestures, two-fisted masculinity, the slickness of a snake-oil salesman, the showmanship of the Mighty Barnum (a role he'd play years later in a television movie), and strong doses of tenderness and intelligence, Lancaster gave a bravura performance. He deservedly beat out four strong nominees for the Best Actor Oscar. But in this year of many exceptional male performances, there was one even better than Lancaster's, by another actor playing a character who isn't exactly who he pretends to be. There have been countless portrayals of maniacs in movie history, but with the possible exception of Peter Lorre's child murderer in *M,* none was played with such skill and imagination, or got under our skins, haunted us, or made us care so much as Anthony Perkins's Norman Bates in *Psycho.*

When he wrote his source novel, Robert Bloch based Norman Bates on Wisconsin's asylum-bound fiend Ed Gein, who indulged in necrophilia, cannibalism, and worse. He provided his Gein-like murderer with a reason for his depravity: a possessive, ruthless, domineering dead mother, whom he now dresses like and becomes whenever an attractive female stops at the Bates Motel. Bloch's Norman is middle aged and balding, and not at all sympathetic. Remember the most unpleasant person who ever sat down next to you in a bus or behind you at a movie, and that's what Bloch's Norman Bates is like. But when Alfred Hitchcock cast Anthony Perkins as Norman the whole concept of the character changed. With the tall, slim, shy, young, boyishly handsome Perkins in the role, we didn't want Norman killed or even injured despite his dastardly crimes. Imagine how bad we would have felt if Norman died at the end! We blamed Mrs. Bates for the murders, and for turning this gentle soul into a hurt, mixed-up killer. Viewers aren't vengeful toward Norman, nor are they, as Perkins told C. V. Drake, fully

Anthony Perkins's Norman Bates has just discovered what "Mother" did to Janet Leigh's Marion Crane in the shower, in *Psycho.*

sympathetic: "[They] want people to understand Norman and to perhaps leave him alone."

Perkins got the role after having played a number of shy, sensitive, confused young men, some of whom have relationships with older women. In *Fear Strikes Out* he was baseball player Jimmy Piersall, who has a nervous breakdown because he never got the full approval of his domineering father. Perkins always claimed that he had no special affinity toward Norman, but he has admitted to a childhood in which "I became abnormally close to my mother. . . . It was the Oedipal thing in a pronounced form. I loved [my father] but I also wanted him to be dead so I could have her all to myself." He also said he didn't have a sexual relationship with a woman until years after he made *Psycho*.

No actor ever got more into his character. Hitchcock wasn't known for listening to actors, but he gave Perkins much leeway with the part. Perkins even came up with Norman's incessant eating of candy (Kandy Korn), which links the adult Norman to his childhood and the character to the movie loonies played by Tim O'Kelly (who eats Baby Ruths) in *Targets* and Robert De Niro (who eats Chuckles and jujubes) in *Taxi Driver*. His performance is beautifully conceived. Just as some people control their anger, Norman controls his insanity. But Perkins lets enough of Norman's abnormality seep through in his conversation with Janet Leigh's Marion—about "personal traps" and why he wouldn't consider putting his mother in a "madhouse"—that when we discover he *is* "Mrs. Bates," we think it makes sense. Perkins doesn't just zero in on Norman's madness, but also exhibits Norman's sweetness, his anguish, his shyness (he can't say the word *bathroom,* much less deal with his sexual perversity), his attempt to be normal (e.g., he changes the motel sheets every day), his amiability, his feeble wit: he tells Janet Leigh's Marion, "There's . . . stationery with BATES MOTEL printed on it in case you want to make your friends back home feel envious"; "My mother . . . she isn't quite herself today."

We feel bad for him when he tries to be friendly to an insurance investigator (Martin Balsam) and Marion's ex-lover (John Gavin), but they won't leave him alone, suspiciously grilling him. Always nervous, now he gets downright jittery, smiles awkwardly, snickers; his jaw muscles quiver from the tension, his eyes twitch, he stutters as he tries to think of responses, he pretends to laugh at their bad humor, his fingers uncontrollably rap against a surface. We can tell by his sorry reactions to hostile questions, and even in the unsure way he walks (often with hands in pockets), that he has spent a lifetime on the defensive, that he has never satisfied anyone.

Because Perkins reveals Norman's admirable qualities, we recognize the great tragedy that has been his life. We admire this boy who defends his mother when Marion suggests she be institutionalized, and who defends his upbringing when Sam questions him: "I had a very happy childhood. My mother and I were more than happy." Although he is appalled by his mother's murders, and his body shakes and he gets sick when he sees what she has done, he covers up her crimes. He'll do *anything* to protect her, yet after the arrest (why has no critic ever mentioned this revealing moment?) the "Mrs. Bates" he remembers and has become immediately tells the police that her son Norman was responsible for her murders. That's the really sad part.

▶ BEST ACTRESS

WINNER:
Elizabeth Taylor *(Butterfield 8)*
Other Nominees: Greer Garson *(Sunrise at Campobello)*, Deborah Kerr *(The Sundowners)*, Shirley MacLaine *(The Apartment)*, Melina Mercouri *(Never on Sunday)*

THE BEST CHOICE:
Jean Simmons *(Elmer Gantry)*
Award-Worthy Runners-Up: Greer Garson *(Sunrise at Campobello)*, Deborah Kerr *(The Sundowners)*, Hayley Mills *(Pollyanna)*

Her name usually doesn't come up quickly when movie fans go on and on about their favorite actresses. And then, it's usually an afterthought: "You know who else I *really* like? Jean Simmons." The first classy name mentioned in at least an hour. The excited response is invariably "Oh, yeah, I forgot about her. I didn't know anyone else *really* liked her." Her name may slip one's mind due to infrequent appearances since semiretirement in the early sixties, but almost everyone who has seen a lot of movies starring the dark-haired, British-born beauty *really* likes her. So why was she never recognized as one of the best leading ladies of her era?

"Jean Simmons has always been taken for granted," wrote David Shipman in his *The Great Movie Stars*. "As a child player in Britain she was expected to be one of the best child players and she was; she was expected to become an international name and she did. In Hollywood for [many] years she was given good roles because she was reliable, and she played them, or most of them, beautifully, and got good notices, and was liked. But she was never a cult figure, or one of those who adorn magazine covers, or someone fan magazines write about all the time. It wasn't . . . that she simply did . . . her job—she's much better than that; she's not a competent actress, she's a very good one—by Hollywood standards a great one, if you take the Hollywood standard to be those ladies who have won Oscars. She wasn't even nominated for a Best Actress Oscar till 1969 [for *The Happy Ending*]. She wasn't nominated even for *Elmer Gantry* (and that year Elizabeth Taylor won). Maybe it doesn't help to have been so good so young."

Elizabeth Taylor won 1960's Best Actress award by taking the sympathy vote. When she almost died from pneumonia in a London clinic, her victory was assured, although it was generally recognized that her portrayal of a doomed call girl in *Butterfield 8* didn't even warrant a nomination. Surely her place on the ballot and at the victory stand should have been taken by Simmons. Though just thirty-one, she'd been impressive since the mid-forties (since 1950 in America) in such films as *Great Expectations, Young Bess* (as Queen Elizabeth), *The Actress, Desiree, Footsteps in the Fog* (opposite then-husband Stewart Granger), *Guys and Dolls, Hilda Crane, This Earth Is Mine,* and future cult films: *Black Narcissus, So Long at the Fair, Angel Face* (as a sweet-faced murderess), and *Spartacus.* But she peaked in *Elmer Gantry,* giving her most self-assured performance in her most difficult role.

In this powerful adaptation of Sinclair Lewis's novel by the actress's soon-to-be new husband, writer-director Richard Brooks, Simmons played twenties evangelist Sharon Falconer, a character inspired by Aimee Semple McPherson. She travels from town to small town converting indigent sinners with sincere sermons about God's love, but she's been too sheltered to have experienced love herself. So when glib, muscular salesman Elmer Gantry (Burt Lancaster) comes on to her, she is swept off her feet. She lets him join her revivalist band and deliver sermons of his own, about how he, a common man who had sinned, found salvation in Jesus. He becomes as powerful as she with imaginative, dramatically delivered sermons full of fire and brimstone, and by taking to the streets with police to shut down speakeasies and brothels. He seduces her. She is happy. But then she must offer blackmail money to prostitute Lulu Banes (Shirley Jones), who has scandalous, recently shot pictures of herself with ex-boyfriend Gantry. Lulu decides to reject the money and give the photos to the newspaper. Then Lulu clears Gantry of any wrongdoing. Sharon would have stuck with him anyway. Sharon's flock returns to her tent-show meeting. She heals a deaf man, the first time she has accomplished a miracle, which doesn't surprise her because she believes she is His instrument. But there is a fire and, refusing to leave the tent, she loses her life. Gantry decides to abandon the revivalist business.

Perhaps Simmons wasn't given proper Oscar consideration because the picture was supposedly dominated by the thunderous Best Actor performance of Burt Lancaster and the sexy Best Supporting Actress portrayal of

Jean Simmons, Dean Jagger (standing), and John McGiver listen while dynamic Burt Lancaster speaks on behalf of her controversial tent show in *Elmer Gantry*.

Shirley Jones. But Simmons was no more dwarfed by Lancaster than Sister Falconer was by Elmer Gantry. Gantry certainly entrances the congregation—and Sharon—with his intense, fiery, hell-and-damnation sermons. Yet Sharon is just as captivating—she even wins over Elmer—with her cheerful, heartfelt sermons about kindness, forgiveness, and love. Gantry sweats and screams and scares: Sharon needs only to smile. As for competing with Lulu on the sexiness scale, Sharon more than holds her own. I think of her dressing-room scene: Sharon, who is dressed revealingly while listening to Gantry's sermon, finds sand in her shoe and pours it into her hand with an ecstatic, sensual look that tells us just how thrilling was her past night's sexual encounter with Gantry on the beach. At this moment we understand why the virile Gantry chooses Sharon over Lulu as his lover.

It is the hard, naughty edge Simmons gives her character that makes her exciting. Sharon's a good person, but she's no goody-goody, and no prude. She has as much fight in her as Gantry. Even before he joined her troupe and ran interference when journalists, politicians, fire marshals, and the police were giving her trouble, she took that role herself, playing hardball and winning. She is attracted to Gantry because they are much alike, striking blows for the Lord; she ain't no lady when she starts kissing him as he drives, thanking him for having made a reporter (Arthur Kennedy) get off her back: "You really are an alley fighter. You hit Brother Jim both sides of the belt. You murdered 'im, baby. You knocked him flat with a celestial bolt, eight, nine, ten, and out. Oh, darling!"

However, it becomes increasingly evident that Sharon isn't just tough, but neurotic as well. She tries to convince herself that she has been touched by God, that she speaks God's words, and that she accomplishes what she does, including her healing miracle, because of her *faith* in

God. But like all those mad scientists in horror movies, she begins to think of herself too highly: "I am Sharon Falconer now. I've made her. I've put her together piece by piece until I've got the right to be her." She does perform that miracle and thanks God for His generosity.

But God—the wrathful God that Gantry spoke of—is so angered by her trespassing in His domain that His fire destroys her empire. Refusing to believe that He doesn't trust her faith in Him, she dies in flames, a sorry end reserved for sorcerers.

1961

▶ BEST PICTURE

WINNER:
West Side Story (Mirisch–B & P Enterprises/United Artists; Robert Wise and Jerome Robbins)
Other Nominees: *Fanny, The Guns of Navarone, The Hustler, Judgment at Nuremberg*

▼

THE BEST CHOICE:
West Side Story (Mirisch–B & P Enterprises/United Artists; Robert Wise and Jerome Robbins)
Award-Worthy Runners-Up: None

For one reason or another *West Side Story* has an important place in many people's lives. As for me: the first time I treated a girl to anything was when I took one to see *West Side Story* in Trenton, New Jersey, in 1962. It surely would have been a better overall experience if another, extremely inconsiderate thirteen-year-old boy hadn't sat *between* me and my date, but I took solace in seeing Natalie Wood on the screen, and I absolutely loved the picture. Even at thirteen I knew it wasn't perfect— Richard Beymer *definitely* had to get his teeth filed—and today it surprises me to see just how flawed it is. Nonetheless, the flaws seem to vanish in a wave of nostalgia (I did manage to pull his arm off her shoulder *before* intermission). And since there were no *great* English-language pictures released in 1961 (though I have much more affection for *Splendor in the Grass*, with Wood at her best), I'll stick with *West Side Story* as Best Picture, if just to acknowledge the numerous moviegoers for whom it has special memories.

In 1957, when low-budgeted troubled-youth pictures were in vogue, *West Side Story* opened on Broadway. It was the idea of choreographer-director Jerome Robbins, who decided to update *Romeo and Juliet.* Arthur Laurents wrote the book, Leonard Bernstein composed the music, and Stephen Sondheim wrote the lyrics that everyone in America would soon be singing. When the motion picture went into production several years later, Robbins was brought in by United Artists to codirect with Robert Wise, who had never made a musical. Robbins directed the prologue and three musical numbers before being dismissed, although he and Wise would share the Academy Award for best direction.

The Jets, a white gang led by Riff (Russ Tamblyn), are angry that the Sharks, a Puerto Rican gang led by Bernardo (George Chakiris), are muscling in on their territory. Blinded by racial hatred, they want to rumble. Bernardo's sister Maria (a dark-skinned Wood) and Tony (Beymer), Riff's best friend and an ex-Jet, attend a dance and immediately fall in love, which infuriates Bernardo. They must have secret rendezvous. Anita (Rita Moreno), Bernardo's girlfriend, finds out about Maria and Tony's relationship but doesn't tell Bernardo. Maria asks Tony to stop the rumble because it will be bad for her people in regard to the police. But his arrival only angers Bernardo further and knives are drawn. Riff runs into Bernardo's knife and is killed. Tony instinctively stabs Bernardo, killing him. But Maria still loves Tony. She sends the unhappy Anita to arrange a rendezvous for her and Tony. But when the Jets insult and maul Anita, she spitefully lies that Maria was shot to death by Chino, a jealous member of the Sharks. When Tony hears this he runs into the streets, calling for Chino to shoot him too. Then he spots Maria. Just as he runs into her arms, Chino kills him. Maria tearfully screams at both gangs. Sad, chastised members of each gang carry away Tony's body.

When *West Side Story* begins, overage, unthreatening-looking actors posing as youth-gang members snap their fingers and half-dance along the street, and Russ Tamblyn starts to sing, you get the feeling that it's going to be difficult going. But *Romeo and Juliet* is irresistible in

George Chakiris and Rita Moreno, who won Supporting Actor and Actress Oscars, lead the dancers in *West Side Story*.

whatever version it appears. Soon you find yourself drawn into the story, enjoying the physical dancing (which is exciting in Panavision), singing along with the classic score, and sadly remembering when you were in that one perfect relationship that had no chance of lasting. There's something primal about this film, something that makes you emotional when you know you shouldn't be. So you'll forgive the miscasting of Richard Beymer (with singing by Jim Bryant) and Natalie Wood (with singing by the ubiquitous Marni Nixon). He's handsome despite the teeth, and she really does see a pretty girl in that mirror there. I like Wise's close-ups as Tony holds Maria's hand to his face, and she holds his to her own, as they sing "Tonight." Wood's Spanish accent doesn't quite make it, but fortunately she only has to say *Buenas noches* a couple of times. There are charming moments when Wood employs exaggerated mannerisms that will remind you of her little girl in 1947's *Miracle on 34th Street*. Tony and Maria's pretend marriage in a bridal shop, when they pledge to love each other "until death do us part," is actually quite touching. So is Tony's death and her horrified reaction, especially when she orders the insensitive policeman away from his body.

There are those who got crushes on Russ Tamblyn from seeing *West Side Story*, but of all the performers, Rita Moreno is the film's class act. Her singing and dancing during "America" is the musical highlight. Moreno won a Best Supporting Actress Oscar, but would leave Hollywood for several years when she was offered only other Latin spitfire parts. Playing Anita proved to be traumatic because of the scene in which the Jets shout racist slurs at her and physically attack her. Interestingly, Moreno felt personally offended and had a difficult time playing it through.

One forgets that in 1961 this film, which pleads for brotherhood, was daring to an uncomfortable degree. Except for Tony, Maria, and the elderly Doc (Ned Glass), the characters are a pretty rotten group. They are all biased. Even Simon Oakland's beat cop, Schrank, is a bigot. When he orders Bernardo and the Sharks from Doc's without reason, he says "I know it's a free country and I ain't got the right. But I got a badge. What do you got?" They've got nothing. Obviously, with such adults running things, none of these kids, white or Puerto Rican, will ever have an opportunity for happiness . . . even in America.

▶ BEST ACTOR

WINNER:
Maximilian Schell *(Judgment at Nuremberg)*
Other Nominees: Charles Boyer *(Fanny)*, Paul Newman *(The Hustler)*, Spencer Tracy *(Judgment at Nuremberg)*, Stuart Whitman *(The Mark)*

▼ ───

THE BEST CHOICE:
Paul Newman *(The Hustler)*
Award-Worthy Runners-Up: James Cagney *(One, Two, Three)*, Albert Finney *(Saturday Night and Sunday Morning)*, Sidney Poitier *(A Raisin in the Sun)*, Anthony Quinn *(The Savage Innocents)*

By the early sixties all the major Hollywood studios were actively pursuing foreign markets, an increasingly important source of revenue. In order that American films might be more welcome abroad, the motion picture industry tried to promote itself as being *international.* The crafty Academy did its part in 1961, when it gave both best-acting Oscars to foreigners. Though Italy's Sophia Loren was the first Best Actress recipient for a foreign-language film, Vittorio De Sica's *Two Women,* her election was less mysterious than Maximilian Schell's in the American-made *Judgment at Nuremberg.* The Swiss-Austrian was excellent as Hans Rolfe, a morally ambivalent, shrewd, often excitable defense attorney for Nazi war criminals, a part he had played in a 1959 television production. It was commendable that the Academy didn't penalize him for playing an unsympathetic character who believes his clients should be freed because they just followed orders during the war, but so influenced was the Academy by Schell's foreignness that they overlooked the fact that his part was really a supporting one (he was fourth-billed among actors).

Schell's victory was an upset. Paul Newman had been the favorite for playing Eddie Felson in Robert Rossen's grim pool drama, *The Hustler.* Ironically, Newman would win his first Oscar for playing Felson, but that would be almost thirty years later, when he re-created the role for Martin Scorsese's "sequel," *The Color of Money.* During that time Newman would be nominated several more times, only to come out empty-handed. They could have saved him a lot of frustration, even embarrassment, if they'd given one to him in 1961: He got it right the first time.

Though still young, Eddie Felson has been traveling around the country for years with his older friend Charlie (Myron McCormick), hustling local hotshots at pool. His goal is to beat the legendary Minnesota Fats (Jackie Gleason), who has sent many a pool hustler home with his tail dragging. Eddie shows that he has more talent than Fats as he wins game after game. But he doesn't know when to quit and gets extremely drunk as they play well into the next day. Fats freshens up and proceeds to win all the money back. The broke and humbled Eddie leaves Charlie. He moves in with Sarah (Piper Laurie), an alcoholic, self-destructive, insecure would-be writer with a limp. They drink and make love. When Eddie soundly

defeats a local pool player, he gives himself away as a hustler. Several thugs break his thumbs. While he is incapacitated, Eddie and Sarah become much closer. They stop drinking and actually talk. She tells him she loves him and wants the same from him. But he says nothing. When he has recovered, Eddie agrees to be managed by Bert Gordon (George C. Scott), a rich bastard who likes "action." Bert thinks Eddie is a "loser"— Sarah disagrees—but knows he has talent. The three go to Kentucky on Derby weekend. Eddie plays billiards with rich James Findley (Murray Hamilton), with Bert bankrolling him. When he falls far behind, Eddie chases Sarah away. Then he thrashes Findley. Feeling gloomy, he walks home. Meanwhile Bert propositions Sarah, lying that Eddie wanted him to pay her off and send her away. Sarah has sex with Bert whom she detests. She then commits suicide. The shattered Eddie tries to beat up Bert. He says he loved Sarah. Eddie slaughters Minnesota Fats at pool. He refuses to give Bert his share of the winnings, saying if Bert doesn't have his thugs kill him, he'll eventually kill Bert. Bert agrees but tells Eddie not to play in any more big-time pool halls.

Blue eyed and handsome, Paul Newman burst onto the scene in the mid-fifties with all indications that he'd be the next Marlon Brando or James Dean (whose death allowed Newman to play Rocky Graziano in *Somebody Up There Likes Me*). But while his talent was evident, his characterizations hadn't either star's fire, emotion, or dangerously exciting unpredictability. His anger seemed forced, he was humorless. At least he never embarrassed himself—other than when toga clad in *The Silver Chalice*—and was a forceful presence in sweaty adaptations of Williams and Faulkner. But he didn't hit his stride until *The Hustler.*

Based on Walter Tevis's short story and novel, this was a low-budget, low-key, black-and-white production. It was a surprise financial success due to writer-director Robert Rossen's tough dialogue and vivid depiction of the seedy poolroom milieu, and the brilliant acting by Newman, Scott, Laurie, and Gleason. Newman created his first compelling screen character. For most of the film he plays what would become the standard Newman part, which Pat McGilligan described as a "heel-hero, a golden boy with the devil's own grin." But in Eddie's relationship with Piper Laurie's Sarah, as when he tells her about his

Neither Paul Newman nor Piper Laurie is satisfied with their troubled relationship in Robert Rossen's *The Hustler.*

love of pool, there are traces of Newman's tender-but-never-a-pansy Rocky Graziano when he is with his sweet wife (Pier Angeli). Fortunately, Newman didn't have to worry about humor, because the film has none. As the brash, smart-ass hustler—a combination of a cocky gunslinger and a boxer willing to sell out friends in order to get a title shot—Newman has surprising authority on the screen, using not only a strong voice and that devil's grin to hold our attention but also a confident pool player's dramatic and imposing body language. For a time Scott, the better actor, steals the film away, just as his devilish Bert Gordon steals Eddie's soul with offers of money and a shot at Fats's throne. But Newman grabs it back at the end, just when Eddie reveals his heart (he loved Sarah) and reclaims his soul. His character is a bundle of energy and anger—he's nicknamed "Fast" Eddie, not "Easy" Eddie—but Newman wisely doesn't try to overpower the role by acting hyper or using too many mannerisms. Except when showing impatience at opposing players' attempts to feel him out before making their opening

wager—he always jumps in with a high bet—his character plays it cool, letting a cigarette dangle from his lips when he speaks, leaning over and surveying the lie of the balls on the table, moving methodically as he plays.

Too bad Eddie's bite isn't as bad as his bark. His trouble is that he doesn't let loose and explode. He shouts a lot, but until he starts pounding on Bert after Sarah's death, he keeps everything locked up, often drinking himself into a stupor. He's afraid of any feelings escaping, which is probably why he closes the top button on his shirt. As much of a masochist as Sarah, he finds excuses to lose at pool (such as getting drunk) because he's afraid to win, to displace the champion. Deep down he knows that his life's goal has no meaning—to win he will have to give up the rest of his humanity, which is what Gordon's Mephistopheles wants. He realizes that to become champion he must be cold and that the part of him that covets the title anesthetizes his emotions. So he refuses to admit his love for Sarah, and eventually sends her away. She is a physical cripple and he is an emotional cripple, playing a game that isn't about winning or losing but beating someone into humiliating, emasculating submission and dehumanizing yourself in the process. The cliché: He is a hustler, but he is only hustling himself.

Only when Eddie's thumbs are broken and he, too, is a *physical* "cripple" can he allow his emotional side to emerge in his relationship with Sarah. That's when Sarah sees a sensitive young man and falls in love with someone she finally can see is a "winner." She knows that winning at pool and making a lot of money isn't what Eddie needs to be a winner—he just needs to play the game that he sees the true beauty in: "It's a great feeling. When you're right and you know you're right . . . You make the shots that nobody's ever made before, you play the game the way that nobody's played." Ironically, the last time Eddie plays, he plays like no one ever has before, soundly beating Minnesota Fats. But he no longer sees the beauty in it. The only beauty in his life—Sarah—is dead. "I loved her, Bert. I traded her in on a pool game." Now it's easy for him to win because he has nothing else to lose.

▶ BEST ACTRESS

WINNER:
Sophia Loren *(Two Women)*
Other Nominees: Audrey Hepburn *(Breakfast at Tiffany's)*, Piper Laurie *(The Hustler)*, Geraldine Page *(Summer and Smoke)*, Natalie Wood *(Splendor in the Grass)*

▼

THE BEST CHOICE:
Natalie Wood *(Splendor in the Grass)*
Award-Worthy Runners-Up: Lola Albright *(A Cold Wind in August)*, Audrey Hepburn *(Breakfast at Tiffany's)*, Piper Laurie *(The Hustler)*, Vivien Leigh *(The Roman Spring of Mrs. Stone)*, Sophia Loren *(Two Women)*, Hayley Mills *(Whistle Down the Wind)*, Marilyn Monroe *(The Misfits)*, Rita Tushingham *(A Taste of Honey)*

After six years of making films in her native Italy, during which time she became Gina Lollobrigida's chief rival, Sophia Loren starred in several British and American pictures that were filmed abroad. She came to Hollywood in 1958, where she was promoted as a sex symbol and miscast in several pictures. This prompted her return to Italy. In 1960 she replaced first choice Anna Magnani in *Two Women,* playing a mother with a teenage daughter in Vittorio De Sica's tragic World War II drama. She was emotional and earthy in giving the best performance of her career, and became the only actress in a foreign-language film to win a Best Actress Oscar. Her award can be attributed to the Academy's desire to honor non-American films in order to give a boost to the Hollywood product abroad; Loren's status as honorary American; and Loren's giving proof, after eleven years, that she was a skilled actress.

Loren's victory came in a year when there were an extraordinary number of superb performances by American and British actresses, despite there not being all that many superb films. The performances I like best were by actresses who played fragile females and had to dig deep inside themselves and reveal their own vulnerabilities and insecurities: Lola Albright in *A Cold Wind in August,* Piper Laurie in *The Hustler,* Marilyn Monroe in *The Misfits,* among others, and my choice for Best Actress: Natalie Wood in Elia Kazan's *Splendor in the Grass.*

William Inge won an Oscar for his first original screenplay, which is set in Kansas in the late twenties. Wood is a poor high-school senior who is head-over-heels in love with rich Warren Beatty (his impressive film debut). He deeply loves her, too, but wishes she would make love to him. Both are sexually frustrated but confused about what to do. Adults aren't at all helpful. Wood's mother (Joanna Roos) keeps badgering her not to go too far until after she's married. Beatty's domineering father (Pat Hingle) tells his son if he gets Wood pregnant he'll have to marry her. Beatty wouldn't mind marrying Wood, but Hingle wants his son to go to Yale for four years first. Beatty breaks up with Wood and takes up with the school slut (Jan Norris). Wood is completely broken, and when Beatty rejects her desperate sexual advances, tries to kill herself. She is institutionalized. Beatty goes to Yale. With the crash of the market, Hingle kills himself; Beatty returns to Kansas to work a small farm. Wood gets better. She falls in love with a patient who recovers, becomes a doctor, and proposes to her. But she isn't sure she is over Beatty. When she is released, Wood visits Beatty. He is married to an Italian woman (Zohra Lampert) he met back east; they have one child and another on the way. Wood finds it strange that she no longer feels the great love she had for him. Now she can marry someone else with no regrets.

Natalie Wood was an inconsistent actress whose bad performances were deserving of the Harvard Lampoon awards given her. But on those rare occasions when she played characters with problems to which she could relate, she opened up as few actresses could, stripped off all her protective pretenses, revealed herself completely, and turned in portraits that were emotionally shattering. Such was the case with her love-struck teenager in *Splendor in the Grass.* Never was she more sensitive, radiant (or sexy), in touch with her character, or revealing of her

own personality. Never did she exhibit such deep *feeling*—down to her rawest nerves—than as this girl in the throes of young love, first love, true love. This is not the puppy love adults suspect. It is a seemingly *eternal* love, which is wonderful but terribly confusing while it lasts, mercilessly cruel just after it ends, and then amazingly fades away with the onetime lovers whole again. It's no wonder that young females identified with her character in the way young males identified with James Dean's confused youth in *Rebel Without a Cause.*

Splendor in the Grass (along with the less impressive but underrated Sandra Dee–Troy Donahue potboiler, *A Summer Place*) was a breakthrough film in that it dared emphasize that teenagers, even girls, are ruled and perplexed by sexual drives. Wood bravely played a girl who has *sexual* desires that are getting out of control—she wants to be good (as does Dee) but it becomes increasingly difficult for her to just say no. Every expression, every movement of Wood's eyes and of her body—she lies down on her stomach with legs spread and a pillow underneath, she automatically pushes her groin into Beatty's, she clutches her mother desperately—reveals that her sexual thoughts are taking over. She worries she's being bad, but she's being normal. *Splendor in the Grass* is, partly, about how Wood's character takes control of her own feelings (and of her life) once she understands them (from talks with the asylum's psychiatrist).

At the beginning she has no control. Her entire, limited life revolves around Beatty. For her, heaven is walking

Attending church services further confuses the sexually confused Natalie Wood and Warren Beatty—who, even here, is being watched accusingly by her mother—in Elia Kazan's *Splendor in the Grass.*

down the crowded school corridor with this handsome hunk at her side. She hasn't let him go all the way, but she begins to waver when she sees him pulling away, saying softly, "I am nuts about you. I would go down on my knees to worship you if you really wanted me to. I can't get along without you . . . and I would do anything you asked me to. I would. I would. Anything." She rolls onto her back and, slightly delirious, waits for *anything*. Hoping to win him back later, she tries to pull him into his car. "I'm not a nice girl," she tries to assure him, ". . . I haven't any pride."

Left on her own the lonely girl walks alone through the corridors, out of synch with all those around her. Then in a brilliantly played, emotionally devastating scene, the tearful Wood interprets a poem of Wordsworth in front of her class, saying words that make it clear to her that her "eternal" love affair has ended. During the initial phase of the breakdown Wood giggles, but soon after she is showing *pain* of loss as few actresses had the ability to do, looking as if she'd been kicked in the gut and is too weak to cry anymore, much less do anything else: "Mom, I can't eat, I can't study, I can't even face my friends anymore. I want to die, I want to die." Wood's great scene comes next, when the girl's anger and first touches of madness emerge together. She soaks in a steaming bath, moving her head back and forth for no

reason as her mother quizzes her about her virginity and says she's going to call Beatty. She sits up and screams in terror, "Don't you dare!" And she doesn't stop screaming, except to submerge her face in the steaming water, telling her mother that she's still "fresh" and "unspoiled" and "virginal like the day I was born." She jumps up, screaming that she hates her mother, and races naked into her room, where she crops her hair. Wow. After being rejected by Beatty, she tries to drown herself. Natalie Wood was terrified of water but played the scene herself. Knowing how this lovely actress would eventually die makes this sequence hard to watch and adds to its already strong emotional intensity.

After time in the institution Wood's character has gained control. Now she can console her mother, instead of the other way around. She is able to visit Beatty without becoming an emotional wreck again. The final sequence perfectly captures the feelings of disappointment and confusion that everyone experiences upon meeting former lovers with whom they were obsessed years before. The adult Wood finds it ironic that she was willing to give so much to, and went through such agony over, someone she no longer feels anything for . . . except as a clouded memory of painful youth. Like Wood we're glad her pain is over, but sad that she will never again have such strong feelings for anyone.

1962

▶ BEST PICTURE

WINNER:
Lawrence of Arabia (Columbia; David Lean)
Other Nominees: *The Longest Day, The Music Man, Mutiny on the Bounty, To Kill a Mockingbird*

▼

THE BEST CHOICE:
Ride the High Country (MGM; Sam Peckinpah)
Award-Worthy Runners-Up: *Lawrence of Arabia* (David Lean), *Long Day's Journey into Night* (Sidney Lumet), *The Man Who Shot Liberty Valance* (John Ford), *The Miracle Worker* (Arthur Penn)

In the sixties, 1962 was, with the possible exception of 1967, the year which produced the most films that had lasting emotional impact on viewers. Such pictures as *Lawrence of Arabia* (which has been reissued in David Lean's longer director's version), *The Longest Day, Lolita, What Ever Happened to Baby Jane?* (which is far better than its camp reputation would indicate), *The Manchurian Candidate, The Man Who Shot Liberty Valance,*

Peeping Tom, and *Ride the High Country* all have fervent followings today, while *The Miracle Worker* and *Long Day's Journey Into Night* have certainly stood the test of time. And many movie fans still remember how moved they were by *David and Lisa, Billy Budd, Days of Wine and Roses, Bird Man of Alcatraz, To Kill a Mockingbird,* and *Sweet Bird of Youth.* (And I liked *Hatari!*) If a poll were taken of critics and film fanatics, all these titles would get votes as 1962's Best Picture. The picture that did win the Academy Award in 1962 was David Lean's antiheroic *Lawrence of Arabia,* with a magnetic star-making performance by Peter O'Toole as T. E. Lawrence (a mysterious British officer who led the Arabs in battle against the Turks during World War I). Scripted by Robert Bolt, it is the rare epic that has exciting adventure, visual grandeur, and interesting psychological complexity. Still, I prefer a much smaller film as 1962's Best Picture, one that few Academy members saw and fewer knew was even eligible for nominations. The glorious *Ride the High Country* is Sam Peckinpah's finest film and one of the best Westerns ever made. It also was a fitting swan song for two of the American Western's icons, Joel McCrea and Randolph Scott.

It's the early twentieth century. Twenty years ago Steve Judd (McCrea) was a lawman who helped tame the West, but he has no place today in what passes for civilization. In a rowdy Western town the overage Judd is hired by the bank to go to Coarse Gold, a mining town, and bring the miners' gold back. Because of robberies on the trail, Judd hires his ex-partner Gil Westrum (Randolph Scott) and young and wild Heck Longtree (Ron Starr) to accompany him. Cynical that civilization has shafted him, Westrum has become a con man and has corrupted Heck. They plan on stealing the gold. Heck wants to kill Judd, but Westrum hopes to convince Judd to join them in the theft. They stop at the ranch of Joshua Knudson (R. G. Armstrong), a strict religious zealot who has kept his grown daughter, Elsa (Mariette Hartley), away from men. Heck is attracted to her but becomes so aggressive that she tells him she's engaged to Billy Hammond (James Drury), who is in Coarse Gold. She runs away from her father and joins Judd, Westrum, and Heck on their trip. When they arrive in Coarse Gold, Elsa marries Billy, but discovers on their nightmarish wedding night that he is a brute. He is even willing to have his brothers (L. Q. Jones, John Anderson, Warren Oates, John Davis Chandler) have their way with her. Judd and Heck rescue her and convince the judge to declare the marriage ceremony to have been illegal. They ride back to town. Heck doesn't want to rob Judd anymore but doesn't want to let down Westrum. Judd catches them with the gold and ties them up. When the Hammonds fire on them, Judd temporarily frees Heck to fight with him, but he hurts Westrum's feelings by not letting him go too. Two Hammonds are killed in the mountains. The other three go to Knudson's ranch, kill him, and wait in ambush. They wound Judd and Heck. Westrum, who had gotten away, rides to the rescue. As in the old days, he and Judd walk side by side, as they take on the Hammonds in a gunfight. The Hammonds are killed and Judd is mortally wounded. Westrum promises to take the gold to the bank—he is touched that Judd doesn't doubt his word. Westrum and Heck and Elsa, who are in love, allow Judd to die alone, gazing at the mountains for the last time.

Sam Peckinpah's second film hasn't the scope of his expensive, expansive, more famous *The Wild Bunch* but it's equally beautiful thanks to their common cinematog-

Old-timers Joel McCrea and Randolph Scott are amused by their young traveling companions, Mariette Hartley and Ron Starr, who will experience the love neither man was fortunate to have had, in Sam Peckinpah's *Ride the High Country.*

rapher, Lucien Ballard, CinemaScope, and breathtaking scenery. It has similar "epic" though past-their-prime characters, but here the camaraderie is more convincing and better explored. While it has adult themes and enough violence to satisfy *Wild Bunch* fans, it also has the humor, tenderness, grace, and lyric qualities of his *The Ballad of Cable Hogue.* Best of all it has McCrea and Scott, two of the Western's supreme stars of the postwar era riding tall in the saddle one final time (though McCrea would star in one more film, in 1976), and immediately instilling the authenticity, physical dimension, and nobleness of character so necessary to heroes in this masculine genre. As the two down-and-forgotten ex-lawmen—one who just wants "to enter His House justified" and the other who has made a pact with the devil—their performances are perfectly in tune with Peckinpah's natural, deceptively simple style. But like the film itself they have immense power: what they do and say has surprising effect on us.

In 1962 some critics contended that this was a Western without a message, believing this was praise. But *Ride the High Country* is several cuts above most Westerns precisely because it has themes important to both the genre and to Peckinpah. In fact, almost every action and line of dialogue has thematic relevance. N. B. Stone, Jr.'s, script is extremely didactic, but his lines are filled with so much wit, warmth, and wisdom that we don't mind. I see the film as a parable in which the corrupted Westrum, novice sinner Heck, and Elsa learn from watching Judd the rewards of leading a moral Christian life. Elsa (a fine performance by Mariette Hartley) was taught by her father to fear a wrathful God who speaks through his slapping hand, but Judd proves to her that God is gentle and forgiving and speaks through the heart. Westrum seems to enjoy playing Mephistopheles to Heck, but he praises Judd so much to the boy that it is clear he wants

Judd, not himself, to be Heck's role model and teach him *decency*. He mocks Judd for his morality, but he allows Judd to serve as his own moral inspiration. He learns how trivial money is in comparison to pride, dignity, loyalty, honest work, the satisfaction of fighting bad men with his best friend, and being redeemed in the eyes of this righteous man. The dying Judd restores Westrum's dignity when he says he has complete faith that he will not steal the gold but bring it to the bank. To Peckinpah, as it is with Westrum, there is nothing more important than dignity. In his films final, dignified acts will absolve men like Westrum of all past transgressions. Through Judd and an opportunity to do good, Westrum regains his morality and is "saved."

There are many memorable scenes: Judd showing up for the bank job and being told he's older than the man they expected; Heck racing a camel against a horse; Judd and Knudson arguing and quoting Scriptures over a tense dinner, while the amused Westrum quotes "Appetite, Chapter I"; the terrified Elsa saying her vows during a tinted, hallucinatory, Felliniesque wedding-orgy scene,

complete with a drunk judge, a fat madam as a brides-maid, whores as flower girls, and the boozing Hammond brothers about to pounce on the bride; Judd and Heck exchanging gunfire with the Hammonds in the wind-swept mountains; Westrum, forgetting his own welfare, riding to the rescue when the Hammonds have Judd and Heck trapped in a ditch. It's then exhilarating to watch the final shoot-out, which is staged like "the gunfight at the O.K. Corral." Judd and Westrum (played by two actors who had both played Wyatt Earp on screen), are like two Wyatt Earps as they walk side by side, heads high and guns blazing, as they'd done in films years before.

Judd's death ranks with the greatest final scenes in movie history. As the wounded man lies on the ground, propped on his left arm, Ballard's ground-level camera is tilted toward God's distant black mountains, which Judd scans for the last time. As he fell gently toward us, dying the most *dignified* of deaths, we realized that he will be riding even higher country. He will enter His House justified. Whenever the last movie Western is made, this is the scene that should put the genre to sleep.

▶ BEST ACTOR

WINNER:
Gregory Peck *(To Kill a Mockingbird)*
Other Nominees: Burt Lancaster *(Bird Man of Alcatraz)*, Jack Lemmon *(Days of Wine and Roses)*, Marcello Mastroianni *(Divorce—Italian Style)*, Peter O'Toole *(Lawrence of Arabia)*

▼

THE BEST CHOICE:
Peter O'Toole *(Lawrence of Arabia)*
Award-Worthy Runners-Up: Kirk Douglas *(Lonely Are the Brave)*, Joel McCrea *(Ride the High Country)*, James Mason *(Lolita)*, Gregory Peck *(To Kill a Mockingbird)*, Robert Preston *(The Music Man)*, Ralph Richardson *(Long Day's Journey into Night)*, Randolph Scott *(Ride the High Country)*, Dean Stockwell *(Long Day's Journey into Night)*

The Academy's choice of Gregory Peck as 1962's Best Actor was extremely popular. Movie fans respected his eighteen-year movie career as a lead actor, although it contained more sturdy than inspired performances. And they suspected that the likable, politically progressive actor was much like his admirable character in Robert Mulligan's *To Kill a Mockingbird,* for which Horton Foote adapted Harper Lee's novel. As 1930s Alabama lawyer Atticus Finch, a widower with two young children and the brave defender of a black man accused of raping a white woman, Peck displayed quiet authority, patience and fair-mindedness, a strong sense of right and wrong, warmth, humility, and courage. He was, as he'd be in other roles, the man you'd want for your father or your president (but not your lawyer, since he loses). But Peck's performance isn't nearly as impressive as we thought at the time. For instance: everyone once praised him for Atticus's deliberate, low-keyed courtroom summation, but today I wish he had more fire in the scene—and that

Atticus had more imagination. He doesn't come across as a particularly competent defense attorney. Justice wasn't done by the jury in the film or by the Academy in regard to the film. Peck was well cast and gave an earnest performance, but there were several actors more deserving of the Oscar. The best performance of the year was by a blond, brainy, blue-eyed British actor who took the world by storm as T. E. Lawrence in David Lean's Best Picture winner, *Lawrence of Arabia.* In his first major role of a lengthy career that has produced many memorable performances and no Oscars, Peter O'Toole played the year's most complex, compelling character and made viewers want to get into the head, not only of Lawrence, but also of the cerebral actor who played him.

Robert Bolt's Oscar-winning script begins with Lawrence's death in England while motorcycling. It then flashes back to World War I, when the educated, idealistic young soldier was stuck behind a desk in Cairo. He was happy to be sent on a mission into the desert to serve as a liaison with the Arab leader, Prince Faisal (Alec Guinness), whose forces were fighting with the British against the Turks. Lawrence surprised Faisal and Sherif Ali (Omar Sharif) and angered the British Colonel Brighton (Anthony Quayle) by honestly stating that the Arabs had to fight for their own concerns or they would permanently become part of the British army. Lawrence devised a "miracle" whereby the Arabs alone would cross a desert and attack the Turks at Aqaba, where the guns faced the Red Sea. The Arabs admired his daring, his bravery, his wearing of native garments, his treatment of Arabs as equals, and his desire to keep Arabia for its inhabitants. His impossible mission succeeded and he became a hero to both the Arabs and British, who ordered him back to organize the Arabs for guerrilla attacks on Turks. Major Lawrence was the one person who could unite Arabs from warring tribes. Lawrence became impressed with his own power and, though he fought it, developed a bloodlust. He asked to be taken off duty because he feared going insane, but he was sent back to war. He ordered and participated in a massacre against retreating Turks. He also led the Arabs into Damascus. The Turks were defeated and Lawrence was no longer needed in Arabia, especially while the British and French divvied up Arab lands, and Arab leaders like Faisal ruled under Western supervision. Shaken by his experiences and cynical about his world-heralded accomplishments, Colonel Lawrence left the land he genuinely loved and returned to England.

Real-life British "adventurer" T. E. Lawrence was the first of Peter O'Toole's brilliant, bigger-than-life, flawed heroes (some would be royalty) who walk the fine line between humanity and godhood, and struggle to rationalize their godlike actions and attitudes. In the case of his Lawrence we see a human being who fancies himself a god (or at very least a Moses)—because no ordinary *man* ever united the Arab tribes, traipsed through such fierce deserts, or proved "what is written" in the Arab books to be wrong—but whose attempts to play god reveal him to be a mad*man*. A madman with delusions of grandeur is exactly the type of soldier the British want to lead the Arabs on their kamikaze missions.

At the beginning of the film those who best knew the dead Lawrence admit that they didn't know him at all, other than that he was "a poet, a scholar, and a mighty warrior. . . . He was also the most shameless exhibitionist since Barnum and Bailey." So O'Toole had the difficult task of understanding and playing a character whom no one else could figure out. Interestingly, his Lawrence is fully aware that no one around him has any idea about what makes him tick, especially his military superiors. He has long ago accepted that "I'm different." So when things start going awry in his head and his feeble attempts to have himself transferred fall on deaf ears, he realizes that he must try to heal himself (which he can't do).

This is the most introspective role in the career of O'Toole, who has often relied on flamboyant gestures, those crazed steel-blue eyes, and intense, scenery-chewing diatribes to carry the day. Except for the massacre scene, in which Lawrence becomes a bloodthirsty maniac (with wide eyes, open mouth, and blood all over), he keeps his Lawrence in check, an excited, passionate man but one whose mind is always at work so that his emotions don't run wild. O'Toole, the actor, is always thinking as he plays Lawrence, who also is thinking. The muscles in Lawrence's face twitch and his eyes reveal great anger, but he doesn't "snap" until the massacre scene, although he senses he is going mad after enjoying executing an Arab. He remains calm and confident, unafraid to speak his mind or undertake a mission even if his life is at stake.

In fact, he relishes defying death, takes pride in his iron will. He tries not to reveal his weaknesses—he won't acknowledge pain when he intentionally burns his fingers or is whipped by Turks who hold him captive; he won't show fear ("My fear is my concern"); when he falters he states, "It will not happen again." But he is thrilled when he shows strength: crossing the desert, leading Arabs into battle, telling British officers of his deeds or power ("*I* did it!" he says after the taking of Aqaba), killing men, being shot and bleeding but not falling over. What humbles him is being whipped and "raped" (this is implied) by a Turkish general (José Ferrer). It then comes as a shock to this would-be god that "any man is what I am." When he was just a man at

Peter O'Toole's blue eyes grow wide and scary as Lawrence thrills to having the power to snuff out human lives in David Lean's *Lawrence of Arabia.*

the beginning, he was better than almost all men (we admired his integrity, and how he defiantly stood up to Ali after the latter killed his Arab companion—"He was my friend!"—for drinking from his well). But he wanted to be more, a god. And of course, this effort took its toll. Having done his part to deliver the Arabs into the hands of the British, which was the antithesis of his personal dream, he realizes that he is no liberator like Moses, no god who can split the Red Sea and have it swallow the oppressors. When he leaves Arabia, with neither Arabs nor British wanting him there anymore, he has been permanently damaged . . . and for nothing. After continuing to speak on behalf of Arab rule this onetime god and permanent legend will die in a common motorcycle accident.

► BEST ACTRESS

WINNER:
Anne Bancroft *(The Miracle Worker)*
Other Nominees: Bette Davis *(What Ever Happened to Baby Jane?)*, Katharine Hepburn *(Long Day's Journey into Night)*, Geraldine Page *(Sweet Bird of Youth)*, Lee Remick *(Days of Wine and Roses)*

▼

THE BEST CHOICE:
Anne Bancroft *(The Miracle Worker)*
Award-Worthy Runners-Up: Bette Davis *(What Ever Happened to Baby Jane?)*, Katharine Hepburn *(Long Day's Journey into Night)*, Shirley MacLaine *(Two for the Seesaw)*

Using the name Anne Marno, Bronx-born Anne Bancroft began her professional acting career in 1950, when she was nineteen. After working in television commercials she spent five years in near anonymity as the female lead in such B pictures as *Gorilla at Large, The Naked Street,* and *The Girl in Black Stockings,* which all look better today because of her presence. Frustrated by Hollywood, she returned to New York in search of meaningful parts. Immediately she won the coveted role of Gittel Mosca in the stage production of *Two for the Seesaw,* and earned her first Tony. Then Arthur Penn cast her as Annie Sullivan, Helen Keller's teacher, and teamed her with young Patty Duke onstage in William Gibson's *The Miracle Worker.* (It had been done on television's *Playhouse 90* with Teresa Wright and Patty McCormack.) She won her second Tony. Still, she was not known to movie audiences, so she was passed over for Shirley MacLaine when *Two for the Seesaw* was filmed in 1962. When Arthur Penn filmed *The Miracle Worker,* however, he insisted that Bancroft play Annie. So Bancroft returned to the movies after five years, in her first lead in an A picture. She deservedly won an Oscar (as did Duke) and this most inspirational of fine movies was a commercial success.

Several months after her birth Helen Keller loses her sight and hearing. Her parents (Inga Swenson, Victor Jory) keep her at home on the plantation rather than send her to an asylum, but she grows up without discipline or the ability to communicate. When she is eleven, her parents decide to hire a teacher—if Helen doesn't improve they will institutionalize her. They are surprised that the teacher, Annie Sullivan, is just out of school and must wear dark glasses because she is nearly blind herself. Annie immediately sees that Helen has tremendous intelligence and curiosity, but Helen literally puts up a fight whenever Annie tries to teach her discipline or to match to specific objects the words she spells with her fingers. Helen keeps running to her parents for protection. Annie doesn't like Helen but she wants her to have every opportunity in the world; she suffers with the memory of her own crippled brother's death when he was Helen's age. When Annie gets Helen to fold her napkin for the first time in her life, Helen's mother is so happy that she agrees, and persuades her husband to reluctantly agree, to Annie's conditions for teaching Helen. For two weeks Annie and Helen live together in a shack on the plantation, while her parents stay away. Helen overcomes her hatred for and fear of Annie and pays attention to her instructions. Although she still puts up a fight, Helen learns how to dress, clean, and feed herself, but still won't make the connection between the signs Annie teaches her on her fingers and the objects Annie has her touch. Annie is upset that she is unable to break through to the girl she has grown fond of. Back with her parents, Helen resorts to her old tricks, testing Annie's authority. When she throws a pitcher of water at Annie, Annie drags her outside to refill the pitcher. When the water from the pump touches her hand, Helen remembers the only word she said as a child: "Water." Suddenly Helen realizes that every object has a word that goes with it. She excitedly has Annie spell on her fingers all the objects she touches. She is ready to learn everything Annie wants to teach her. That night Helen crawls into Annie's arms and kisses her. Annie spells out, "I love Helen."

The Miracle Worker is an extremely powerful movie

Anne Bancroft's Annie Sullivan drags Patty Duke's Helen Keller into the yard to retrieve water in Arthur Penn's *The Miracle Worker.*

that should be more significant in feminist film criticism. Because one character is a child, many viewers overlook the fact that this is one of the first films about one female helping another to achieve something. At first there is a battle of wills between these stubborn females, later to be replaced by a partnership based on love, understanding, and mutual respect. Refusing to be handicapped by her own near-blindness or her sex, Sullivan strives to reach her potential in her profession—as she insists, she won't "give up." She won't even accept praise when she realizes that she hasn't accomplished what she expects from herself. To achieve her own goals she knows she must help Helen overcome her physical problems, use her brain, become independent of her parents, and reach her full potential. This is a film about liberation, how Helen's breakthrough also frees Annie from her self-doubts and guilt (she could do nothing to help her brother) and allows Helen's mother to achieve equal standing with her authoritarian husband ("All right," he says, "I'll consent to everything").

What were the odds that Anna Maria Louise Italiano would be the ideal choice to play Annie Sullivan? But for a brief period in the sixties there was no one better than Anne Bancroft at playing strong-willed, self-confident, and defiant women, perhaps because that pretty much described the actress herself. And this is what bonded the actress to the determined, resilient, fiery Irishwoman whose "idea of the Original Sin [is] giving up." Bancroft

plays Annie with passion, spirit, warmth, humor, strength, no-nonsense honesty, and much physical prowess. In this demanding role she must deliver many lines while in the midst of wrestling Duke. Their knock-about battles are long and complexly choreographed, but Bancroft and Duke handle them with the skill of great silent comediennes doing wild, intricate slapstick. Even when not tumbling on the ground Bancroft can rarely relax because Annie's admirable patience is constantly in conflict with her Irish temper.

We inevitably cry happily at the end of *The Miracle Worker,* but I don't think the reason is merely that Helen says "water" and Helen and Annie express love for each other (though these are emotionally powerful moments). I think the reason is unusual and has to do with our thankful response to a woman who had more fight than we have ourselves. We respect the mettle, the pugnacity, the grit, and the guts of Bancroft's determined character. We cry at the end because Annie fought so hard, and went far beyond the call of duty, to help Helen, and her efforts were rewarded . . . with a miracle. We realize that only someone with the fight to match Helen's could have reached her. Annie is the rare person who was willing to endure bumps, bruises, and insults for even minor triumphs: "The room's a wreck but her napkin is folded." Nearly blind herself, one disrespectful remark away from having Captain Keller fire her, hearing Helen's older half-brother (Andrew Prine) mock her efforts, and enduring Helen's own contempt, she never backed down. She just got stronger and more dedicated: "I treat her like a seeing child because I ask her to see, I expect her to see. Don't undo what I do!" She fought for Helen, as well as for herself, putting herself in front of the firing squad in the knowledge that she was Helen's only hope. She asked for no pity and didn't waste the precious time she had with Helen trying to get the parents' understanding of her harsh "tough-love" technique. Helen's future was at stake.

I like Bancroft's slight smiles, hints that Annie knows she has a touch of madness. That's fine with her because, as she tells the Kellers, the madness is part of the strength she developed while growing up in an asylum. Only a slightly mad woman would speak to her employers as bluntly as she does. When, for instance, the angry father yells, "If you want to stay, there must be a radical change of manner!" she replies: "Whose?" Obviously, this is the one person in the world who has the fortitude to help Helen. Of all the people in the world, *she* was the one who arrived to be Helen's teacher—that was the first miracle.

1963

▶ BEST PICTURE

WINNER:
Tom Jones (United Artists–Lopert; Tony Richardson)
Other Nominees: *America, America; Cleopatra; How the West Was Won; Lilies of the Field*

▼

THE BEST CHOICE:
None
Award-Worthy Runners-Up: None

Every time there is a presidential election, a great many of us wish we could mark a box on the ballot for None of the Above. That's how the Academy should have voted in the 1963 Best Picture race. It's true that at the time, *Tom Jones,* British director Tony Richardson's adaptation of Henry Fielding's bawdy Restoration comedy, was extremely popular, as was most everything British. It certainly was more enjoyable than the other sorry films nominated for Best Picture. But Richardson's directorial impositions no longer seem fresh, star Albert Finney has been much more impressive in other roles, and the tone of the film now comes across as smug rather than cheery. And since 1963 we've also had our fill of bawdy period pieces—prurient European costume dramas (with much nudity) have provided cable television with unlimited late-night product.

Despite the five nominees, 1963 wasn't the worst year for films. I have several favorites: *The Birds, The Haunting, The L-Shaped Room, Jason and the Argonauts, Shock Corridor, The Nutty Professor, Dr. No* (which premiered in Britain in October 1962), and *From Russia with Love.* And there are staunch admirers of such films as *Hud, It's a Mad Mad Mad Mad World, The Great Escape,* and *Lord of the Flies,* among others. No, it wasn't such a terrible year, but no film had the stature or emotional impact to be worthy of a Best Picture Oscar.

▶ BEST ACTOR

WINNER:
Sidney Poitier *(Lilies of the Field)*
Other Nominees: Albert Finney *(Tom Jones)*, Richard Harris *(This Sporting Life)*, Rex Harrison *(Cleopatra)*, Paul Newman *(Hud)*

▼

THE BEST CHOICE:
Jerry Lewis *(The Nutty Professor)*
Award-Worthy Runner-Up: Rex Harrison *(Cleopatra)*

Sidney Poitier's selection as 1963's Best Actor for Ralph Nelson's *Lilies of the Field* marked only the second time a black performer had won an Academy Award and the first time since Hattie McDaniel was voted Best Supporting Actress in 1939 for *Gone With the Wind.* Coming at a time when millions of whites across America were deeply involved in the Civil Rights movement and new president Lyndon Johnson was launching his "Great Society," the award to Poitier couldn't have been more appropriate. But was it given because Academy voters were suddenly color blind and sincerely believed that Poitier gave the year's best performance? Or because they felt pressured to show the world they were willing to give their major awards to blacks? Since beginning his film career in 1950 Poitier had given consistently excellent performances; extremely charismatic, he became the one black star of the era, securing his place in movie history. Undoubtedly Poitier should receive a career Oscar for what he did on screen and what he represented, but with the possible exception of his performance in *A Raisin in the Sun,* he was never worthy of a Best Actor Oscar. He is likable as Homer Smith, a handyman who helps refugee nuns build a chapel, in the pleasant but unremarkable *Lilies of the Field,* but Homer is one of Poitier's least interesting and least complex characters. Also, Homer is his least threatening character—he can even take off his shirt around nuns. Maybe the Academy saw the chance to remove the onus of never having given a major acting award to a black before, because this was no Oscar-winning performance. Anyway, that no blacks had ever won a major acting statue reflected less on the rank-and-file Academy voters than on the Hollywood power structure that had traditionally denied lead roles to blacks. Poitier's Oscar actually had a deleterious effect in that it gave the false impression that there was now unlimited opportunity for blacks in Hollywood. Public outcry on behalf of all black actors was temporarily silenced. I think it would have been more beneficial if the 1963 Oscar had been given to someone else.

But not many will agree with my alternate choice. Jerry Lewis? He gets awards only in France. In his more hostile native country one can't imagine him even being nominated for an Oscar. But I think that in his wildly inventive Jekyll-and-Hyde variation, *The Nutty Professor,* he gives a brilliantly conceived, quite hilarious, and daring comedic performance, worthy of consideration.

Lewis plays Julius Kelp, an intelligent but weak, buck-toothed, and myopic college chemistry teacher. His science experiments tend to end with explosions. Julius is attracted to a beautiful student, Stella (Stella Stevens), but he doesn't think he's much competition for the football players she dates. He takes a muscle-building course at Vic Tanny's but all he does is lose two pounds. So he elects to change himself with chemicals. He drinks a vial containing a potent formula and his body undergoes tremendous change. He becomes handsome Buddy Love, the coolest swinger around, and the most egotistical. The suave Buddy charms all the students at the Purple Pit with his singing and piano playing. He also sweeps Stella off her feet. She finds him irresistible while detesting his narcissism. Every time Buddy is about to make his move on Stella, however, the formula wears off, his voice grows nasal, and he must rush off before turning back into Julius. When Buddy performs at the prom, the formula wears off while he is onstage, and before the eyes of the crowd he is transformed into Julius. Julius apologizes to all the students, telling them the lesson he has learned: "You may as well like yourself: if you don't think too much of yourself, how do you expect others to?" Stella tells Julius that she loves him and not Buddy.

Much credit for Jerry Lewis's best film goes to Lewis's innovative direction and the witty screenplay he wrote with Bill Richmond. But the film also contains Lewis's most impressive performance, as he plays two memorable figures. Eccentric scientist Julius Kelp is a typical Lewis creation. He has buck teeth, oddly shaped glasses, hair on his forehead. He is the weakest person in the film, male or female. He has a nasal voice, licks his lips when he speaks, babbles in circular sentences that quickly bore the listener. He walks awkwardly, using small steps, with his head pushed forward, stomach caved

An unusual but successful romantic pairing, Jerry Lewis and Stella Stevens in *The Nutty Professor.*

in, his back curved. He dances spastically but imaginatively. He is so smitten by pretty Stella that he puts the sleeve of his white tuxedo into the punch bowl as they chat. He is mild mannered and seemingly harmless but is terribly destructive. He's the standard Lewis underdog who tries so hard that he messes up everything.

On the other hand, Buddy Love is "perfect"—except for the fact that he knows and brags that he's perfect. He is so conceited that he is a monster. By design, it is actually uncomfortable watching Buddy, seeing him humiliate other people, seeing him win sweet Stella's affection, seeing him kiss his own hand. For Lewis to play such a despicable character took guts because he risked turning off the kids who always were his greatest supporters. His own children weren't even allowed to see the film because Lewis was playing, as he said himself, "the worst human being I've ever seen in my life." I used to think Lewis modeled Buddy on his vain, romantic, boozing, singing ex-partner, Dean Martin. But after enduring Jerry Lewis on his telethons, I now think Buddy Love was the alter ego of Jerry Lewis, the part of himself he once tried to suppress.

Lewis shines in a number of amusing sequences. Among my favorites are when Julius meekly shuffles into the dean's office and sinks deep into a chair before being reprimanded for his latest explosion; and when underhanded Buddy (this is Buddy's only *funny* scene) gets into the dean's good graces by complimenting him on his suit and flattering his acting ability, coaxing him into reciting Hamlet's soliloquy while standing on top of a table and wearing the weird attire that Buddy hands him every time he tries to begin. But the wittiest sequences are those with no dialogue. Actually, he babbles amusingly during the hilarious Vic Tanny sequence, but we laugh at the sight gags: Julius gets knocked over when entering the gym; hit on the shoulder, he flies onto a trampoline, readjusting his glasses between bounces ("If you would say that a man with an ulcer [and] a nail in his shoe and a splinter in his finger was then struck by lightning—if you could say that man was not hurt, then yes, you could say that I'm not hurt"); he repeatedly flies backward into the wall while using pulleys ("Oh, that's very invigorating"); and in a cartoonish bit, his arms stretch to the floor when he's handed heavy barbells (that night he can scratch his feet without bending over).

Lewis's critics often wonder why the French adore him so much. When one watches *The Nutty Professor,* one can see the answer: Lewis's comedy was less influenced by American comics than by revered French comedian-director Jacques Tati. Like Tati, Lewis does pantomime, devises routines in which sight gags are used in conjunction with the music and noises he later places on the soundtrack, injects surreal humor into his films (which of course the French surrealists love), and plays a character who destroys every environment he enters (and tries to sneak away undetected). Lewis actually goes farther than Tati when he uses the soundtrack to make his "silent" humor work. In one great bit he sneaks down a dark hallway. He removes his sneakers to stop the loud squeaking, only to discover that it's his feet making the noise. In another amusing bit Julius comes to class with a terrible hangover. Every sound he hears—pencils clicking, chalk squeaking, gum being chewed—is magnified to such a degree that it's as if cannonballs were exploding in his head. The humor comes from watching Julius's face contort in reaction to the booming soundtrack. Also funny is when Julius stands at the end of a faculty greeting line at the prom, and can't help but move and groove—arms and legs flailing about—to the band.

Then there is a bit where Buddy speaks but it isn't the words that have importance but the *sound* of the voice, which grows nasal as he transforms back into Julius. It is odd hearing that silly sound emanate from the seductive Buddy. It's also interesting watching Lewis use his comically pitched voice while in his Julius makeup, then his natural voice when he plays Buddy, and, finally, the nasal voice rising in Buddy as he is transformed onstage into Julius. It's surprising because you think the Julius voice is wedded to the Julius character. Lewis, using that voice when looking like himself, immediately wins our sympathy. With a similar motivation he often reverts to his "kid" persona on the telethon, when desperate for laughs. At the end of *The Nutty Professor* the funny-voiced, funny-looking Julius survives and the dashing but obnoxious Buddy disappears. One wonders what Lewis, the director-writer-actor, was saying about himself.

► BEST ACTRESS

WINNER:
Patricia Neal *(Hud)*
Other Nominees: Leslie Caron *(The L-Shaped Room),* Shirley MacLaine *(Irma La Douce),* Rachel Roberts *(This Sporting Life),* Natalie Wood *(Love with the Proper Stranger)*

▼

THE BEST CHOICE:
Leslie Caron *(The L-Shaped Room)*
Award-Worthy Runners-Up: Shirley MacLaine *(Irma La Douce),* Patricia Neal *(Hud)*

From 1949 until the mid-sixties, when a stroke almost took her life and altered the course of her career, Patricia Neal was a different kind of leading lady. She starred in such films as *The Fountainhead* (she'd have a crushing, much-publicized three-year affair with Gary Cooper), *The Breaking Point, The Day the Earth Stood Still, Diplomatic Courier,* and *A Face in the Crowd,* and one always knew that no other actress would have played the parts as she did. Neal was a smart, forceful screen presence. She had a sexy Southern drawl and an erotic face with a sly, full-face grin and eyes that expressed excitement about the dangerous men standing before her and self-mockery that she should be so attracted to them. Her smart, aggressive, sensual women risk getting involved with troubled or troublesome men, often get hurt, and try to work through the confusion and pain. At thirty-seven Neal was certainly sexy enough to play opposite Paul Newman in Martin Ritt's modern-day western, *Hud.* She played a lusty, strong-willed, once mistreated housekeeper who is aroused by Newman's constantly-on-the-make cowboy (the son of her employer, Melvyn Douglas), but tries to discourage this cad: "I've done my time with one cold-blooded bastard and I'm not looking for another." ("It's too late, honey, you've already found him," Hud responds). Neal gave the year's best performance, male or female, but since her part wasn't that substantial, I think she should have been in the Supporting Actress category (along with Rachel Roberts, who didn't have much screen time in *The Sporting Life*). That's the reason Neal is my second choice for the Best Actress award, behind Leslie Caron, who broke out of her Hollywood shackles with a bold performance in the British drama *The L-Shaped Room.*

The winner of the British Film Academy Award for this role, Caron played Jane, an insecure twenty-seven-year-old Frenchwoman, who leaves her unsupportive parents' home and moves into an L-shaped room in a cheap London boardinghouse. She is two months pregnant from her only lover, but she doesn't want to marry him. When she has an upsetting visit with an unfeeling doctor, she decides that she wants to keep the baby. She becomes friends with her neighbors: Toby (Tom Bell), an unpublished writer, Johnny (Brock Peters), a Caribbean-born jazz trumpeter, and Mavis (Avis Bunnage), an aging lesbian, who once was a music hall performer. She and Toby fall in love, but when Johnny tells Toby she's pregnant, Toby turns away from her, hurting her terribly. Everyone wants her to have an abortion but she stands firm. Toby again becomes her lover, but he's so upset about having no money that he can't handle the relationship. Jane has a baby, which is delivered by a kind doctor. Toby visits her in the hospital and gives her a short story he's written called "The L-Shaped Room." On leaving the hospital she heads back to her parents, but stops off at the boardinghouse. Toby isn't there, but she leaves his manuscript on his typewriter with a complimentary note saying that she awaits his story's ending.

Today films about single pregnant women who decide to keep their babies reflect a conservative Hollywood that is afraid to offend the pro-life forces. But in its day Bryan Forbes's *The L-Shaped Room* was quite daring because it broke away from the tradition of having the pregnant woman either suffer a miscarriage, give birth to a stillborn baby, or die herself—a payback for having "sinned." Moreover, in sixties movies a single woman who shamelessly had a baby out of wedlock and kept it defied the established order. Caron's Jane doesn't have the baby because she is against abortions per se (at one time she takes pills to cause a miscarriage) but because her baby's birth will be a means of injecting "life"—figuratively and literally—into her dreary existence. She loves the people in her boardinghouse, but they are all lonely, unfulfilled,

and unhappy. Pretty much *dead*beats. To Toby, who loves Jane and is sickened by the thought of another's child in her belly, to the lesbian Mavis, who never had a relationship that could produce a child (her "child" is a cat), and to Johnny, who sees the baby as proof that the unmarried Jane is a "whore" (especially when she becomes Toby's lover), the baby represents something scary and disruptive—its birth will cause them to confront themselves. So they want Jane to have an abortion, adding more death to their lives. Jane stands firm, refusing to allow them to dictate her future. Ironically, with the baby's birth her friends start to break out of their respective shells. The baby is a life force for them as well.

Part of Caron's appeal in her MGM days was that her characters never came across as innocent as they were on the surface. By design MGM gave her young characters a sexual edge in such pictures as *An American in Paris* (an older man has been taking care of her *before* Gene Kelly discovers her), *Lili* (she is almost raped, and then is willing to give herself to the older man who rescues her), and *Gigi* (she grows up right before Louis Jourdan's excited eyes). Yet in *The L-Shaped Room* Caron revealed a sexual maturity that her fans were unprepared for. Without the Hollywood beauty treatment she looked like a real woman for a change, and she was more appealing than ever. And, in 1963 there was something enticing as well as admirable about this woman who refuses to marry the man who impregnated her, or let a quack male doctor give her an abortion so he can pay his bills, or get an abortion though it would guarantee the love of Toby, the man she loves.

In past years I have tended to give Alternate Oscars to women playing extremely strong characters, but what makes Caron's Jane so affecting is that she does strong things despite being extremely vulnerable and lacking self-esteem. Of going it alone she says simply, "I don't have any choice." She tells Toby, "I'm not your responsibility—I'm not anybody's but mine." People give her bad advice (which will help them more than her), let her down, and put pressure on her. But despite the occasional lapse of confidence in her own decisions—she takes the pills, cries, has tantrums, chops off her hair in a moment of self-hatred—she remains firm. She must protect herself, as when she tells off Toby for trying, unsuccessfully, to make her feel like a whore ("All I've had is two men. I'm twenty-seven and only twice, that's all it's ever happened. So what does that make me?"). And she must find the way to replenish her sapping strength and achieve her own happiness. It's wonderful to see Caron manage a rare smile! She does this when she makes love to Toby, when she recovers after the miscarriage attempt fails ("I have a lot to be thankful for"), when she receives a baby crib from Johnny, and when she learns from the kindly doctor that her baby has been born: "He's a girl!" After the baby is born, Jane's life is far from perfect—she must go live with parents who don't understand her—but at least she's truthful when she says, "I couldn't be better." For once, a Caron character is living in the real world, where there aren't many fairy-tale endings.

Leslie Caron falls in love for the first time, with Tom Bell, but she carries another man's baby in *The L-Shaped Room*.

1964

▶ BEST PICTURE

WINNER:
My Fair Lady (Warner Bros.; George Cukor)
Other Nominees: *Becket; Dr. Strangelove: or, How I Learned to Stop Worrying and Love the Bomb; Mary Poppins; Zorba the Greek*

▼

THE BEST CHOICE:
Dr. Strangelove: or, How I Learned to Stop Worrying and Love the Bomb
(Columbia; Stanley Kubrick)
Award-Worthy Runners-Up: *A Hard Day's Night* (Richard Lester), *The Servant* (Joseph Losey), *A Shot in the Dark* (Blake Edwards)

George Cukor's film version of Lerner and Loewe's *My Fair Lady,* itself a musical adaptation of Shaw's *Pygmalion,* became Warner Bros.' top-grossing film and copped eight Oscars, including 1964's Best Picture, Best Director, and Best Actor (Rex Harrison). *My Fair Lady* is only a *fair* film at best, and as a movie musical it is a failure. Even those songs that haven't grown tiresome over the years can't salvage the poorly conceived production numbers. If you can call them that. For this big-budget musical doesn't have any large-scale production numbers. When Audrey Hepburn's Eliza Doolittle sings *to herself* "I Could Have Danced All Night," all she's referring to is taking one or two turns around the parlor with Rex Harrison's stuffy Professor Higgins. That's it. Most of the numbers seem to have been performed on a confining stage since Cukor made no effort either to enhance them or to mask their deficiencies with cinematic touches. Furthermore, the postproduction dubbing of the songs is woeful, and even when Hepburn's lips are in synch with Marni Nixon's voice, the substitution is so obvious that one can't help wishing Jack Warner hadn't snubbed Julie Andrews, who played Eliza on Broadway. Besides singing herself, Andrews might have given more strength to Eliza. Hepburn's Eliza is too weak—the viewer is annoyed to find her so happy to give up her freedom for marriage with a dull, older man who has treated her with condescension.

The year's best movie musical was *A Hard Day's Night,* with the Beatles. It had more humor, more interesting characters, better cinematography, more imaginative direction, and a far better soundtrack than *My Fair Lady.* It's the film I most enjoy from 1964, but another outstanding picture is more deserving of the Oscar because of its lasting impact: Stanley Kubrick's brilliantly scripted and acted "nightmare comedy," *Dr. Strangelove: or, How I Learned to Stop Worrying and Love the Bomb.* It was the period's most controversial film, both vilified and praised for being the first satire that dared attack (in both comical and serious ways) the nuclear irresponsibility of America's politicians and military leaders. It spoke for the entire paranoid generation. Today, the film is even more timely. Considering all the impossible events that have taken place since 1964 (from Watergate to the Iran-Contra affair to the Persian Gulf War), and all the crooked politicians, loose-cannon military men, and ninnies, incompetents, and right-wingers in power who have populated the political arena, one no longer considers the strange events or berserk characters in *Dr. Strangelove* as being too farfetched. As long as there remains the very real threat of someone starting a nuclear war, *Dr. Strangelove* will be our best comic release. Perhaps we laugh at ourselves for living in a world whose fate is in the hands of wild men and clowns.

Kubrick originally intended to keep the serious tone of the source novel, *Two Hours to Doom* (titled *Red Alert* in America), which was written by ex–RAF officer and former British intelligence agent Peter George, using the pseudonym Peter Bryant. (After writing one more nuclear thriller George committed suicide.) But while adapting George's tense story about how a liberal American president tries to abort a mistakenly initiated nuclear-bomb mission on Russia—even giving the Russians data that will allow them to shoot down our planes and nuke one of our cities if a Russian city is bombed—Kubrick decided that all the absurd things he was keeping out of his script were the most truthful. So with the help of Terry Southern and star Peter Sellers, who devised three comic characterizations, Kubrick vented his rage by making his story and the characters who populated it outrageous.

For starters, George's General Quinten, a contemplative, fatally ill, deranged officer who initiates the bombing mission in the belief that a limited nuclear war will result in lasting peace, became the ripsnorting, paranoid, off-his-rocker General Jack D. Ripper (a frighteningly hilarious portrayal by Sterling Hayden), who wants to wipe out the commies for sapping America's precious bodily fluids and making him impotent. General Keppler, a

In the War Room, Peter Bull's Russian ambassador is quite disturbed to learn from Peter Sellers's American president that the U.S. has mistakenly launched a full-scale nuclear attack on the Soviet Union in Stanley Kubrick's doomsday comedy, *Dr. Strangelove: or, How I Learned to Stop Worrying and Love the Bomb.*

minor character in the book who has a brief verbal altercation with the Russian ambassador, became George C. Scott's ignorant hawk, General Buck Turgidson, who *never* admits mistakes and always tries to turn strategic blunders into military advantages (he wants the attack to proceed in order to catch the Russians "with their pants down"). Captain Clint Brown, the dedicated, patriotic flight commander of the *Alabama Angel,* became Slim Pickens's jingoistic, glory-hungry flight commander–cowboy of the *Leper Colony,* Major T. J. "King" Kong, who literally rides the bomb to the ground. Quinten's intelligent executive officer, Major Paul Howard, became Sellers's Lionel Mandrake, a veteran, stiff-lipped British officer—he may be the film's only rational character but he is reduced to trying to make a collect call to the president from a phone booth. The strong-willed, nameless president of the book became Sellers's short, bald, well-meaning but ineffectual Merkin Muffley (meaning "stupidity"). Sellers's unforgettable title character, a grotesque, wheelchair-bound German scientist, is one of Kubrick's many fabrications. That this amoral ex-Nazi, who automatically salutes Hitler with his uncontrollable right arm and tries to keep from strangling himself with his gloved right hand (none of the weirdos around him thinks this strange) has become America's director of weapons research and development is a chilling thought, but it's believable considering some of the scoundrels who became "friends" of America during the Cold War.

Kubrick pretty much agreed with George's interpretation of American generals as "war-hungry psychopaths on the lunatic fringe." But where George was respectful of American politicians, American emigré Kubrick makes the point that if America's military gets us into trouble, America's inept, confused politicians (including the pres-

ident) will have no idea how to get us out of it. Kubrick also introduces a sexual subtext into the story, making the point that playing power politics and making war are male games, extensions of our leaders' sex lives. Turgidson, Russian Premier Kissoff, and the *Leper Colony* fliers have their sex lives interrupted by the crisis; Ripper, Muffley, and Dr. Strangelove are incapable of having sex. In this film where the props and weapons are aggressive and phallic, the Russians' doomsday device (a Kubrick invention), which explodes automatically when America's bomb lands on Russian soil and destroys the world (an incident absent from the book), is their mutual "sexual" climax.

In Kubrick, men have become prisoners of science, an extension of its fallible machines. Unable to communicate with sincere words or feelings, they fight and build bombs to express what they are thinking. It's appropriate that everyone in the film is a caricature because, as Turgidson admits to Muffley, "The human element seems to have failed us here." When even the president starts listening to the Nazi Strangelove's proposal that the government elite move into mine shafts, where there will be ten women for every man in order to populate post-nuclear America, we see that this is no Age of Reason. And in an unreasonable age, where there is no such thing as a fail-safe system, we can't consider bombs deterrents to war, but potential instruments of annihilation. Oddly, there's something wonderfully cathartic about watching our world blown to smithereens by the dummies in this film, as Vera Lynn sings "We'll Meet Again." See? Our paranoia has been validated. And then we stand up in the theater and go home, laughing as we face another scary day.

▶ BEST ACTOR

WINNER:
Rex Harrison *(My Fair Lady)*
Other Nominees: Richard Burton *(Becket)*, Peter O'Toole *(Becket)*, Anthony Quinn *(Zorba the Greek)*, Peter Sellers *(Dr. Strangelove: or, How I Learned to Stop Worrying and Love the Bomb)*

▼

THE BEST CHOICE:
Peter Sellers *(Dr. Strangelove: or, How I Learned to Stop Worrying and Love the Bomb)*
Award-Worthy Runners-Up: Dirk Bogarde *(The Servant)*, Sean Connery *(Goldfinger)*, Peter O'Toole *(Becket)*, Anthony Quinn *(Zorba the Greek)*, Tony Randall *(The 7 Faces of Dr. Lao)*, Peter Sellers *(A Shot in the Dark)*

The "British invasion," led by the Beatles in music and James Bond in the movies, was in full force by early 1965, when the Oscar nominations were announced. Four British actors vied with Mexican-born Anthony Quinn for the Best Actor statue, the first time that there was a category in which none of the nominees was born in America. Would Quinn, the sentimental choice for his earthy, lively portrait of *Zorba the Greek,* have stood a chance if Zorba were a Brit? As it was, Rex Harrison, who was the best thing about *My Fair Lady,* was selected Best Actor, and Quinn and his fellow losers were well on their way to being pointed to as prime examples of deserving actors who never won the coveted prize. In much more challenging roles than Harrison's Henry Higgins (which he'd played over a thousand times onstage), Richard Burton was very good as Archbishop of Canterbury Thomas à Becket and Peter O'Toole was even better as Henry II in the dramatic powerhouse, *Becket.* But Peter Sellers bettered all three of them by playing three roles to perfection in Stanley Kubrick's apocalyptic comedy, *Dr. Strangelove: or, How I Learned to Stop Worrying and Love the Bomb.* His portrayal of three characters in one film underlined the fact that Sellers was everywhere in 1964 (his frenetic pace brought on a heart attack): he was an eccentric pianist in *The World of Henry Orient* and played, for the first two times, his inimitable Inspector Clouseau in *The Pink Panther,* a supporting role to David Niven's jewel thief, and *A Shot in the Dark,* in which he gave one of the cinema's most hilarious and innovative comic performances, now in the lead role. But as wonderful as Sellers was as the inept French detective in *A Shot in the Dark,* it was his three masterful creations in *Dr. Strangelove* that should have added up to an Oscar.

Many critics, especially in England, despised Sellers because they didn't consider him a good comic actor, but simply a mimic. Even if he was just a mimic—and I think he was also a skilled physical comic—that talent was sufficiently brilliant to have given the world a host of unforgettable characters. In *Dr. Strangelove,* where, as Kubrick stated, "much of the impact hinged on the dialogue, mode of expression, and euphemisms employed," Sellers is at his peak.

One of his characters in Lionel Mandrake, a British officer whose thick mustache hovers over his stiff upper

Peter Sellers as the unforgettable title character in *Dr. Strangelove.*

lip. Mandrake is attached to Burpleson Air Force Base, from which insane General Jack D. Ripper (Sterling Hayden) gives the order to an airborne division to drop a nuclear bomb on Russia. Mandrake tries to calmly cajole Ripper into giving him the recall code to prevent nuclear war. Sellers plays Mandrake like a cross between stalwart Trevor Howard–David Niven RAF officers and a very subdued and subtle Terry-Thomas. He's very British: he won't yell at his superior officer or even at the telephone operator who refuses to put his emergency world-saving call through to the president unless he inserts correct change. When he learns that war has begun, he says simply, "Oh, hell . . ." The lone British character in the British-made film is the only character who uses his intelligence. However, if he were only as frantic as some of the Americans in the film, he might get something accomplished before it's too late.

Even better is Sellers's American president, Merkin Muffley. Sellers plays him as a fifties-style Adlai Stevenson Democrat. He wears glasses, is almost completely bald, has no charisma, no personality, no charm, no strength, no initiative. You have to wonder about the fellow he beat to be elected. Throughout the film Muffley struggles to keep his composure while everyone around him acts like an ass. When General Buck Turgidson (George C. Scott) actually tackles the Russian ambassador (Peter Bull), Muffley simply admonishes them: "You can't fight here—this is the War Room!" It's also most amusing when he struggles to keep his temper as a president should, speaking through tight lips and measuring his words while the slightly embarrassed Turgidson explains how it was possible for Ripper to launch a nuclear attack without presidential authorization; and later while Turgidson recommends that the United States launch a full-scale sneak attack on Russia *immediately,* so it will suffer only "modest and acceptable civilian casualties—no more than ten to twenty million killed, tops, depending on the breaks." Sellers's finest moment as Muffley is a classic Bob Newhart–like solo "hot line" phone conversation, in which, speaking calmly, he informs Premier Kissoff that the United States has launched a nuclear attack on Russia. He's like a teenage boy trying to explain delicately to a female cousin why he's changed his mind and is taking someone else to the big dance, while waiting for her blowup.

Sellers's weirdest creation is Dr. Strangelove, a sickening parody of Wernher von Braun. He fits into the tradition of vile, mad (often crippled) German scientists that dates back to the silent era. He has a thick German accent, a shaky voice that isn't to be trusted, a pervert's grin; wavy, dead-looking hair; dark glasses; a double chin; paralyzed legs; and a gloved hand that alternately shoots out into a "Heil Hitler" salute and tries to strangle him. He is part broken man and part broken machine, an extension of his wheelchair. And he's a member of the U.S. government's high command!—the director of weapons research and development, of all things. He salivates over a plan according to which all top men in government and the military will escape the nuclear war by withdrawing into mine shafts, where women will outnumber men ten to one. So excited is he about his filthy plan that he rises from his chair and spouts the film's last line: "Mein Führer, I can walk!" We worry what this wretch is capable of now that he's back on his feet. That's why we don't feel upset when in the next instant the world blows up.

▶ BEST ACTRESS

WINNER:
Julie Andrews *(Mary Poppins)*
Other Nominees: Anne Bancroft *(The Pumpkin Eater),* Sophia Loren *(Marriage Italian Style),* Debbie Reynolds *(The Unsinkable Molly Brown),* Kim Stanley *(Seance on a Wet Afternoon)*

THE BEST CHOICE:
Paula Prentiss *(Man's Favorite Sport?)*
Award-Worthy Runner-Up: Anne Bancroft *(The Pumpkin Eater)*

Playing P. L. Travers's "practically perfect" nanny in Walt Disney's expensive musical *Mary Poppins* was originally just a consolation role for Julie Andrews, who had been rejected for *My Fair Lady.* Andrews had created Eliza Doolittle on Broadway, but since she'd never been in a film and had no box-office clout, Jack Warner gave Audrey Hepburn the coveted part, although her singing would have to be dubbed (by Marni Nixon). Academy members voted *My Fair Lady* Best Film, and Rex Harrison Best Actor, but, in response to Warner's snub of Andrews, snubbed Hepburn when handing out nominations. Andrews not only was nominated for her debut in *Mary Poppins* but was voted Best Actress. She was much better opposite James Garner in the black comedy *The Americanization of Emily,* which also was released in 1964, but no one saw that picture, while *Mary Poppins* was an enormous hit. Andrews's singing and natural charm didn't quite make up for her being miscast in a role that required her to suppress her energy and cheery humor. There is nothing special about her performance. More-over, Andrews disappears for such long, pivotal stretches of the movie that her part nearly becomes a supporting one.

Nineteen sixty-four didn't contain many memorable showings by actresses. In fact, my choice for best performance, Paula Prentiss in *Man's Favorite Sport?,* is one that is almost forgotten—if it was noticed in the first place. I am among those many movie fans who noticed something special about Prentiss. Beginning with *Where the Boys Are* this tall, lanky Texas-born brunette gave terrific, offbeat, usually comic performances in several fringe pictures of the early and mid-sixties, before her roles got smaller and her films became more serious. I think her best role was in Howard Hawks's sex comedy, opposite a surprisingly funny Rock Hudson.

Prentiss plays the single Abigail Page, who works as publicist for a lodge on Wakapoogee Lake, which is holding its annual fishing contest. She convinces the manager (John McGiver) of Abercrombie & Fitch in San Francisco to enter its fishing-expert salesman Roger Willoughby (Hudson). It will be a boon to the contest to have a famous fishing writer and authority participating in the event. The aggressive Abigail forces the reluctant Roger to agree. But he confides that he has never been fishing in his life. In a week's time she tries to teach him how to fish—he almost drowns. She finds herself attracted to Roger, but realizes she drives him crazy. Besides, he's engaged. Still she pursues him . . . until he responds—then she gets scared and runs away. By fool luck Roger wins the contest. He gives up the trophy because he doesn't want to have won under false pretenses. By then Roger's jealous fiancée has left him and he realizes he loves Abigail. He pursues her to her campsite. She tries to chase him away, but he crawls into her sleeping bag. They wind up floating in the middle of the lake. When they kiss, it's like two trains colliding.

Hawks's sex comedy has some hilarious sight gags and a few funny lines of dialogue, but that it is anything special is due to the appeal of Prentiss and Hudson, who compensate for their lack of sexual chemistry by having fun on screen. Hawks intended his picture to be a throwback to his thirties screwball comedies, like *Bringing Up Baby,* with Prentiss and Hudson playing the Katharine Hepburn and Cary Grant parts (indeed he originally wanted those two actors for the roles). Like Hepburn, Prentiss covers her insecurities by acting aggressively. She overwhelms Hudson, just as Hepburn overwhelmed Grant, pursuing him relentlessly, keeping him off balance with illogical responses to his questions, tactlessly laughing at him when he does something foolish (like unknowingly eating a salad after a caterpillar fell in it), physically wearing him down, almost causing him to drown. Since he pretends no interest in her, she takes the initiative and, like other Hawks women, usurps the "male" role in the romance. Extremely pushy, she kisses him when he's unconscious, she visits his cabin late at night while wearing short pajamas, she crawls into his bed (while he's away) and falls asleep, she starts a leading conversation about kissing ("Roger, I have to ask you a question—would . . . you . . . please . . . like to kiss me? Would you?"), and she teaches him fishing . . . until she's got him, hook, line, and sinker.

In the opening titles Hawks presents a montage of photos of beautiful James Bond–like women; the other two actresses in the film, Maria Perschy and Charlene Holt, are extremely beautiful, play sexy characters, and are seen in various states of undress. It's as if Hawks intended to undermine his tomboyish, familiarly attractive female lead. However, Prentiss is the one who catches our eye and Hudson's as well. It's evident that she is *different.* Hudson insists that he hates "domineering females," but he appreciates that she makes a play for him, when he wouldn't feel at ease chasing her. He complains, "Everything you do makes trouble," but it's the trouble he finds fascinating: "I never know what you're going to do next . . . living on the slopes of a live volcano. I mean you're exciting."

As it was with Hepburn in *Bringing Up Baby,* Prentiss is her own worst enemy. She wishes she weren't so

Paula Prentiss can't be stirred from Rock Hudson's bed in Howard Hawks's *Man's Favorite Sport?*

pushy, so obvious with her ambushes, so talkative. She even tries to cool it with Hudson, once she realizes that she is wrecking his life. However, she's like a schoolgirl who can't control herself because she's too much in love. I love her excitement when she realizes that he might be attracted to her too. "There are times—" he says, only to have her interrupt impatiently, "What kind of times?" Her heart beating wildly, she constantly interrupts him as he tries to explain how he finds her "strangely attractive," like "a bird watching a snake"—an image she nervously creates with a grasping hand and a zapping noise. "There are times when I like you," he finally admits. "Is this one of them?" she asks eagerly. "I guess it must be, because right now"—he stammers—"I'm wondering what it would be like if I kissed you?" "You're wondering?" she asks incredulously, forcing the issue. They kiss and Hawks cuts to two trains colliding and then back to Prentiss, who has one of the funniest facial responses to the perfect kiss in movies. It's a fitting climax to a great romantic scene.

Prentiss is funny throughout the film, whether slapping her hand down on a table and sending an ashtray flying through the air and into a fish tank, giving Hudson motorboat instructions that send him flying into the water ("You just yank that back as hard as you can . . . but *before* you do that . . ."), laughing about Hudson's caterpillar salad, laughing at the way his jealous fiancée storms out until she sees his unamused response ("She was just about the maddest woman I've ever seen. . . . Don't hit me, Roger"), or having crying fits (a reminder to Hudson that she is *female*).

Paula Prentiss could have used an Oscar in 1964, because for the next few years she didn't have the pull to get the parts that her talent warranted. Briefly, she displayed her unique blend of wacky and sophisticated humor on television, opposite husband Richard Benjamin in *He and She.* But in films she was soon reduced to supporting roles, most effectively in *The Parallax View* and *The Stepford Wives.* Not until 1980's *The Black Marble,* a romantic comedy–police drama, did she again have a strong lead. And she still sparkled.

▶ BEST PICTURE

The Sound of Music (20th Century–Fox; Robert Wise)

Other Nominees: *Darling, Doctor Zhivago, Ship of Fools, A Thousand Clowns*

▼

THE BEST CHOICE:

Repulsion (Compton-Cameo; Roman Polanski)

Award-Worthy Runners-Up: None

The race for Best Picture of 1965 was between Robert Wise's *The Sound of Music* and David Lean's *Doctor Zhivago.* Both were slickly made, tasteful, and exceedingly commercial. Both featured engaging lead performances by attractive blondes from Britain named Julie, who had zoomed to box-office prominence: the wholesome Julie Andrews had been the previous year's Best Actress for her debut in *Mary Poppins* and was the favorite to repeat for *The Sound of Music,* taking care of even more children; the sexy Julie Christie would defeat Andrews for Best Actress for *Darling.* It's likely the Academy selected *The Sound of Music* as its Best Picture because it was, quite simply, a full-scale *Hollywood* production (despite Andrews's presence) and voters didn't want it to come off second best to a British film. National pride aside, I think the Academy made the correct choice between the two. *The Sound of Music* is shamelessly syrupy and manipulative and was calculated to make a fortune, but after all these years it still affects millions of viewers emotionally, thanks mostly to Andrews. *Dr. Zhivago* comes across as lumbering, pedestrian, and artificial. Also, Omar Sharif's heart attack sequence is the most wretched in film history.

My choice for Best Picture is Roman Polanski's unnominated black-and-white *British*-made *Repulsion,* with another blonde, France's Catherine Deneuve. While Andrews brought sunshine into people's lives on- and offscreen, Deneuve gave the year's darkest portrayal as a psychotic young woman who literally tries to brush sunlight away.

Originally from Brussels, Deneuve's shy, sensitive Carol is a young manicurist who lives in a London flat with her older sister Helen (Yvonne Furneaux). She is disturbed by the frequent visits of Helen's married boyfriend, Michael (Ian Hendry). Their lovemaking each night upsets this young woman, who is both repulsed by sex (and men) and obsessed with it. She is courted by a nice, handsome young man, Colin (John Fraser), but she keeps putting him off. She allows him to kiss her, but then rushes to her apartment to brush her teeth and wash out her mouth. She throws out Michael's toiletries. Helen and Michael go to Italy, leaving Carol alone. She becomes increasingly withdrawn. Each night she has sexual fantasies in which strange men break into her room and rape her. She fades in and out, loses track of time, leaves food out to rot, rips out her telephone cord, stops going to work, and continues to have violent sexual fantasies. Colin breaks into the apartment to find out what has happened to her. She bashes in his head with a candlestick and puts his body in the water-filled bathtub. She boards up the door, but the landlord breaks in to collect overdue rent. Seeing her in her nightdress, he forces himself on her. She slashes him to death with a razor. Helen and Michael return to the flat. Neighbors also wander in. The corpses are discovered. Michael carries the catatonic Carol to an ambulance.

When *Repulsion* was released it was considered by many—including young women who related to the sexually repressed Carol and her dangerous fantasies—to be more frightening than *Psycho.* Today, it seems more unnerving than terrifying—although viewers still jump when they see the fantasy man's reflection in the mirror. Yet it remains fascinating as an erotic psychological thriller; an enigmatic portrait of a woman who sinks into madness; and an early look into the macabre mind of Roman Polanski.

According to his autobiography Polanski based his heroine on a woman he knew, who seemed quiet but was prone to inexplicable moments of violent behavior. As he would do in later films, the Polish-born director, whose one previous feature was *Knife in the Water,* placed his main character in a bewildering, inhospitable setting. The hostile world in which his fragile heroine sleepwalks is fit landscape for a breakdown. She's a foreigner living in London, unknown to her snoopy, much older neighbors, and even to her landlord. She's close to her older sister, but Helen isn't at all like her, doesn't know anything about her it turns out, and is

A study in isolation: Catherine Deneuve in Roman Polanski's *Repulsion*.

spending all her time with her boyfriend, Michael. At a cosmetics clinic she is employed by an ugly, older woman to give manicures to equally grotesque, equally old women whose faces are covered with grease and mud. She's the only one who leaves the beauty shop looking beautiful. She can't deal with sex, yet everything she hears in the shop is about men (being beasts) and everything she sees has sexual connotations. The men in her life are: a construction worker who makes remarks to her as she passes him in the street; Michael, who is stepping out on his wife; Colin, who is well meaning but never stops making a play for her; and her landlord, who tries to rape her as soon as they meet. They're not a great lot. During the film everyone gets the urge to take care of Carol, as if she were a child, but at one point they each (except for her work friend, Bridget) in some way turn against her or become aggressive toward her. Her employer admonishes her, her sister yells at her for protesting her affair with Michael, both Colin and the landlord break through her front door, the landlord forces himself on her, et cetera.

It's a sad world in which no one offers help, in which no one recognizes Carol's problem or makes a real attempt to understand what is wrong. Carol can't think clearly as Polanski fills the frame with sexual imagery and the soundtrack with the bells of the convent, shrill rings of the telephone and doorbell, dripping tap water, traffic noises, Helen's love moans, the weird song of the three street musicians, and the harsh complaints by the aged women customers about men. It's an illogical world where the giddy nuns next door play schoolyard games, where a musician walks backward down the street, where the beautiful Carol has never had a lover. Little wonder that reality and illusion merge in Carol's troubled mind.

Deneuve is convincing as the lonely, unformed young woman who is drifting into insanity, whose mind is deteriorating while the food around her rots. She gets to laugh and smile only once in the film, when Bridget talks about *The Gold Rush* (apparently Polanski believes only Chaplin could cheer up someone having a nervous breakdown). At other times her Carol is withdrawn, frightened, guilty (her violent nightmares reflect that she wants to be punished for her sexual desires). She just pulls into herself, to where she can't be reached. It's spooky. Some critics chastised Polanski for his depiction of "woman as man-killing monster," but Carol doesn't represent evil. Polanski treats her extremely sympathetically. Interestingly, even male viewers identify with Deneuve rather than with her male victims, whereas while watching *Psycho,* everyone identifies with the psychotic's victims. Carol's hallucinations/nightmares are full of erotic images—it's a sexy film—but Polanski doesn't want us to become aroused when she is raped and ravaged by her imagined male intruders. Significantly, we are disturbed by the attacks because we know Carol is suffering without achieving any kind of sexual satisfaction or liberation. We realize that she can't cope with the sexual confusion.

Most critics were annoyed because they believed Polanski should have explained the reasons for Carol's breakdown. Well, he does. At the end Gilbert Taylor's camera finds a photo of Carol as a little girl as she stands behind her seated family. The sad-eyed girl doesn't look at the camera but to her left, at the man who is presumably her father, the only other lit figure *before* Taylor's camera moves into a close-up of the girl's face. It's Polanski's "Rosebud" shot, giving us the evidence as to what (in this case, who) caused Carol's enormous sexual problems and the Revulsion (the film's original title) toward men, which have led to her disintegration. Here Polanski exonerates *her* from all guilt for her actions. And he fully reveals his affection for her. Like the film's characters, and like ourselves in the audience, he wants to protect her and take care of her, but knows he can do nothing to help. It is many years too late.

▶ BEST ACTOR

WINNER:
Lee Marvin *(Cat Ballou)*
Other Nominees: Richard Burton *(The Spy Who Came in from the Cold)*, Laurence Olivier *(Othello)*, Rod Steiger *(The Pawnbroker)*, Oskar Werner *(Ship of Fools)*

▼

THE BEST CHOICE:
Sean Connery *(The Hill)*
Award-Worthy Runners-Up: Ivan Dixon *(Nothing But a Man)*, Laurence Olivier *(Othello)*

In most cases a comic actor has to play a serious part before receiving Academy Award consideration, but in 1965 tough guy Lee Marvin showed he could play wild comedy in the Western parody *Cat Ballou* and rode off with an Oscar. He played both Kid Shelleen, the alcoholic gunslinger Jane Fonda hires, and the deep-voiced, nose-less villain who killed her father. Marvin has one of the great scenes of his career: Kid literally can't hit the broad side of a barn or make any sense until he has a swig of liquor, and suddenly he's hitting bull's-eyes and delivering a long soliloquy about gunfighters and the old days in Tombstone. Too bad Marvin didn't expand this routine into a one-man stage show. Marvin also is amusing when he readies himself for a showdown, dressing for success. Surely Marvin gave an Oscar-worthy performance, but despite playing two characters, he actually has only a *supporting,* tangential role. In fact, from a story standpoint, his Kid Shelleen could easily be excised from the film, although his loss would leave very little humor behind. So I would opt for Sean Connery, who never received a Best Actor Oscar despite having a marvelous career and making a strong impact on our lives. He gave a powerful dramatic performance in *The Hill,* but since he was still only the actor who played James Bond in the myopic eyes of the Academy voters, he wasn't taken seriously enough even to be given a nomination.

Sidney Lumet's unrelentingly intense drama is set in a British desert prison camp for military insubordinates. Connery (as Trooper Roberts) is one of several new prisoners. He was found guilty of knocking out his officer's teeth when he ordered Connery to lead his men into battle—he won't reveal until later that he attacked the officer after he had already returned from battle with half his men dead and the officer insisted he take them out again and be massacred. The ineffectual commandant is usually cavorting with prostitutes, so the camp is run by a dictatorial sergeant major (Harry Andrews), a career soldier who rules with an outdated book on military conduct. He believes the prisoners must suffer in order to improve and keeps them on a steady diet of discipline and punishment. He is proud of a steep dirt hill he had the prisoners build in the middle of the courtyard. Prisoners, including Connery and the newcomers who share his cell, must run up and down it until they collapse. Andrews's sadistic chief officer (Ian Hendry)

carries out all discipline, and relishes the assignment. Andrews and Hendry have it in for Connery because they think him a coward and punish him severely. But a cellmate (Alfred Lynch) suffers worse treatment and though he is very ill, Hendry continues to punish him. He dies. After Andrews and Hendry cover up their crime, Connery and Ossie Davis, a prisoner who is constantly insulted because he is black, state that they want to make a report against Hendry to the commandant. Hendry and two men beat up Connery, breaking his foot. But he won't change his mind. Andrews and Hendry don't worry about him or Davis, but the medical officer (Michael Redgrave) and another officer (Ian Bannen) unexpectedly support the prisoners. Connery realizes that the reign of Andrews and Hendry is over. When Davis and another prisoner (Jack Watson) beat up Hendry, Connery cries for them to stop, saying that they already have won. But they continue their punishment.

It took years before any critic recognized that Sean Connery wasn't merely well cast as the handsome, suave James Bond but was actually doing an excellent job in a difficult role. Connery was eager to take roles other than

Sean Connery learns from Harry Andrews that he'll be educated in strict military discipline while confined to prison in Sidney Lumet's *The Hill.*

Bond, both to prevent himself from being typecast and to prove he was a skilled, versatile actor. He had been in Hitchcock's *Marnie,* but *The Hill* was the picture Connery had been waiting for. In an early scene Connery responds to Andrews's boasting about the prisoner-built hill, with a sarcastic "That's marvelous, sir, a great construction." In the Bond films the secret agent's archvillains would have reacted with impressed amusement at Bond's bold humor. But in *The Hill* Andrews doesn't give Connery's character such satisfaction because there is no place for humor in the deadly business that begins between them. There is no mutual respect or enjoyment in matching wits with an equal. All Andrews wants to do is break Connery, whom he considers his inferior. Connery immediately realizes this too; speaking of the hill he remarks, "I can do without it, sir, but I think you've got other plans for me." So much for Connery's Bond-like humor for the rest of the film.

Connery's character is a brave man, willing to take physical abuse, to be insulted for his supposed cowardice on the battlefield without thinking it necessary to set one story straight and to put himself on the line for justice. Unlike the others in his cellblock—particularly Davis—he doesn't sour on the military because of their mistreatment in this prison. He accepted his imprisonment be-cause he knew there would be dire consequences for clobbering his officer—he reasons that a military tribunal had to punish him, or no soldier would respect discipline and the military would cease to function. What he doesn't accept is that the sadistic Andrews runs the camp as if it were the nineteenth century, making a mockery of the type of discipline all soldiers will respect. He doesn't want to destroy the system but to *reform* it from, literally, within. He wants to go through the proper military channels. One wonders: would Connery have joined Davis and Watson in their final anarchic act, beating up Hendry, if this film had been made a few years later, when the Vietnam War had intensified and the younger movie audience cheered full-fledged rebels?

The film's best scene takes place in the courtyard, when Connery and Andrews (a great performance) angrily debate the merits of punishing prisoners in the Victorian-age manner. Connery repeatedly falls because of his broken foot, hears Andrews's order to rise, and immediately gets up, defiantly, to resume his emotional screaming at a man who refuses to listen. In subsequent years Connery would amass such impressive credits that everyone would agree he is a marvelous actor—but I don't think he ever was better than at this moment.

▶ BEST ACTRESS

WINNER:
Julie Christie *(Darling)*
Other Nominees: Julie Andrews *(The Sound of Music),* Samantha Eggar *(The Collector),* Elizabeth Hartman *(A Patch of Blue),* Simone Signoret *(Ship of Fools)*

▼ ───

THE BEST CHOICE:
Julie Andrews *(The Sound of Music)*
Award-Worthy Runner-Up: Julie Christie *(Darling)*

Julie Andrews was single-handedly responsible for *The Sound of Music* becoming the most profitable musical in history and winning 1965's Best Picture Oscar, yet the Academy didn't vote her Best Actress. She'd won the award the year before for *Mary Poppins,* so even though she was infinitely better in Robert Wise's lavish musical, she was considered old hat by the voters. Especially with a new star, a sexy, more vivacious blonde from Britain named Julie Christie, taking the world by storm. The Academy figured Andrews would be satisfied with her new designation as the world's box-office queen, and gave the Oscar to Christie. In John Schlesinger's ultrahip *Darling* Christie played a swingin', smart but superficial, "modern" young woman whose reckless pursuit of excitement and sexual pleasure breaks hearts and costs her all chance for contentment. Today, Christie so avoids commercial projects—and avoids Hollywood as well—that we might suppose that, in 1965, the Academy went against tradition, picking an out-of-the-mainstream actress over one with mass appeal. But with *Darling* and *Doctor Zhivago* both in release by Academy Award night, Christie was a household name, a big star, the sexy alternative to the wholesome Andrews. Her model's beauty, sexuality, and vital screen personality had immense impact on viewers, especially Americans turned on by anyone young, sexy, and British. She was unlike anyone else in the cinema. Pauline Kael was among those who immediately found her "extraordinary—petulant, sullen, and very beautiful." But once we saw Christie shine in such later films as *Petulia* and *McCabe and Mrs. Miller,* we realized that she hadn't been given full opportunity to reveal her dramatic or comic talents in *Darling.* She'd gotten by mostly on looks and personality. Her wonderful, flabbergasted reaction on the podium upon winning the Oscar so soon after breaking into movies was almost enough to justify her winning. But the award

Julie Andrews wins over the troublesome children by singing away their fears in Robert Wise's *The Sound of Music.*

should have gone to Andrews. So confined in the dreary *Mary Poppins,* she came alive in *The Sound of Music.*

In a role created by Mary Martin on Broadway, Andrews played Maria, a nun-in-training in Austria, prior to World War II. Lovable but too stubborn and independent to follow convent rules, she is sent to be governess to the seven incorrigible, motherless children of Captain Von Trapp (Christopher Plummer). She discovers that they are nice children, just love-starved. The Captain believes the children need discipline—she gives them love, and, beyond instilling good manners, teaches them to sing and play. At first the Captain is angered by her unwillingness to follow orders, but when she brings music back into the house, he is overcome with emotion. He and his children show affection to each other for the first time since the death of the Captain's wife. Maria and the Captain try to ignore their growing love for each other. Maria goes back to the convent, but decides to give up being a nun and return to take care of the children. The Captain's fiancée (Eleanor Parker) realizes that the children and the Captain love Maria more than they do her. She leaves. The Captain and Maria marry. They perform as the Trapp Family Singers. During the Salzburg Folk Festival they escape the Nazis in the midst of a performance. They climb the mountains and flee over the border. This family will perform all over the world.

Not everyone was taken by Julie Andrews in *The Sound of Music,* who gave new meaning to the words *wholesome* and *goody-goody.* Critic David Thomson, for instance, wrote that "for myself, I find that Julie Andrews curdles the milk of kindness quicker than any actress around." But even he admits that she is the reason that "all over the world, people have returned to *The Sound of Music* time and time again. . . . The almost instant buckling of the Andrews charm under serious critical inspection is a small thing measured against the pleasure or solace she brings so many people. And one should reject the immediate temptation to deride that pleasure or caricature such people."

The Sound of Music is a sickeningly sugary and manipulative movie, but Andrews is so captivating that it is quite watchable. It's hard not to react positively to infectious energy, warmth, and exuberance. She can sing about such things as "raindrops on roses and whiskers on kittens" and make you want to sing along instead of throw up. Her voice is superb, she injects humor into her delivery, and she's as good as Barbra Streisand at *acting* while singing. Her Maria is sweet and charming, but she's also outspoken and defiant enough of authority figures to please the most rebellious of viewers. Plus she's brave. Maria reminds me of those fearless abducted women in adventure movies who slap or spit at frightening pirates or Indians, motivating these abductors to say, "I like her spirit." Andrews's Maria charms the socks off everybody. She can sing, dance, climb trees, be funny, take care of the kids, give good advice, even convince the Captain that he's been wrong about the way he's brought up his children. Out of green curtains she sews for the children some of the most hideous outfits ever seen on the screen, but otherwise she has fewer deficiencies than the "practically perfect" Mary Poppins. "My dear, isn't there anything you can't do?" is the rhetorical question asked by her romantic competitor, who realizes she has no chance against Maria.

True, Andrews's sunny, uplifting, high-energy performance lasts only until the second, more serious half of the film. But by that time she's made us feel so cheery that we can handle the romance, troubles with Nazis, and the newly sentimental Plummer's eyes watering in every other scene.

When Andrews didn't win her second consecutive Oscar she joked that she wouldn't fall victim to the curse begun by Luise Rainer, whose career went downhill after she pulled off that feat. Nonetheless, Andrews still proceeded to star in flop after flop, ending up as box-office poison. She would be impressive in nonvirginal, image-changing roles in husband Blake Edwards's *The Tamarind Seed, "10", Victor/Victoria,* and *S.O.B.*—baring her breasts!—but she'd never again achieve the popular success she had in the mid-sixties. Yet her lilting performance in *The Sound of Music* endures.

1966

▶ BEST PICTURE

WINNER:
A Man for All Seasons (Columbia; Fred Zinnemann)
Other Nominees: *Alfie; The Russians Are Coming, The Russians Are Coming; The Sand Pebbles; Who's Afraid of Virginia Woolf?*

▼

THE BEST CHOICE:
Cul-de-Sac (Compton-Tekli; Roman Polanski)
Award-Worthy Runners-Up: None

For the second straight unimpressive year for movies, my choice for Best Picture is a low-budget, black-and-white, bizarre British film directed by Roman Polanski. *Cul-de-Sac* came from an original script by Polanski and Gerard Brach (also his collaborator on *Repulsion*), incorporated improvisation by Donald Pleasence, Lionel Stander, Françoise Dorleac (the ill-fated real-life sister of *Repulsion* star Catherine Deneuve), and other actors, and paid homage equally to movies and to Pinter and Beckett (it was almost called *Waiting for Katelbach*). Neither widely screened nor appreciated in America—even by those critics I most admired—it went unnominated. Meanwhile, the Best Picture race became a toss-up between two play adaptations: Mike Nichols's *Who's Afraid of Virginia Woolf?* for which Ernest Lehman adapted Edward Albee, and Fred Zinnemann's *A Man for All Seasons,* for which Robert Bolt won an Oscar for adapting his own work.

Nichols's film, with an intentionally overweight Elizabeth Taylor and husband Richard Burton as Albee's self-destructive married couple, received thirteen nominations and won five Academy Awards, including one for Taylor. But in the Best Picture competition its forced hysteria lost out to the strained politeness of Zinnemann's classy but strangely dispassionate work about how Sir Thomas More (an Oscar-winning Paul Scofield) chose to give up his life rather than sanction Henry VIII's divorce from Catherine of Aragon and remarriage to Anne Boleyn. Like both films *Cul-de-Sac* contains scene after scene of confrontational, power-play conversations; like *A Man for All Seasons* it is, in a distorted way, about a man who loses everything while battling for his integrity (Scofield's hero maintains it, Pleasence's "hero" makes a last-ditch effort to reclaim it); and like Nichols's work it uses the catalystic appearance of intruders/visitors into a couple's home to cause them to confront what's drastically wrong with their marriage. However, *Cul-de-Sac,* the most peculiar, unpredictable, hilarious, and emotionally wrenching of black comedies, isn't at all like

either film or anything else released in 1966. While it recalls movie melodramas in which gangsters hide out in innocent people's homes and anticipated Sam Peckinpah's *Straw Dogs,* it fits snugly into Polanski's eccentric collection.

In Polanski's first film, *Knife in the Water* (made in his native Poland), it is a handsome young hitchhiker who disrupts the superficially complacent lives of a man and his younger wife as they holiday in near isolation on a yacht. In *Cul-de-Sac* a burly older gangster, Dickie (Stander), disrupts the superficially complacent life of the bald, middle-aged, retired George (Pleasence) and his beautiful, much younger wife, Teresa (Dorleac), when he hides out in their isolated island castle in Northumberland. Fleeing a botched crime, he and his wounded partner, Albie (Jack MacGowran), come upon the castle

Lionel Stander, Françoise Dorleac, and Donald Pleasence are the three leads in Roman Polanski's peculiar *Cul-de-Sac.*

while driving upon a road that is covered by water during high tide. Dickie first spots the half-naked Teresa frolicking with a young man who is the son of neighbors visiting George. That night Teresa dresses George in her nightgown and marks his face with lipstick and liner, but their kinky game is interrupted by Dickie. He is at times a complimentary guest, but for the most part he bosses them around, pushes them about, and insults them. Teresa becomes angry at George for not being "man" enough to stand up to Dickie. Dickie expects that his boss, Katelbach, will soon be sending a car for himself and Albie. Albie dies. And Katelbach never shows up. Dickie forces George to drink alcohol despite his ulcer. In a drunken state George confesses to the sympathetic Dickie his unhappiness over his young wife and his expensive castle retreat. George's longtime friends—a middle-aged couple with an obnoxious child—and other guests show up unexpectedly to meet his new wife. Dickie pretends to be their gardener. He is as uncivil as the snobby guests deserve. Teresa tries to boss Dickie around, but he doesn't go for it. When the annoying little boy shoots a gun that breaks a priceless stained-glass window, George loses his temper and orders everyone away. He tells the couple that they also interfered in his relationship with his first wife, Agnes. Dickie tells Teresa's young lover to leave. Teresa steals Dickie's gun and gives it to George, telling him Dickie sexually attacked her. He wildly shoots it, mortally wounding Dickie. When a car drives up, the crazed George thinks it's Katelbach and takes a fighter's position in front of it. But it is a male guest returning. George packs Teresa's belongings and sends her away with him. He then sits crying on a rock as the water rises around him, calling for Agnes.

Cul-de-Sac fits in with Polanski's other films about lonely, alienated, humiliated characters who are driven to violence and/or madness. We get only hints about George's past, but we can surmise that during the war he probably sat behind a desk, although he certainly has embellished his insignificant record for Teresa's benefit; that he successfully ran a factory; that he left a wife and children for his young second wife. Although he is a weakling, he was, oddly enough, in positions of power throughout his life. Now he finds himself devoting his life to the trampy Teresa, buying her the castle, painting countless pictures of her, letting her humiliate him sexually (the king of the castle happily becomes the queen), looking the other way when she's off with the young neighbor. He worships her, so he'll put up with anything. But it's hard on him to be humiliated by another man in front of her, to be called "a fairy," to allow Dickie to insult her, to be shown up as a coward. He makes weak gestures to assert himself, but he can't look Dickie in the eye because Dickie's too tall and ignores him anyway. Dickie is more worthy than he of being boss in this castle, where Sir Walter Scott created *Rob Roy*. George doesn't drink because of his ulcer (signifying he isn't a happy man), but when Dickie forces him to get drunk he talks clearly for the first time, bonding with his new male drinking buddy (in a fabulous, lengthy, one-take improvisational scene on the beach) and confessing his discontent with his life to a sympathetic ear.

Dickie sees through Teresa ("I don't dig chicks like you") and helps George face up to what she's really like. The most moral character in the film, Dickie protectively chases away her young lover: "Can't you understand that madam doesn't feel like going shrimping with you!" He tries to be straight with George and, though he can never fully respect him, grows to like him and talks to this little fellow he once called "fairy," man to man. Everyone else is dishonest with George, patronizing him, teasing him, making him feel small. He chases everyone else away but feels so comfortable in Dickie's presence that he can nap with him on the terrace. It's a shame that Teresa comes between the two friends, lying to George that Dickie sexually attacked her and appealing to George's budding masculine pride, coaxing him to shoot Dickie. The dying Dickie feels betrayed by George's action, especially in that George shot him to impress the unworthy Teresa, who has been cheating on him. As his last gesture Dickie grabs a machine gun and shoots up their world. But the fortress no longer has significance for George. Having been forced to act like a "man" by his young wife, George has no more need for her, just as the once cowardly Dustin Hoffman pushes away Susan George after proving himself with a gun in *Straw Dogs*.

The Polish Polanski's British-made picture, which brings together a Brit, an Irishman, an American, a French actress, and assorted types, is written, directed, and played to great comic effect. The then little-known Pleasence (who resembles Gandhi here) and the great character actor Stander make a surprisingly funny comic duo. Stander is wonderful in the role he played best: a well-dressed (he wears a Christian Dior tie), well-mannered (I love it when he goes through the bedroom and bathroom saying, "Very nice" and "Very classy"), sensitive brute. But at its heart Polanski's *Cul-de-Sac* is a sad, touching film about an alienated individual who has frightening insecurities and weaknesses common to most men. When he sits on the rock in a fetal position, the water rising around him, and calls for his past ("Agnes!"), the long-lost security and self-respect he threw away for sexual excitement, there are many men who would ask him to move over and make room.

▶ BEST ACTOR

WINNER:
Paul Scofield *(A Man for All Seasons)*
Other Nominees: Alan Arkin *(The Russians Are Coming, The Russians Are Coming)*, Richard Burton *(Who's Afraid of Virginia Woolf?)*, Michael Caine *(Alfie)*, Steve McQueen *(The Sand Pebbles)*

▼

THE BEST CHOICE:
Richard Burton *(Who's Afraid of Virginia Woolf?)*
Award-Worthy Runners-Up: Michael Caine *(Alfie)*, Sean Connery *(A Fine Madness)*, Zero Mostel *(A Funny Thing Happened on the Way to the Forum)*, Donald Pleasence *(Cul-de-Sac)*, Paul Scofield *(A Man for All Seasons)*, Lionel Stander *(Cul-de-Sac)*

Those who expected it to happen were sure it would be special: for giving the performance of his movie career in *Who's Afraid of Virginia Woolf?* Richard Burton would finally win the Best Actor Oscar, after three previous nominations, and he'd win it on the same night his costar and wife, Elizabeth Taylor, was selected Best Actress. Well, Taylor got her Oscar but her victory was spoiled by Burton's third failure in three years—an embarrassment that would be repeated two more times in Burton's career. (He expected to lose in 1966, so the couple stayed away from the ceremony.) Burton was defeated by fellow Britisher Paul Scofield, who played sixteenth-century English chancellor Sir Thomas More in Fred Zinnemann's Best Picture winner, *A Man for All Seasons.* Reprising the role he had played on the stage in London and New York, Scofield gave a disarmingly dignified performance, quite unlike what moviegoers were used to in historical dramas. Until More's outburst at his trial for treason (he won't publicly endorse Henry VIII's divorce and remarriage), Scofield delivers almost all of his lines quietly, with patience and restraint. Yet his every word has both eloquence and force. It was the kind of hypnotic performance that we'd long expected of Burton. Until we gave up on him in the early sixties.

By that time we'd come truly to disrespect Burton's film acting; David Shipman wrote revealingly, "His stock-in-trade is to gaze mournfully just to the right or left of the camera and let his great actor's voice bark at some hapless fellow performer." But the great underachiever then hit his stride with impressive Oscar-nominated performances in *The Spy Who Came in from the Cold* and *Becket,* opposite Peter O'Toole's Henry II. And then came Mike Nichols's *Who's Afraid of Virginia Woolf?,* a misguided movie that, nevertheless, provided Burton with a marvelous ambiguous character and great lines of dialogue that allowed him tremendous freedom. As great as Scofield was in *A Man for All Seasons,* Burton matched him, particularly in the *reading of lines*—an art most movie stars are not required to master. I'd be content with Scofield's victory if, after winning the Oscar, he hadn't completely turned his back on movies and returned to the stage. That he has an Oscar is of little satisfaction to movie fans, particularly since he won it for a role he created onstage. So his Oscar goes to Burton.

Yes, Burton made more than his share of clinkers and should have been fined for some of his lame performances, but at least this heralded stage actor made *movies,* lots of them. Besides, it really would have been special if Burton and Taylor (to whom I'm also giving an Oscar) had been the first and only married couple to have won acting Oscars for the same film.

Burton and Taylor were known to squabble, but not nearly to the destructive degree of George and Martha in Albee's play, adapted for the screen by Ernest Lehman. George, only an associate professor after twenty years in the history department at a small college, and Martha, the daughter of the college president, scream at and insult each other all the time, even during this night when Martha invites a new young biology teacher (George Segal) and his mousy wife (Sandy Dennis) over for a visit. He criticizes her for being loud, vulgar, overweight, and alcoholic. She believes he is ineffectual and a flop. They seem intent on destroying each other, and when they're not insulting each other directly, they're doing it through their uncomfortable guests, revealing the most intimate secrets. The two guests, who also end up airing their dirty laundry during the chaotic all-night "party," can't figure out the truth about George and Martha. And since we don't know, until near the end, that the son they mention is imaginary, we can't figure out why they should have stayed together so long; whatever love and respect they had for each other must have disappeared many years ago.

All eyes were on Elizabeth Taylor when *Who's Afraid of Virginia Woolf?* was released, because no one could picture the lovely, young-voiced actress whom they'd watched grow up, play the vulgar Martha. Her performance is so ostentatious (both those who admired and attacked it will agree on that) that it takes a while to realize that the comparatively subdued Burton is giving a brilliant characterization. But when George loses his cool, Burton heats up, displaying, as Andrew Sarris wrote, "electrifying charm." We are transfixed by his every movement, dazed by his wise yet not always logical remarks, kept off balance by his secretive smiles and powerful gazes, knocked backward by his every shout. He doesn't look to the left or right of Haskell Wexler's camera, but directly into the eyes of Martha during their

Not as loving as they look, Richard Burton's George and Elizabeth Taylor's Martha are actually insulting one another in Mike Nichols's *Who's Afraid of Virginia Woolf?*

her questions and respond to her insults with insults of his own ("You're going bald"/"So are you") without listening to what she said in the first place. (Nor does he *listen* to his guests, answering his own questions to them before they have time to respond.) He tries to blank out or drown out Martha's vicious words (and the meaningless conversation of his unimportant guests) with the long-winded observations of a history professor. But after twenty years she can still hit nerves if she screams loudly enough and blasts him with the appropriate cruel words, some of which he supplies to her himself. She knows that despite his professed boredom, he won't back away when she initiates their horrible nightly games, allowing her to change the rules every night on him. As she starts to go too far and really hurt him, he warns, then threatens her ("Be careful, Martha, I'll rip you to pieces"), and finally he nearly kills her with his hands and destroys her with his words about their "son" ("Martha, I have some terrible news"). Yet, when he goes to sleep each night, he is with the woman he loves. Their battles are what keep them both stimulated and spare them from dealing with what is really wrong with their lives. Unlike Martha the intellectual George is amused by the irony of their covering real pain with fabricated pain and filling their empty lives with muck. He gets a kick out of this, and often can't stop himself from grinning or laughing at their sorry syndrome. It's all he can do, because—as we gradually find out—he, and not Martha, is the strong one in this relationship. He must remain solid if Martha, who turns out to be weak, is to be protected. The years of combat have taken their toll on George, but it is still through his strength that this shaky marriage survives. And it is Burton's strong performance that gives the film its anchor.

razor-sharp arguments, or at his guests—without really seeing them—or off into space, in search of the past for an explanation for his present circumstances. At times it seems as if bad memories intrude immediately upon his line of vision.

Burton's George is a man who has long been worn out. We can imagine his having squabbled with the inexhaustible Martha night after night for the past twenty years. On automatic pilot, he has learned how to answer

▶ BEST ACTRESS

WINNER:
Elizabeth Taylor *(Who's Afraid of Virginia Woolf?)*
Other Nominees: Anouk Aimée *(A Man and a Woman)*, Ida Kaminska *(The Shop on Main Street)*, Lynn Redgrave *(Georgy Girl)*, Vanessa Redgrave *(Morgan!)*

THE BEST CHOICE:
Elizabeth Taylor *(Who's Afraid of Virginia Woolf?)*
Award-Worthy Runners-Up: Anne Bancroft *(Seven Women)*, Lynn Redgrave *(Georgy Girl)*, Tuesday Weld *(Lord Love a Duck)*

The year 1966 was so horrendous for lead actresses in American films that two of the Academy's nominees for Best Actress, France's Anouk Aimée and Czechoslovakia's Ida Kaminska, starred in foreign-language films, and two others, sisters Lynn and Vanessa Redgrave, were in British films. It's scary to think that Raquel Welch in *Fantastic Voyage* and Debbie Reynolds in *The Singing Nun* gave what were, by default, among the best six or seven lead performances by an American actress. It is only under

those circumstances that I'll go along with the Academy's choice of Elizabeth Taylor as Best Actress for *Who's Afraid of Virginia Woolf?* although I don't completely disagree with the many critics who weren't impressed by her. I think Lynn Redgrave gave a more accomplished performance than Taylor, but Taylor's failed performance was, and still is, more interesting than Lynn Redgrave's success. Ironically, like Taylor, Redgrave put on extra weight to play her lovesick character—but since we had never seen

It's a typical stormy night for Elizabeth Taylor's Martha in *Who's Afraid of Virginia Woolf?*   (Photo credit: Mel Traxel)

her before *Georgy Girl,* we were aware only of Taylor's sacrifice, which, like Robert De Niro's weight gain for 1980's *Raging Bull,* added to her Oscar credentials.

Husband Richard Burton convinced Taylor to play Martha opposite his George in director Mike Nichols and producer-writer Ernest Lehman's movie of Edward Albee's controversial work, which at the time was regarded by many as America's greatest play. The former child actress had finally established a mature image in *Cat on a Hot Tin Roof; Suddenly, Last Summer; Butterfield 8; Cleopatra,* and two films with Burton, *The V.I.P.'s* and *The Sandpiper,* but she'd never been required to show much dramatic range. And this time she couldn't fall back on her beauty and sex appeal to win audience sympathy, because her Martha would be older, overweight and obnoxious, even offensive—none of her adult parts had prepared her public for Martha's vile cursing. It was bad

enough that her acting ability would be subjected to such close scrutiny, but in addition she was saddled with a character whose repulsive behavior ("There isn't an abomination award you haven't won," contends George) might cause the less sophisticated among Taylor's fans to respond negatively to the actress playing her. So I think that it really was a risky undertaking for Taylor.

Taylor used a huskier voice than usual to play the booze-soaked Martha, yet, as many critics complained, the character is too shrill, pretty much like Natalie Wood at her worst. Martha should overpower George with well-chosen, snidely delivered words, but Taylor's Martha too often tries just to shout George into submission. Martha should appear to be strong for most of the play/film, rather than just loud and irritating, so that we'll be the more surprised when her weakness becomes evident—and we realize that George, who we'd wrongly assumed was ineffectual, is the only one capable of keeping the marriage intact. Andrew Sarris suggested that Patricia Neal would have been ideal as Martha, playing opposite Burton. It would also be interesting to have seen Elizabeth Ashley or, perhaps, even Susan Hayward in the part. But despite her deficiencies Taylor does an adequate job. Her detractors claimed that her every gesture and line delivery was calculated, but aside from the times Martha talks in rhythm to her gyrating dancing, I don't sense any self-consciousness on her part. Anyway, it's hard to tell if it's the actress or the character who is being calculating, because, remember, Martha never stops acting her part in the brutal humiliation "game" she and George have been playing ad nauseam during their twenty-year marriage.

If Taylor doesn't come across as being natural or at ease, at least give her credit for attempting to *act* rather than just inhabit a character. She should be commended for the physicality of her performance, using her newly plump body—evidence that the once-beautiful Martha has gone to seed—as effectively as her cruel remarks. Her foul language is no more obscene than her body language. Surprisingly, Taylor has her best moments when the camera is directly on her, when the furious Martha argues with George, flirts with the handsome young biology teacher who visits them (George Segal), admits to the teacher that only George can make her happy (though she doesn't want to be happy), and, upon George's insistence, sadly concedes that their son (an imaginary child) is "dead." Only at the end, when Martha's anger is spent and her weakness comes through—and Taylor seems to bond with her unfortunate character—do we feel sympathy for her. She may have failed Martha in many ways throughout the film, but when it really counts Taylor makes us understand this troubled woman. And we are moved considerably. For a minute there we respond to Taylor as we did when she faced problems in *National Velvet* and *Father of the Bride.*

1967

▶ BEST PICTURE

WINNER:
In the Heat of the Night (Mirisch/United Artists; Norman Jewison)
Other Nominees: *Bonnie and Clyde, Doctor Dolittle, The Graduate, Guess Who's Coming to Dinner*

▼

THE BEST CHOICE:
Bonnie and Clyde (Warner Bros.–Seven Arts; Arthur Penn)
Award-Worthy Runners-Up: *Chimes at Midnight/Falstaff* (Orson Welles), *The Graduate* (Mike Nichols), *Point Blank* (John Boorman), *Two for the Road* (Stanley Donen)

The Academy felt proud and in tune with changing America when it gave its Best Picture award to Norman Jewison's *In the Heat of the Night,* a film that dealt with black-white relations. That it gave the Oscar to a film in which Sidney Poitier's character *works* with a white man instead of one in which his character marries a white woman is probably revealing of the voters' weak knees, but to be fair, *In the Heat of the Night,* as muddled a mystery as it is, is a much better picture than Stanley Kramer's *Guess Who's Coming to Dinner.* Both pictures were noncontroversial "controversial" films, but at least Jewison's film had some bite to it, provided by Poitier as a surly cop from Philadelphia and Rod Steiger as the redneck sheriff with whom he forms an uneasy alliance in racist Mississippi. It had the distinction of being the first whodunit to win the Oscar. But *In the Heat of the Night* wasn't deserving of it in a year containing two landmark films, Arthur Penn's *Bonnie and Clyde* and Mike Nichols's *The Graduate,* as well as John Boorman's stylized gangster film, *Point Blank,* and Stanley Donen's *Two for the Road,* one of the most observant American films about marriage.

The Graduate struck a responsive chord in college-age viewers, and had more impact on them than any other film of the era, with the possible exception of *Easy Rider.* Everyone seems to remember when they saw it for the first of many times, and with whom. But *Bonnie and Clyde* also caused a major stir, and not only in setting new fashion trends. It was a groundbreaking American movie that thrilled those turned on by action, sex, and fast cars. Young viewers also could identify with anarchic characters whose impulsive freedom-seeking acts result in their being further trapped. Equally significant, it excited those of us who were intrigued by the filmmaking process. *Bonnie and Clyde,* which broke many conventions, was directly responsible for *many* people becoming fanatical about film.

Penn's picture borrowed from past couple-on-the-run films like Fritz Lang's *You Only Live Once,* Joseph H. Lewis's *Gun Crazy,* and Nicholas Ray's *They Live by Night,* and energetic B gangster pictures from the fifties like *The Bonnie Parker Story.* But it's likely that his main inspiration was Jean-Luc Godard's French "New Wave" classic *Breathless,* an offbeat gangster film with free-form storytelling and cinematic devices (including crosscutting), and an attractive criminal couple, played by charismatic actors. (Interestingly, Godard was an early choice to direct this film.) We feel the same sexual charge watching Warren Beatty's Clyde Barrow and Faye Dunaway's Bonnie Parker as we do watching Jean-Paul Belmondo and Jean Seberg, especially in their bedroom scenes (when Clyde gently puts his hand over Bonnie's face)—which is incredible considering that Clyde is impotent for most of the film. In Godard's film Seberg betrayed Belmondo to the police; Penn would have none of that. His female lover sticks with her man until they both really are breathless.

On several occasions Penn has told stories that are part history and part myth, and that deal with outsiders (Billy the Kid, Annie Sullivan, Arlo Guthrie, Little Big Man) who are in conflict with society or oppressive historical forces. Here the story is against an authentic, barren Depression-era America, hauntingly photographed by Burnett Guffey (who deserved his Oscar); yet the brilliant script by David Newman and Robert Benton (which has none of the irritating self-conscious humor of, say, *Butch Cassidy and the Sundance Kid*) romanticizes the gangster couple. Penn doesn't apologize for his approach. Instead he defends it within the film, showing that their lives were romanticized in their own time by the press, the law (which built them up to the public), and the couple themselves with their own still camera (they posed for outrageous "gangster" photos) and Bonnie's poem. Penn doesn't glamorize their crimes—they are basically bumblers—but he reveals his own excitement in their unique love. Lost by themselves, they thrive in each other's company. We like them together from the great first scene: they meet when she's horny and naked in her bedroom and calls down to him in the street where he's stealing a car; and moments later they stroll together, he letting her feel his pistol before really impressing her by robbing a store and driving her away to a more exciting life. Their love intensifies as they commit crimes together, fight police together, bleed from wounds at the same time. Of course, they are killed together. Their crime family includes Clyde's brother Buck (Gene Hackman), his hysterical wife, Blanche (Estelle Parsons won the Best Supporting Actress Oscar), and young driver C. W. Moss (Michael J. Pollard), but the two of them are already a family, united against the world. Our sympathy for them is great because of the dynamic performances by the leads. Dunaway (in her least mannered performance), with wild hair under a beret and sexually hungry eyes, and Beatty, who seduces this female with charm and sincere compliments instead of sexual prowess, truly care about these characters who don't stand a chance. They display amazing emotional intensity in their scenes together (especially when she insults his sexual capabilities and then apologizes). So we can understand the depth of their characters' love and need for each other.

"We rob banks!" they brag, proud that they have a *job*, an *exciting* job, during the vapid Depression. Their crimes are about the only signs of life and energy in this America that has been anesthetized by poverty; and unfortunately, the only acts of rebellion against an impersonal bank- and police-run country (their crimes have only an instinctual political basis). For Bonnie and equally passionate but sexually impotent Clyde, robbery is their emotional release and, for a time, an (insufficient) replacement for sex. They are happy that they have work to do together and feel fortunate for a chance at fame of any kind. They're friendly, trusting, uneducated, and decent, if reckless, people: "real folks" who have no animosity toward anyone and can't comprehend why there is so much machinery working against them. The

Warren Beatty, Faye Dunaway, and Michael J. Pollard narrowly escape the police in Arthur Penn's *Bonnie and Clyde*.

incredibly well-staged and -edited gun battles between the police and the gang are tantamount to small wars, with machine guns blasting, blood gushing Sam Peckinpah style, armored cars, even grenades.

We are disturbed that Bonnie and Clyde are so casual about committing violent acts, but we are shocked at the violence launched against them. The direction and editing (Dede Allen's finest moment) of their death by ambush—a classic sequence in which they each are riddled by about fifty bullets—is astonishing. It is because this picture has so much wit (Gene Wilder debuted in the film's most comical sequence), joviality, lyricism, cheery music (Flatt and Scruggs's "Foggy Mountain Breakdown" plays during car chases), and romance (as well as sex), that the downbeat finale is so devastating. Bonnie and Clyde may have been criminals, but they didn't deserve this.

▶ BEST ACTOR

WINNER:
Rod Steiger *(In the Heat of the Night)*
Other Nominees: Warren Beatty *(Bonnie and Clyde)*, Dustin Hoffman *(The Graduate)*, Paul Newman *(Cool Hand Luke)*, Spencer Tracy *(Guess Who's Coming to Dinner)*

▼

THE BEST CHOICE:
Orson Welles *(Chimes at Midnight/Falstaff)*
Award-Worthy Runners-Up: Dirk Bogarde *(Accident)*, Albert Finney *(Two for the Road)*, Dustin Hoffman *(The Graduate)*, Lee Marvin *(Point Blank)*, James Mason *(The Deadly Affair)*

It's hard to fathom today, but for a brief time in the mid-sixties, beginning with an uncharacteristically restrained performance in *The Pawnbroker,* Rod Steiger was considered by many to be America's foremost movie actor. The egotistical actor himself believed this and, taking charge of his career, promptly drove it into the ground, giving himself a heart attack in the process. Steiger was at the height of his glory when he costarred in Norman Jewison's Best Picture winner, *In the Heat of the Night,* playing a bigoted redneck cop who begrudgingly works with Sidney Poitier's surly black Northern policeman to solve a murder. Steiger was well cast and forceful as usual, but as Academy voters and many of us viewers at the time failed to notice, he used a combination of (undeniable) talent and bluster to cover up a lazy, shallow portrayal of a potentially fascinating character. If he'd only stopped shouting and calmed down for a moment.

Orson Welles also had a tendency to overact, particularly late in his career when he found himself in projects that he didn't care about. Or perhaps it is more accurate to say that he never felt the necessity to tone down his performances so that they wouldn't overwhelm costars with less screen presence. Even if this made him seem like a ham. Overweight and reduced to doing cameos, the onetime leading man eventually lost the fine acting reputation he had earned in the forties and fifties. But in 1966 and 1967 he had a brief resurgence, reminding viewers that he wasn't a great talent only behind the cameras. He was marvelous in the small role of Cardinal Wolsey in Fred Zinnemann's *A Man for All Seasons,* but that was just a prelude to his magnificent, witty, yet poignant interpretation of Falstaff, the robust lead character of his own, even more impressive historical drama, *Chimes at Midnight.* Made with French and Spanish backing, Welles's low-budget adaptation of Shakespeare was completed in 1966 but didn't play in America until 1967. A vicious review by Bosley Crowther in *The New York Times* killed its chances for getting more than minor distribution. Even the most fanatical movie fans, including Welles's most ardent admirers, were unable to see Welles's final masterpiece—and possibly his greatest film (despite some shoddy production values)—and Welles, the actor, at his peak.

Another of Welles's many movies dealing with the betrayal of friendship, *Chimes at Midnight/Falstaff* began as a play, which he produced in Belfast in 1960. It was taken from Shakespeare's *Henry IV Parts 1 and 2,* with bits from *Henry V, The Merry Wives of Windsor,* and *Richard II;* Raphael Holinshed's *Chronicles* was the source of the narration. Rather than have Henry IV (John Gielgud) or Prince Hal/Henry V (Keith Baxter) as his protagonist, Welles gives that role to Falstaff, no royal figure but merely the surrogate father to Hal while his real father, Henry IV, wears the crown. Falstaff was more clownish in Shakespeare, but it is still disconcerting to see this obese, lying, bawdy coward as the hero of an historical drama. Moreover, we're not used to having our tragic heroes depicted as being so entirely good. This hero's tragic flaw is actually a positive attribute: he is so pure and innocent that he cannot believe Hal would betray their friendship once he becomes king. When the young man severs all ties with him after ascending the throne, the emotional Falstaff is shocked and humiliated. He literally dies of a broken heart.

Welles's Falstaff certainly isn't the sort the new king

Orson Welles's Falstaff is the fat coward in the heavy armor who avoids combat in the amazingly filmed battle sequence in Welles's *Chimes at Midnight.*

would want to bring to a courtly function, but he's a great, reliable pal. Though he fibs constantly, he is totally honest; though he rubs shoulders with the town dunce and senile old men, he alone has knowledge about what is most important in life: love, loyalty, friendship, good conversation with tall tales and laughter, a wild roll with a wench, overeating and drinking, and a satisfying bowel movement. Welles plays Falstaff with tremendous warmth because he knows this man is special: he represents goodness in an otherwise heartless world. In his perceptive book *Orson Welles* Joseph McBride quotes Welles's profound description of his character: "What is difficult about Falstaff, I believe, is that he is the greatest conception of a good man, the most completely good man, in all drama. His faults are so small and he makes tremendous jokes out of little faults. But his goodness is like bread, like wine. . . . And that was why I lost the comedy. The more I played it, the more I felt that I was playing Shakespeare's good, pure man."

Even when playing the "heavy" in such films as *Citizen Kane, The Third Man,* and *Touch of Evil,* Welles took on the role of "victim" in regard to betrayed friendships. This time, he played a good man whose closest friend proves disloyal. Welles always found more security in being an unsympathetic character, but he found his perfect screen match in Falstaff and was completely comfortable. Warts and all, Falstaff is the character closest to the real Welles. That's why you may think you see something in the actor's manner that suggests he—as well as the character—takes Hal's rejection of his old friend so personally. (I think Hal reminded Welles of the many young talents he helped nurture, who ignored him once they'd made it and he had fallen on hard times.) In Shakespeare the new king's banishment of Falstaff is seen as the sad but mature and necessary act of a man with grave responsibilities. But in Welles's version there is no excuse for Hal's dastardly act—he doesn't gain dignity by ridding himself of Falstaff, but loses his sense of decency.

▶ BEST ACTRESS

WINNER:
Katharine Hepburn *(Guess Who's Coming to Dinner)*
Other Nominees: Anne Bancroft *(The Graduate)*, Faye Dunaway *(Bonnie and Clyde)*, Dame Edith Evans *(The Whisperers)*, Audrey Hepburn *(Wait Until Dark)*

▼

THE BEST CHOICE:
Audrey Hepburn *(Two for the Road)*
Award-Worthy Runners-Up: Anne Bancroft *(The Graduate)*, Faye Dunaway *(Bonnie and Clyde)*

The wrong Hepburn won the Best Actress Oscar in 1967. It's hard to begrudge the Academy for giving the award to the incomparable Katharine Hepburn in any year she appeared in a movie, but in this year, when she was only in Stanley Kramer's dismal interracial-marriage comedy-drama, *Guess Who's Coming to Dinner,* the winner should have been Audrey Hepburn. And if not her, Anne Bancroft for her Mrs. Robinson in *The Graduate;* or Faye Dunaway for her exciting portrayal of gangster Bonnie Parker in *Bonnie and Clyde.* But Academy members were swayed to vote for Katharine Hepburn because she was returning to films after a five-year absence, hadn't won the Oscar since 1932–33 for *Morning Glory* despite many splendid performances, and her costar and longtime lover, Spencer Tracy, had died ten days after filming ended—an Oscar for her would be an award for both of them. Unfortunately, Hepburn's portrayal of a patient housewife who is married to conservative Tracy—they must come to terms with daughter Katharine Houghton's decision to marry black scientist Sidney Poitier—was the blandest of her career. You keep expecting her to have a tremendous scene all to herself, but it never happens. Maybe the Academy wouldn't have voted for her if they knew they'd give her the award the following year, for a more deserving performance in *The Lion in Winter.*

Audrey Hepburn was nominated for her menaced blind woman in *Wait Until Dark,* but her Oscar-worthy role was in *Two for the Road,* in which she and Albert Finney are a wonderful romantic team. Stanley Donen's wry, insightful look at marriage was warmly received when it was released but no one made very much of it. Yet within a few years it developed a fervent cult among romantics, and Hepburn's performance, which was pretty much neglected in 1967, became—along with her Holly Golightly in *Breakfast at Tiffany's*—the most appreciated of her career. I didn't agree with the Academy's decision to give the Oscar to Hepburn for her 1953 American debut, *Roman Holiday,* because I thought the chic young actress, with the elegant manner, skinny body, swanlike neck, and delicate, beautiful features hoped to charm viewers rather than impress them with her acting. She had matured as an actress long before making *Two for the Road,* but she'd rarely gotten roles where it made much difference. Joanna in *Two for the Road* was one of the few women she ever played who is somewhat real

and not just a character found in Hollywood fairy tales. Joanna is especially memorable because the older, more experienced Hepburn finally had to dig into herself to understand and play a character. She gives a mature, perceptive performance, without sacrificing any of the charm that always made viewers automatically love her.

The exceptional original script by Frederic Raphael *(Darling)* is about a successful architect, Mark (Albert Finney), and Joanna (Hepburn), his wife of twelve years. Though they love each other, they constantly bicker, feel resentment toward each other, and admit that they aren't particularly happy. They wonder how their marriage has managed to last so long when, as they've come to believe, their life together has been miserable since the start. We go back in time and see the couple at various points in their relationship, as they travel together through Europe. They fall in love after meeting and hitchhiking together, and though he's been speaking badly of marriage, he proposes; they travel with Mark's ex-girlfriend (Eleanor Bron), her fastidious husband (William Daniels), and

Audrey Hepburn and Albert Finney are on one of their frequent trips in Stanley Donen's bittersweet comedy-romance, *Two for the Road.*

bratty little girl; they travel alone—Joanna announces her pregnancy, Mark gets his first rich client; and so on. Mark's success goes to his head. At one point Mark has a one-night stand. The marriage strained, Joanna has an affair with David (Georges Descrières), but she returns to Mark because David was too serious and she missed her husband. Throughout the film we watch Mark and Joanna intentionally hurt each other, suffer as individuals and as a couple, get on each other's nerves, disappoint each other, be insensitive to each other's needs, criticize each other, and argue. That's all the two of them remember when things are bad. But we also see them laugh together, be playful, make love a great deal (they never turn each other down or tire of one another sexually), appreciate and love each other. We come to like them as a couple more than they do themselves—and we can understand why their marriage has lasted and will survive. They are good together—no couple is perfect—and, even after a dozen years, exciting.

Oddly, Hepburn's longtime marriage to Mel Ferrer was falling apart at the time she made this film about a marriage that withstands all difficulties. Her Joanna is the glue that holds the marriage together. She puts up with Mark's bad moods, his insensitivity, his insufferable egotism, his griping, his snide remarks (which she can match), his pessimism about their marriage. Repeatedly, she is the one who relaxes and comforts him with her words, cheery expressions, humor (Hepburn is funny), *and* her presence (she has not run away); makes love to him while the world around them disappears; assures him of her love and that he hasn't disappointed her by not giving her what he assumes she needs. When his spirits are low, she smiles, says something funny, or acts

silly, and the sun shines briefly. She is always direct with him. She is never too shy or demure to yell back at him, tell him she loves him, or tell him what she wants (because it is never more than he can give her). He's really not the ideal husband, but Joanna brings out all that is good in him . . . and he knows and appreciates this. Early on he asks, "Who are you?" and she responds, "Some girl." But even then he suspects that she is the *only* one for him in the entire world, that he has lucked onto the best woman he could ever find. Even then he seems to know that he needs her: "If there's one thing I despise it's an indispensable woman." But Joanna gets tired of doing it on her own. Not the perfect wife and incapable of keeping all her promises (for instance, "I won't ever let you down"), she almost ends the marriage herself when she has an affair with David. It isn't Mark's words that make her return. As usual she does it on her own—after fading out on David and drifting into happy memories of Mark.

Hepburn and Finney have many special moments together, including those when they argue. But the highlights are undoubtedly those scenes in which they are romantic. From Hepburn's eyes and expressions in moments of intimacy, we have knowledge of Joanna's deep feelings for Mark. And we can see why Mark would love her so much. It seems ridiculous to propose that Hepburn earned the Oscar just by the way she says, "I love you," in this film, but every fan of the movie would agree that no actress ever said it with such conviction. (No wonder it was rumored Finney and Hepburn were having an affair.) Each time her Joanna says "I love you" to Mark, emotionally and while looking him in the eye, we can't help thinking along with him that he's one lucky guy.

▶ BEST PICTURE

WINNER:

Oliver! (Columbia; Carol Reed)

Other Nominees: *Funny Girl; The Lion in Winter; Rachel, Rachel; Romeo and Juliet*

▼

THE BEST CHOICE:

2001: A Space Odyssey (MGM; Stanley Kubrick)

Award-Worthy Runners-Up: *Oliver!* (Carol Reed), *Petulia* (Richard Lester)

The Academy's conservative choices for 1968's Best Picture—four play adaptations, two of them musicals and two historical costume dramas—didn't reflect the di-

verse, offbeat, and definitely more personal product that made this such an interesting year for movies. Among the films that were, at least in theory, eligible for the

Oscar were Roman Polanski's *Rosemary's Baby,* Richard Lester's *Petulia,* Peter Bogdanovich's *Targets,* Michael Reeves's *The Conqueror Worm,* John Cassavetes's *Faces,* Mel Brooks's *The Producers,* Noel Black's *Pretty Poison,* Karel Reisz's *Isadora,* Sergio Leone's *The Good, the Bad, and the Ugly,* Peter Yates's *Bullitt,* Ralph Nelson's *Charly,* Jean-Luc Godard's *Weekend,* Luis Buñuel's *Belle de Jour,* and best of all, Stanley Kubrick's colossal *2001: A Space Odyssey.* Unfortunately, the Academy continued to show bias against science-fiction pictures, giving only a special-effects Oscar to the year's most ambitious, controversial, visually impressive, and, among college-age viewers, popular film. Its embarrassing failure even to nominate *2001,* despite nominating Kubrick for Best Director, was taken as an insult by perceptive young filmgoers, who got a new perspective on the types of films "allowed" to win major awards. At the time many *2001* fanatics reflexively scorned the Academy's choice, Carol Reed's *Oliver!.* I happen to have loved *Oliver!,* the best, most imaginative musical in years and an improvement on David Lean's 1948 drama, *Oliver Twist,* and saw it almost as many times as I did *2001.* But in 1968 every film was dwarfed by Kubrick's monumental achievement.

It's hard to impress on people who weren't there just how thrilling it was to see *2001* when it was released in 1968 at New York's Cinerama Theatre. One sat up close and with eyes wide during the "Dawn of Man" sequence, the stunning fifteen-minute "star-gate" sequence that was conceived by special effects wizard Douglas Trumbull; the finale when the enormous baby (the new "Jesus"?) drifts toward earth; and so many other scenes. I remember when my college film society voted the next year not to book the film because it would have been shown in 35mm and we worried that those who saw it for the first time would be gypped. Today, people routinely watch it on their twelve-inch televisions. Which I guess proves the film has tremendous visual power even when you can barely see it; and that it remains the most enticingly cerebral of science-fiction films.

2001 is about our evolution from ape to ape-man to dull human being (us) to civilized man to angel. That evolution is influenced/determined by a superior alien intelligence that made contact with our ape ancestors and through "race memory" became God to the earthlings that followed. Kubrick and Arthur C. Clarke adapted Clarke's 1951 short story "The Sentinel," which had an American astronaut discovering a black monolith that was left on the moon by a super intelligence. It has served as a beacon through the ages, sending a signal to those who left it. When the earthlings dismantle it, the transmission stops, letting the alien intelligence know that man has evolved enough to travel to the moon. So the worried earthlings wait for the return of the ancient race. In the film it is the aliens who wait for us to evolve enough to come to them.

Evolution begins four million years ago, when a black monolithic slab appears to a family of vegetarian apes led by Moonwatcher, whose curiosity (he looks to the skies) is rewarded. His ape family evolve into *ape-men,* who

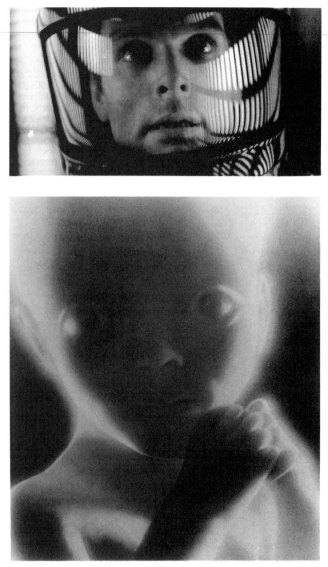

In Stanley Kubrick's monumental *2001: A Space Odyssey* American astronaut Keir Dullea evolves through contact with aliens from man to star child.

become predators, use bones as weapons, eat meat, and stake out territory. These are the grunting ancestors of the barely communicative, hostile human beings who inhabit the earth and travel in nuclear-powered spacecraft in the year 2001. According to Kubrick evolution has been a failure. Unworthy of their own technical achievements, human beings have become the equivalents of robots, showing little emotion or imagination, eating synthetic food, separating themselves from their families, sending shallow messages through space, and among government/military officials, exchanging untruths with those representing other nations (Russia and America still mistrust and compete with each other). When Americans, under the supervision of the boring Dr. Heywood Floyd (William Sylvester, a bloodless Hugh Beaumont), discover a black monolith on the moon, they keep the discovery to themselves, somehow proud to have found an artifact created by an intelligence that makes them seem like peabrains in comparison. The monolith starts emitting a piercing signal toward Jupiter, and the aliens know that the earthlings will attempt to follow the signal. Kubrick has no respect for man in general but admires his insatiable curiosity to make discoveries that may even lead to "culture shock."

Not that the two human, look-alike astronauts, Keir Dullea's Dave Bowman (Bow-man has evolved from ape-man) and Gary Lockwood's Frank Poole, display much curiosity as they make their half-billion-mile journey to Jupiter on the *Discovery*. They don't even look at the stars from their craft's windows, preferring to jog endlessly, watch television, or keep the HAL 9000 company. HAL is a supersophisticated talking computer that virtually controls the ship. Some critics complained that the neurotic HAL, which tries to sabotage the mission and kill Bowman and Poole (after doing just that to the three scientists in deep freeze), has more personality than the two astronauts. That was Kubrick's point. He wanted to express the irony of increasingly mechanized human beings creating machines (like HAL) that show a complete range of human emotions. Human beings have created machines to make all the judgments—Bowman and Poole are virtual maintenance men—and to oversee mankind

in the fashion of Orwell's Big Brother. Only when Bowman confronts HAL in an unforgettable life-and-death battle does the human being display human traits, specifically fear, sorrow (when he dismantles the computer that pleads pathetically for its life), and the need for self-determination. So by breaking off his shackles Bowman proves to the aliens that he is the one human being worthy of coming to them. In the incredible star-gate sequence Bowman travels through space (and time?) in a small capsule, ending up in a timeless white chamber, a terrarium where he is observed by the alien creatures (we don't see them because they have evolved into a more efficient energy life force, but we hear their "laughter"). His life passes in a flash and, dying, he looks into a black monolith. We next see the star child—a new Jesus?—who resembles Dave, drifting in its embryonic state toward earth. The evolution is complete. Man has seen his origins and come back in a higher form to begin the second millennium. The most awesome, beautiful (Geoffrey Unsworth's visuals, the classic music on the soundtrack), and mentally stimulating science-fiction film of all ends with an image and concept that jarred us in 1968 and remains firmly in our minds and memories as we move perilously closer to the year 2001.

▶ BEST ACTOR

WINNER:
Cliff Robertson *(Charly)*
Other Nominees: Alan Arkin *(The Heart Is a Lonely Hunter)*, Alan Bates *(The Fixer)*, Ron Moody *(Oliver!)*, Peter O'Toole *(The Lion in Winter)*

▼
THE BEST CHOICE:
Steve McQueen *(Bullitt)*
Award-Worthy Runners-Up: Ron Moody *(Oliver!)*, Peter O'Toole *(The Lion in Winter)*, Vincent Price *(The Conqueror Worm/The Witchfinder General)*, Cliff Robertson *(Charly)*, George C. Scott *(Petulia)*, Peter Sellers *(The Party)*, Richard Widmark *(Madigan)*

Cliff Robertson was a competent, likable leading man of very little distinction, beyond his role as John Kennedy in *PT 109* and as a loser who takes on the mob in Sam Fuller's cult B melodrama, *Underworld, USA*, before he hit paydirt as the title character in *Charly*. Daniel Keyes's prize-winning short novel about a mental retardee who becomes a genius after a radical scientific experiment—only to discover that the change is temporary—had been adapted for television with Robertson in the part. Robertson then bought the movie rights and worked tirelessly to get it produced, with himself in the lead. Directed by Ralph Nelson, the movie received fine notices and Robertson was nominated for best actor. He then proceeded to wage one of the Oscar's most shameless self-promotion campaigns, filling the trades with endorsements for the film and his performance. Oddly, his strategy paid off. I don't think the Academy was manipulated by the

quotes into believing his performance was better than it actually was. But only then did they begin to think of Robertson as an Oscar candidate. They had genuinely been touched by his sweet, moving characterization, playing essentially two characters. My one real complaint is that too often Robertson's genius Charly responds to something with a blank expression and viewers automatically read every emotion behind his facade. It's too easy a performance.

Looking back, it's surprising that Academy voters didn't select Peter O'Toole for his thunderous, high-comedy portrayal of Henry II in *The Lion in Winter*, especially since the best actor of the sixties hadn't yet won the award. Perhaps they reasoned that O'Toole, who had played this character in *Becket*, could act such parts in his sleep. (I think they underestimated the part and the performance.) If the Academy was looking for a more

Steve McQueen is a San Francisco homicide detective in *Bullitt,* arguably his best film.

restrained performance than O'Toole's, I think they should have bypassed Robertson for the era's definitive low-key actor, Steve McQueen. After a series of fine, restrained performances in *Hell Is for Heroes; The War Lover; The Great Escape; Soldier in the Rain; Love with the Proper Stranger; Baby, the Rain Must Fall; The Cincinnati Kid,* and *The Sand Pebbles*—for which he received his only Oscar nomination—McQueen peaked in Peter Yates's exciting cop drama, *Bullitt.* For those who think the underrated actor deserved Oscar recognition, this is the film to point to.

McQueen plays Frank Bullitt, an honest, dedicated San Francisco homicide detective. He is assigned to protect a witness who has come from Chicago to testify against the mob. The gangster's appearance will be a boon to the career of an opportunistic senator (Robert Vaughn), who is heading the crime investigation. Vaughn puts much pressure on McQueen to deliver his witness safely. But the witness is killed by professional hitmen, after he unlocked the door to his room to let them in. The witness dies in the hospital, but McQueen whisks away the body so Vaughn doesn't know he's dead—he needs time to investigate. He discovers that the dead man was only a look-alike for the embarrassed Vaughn's witness—he was set up to be killed while the real witness flies away with

mob money. But just before his plane takes off for Europe, McQueen arrives at the airport . . . leading to a gun battle.

Sharply directed and edited, filled with energy and style, and containing several exciting action sequences—including a classic fifteen-minute high-speed chase on San Francisco streets—*Bullitt* was one of the best genre pictures of the era. Thanks to McQueen it had one of its most memorable heroes, a counter to Clint Eastwood's Dirty Harry Callahan. McQueen's "invisible" acting style in the Gary Cooper–Spencer Tracy tradition had always kept him from receiving the critics' praise his devoted fans knew he deserved. But he finally got praise—though the Academy didn't seem to notice—as Bullitt, whose inability to show emotion perfectly suited McQueen's nonexpressive acting style. Bullitt has become so matter-of-fact when dealing with brutal murders that—as his uptown girlfriend, Jacqueline Bisset, protests—he now has difficulty showing his feelings in his personal life. Even when she tells him this, he is at a loss how to respond. One might think he is as devoid of feelings as Lee Marvin's gangster in *Point Blank*—whom Angie Dickinson slaps repeatedly without getting a reaction—but when we look into McQueen's soft blue eyes, notice his subtle expressions, and listen to his voice, we are aware of his pain, his sensitivity, and his gentleness. We know he wants to try to thaw out, but fears that will keep him from coping with his job, which means a lot to him: he realizes that someone has to do it, and no one can do it better than he. So we are touched when he makes his feeble attempt at the end of the film: before joining Bisset in bed, he washes his hands and takes a deep, sorrowful look in the mirror at the face of a man who has just killed another man in the line of duty.

McQueen is fun to watch as he does bits of business that reveal much about this character. I like it when he wakes up, slow and cranky, walking across the floor as if it were covered with broken glass; when he completes his grocery shopping by buying a half-dozen TV dinners without bothering to see what is in each package; when he can't find a dime so sneaks a newspaper from its machine without paying; when he listens to slimy Vaughn's orders and then ignores them; when he silently drinks coffee and snacks while both he and a skilled black doctor overhear Vaughn arranging for the doctor to be replaced—his expression doesn't change, but it's obvious that through eye contact he and the doctor have formed a bond, respecting each other for being on Vaughn's shit list.

But McQueen is at his best in action sequences. Chasing an assassin through the hospital, chasing the chief villain on an airport runway and inside the terminal, and, seated in a sportscar, chasing the two assassins in that influential, dizzying sequence that was shot on location—with McQueen doing his own driving—up and down the steep streets of San Francisco. He's exciting to watch. If Bisset also could see her man at work, in action, she wouldn't complain—she'd only love him more.

▶ BEST ACTRESS

WINNER:
Katharine Hepburn *(The Lion in Winter)* and **Barbra Streisand** *(Funny Girl)*
Other Nominees: Patricia Neal *(The Subject Was Roses)*, Vanessa Redgrave *(Isadora)*, Joanne Woodward *(Rachel, Rachel)*

▼
_____

THE BEST CHOICE:
Tuesday Weld *(Pretty Poison)*
Award-Worthy Runners-Up: Julie Christie *(Petulia)*, Katharine Hepburn *(The Lion in Winter)*, Barbra Streisand *(Funny Girl)*, Joanne Woodward *(Rachel, Rachel)*

The most heated contest for Best Actress in Academy history took place in 1968, resulting in a revered movie veteran and an exciting movie newcomer sharing the honor. Katharine Hepburn was awarded her record third Oscar (it was her record eleventh nomination) for her fiery Eleanor of Aquitaine in *The Lion in Winter,* and Barbra Streisand won for her much anticipated movie debut as Fanny Brice in *Funny Girl,* reprising her Broadway success. They defeated Patricia Neal, whose role in *The Subject Was Roses* was her first since suffering several debilitating strokes; Vanessa Redgrave, whose chances for winning for her erratic performance in *Isadora* dwindled when the single actress announced her pregnancy and spoke out against the Vietnam War; and New York Film Critics winner Joanne Woodward, who was outstanding in the Paul Newman–directed *Rachel, Rachel,* but probably lost her shot at the Oscar when she protested her husband's exclusion in the Best Director category. All five nominees received special attention, as did *Rosemary's Baby*'s Mia Farrow. In contrast Tuesday Weld's super performance in *Pretty Poison* received praise only from the few hip critics who rushed to see Noel Black's low-budget black comedy before it vanished. The very idea of Tuesday Weld winning a Best Actress Oscar over the 1968 nominees would have made the prestige-conscious Academy voters squirm. But I think it would cause many movie cultists to smile (laugh?) with approval, as this inimitable actress has a strong, loyal following. Besides, for *Pretty Poison* she deserved it. Hers is the one performance of 1968 that still seems fresh and exciting.

Imagine *The Bad Seed*'s diabolical eight-year-old Rhoda Penmark grown up. That's who Weld's immoral seventeen-year-old high school majorette Sue Ann Stepanek will remind you of. She lives in a small town with her strict mother (Beverly Garland is particularly nasty), craving excitement. She meets Anthony Perkins's Dennis Pitt, who has just started working at the lumber company, a job he got through his probation officer, Azenauer (John Randolph). Dennis has just been let out of an institution: as a boy he spitefully burned down his aunt's house, not knowing she was still inside. To attract Sue Ann, Dennis pretends to be a CIA agent, on a secret mission having to do with the poisoning of America's water supply. The excited girl agrees to work with him, sealing their pact by making love to him. Afterward she wants to do something really exciting. At some point she realizes he's too clumsy, too frightened, and too much of a loser to be a secret agent. But she leads him on, hoping he'll be the means for escaping her mother's control. At night she goes with him to the lumber mill, where he—pretending to be doing spy business—unscrews the bridge supports from which pollutants flow into a small river. When the night watchman turns up, Sue Ann calmly kills him, stealing his gun. She tells Dennis she wants to run away with him, but while he anxiously waits for her to pack, which she does slowly, her mother "unexpectedly" returns. Sue Ann shoots her mother. Later she tells

Tuesday Weld becomes lover and accomplice of Anthony Perkins in the quirky black comedy *Pretty Poison.*

the police that Dennis did it. The police believe the tearful girl. Dennis goes to jail. He tells Azenauer to watch Sue Ann. A year later, when Sue Ann meets a new worker at the lumber mill, they plot how to get her freedom from the strict people she now lives with. Azenauer secretly observes her.

Weld's Sue Ann comes across as a typical American teenage innocent, a pretty, high-spirited blonde, who is on the honor roll, takes hygiene classes, and carries the American flag while marching with her school band. But to director Noel Black and screenwriter Lorenzo Semple, Jr. (who adapted Stephen Geller's novel), she represents the pretty poison that festers in our heartland, while paranoid Americans worry about being infected by outsiders and foreigners. She blames an outsider for her crimes and is believed. As Sue Ann grew up she refined, even perfected, her evil, keeping it veiled under a cheery veneer. It now corresponds with her sexual amorality. It's fun watching Weld be amoral. When she drowns the mortally wounded night watchman by sitting on his back, while letting her dress ride up, she is likely bucking herself to an orgasm. After she kills him and after she kills her mother, she immediately wants to have sex with Dennis, who is too shocked to do anything. She speaks of her two murders with almost clinical detachment. "I hit him *twice*—you see, he started to go down and I bopped him on the side of the head"; "she wasn't frightened at all, just a little surprised." But she enjoys

the acts immensely, licking her lips while she plugs her mother, smiling with fulfillment after doing in the old man: "God, what a night!" She is always so happy that she is, oddly, the ideal date . . . as long as the guy is willing to commit crimes to please her. She is quite an attraction for the masochistic Dennis.

This picture is full of dark, ironic humor, and Weld gives Sue Ann the comic edge to match Perkins's oddball Dennis. No matter what ludicrous ideas Dennis cooks up, Sue Ann is willing; in fact, she's one scheme ahead of him. Like Weld's thirteen-year-old who schemes to get a strapless gown in her 1956 movie debut, *Rock! Rock! Rock!,* her memorable, money-hungry Thalia Menninger on television's *The Many Loves of Dobie Gillis*—her prototypical role—and her manipulative teenager in *Lord Love a Duck,* Weld's greedy, egocentric Sue Ann delivers such a seductive I-need-something spiel that men will do anything to satisfy her. No one is better than Weld at showing excitement at acquiring things. Sue Ann's eyes light up, she squeals, she rubs her body against Dennis. She's like a youngster on her birthday. Dennis can't resist pleasing her. Unfortunately, in order to give her the freedom she desires for a present (freedom for her means the potential for excitement), he is willing to give up his own. She doesn't even thank him for taking the rap and going to prison. And, of course, it's of no solace to him when she tells the police, "I feel a little bit responsible for Mom's death myself."

▶ BEST PICTURE

WINNER:
Midnight Cowboy (United Artists; John Schlesinger)
Other Nominees: *Anne of the Thousand Days; Butch Cassidy and the Sundance Kid; Hello, Dolly!; Z*

▼

THE BEST CHOICE:
Once Upon a Time in the West (Paramount; Sergio Leone)
Award-Worthy Runners-Up: *Medium Cool* (Haskell Wexler), *They Shoot Horses, Don't They?* (Sydney Pollack)

Nineteen sixty-nine was a watershed year in the cinema, as sex, left-of-center politics, and disenfranchised characters began to dominate the screen; the big-budget musical was having its last gasp and the Western its last hurrah. For the first time Woody Allen wrote, directed, and starred in a picture, *Take the Money and Run,* and Paul Mazursky wrote and directed the "topical" wife-swap comedy *Bob & Carol & Ted & Alice,* but most 1969

movies were extremely cynical and had depressing endings. The MPAA introduced its ratings system and United Artists's *Midnight Cowboy* became the first X-rated picture to be released by a major studio and the only one to win a Best Picture Oscar. Along with *Butch Cassidy and the Sundance Kid* and *Easy Rider,* John Schlesinger's drama also introduced the "buddy picture." *Butch Cassidy* was the most successful film of the year but *Easy*

Charles Bronson and Henry Fonda in the final showdown in Sergio Leone's masterpiece, *Once Upon a Time in the West.*

Rider made so much money on a low investment that all studios decided to bankroll small-budget, personal films with antiestablishment themes. Paramount took off its shelf Haskell Wexler's *Medium Cool,* the most political narrative film yet released by a studio (officially, it got its X rating because it was the first American studio film with full-frontal nudity, but more likely it was because of its leftist slant). In fact, young viewers were so hungry for pictures with political themes that *if . . .* , from Britain, and *Z,* a French-Algerian film, were financial successes in America. Surely, Costa-Gavras's political thriller, about a high-level conspiracy to assassinate a leftist leader in Greece, was the most radical picture yet to receive a Best Picture nomination—it won as Best Foreign Film.

Midnight Cowboy featured great performances by Jon Voight, as a Texas hick who becomes a Forty-second Street hustler, and Dustin Hoffman, as the gimpy Times Square sleazo he moves in with when penniless, but the film was marred by too many technical impositions and the British Schlesinger's obvious enjoyment in victimizing his two down-and-out characters in the name of America. For the best picture of the year I endorse a real *cowboy* movie. Not George Roy Hill's self-consciously hip *Butch Cassidy,* or the enjoyable but unremarkable *True Grit,* which won John Wayne his only Oscar, or the film many viewers would rate the year's best, Sam Peckinpah's *The Wild Bunch,* a war movie posing as a Western. My choice is *Once Upon a Time in the West,* the last in the line of those classic Westerns it both emulates and subverts.

This baroque epic Western was directed by the bold Italian stylist Sergio Leone, who had made Clint Eastwood a star with the violent "Man with No Name" spaghetti westerns, *A Fistful of Dollars, For a Few Dollars More,* and *The Good, the Bad, and the Ugly.* Leone wrote the story with Bernardo Bertolucci and Dario Argento (two men who would gain international prominence as directors); Tonino Delli Colli was responsible for the stunning wide-screen cinamatography; and the peerless Ennio Morricone, whom Leone made famous, provided the

haunting melodies, musical motifs, theme songs, and choral numbers that comment on the action, add humor, and help move the story forward.

As in the Eastwood movies Leone presents an historical, civilized West overlapping the mythological one, where the last battles take place between superwarriors (the superheroes are as ruthless as the supervillains) with nearly godlike skills of combat. Charles Bronson's "The Man" (Leone's "good" personification in a world where others are worse) arrives in Flagstone to kill Henry Fonda's dressed-in-black gunslinger, Frank (Leone's "bad" personification). Frank and his men are in the desert on Brett McBain's land, Sweetwater, massacring McBain and his children (in a scene inspired by *The Searchers*), and implicating Jason Robards's witty, chatty outlaw, Cheyenne (Leone's "ugly," or *flawed* superwarrior). Frank wants McBain's fertile desert land for his railroad baron boss, Morton (Gabriele Ferzetti), who intends it for a station. But McBain married a New Orleans prostitute, Jill (Claudia Cardinale), who arrives in town and claims the land. Cheyenne befriends Jill. The Man befriends Jill. Frank seduces Jill. He forces her to auction her land so he can acquire it "legally." Cheyenne rescues the Man from Frank, but the Man turns him in for the bounty so he can buy the land at the auction. He returns the land to Jill. As he expects, Cheyenne escapes. Cheyenne kills Morton. The Man kills Frank in a gunfight, explaining that he has chased Frank because Frank murdered his brother many years before. Jill is sad to see Cheyenne and the Man leave. Rich, she will remain in town to watch it grow. Once out of her sight, Cheyenne dies of wounds suffered while attacking Morton's train. The Man rides off leading Cheyenne's horse, with Cheyenne draped over its back.

Once Upon a Time in the West is Leone's elegy to the masculine, mythological, precivilization West of many movie Westerns. It is his sorrowful, angry gaze at the advent of civilization in the real American West, which he believes was marked by the birth of matriarchy (the prostitute becomes a wife and businesswoman) and the coming to power of corrupt, wimpy men who had money to employ the once-independent gunmen (even superwarriors like Frank) to protect their empires. There are many killings in Leone's Westerns but they have thematic purpose: each time someone is killed, someone else in capitalist America will profit financially. Only the Man is driven by revenge, the one pure motive (other than self-preservation) in a Leone film.

The lengthy finale, the inevitable shootout between the Man and Frank, is one of several amazingly staged scenes in the movie. The elaborate title sequence in which three gunmen (including Jack Elam and Woody Strode) wait for the Man at a train station and are killed by him is equally memorable. (The only scene I like better is Frank's easy seduction of the lustful Jill.) His audaciously staged, ritualistic gunfights, during which he intersperses tight shots of eyes and hands in relation to guns, and moves the opponents—one in close-up and one in long shot—in and out of his wide frame, both build tension and provide the humor that is essential to Leone's work. No one was better at using the wide screen, whether to show us a wide-brimmed hat extending from one side of the frame to the other, a majestic Western landscape, or a close-up of one of his characters, all of whom have interesting faces. He also loved to show his actors walking across the large frame, particularly Fonda, his favorite actor as a boy.

Before his untimely death Leone directed only five Westerns (including *Duck, You Sucker,* which is actually set during the Mexican Revolution) and the gangster film *Once Upon a Time in America.* I think *Once Upon a*

Time in the West is his masterpiece, his most beautifully shot, ambitious, humorous, erotic, and psychologically compelling work. It was ignored by most everyone in America when it played here briefly in a truncated version; and for many years its full-length 165-minute version was available only in 16mm prints. Now fully restored in 35mm, it is regarded as a masterpiece. You'll really have to be patient for it to turn up on a big screen, though, which is how it must be seen. At least, it's worth a long wait. I've known it to convert skeptics into liking Westerns.

▶ BEST ACTOR

WINNER:

John Wayne *(True Grit)*

Other Nominees: Richard Burton *(Anne of the Thousand Days),* Dustin Hoffman *(Midnight Cowboy),* Peter O'Toole *(Goodbye, Mr. Chips),* Jon Voight *(Midnight Cowboy)*

▼

THE BEST CHOICE:

Dustin Hoffman *(Midnight Cowboy)*

Award-Worthy Runners-Up: James Caan *(The Rain People),* Steve McQueen *(The Reivers),* Jon Voight *(Midnight Cowboy),* John Wayne *(True Grit)*

It took donning an eye patch and playing a boozy, overweight, cantankerous old lawman to win John Wayne his long-overdue Oscar. At the time we Wayne fanatics were happy that he'd finally gotten the award and thought he did an admirable job as Rooster Cogburn in Henry Hathaway's down-and-dirty, but amusing, Western, *True Grit.* But we resented that he had to play a buffoon and spoof himself in order to get Academy validation—as it had been with Humphrey Bogart's alcoholic skipper in *The African Queen.* And we really didn't like the Academy's false message that if only Wayne had been offered such meaty roles earlier, we would have known he had exceptional acting talent. It was as if he'd never made *Stagecoach, The Long Voyage Home, Angel and the Bad-man, Fort Apache, Red River, She Wore a Yellow Ribbon, The Quiet Man, Hondo, The Searchers, Rio Bravo, The Man Who Shot Liberty Valance,* and *El Dorado,* among others. Wayne had given terrific performances for three decades, but the Academy's refusal even to nominate him for an Oscar (except for *Sands of Iwo Jima*) helped perpetuate the myth that he wasn't really an actor at all, that "he was only playing himself." Hathaway was a talented old-time director, but it would have been more appropriate if Wayne had won his Oscar for a film directed by John Ford or Howard Hawks.

Wayne's only serious challenger in 1969 was Dustin Hoffman from the non-Western *Midnight Cowboy,* in which Jon Voight cites Wayne to disprove Hoffman's theory that all "cowboys are fags." Despite numerous flaws *Midnight Cowboy* was selected Best Picture on the

strength of the outstanding performances by Hoffman and Voight. I choose Hoffman over Voight as the year's best actor only because of the consistency of his performance. Voight's character seems to change a bit from scene to scene, as does the thickness of his Texas accent.

Enrico "Ratso" Rizzo (Hoffman) doesn't turn up in *Midnight Cowboy* until after Joe Buck (Voight) has taken a bus from Texas to New York to try to make it as a "hustler." He's already spent time in the unfriendly city and is low on money. A lowlife con man, with a gimpy leg and a heavy cough, Ratso convinces the gullible Joe to let him be his manager. He takes twenty dollars from Joe to introduce him to a connection who, he promises, will introduce him in turn to rich lady clients. But the man turns out to be a religious fanatic, not a connection. Ratso takes off with the twenty dollars. Joe eventually runs into Ratso again, but Ratso has spent all the money. Ratso invites the broke Joe to share his decrepit apartment in a condemned building. Ratso does the cooking and teaches Joe how to pull off petty crimes so they can eat occasionally. Their situation seems hopeless, but they grow close. The sick Ratso dreams of going to Florida. Joe and Ratso are invited by chance to an ultrahip party, where Joe meets a woman (Brenda Vaccaro) who will pay for his services. She promises to introduce him to other women. Joe is delighted by his prospects, but Ratso is deathly ill. Joe wants to take him to Florida. He goes with an elderly gay man (Barnard Hughes) to his hotel. When the man tries to send him away without much money, Joe robs him and pushes a phone receiver into

Dustin Hoffman's Ratso Rizzo primes
Jon Voight's Joe Buck for a
big date in *Midnight Cowboy*.

his mouth. Joe takes Ratso by bus to Florida, but Ratso dies just before they reach Miami.

I still remember how surprised I was that Hoffman could effectively play someone so different from Ben in 1967's *The Graduate*. The Mike Nichols film gave Hoffman his first real exposure, and though he made us laugh with his deadpan style, we weren't sure if he had any versatility. His Ratso Rizzo in *Midnight Cowboy* was startling. His performance made us realize how impressive his taken-for-granted performance in the earlier film had been.

Hoffman considered Ratso an easy role, but I don't think other actors would have played him in the difficult manner Hoffman chose. More likely, they would have cashed in on the sympathy the gimpy, broke, sickly Ratso could easily have elicited, making us see warmth under his sleazy facade right from the beginning. But Hoffman instead lets us get to know the repellent side of Ratso. A horror-movie maxim is in effect: A grotesque-looking figure will eventually act in a grotesque manner. With an unwashed body, greasy hair, rotten teeth, ugly stubble, a phlegmy cough, a limp, a cigarette butt dangling from his chapped lips, and an irritating nasal voice, Ratso acts like the worm he feels he has become after years on the streets. Only Joe, the nicest, most innocent guy in the world, can stand to be around him.

If Joe's loyalty isn't enough to help Ratso rise above worm status, it is enough to get him to reveal his human qualities. Hoffman is more interested in Ratso's recovery of his long-lost *dignity* through a platonic "love" bond with Joe than in winning our sympathy for his character. One of America's forgotten, penniless men, Ratso, like Chaplin's Tramp, fights to maintain his pride despite his desperate situation. Refusing to be beaten down, Hoffman's Ratso yells at disrespectful cabdrivers ("I'm walk-

ing here!" he improvised at a real cabbie who almost ran him down) and everyone else who crosses his path, and, with hands and feet constantly moving, slaps and kicks his way past inanimate objects to wherever he's going. He won't acknowledge that his apartment isn't fit for a rat, much less Ratso and his roommate. Even to Joe he has a hard time admitting his failings . . . until he is deathly ill. For instance, after falling down a long flight of stairs, he insists to Joe he is all right. In his daydreams he sees himself an important man in Miami: fancily dressed, with no limp, known by women, and respected by the men with whom he gambles.

But in New York, where he knows he's a nobody, his lone source of pride is his crafty "management" of Joe, whose handsome "stud" body gives him opportunities Ratso could never have himself. He takes care of Joe, giving him a place to sleep, advising him, cooking for him, washing his clothes, shining his boots, sprucing him up so he can ply his trade. What pride he has watching the spiffy Joe enter a fancy women's hotel to pick up a pretty date, even while he himself must stand in the darkness dressed like a bum. Joe becomes part of him. And, much to his own surprise, Ratso also becomes a welcome part of Joe, who happily shares all his fortunes with his friend. Joe is too nice to overlook what Ratso has done for him. He helps Ratso realize his dream by taking him to Florida—committing a horrible crime to get the bus fare. And after Ratso admits he wet his pants, Joe cheers him by saying it's nothing. Then Joe dresses him in a new outfit. He allows Ratso to die with the dignity he fought for. As Hoffman intended, we don't feel sorry for Ratso even in death. Instead we are happy he is finally at peace, with his best buddy's arm wrapped comfortingly around his shoulder.

► BEST ACTRESS

WINNER:
Maggie Smith *(The Prime of Miss Jean Brodie)*
Other Nominees: Genevieve Bujold *(Anne of the Thousand Days)*, Jane Fonda *(They Shoot Horses, Don't They?)*, Liza Minnelli *(The Sterile Cuckoo)*, Jean Simmons *(The Happy Ending)*

▼

THE BEST CHOICE:
Shirley Knight *(The Rain People)*
Award-Worthy Runners-Up: Genevieve Bujold *(Anne of the Thousand Days)*, Jane Fonda *(They Shoot Horses, Don't They?)*

It appeared that Shirley MacLaine was finally in line for a Best Actress Oscar when she signed to play the lead in Bob Fosse's musical, *Sweet Charity*, taking the part Gwen Verdon played in Fosse's stage hit. As a big-hearted girl who always gets shafted in love, MacLaine would sing and dance and do what she did better than anyone, attempt to smile while her heart was breaking. MacLaine had some great moments in this underrated musical, but she mugged her way out of contention. Her place among the nominees was taken by Liza Minnelli, who in *The Sterile Cuckoo* played an even more pathetic jilted female. In the Best Actor category John Wayne had captured America's sentimental vote, but neither America nor the Academy had any emotional investment in regard to who prevailed as Best Actress. So amid the apathy Britain's Maggie Smith sneaked to a surprise victory as Muriel Spark's eccentric teacher in *The Prime of Miss Jean Brodie*. Smith's performance was too mannered and theatrical for my tastes, but she exhibited such talent that no critics of the day bothered to criticize her—especially after their colleagues sang her praises. Oddly, even the Oscar didn't help Smith receive film offers worthy of that talent.

My choice for Best Actress is Shirley Knight, who played a pregnant woman who leaves her husband in Francis Ford Coppola's *The Rain People*. Coppola's ahead-of-its-time feminist drama got little distribution when released, and most of those relatively few people who have since tracked it down didn't see it until years later, after Coppola's reputation had been established with *The Godfather* and other films. Even today, Knight's compelling performance remains a well-kept secret.

Knight plays Natalie Ravenna, a childless Long Island housewife, who leaves her husband, Vinny, one rainy morning while he sleeps. She drives without direction along America's turnpikes, calling Vinny often, assuring him she is safe, and telling him she wasn't much of a wife. She informs Vinny that she is pregnant, but isn't sure if she wants the baby. At first he warns her not to have an abortion, but as time goes on, he tells her to have it if she'll just return to him. Thinking she wants a sexual experience with someone other than her husband, Natalie picks up a hitchhiker. But "Killer" Kilgannon (James Caan) turns out to be an injured ex–football player who wears a plate in his head and has the mind of

a child. "Killer" becomes attached to her. She feels responsible for him, yet resents his intrusion on her life. She tries often to abandon him but keeps retrieving him from horrible situations. Natalie accepts a date from Gordon (Robert Duvall), an aggressive motorcycle cop, who takes her to his trailer. When she changes her mind about sleeping with him, Gordon becomes furious and they struggle. "Killer" breaks in and beats up Gordon, whose terrified young daughter picks up his gun. She shoots "Killer." Natalie tells "Killer" that she and Vinny will always take care of him—but he is dead.

Like Maggie Smith, Shirley Knight had more success on the stage than the screen. She was attractive and undeniably talented, but neither her looks nor her cerebral acting style—her characters don't reveal themselves through dialogue—were typical of Hollywood leading ladies. Denied choice parts, she fled Hollywood in the early sixties. Her one significant lead had been in *Dutchman*, which was filmed in London. In it she played a wicked prostitute who mercilessly goads a seemingly mild-tempered black man aboard a New York subway train. Although she hadn't much of a track record, Coppola wrote his script for *The Rain People* (which he based on a story he wrote in college) specifically for Knight. Knight gave, despite some conflicts between

Shirley Knight and Robert Duvall in Francis Ford Coppola's early feminist film, *The Rain People*.

them, the great performance he had expected. As a woman whose words don't reflect her innermost feelings (which she hides even from herself), Knight again expressed what we needed to know about her character through expressions, gazes, body movements, speech patterns, even degrees of fatigue. For instance, she doesn't say a word in the opening scene in which she wakes up under her husband's heavy arm, takes a liberating shower, and sets the silverware for his breakfast as the "perfect wife" would do. But as we watch Knight we realize that Natalie *must* leave or go crazy. And later in a motel, Knight lets us know how important freedom is to Natalie simply in the way she makes coffee for herself for a change. Knight projects the disorientation, confusion, loneliness, and self-hatred that weighs so heavily on this woman who has just left her good husband for no good reason she can think of—she assumes it's because she wants sexual excitement, but discovers that's not the case.

All the time, Knight lets us feel Natalie's shame for not having fulfilled her wifely obligations. *That* is what this film is about. Natalie considers herself the only woman in the world with misgivings about marriage and a child. The women's movement wasn't in full swing when this picture was made—otherwise Natalie might seek support from women with similar fears. Alone and wrongly hating

herself, she becomes self-destructive and ends up in serious trouble.

Natalie's early marriage stifled her maturation, so at times she comes across as a reckless young girl. Watch how Knight puts on makeup before Natalie's "heavy date" with Gordon. She reveals motherly instincts with "Killer," but they're so sporadic that it's clear that she must grow up and become strong within herself before she'll be ready to have a child of her own.

Natalie tells Vinny, "If you knew me, you'd hate me." But no one knows Natalie, not even Natalie. After being the same boring wife, day after day, year after year, Natalie has broken free and now seeks to forge an identity for herself. She evolves at an extremely rapid pace, fumbling along, making correct choices and all kinds of mistakes and miscalculations, even about herself. Knight's performance is deeply affecting because she struggles along with her character, suffering through her mistakes and agonizing in her confusion. I assume Knight identifies with much of what Natalie goes through. Knight seems to be forcing Natalie to define herself, understand herself, be easier on herself. Only then can the character and the immersed actress breathe sighs of relief. Unfortunately, the film's resolution doesn't allow for such comfort.

1970

▶ BEST PICTURE

WINNER:

Patton (20th Century–Fox; Franklin Schaffner)
Other Nominees: *Airport, Five Easy Pieces, Love Story, M*A*S*H*

▼

THE BEST CHOICE:
Five Easy Pieces (BBS/Columbia; Bob Rafelson)
Award-Worthy Runners-Up: *The Ballad of Cable Hogue* (Sam Peckinpah), *Burn!* (Gillo Pontecorvo), *The Honeymoon Killers* (Leonard Kastle), *Little Big Man* (Arthur Penn)

Considering that many of the young viewers who comprised Hollywood's target audience in 1970 were part of the antiwar movement, one might assume today that 20th Century–Fox went out on a broken limb when it made Franklin Schaffner's big-budgeted, 170-minute *Patton,* with George C. Scott essaying the part of America's intrepid World War II general George S. Patton. But at the time Robert Altman's irreverent Korean War comedy, *M*A*S*H,* was considered far more controversial. The

1970 Best Picture winner was geared to be, politically speaking, a middle-of-the-road film that wouldn't offend anyone, and it was rewarded with across-the-board popularity. It became the favorite movie of hawkish presidents and military men, who jotted down every quote the aggressive general uttered about the nature of war and the responsibilities of the officers and soldiers who fought it. Those who insisted the Vietnam War was being lost because sound military strategy was being compromised by diplomacy, discovered in this film the historical figure they wanted our generals to emulate. War protesters didn't lash out at the film, either, much to Twentieth's relief. That's because it was set during a "just war"; and—as calculated by young coscreenwriter Francis Ford Coppola—Patton was appealingly presented as a nonconformist within the military, a poet and historian who often speaks his mind against authority figures. Also, many young men saw their own obstinate, authoritarian fathers in Scott's character. Moreover, any time Patton says something that might have raised the ire of college-age viewers, Coppola and Edmund H. North wisely have Karl Malden's Omar Bradley counter with a more reasoned statement, as if he and not Patton represented the thinking of the filmmakers.

Patton contains a great performance by Scott and holds up fairly well as a biography and as a war movie. But under close scrutiny you'll notice that this film has a flimsy structure, with five or six basic scenes that are repeated over and over in different settings, as the war progresses. Repeatedly, Patton startles officers with his idiosyncrasies, frightens soldiers with his discipline, shows (when his guard is down) that he really cares about the men who serve under him, gets into trouble for being outspoken, and so on. Also annoying is that every time Coppola and North want us to know what a military genius Patton is, we cut to German headquarters, where we hear their top brass exalting him.

For 1970's Best Picture I much prefer another, much different character study, Bob Rafelson's *Five Easy Pieces,* featuring a star-making, Oscar-nominated performance by Jack Nicholson.

Nicholson's Bobby Dupea works on an oil rig, lives with a sexy, sweet, but not very smart country-singing waitress, Rayette (Karen Black was nominated for Best Supporting Actress). He bowls, plays poker, and sleeps around with floozies. He feels trapped, especially when Rayette becomes pregnant. He loves her but can't conceive of spending his life with someone so different from himself. Everything goes wrong: His best friend (Billy Green Bush) is thrown into jail for violating his parole, leaving behind his wife and baby, and Bobby himself is fired. Learning that his father has had a series of strokes, he returns home to Puget Sound after a few years. We are surprised to find that he came from a rich, cultured background. He had once studied to be a classical pianist (as a kid he studied "Five Easy Pieces"), as did his brother (Ralph Waite in a neck brace) and emotionally shaky sister (Lois Smith). He hadn't gotten along with his father, a stern orchestra conductor. Putting Rayette in a motel, he aggressively pursues a beautiful young pianist, Catherine (Susan Anspach), whom his brother expects to marry. They sleep together but she rejects a long relationship because, she says, he has no love or respect for himself and has no right to ask that from others. Driving back home, Bobby and Rayette pull into a truck stop. He gives her his wallet so she can grab a bite to eat. While she is away, he hitches a ride with a trucker heading to the frozen north.

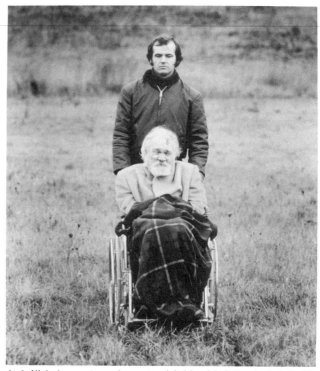

Jack Nicholson returns home to visit his sick father in Bob Rafelson's *Five Easy Pieces.*

It is to the Academy's credit that it even nominated *Five Easy Pieces* for Best Picture along with such conventional commercial choices as *Patton, Love Story,* and *Airport* (which started the big-budget disaster-film craze). Existential road pictures (of which it was the best) never got much Oscar consideration. Today this open-ended film would have no chance of being financed by a major studio, but it was one of the era's landmark counterculture pictures. We were excited by Rafelson's free-wheeling, low-budget time-piece that had an incisive, bitter, and witty script by Adrien Joyce (and Rafelson), evocative cinematography by Laszlo Kovacs, sex, arguments, Tammy Wynette songs, and superb acting by Nicholson, Black, Anspach, and others in the starless cast. And though Bobby Dupea was not like anyone with whom we associated, we responded to his strong sense of alienation. And to his rebelliousness and frustration, which result in some classic Nicholson outbursts of temper, like the one scene in which he blows his stack at an obnoxious truck stop waitress who won't allow him "substitutions" in his order. How could we not like a guy Patton might have slapped for insubordination, dereliction of duty or, more likely, desertion?

The picture is full of odd, funny moments (like the memorable waitress scene) and unusual movie characters, including Black's Rayette, Sally Struthers's floozy Shirley ("but they call me Betty") and Helena Kallianiotes's constantly complaining hitchhiker Palm Apodaca: "Dirt isn't bad—it's filth. Filth is bad. That's what starts maggots and riots. . . . I've seen filth like you wouldn't believe." But the humor is cut by Tammy Wy-nette's shattered-dreams songs on the soundtrack and an assortment of pathetic characters who are trapped in wheelchairs, neck braces, and behind bars, or by their own insecurities or circumstances. We don't admire Bobby for escaping his trap, life with the likable but annoying Rayette (who often sings Tammy's "Stand By

Your Man"), but we understand that he would suffocate if he committed himself to her. So we accept his running away because it is for her benefit more than his own. He has no money and not even a jacket, as he heads to the cold north, fleeing, maybe even dropping out of the world, yet, as many of us felt about our own directions back then, going nowhere.

▶ BEST ACTOR

WINNER:
George C. Scott *(Patton)*
Other Nominees: Melvyn Douglas *(I Never Sang for My Father)*, James Earl Jones *(The Great White Hope)*, Jack Nicholson *(Five Easy Pieces)*, Ryan O'Neal *(Love Story)*

▼

THE BEST CHOICE:
Jack Nicholson *(Five Easy Pieces)*
Award-Worthy Runners-Up: Peter Boyle *(Joe)*, Marlon Brando *(Burn!)*, Ben Gazzara *(Husbands)*, Dustin Hoffman *(Little Big Man)*, Tony Lo Bianco *(The Honeymoon Killers)*, Jason Robards, Jr. *(The Ballad of Cable Hogue)*, George C. Scott *(Patton)*, George Segal *(Where's Poppa?)*, Gene Wilder *(Start the Revolution Without Me)*

George C. Scott's tour-de-force performance as America's controversial World War II general George S. Patton, in Franklin Schaffner's Best Picture winner, *Patton,* overwhelmed everyone in 1970. His blunt, imposing opening speech in front of a huge American flag became an instant classic—he could have stopped right then and won the Oscar. It leads me to believe that Scott would have been even more effective in a one-man show about Patton, because the other characters and repetitive scenes and conversations get in the actor's way. Still, for giving one of the cinema's most forceful and memorable characterizations of an historical figure, he certainly was worthy of the award the Academy wanted to give him. But Scott didn't show up to claim his Oscar, saying he didn't want to compete with other actors. If he didn't want the real Oscar, I'd wager he wouldn't be excited by an Alternate Oscar either. So I'll give 1970's Alternate Oscar to someone who never turned down an award: Jack Nicholson, who gave a performance equal to Scott's in Bob Rafelson's *Five Easy Pieces,* my choice as the year's best picture.

Nicholson had toiled in B pictures for more than ten years when he lost his anonymity as the amiable and philosophical Southern ACLU lawyer in *Easy Rider.* That earned him the lead in *Five Easy Pieces,* playing cultural misfit Bobby Dupea, the role that proved he could be a handsome, virile leading man and shot him to stardom. Overloaded with pent-up energy, ready with the quick snide remark, soft spoken until he can no longer suppress his temper, Nicholson made a startling impression. When we first see Bobby, he works on an oil rig, and lives with a sexy, not-too-bright waitress, Rayette (Karen Black), who constantly sings country songs and wants affection. He tries to lead a simple, easygoing life, work-

ing, playing cards, bowling, and sleeping around, but everything and everyone he meets drives him up the wall: Rayette; a weird, filth-despising hitchhiker (Helena Kallianiotes); a waitress who won't serve him what he wants ("No substitutions," she insists); a snobby intellectual woman who has the audacity to patronize and belittle Rayette. His world is as full of aggravation as W. C. Fields's, and at times is just as funny. Nothing goes as he wants, no one will leave him alone. This leads to angry outbursts: slamming his hands on the inside of his car, which won't start and allow him to flee Rayette (a great

Jack Nicholson makes a play for Susan Anspach in *Five Easy Pieces.*

Nicholson moment); yelling at Rayette and hurting her feelings; telling off the snob for not knowing how superior Rayette is to her; telling the waitress to stick a chicken between her legs and knocking everything off the table—still the most famous of Nicholson's many screen tantrums.

Whereas Scott's Patton, despite his self-acknowledged flaws, is content with who he is, Nicholson's Bobby Dupea has no idea who he is anymore. Everything he has experienced in his adult life has been his escape from his earliest identity: he comes from a rich, educated, classical-music background that he wants nothing to do with. His modus operandi is to travel around the country taking different low-paying jobs; and when things get too heavy, to escape from the person he has become and no longer wants to be. Now he wants to escape his confining, mismatched relationship with the pregnant, well-meaning, but suffocating Rayette. He wants to run off with his brother's fiancée (Susan Anspach), a smart, classy pianist, whom he meets when he returns home after a few years

to see his father. When she won't have him, Bobby goes off alone, aimlessly up north, deserting Rayette at a truck stop.

As disaffected a character as Bobby Dupea is, he was sort of an Everyman in 1970. Young viewers in the counterculture realized that Bobby didn't share their discontent with the political state of America, and they didn't relate to his present or past lives, but they did identify with Bobby's outsider status; restlessness; fury and irritation when pressured; sexual energy; inability to fit comfortably into marriage, parenthood, or other niches; need to keep the exit door within sight; disappointment in himself; and desperation to mend and give meaning to his life. Surely, we could relate to his feeling that nothing in America worked properly, that everything was geared to drive a person crazy. Best of all: when he takes on the waitress superior, he becomes our champion. As he shows in the diner sequence and throughout *Five Easy Pieces,* no actor was better at playing volatile confrontation scenes than Jack Nicholson.

▶ BEST ACTRESS

WINNER:
Glenda Jackson *(Women in Love)*
Other Nominees: Jane Alexander *(The Great White Hope),* Ali MacGraw *(Love Story),* Sarah Miles *(Ryan's Daughter),* Carrie Snodgress *(Diary of a Mad Housewife)*

▼

THE BEST CHOICE:
Glenda Jackson *(Women in Love)*
Award-Worthy Runner-Up: Barbara Loden *(Wanda)*

It seemed ironic and a sign of the times that Ken Russell directed a film titled *Women in Love,* adapted from D. H. Lawrence's novel about two sisters who venture into intense romances, yet gave top billing to two actors, Alan Bates and Oliver Reed, perhaps their reward for doing a stupefyingly silly full-frontal nude wrestling match. But no matter: third-billed Glenda Jackson won an Academy Award for Best Actress and the men went unnominated. Looking back at the seventies, I find myself agreeing with the Academy's choices for Best Actress to an alarming degree—though I note that the lack of strong women's roles in the decade resulted in there being only one or two strong female performances in most years. I even go along with the selection of Jackson, never one of my favorites, in a year with so few impressive performances that Ali MacGraw was nominated for Best Actress for *Love Story!*

In Larry Kramer's faithful adaptation of Lawrence—which Russell almost ruins with overly flamboyant visuals—Jackson played Gudrun Brangwen. She and her younger, more demure, less intellectual sister, Ursula (what ever happened to Jennie Linden after this appeal-

ing performance?) live in Beldover, a mining town in the Midlands. Gudrun is a sculptress and Ursula a teacher. In their twenties, they wonder about the nature of love. While Ursula becomes romantically involved with Bates's cynical school inspector, Rupert, Gudrun chances an affair with Reed's volatile Gerald, the son of a wealthy mineowner and Rupert's close friend. Their stormy affair is full of passion, but Gudrun resents Gerald's inability to love women. On vacation in the Alps, she breaks off with him. Angered at her friendship with a homosexual (Vladek Sheybal), Gerald nearly strangles her to death. He then wanders off into the snow to die. While Ursula settles into marriage with Rupert, who longs for his male friend to make his life fuller, the free Gudrun excitedly looks toward her unpredictable future.

The thirty-two-year-old daughter of a bricklayer, Jackson had first received attention in her native England as part of Peter Brook's Theater of Cruelty revue, which performed under the auspices of the Royal Shakespeare Company. She made a strong impression as the crazed Charlotte Corday on the stage in London and New York in Brook's *Marat/Sade,* and made her movie debut in the

Glenda Jackson's Gudrun is unhappy with her turbulent love affair with Oliver Reed's Gerald in Ken Russell's adaptation of D. H. Lawrence's *Women in Love*.

role when Brook adapted his production for the screen. After Brook's experimental *Tell Me Lies* and Peter Medak's perverse, and equally obscure, *Negatives*, Jackson got to play Lawrence's complex heroine in *Women in Love*. This was Ken Russell's breakthrough film, his third directorial effort, and one of his most controlled, well-received projects. She became an instant international star—it was released in 1969 in England, in 1970 in America—and probably would have won the Oscar even if the competition had been stronger.

Jackson impressed everyone, including me in 1970, because she was much different from other leading actresses of the day. Here was an actress who came across as extremely intelligent, forceful, defiant, and witty and could convincingly play women with similar traits without turning off viewers to herself or the characters. In the past, viewers rarely warmed to intellectual female characters, but Jackson showed that brainy women like Gudrun are capable of tremendous passion, even heightened sexuality because of their curiosity. Jackson wasn't as pretty as typical leading ladies, yet in the erotic *Women in Love* (and subsequent films) she was a turn-on in daring, intense sex scenes. For her Gudrun makes love with her head as well as her body, exploring the mental and spiritual as well as the physical aspects of sex. Gudrun sees sex as an act that simultaneously bonds a woman to her lover and liberates her. She wants much from Gerald—that he attempt to understand her, that he love her—but she seems almost relieved that he can't give it to her. This woman who announces, "I am a new creature stepping into life," wants most of all to be a *free*

woman—which, I assume, is why many female viewers responded favorably to her in 1970.

Jackson gives a bold performance, making no attempt to cover those traits that might diminish Gudrun's appeal. Aside from barroom floozies in Westerns and B melodramas, Gudrun is one of the few sympathetic female leads with more than a touch of arrogance. She isn't just highly spirited or headstrong or even aloof—she is arrogant. This doesn't come across through meanness (though there is slight insensitivity on her part) or condescension. It comes across in her refusal to conform or compromise; or—and this drives macho men like Gerald crazy—to reveal her weaknesses or dependence on men. Through Jackson we see that Gudrun—who does have annoying imperfections—has too much going for her and too much of the world to explore to settle for Gerald or any other man.

Women in Love opened the doors for Jackson to make other major films throughout the seventies, including the contemporary drama *Sunday Bloody Sunday*, the American comedy *A Touch of Class* (winning her second Oscar), and several historical dramas, often playing royalty. During this time she may have been the cinema's most respected actress. For the most part I found her mannered, and hated her viper tongue and the way she seemed always to be projecting for the person in the last row of the theater. It wouldn't be until 1985's low-key British sleeper *Turtle Diary* that I would again appreciate Jackson as much as I did when she captivated us all in *Women in Love*.

▶ BEST PICTURE

WINNER:
The French Connection (20th Century–Fox; William Friedkin)
Other Nominees: *A Clockwork Orange, Fiddler on the Roof, The Last Picture Show, Nicholas and Alexandra*

▼

THE BEST CHOICE:
McCabe and Mrs. Miller (Warner Bros.; Robert Altman)
Award-Worthy Runners-Up: *Dirty Harry* (Don Siegel), *Klute* (Alan J. Pakula), *The Last Picture Show* (Peter Bogdanovich), *Macbeth* (Roman Polanski), *Walkabout* (Nicolas Roeg)

It is well known that, with few exceptions, Academy voters have distanced themselves from comedies, Westerns, war films, musicals, and horror and science-fiction movies. But it's surprising that their long-standing prejudice against non-"prestige" genres extends to "crime" movies. Until Best Picture winners *In the Heat of the Night* in 1967 and *The French Connection* in 1971, no film with a policeman as the lead character had even been nominated for Best Picture since *The Racket*, in 1927–28, the first year of the Academy Awards. Other than a few "trial" films—*Witness for the Prosecution, 12 Angry Men, Anatomy of a Murder*—no Best Picture nominee since 1947's *Crossfire* (in which Sam Levene did have a strong though supporting role as a cop) was about the solving of a crime. No nominee had even featured a *private* detective since Humphrey Bogart's Sam Spade tried to get his hands on *The Maltese Falcon* in 1941. No caper film had been nominated for Best Picture; and there were no nominees between *The Racket* and *The French Connection* that had to do with gangsters. William Friedkin's *The French Connection,* about New York cops taking on international heroin smugglers, was a new kind of police-versus-gangster film. If it feels dated it is because it spawned countless cop films, all with brutal action, morally ambiguous heroes, morally vacuous villains, and razzle-dazzle car chases. While it no longer seems to be of Best Picture caliber, its action scenes remain exciting and we can still see why Gene Hackman became a star (he also was voted Best Actor) for his authentic (he's obsessive and violent) portrayal of real-life police detective Jimmy "Popeye" Doyle.

Nineteen seventy-one, the last year in which British films flooded the American market, saw the release of an inordinate number of unusual pictures that had lasting impact on viewers. Titles included *Carnal Knowledge; Straw Dogs; The Boy Friend; Willy Wonka and the Chocolate Factory; Sunday, Bloody Sunday; The Go-Between; Klute; The Hospital; Dirty Harry; Shaft; Play Misty for Me; Harold and Maude; Bananas; Macbeth; Two-Lane Black-*

top, Walkabout; Best Picture nominees *A Clockwork Orange* (the most controversial film of the year) and *The Last Picture Show* (the most respected film of the year); and my choice for Best Picture, *McCabe and Mrs. Miller* by Robert Altman. The Academy's aforementioned bias against Westerns prevented Oscar consideration for Altman's follow-up to *M*A*S*H*—Julie Christie received the film's only nomination—although it's so unlike all other Westerns (in terms of its premise, characters, and dialogue) that one wonders if it really is one.

Based on Edmund Naughton's novel, *McCabe,* the picture takes place in a Washington state mining community around the turn of the century. Presbyterian Church consists of only a few wood buildings scattered around the saloon where John McCabe (Warren Beatty) first makes his appearance. Rumor has it that he used a derringer to kill someone named Bill Roundtree, but no one saw the event and McCabe will neither confirm nor deny it. He's no gunman, he insists, but a gambler and businessman. He turns a tidy profit as pimp to three not very good-looking women. Then he goes into partnership with Christie's Mrs. Miller, an ambitious and tough English madam (and high-priced whore), who brings in her own women and sets up a "high-class" brothel. The town expands and McCabe and Mrs. Miller prosper. A mining company offers to buy out McCabe but he turns it down, not realizing that he's done a dangerous thing. The company sends a hired gun, Butler (Hugh Millais), a punky Kid (Manfred Schulz), and an Indian, Breed (Jace Vander Veen), to Presbyterian Church. Mrs. Miller tells McCabe to flee, but after speaking to a lawyer (William Devane), he decides to stand up for all small businessmen. On a snowy morning he takes on the three intruders. He shoots Kid and Breed in the back. After being mortally wounded by Butler, he kills him . . . with a derringer. As he dies in the snow, the townspeople are busy extinguishing a fire in the church, and Mrs. Miller sleeps in an opium den.

A bawdy bad joke about "free" enterprise, big busi-

Offscreen lovers Julie Christie and Warren Beatty costarred in Robert Altman's offbeat Western, *McCabe and Mrs. Miller.*

ness, and the growth of America, Robert Altman's revisionist, rule-breaking Western throws viewers completely off balance. Nothing is what it seems, nobody is who you think he is, everything that happens is unexpected. The picture has a humorous tone, but even before the finale it is full of casual violence that is extremely brutal: a crib whore stabs a client, a jealous husband gets his head bashed in during a fight, a gentle cowpoke (Keith Carradine) is gunned down for no reason by the bullying Kid in a horrifying scene. The film is beautifully, hauntingly photographed (by Vilmos Zsigmond) but the images are all ugly. The staging of scenes has background characters in the foreground. In an ironic finale everyone in town rallies to save the church from a fire, but while they celebrate, these Christians allow McCabe, the man responsible for the town's growth, to fight alone and die alone.

Our lead characters, McCabe and Mrs. Miller (excellently played by Beatty, who wrote much of his own dialogue, and Christie), are not at all sympathetic. They are opportunists and exploiters interested only in making money. Beatty described his character as a "cocky schmuck," who does nothing positive for anyone. He burps a lot, he rarely bathes, he gets drunk, he tells dirty jokes. The best that can be said of him and Mrs. Miller is that they treat their customers fairly, never cheating them of their money. Since they are played by two sex symbols who were offscreen lovers and have electricity between them on screen, we expect McCabe and Mrs. Miller to become passionate lovers themselves, especially in the rare Western to have sexual content and a distinct *romantic* feel. But while they grow fond of each other (they may even fall in love), he must pay her for sex and we

never actually see them making love. We think that when the chips are down, she will be the brave one and he will show himself to be a coward—just the opposite happens.

It's interesting how Altman introduces McCabe, with men gossiping that he was the one who shot Bill Roundtree with a derringer. We don't believe the idle chatter or even that there was a Bill Roundtree any more than we believe the other part of the rumor: that Beatty's McCabe used to be nicknamed "Pudgy." When the lying Butler contends to McCabe that Bill Roundtree was the best friend of his best friend, McCabe reacts with cowardice, leaving the saloon as Butler ordered. Butler then announces to the men around him that he never heard of Bill Roundtree and that he is positive that McCabe never shot anyone. We are now fully convinced that McCabe didn't kill anyone. When McCabe kills Kid and Breed, he shoots them in the back (some hero), which doesn't change our minds about Bill Roundtree. But when Butler approaches McCabe for the final kill, McCabe shoots him between the eyes. With a derringer! Just how he *definitely* killed Bill Roundtree! His final act—like Elliott Gould's unexpected final act with a gun in Altman's *The Long Goodbye*—shows that McCabe is not as far out of his league dealing with these villains as we'd assumed. As we watch the snow covering him as he dies—burying him and purifying him—we reevaluate him, looking back on his actions in a different light. There was more to McCabe than met the eye.

As many critics of the day contended, *McCabe and Mrs. Miller* was one of the best films of the decade. It still has no equivalent in the cinema. However, even the best films have flaws. If you aren't one of singer-composer's Leonard Cohen's eleven fans, beware of the soundtrack.

▶ BEST ACTOR

Gene Hackman *(The French Connection)*
Other Nominees: Peter Finch *(Sunday Bloody Sunday)*, Walter Matthau *(Kotch)*, George C. Scott *(The Hospital)*, Topol *(Fiddler on the Roof)*

▼

THE BEST CHOICE:
Malcolm McDowell *(A Clockwork Orange)*
Award-Worthy Runners-Up: Gene Hackman *(The French Connection)*, Jack Nicholson *(Carnal Knowledge)*, George C. Scott *(The Hospital)*

Best Picture winner *The French Connection* owed much of its appeal to the filmmakers' striving for authenticity. It was filmed not on a studio backlot but on the streets of New York City and the actors—Gene Hackman and Roy Scheider, who played the real-life narcotics detectives battling international drug smugglers—were not handsome young superstars, but common-looking men unknown to the general public. The forty-year-old Hackman had been an effective supporting player the past seven years, even earning Oscar nominations for *Bonnie and Clyde* and *I Never Sang for My Father*, but it was *The French Connection* that proved he could be a strong, if unlikely, leading man. He was riveting as the brutal, driven Jimmy "Popeye" Doyle, one of the first cops in American films who is anything but wholesome. However, taking nothing away from Hackman's performance—and taking into consideration my intention to give him the Best Actor Oscar in 1974 for *The Conversation*—I think that the most dynamic performance of the year was delivered by unnominated British actor Malcolm McDowell in Stanley Kubrick's much-debated *A Clockwork Orange*. A onetime coffee salesman, McDowell had made a big impression as a rebellious, insolent student in Lindsay Anderson's *if. . . .*; in the climactic surrealistic sequence he shoots some of the teachers of his oppressive school, much to the approval of anarchist viewers all over the world. Kubrick said that he wouldn't have made a film of Anthony Burgess's disturbing futuristic fable if the charismatic McDowell hadn't been available to portray the teenage protagonist.

McDowell is Alex, a young hood in the near future. He routinely plays hooky from school while his parents are at the factory, picks up teenage girls for sex, listens to Beethoven, and spends nights with his three "droog" friends practicing ultraviolence: beating, raping, robbing, terrorizing citizens, and brawling with the other gangs that control the streets. The four droogs beat wealthy writer Mr. Alexander (Patrick Magee) and rape his wife, while Alex warbles "Singin' in the Rain." The droogs also pay a surprise visit to a snobbish lady with cats. Alex kills her. But he can't escape because his droog pals are angry at him and knock him out. Caught at the murder scene, he receives a lengthy prison term. He convinces the Minister of the Interior to let him be the first subject of

the controversial Ludovico technique, which will restrain his criminal impulses. He receives injections and is forced to watch violent films, while Beethoven plays in the background. When released, he becomes nauseated around any violence or when he hears Beethoven. He can't fight back when he is attacked. He takes refuge in Alexander's house. They don't recognize each other until Alex breaks into "Singin' in the Rain." Alexander locks him in a room and starts playing a recording of Beethoven. Alex attempts suicide. He wakes up in a hospital. The government condemns the doctors for the treatment. After a time in the hospital, recuperating, Alex has evil thoughts once again.

Technically brilliant but thematically controversial, *A Clockwork Orange* was the most argued-about picture of

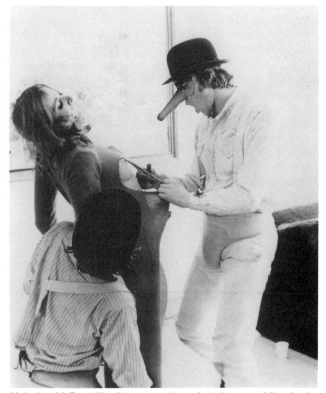

Malcolm McDowell's Alex commits a brutal rape while singing "Singin' in the Rain" in Stanley Kubrick's *A Clockwork Orange*.

the seventies. I agreed with those who thought that it was too cold and fascistic, catering to violence-prone youths and reactionaries. Which isn't to say that I wasn't as enthusiastic about McDowell's performance as Kubrick intended I should be, and I kind of resented it. Kubrick wants to manipulate us viewers into siding with "poor" Alex, vindicating him despite his cruel acts so that we'll agree with the movie's theme: that it's better to allow even a young thug to have free will than to transform him into a gentle "clockwork orange": human on the outside and mechanized on the inside. Kubrick wanted us to identify with Alex, even at his most savage moments. So he stylized all of the violence Alex perpetrates, while rendering realistically all the violence Alex is subjected to; and he altered the victims from their characterization in the book so that we aren't so appalled by what happens to them. And, most significantly, he cast McDowell as Alex. The slim, athletic, light-haired young Brit is instantly likable. As Alex he excites us with his good looks, charm, aggressiveness, and intelligence. He's as fearless and energetic as a young Jimmy Cagney and, like him, seems to be dancing as he moves across the screen. He is the only actor with an infectious smirk and a sexy wicked gleam in his eye. McDowell acknowledged that his character is a "force of evil" but, as Kubrick figured, we'd like even the devil if McDowell played him with the same joy he conveys in his Alex, the happiest of all Kubrick's characters. McDowell delivered the characterization that Kubrick wanted and his Alex became in succeeding years the hero to the punk-thug element of the midnight movie crowd. Only those who could separate McDowell from the less appealing Alex realized that Alex is no rebel. He doesn't exercise free will even before his alteration under the Ludovico treatment. My guess is that he once committed crimes to lash out at the society that would let him act in such an obscene manner, but by the time the film story begins he has become so *conditioned* by past violence that his criminal behavior has become reflexive, instantly accomplished and forgotten. Long before Alex was subjected to the Ludovico treatment, he already was a "clockwork orange."

▶ BEST ACTRESS

WINNER:
Jane Fonda *(Klute)*
Other Nominees: Julie Christie *(McCabe and Mrs. Miller)*, Glenda Jackson *(Sunday, Bloody Sunday)*, Vanessa Redgrave *(Mary, Queen of Scots)*, Janet Suzman *(Nicholas and Alexandra)*

▼

THE BEST CHOICE:
Jane Fonda *(Klute)*
Award-Worthy Runners-Up: Jenny Agutter *(Walkabout)*, Verna Bloom *(The Hired Hand)*, Julie Christie *(McCabe and Mrs. Miller)*, Ruth Gordon *(Harold and Maude)*, Glenda Jackson *(Sunday Bloody Sunday)*, Jessica Walter *(Play Misty for Me)*, Kitty Winn *(Panic in Needle Park)*

It seems implausible today, but Jane Fonda's reputation as a movie star changed almost overnight from near-laughingstock to, as her father Henry attested, "the best actress of her generation," and the change coincided with her becoming a vocal feminist and antiwar activist. Her 1968 appearance in then-husband Roger Vadim's futuristic sex farce, *Barbarella,* almost single-handedly erased the progress she'd made as an actress from her shaky beginnings in the early sixties. But she came back stronger than ever, truly shocking us with her talent and style as a marathon dancer in 1969's depressing Depression drama, *They Shoot Horses, Don't They?* She received an Oscar nomination and was voted Best Actress by the New York Film Critics. Full vindication wouldn't come, however, until two years later when she deservedly won the Best Actress Oscar (and another New York Film Critics award) for her next film: Alan J. Pakula's erotic and tense psychological thriller, *Klute.* Her uninhibited, every-feeling-and-thought-exposed portrayal of New York call girl Bree Daniels—a part other actresses would have been terrified to play—caused all of us to shake our heads in amazement. The seventies were filled with exciting performances by actresses—including others by Fonda—but there was none any better than this.

Bree wants to stop being a call girl and become a model or actress, but to make ends meet she continues to service businessmen passing through town. With these men she seems at ease, in complete control, but when alone she is paranoid. Donald Sutherland's John Klute, a humorless small-town Pennsylvania investigator, comes to New York to search for his missing friend, whose disappearance is connected to the murder of one of Bree's prostitute friends. Bree is now being threatened by the same sadist who killed her friend and is extremely scared. At first she is cold to Klute, but she comes to trust and need him—which, she tells her therapist, frightens her. They become lovers. She tries to push Klute away and at one point returns to her former pimp (Roy Scheider). The killer (Charles Cioffi)—the missing (dead) man's business partner and the man who sent

Jane Fonda and Donald Sutherland in Alan J. Pakula's psychological sex thriller, *Klute.*

Klute to New York—corners Bree when she is alone. He knows Bree can identify him. He tries to strangle her, but Klute arrives. The killer falls to his death. Bree leaves for Pennsylvania with Klute, not knowing if she'll return.

Like most of Fonda's best characters Bree changes (wises up) during the course of the film as she analyzes herself, breaks ties, takes chances. What makes figuring out Bree such an interesting undertaking is that Fonda herself is trying to get deep into the mind of this complex character. As it is with those other Fonda women, Bree is still evolving and still trying to solve her problems when the film ends: "I have no idea what I'm going to do." In midfilm Bree tells her therapist that being a prostitute is liberating because she—meat when auditioning for legitimate acting jobs—feels in *control* of her life only when turning tricks: "When you're a call girl, you control it. I know I'm good. I'm not nervous. For an hour I'm the best actress in the world—you don't have to feel anything, you don't have to care about anything, you don't have to like anybody. . . ." Obviously, she is in control only in her fantasy life. In real life she sits in her apartment behind several locks, terrified of a knock on the door or the ringing phone. Her movement toward real-life liberation comes when she learns to trust Klute and realizes that she enjoys making love to him. She tells her therapist, "He's seen me horrible—he's seen me ugly, he's seen me mean, he's seen me whorey—and it doesn't seem to matter and he seems to accept me." She comes to realize that being in love with a man she has sex with doesn't mean she has to relinquish control. She comes to realize that the gentle, considerate Klute (who seduces her by touching her face) is different from the men she is used to dealing with, particularly the sadistic murderer who seeks to reverse the control that hookers like Bree try to have over clients.

Oddly, we come to share the killer's contempt for hookers from watching Bree in action. She is dishonest and manipulative in her work. She is quite seductive, pretending to be excited by whatever the man suggests they do: "That sounds fantastic. Oh, that's so exciting . . . but it's going to cost you more. That's fantastic. I like your mind." And in bed she pretends to be having an orgasm when she's actually checking her watch (an indelible image). Bree is intelligent (she even mentions Yemen in conversation), educated, clever, and beautiful but still has such lack of self-esteem that she thinks being a desirable hooker is proof of her worth. Unlike the killer, who sees only one side of Bree (and other hookers), we see all the facets of her life—her humiliating audition rejections, her therapy sessions, her fear of the dark—and feel sympathy for her, as does Fonda.

In 1971 Fonda's performance was different from anything else on the screen. It was convincingly real. Fonda held nothing back in her portrait of a hooker, fearlessly using vulgar language and, when being seductive, using her body and voice in a lewd manner. In those scenes that have no dialogue, Fonda keeps us entranced with her face, eyes, and movements. My favorite moment has her lovingly latch on to Klute's jacket as they walk through the crowded streets, a gesture that conveys so much. Another highlight is when the stoned Bree walks across the floor of a club, uninhibited with her mouth and body, kissing and hugging men, sweating, sitting with her pimp as if she were a cat curling up with its owner. But it is in those scenes with dialogue that Fonda really stood apart from other actresses. We weren't used to such a direct style. When she speaks revealingly to her therapist she faces the camera (as her disturbed woman did in *The Chapman Report*) and because she hesitates between words, leaves sentences incomplete in order to begin new thoughts, and allows her voice to waver and tears to fall, we believe that the person we see on screen is improvising and what she's saying is from the gut. In 1971 we believed that through Fonda we were being given the chance to explore a female character's psyche to a much larger degree than we had in a lifetime of moviegoing.

▶ BEST PICTURE

WINNER:
The Godfather (Paramount; Francis Ford Coppola)
Other Nominees: *Cabaret, Deliverance, The Emigrants, Sounder*

▼

THE BEST CHOICE:
The Godfather (Paramount; Francis Ford Coppola)
Award-Worthy Runners-Up: *Cabaret* (Bob Fosse), *Deliverance* (John Boorman), *Play It Again, Sam* (Herbert Ross)

The Godfather, Francis Ford Coppola's thrilling adaptation of Mario Puzo's best-seller, scripted by Coppola and Puzo, more than lived up to its hype. Grand-scale, without the self-importance or artistic pretensions that have characterized Coppola's overblown sequels, this imaginatively conceived and extraordinarily executed piece of filmmaking appealed to just about everyone who liked *movies,* and became the highest-grossing picture of all time. And despite formidable competition from *Cabaret* (which won eight Oscars) and *Deliverance,* it deservedly was voted Best Picture by the Academy.

The Godfather revealed that the public had a previously unsatisfied curiosity about the workings of the Mafia. In taking us behind the closed doors of the powerful Corleone crime family, Puzo and Coppola wanted to impress upon us the idea that organized crime is just another corrupt American corporation, another business that flourishes specifically because of America's free enterprise system. Only, in this business, power plays and takeover attempts result not just in financial ruin for the losers but in violent death.

The film opens in the mid-forties, when Italian godfather Vito Corleone (Marlon Brando, with cotton stuffed in his cheeks) hosts the lavish wedding of his daughter (Talia Shire, Coppola's sister). This united his three sons: hot-tempered Sonny (James Caan), weak Fredo (John Cazale), and smart returning war-hero Michael (Al Pacino). Michael plans to stay out of crime and marry WASP teacher Kay (Diane Keaton). We also meet the many people in Corleone's immediate and extended family, as well as his soldiers. Everyone is Italian except family lawyer Tom (Robert Duvall), who is like Corleone's fourth son. At this wedding we learn that Don Corleone rules his empire as much with intimidation as with violence. His ironic catchphrase is "We'll make him an offer he can't refuse."

The picture takes place over about ten years, has key sequences in New York, Los Angeles, Las Vegas, and Italy. It tells the story of the Corleones' efforts to reestablish themselves as New York's top crime family by going to war with other families and rooting out those within their own circle who have turned traitor. The Corleones succeed because they are as vicious as their opposition, but shrewder, and because the Corleones have an admirable sense of loyalty and familial obligation. For instance, when Vito Corleone is incapacitated after an assassination attempt, Michael, the cleverest and most sensitive of his sons, steps in to prevent the family from going under, committing himself to the ways of his father despite his longtime desire to be respectable. Michael may pretend that he wants only to help his father and brothers, but he is seduced by power and the mechanics of planning and carrying out violent crime.

In addition to the lengthy, opulent wedding, there are numerous classic sequences: Michael rescues his father from a second assassination attempt at a deserted hospi-

The Corleone clan—Marlon Brando and sons Al Pacino, James Caan, and John Cazale—in Francis Ford Coppola's Oscar-winning blockbuster, *The Godfather.*

tal; Michael assassinates a tough crooked cop (Sterling Hayden) and a rival mobster at a restaurant; Sonny brutally beats his sister's abusive husband in the street; Sonny is mowed down at a tollbooth; a surly Hollywood executive (John Marley), who assumes he can stand up to the Corleones, thinks differently when he wakes up with the head of his $500,000 horse in his bed; Corleone's most rugged henchman (ex-wrestler Lenny Montana) is unexpectedly garrotted; Michael, living in exile in Italy and married to a young Italian, watches her die when she turns on the ignition of his car; Don Corleone dies from a heart attack while playing with his grandchild; and, in a brilliantly edited sequence, enemies of the Corleones are massacred in several locations at the same time. In 1972 it was exciting watching several cast members become stars—Pacino, Caan, Keaton, Duvall, and, to a lesser degree, Shire and Cazale—despite Brando's dominating presence. And it was fascinating to get a look at the Mafia's dirty laundry and to witness the film's savage violence.

I wouldn't argue with Bob Fosse's selection as Best Director for *Cabaret*, but Coppola had a much more difficult project. It is impressive that he was able to make every death scene exciting yet not let violence so overwhelm the film's romance that we wouldn't care about the relationship of Michael and Kay. And I find it amazing that he kept his story from becoming muddled and losing momentum during its 175-minute duration—especially since the film takes place over a decade, features action in several different settings, and includes numerous characters. One trick Coppola used to keep our interest was to employ different styles of cinematography and music according to the time and location. When casting, he wisely chose actors with distinctive looks and voices so that we can recognize them in later scenes although their initial appearances were brief. Also to limit the confusion, Coppola decided not to squeeze in everything from Puzo's book but to have fewer scenes and give each added substance and impact. In those scenes he makes it clear who his characters are, how they relate to each other, and what their allegiances are, providing even his less important characters enough time to make strong audience impressions. So when someone later threatens the Corleones, or someone turns traitor, or someone is killed, we know who he is and can take a rooting interest. Of course, we always end up rooting for the Corleones, who are among the most peculiar of movie "heroes." In their sinister section of the world—while they determine much in our lives, we don't see them—these monsters are the nicest guys around.

▶ BEST ACTOR

WINNER:
Marlon Brando *(The Godfather)*
Other Nominees: Michael Caine *(Sleuth)*, Laurence Olivier *(Sleuth)*, Peter O'Toole *(The Ruling Class)*, Paul Winfield *(Sounder)*

▼

THE BEST CHOICE:
Woody Allen *(Play It Again, Sam)*
Award-Worthy Runners-Up: Robert Duvall *(Tomorrow)*, Stacy Keach *(Fat City)*, Peter O'Toole *(The Ruling Class)*, Al Pacino *(The Godfather)*, Jon Voight *(Deliverance)*

Marlon Brando had been working steadily on the fringes, but *The Godfather* was heralded as his comeback film, and his subsequent Best Actor Oscar was indication that Hollywood was welcoming his return. Brando had presence, of course, and it's hard today to picture anyone else as Vito Corleone, but his characterizations had been far more interesting in such recent sleepers as Hubert Cornfield's *Night of the Following Day*, Gillo Pontecorvo's *Burn!*, and Michael Winner's *The Nightcomers*. Although he played the title character, his screen time was limited (he should have switched categories with Supporting Actor nominee Al Pacino) and he was quite hammy. Had his jowls not already been puffed out with cotton, it would have been more obvious that he was playing the part with tongue firmly in cheek. Those who recognized this and still voted for him might have done better by selecting Woody Allen, whose humor wasn't disguised in *Play It Again, Sam.*

Although Allen wrote the script, which he adapted from his play, the director of *Play It Again, Sam* was Herbert Ross. At this point in Allen's career another director was probably a good idea, because Allen gave his most controlled performance to date and the film was much more cohesive and real than his own efforts would have been. Woody plays Allan, a San Francisco film critic who is neurotic and helpless in romance. His idol is Humphrey Bogart, who had it all together and knew how to treat women. Allan's wife (Susan Anspach) has just dumped him, so his married friends Dick (Tony Roberts) and Linda (Diane Keaton) set him up on several blind dates. Beyond nervous, Allan blows it every time, repeatedly making a fool of himself. The only woman he can be natural around is Linda. Because Dick is obsessed with his work, Linda spends more and more time with Allan and finds herself attracted to him and jealous of his dates. When Dick goes to Cleveland, Linda comes to

In *Play It Again, Sam* Woody Allen coolly demonstrates for an unimpressed Diane Keaton (back turned), Tony Roberts, and blind date Jennifer Salt how to shovel rice into his mouth efficiently.

Allan's for dinner. With Bogart (Jerry Lacy) urging him on, Allan makes a play for Linda. She rushes out, but returns. They sleep together and it is wonderful. They debate how to break the news to Dick. Dick confides to Allan that he thinks Linda is having an affair. He says he'll kill himself it it's true. Dick confronts Linda at home, but she says nothing. Dick leaves for the airport. Linda follows. Allan brings up the rear. Allan and Linda maturely agree that they must break off and that Linda should stay with the husband she loves. Like Bogart in *Casablanca* Allan gallantly lies to the husband that he tried to seduce his wife, but she was loyal. Dick and Linda fly to Cleveland together. Allan walks off alone, realizing that he doesn't need Bogart anymore because he has his own style.

It's hard to adjust to a Woody Allen character living not in New York City but in San Francisco, but Allan Felix certainly fits the Allen image. In fact, being *real*, he was Allen's first movie character who gave us insight into the actor-comic-writer-filmmaker. Allan was neurotic, depressed ("I chuckle, I giggle," he protests, "I guffaw occasionally"), insecure, sex crazed, movie crazed. We wondered if the real Allen really wore a shower cap. And if, after tasting a bourbon, he spit it all over the bar, jerked his head in all directions, and passed out with a thud. Allan has some funny Allen-like one-liners: explaining why Bogart is his hero, he says, "Look, if [I'm] going to identify, who am I going to pick, my rabbi?"; when Bogart assures Allan that he's also been slapped by women, Allan counters with "Your glasses never fly across the room." And when he tries to get a date with a depressed woman at the art museum: finding out she plans suicide on Saturday, he asks if she's available Friday. I also like his witty and warm romantic interludes with Keaton's Linda.

But the comic highlights are his disastrous blind dates. A nymphomaniac (Viva), who admits she has slept with *everybody*, is insulted when Allan takes her in his arms; a sluttish date (Joy Bang) is whisked away by Hell's Angels types. The film's funniest sequence is Allan's first date, which is filled with nonstop gags. Nervously putting aftershave all over his body in preparation for her arrival, he unthinkingly takes a sip from the bottle and gags; he loses control of his electric hair dryer, knocking almost everything out of his medicine cabinet; he can do no more than grunt when he is introduced to Sharon (Jennifer Salt); he knocks over and breaks almost everything in his apartment; he screechingly slides the phonograph needle across his record and, swinging his hand, watches the disc fly out of the album cover he's holding and crash into the wall; with much pride he makes a self-consciously intellectual statement about rain; at a Chinese restaurant he demonstrates the fine art of shoveling rice into his mouth; and when Sharon excuses herself in disgust, he confidently announces, "She likes me."

In later films Allen would tone down his on-screen personality and do more character comedy. And he would improve as an actor (justifiably being nominated for Best Actor for *Annie Hall*). But it's a treat looking back at this film to see Allen play a nutty neurotic and do a lot of slapstick—because one forgets how adept he was. And how can we not smile when Allan walks off at film's end, giving up his tough guy idol and saying, "I'm short and ugly enough to succeed on my own"? Allen, who would soon be back in the director's chair, certainly got that right.

▶ BEST ACTRESS

WINNER:
Liza Minnelli *(Cabaret)*
Other Nominees: Diana Ross *(Lady Sings the Blues)*, Maggie Smith *(Travels with My Aunt)*, Cicely Tyson *(Sounder)*, Liv Ullmann *(The Emigrants)*

▼

THE BEST CHOICE:
Liza Minnelli *(Cabaret)*
Award-Worthy Runners-Up: Shirley MacLaine *(The Possession of Joel Delaney)*, Barbra Streisand *(What's Up, Doc?)*

In a movie career that stretched over twenty-five years, the only Oscar Judy Garland received was a "special" one for "best juvenile performance of the year" for her Dorothy in 1939's *The Wizard of Oz*. She shone in many later musicals but the Academy, which in Hollywood's Golden Age bypassed performances in musicals, nominated her for Best Actress only for her last Hollywood musical, 1954's *A Star Is Born*. She deserved the Academy Award for that role, but lost to twenty-six-year-old Grace Kelly for *The Country Girl*. Liza Minnelli was nominated for a Best Actress Oscar for what was only her second film, *The Sterile Cuckoo*, which she made at the age of twenty-three in 1969, the year her mother died. She was twenty-six when she starred in her first movie musical,

Liza Minnelli had her one great screen role in Bob Fosse's *Cabaret,* winning the Best Actress Oscar that had been denied her mother, Judy Garland.

Bob Fosse's *Cabaret,* for which she was selected Best Actress. It's possible that she would have won with just a mediocre performance because the Academy wanted to make up for its slight of her mother. But Minnelli gave such a dynamic performance that no one questioned her victory over a weak field of nominees. On the podium she thanked the Academy voters for giving the statue to *"me."*

Fosse's stylish political musical was adapted by Jay Presson Allen (and Hugh Wheeler) from John van Druten's play *I Am a Camera*—filmed in 1955 with Julie Harris!—which was based on Christopher Isherwood's autobiographical *Goodbye to Berlin* stories. It is set in Berlin in 1931, when the once-mocked Nazis are an emerging and frightening political force. Minnelli is American Sally Bowles, who dreams about being a great actress but for now sings and dances in a cabaret. She will sleep with anyone whom she thinks can further her career. She becomes best friends with Michael York's Brian Roberts, a young British scholar who moves into her boardinghouse and works as an English tutor. They become lovers—she is the first woman he's ever had success with in bed. Friction develops between them when the corruptible Sally begins flirting with the aristocratic Maximilian (Helmut Griem) and the three of them spend decadent time together. They both sleep with him. Sally becomes pregnant. Brian promises to marry her and raise the child, even though they aren't sure it's his. But Sally has an abortion. She doesn't want to move to Cambridge and be a housewife, because she still dreams of being a star. As the Nazis take control in Berlin, Brian goes back to England. Sally stays on at the cabaret.

With those big, soulful eyes that flood her face with tears without need of a cue, a stunned, open-mouthed, little-girl pout, and a tries-too-hard-and-makes-a-fool-of-herself manner, Liza Minnelli was peerless at seducing audience pity for her characters. She had done that to best effect in *The Sterile Cuckoo* and would do it again in 1977's *New York, New York,* making misty-eyed viewers lose sight of the fact that she was the insensitive villain in her marriage to Robert De Niro, and not he. In *Cabaret* we realize that her Sally Bowles is troubled, could use someone to take care of her, needs love more than the fame she covets, and will be hurt repeatedly as she stumbles through life. And we are moved as, in the tradition of her mother's characters, she smiles and laughs in the midst of humiliation and when her heart is breaking in two. However, Minnelli won't let us pity Sally—or not too much anyway. Sally determines her own fate, yielding to her delusions about rich lovers and a future of stardom. Not that she should, but she makes no effort to reform, although she herself is sometimes annoyed by her flawed, somewhat disgraceful personality. We admire her for being able to withstand constant pain and disappointment to go after her infantile dreams.

Extravagant herself, Minnelli found her ideal role in the outrageous, affected, show-bizy Sally, who has a Louise Brooks hairdo, wears bright lipstick and shocking nail polish, and, strictly for effect, drinks, smokes, flirts ("Have you a cigarette, I'm desperate" is her come-on), talks incessantly, curses openly, puts on airs ("I find it *très amusant*"), and professes confidence ("I'm going to be a great film star; that is if booze and sex don't get me first. Do I shock you, darling?"). Brian is the only one to see the real, vulnerable Sally—and he likes what he

discovers. He's also the only one who tells her that she needn't give way to pretense to compensate for what she fears is lack of talent (she thinks she's just biding time as a performer while waiting to become an actress). He has seen Sally at the cabaret and, like us, realizes that she has remarkable talent, more than enough to lead her to stardom as a performer if she would be satisfied with that.

It is during Fosse's stylized musical numbers that Minnelli completely amazes us, whether singing marvelous solos, or duets with Joel Grey (the deserved Best Supporting Actor for his perverse cabaret emcee). We are jolted by these performances, suddenly remembering that her acting, as fine as it is, is only her second-best talent. As we watch her sing the climactic part of the finale—the great title song—marching directly away from the camera and then, in an exciting moment, turning around into an exhilarating close-up, we recognize that we are seeing a rare, bona fide STAR.

1973

▶ BEST PICTURE

WINNER:
The Sting (Universal; George Roy Hill)
Other Nominees: *American Graffiti, Cries and Whispers, The Exorcist, A Touch of Class*

▼

THE BEST CHOICE:
American Graffiti (Universal; George Lucas)
Award-Worthy Runners-Up: *Bang the Drum Slowly* (John Hancock), *The Long Goodbye* (Robert Altman), *Mean Streets* (Martin Scorsese), *The Way We Were* (Sydney Pollack)

In the year between the two *Godfather* victories, the Academy's Best Picture selection, George Roy Hill's *The Sting,* portrayed crime of a much more benevolent sort: two likable scam-artists (Robert Redford and Paul Newman) pull a fast one on a cruel con-man (Robert Shaw). In a year in which controversy centered around William Friedkin's graphic rendering of William Peter Blatty's *The Exorcist* and Bernardo Bertolucci's sexually graphic *The Last Tango in Paris,* featuring middle-aged Marlon Brando being kinky with Maria Schneider, the Academy opted for the year's least controversial film. A great date movie and cheery commercial film, *The Sting* appealed to most everyone. It had a slick and tricky script by David Ward, catchy Scott Joplin ragtime music, and best of all the engaging camaraderie between the current cinema's

top male hearthrob and his immediate predecessor. It fit into the "buddy" or "male-bonding" category that had been initiated by Redford and Newman in *Butch Cassidy and the Sundance Kid* in 1971; but that category in 1973 included three pictures more exciting and rewarding than the Oscar winner: Hal Ashby's *The Last Detail* (with Jack Nicholson, Otis Young, Randy Quaid), Martin Scorsese's breakthrough film, *Mean Streets* (Harvey Keitel, Robert De Niro), and my favorite baseball film, John Hancock's *Bang the Drum Slowly* (Michael Moriarty, De Niro).

These male-friendship films were some of the many pictures released in 1973 that were about relationships. There were many films about men and women *(Last Tango in Paris, The Way We Were*—also with Redford—

At the conclusion of George Lucas's *American Graffiti,* Richard Dreyfuss (with back turned) bids farewell to (L–R) Cindy Williams, Ron Howard, Charles Martin Smith, and Paul LeMat.

Cinderella Liberty, Blume in Love, A Touch of Class, et cetera)—and even a film or two about the relationship between a father and young daughter *(Paper Moon),* between a mother and young daughter *(The Exorcist),* and between women (Ingmar Bergman's *Cries and Whispers*). But only one picture dealt with the relationships between teenage boys and girls: George Lucas's *American Graffiti.* Because of this seminal youth film the next two decades would be overrun with pictures about overly worried or overly excited teenagers (who are usually having sex and/or getting their heads chopped off), but none would be such labors of love. None would have the sense of fun, humor, warmth toward characters, or genuine nostalgia that is evident in Lucas's every shot and line of dialogue. *American Graffiti* was an instant classic, a smash hit, a vehicle that helped launch numerous careers (even Harrison Ford has a small part), and my choice for 1973's Best Picture.

Produced by Francis Ford Coppola's American Zoetrope (Coppola and Gary Kurtz were credited as producers), this was a film made by a director who had freedom to get across his vision (not to mention the go-ahead to pay $80,000 for song rights for the first golden-oldies soundtrack). And what a sweet vision it was. Made in a cynical era, it is Lucas's idealized remembrance of an innocent time, before Kennedy's assassination, Vietnam, the Beatles, social unrest and politicization of white middle-class kids, and the sexual revolution. It is set in Modesto, California, on prom night 1962. Our heroes are three graduating high school students, Ron Howard, Richard Dreyfuss, and Charles Martin Smith, and the slightly older Paul Le Mat. Lucas moves smoothly back and forth between their story lines—as he would with his characters in *Star Wars*—which at times overlap.

Wolfman Jack plays rock classics on the radio. Meanwhile, Howard thinks about going away to college, but longtime girlfriend Cindy Williams, only a junior, is upset when he suggests they date others during the year. They spend the night arguing, realizing how much they need each other, and reevaluating their futures—Howard decides not to go away. Dreyfuss spends his last night with three much tougher guys (becoming one of the gang) and trying to find a sexy blonde (Suzanne Somers) who flirted with him from a passing car. Reluctant to go away, he changes his mind during the night. Nerdy Smith (a terrific actor) hits the jackpot when he picks up "fast" blonde Candy Clark, sparking her interest by suggesting she resembles Connie Stevens. She's been around but he impresses her with a wild night on the town. Le Mat, "cool" twenty-two-year-old local dragster champ, also picks up a girl (Mackenzie Phillips), but he discovers when she climbs into his car that she's only twelve. At first he's embarrassed to be seen with her, but later discovers that she's a terrific companion—even if she does like the Beach Boys.

Lucas didn't want to make a teen-sex movie. Instead, he made the most romantic of teen movies, culminating with Ronny Howard and Cindy Williams's slow-dancing to the Platters' "Smoke Gets in Your Eyes," which should remind viewers of the most emotional single dance they had in their youth. In the absence of sex we are excited by memory-jarring images of teens hanging out at the drive-in, checking out the opposite sex, and downing malts and greasy food; cruising; drag-racing; making out; dancing; playing pranks on cops; and listening to rock music on the radio—everyone was bonded because they all listened to the same station. And on prom night they are worrying about their futures. If only they knew what we do about the upcoming years.

The characters in *American Graffiti* are well drawn, well played, and familiar; the dialogue by Lucas and Gloria Katz and Willard Huyck is witty, clever, and accurate; and the movie moves as quickly as the cars that zip up and down the main strip. The exuberance of those in back and in front of the cameras is truly infectious, even today. When this film was released it made us feel nostalgia for a bygone era, but today it makes us nostalgic for 1973, when all these unknown future stars could still play teenagers. As their careers progress, they have aged before our eyes and made us feel old in the process. At least the oldies on the soundtrack never age.

▶ BEST ACTOR

WINNER:
Jack Lemmon *(Save the Tiger)*
Other Nominees: Marlon Brando *(Last Tango in Paris)*, Jack Nicholson *(The Last Detail)*, Al Pacino *(Serpico)*, Robert Redford *(The Sting)*

▼
___

THE BEST CHOICE:
Marlon Brando *(Last Tango in Paris)*
Award-Worthy Runners-Up: Divine *(Pink Flamingos)*, Malcolm McDowell *(O Lucky Man!)*, Robert Mitchum *(The Friends of Eddie Coyle)*, Michael Moriarty *(Bang the Drum Slowly)*, Jack Nicholson *(The Last Detail)*, Robert Redford *(The Way We Were)*

Jack Lemmon was responsible for getting financial backing for the Steve Shagan–scripted *Save the Tiger,* which allowed him to play his first serious role since 1962's *Days of Wine and Roses.* In the earlier film he was an alcoholic and got an Oscar nomination; this time he won an Oscar for playing a middle-aged dress manufacturer who is on the verge of a breakdown. It was an award he was denied for his more deserving comedy roles. I think Lemmon's performance in this pretentious drama is too mannered and self-conscious, as he tends to be in other dramatic films in which his characters have anxiety attacks and emotional outbursts while losing their grip on their lives. Besides, also playing a man in midlife turmoil, forty-nine-year-old Marlon Brando gave a much better performance in Bernardo Bertolucci's then-scandalous *Last Tango in Paris.*

Brando had returned to the movie spotlight in *The Godfather,* winning 1972's Best Actor Oscar. As the aged but still imposing Don Corleone he proved that he still had the incredible magnetism he once displayed in the 1950s. Still no one was prepared for him in the X-rated *Last Tango,* when, despite graying hair and a pot belly, he proved he was still capable of being a virile, romantic—or, better, *sexual*—lead, opposite twenty-one-year-old Maria Schneider.

The setting is Paris. Brando is an American, Paul, a flophouse owner who is devastated by his unfaithful wife's unexpected suicide. Twenty-year-old Jeanne (Schneider), who is engaged to a young documentary filmmaker, Tom (Jean-Pierre Léaud), arrives to look at a vacant apartment at the same time Paul comes there. The strangers immediately make mad, passionate love. They agree not to reveal their names or discuss their lives outside the apartment. They return repeatedly for increasingly perverse sexual encounters. He dominates her, making her do his bidding, breaking down her sexual barriers. She tries to get him to talk about himself. He talks of his childhood, but then won't admit what he's said is true. She becomes dependent on him, even coming to him in her wedding gown although she insists she loves Tom. After his wife's funeral Paul doesn't return to the apartment. He comes up to Jeanne on the boulevard. She now insists that the relationship is over. He won't accept her decision and now tells her about himself.

They spend the day together, getting drunk in a café where a tango contest is being held. She says she loves him but then runs off, saying she is through with him. He chases her into her apartment. She tells him her name and kills him with her father's gun.

Its controversial aspects aside, *Last Tango in Paris* broke ground by having characters communicate through sex. Yet it is not about sex per se, but about a man who uses sex as an escape from his despair. He

The despairing Marlon Brando is about to begin an intense sexual relationship with young stranger Maria Schneider in Bernardo Bertolucci's barrier-breaking *Last Tango in Paris.*

attempts a relationship with a stranger because he doesn't think he'll have to deal with it on an emotional level. His wife's unexpected suicide makes this angry, guilty, rejected man want to escape the real world and rest his emotions for a time. He tries to slip into a "sexistential" world where his recent past, present, and future no longer exist because he has no identity. He discovers that he wants to block out only his adulthood, not his youth. Outside the apartment Paul also goes through a childish period: he has temper tantrums and crying fits, throws and breaks things, slams doors, turns out lights, even bites his mother-in-law's hand. His relationship with Jeanne becomes like a young boy's with a naughty neighbor girl. They play childish adult games, a sophisticated, perverse version of little kids playing house. There is pretense in everything they do. Because she fears aging herself, Jeanne is the perfect companion for his kid's world—he allows her to be *a child without sexual inhibitions,* getting her to reject her bourgeois shackles. He keeps digressing, pulling down his pants at the tango contest, sticking his chewing gum on Jeanne's balcony railing before he dies, dying in the fetal position.

Bertolucci decided he wanted Brando as his lead when he saw a painting by English artist Francis Bacon of "a man in great despair, who had an air of total disillusion-

ment." (The painting is seen in the film's credit sequence.) Brando accepted the part after seeing the painting, not even reading the script. He knew he'd rewrite much of it himself, and improvise when necessary. It's fascinating watching Brando's performance because there are long stretches where it seems like he's improvising, or searching the ceilings, floors, walls, and even Schneider's body for his lines. He has many memorable—erotic or raunchy—moments with Schneider, but my favorite scene has him sitting alone with his wife's body. He cruelly curses her, cries himself into a daze, and unthinkingly calls her "sweetheart" (the way he really feels for her). We feel his anguish. Throughout the film he dazzles us, never boring us: Paul is alternately savage and tender, confident and perplexed, touching and pathetic, tense and wickedly funny. At his best Brando plays this broken, confused man with feelings that come from deep inside. Feminist critics correctly berated Bertolucci for not using scenes he filmed of Brando naked while keeping many nude scenes of Schneider, but no one disputed that this is the film in which Brando most *reveals* himself, dark side and all. The film may deal with Jeanne breaking through sexual barriers, but viewers thrill more to watching Brando strip away all that protects both his character and himself.

▶ BEST ACTRESS

WINNER:
Glenda Jackson *(A Touch of Class)*
Other Nominees: Ellen Burstyn *(The Exorcist)*, Marcia Mason *(Cinderella Liberty)*, Barbra Streisand *(The Way We Were)*, Joanne Woodward *(Summer Wishes, Winter Dreams)*

▼

THE BEST CHOICE:
Barbra Streisand *(The Way We Were)*
Award-Worthy Runners-Up: None

In 1973 Glenda Jackson starred in her first comedy, Melvin Frank's *A Touch of Class,* opposite George Segal. The between-the-sheets, battle-of-the-sexes comedy was praised as a sophisticated screwball laugh riot that harked back to the comedies of Hollywood's Golden Age. It received an Academy Award nomination for Best Picture and Glenda Jackson won her second Best Actress Oscar in four years. I think the mean-spirited comedy was as funny as a crutch and the constantly sniping Jackson—who could do no wrong according to her theater-matinee-type fans—gave a performance that really tested one's nerves. That said, I admit that my choice for Best Actress of 1973, Barbra Streisand, gave a performance in *The Way We Were* that many viewers of the day disliked as much as I did Jackson's. At the time it was a chancy proposition to admit you were fond of the sentimental Streisand–Robert Redford movie, which got much worse reviews than *A Touch of Class.* But a cult developed

around the film among romantics, and in time many of its initial detractors were struck by its spell. And now not only Streisand's diehard fans have warmed to her performance, which I think is the best of her career, but many others appreciate it as well.

Sydney Pollack directed Arthur Laurents's adaptation of his deeply affecting novel. Streisand is Katie Morosky. The Jewish Katie was the campus radical in the thirties when she got a crush on apolitical, gentile All-American boy Hubbell Gardner (Redford). She thought him too frivolous, and he thought her too serious. She encouraged him to become a writer. During World War II Katie works in a radio station in New York, doing political activity on the side. She runs into Hubbell, who is now in the navy. She has read his first novel and encourages him to write a second one. They become lovers. She loves him deeply but detests his carefree friends. He loves her deeply but can't put up with her being so serious about

At the big college dance Barbra Streisand thrills to a dance with handsome Robert Redford, while jealous James Woods (the blurry figure in the background) looks on, in the most romantic film of the seventies, *The Way We Were.*

political issues. They break up. She convinces him she will stay out of politics. They marry and go to Hollywood, where Hubbell adapts a screenplay based on his first novel and works on his second novel. Katie works as a reader. She becomes pregnant. The marriage is strained when Katie goes to Washington on behalf of the blacklisted Hollywood Ten. Meanwhile Hubbell agrees to commercialize his script so that a philistine director will accept it. He also gives up the idea of being a novelist. He sleeps with his college girlfriend (Lois Chiles), who is breaking up with his friend (Bradford Dillman). Katie criticizes the movie of his script. She also says she knows about his infidelity. He says that their problems have nothing to do with his one-day affair, but her return to politics and her insistence on pushing him to be a serious writer. Katie asks him to stay with her until their daughter is born. She returns to New York and eventually marries another man. In the fifties they run into each other when Hubbell comes there to write for television and she's on the street getting signatures to ban the bomb. They embrace one last time, still feeling tremendous love for one another.

Few screen couples have achieved the amazing chemistry Streisand and Redford have in *The Way We Were.* So much of the picture is shot in close-up with the two of them looking into each other's eyes and reacting to each other's gaze and words with love and appreciation (he sees her beauty, where others have missed it). In close-up Streisand, whether crying or smiling or joking or lecturing or gabbing or just yearning, reveals so much, not just of Katie but of herself (ex-husband Elliott Gould told me that when he saw Katie he said, "That's Barbra"). Streisand is at her most lovable and vulnerable, playing this woman who has such heart, such sensitivity, such dedication to unpopular causes. As Hubbell complains, Katie never lets up for a minute, never relaxes just to

enjoy life, never stops trying to better the world and their relationship, and never stops prodding him to fulfill his early ambitions to be a novelist. Our reaction is to feel emotionally drawn to her *every* moment she is on the screen—after all, she's always walking a high wire and Hubbell has taken away the net. One night at college the nervous Katie twice told Hubbell about how the Duke of Windsor had just married Mrs. Simpson—the implication being that Katie sees herself as a commoner in relation to Hubbell, campus royalty. To her the "gorgeous" Hubbell (he looks like Robert Redford!) is a dream. Yet years later this gawky, funny-looking Jewish girl will sacrifice everything, including dream-lover Hubbell, to follow her convictions; while Hubbell, the attractive, All-American WASP, will, like many of Redford's characters, sell out his good values and talent to make it as a hack Hollywood writer. He always worried that he was a fraud—she thought differently, but lost her gamble.

When they split up, we feel as bad as they do themselves because we understand their need for each other—he knows he'll never find anyone who, as she says, "[is] as good for you as I am, to believe in you as much as I do, or love you as much." Yet we agree that the reasons they quarrel—for once a couple's problems have a political basis—will never go away. He can never meet her high standards for him, she'll never lower her standards to suit him. "You really think you're easy?" he asks her. "Compared to what? The Hundred Years War? You're so ready to fight, you don't have time to understand anything. Counterattack, politics, revolution, cause. That's fine. It's all fine—for you. So do it, stay with it. I admire it. . . ." "Up to a point!" she says, explaining their vast differences with those few words.

Streisand has an extraordinary number of wonderful, truly memorable moments in just one film. For instance, there's a scene in college writing class: Katie is ripped apart when the professor doesn't choose to praise or read aloud her much-suffered-over essay, yet despite her own disappointment she still listens to the professor praise and read Hubbell's introspective story and looks at Hubbell with new appreciation and understanding. Later on, I love Streisand's expressions when she realizes that the drunken Hubbell, whom she has not seen in seven years, has crashed in her bed. She daringly strips and climbs in next to him, thrilling to the ultimate guilty pleasure. Following a great scene in which she—babbling nonstop—insists he stay for dinner although she's not making her specialty, pot roast, there's another, a very romantic and erotic scene in which for the first time she makes love to the *sober* Hubbell. She closes her eyes, they tell each other they're beautiful, she touches his face, they kiss softly, they look into each other's eyes. Streisand's most emotional scene—and my favorite—has Katie calling Hubbell after their first breakup and tearfully explaining she has to talk to her best friend and that's him. Forget Luise Rainer's classic tearjerking phone conversation in *The Great Ziegfeld,* because this one has that beat. Also emotional is the screening-room scene, when Katie confronts Hubbell about his affair and his trashy movie: "Why did you have to go with her? Tell me I'm not good enough. Tell me you don't like my politics. Tell me I talk too much. You don't like my perfume, my family, my pot roast. . . . I hate what you did to your book. I hate the picture. I hate those people. I hate the palm trees. I wish it would rain. Oh, I want . . . I want . . . I want us to love each other."

Also bound to cause tears is their brief reunion that ends the picture. They look at each other with undiminished love and admiration and just as it was when they held each other years before, Katie closes her eyes when they embrace. From Streisand's expression we feel all Katie's sensations. As the end titles roll, and we hear Streisand's emotionally charged vocal of Marvin Hamlisch's sentimental title song, all those memories of the way they were race through our minds. We remember their words when they broke up in California: "But it was lovely, wasn't it?" Katie asks. "Yes, it was lovely," he says. We're comforted that Streisand's Katie, who deserved so much more, at least had that.

1974

▶ BEST PICTURE

WINNER:
The Godfather, Part II (Coppola Company/Paramount; Francis Ford Coppola)
Other Nominees: *Chinatown, The Conversation, Lenny, The Towering Inferno*

▼

THE BEST CHOICE:
Chinatown (Paramount; Roman Polanski)
Award-Worthy Runners-Up: *Alice Doesn't Live Here Anymore* (Martin Scorsese), *Monty Python and the Holy Grail* (Terry Gilliam and Terry Jones), *The Parallax View* (Alan J. Pakula), *Thieves Like Us* (Robert Altman)

When production of *The Godfather, Part II* was announced, most everyone was skeptical that director Francis Ford Coppola and his coscreenwriter, Mario Puzo, could duplicate the success of their 1972 Best Picture winner, especially since this time they wouldn't have a Puzo best-seller from which to take their story. But it turned out to be even more highly regarded than *The Godfather*. That's because it was the rare sequel that was more ambitious than the original. It didn't simply use crowd-pleasing violence to fill the void left by the deaths of Marlon Brando's Vito Corleone and James Caan's Sonny Corleone in the first film. Instead it continued to deal with the personalities in the Corleone family— giving us parallel stories of the young, immigrant Vito (Robert De Niro), as he builds his empire in the early twentieth century, and of Michael Corleone (Al Pacino), as he consolidates, in the 1950s, the crime empire he inherited from his late father. And it went a step farther by exploring the link between organized crime and politicians—which was certainly a topical theme in light of the Watergate scandal. It, too, had tremendous financial success and won a Best Picture Oscar.

I liked that *The Godfather, Part II* was political and high minded. I also admired Robert De Niro in the flashback sequence. But I thought that Pacino's Michael was a brooding bore this go-around, that the direction was self-consciously arty and self-important, and that the major scenes were calculated for audience response—in fact, several scenes in the 1950s section come across as phony imitations (using the film's characters) of familiar real-life scenes that we'd seen on television (the Senate crime hearings, Jack Ruby's public assassination of Lee Oswald). Many viewers preferred Coppola's other 1974 nominated picture, *The Conversation,* another film that reflected the nation's Watergate sensibility, but I also find that critically acclaimed picture too pretentious to be regarded as Best Picture. My choice is another nominee and still another film that deals with political corruption. The fascinating Jack Nicholson detective classic *Chinatown* is the third Roman Polanski film in a decade to win my Alternate Oscar, following 1965's *Repulsion* and 1966's *Cul-de-Sac.* I think it is Polanski's masterpiece.

Robert Towne wrote the dazzling Oscar-winning script that has a terrific hero (brilliantly played by Nicholson, who emphasizes shrewdness rather than explosiveness), other fascinating characters with fascinating problems, menacing villains, sensational dialogue ("You can't eat the venetian blinds, I just had them installed on Wednes-

Private eye Jack Nicholson and rich
and troubled widow Faye Dunaway are
untrusting lovers in Roman Polanski's
Chinatown.

day"), and *two* intriguing mysteries, one involving a water-land swindle, the other incest. It is set in late-thirties L.A., which Polanski re-creates through props, costumes, buildings, automobiles, and music (by Jerry Goldsmith). This is the surreal night world and equally sinister, sun-drenched day world that Philip Marlowe and Mike Hammer once staked out. It is a world where everyone has secrets, no one is trustworthy, and people are vicious; where corruption flourishes and no one seems to care . . . except for our hero. Nicholson's J. J. Gittes is this noir throwback's "lone moral force in the universe," despite the fact that he makes his living as a lowly "bedroom dick," taking photos of unfaithful husbands and wives. "I make an honest living," he argues. He quit being a cop in Chinatown because cops were expected to do "as little as possible" in fighting crime and corruption. As a private eye a few years later, he sees that L.A. proper has become just as contaminated and that the "pure" desert land outside the city is endangered. He hopes to stop this corruption by finding out who drowned the honest water commissioner, Hollis Mulwray (Darrell Zwerling). Mulwray discovered a scheme to induce officials to support a measure to incorporate the San Fernando Valley into the city; someone was creating a fake drought in L.A. by secretly diverting water onto Valley land he had purchased. (This premise has a basis in fact.) While Gittes has an affair with his client, the dead commissioner's icy, neurotic widow, Evelyn (Faye Dunaway), he begins to suspect that her rich, ruthless father, Noah Cross (John Huston), Mulwray's ex-partner, is behind the land swindle, and possibly the murder. Gittes should get off the case but he wants to clear his name, having been made a fool of when originally hired to dig up dirt on Mulwray. He had photographed Mulwray with a young mystery woman (Belinda Palmer as Katherine) after having been hired by someone (Diane Ladd as Ida Sessions) only pretending to be Evelyn Mulwray.

In the film noir tradition the entire movie is shot from Gittes's perspective. We follow him around as he does his snooping and interrogating, and we realize that most of those classic detective movies didn't bother to show us the hero doing his job. It's truly engrossing watching Gittes unravel the fascinating mystery that Towne has created, step by step and clue by clue. He makes mistakes and misjudgments, but he is an extremely skilled sleuth. Unlike Bogart's Sam Spade in the Huston-directed *The Maltese Falcon,* Gittes doesn't enjoy dealing with the weird and dangerous characters who inhabit his menacing world—including Huston's Noah Cross and the sadistic little weasel (played by Polanski) who slices Gittes's nose—but he has Spade's bravado and like Spade knows that in order to survive he must talk tough and be sarcastic even when in danger. He knows when to be polite, solicitous, tough, and even annoying.

If he weren't moral, Gittes would be linked less to Philip Marlowe than to Ralph Meeker's Mike Hammer in 1956's bizarre *Kiss Me Deadly.* Meeker's equally cocky (but nonmoral and fascistic) bedroom dick also gets in way over his head by sticking it where it shouldn't be, into a case involving the FBI and a stolen nuclear bomb. The reckless Gittes always dives in headfirst when conducting his investigation of the water swindle, and he figuratively drowns in a case involving government officials and the powerful Cross. Hammer's interference in the FBI investigation and refusal to cooperate don't benefit anyone: the film ends with a nuclear explosion that probably destroys the world. For all his efforts to do good, Gittes still gets Evelyn killed (in the only scene set in Chinatown), doesn't prevent the land fraud, and watches helplessly as his lover's corrupt, murderous father slips away with the weeping, screaming Katherine, whom he fathered incestuously. It's a shattering ending.

More than fifteen years later Nicholson would reprise Gittes in *The Two Jakes,* which he directed. However, the character works much better as a relatively young man, who is cynical but not wise enough to be defeatist. Only at the end of *Chinatown* does he have his worst fears confirmed: no one is more impotent than one moral man without power.

▶ BEST ACTOR

WINNER:
Art Carney *(Harry and Tonto)*
Other Nominees: Albert Finney *(Murder on the Orient Express)*, Dustin Hoffman *(Lenny)*, Jack Nicholson *(Chinatown)*, Al Pacino *(The Godfather, Part II)*

▼

THE BEST CHOICE:
Gene Hackman *(The Conversation)*
Award-Worthy Runners-Up: Warren Beatty *(The Parallax View)*, Art Carney *(Harry and Tonto)*, Keith Carradine *(Thieves Like Us)*, Divine *(Female Trouble)*, Richard Dreyfuss *(The Apprenticeship of Duddy Kravitz)*, Jack Nicholson *(Chinatown)*, Gene Wilder *(Young Frankenstein)*

The sweetest road movie to come down the pike, Paul Mazursky's *Harry and Tonto* was written specifically for James Cagney. But the seventy-five-year-old Cagney refused to end his thirteen-year retirement to play a crusty New York widower who, when his apartment building is knocked down, takes a transcontinental journey with his cat, Tonto, meeting relatives and a strange assortment of characters along the way. Fifty-six-year-old Art Carney stepped in and gave a fine performance, revealing unsuspected dramatic skills and proving that he could command our attention on the big screen as a leading man just as surely as when he charmed us as Ed Norton on the small screen's *The Honeymooners,* supporting Jackie Gleason. He became the oldest Best Actor victor since sixty-three-year-old George Arliss won for 1929's *Disraeli.* Carney was a popular choice—although there were many who favored Jack Nicholson for *Chinatown*—but in hindsight his victory is of little satisfaction for movie fans because with the exception of *The Late Show,* opposite Lily Tomlin, Carney's later contributions to movies were negligible. He remains a television star—his winning an Oscar is no more meaningful than Jack Nicholson winning an Emmy would be if he should make a rare television appearance. Carney should get Emmys, Brando should get Oscars. Anyway, we gave Carney too much credit for making Harry seem, refreshingly, so much younger than his years, forgetting that a much younger actor was in the part.

In a year that saw many award-worthy performances by actors—Nicholson is my choice among the nominees—I will give the Alternate Oscar to Gene Hackman, who played another Harry, in Francis Ford Coppola's intricate paranoia drama, *The Conversation.*

Hackman is Harry Caul, a private surveillance expert, the most famous in his field. He lives alone in a small San Francisco apartment and has essentially no private life. Years ago he turned secret recordings over to a client, and a couple and their child wound up murdered. He doesn't want that to happen again. He is hired by a powerful magnate (unbilled Robert Duvall) to tape a conversation between his young wife, Ann (Cindy Williams), and her lover, Mark (Frederic Forrest), one of his executives. As they walk in circles in a nearby park, Harry records them using three directional microphones and one microphone planted on an assistant. Not all their conversation is recorded clearly, but Harry deduces that they are nice people, who are deeply in love but worry that they will be killed if her husband finds out. Mark tells Ann about a particular hotel room and gives a specific time. Harry assumes they will have their next romantic interlude there. Fearing for them, Harry refuses to turn over the tapes, despite warnings from the magnate's chief executive, Martin (Harrison Ford). Harry suspects he's being followed, maybe even bugged. Wor-

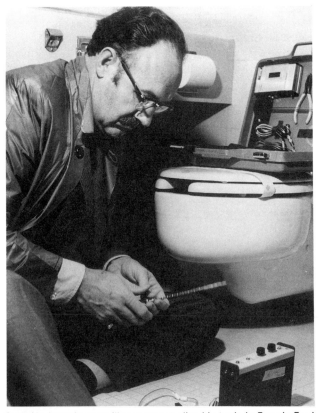

Gene Hackman's surveillance expert plies his trade in Francis Ford Coppola's paranoia film, *The Conversation.*

ried and guilty, he is seduced by a woman (Elizabeth MacCrea) who works for his chief competitor (Allen Garfield at his sleaziest). When he awakens, he discovers that the tapes are gone. The magnate has the tapes; he pays Harry his fee. But guilty Harry isn't through. He checks into the hotel room next to the one he heard Mark mention. He overhears Ann scream and imagines that she is being killed. Later he discovers blood in the room. But the next day he sees Ann and reads in the paper that her husband has supposedly been killed in an auto crash. Ann will get all his vast property and stock holdings. Harry now realizes that Ann lured her husband to the hotel room and Mark murdered him. Martin calls Harry. He says they'll be listening to Harry to make sure he hasn't told anyone what he knows. Harry strips down his apartment looking for hidden microphones.

Although it had the good fortune to be released when Watergate and wiretapping were hot topics, Coppola's low-budget paranoia drama was drowned under the great wave of publicity for his *The Godfather*. Many critics preferred it to *The Godfather* and it made several Top Ten lists. It was voted Best Picture at Cannes. I think the picture is extremely flawed—Coppola's worst mistake is to delve into pretentious fantasy (Harry's nightmares) and arty images when realism is the picture's strongest suit—but if it didn't have a chance at box-office success it is because it is a character study instead of the political thriller viewers expected. As a character study it works quite well, because Gene Hackman is brilliant at portraying a unique movie protagonist.

Whereas Hackman was tough and virile in his Academy Award–winning role of policeman "Popeye" Doyle in 1971's *The French Connection,* this time he is far from intimidating: he has a receding hairline, a wimpy mustache, and the glasses of someone who has spent more time in a library than a gym. Despite his expertise at espionage the forty-four-year-old Harry is quite bland. He is unmarried and lives alone, his only hobby playing the sax along with jazz records. He is secretive, increasingly paranoid, depressed, and guilty. His guilt stems from his being a moral Catholic whose work is sleazy and unethical. He's the type who feels it necessary to reveal in confession that he sometimes takes newspapers without paying for them and that he has impure sexual thoughts; so how he must suffer when he thinks his work may cause people to be murdered. He agonizes about his complicity in a sin. Hackman's biggest success was to figure out exactly how much of a stuffed shirt Harry should be. Because of the nature of Harry's job and the people he meets, Hackman can't make him a complete innocent, but does make him uncomfortable and awkward except when working. He has trouble communicating with either men or women, because he feels everyone is prying into his life. It's clear he's no virgin and that women arouse him, but he's such a lousy kisser that it's equally obvious he hasn't had much experience and that women wouldn't flip over him. Because he has trouble with people, he tries to keep his gadget-dominated work as impersonal as possible: "Listen, if there's one surefire rule that I have learned in this business it's that I don't know anything about human nature, I don't know anything about curiosity. That's not part of what I do." When he brings the human element into this thinking and starts feeling sorry for Ann and Mark (a big mistake!), Harry becomes sloppy in his work—the world's greatest surveillance expert allows tapes to be lifted from him.

Hackman's guilt-ridden Harry spends the entire film repressing emotions, trying not to reveal what is on his mind, trying to keep calm as things go awry, trying to deal with his fear, trying to keep his temper. And this takes its toll. He sweats, he circles a room like a caged tiger, he has attacks of guilt, he becomes increasingly paranoid. He's pretty much over the edge by the time he starts ripping up his walls and floor to search for a nonexistent wiretap in his apartment. He's like the guy in "The Tell-Tale Heart" who obsessively tries to wipe away evidence of his murder. Significantly, Hackman doesn't participate in any action scenes, but just watching and listening to him is exciting.

▶ BEST ACTRESS

WINNER:
Ellen Burstyn *(Alice Doesn't Live Here Anymore)*
Other Nominees: Diahann Carroll *(Claudine)*, Faye Dunaway *(Chinatown)*, Valerie Perrine *(Lenny)*, Gena Rowlands *(A Woman Under the Influence)*

▼
THE BEST CHOICE:
Ellen Burstyn *(Alice Doesn't Live Here Anymore)*
Award-Worthy Runners-Up: Diahann Carroll *(Claudine)*, Shelley Duvall *(Thieves Like Us)*, Goldie Hawn *(The Sugarland Express)*

Liv Ullmann, arguably the best, most important actress of the era, was justifiably declared Best Actress of 1974 by the New York Film Critics for her shattering performance in Ingmar Bergman's domestic epic, *Scenes from a Marriage.* But she was denied a chance to repeat her victory in the Oscar race, when the picture was declared ineligible for Academy consideration in all categories. Apparently there was a rarely enforced Academy rule that a TV presentation—*Scenes from a Marriage* was originally a six-part series on Swedish television in 1973—was required to play in theaters in the same calendar year it was telecast. Several actresses, including the soon-to-be nominated Ellen Burstyn, Diahann Carroll, and Gena Rowlands, wrote a letter urging the Academy to revise its policy so Ullmann would be allowed to be nominated. But the Academy stood firm. With Ullmann out of the running Burstyn had clear sailing in the Oscar race for her fine, disarming performance in the popular *Alice Doesn't Live Here Anymore*. (Gena Rowlands had incredible moments as a woman having a nervous breakdown in husband John Cassavetes's *A Woman Under the Influence,* but overall her performance was too erratic to be Oscar worthy.) A respected, very likable actress playing a very likable character trying to earn respect was a difficult combination to beat. It also didn't hurt Burstyn's chances that this film, with "feminist" underpinnings, about an unmarried woman existed because Burstyn had brought Robert Getchell's script to Warner Bros. and secured financing, wrote and improvised some of the dialogue, recruited much of the cast and crew, and hired director Martin Scorsese. Oddly, she was the only one of the nominees not present at the Academy ceremony.

Burstyn played Alice Hyatt. When she was a child in Monterey, California, she wanted to be a singer, but gave up her career to get married. Now thirty-five, she lives in New Mexico with her unappreciative husband (Billy Green Bush) and sweet, nutty, and argumentative son, Tommy (Alfred Lutter). When her husband is killed, she and Tommy drive toward Monterey. She promises him that she will have him there in time for school in September but must find work along the way as a singer. In Phoenix they check into a motel. Alice works as a singer in a bar. She has an affair with a younger man, Ben (a frightening performance by Harvey Keitel), but when it turns out he is a married psychotic, Alice and Tommy get back into the car and speed away. In Tucson, Alice settles for a waitressing job at Mel and Ruby's Café. After a rough start she befriends another waitress (Diane Ladd), filling a need in her life. She falls for a handsome, divorced rancher, David (Kris Kristofferson). David and Tommy get along, until David can no longer tolerate how spoiled he is and spanks him. This prompts Alice to break off their relationship. David comes to the diner and before everyone tells Alice that he wants her back. He promises he won't try to stop her plans to sing or go to Monterey. When he says he'll give up his ranch for her, Alice knows she has found the right man. She tells Tommy they won't be going to Monterey as she'd promised him. Tommy is delighted to stay in Tucson to be near his precocious friend Audrey (Jodie Foster). He even admits he likes David, just not his taste in country music. Alice and Tommy walk together down the highway . . . toward a restaurant lounge called "Monterey."

Alice Doesn't Live Here Anymore received excellent reviews when released, including an endorsement from *Ms.* magazine, but there was debate about whether it lost

Ellen Burstyn briefly realizes her ambition, when she works as a lounge singer in Martin Scorsese's *Alice Doesn't Live Here Anymore.*

its claim to being feminist when Alice cancels her plans to go to Monterey to settle down with David in Tucson. It was disturbing to read righteous male critics taking a feminist position and complaining that Alice's decision to stay proved she wasn't strong enough to live without a man. I think such critics were being too judgmental toward Alice, preferring she make the wrong choice if it proved to them she was strong. Alice's decision to stay with David doesn't mean that she would stay with any man just to be with a man—it just means she would stay with David, and that decision isn't written in stone or on a marriage certificate. She still seeks a singing career to make her independent and prepare her for a time when and if she and Tommy are on their own again.

Is Burstyn's Alice weak? She cries, makes irrational decisions, is confused about her future, can't control her son, lacks confidence in her talent, is lonely; she worries constantly about whether she can make money and whether she is a good mother. But despite everything she accomplishes much, conveying the theme of the film: it isn't only the strongest women who can reveal strength when they are on their own. What's admirable is that Alice deals with her fears head-on, despite her insecurities. She gains strength by facing adversity on her own and being responsible for her own life and that of her son. So when she decides to stay with David, it is not a decision made through weakness.

Alice Doesn't Live Here Anymore capped an extremely productive period for Ellen Burstyn, who had already given terrific performances in *Tropic of Cancer*—doing one of the American screen's first full-frontal nude scenes—*The Last Picture Show, The King of Marvin Gardens,* and *The Exorcist.* She was forty-two when she played the thirty-five-year-old Alice. Much of her success in the role was due to her getting into the skin and into the mind of Alice, becoming so comfortable that she felt she could improvise lines for the character. After three unsuccessful marriages the unmarried Burstyn said she understood much of what her character goes through— I assume she was referring to Alice's striving for independence while fearing to be without a protective man.

In a superb, thoroughly convincing characterization Burstyn lets us see many facets of Alice, the bad as well as the good, the fragile and the resilient. At various times she is funny, goofy, angry, scared, sexy, pathetic, calm, hysterical, optimistic, pessimistic, patient, intolerant, hard (not too often), and soft (e.g., when she asks to touch David's beard). There is one consistency: Alice always reacts emotionally to *anything* anyone says or does. Nothing passes her by, nothing is taken casually. For a woman who is trying to put together her life and forge her own identity, there is nothing insignificant. So Burstyn conveys the sense that every line of dialogue, every

gesture, and every expression has special meaning. She gives as much to the briefest, nondramatic scenes as to the most powerful sequences—in fact, she probably won the Oscar because she is so appealing in the movie's small moments. Particularly memorable are Burstyn's many one-on-one scenes with the other actors: the talented, witty Lutter (humorous, believable, precious scenes between mother and son), Keitel, Ladd (at first they feud, later the new friends exchange confidences), Kristofferson, and others. Burstyn's Alice responds in various ways to the people in her life, but her responses are always honest (the actress has an honest face) and open and help us gain insight into her. We learn so much about her in this way that by film's end, we want to join the diner customers who cheer her—as she breaks through to at least temporary happiness.

1975

▶ BEST PICTURE

WINNER:
One Flew Over the Cuckoo's Nest (Fantasy Films/United Artists; Milos Forman)
Other Nominees: *Barry Lyndon, Dog Day Afternoon, Jaws, Nashville*

▼

THE BEST CHOICE:
The Man Who Would Be King (Columbia/Allied Artists; John Huston)
Award-Worthy Runners-Up: *Jaws* (Steven Spielberg), *One Flew Over the Cuckoo's Nest* (Milos Forman)

Adapted from Ken Kesey's 1962 cult novel and a subsequent play, *One Flew Over the Cuckoo's Nest* was considered a chancy film project. Kirk Douglas, who produced the flop Broadway play, had spent thirteen frustrating years trying to get studio backing before turning over the rights to his son, Michael Douglas. By getting Jack Nicholson to agree to play the lead, R. P. McMurphy—disruptive, nonconformist patient in a mental hospital—Michael Douglas was able to secure $3 million, a third of which went to his star. Only after the film was made did Douglas get a distributor, United Artists. It was an unexpected financial success and swept the Oscars, winning the statues for Best Picture, Best Director (Milos Forman), Best Actor (Nicholson is fabulous), Best Actress (Louise Fletcher as the heartless Nurse Ratched, McMurphy's nemesis), and Best Adapted Screenplay (Lawrence Hauben and Bo Goldman). The Academy had no reservations about honoring it because in addition to being a critical and popular success, it wasn't nearly as controversial as

had initially been feared. First of all, Forman's depiction of mental patients was sensitive. More important, though it took an antiauthoritarian stance, the film's target was not the government, police, military, or CIA/FBI, but just the staff, particularly one nurse, of a mental hospital off in the Northwest, back in 1963. Even McMurphy's ploys against Nurse Ratched aren't that subversive. So to the surprise of fans of the book, this movie adaptation was palatable to middle-of-the-road audiences. Which doesn't mean that my opinion of it is low. In fact, the only Oscar nominee I prefer to it, Steven Spielberg's *Jaws,* was geared specifically for the masses, a pure popcorn thriller (though it had a minor government-cover-up theme) that temporarily became the all-time box-office champ.

While viewers flocked to *One Flew Over the Cuckoo's Nest* and *Jaws,* they ignored *The Man Who Would Be King,* although it was directed by John Huston and starred Sean Connery and Michael Caine. Even today, Huston's adaptation of Rudyard Kipling's marvelous short story is vastly underappreciated and rarely screened. I think it's one of the screen's greatest adventure yarns and my choice as 1975's Best Film.

Huston and Gladys Hill faithfully adapted the story that Kipling wrote when he was a young journalist in India in the 1880s. One change they made was to insert Kipling as a character, the person to whom Peachy Carnehan (Caine) tells his incredible story. Peachy first met Kipling (Christopher Plummer) in an India railroad station, when he stole Kipling's watch. But upon discovering that his victim was a Mason, as were Peachy and his bosom buddy, Daniel Dravot (Connery), he returned it. Peachy and Danny were once gallant British soldiers in India but had become petty criminals and an embarrassment to British officials there. They told Kipling that they would make the impossible journey to Kafiristan, following in the steps of Alexander the Great. Once there, they planned to use their military skills to make a minor local ruler into a great conqueror, and then usurp his throne, ruling as kings themselves and becoming wealthy. Three years later the half-mad, physically ravaged Peachy returns to tell Kipling what happened. They had succeeded in their venture: after arriving in Kafiristan, they led the troops of Ootah (Doghmi Larbi) of Er-Heb to victories over his primitive enemies. When Danny was shot with an arrow, he didn't bleed—as it actually struck his bandolier—so everyone assumed he was a god. Peachy and their new friend, Billy Fish (Saeed Jaffrey), a Gurkha warrior who learned English while serving the British, suggested he keep up the guise. Ootah was disposed of by his people, and Danny became king, receiving wealth from all tribes. He was summoned to the holy city of Sikandergul (a Huston addition). The priests wanted to see if he was truly divine, but before they shot arrows into him by way of a test, they noticed he carried an amulet with a Masonic design identical to that of their own god. They, too, were Masons. They believed Danny was the son of the god Alexander and gave him all the wealth they had kept for his "father." Danny and Peachy planned on taking the fortune and returning home in several months, but Danny became convinced that he indeed was a god, and decided to remain and rule. He chose a young bride (Shakira Caine). She was so frightened that she'd catch fire if she made love to a god that she scratched him. He bled. Seeing Danny wasn't a god, the priests swarmed upon him, and his men. Billy was killed, the other soldiers captured. Danny died gallantly, falling from a rope bridge he had built. Peachy was crucified, but surviving the night, he was let go. His story finished, Peachy says farewell to Kipling and departs on "urgent business," leaving behind Danny's mummified head.

Huston had wanted to make *The Man Who Would Be King* many years before, using Humphrey Bogart and Clark Gable, but it wasn't until he was seventy that he undertook his only epic. His amazing accomplishment at an advanced age is akin to Akira Kurosawa's making *Ran* when approaching seventy-five. It is an epic like no other, set in a distant, haunting world that has no equivalent in film. Difficult filming was done in remote sections of Morocco and it's as if Huston, cinematographer Oswald Morris (who deserved an Oscar), and the cast and crew happened through a time warp, finding the mysterious people who populate the film and awesome sights not seen by white intruders since Alexander crossed the same misty, snow-covered mountains. Who designed the Er-heb fort-town that is built on uneven ground, and the mystical Sikandergul, which is perched high on a mountaintop? And it's hard to believe Edith Head, who designed clothes for Grace Kelly, provided the gowns and garments for these ancient people. Interestingly, Huston cast the soldiers, crowd participants, and bald, eerie priests with natives of the Atlas Mountains who spoke only Berber—the hollow-cheeked old man who played the High Priest was well over a hundred. (One reason we feel on edge is that we worry the filmmakers and cast will meet the fate of Danny and Peachy among these spooky people, in this out-of-the-way locale.) What strange images: priests with their eyes closed (so they won't see anything bad) marching across the desert, and opposing armies falling to the ground until they pass; polo-playing Er-Hebians using decapitated heads for balls; two large, imposing white men in bright red British army jackets leading primitive people in battle; a thousand angry priests attacking the fraudulent god and Peachy—imagine a thousand pissed-off Hari Krishnas!

The story itself is a pip, a wonder-filled adventure and a wry comment on arrogant British imperialism that culminates with Danny, embodying the declining British empire, plummeting for hours from a destroyed bridge that he'd built to link the new and old worlds, his crown just out of his grasp. As Huston said (quoted by Gerald Pratley) of Kipling's story, the film "contains everything a good story should have: excitement, color, spectacle and humor, adventure, high drama, tragedy, good conversation . . . truth and irony." It also has two lovable rogues

Sean Connery and Michael Caine are excited by the wealth given them by the holy men who believe Connery is the son of Alexander the Great in John Huston's unsung epic, *The Man Who Would Be King*.

as its heroes, played splendidly by Caine and Connery. They are tremendously flawed individuals—they admit they've never done a good deed and won't be wept for once they die—who are not particularly intelligent and are even racists, but they have immense appeal (especially with these two actors in the parts). We are to admire their resourcefulness, sense of purpose, fearlessness, calm strategy-making prior to conflict ("the problem is how to divide five Afghans from three mules and have two Englishmen left over"), and gallantry during battle. And we are taken with their tremendous spirit, humor (this is a funny film), and most of all their camaraderie. After many years together the two are like halves of the same person, finishing each other's sentences, not bothering to see how the other is doing in battle because

they know exactly. They split apart only briefly, when Danny takes to believing he is a god. He will learn his lesson at the end and apologize, upset that he has gotten Peachy into trouble with him. But Peachy wouldn't have it any other way. They stand back to back—smiling and singing—as the priests close in. And when Danny is ordered to the middle of the bridge, and priests cut the ropes, Danny and Peachy sing together, very loudly and defiantly. Supportive friends to the end—no blades can cut their bonds. This is such a great, emotional scene that every time I see it, I wish I knew the words to their song so I could join in, to lend them support, and, like them, drown out my own sorrow that a unique friendship is ending.

▶ BEST ACTOR

WINNER:

Jack Nicholson *(One Flew Over the Cuckoo's Nest)*
Other Nominees: Walter Matthau *(The Sunshine Boys)*, Al Pacino *(Dog Day Afternoon)*, Maximilian Schell *(The Man in the Glass Booth)*, James Whitmore *(Give 'Em Hell, Harry!)*

▼

THE BEST CHOICE:

Jack Nicholson *(One Flew Over the Cuckoo's Nest)*
Award-Worthy Runners-Up: Michael Caine *(The Man Who Would Be King)*, Sean Connery *(The Man Who Would Be King)*, Tim Curry *(The Rocky Horror Picture Show)*, Gene Hackman *(Night Moves)*, Walter Matthau *(The Sunshine Boys)*, Robert Mitchum *(Farewell, My Lovely)*

In 1975 the Academy belatedly recognized Jack Nicholson as the cinema's top male star, giving him an overdue Oscar. In 1970 Nicholson was satisfied just to have been nominated for Best Actor for his misfit Bobby Dupea in *Five Easy Pieces,* his first lead in a major film. He knew everyone was going to vote for George C. Scott for *Patton.* But in 1973, when he was nominated again for his foul-mouthed navy lifer Badass Buddusky in *The Last Detail,* he admitted disappointment after he lost to Jack Lemmon for *Save the Tiger.* And the following year he couldn't have been too happy when his terrific nominated performance as private eye Jake Gittes in *Chinatown* failed to beat out Art Carney in *Harry and Tonto.* But in 1975, playing Randle Patrick McMurphy, a mental hospital's renegade-at-large in Milos Forman's Best Picture winner, *One Flew Over the Cuckoo's Nest,* victory was assured. So brilliant was his performance and so unexpectedly popular was the film version of Ken Kesey's controversial cult novel that this time the image-conscious Academy had no choice but to give Nicholson the Oscar, whatever their reservations had been in the past.

Oregon, 1963. R. P. McMurphy feigns insanity in order to get transferred to a mental hospital from a work farm, where he's serving time for having had sex with a fifteen-year-old. He is placed in a ward with seventeen other

male patients, of whom nine seem to be totally withdrawn. The others are all controlled by the authoritarian nurse who heads the ward, Mildred Ratched (Louise Fletcher was selected Best Actress). They obediently take medicine that dulls their senses and fearfully let her manipulate them into docility. The daily group therapy sessions invariably result in Ratched's making the men lose self-esteem. A free spirit who only pretends to take his medicine, McMurphy gets the men to think for themselves and question Ratched's authority. They all respond to this charismatic newcomer, even a 6'5" Indian, Chief Bromden (Will Sampson)—the novel's narrator—who pretends to be deaf and dumb. Ratched resents the influence McMurphy has over the men and seems determined to break his rebellious spirit. She insists that he not be transferred from her ward. After he fights with a guard, she sends him for shock treatments. Realizing that he can't survive under Ratched's thumb, McMurphy plans to escape. But first he holds a wild Christmas party for the men, bringing in two female prostitutes. One sleeps with a young patient, Billy (Brad Dourif). When Ratched catches them, she threatens to tell his mother, her friend. Billy commits suicide. Rather than escaping out an open window, McMurphy tries to strangle Ratched. Afterward, he is lobotomized. Chief Bromden puts him out of his

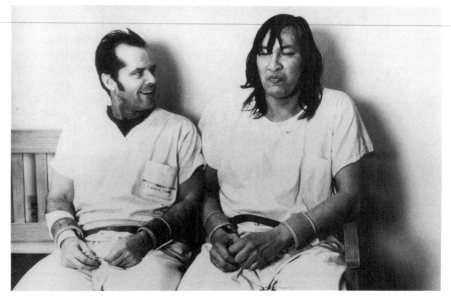

In Milos Foreman's multiple-Oscar–winner, *One Flew Over the Cuckoo's Nest,* Jack Nicholson's R. P. McMurphy, who doesn't know he is about to receive shock treatment, chats with Will Sampson's Chief Bromden, the narrator in Ken Kesey's novel.

misery by suffocating him with a pillow. Then the big Indian breaks through a window and escapes the cuckoo's nest, as the other patients cheer.

Never known for low-key performances, Nicholson was perfectly cast as this man who pretends to be mad and who, if we equate rebellion with abnormality, may in fact be so. He certainly fits in better with the mental patients than with those who run the asylum. His McMurphy is always wild, always in a party mood, and is a human injection of life, of entertainment, into the other patients' dull, regimented lives. He laughs loudly, talks nonstop, plays games (poker, basketball), steals a bus and takes everyone fishing, shoots water at them, leads the patients in cheering a nonexistent World Series game he narrates as they stare at a blank television screen (when Ratched won't turn on the actual game), stands up to Ratched, breaks her rules. How Ratched detests this man with the lunatic grin and laugh, who sees through her, who makes her blush with his crude language ("Next woman takes me on is gonna light up like a pinball machine and pay off in silver dollars"), who makes himself a thorn in her side but pretends innocence—as Molly Haskell suggests, Nicholson plays McMurphy with "ironic self-awareness"—and who is capable of doing anything to undermine her authority.

The rambunctious Irishman is probably Nicholson's sweetest, most caring character. We even accept his explanation as to why he couldn't help having sex with a fifteen-year-old. Unfortunately, he fits into the line of Nicholson's well-meaning idealists whose attempts at doing something of value are futile, who end up failures despite impressive accomplishments. Fighting Ratched for the other patients' minds and souls, he manages to improve their outlooks on life and to see Ratched as the monster she is, he inspires Chief Bromden's escape, and he has the satisfaction of putting Ratched in a neck brace. However, his actions and attitude result in Chief Bromden

and another patient joining him in receiving shock therapy; Billy ending up dead (although Ratched was directly responsible); and his having a lobotomy and ending up dead.

When Kirk Douglas originally bought the movie rights to Kesey's novel, he wanted to play McMurphy himself, but gave up the idea when he became too old for the part. Like Nicholson he intended to tone down McMurphy from the bigger-than-life symbol-figure (an angel?) he is in the novel, and make him fully human. However, Douglas wanted to retain the sexual element present in the book, where McMurphy despises but is sexually attracted to the big-breasted Nurse Ratched, and the sexually repressed Ratched is determined not just to control her male patients, including McMurphy, but to emasculate them. At the conclusion Douglas wanted his McMurphy to rape Ratched, not merely attempt to strangle her. Interestingly, McMurphy's ploys against Ratched are not at all sexual, though he is a very sexual person. And they are no more subversive than the hijinks pulled by the unruly frat kids against the dean in *National Lampoon's Animal House.* The most effective thing he does is attempt to be the patients' role model—repeatedly, he bets them he can break rules; when he fails, he says, "But I tried, didn't I, goddammit. At least I did that." At first he can't really see inside the soft-voiced, unemotional Ratched. He can only tell her superiors that "she ain't honest . . . she likes a rigged game." Later he sees her for the dangerous witch she is. Only too late does he realize that Ratched will do anything to maintain authority in her world. Like most Nicholson characters he underestimates the predicament he's in and the power of his enemies. And just when he seems victorious, something backfires, and he fails miserably, losing everything. At least McMurphy was Nicholson's first loser to win him an Academy Award.

▶ BEST ACTRESS

Louise Fletcher *(One Flew Over the Cuckoo's Nest)*
Other Nominees: Isabelle Adjani *(The Story of Adèle H.)*, Ann-Margret *(Tommy)*, Glenda Jackson *(Hedda)*, Carol Kane *(Hester Street)*

▼

THE BEST CHOICE:
Isabelle Adjani *(The Story of Adèle H.)*
Award-Worthy Runners-Up: Louise Fletcher *(One Flew Over the Cuckoo's Nest)*, Carol Kane *(Hester Street)*

As part of the *One Flew Over the Cuckoo's Nest* sweep, Louise Fletcher became the least known Best Actress winner. Previously, the forty-one-year-old character actress had nothing more significant than a supporting role in Robert Altman's sleeper, *Thieves Like Us.* Her lack of an image was to her advantage, because when she played the evil Nurse Ratched viewers didn't know what to expect. Ratched's villainy is blatant in Ken Kesey's novel, but Fletcher is subtle, playing her as a soft-spoken, insincerely friendly control freak who is determined to maintain her authority over her male patients at all costs (she does it best through fear, humiliation, and sense-dulling drugs). Look into her emotionless eyes and you realize she has no soul! As effectively hateful as is Fletcher's Nurse Ratched—indeed she is one of the cinema's great villainesses—it is still a one-dimensional role that doesn't let us see if Fletcher has much range. In subsequent films she proved to be no better than an adequate actress who had the bad habit of inventing one or two personality traits for her characters and making them the key to her entire performance—the result has been other insufficiently developed characters.

This was a weak year for American leading ladies, as was reflected in the nominations for Best Actress. The Academy even nominated, for only the third time, a foreign actress in a foreign-language film, France's Isabelle Adjani for François Truffaut's *The Story of Adèle H.,* passionately playing Victor Hugo's tormented daughter. Her surprising nomination allows me to consider her for an Alternate Oscar, which she richly deserves for one of the truly unforgettable performances of the decade.

In 1863 Adèle Hugo arrives in Halifax from Guernsey. Already mentally unstable, she has come to rekindle her romance with a young soldier, Lieutenant Pinson (Bruce Robinson), whom her famous father had selected as a marital prospect for her. But this carouser wants nothing more to do with her. Desperately in love, she can't accept his rejection. She fills her journal with romantic flights of fancy and writes home about the budding romance she has with Pinson, and then of their marriage. Meanwhile, she tries to win him back. She spies on him making love, she sends him prostitutes, she gives him money, she puts notes in his uniform, she lies to Pinson's father that she is pregnant. She has no sense of pride. She becomes desperately ill, sleeps in a flophouse, goes insane. Even

when she can no longer recognize Pinson's face, she continues her quest. She even follows him to Barbados. Completely shattered, she is sent home to recover.

At twenty-one Isabelle Adjani was the youngest Best Actress nominee in history. Already heralded as France's most exciting young stage actress, she rejected a twenty-year contract with the Comédie-Française to appear in Truffaut's film, a smart move that resulted in her becoming an international film star. Whereas Louise Fletcher won the Oscar playing a middle-aged, sexually repressed woman who smothered all her emotions, Adjani understandably made a greater impact as a young, sexually willing yet frustrated woman who is all emotion. Truffaut's characters are driven by their hearts rather than reason and typically love those who don't love them equally or at the same time. His heroes who experience

Isabelle Adjani is the love-obsessed daughter of Victor Hugo in François Truffaut's *The Story of Adèle H.*

unrequited love—for example, Jean-Pierre Léaud's characters in *Stolen Kisses* and *Two English Girls*—are stoical as they continue their obsessive pursuits. But this time, when Truffaut tells a true story inspired by Adèle's journal, he really explores the pain and humiliation one might endure when deep love is unfulfilled.

For viewers it's hard enough watching death-courting, destructive male characters obsessively pursue unattainable women—as it is with James Stewart in *Vertigo* and John Moulder-Brown in *Deep End*—but it's absolutely devastating watching Adjani's lovely young Adèle sink into humiliation and madness as a result of her abandonment; heartbreaking to see her beautiful face (which Truffaut keeps in long close-ups) with bloodshot eyes and a river of tears streaking her cheeks—or with happy eyes and excited expressions as she fabricates romantic lies for her journal and letters. She recalls spinster Olivia de Havilland in *The Heiress,* whose one lover, handsome Montgomery Clift, proves to be a fraud interested only in her money. Like de Havilland, Adèle's need for love from her suitor is rooted in her need to escape the house of her unloving father, to prove to him she is worthy of love. Ironically, becoming slave to another man is her way of achieving freedom from her father. What's so sad is that Adèle is beautiful, passionate, and clever enough to win many hearts, but she pursues a man who she realizes is a rat. She simply gives up trying to control her heart, which acts independently from her brain and has more power.

Caught up in her obsession, Adèle separates the idealized lover about whom she rhapsodizes in her writings from the real Lieutenant Pinson, not even recognizing him as they pass on the street. Like other Truffaut char-

acters she communicates her feelings through writing, and not in person. The fabricated world she writes about in which she and her lover live happily is her necessary escape from the heartless world outside her door. In that world she is miserable and insane. Truffaut wanted to make the rare "film about love involving one person." Such a love will consume the one whose passion isn't returned, which is what happened to the real Adèle Hugo. As she would do years later in the role of Rodin's lover, the sculptress *Camille Claudel*—another woman driven mad by rejection and isolation—Adjani played a woman in pathetic circumstances who could very easily have won every viewer's complete sympathy. But she instead takes Adèle so far over the edge (as she would Camille) that we have no more tolerance for her than we do for any beautiful but dangerous loony talking angrily to herself on a street corner. As Frank Rich commented in Annette Insdorf's book, *François Truffaut,* "If Truffaut had wanted to tear our hearts out, he could have provided a soft-featured, soft-spoken goddess, a latter-day Lillian Gish, but . . . Adjani's face tells us more about her burning soul than is comfortable—she's so intense it's intimidating—and rather than identifying or sympathizing with her, we recoil in vague annoyance." By the time Adèle has taken to walking catatonically through the streets—as in her trancelike walk in *Nosferatu,* Adjani's ethereal quality comes into play—we've shared so much of her misery that we're relieved she is no longer aware of her suffering. Only an actress with Adjani's extraordinary gifts for conveying what Truffaut called "inner violence, emotional violence," could so thoroughly wear us out that we'd recognize her new condition as a sign of improvement.

1976

▶ BEST PICTURE

WINNER:
Rocky (United Artists; John G. Avildsen)
Other Nominees: *All the President's Men, Bound for Glory, Network, Taxi Driver*

▼

THE BEST CHOICE:
The Front (Columbia; Martin Ritt)
Award-Worthy Runners-Up: None

Everyone loves an underdog. That's why audiences loved *Rocky,* a movie about a club boxer who has enough heart to go the distance against the heavyweight boxing

champion, and why everyone was happy when this small, unpolished film starring an essential unknown, Sylvester Stallone, won the Best Picture Oscar over several heavy-

In a serious role Woody Allen guarantees himself a jail sentence by defying a committee seeking out communists in television at the climax of Martin Ritt's *The Front*.

weight contenders, including *All the President's Men,* with Robert Redford and Dustin Hoffman, and *Network,* for which Faye Dunaway and Peter Finch won Oscars. *Rocky* still has undeniable appeal, and if it had served as inspiration for anything more than progressively inferior sequels, I might want it to keep its Oscar. But my choice for Best Picture is another sleeper, Martin Ritt's *The Front,* a disarmingly genial picture about a serious subject: the blacklisting of suspected communists in the entertainment field in the fifties.

The hero of *The Front* is different from the one in *Rocky,* though he, too, proves true to himself. He's a little fellow with intellect instead of brawn, played by Woody Allen. Howard Price is a low-salaried cashier at a New York bar, and is always in debt because he consistently makes terrible sports bets—he's the type who would have bet a wad of money on Rocky to have *beaten* Apollo Creed. Television writer Alfred Miller (Michael Murphy), his lifelong friend, has been blacklisted for being a communist sympathizer, and the apolitical Howard agrees to be his "front." Alfred will write scripts for a popular show called *Grand Central,* and, for ten percent, Howard will sell them under his own name. The show's producer, Phil Susman (Herschel Bernardi), script supervisor, Florence Barrett (Andrea Marcovicci), and popular costar, Hecky Brown (Zero Mostel), marvel at Howard's work, not knowing he didn't write it. Howard and Florence start dating. Howard and Hecky become friends. Howard becomes the front for two more leftist writers. So he makes good money and becomes famous—he has the audacity to tell the writers to do rewrites when their material doesn't meet his standards. But the show is being watched carefully by investigators looking for communist subversives. Susman is forced to fire Hecky because he once marched in a May Day parade and now

can't name others who were present. Hecky can't get work. Meanwhile, Florence becomes so angered that Phil won't stand up against the blacklist that she quits the show. She wants Howard to write a pamphlet against the blacklist, which she'll edit. When he won't agree to give up his career, she breaks up with him. Hecky commits suicide, an event that affects Howard deeply. Howard confesses to Florence that he didn't write the scripts. He wants her to love him for himself, not because he is an artist. He tells her he will prove his integrity. Called before HUAC, Howard is told to name one name or go to jail for once having been a bookie. The committee says he can name Hecky. But he tells the committee to "fuck" itself—which is why the film almost got an R rating—and goes to jail, a hero to Florence, Alfred, and protesters.

When released, *The Front* was greeted with confusion. Some couldn't see it as a serious film because of its gentle tone, the casting of Allen, and Howie's spouting of some funny "Allen-like" lines: "In my family the biggest sin was to buy retail"; "I feel if you're going to write about human beings," he bluffs in response to Florence's flattery, "you may as well make them human beings"; "Swimming isn't a sport—swimming is what you do so you shouldn't drown." (My favorite comic moment is when Howie tries to pick up a woman by saying, "I'm a dentist," and she asks, "Professionally?") For instance, Pauline Kael commented, "The writer, Walter Bernstein, had a nifty comedy idea . . . but he didn't develop its comic potential." That's because Bernstein didn't want to.

This is not a comedy. Howie has funny lines simply because Howie is a funny guy, which makes him appealing to both Florence and Hecky. Ironic humor is used to call attention to the absurdity of the situation, where even the apolitical, innocent "front" for blacklisted writers is subpoenaed by HUAC, where a man's career is ruined because he joined a May Day parade in order to march with an attractive woman, and where a man can be blacklisted because he has the same name as a communist sympathizer and can't clear himself unless he can name names. The rest of the humor and the friendly tone serve only to temper the rage. We still get a sense of the very serious paranoia, desperation, and insanity of the McCarthy era, and come to understand why those who were blacklisted—including Ritt, Bernstein, Mostel, Bernardi, and supporting players Joshua Shelley and Lloyd Gough—still detest both those producers like Susman who didn't stick up for them against the network and sponsors, and those who testified before HUAC.

The film is a tribute to those who took moral stands during that scary period. It contends that while the committee forced some real leftists to become turncoats, its disturbing actions actually politicized others. Howard is completely apolitical prior to two jolting events: Florence's exhibiting her idealism by quitting her high-paying job, and Hecky's taking his own life. Price is interested only in making money (to pay off debts) and in his budding reputation. (Ritt claimed he once saw an untalented front resembling Howie—"I couldn't write a grocery list"—tell a veteran blacklisted writer that his script "is not up to my usual standard. I'm not going to turn it in.") There's about as little chance of Howie's not cooperating with the imposing HUAC as there is of Allen idol Humphrey Bogart's risking his life to help Paul Henreid escape at the end of *Casablanca*. But Bogart came through and so does Howie. Allen is terrific in this picture, but he saves the best for the end. I love Howie's double-talking testimony to the smug committee ("When you say *know*—can you ever really *know* a person? I grew up with an Alfred Miller. But did I *know* him. . . . In a biblical sense? *Know* him? Am I right?") When they demand Hecky's name he rises, the anguish leaving his face, and walks toward the door, disrespectfully calling the members "fellahs." He's not afraid—we don't need his profanity to tell us that—although he knows he'll go to jail. Howard proves to us that brave acts reflecting integrity aren't reserved only for heroes.

▶ BEST ACTOR

WINNER:
Peter Finch *(Network)*
Other Nominees: Robert De Niro *(Taxi Driver)*, Giancarlo Giannini *(Seven Beauties)*, William Holden *(Network)*, Sylvester Stallone *(Rocky)*

▼

THE BEST CHOICE:
Robert De Niro *(Taxi Driver)*
Award-Worthy Runners-Up: Woody Allen *(The Front)*, Giancarlo Giannini *(Seven Beauties)*, William Holden *(Network)*, Walter Matthau *(The Bad News Bears)*, Sylvester Stallone *(Rocky)*, John Wayne *(The Shootist)*

Peter Finch was scheduled to promote himself for a Best Actor nomination and his film *Network* for a Best Picture nomination on *Good Morning America* on the morning he died of a heart attack. There were those who whispered the "Oscar Curse" was at work, but more likely it was the television gods who resented his appearance on the small screen to praise a film that railed against the boob tube. Finch, who died at sixty after having appeared in movies for forty years—in his native Australia, England (where he later resided), and the U.S.—became the first Best Actor to be given the award posthumously. In the Paddy Chayefsky–scripted, Sidney Lumet–directed drama, Finch played Howard Beale, a once serious newscaster who has a breakdown and becomes "The Angry Messiah of the Airwaves," host of his network's highest-rated program. As Beale, Finch got to deliver the still much-quoted battle cry "I'm mad as hell and I'm not going to take it anymore!" Yet Finch doesn't convince me that his Beale has enough charisma to catch the fancy of the public as did Andy Griffith in *A Face in the Crowd*. Anyway, Finch's role is a supporting one—he turns up every twenty minutes or so to rant and rave on television and then he disappears. William Holden, as Beale's best friend, is *Network*'s leading man and a much more legitimate candidate for Best Actor.

I suspect that if Finch's tragic death hadn't guaranteed him the sentimental vote, Sylvester Stallone would have prevailed as Best Actor. His shrewd, touching, and physical performance was chiefly responsible for *Rocky*'s amazing popularity. Also, one couldn't overlook his success at having created a hero for the masses, a character who would become a lasting part of our pop culture.

Nevertheless, I think the best performance of the year was by an actor playing not just another outsider, but a sociopath: Robert De Niro in Martin Scorsese's *Taxi Driver*. On the heels of *The Godfather, Part II,* for which he was voted Best Supporting Actor, De Niro's portrayal of Travis Bickle made him a full-fledged star.

Ex-marine Travis Bickle suffers from terrible headaches and stomach pains. Because he can't sleep he takes a job as a New York cabbie, driving endless hours to even the most dangerous parts of the city. He has no friends and spends his free time alone, watching soaps or porno movies, or writing in his journal about what a sewer the city is. He gets a crush on Betsy (Cybill Shepherd), a beautiful blonde who works on the presidential campaign of Charles Palantine (Leonard Harris). He convinces her to have coffee with him and later go to a movie, but when he takes her to a porno film, she walks out in disgust. When he goes to her office, her coworkers must drag him out. He screams that she'll die in hell. He tells an older cabbie (Peter Boyle) that he's getting funny ideas in his head. He buys several guns. He decides that he must get a twelve-year-old prostitute, Iris (Jodie Foster), away from her pimp, Sport (Harvey Keitel), and return her to her parents. Travis goes through rigorous physical training. He kills a holdup man. He decides to assassinate Palantine at a rally, but looks suspicious in his new mohawk and is chased away by secret service agents. He then "rescues" Iris, killing Sport and two other men. He is shot himself and spends time in a coma. The media concludes he is a hero. He is now at peace with himself. When Betsy hints she's interested in him now, he drives off into the night.

Screenwriter Paul Schrader based Travis on real-life diary-writing assassins, sociopaths in other movies, and

Robert De Niro is an alienated Vietnam vet who is driven to senseless violence in Martin Scorsese's *Taxi Driver.*

the impression the actor is improvising. Schrader says he often gets credit for De Niro's most famous improvised line, which is heard when Travis challenges a fantasized opponent in the mirror—"You talkin' to me?" As in *Mean Streets* his spontaneous verbal sparring with Harvey Keitel—here they play two lowlifes—is great; it is full of wit but is unnerving because we know there is a good chance for violence. Although the scene is ridiculous and I don't know if any of it was improvised, I also like Travis's annoying, overly friendly chat with Palantine's serious secret service agent, and how he smilingly introduces himself as Henry Kinkle.

We hear through Travis's narration what he writes in his journal, but it's surprising how much of the time Travis is silent on screen, even when driving passengers—his solitude might explain why he is so foolishly gabby in the company of Betsy and Iris. As we can tell from observing Travis as he sits and says nothing, listens to his passengers, observes what mayhem goes on outside his cab, trains for his assassination attempt, and conducts his rescue of Iris, De Niro doesn't need dialogue to grab hold of us, to draw us into his character's unhinged mind. His dimpled, insincere smile, his suspicious eyes (which he finally hides under shades), and his seemingly relaxed but actually primed-for-action body give us a creepy feeling. We await the explosion. Unlike a Jack Nicholson or Marlon Brando, De Niro's characters are too inarticulate to be effective if they explode verbally. So they must become physically destructive. It's hard not to respond with excitement to Travis's final rampage because the charismatic De Niro is in the part, Travis is so daring, and three vermin are wiped out. Unfortunately, the New York media in the film wasn't alone in thinking Travis a hero for his actions. Some viewers felt the same way. The filmmakers didn't make it clear enough that De Niro's racist, misogynist, fascist protagonist was not to be cheered. Hey, I even find myself every now and then leering cockily into a mirror with a pointed toothbrush in my hand and saying, "You talkin' to me?"

himself, while he was going through an isolated, alcoholic period. Still, there's much that is difficult to believe about Travis. This, along with its gruesome violence and unsavory subject matter, is a reason why the film was so controversial—even before we knew about John Hinckley's dangerous fixation on Jodie Foster. It's one thing to be irrational, it's another to be stupid, as Travis too often is. But my gripes about Travis's character have only to do with the script, not De Niro's performance.

This was De Niro's second film for Scorsese, following *Mean Streets,* in which he played Harvey Keitel's undisciplined friend, Johnny Boy. In that film he was an exciting presence; here he is mesmerizing. He has great dialogue scenes scattered through the picture in which his repeated phrases and questions—standard Schrader dialogue for inarticulate men in a Scorsese film—give one

---

▶ BEST ACTRESS

WINNER:
Faye Dunaway *(Network)*
Other Nominees: Marie-Christine Barrault *(Cousin, Cousine),* Talia Shire *(Rocky),* Sissy Spacek *(Carrie),* Liv Ullmann *(Face to Face)*

▼

THE BEST CHOICE:
Sissy Spacek *(Carrie)*
Award-Worthy Runners-Up: Faye Dunaway *(Network),* Audrey Hepburn *(Robin and Marian),* Glynnis O'Connor *(Ode to Billy Joe),* Liv Ullmann *(Face to Face)*

Eight years after bursting onto the scene with her best performance in *Bonnie and Clyde,* Faye Dunaway won

her only Oscar to date for her ambitious, ruthless, and brilliant television executive in *Network,* who talks shop

The three faces of Sissy Spacek as the ill-fated title character of Brian De Palma's *Carrie,* from the Stephen King novel.

while having sex and admits, "All I want out of life is a thirty share and a twenty rating." She gave one of her wittiest, sexiest, and—this was her specialty—coldest portrayals, and I think she was less mannered—her worst tendency—than her critics griped. I don't disagree with those who contend the Academy waited to give her an Oscar for playing an independent woman who is a monster—a slap at the women's movement—because that likely was one reason Louise Fletcher had received an Oscar for her Nurse Ratched the previous year. However, I won't make too much of that, since my own choice for Best Actress, Sissy Spacek, plays something akin to a monster (a freak?) in Brian De Palma's *Carrie.*

In De Palma's lively, terrifically cast adaptation of Stephen King's book (with a script by Lawrence Cohen), Spacek plays Carrie White, a teenager with secret telekinetic powers. Spacek is a painfully shy high school student living with her religious zealot mother (Piper Laurie), who constantly punishes her daughter and tells her to be wary of males. At school the naive Spacek is the butt of other girls' jokes and is ignored by the boys. Her sympathetic gym teacher (Betty Buckley) punishes several girls for teasing Spacek. One (Nancy Allen) vows revenge and enlists the aid of her stupid boyfriend (John Travolta). Another (Amy Irving) feels so bad that she convinces her handsome boyfriend (William Katt) to invite Spacek to the prom. The surprised Spacek is suspicious at first but agrees to the invitation, refusing to

listen to her mother's protests. She has a wonderful time at the prom and is thrilled when she is voted prom queen. But Allen and Travolta drop pig's blood on her as she's standing there on the stage. Humiliated and vengeful, Spacek uses her powers to lock the school doors and start a huge electrical fire. She kills Allen and Travolta as she walks home. At home she and her crazed mother fight it out, with both dying. Irving has nightmares about the dead girl pulling her into her grave.

As Carrie White, Spacek gave what remains the best performance in either teen pictures or teen horror films. However she had no hope of winning an Oscar because she was a virtual unknown appearing in a film that was a combination of two genres always ignored by the Academy. That she was nominated at all is quite remarkable and was the direct result of word spreading through Hollywood about De Palma's exciting "sleeper" (remember, neither he nor King was known to the masses yet) and a fascinating lead performance by that tiny, quirky Texas gal who had given a haunting portrayal a few years back in the cult favorite, *Badlands.*

Spacek was splendid as the sad, bewildered, insecure Carrie White, who is victimized by both her crazy, abusive mother and her cruel classmates. To play this isolated girl, Spacek supposedly stayed away from the others in the cast. On screen, it's painfully clear that the shy, troubled Carrie doesn't feel she fits in. She looks downward, hides herself behind messy hair, books, and sweaters, and whispers when she talks as if she's afraid she'll be yelled at or mocked. Spacek said she saw King's horror story as that of "a secret poet," who is unable to express herself verbally after so much mistreatment. Because she tries to suppress her need to communicate as well as her anger, and hasn't the courage or wherewithal to act on her desires (sexual, too, now that she has had her first period), she develops strong telekinetic powers. At last she can be aggressive and fight for herself. We're actually glad she has some means to seek revenge when the one happy night of her life is ruined by her mother and classmates.

My favorite scene in this perverse Cinderella tale is at the prom as Carrie dances with her handsome date and sits talking with him. Relaxed and being herself, and feeling pretty, she glows. Katt looks at her for the first time and is surprised to discover that his date is special, the gem among the clones. His response to Carrie reflects our own response to the young Sissy Spacek, who suddenly emerged in *Carrie*—a low-budget horror film—as one of the most gifted and unusual leading ladies of the era. We eagerly anticipated future roles . . . and she didn't disappoint us.

▶ BEST PICTURE

WINNER:
Annie Hall (United Artists; Woody Allen)
Other Nominees: *The Goodbye Girl, Julia, Star Wars, The Turning Point*

▼

THE BEST CHOICE:
Annie Hall (United Artists; Woody Allen)
Award-Worthy Runners-Up: *Close Encounters of the Third Kind* (Steven Spielberg); *Julia* (Fred Zinnemann), *Three Women* (Robert Altman)

Woody Allen's *Annie Hall* overcame the Academy's long-standing bias against comedies when it became the first to win the Academy Award for Best Picture since *Tom Jones* in 1963 and the first out-and-out American comedy to win it since *You Can't Take It with You* in 1938. And despite the film's anti–Los Angeles sentiment it also overcame the Academy's prejudice against New York films and filmmakers—although its New York cinematographer, Gordon Willis *(The Godfather, All the President's Men),* again was bypassed for a nomination. For the first time since 1967 the Academy agreed with the New York Film Critics on Best Picture. Allen was already the darling of New York critics, but the Academy's uncourted stamp of approval was the final confirmation that with *Annie Hall* he had moved in *everyone's* opinion into the highest echelon of filmmakers.

By picking this small character comedy that was only a modest box-office success, the Academy turned its back on George Lucas's operatic SF adventure, *Star Wars,* which had become the most popular film of all time and would change Hollywood product (in mostly bad ways) for years to come. A more legitimate contender for Best Picture would have been Steven Spielberg's SF epic, *Close Encounters of the Third Kind,* which glorified peace rather than war. But it went unnominated, perhaps to punish Columbia Studios after actor Cliff Robertson had correctly accused studio president David Begelman of signing bogus checks. Anyway, Spielberg's 1980 revision, with *The Special Edition* added to the title, is more deserving of a Best Picture Oscar. I think the one picture that rivaled *Annie Hall* was Fred Zinnemann's tense political drama *Julia,* with Jane Fonda as Lillian Hellman and Vanessa Redgrave as her fascist-fighting best friend. But it would be almost criminal to take the award away from one of the most beloved films ever made.

Comic Alvy Singer, a neurotic, cynical New York Jewish intellectual, looks back on his relationship with aspiring singer Annie Hall (Diane Keaton won an Oscar), a neurotic and naive WASP from Wisconsin. Interestingly, the Oscar-winning script by Allen and Marshall Brickman was much shorter than their shooting script. Much more material was shot. The film (originally titled *Anhedonia*) was intended to be an autobiographical, Felliniesque exploration of Alvy's life, in which this always unhappy writer evaluates his work and past and current life, including romances. But extensive editing was done (mostly of surreal episodes), cutting the film down to just ninety-three minutes (making it the shortest Best Picture winner). What remained was a bittersweet remembrance of the failed romance between Alvy and Annie—which was meant to parallel that between onetime lovers Allen and Keaton—and a thank-you tribute to Annie/Keaton. True, Allen retained scenes of Alvy with his two former wives (played by Janet Margolin and Carol Kane) and with a strange humorless date (Shelley Duvall), and scenes of young Alvy with his bickering parents, but only so we understand Alvy's expectations from women and marriage at the time he falls for Annie.

Few relationships in film are explored with as much humor, emotion, and perception as that between Alvy and Annie. We see it from Alvy's perspective, but often Allen the filmmaker reveals what Alvy doesn't see. Alvy remembers the wonderful moments of awkward courtship, the romance (I love it when, early on their first date, Woody stops Annie on the street and kisses her so they won't be anxious about doing it later), the laughter, the support, the rejection, the zaniness, the tears, the vulnerability, the loss of passion and intensity on her part, the enduring love. They were a couple doomed by sexual hangups, misunderstandings, disappointments, Alvy's jealousy and possessiveness, and mutually neurotic, irrational behavior. They could never relax. Significantly, when Alvy looks back he blames himself and not Annie for what went wrong—similarly, the noncritical Allen is more interested in making us see why Annie/Keaton was so lovable than in emphasizing her contribution to the

Woody Allen returns to his childhood, with Tony Roberts and Diane Keaton as companions, in *Annie Hall*.

breakup. Alvy's crime was to refuse to change himself (to forget his death phobia for just a minute, to be less demanding of her) while insisting on improving the *perfect* Annie. Like many intellectual males he played mentor to a naive female pupil, making her feel insecure about her lack of knowledge. But when she had learned enough, she wisely broke free from his destructive hold on her. It's touching that Alvy has no animosity toward her and is glad he knew her. He tells us that relationships are "irrational, crazy, and absurd," but they're worth any suffering they cause. Annie was worth it.

It was a sweet touch that Allen named the film *Annie Hall* (Keaton's real name is Diane Hall, and her nickname Annie) instead of "Alvy Singer" or even "Alvy and Annie." It almost made up for Allen's need to be in almost every shot—even when Annie goes to her psychiatrist, Allen splits the screen so we see Alvy with his own psychiatrist. At least, Allen was willing, for the first time, to let his other actors, especially Keaton, *act,* and be funny on their own. Keaton had been funny in both *Sleeper* and *Love and Death,* but this was the first time that her humor came from herself and not from Allen. This was a significant breakthrough for Allen in working with actresses.

With *Annie Hall* Allen became a more imaginative, technically proficient filmmaker and a more sophisticated writer-director. He was now secure enough to cut back on easy laughs and outrageous sight gags. Now instead of making us laugh by presenting us with preposterous characters and completely absurd situations, he did so by showing real people acting in preposterous ways and by revealing the absurdity of life and relationships. He even toned down his own character, presenting the figure that most Allen fans think is closest to Allen. Annie, too, is slightly off the wall, but despite her unusual attire and her ordering corned beef with white bread and mayonnaise, she is real and endearing. We take the

relationship between Annie and Alvy seriously because they are real people. And we feel very sad when they split up.

But we laugh through it all. There are many memorably hilarious moments in *Annie Hall.* There's the scene in which Annie sends Alvy to her tub to kill a spider that he thinks "is as big as a Buick." I love, too, Alvy's expression as he's being driven to the airport by Annie's weird brother (Christopher Walken), who recently confessed to him that he's been tempted to provoke a head-on collision. And when Shelley Duvall tells the sore-jawed Allen that "sex with you is a Kafkaesque experience. . . . I mean that as a compliment." Perhaps the best scene in the movie has the flirting Annie and Alvy trying to fake through an intellectual conversation on photography, while Allen's subtitles reveals Annie thinking, *He probably thinks I'm a yo-yo,* and Allen thinking, *I wonder what she looks like naked.*

Then there's the moment when Grammy Hall looks at Alvy and, Allen shows us, sees him as an Hassidic Jew, with a long black beard, curls, black hat, and black frock coat. Everyone loves another surrealistic moment when Alvy pulls Marshall McLuhan from behind a poster to refute the absurd interpretation of his work being given by a blowhard professor in a movie line. "If life were only like this," says the triumphant Alvy. In the movie Allen also makes cracks about life, death, art, drugs (he sneezes $2,000 worth of cocaine across a room), health food (in California he orders mashed yeast), sex, therapy, New York culture, and Los Angeles "culture." His view of Los Angeles, with its blinding sun and mellow, lamebrain types, is so devastating that it's a wonder Academy voters took it so good-naturedly. Alvy gets physically sick while going to L.A. to pick up an award. Which may explain why on Academy Award night, Allen was back in New York.

▶ BEST ACTOR

WINNER:
Richard Dreyfuss *(The Goodbye Girl)*
Other Nominees: Woody Allen *(Annie Hall)*, Richard Burton *(Equus)*, Marcello Mastroianni *(A Special Day)*, John Travolta
(Saturday Night Fever)

▼

THE BEST CHOICE:
John Travolta *(Saturday Night Fever)*
Award-Worthy Runners-Up: Woody Allen *(Annie Hall)*, Richard Dreyfuss *(The Goodbye Girl)*, Paul Newman *(Slap Shot)*, Craig
Russell *(Outrageous!)*

Short in size but large in stature, Richard Dreyfuss has been one of our most appealing, offbeat leading men for two decades. In 1977 he had his most successful year, winning the Best Actor Oscar for Herbert Ross's *The Goodbye Girl* and starring in one of the most profitable films of all time, Steven Spielberg's *Close Encounters of the Third Kind*. If his worst moments had been excised from both films, he'd have deserved two Oscars—in fact, Spielberg cut out his aggravating Jack Lemmon–like destruction scene for his film's 1980 "Special Edition." As they stood, however, I'm not sure he deserved one for either film. He does have great comic moments in the Neil Simon film, as a struggling actor who moves in with single mother Marsha Mason and her child, Quinn Cummings. But there are some moments when he seems to be acting on a stage, others when he's mannered, and others when he is obviously loving his own performance—at those moments he's even more obnoxious than his tactless character at his worst.

My choice for Best Actor of 1977 is John Travolta, who, like Dreyfuss, starred in what is now a dated film, *Saturday Night Fever*. The last thing I want to do is remember the disco craze, but Travolta's performance is still electrifying.

Produced by Robert Stigwood and directed by John Badham, *Saturday Night Fever* was based on a *New York* magazine article titled "Tribal Rites of the New Saturday Night," about Brooklyn youths who spent weeknights dancing to the disco beat. Travolta is Tony, a nineteen-year-old Catholic who works in a paint store, wastes time with his unmotivated, high-energy, girl-crazy male pals, and spends all his money at the 2001: Odyssey nightclub, where he is the king of the dance floor. His home life is a mess, with his critical father out of work and his mother always complaining, so he finds his rewards at the 2001. He wants to escape Brooklyn and make it big, but without an education, he thinks dancing is his only hope. He wants to win a prestigious dance contest at the 2001. He becomes partner to the classier and slightly more knowledgeable Stephanie (Karen Lynn Gorney). She mocks him at first, calling him a cliché, but eventually discovers his good qualities. They learn to respect each other. They win the contest, but Tony knows it was only because the runners-up are outsiders, and he gives the first-prize

trophy to them. When Tony tries to force himself on Stephanie she breaks off their relationship. Tony becomes fed up with his friends' sexual antics and mindless gang-fights and is upset when one falls to his death. He flees to Manhattan to see Stephanie. He says he wants to find work there and will need her to be his friend. She agrees to be his friend.

There was doubt that Travolta could make the transition from television, where he'd built up a following as Vinnie Barbarino in the high school comedy *Welcome*

John Travolta, dancing with Karen Lynn Gorney, caused a sensation in *Saturday Night Fever,* his first starring role.

Back, Kotter. But in his first movie lead (he'd been funny in a secondary role in *Carrie*) he became the sensation of the year, a magazine cover boy and sex symbol. The movie is shallow and the leading lady can't act, but Travolta is an exciting presence. He's great out on the dance floor, making sexual moves to the Bee Gees that have the females in the 2001 sighing, but he's just as much fun to watch while strutting down the street as if he knows everyone is watching, or gazing at himself in the mirror—a moment of narcissism for a young boy without much self-esteem. Although he plays someone whose cocky attitude takes getting used to—"You make it with some of these chicks, they think you gotta dance with them"—Travolta is completely captivating. He has sweet, puppy-dog eyes, a sheepish face, and a delivery that starts out aggressive but ends up sounding hurt or defensive, as if he expects to be put down. And he smiles so appreciatively if he gets a compliment, as when his boss gives him a raise, and when Stephanie admits he's interesting and even intelligent. We empathize with him

for feeling his depth of knowledge is mighty shallow (he pretends to know Laurence Olivier, saying "Oh, *him*— oh, he's good") and for his fears that he won't be able to realize his dreams because his only skill is dancing. Whereas most male directors concentrate only on female dancers' physicality, Badham wasn't ashamed to exploit Travolta's sexual appeal in the same manner in which Emile Ardolino would exploit Patrick Swayze's in *Dirty Dancing* ten years later. But I'm equally glad that he also explored Travolta's sensitivity, which remains his most appealing trait. For those who still missed James Dean and Montgomery Clift, it was good to see an emotional young actor on the screen again.

Travolta had two more major successes, *Grease* and *Urban Cowboy,* which also exploited his youth, lithe body, sensitivity, and dancing skills, before a string of box-office failures turned him into a young has-been. Today John Travolta is middle aged, dating us all. It's just hard to believe that so many years have passed since he gave everyone an infectious dose of *Saturday Night Fever.*

► BEST ACTRESS

WINNER:
Diane Keaton *(Annie Hall)*
Other Nominees: Anne Bancroft *(The Turning Point),* Jane Fonda *(Julia),* Shirley MacLaine *(The Turning Point),* Marsha Mason *(The Goodbye Girl)*

▼

THE BEST CHOICE:
Diane Keaton *(Annie Hall)*
Award-Worthy Runners-Up: Anne Bancroft *(The Turning Point),* Shelley Duvall *(Three Women),* Jane Fonda *(Julia),* Diane Keaton *(Looking for Mister Goodbar),* Shirley MacLaine *(The Turning Point),* Sissy Spacek *(Three Women)*

The nominations for Best Actress in 1977 were the strongest of the decade, with former winners Jane Fonda and Anne Bancroft competing with the too-long-neglected Shirley MacLaine and two of the most popular and respected actresses of the period: Diane Keaton and Marsha Mason. Brilliant performances in Robert Altman's perplexing *Three Women* by Sissy Spacek and, even better, Cannes Festival winner Shelley Duvall—as a chatterbox without any personality who has her identity stolen by the admiring Spacek—couldn't even make the Academy's list. There was even another unnominated performance that was at least equal to Diane Keaton's Oscar-winning portrayal in *Annie Hall.* Oddly, it was also by Keaton, in *Looking for Mister Goodbar.* Keaton's sexually uninhibited, all-nerves-bared portrait of a self-loathing, doomed singles-bar swinger was stunning, but she wasted the effort because Richard Brooks's film of Judith Rossner's sensational best-seller fell apart around her. Anyway, moviegoers who were so charmed by *Annie Hall* and her performance as the title character want to identify Keaton more with the Woody Allen comedy than

with a messy drama in which her character is knifed to death.

Annie Hall has come to New York from Wisconsin. She hopes to be a singer but has no confidence. Single and lonely, she is excited to meet Jewish comedian Alvy Singer. She is at a loss over what to say or do when he comes to her apartment. He is completely taken with her. They become a couple and move in together. He encourages her singing, which improves. He also pressures her into reading books and seeing movies about death (his obsession), seeing a therapist, and attending adult-education classes. She feels that he doesn't think her intelligent or knowledgeable enough for him. Her interest in sex wanes, much to his chagrin. She senses that he wants to control her so much that she won't even have her own feelings. At one point she breaks up with him, but gets lonely and asks him back. They go to Los Angeles. He hates it, she loves it. Afterward they decide to split up. She goes back to Los Angeles to work on an album. He misses her so much that he goes there after her. She tells him she isn't sure she loves him anymore. He returns to

Diane Keaton and Woody Allen are a loving but mismatched couple in *Annie Hall*.

New York alone. She will eventually move back to New York and they'll have a comfortable reunion. But they won't get back together. Alvy still feels lucky he knew her.

Diane Keaton's Annie Hall was the first multidimensional woman in Allen's work. At the beginning of the relationship Annie was an unformed character, as is reflected in her mismatched men's clothing—a polka-dot tie, vest, a loose-fitting shirt and baggy chinos, and funny hat. Keaton shows us that she is insecure about her singing talent and her level of intelligence when she enters a relationship with Alvy. Then she lets us see that he has initiated positive changes in her, making her more confident, knowledgeable, and independent. But then he starts to feel insecure himself, and abandoned, and tries to reel her in and take control again. The "improved," wiser Annie knows better than to stay in a stifling, argumentative relationship with a man who has a death phobia and refuses to enjoy life, even if he does provide her with security. Although it makes us sad, we support Annie's decision to break free and begin a new, less pressured life of her own, in which she's entitled to make mistakes, and her body and her feelings are her own. We support Annie because the likable Keaton makes us trust her motives. It takes Alvy time to come around, but even he eventually concedes that she made the right decision.

Keaton had been sexy and funny in her previous films with Allen, *Play It Again, Sam* (directed by Herbert Ross), *Sleeper,* and *Love and Death,* but in *Annie Hall* she finally emerged to the forefront. Allen had learned to trust her

so completely that he let her contribute much to Annie's character and humor. He was even willing to play straight man to her in several scenes: when Annie clumsily asks Alvy if he wants a ride home from the tennis club; when she tells a long, inappropriately jolly story about her narcoleptic relative who fell asleep and died. Annie was the first truly complex woman in Allen's work. Since he based her on Keaton at the time of their romance—Keaton's real name is Diane Hall and her nickname was Annie—she felt confident to contribute ideas to the characterization. Whereas in earlier films she simply played parts for Allen, this time she invested herself in Annie, providing her not only with wit but also with vulnerability, insecurity, naiveté, and quirkiness. She's nice, unprejudiced, klutzy, and so neurotic that her therapist wants to see her daily.

Annie is one of the most endearing of screen heroines. You'll take to her just watching her express herself to Alvy: she looks every which way as she babbles, starting sentences but dropping them after a few nonsensical words and trying again, admonishing herself for her inability to communicate, tossing in "God!" and "Yeah" and "Oh, dear," and Grammy Hall's "La-dee-dah," her arms akimbo; she never curses, she says things are "neat." Allen lets us see Keaton at her most beautiful and lovable, revealing those idiosyncrasies, mannerisms, and expressions he adored. He makes us understand why Alvy would love her so much—and why he thought any man would fall in love with Diane Keaton.

1978

▶ BEST PICTURE

WINNER:
The Deer Hunter (EMI Films/Universal; Michael Cimino)
Other Nominees: *Coming Home, Heaven Can Wait, Midnight Express, An Unmarried Woman*

▼

THE BEST CHOICE:
Coming Home (United Artists; Hal Ashby)
Award-Worthy Runners-Up: *Go Tell the Spartans* (Ted Post), *Interiors* (Woody Allen)

By 1978 sufficient time had passed since the end of the Vietnam War for weak-kneed Hollywood studios finally to make films about it. Written by Wendell Mayes during the war, the rarely screened sleeper *Go Tell the Spartans,* set in 1964 before America's escalated involvement, is still, with the possible exception of *Platoon,* the best anti–Vietnam War film showing our soldiers in combat. Conceived before the conclusion of the war, Hal Ashby's *Coming Home,* a cross between *The Best Years of Our Lives* and *Born on the Fourth of July,* is still the best anti–Vietnam War film about returning vets. But the Best Picture award went to Michael Cimino's apolitical con-job, *The Deer Hunter,* which for some reason many viewers considered an eye-opener about the war, when even Cimino admitted it was an "unreal," surreal portrait. In fact, Cimino's film is condescending to its three white characters (we're supposed to understand better what happens to onetime POWS Robert De Niro, Christopher Walken, and John Savage than they do themselves) and racist toward all Vietnamese; moreover he uses a false event—the Cong guards force the three friends to play "Russian roulette"—to give us our impression of the hellish war. None of the men has his political consciousness raised, and the same goes for people who watch this film ("war is harrowing," and "the Vietnamese are savages" is all one comes away with). On the other hand, *Coming Home,* my choice for Best Picture, deals with issues that are still timely, such as our government and military's insensitivity and indifference toward Vietnam vets with physical and/or psychological problems.

It is 1968 in California. Jane Fonda is the straitlaced, obedient wife of a chauvinistic, hawkish career marine, Bruce Dern. When he excitedly goes to Vietnam, expecting to be a hero, she becomes a volunteer at a veterans' hospital, although she knows Dern would object. She is shocked at how inadequate is the care and concern for these men who were physically or psychologically damaged in combat. Jon Voight is a wheelchair-confined paraplegic she tends. He believes U.S. involvement in the war is wrong and not worth the damage being done to young men, and that the returning vets are being ignored by the system. Fonda and Voight are attracted to each other, but she remains true to her husband. She goes to Hong Kong to visit Dern when he has leave. He is disillusioned by this "boring war" in which his men act like animals and there is no attempt by the military to achieve victory. He is jealous because she is working with men in the hospital. Both have changed and there is a wall between them. Fonda returns to California on the night Voight is arrested for chaining himself to a Marine recruitment center gate to protest the suicide of a friend at the hospital. She wants to make love to him. She has her first orgasm. Fonda and Voight fall in love, but when

Jane Fonda is the straitlaced wife of career soldier Bruce Dern in Hal Ashby's *Coming Home.*

Dern returns, she goes back to him. Dern is completely unprepared for civilian life, especially considering that he never did have the chance to be a hero. Dern is informed by the FBI of his wife's affair with Voight. Confused and disoriented, he threatens to shoot them both, but Voight talks him out of it. While Voight speaks to high school kids about why they shouldn't enlist, and Fonda goes shopping for her dinner with Dern, Dern walks into the ocean and drowns.

Waldo Salt and Robert C. Jones won an Oscar for their screenplay for *Coming Home,* although Nancy Dowd, who got "story" credit, vocally complained to anyone who would listen that Fonda (whose IPC company produced the picture) destroyed her original script. Dowd said her original was much more political, which I assume means it didn't allow the focus of the film to drift from the government's mistreatment of disabled vets to the love story of Fonda and Voight. But I think the film is powerful enough still to have tremendous impact more than a dozen years later, and quite brave considering it was Hollywood's first anti–Vietnam War film. It's hard not to be deeply affected when Voight sits in his wheelchair telling young high school kids—crying at one point—that he doesn't want them to be fooled by marine recruiters like he was at their age: "I have killed for my country . . . and I don't feel good about it. 'Cause there's not enough reason. . . . And there's a lot of shit that I did over there that I find fuckin' hard to live with. . . ." One might have thought Voight, who didn't fight in the war, was just a propaganda mouthpiece, if one hadn't seen the wrenching documentary *Winter Soldier,* in which similar weeping, guilty Veterans Against the Vietnam War confess the war crimes they and their fellow soldiers committed in the name of America. The point made is that no one can justify a war that is condemned by physically or psychologically disabled vets like Voight, the ones who most need to know that their participation wasn't for nothing. "If we want to commit suicide we have plenty of reasons to do it right here at home," he says. "We don't have to go to Vietnam and find reasons for us to kill ourselves. I just don't think we should be over there. . . ."

Significantly, *Coming Home,* like the antiwar movement itself, was not against U.S. *soldiers,* even against hawks like Dern. The film is against the military brass and government who show concern for our young men only during the recruitment and training processes. It is a persuasive plea for more caring treatment for *all* returning soldiers, whether they are physically injured, thoroughly disillusioned by their war experiences, or having difficulty adjusting to wives, the changing rhythm of civilian life, and a country filled with war protestors. Startlingly, we end up with more sympathy for Dern—his *pain* breaks your heart—than for anyone else. Unlike

Voight, whose anger was tempered by Fonda's understanding, Dern hurts too much to wait patiently for Fonda to heal him.

Long-haired Hal Ashby, a terrific, too-often-forgotten major director of the period *(Harold and Maude, The Last Detail, Shampoo, Bound for Glory, Being There),* makes sure we aren't passive viewers. As we watch, we imagine the smells that permeate every setting; and we imagine sharing whatever body sensations the characters on screen are having, whether painful or sensual. Everything in this movie is physical. Ashby made this film with characteristic sensitivity and without a trace of the condescension toward its characters that marred *The Deer Hunter.* (One exception: his dim view of the prim and too-proper soldiers' wives who reject Fonda's suggestion to include an article about the mistreatment of disabled vets in the base newspaper.) Ashby got believable, heartfelt, deeply moving performances from all his actors (Penelope Milford, as Fonda's hippie friend, was nominated for Best Supporting Actress). It's obvious that he feels tremendous warmth for the characters played by Voight and Fonda, who use each other's unexpected love to help them break their respective bonds (the stigma of being in a wheelchair, a repressive marriage) and achieve self-esteem. Significantly, we readily accept the increasingly liberated Fonda having an adulterous affair. We don't condemn her for seeking happiness. The Voight-Fonda love scene is justifiably famous, for it remains one of the two or three most erotic in movie history. *Both* the naked Voight and Fonda look beautiful and sexy. She turns off the light, he tells her to turn it on: "I want to see you." She asks, "What should I do?" He answers calmly, "Everything. I want you to do everything." What he can't feel, he explains, he sees, and that excites him. It is exciting to us that they talk and they explore. And, as he performs cunnilingus, Fonda has her first orgasm. Her acting's so convincing when expressing sexual excitement and satisfaction, that one can't help—at least I can't—wondering how the actress's offscreen lovers have been affected when they see this scene.

While the issue of inadequate care provided to Vietnam vets has not disappeared, *Coming Home* sends one back in time. Ironically, the blaring music on the soundtrack—a lot of Stones, some Beatles, the Chambers Brothers, et cetera—and the loose, fast cinematography by Haskell Wexler, doesn't zoom us back to 1978, when the film was made, but to a few years earlier, when the war was being fought. *Coming Home* was slightly dated when it came out a few years after it should have been made. But now, if we look at the screen rather than the release date, we assume that it's the only Hollywood movie that accurately documented that momentous time in America as it was happening.

▶ BEST ACTOR

WINNER:
Jon Voight *(Coming Home)*
Other Nominees: Warren Beatty *(Heaven Can Wait)*, Gary Busey *(The Buddy Holly Story)*, Robert De Niro *(The Deer Hunter)*, Laurence Olivier *(The Boys from Brazil)*

▼

THE BEST CHOICE:
Jon Voight *(Coming Home)*
Award-Worthy Runners-Up: Gary Busey *(The Buddy Holly Story)*, Dustin Hoffman *(Straight Time)*, Harvey Keitel *(Fingers)*, Tim McIntire *(American Hot Wax)*

Paraplegic ex-marine Luke Martin in *Coming Home* was one of the first movie heroes to voice disapproval of United States involvement in the Vietnam War. Because it would be a controversial part, United Artists wanted to cast an extremely popular actor so that even conservative audiences would tolerate his viewpoint. Jack Nicholson, Al Pacino, and Sylvester Stallone, fresh from his *Rocky* success, were approached but no deal was consummated. That's when Jane Fonda, whose IPC company was producing the film, and producer Jerome Hellman, who'd made *Midnight Cowboy* with Jon Voight, asked UA executive Mike Medavoy to accept Voight in the role. It was a few years since *Midnight Cowboy* and *Deliverance,* and Voight's star was in one of its periodic declines, which is why Medavoy offered extra money to persuade them to find another leading man. But Fonda and Hellman stuck with Voight because they realized that his strong antiwar credentials bonded him with Luke and that his dedication to his craft guaranteed he'd do the research necessary to both get into the head of and physically function as this angry wheelchair-bound vet. Voight rewarded their confidence with one of the best performances of the decade, earning him 1978's Best Actor Oscar.

Luke was a high school quarterback when he was convinced by marine recruiters to enlist and do his tour of duty in Vietnam. He doesn't tell old war stories, just saying his debilitating injury happened "a long time ago." But he is angry that he gave up his body in a war that he now believes America shouldn't be participating in. And he is angry at the inadequate treatment provided for him and the other patients at a California veterans hospital. In fact, he has tantrums. Luke's anger is softened by a caring volunteer nurse, Sally Hyde (Fonda), whose hawkish marine husband, Bob (Bruce Dern), is off in Vietnam. They become lovers and his life has new meaning. Then Bob returns and Sally goes back to him. But Bob has psychological problems, and when he finds out about the affair, he almost shoots Sally and Luke. But Luke talks him out of it, saying that won't solve his problems. Luke leaves. He goes to high schools and tries to tell students they shouldn't enlist. Unable to adjust, Bob kills himself.

Voight plays his character with intelligence, sensitivity, honesty, an amazing degree of restraint, and dignity. The role was hard to play for several reasons. Luke is in a wheelchair yet must come across as physically fit and sexually desirable. He must display hostility and rage, yet still seem reasonable and not scare viewers into thinking he shouldn't be welcomed back into society. He must elicit audience sympathy for all disabled vets by complaining about his own treatment, yet not display self-pity. He must cry and make it seem like a *strong* act. He is not, as we first assume, completely self-absorbed, but a very compassionate man. Voight manages control over this character who fights for self-control. Actually, what Luke needs is recognition that he is still a human being, a man, someone who can give other patients good support, give youngsters good counsel, and give Sally good

Jon Voight's Luke Martin and Jane Fonda's Sally Hyde spend their final, tearful moments together before her husband's return from the war in *Coming Home.*

loving. He turns out to be one of the nicest, most admirable, most desirable of movie heroes.

Voight catches your attention with his ranting and his racing about in his gurney and, later, his wheelchair. But his finest moments come when he is still and composed, being thoughtful and caring: when he visits Sally's for dinner, and has her confirm her invitation had nothing to do with charity, he smiles and says, "I'm just very happy to be *here*"; and when they sit outside, she on the ground in front of his chair, he tells her of how he still walks in his dreams; and when Bob points a gun at his head, demanding, "Say something else, fuck!" in a way that lets you know he will shoot Luke if he doesn't say exactly the correct words, Luke calmly—without patronizing Bob—says exactly the correct words: "I'm not the enemy. You know the enemy is the fucking war." It's a great moment, when two seemingly different men completely understand each other, and even like each other (despite being romantic rivals) because they have had a horrible shared experience. Voight's final great scene is his talk to high school students about how the Vietnam War "ain't like in the movies." He cries about what he saw and what he did and has to live with, but tells them that he doesn't feel self-pity, just worry that they will believe recruiters and go to war and also suffer. So convincing is Voight—who speaks from the heart for all the vets he met while researching the role—that this clip should be part of every high school's recruitment-day program.

On Academy Award night the camera caught Voight in the audience being completely blown away by Laurence Olivier's beautifully delivered, if nonsensical, acceptance speech for a Life Achievement Award. It must have seemed strange to Voight to defeat Olivier soon after in the voting for Best Actor. But for the performance Voight gave in *Coming Home,* probably even the great Olivier was in awe.

▶ BEST ACTRESS

WINNER:
Jane Fonda *(Coming Home)*
Other Nominees: Ingrid Bergman *(Autumn Sonata),* Ellen Burstyn *(Same Time, Next Year),* Jill Clayburgh *(An Unmarried Woman),* Geraldine Page *(Interiors)*

▼

THE BEST CHOICE:
Jill Clayburgh *(An Unmarried Woman)*
Award-Worthy Runners-Up: Jane Fonda *(Coming Home),* Melanie Mayron *(Girlfriends)*

Many Hollywood insiders predicted that Ingrid Bergman would be selected Best Actress of 1978 for Ingmar Bergman's mother-daughter (Liv Ullmann) talkfest, *Autumn Sonata.* Bergman had won the New York Film Critics award. However, it appeared from the start that the real Oscar competition was between Jane Fonda for Hal Ashby's *Coming Home* and Jill Clayburgh for Paul Mazursky's *An Unmarried Woman.* Just as the Academy in 1956 gave Bergman an Oscar for *Anastasia* to confirm that Hollywood, which had demeaned and banished her, had finally forgiven Bergman for her illicit affair with Roberto Rossellini, the current Academy members gave the Oscar to Jane Fonda to show Hollywood was no longer hostile to the actress whom many had called a traitor during the Vietnam War. That she had starred in a film dealing with Vietnam made her award that much more gratifying to her, perhaps as vindication of her antiestablishment stance in the light of the Pentagon Papers revelations and Watergate. But would she have won if Clayburgh weren't a New York actress and *An Unmarried Woman* hadn't been a distinctly New York film? And did it make a difference that Fonda's character returns to her soldier husband despite loving someone else, while Clayburgh's character refuses to take her roaming husband back now that she is having an affair of her own? And did it make a difference that Clayburgh's character won't even settle down with the artist with whom she has an affair? Considering all the male voters in the Academy, I suspect that it did.

Erica (Clayburgh) and Martin (Michael Murphy) are a middle-class New York couple who have a fifteen-year-old daughter, Patti (Lisa Lucas). Erica is content, working in an art gallery, having lunches with her three female friends, being mother to a funny, savvy teenager, and having the security of a man who makes a good living, still loves her, and is a good sexual partner. But he unexpectedly admits he's having an affair with a twenty-six-year-old, whom he wants to marry. He moves out. Erica is crushed. She is depressed, lonely, furious, and disoriented. She can't stand men, especially those who make passes at her. She even kicks Patti's boyfriend out of the apartment, while in a fit of hysteria over a man who made a pass earlier—and feeling jealous, too, over her daughter's relationship. She goes to a therapist, where she has many tearful sessions. Her therapist convinces her to get back into the flow of life, and to date again. After a one-nighter she has an affair with Saul (Alan Bates), a divorced British artist with two children. He is a

Jill Clayburgh has found an ideal lover in Alan Bates's artist, but isn't sure whether to remain single or commit herself to him in Paul Mazursky's *An Unmarried Woman.*

nice man, a good lover, and treats her with respect. She rejects Martin when he wants to come home. Still, she won't commit herself to Saul. She wants time alone to feel what it's like to be independent. They amicably part for the summer.

I first saw and was impressed by Jill Clayburgh when she played a young, endangered New York streetwalker in a powerful made-for-television movie, *Hustling.* She was so convincing that I, not knowing she came from a wealthy family and went to Sarah Lawrence, couldn't imagine her doing comedy, being glamorous, or playing an educated, responsible middle-class wife and mother. But in the female leads that followed—the truly lousy *Gable and Lombard, Silver Streak* with Richard Pryor and Gene Wilder, and *Semi-Tough* with Burt Reynolds and Kris Kristofferson—she proved she could do all of this; and as Erica in *An Unmarried Woman* she did do all of this exceptionally well.

Mazursky's seriocomedy was hailed as a groundbreaking feminist film—an easy tag to put on a picture about a woman achieving independence—but considering that the women's movement had been going strong for a good eight years, its long-overdue theme was daring only by Hollywood standards. (*Alice Doesn't Live Here Anymore* would have qualified in 1974 if Ellen Burstyn's widow didn't decide to stay with Kris Kristofferson's rancher.) According to Mazursky (in an interview with Terry Curtis Fox), "*An Unmarried Woman* is about the subtle place a lot of women find themselves in. I wanted to do a movie about the middle-class women who have happy lives, a lot of opportunity, for whom things are good—but who in essence, are psychological slaves. They

really live through their husbands, through the man. . . . *An Unmarried Woman* is . . . about accepting being on your own. It doesn't mean being lonely, or being alone forever. It's accepting that it's okay in this society to be on your own."

It takes months of repairing the damage left by her husband's sudden departure before Erica is happy to be alone. Clayburgh makes us feel her confusion and humiliation; her anger; her loneliness; her initial hatred and distrust of all men; her irrational jealousy toward her daughter for having a boyfriend, and her worry that her "baby" is getting involved with someone of the heartless gender; her desperate need to work herself out of her dark abyss by seeing a therapist; her timidity and distrust around new men; her curiosity about how she'll respond sexually to a new man after seventeen years with one lover, and her improved self-image when she proves a good lover to a one-night stand (Cliff Gorman); her realization that she is a desirable woman because of her mutually satisfying relationship with a friendly, handsome artist, Saul (Alan Bates)—she walks through his loft, amazed that "I'm happy!"; and her final delighted discovery that she has gained control of her life for the first time and that being alone and single is scary but exciting. Many viewers couldn't understand why Erica wouldn't marry Saul, when he (as played by Bates) seems like the man of most women's dreams. But we agree with her decision to be independent because we see she has blossomed while alone. Though she hadn't noticed, we could tell that her role in her marriage was not enviable. When Michael steps in dog shit and she cleans his sneaker, you know something's drastically wrong.

Except for when Erica gets the urge to dance around her apartment in her underwear, and her tearful therapy sessions, Clayburgh doesn't have any big moments. But she is good in scene after scene, revealing more and more of her character. Erica is flawed but learns to accept her imperfections. She's also funny, so strong willed that she won't say yes to Saul, and so sexy that we find her enticing several moments after she throws up on screen (when Martin breaks the bad news). Clayburgh makes the one-night-stand sequence—during which Erica is too embarrassed to strip with the lights on, and she bursts out laughing upon being touched, only to quickly respond with passion—painful, humorous, and erotic. It's the scene in which Erica breaks out of her depression and Clayburgh completely wins us over.

I think the performances by Clayburgh and Fonda were of equal quality. But I wish Clayburgh had won the Oscar. Not only for playing what was considered a pivotal woman's role of the era, but also because Clayburgh's stay at the top was so brief (her films went downhill after *Luna, Starting Over,* and *It's My Turn*) that the award would be a strong reminder that she was there at all.

1979

► BEST PICTURE

WINNER:
Kramer vs. Kramer (Columbia; Robert Benton)
Other Nominees: *All That Jazz, Apocalypse Now, Breaking Away, Norma Rae*

▼

THE BEST CHOICE:
Manhattan (United Artists; Woody Allen)
Award-Worthy Runners-Up: *Breaking Away* (Peter Yates), *Norma Rae* (Martin Ritt)

Nineteen seventy-nine was an unusually fine year for movies. While I think only three films were special enough to be considered for Best Picture—*Manhattan, Breaking Away,* and *Norma Rae*—there were several that I rank only a notch or two below them in quality: *Kramer vs. Kramer,* which was the Academy's Oscar winner, *The China Syndrome, Being There, The Black Stallion, A Little Romance, "10", Alien, Agatha, Over the Edge, Quadrophenia, The Onion Field, Saint Jack,* and *North Dallas Forty.* Even *The Wanderers, The Warriors,* and *The Europeans* (not a gang picture) deserved honorable mention. And *All That Jazz,* Bob Fosse's stylized autobiographical musical, and *Apocalypse Now,* Francis Ford Coppola's overblown Vietnam saga, had many admirers. In fact, both were nominated for the Oscar, but lost to Robert Benton's simpler drama. *Kramer vs. Kramer,* about a self-obsessed man who finds happiness raising the child he doesn't know after his wife leaves him, benefited from fine acting by Dustin Hoffman (Best Actor) and Meryl Streep (Best Supporting Actress). But it is annoying how it goes overboard in championing this man who simply does what women do as a matter of course. The Academy felt it had done its bits for Woody Allen in 1977, when it gave its Best Picture Oscar to the New York filmmaker for *Annie Hall.* Perhaps because he did include a sequence in Los Angeles, even if it was derogatory. However, a movie titled *Manhattan,* made in black and white—maybe a backhanded slap at commercial Hollywood—didn't stand a chance.

Manhattan received only one nomination, for the original screenplay written by Allen and Marshall Brickman (who had won for *Annie Hall*). Their story's central character is Allen's Isaac, a lifelong New Yorker whose great love for the city is tempered by his troublesome love life. He's twice divorced and his young son is being raised by his second wife, Jill (Meryl Streep), and the woman she left him for—and now Jill has written a scathing tell-all book about their marriage and there's movie interest in it. He's forty-two, but his girlfriend,

Tracy (Mariel Hemingway), is a seventeen-year-old high school student. He has fun and is comfortable with her but doesn't want to take the romance as seriously as she does. His anxiety increases when he quits his job as a comedy writer on an irrelevant hit show and decides to write a book. His married best friend, Yale (Michael Murphy), is having an affair with Mary (Diane Keaton), an intellectually pretentious neurotic. Isaac despises Mary, but when Yale ends the affair, he starts dating her. He breaks up with Tracy, who is heartbroken. Isaac thinks things are working out with Mary, but one day she tells him she and Yale are back together. Yale leaves his wife. Isaac realizes how much he misses Tracy and that he was happier with her than all other women. He runs to her

Woody Allen and Diane Keaton enjoy New York's pleasures and fall in love in *Manhattan.*

apartment. She is about to leave for school in London for six months. He worries she'll forget about him in that time. She tells him to have faith in her. He smiles.

Annie Hall is Allen's most adored movie, and the pivotal film in his career. Yet as much as I love that film, I prefer *Manhattan*. It's a gloriously photographed love poem to the city he "romanticizes . . . all out of proportion—to him, no matter what the season was, this was still a town that existed in black and white and pulsated to the great tunes of George Gershwin." And it's a bemused, sometimes cynical look at the clumsy people who inhabit this perfect town and have imperfect love lives. It showed a definite maturity in Allen as a filmmaker and an artist. Isaac is certainly neurotic, insecure, and loaded with phobias, but he's not the basket case that Allen played in the past. He still has trouble with women, but he no longer doubts his ability to attract them. And when he breaks up with Tracy, it's the first time Allen let his character actually be mean to someone, and not be the victim. Significantly, not all scenes are played for humor. In past films Allen hogged center stage—even in *Annie Hall,* where he finally allowed his female character to say lines that reflected her thinking more than his own, he wouldn't let Keaton have scenes without him. This film he made more into an ensemble piece, allowing time for the Keaton-Murphy story line. Keaton seems to have more freedom than before, and though her character isn't nearly as lovable as Annie Hall, she may be better in this film. Allen is very patient with all his actors, including himself, and consequently there are several lengthy, extraordinarily well played, intricately written dialogue scenes (most with characters walking) that have no cuts—here Keaton shines. Allen even attempted his first sexual-tension sequence, as Isaac and Mary move through the dark planetarium, obviously feeling urges to kiss and embrace for the first time (later he tells her, "I had a mad impulse to throw you down on the lunar surface and commit interstellar perversion with you.")

There are many laugh-out-loud moments: Isaac reveals that his book is an expansion of a short story about his mother, "The Castrating Zionist"; Isaac discovers in Mary's fridge "a corned beef sandwich from 1951"; as they walk through a quiet museum, Mary loudly announces to Isaac that "my problem is I'm both attracted and repelled by the male organ"; Isaac is infuriated that his new apartment has brown water and that the loud noises he constantly hears sound like a man is either "sawing a trumpet" or "strangling a parrot"; enjoying a romantic rowboat ride with Mary in Central Park, Isaac lets his hand float through the water—and it comes up covered with sludge; Isaac meets Mary's ex-husband, whom she's always described as a sexual animal with a devastating effect on women, and he turns out to be a little weasel (played by Wallace Shawn); Isaac tells Tracy that as long as their affair lasts he wants her to enjoy "my wry sense of humor and astonishing sexual technique"; Isaac takes his son for a walk and we watch from a distance as they window-shop, Isaac pointing emphatically to a small toy boat and his son pointing emphatically to one twice as big and expensive; Isaac gets annoyed when Yale and Mary list overrated people in music, literature, and film, and when Mary pronounces "Van Gogh" as if she were clearing her throat.

But there are just as many memorable sweet moments, most having to do with Tracy. The sweetest, most tearful moment in all of Allen's work is when Isaac lists into his tape recorder all the things that make his life worth living and after mentioning Gershwin, Brando, Groucho Marx, the Second Movement of the Jupiter Symphony, he suddenly says, "Tracy's face." I love the final scene when he runs block after exhausting block to Tracy's apartment and sees her again, telling her she's not so young after all, and smiling when he realizes that even in London for six months, this wonderful girl (now a young woman at eighteen) will be faithful to him. It's truly a romantic moment, when at last his love for a lovely, rewarding city is matched by his love for a lovely, responsive young woman.

▶ BEST ACTOR

WINNER:
Dustin Hoffman *(Kramer vs. Kramer)*
Other Nominees: Jack Lemmon *(The China Syndrome)*, Al Pacino *(. . . And Justice for All)*, Roy Scheider *(All That Jazz)*, Peter Sellers *(Being There)*

▼————————————————————————————

THE BEST CHOICE:
Ben Gazzara *(Saint Jack)*
Award-Worthy Nominees: Woody Allen *(Manhattan)*, Dennis Christopher *(Breaking Away)*, Phil Daniels *(Quadrophenia)*, Dustin Hoffman *(Kramer vs. Kramer)*, Ron Leibman *(Norma Rae)*, Dudley Moore *("10")*, Nick Nolte *(North Dallas Forty)*, Richard Pryor *(Richard Pryor Live in Concert)*, Burt Reynolds *(Starting Over)*, Peter Sellers *(Being There)*

Twelve years after he leapt to stardom in *The Graduate* and received nominations for that film, *Midnight Cowboy,* and *Lenny,* Dustin Hoffman finally won a Best Actor Oscar for *Kramer vs. Kramer.* The Academy hadn't been so eager to give the statue to the actor who once termed the Oscar ceremonies "dirty and obscene and no better than a beauty contest" and had in fact not nominated him for other deserving performances. But in 1979 the time had come to recognize his talent—and the Academy was relieved that Hoffman delivered a conciliatory acceptance speech. Hoffman was excellent in writer-director Robert Benton's film of Avery Corman's novel, playing a father who must take care of the son he doesn't really know after his wife walks out. I like the way Hoffman's Ted Kramer is confused, nervous, and flawed throughout, but becomes more human as a result of being with his son—for him parenthood is liberating. My only gripe with Hoffman's selection is that his characterization is too conventional in a year that featured many terrific off-center performances by actors. That he wasn't even nominated for his disreputable character in the previous year's sleeper, *Straight Time,* yet would win for the pat and polished but less daring *Kramer vs. Kramer* pretty much explains the Academy's thinking.

Having already given Hoffman an Alternate Oscar for *Midnight Cowboy,* I'll bypass him now. I'm tempted to give the award to Richard Pryor for *Richard Pryor Live in Concert,* making him my first black winner, but as riveting a presence as he is, and as much *acting* as he does in his hilarious routines, I don't want to award a live-concert performance. However, if the Academy can nominate James Whitmore for *Give 'Em Hell, Harry,* then I can at least nominate Pryor. My choice, though, is the unnominated Ben Gazzara in Peter Bogdanovich's *Saint Jack,* giving one of those terrific off-center performances I just mentioned.

Gazzara is American Jack Flowers, a well-educated Korean War hero, who's a pimp and wheeler-dealer in Singapore in the early seventies. He caters to American soldiers and English-speaking businessmen. He knows everyone, but his only good friend, William Leigh (Denholm Elliott), is a gentle British businessman who wants nothing to do with the sleazy side of Singapore. Jealous local brothel owners want to close down Jack's operation. He is abducted and has threats tattooed on his arms. His days as a pimp are over. Jack is saddened by the heart-attack death of Leigh. He still makes a little money selling contraband, but he accepts $25,000 from an American (Bogdanovich) to secretly photograph a visiting senator (George Lazenby) having sexual relations with a boy prostitute. He can use the money to leave Singapore and return to America. He takes the pictures but, thinking about the uncorruptible Leigh, throws them into the river.

Saint Jack was a pleasant surprise because we thought at the time that Peter Bogdanovich wanted to make only commercial films, to salvage his troubled directing career. Instead he chose to film a talky, complex character study, which he, Howard Sackler, and Paul Theroux adapted from Theroux's novel. And for his lead he picked Ben Gazzara, who had no box-office pull whatsoever. In the late fifties Gazzara was expected to become a major movie star following his first two films, *The Strange One*

Ben Gazzara welcomes three friendly American soldiers to Singapore in Peter Bogdanovich's sadly neglected *Saint Jack.*

and *Anatomy of a Murder,* but his film career stalled and in the sixties he found success on television, particularly in *Run for Your Life.* Other than playing the title role in *Capone,* the only movies of significance that he made in the seventies were for his friend John Cassavetes—*Husbands, The Killing of a Chinese Bookie,* and *Opening Night*—which the mass audience avoided like the plague. *Husbands* contained his best performance prior to *Saint Jack.*

Gazzara creates a vivid personality. Jack Flowers drinks Scotch, smokes cigars, wears colorful shirts outside his pants, and walks through the sinful streets, brothels, and hotels, acknowledging prostitutes and other acquaintances—he remembers everyone's name—and chatting with strangers. So comfortable is Gazzara wandering through Singapore that it's hard to believe he doesn't really live there. Jack works in a sleazy business, but he tries to give all his customers their money's worth and puts up with their indulgences. He is always calming people down, picking up the pieces. He's easygoing, not the type to be intimidated; about to be attacked by several young men who work for a dwarf gangster, he says, "All right, boys, let's get it over with before I drop-kick this little cocksucker down the hill." Afterward, he simply drinks away the pain. Until William's death Jack tries not to let anything bother him, even his own torture and the collapse of his business. He simply smiles at life's ironies.

Jack's actually a nice, friendly guy, who can tell a good story—dirty and otherwise—and has an odd assortment of knowledge stored away. He's street smart and tough, and has a sixth sense for danger. He can also see through anybody. He seems to know everybody and everyone seems to like him. Yet he is afraid of committing himself to a woman (alibiing that marriage ruins his sense of humor), and he has no good friends until he meets William, the rare ethical, gentle man to visit Singapore. William is the only man who seeks Jack's friendship rather than favors. (Their scenes together, during which friendship and respect develop, are beautifully acted and genuinely touching.) It makes sense that Bogdanovich includes many lengthy close-ups of Gazzara, a very introspective actor, for Jack has no one to whom he can reveal his deepest thoughts. The carnival-like world in which he lives and spends time with temporary lovers while helping others (for a price) have their sexual desires met, keeps him temporarily stimulated and so occupied that he isn't often pained by his sorry life. But when Singapore turns mean—he is abducted and tortured by his competition; stoned, combat-fatigued American soldiers are frightening visitors; he is asked to commit a despicable act for money—he realizes that it's time to get out and go home to America. Throughout the film Flowers shows us he is a decent, moral, responsible man and we can't imagine him sinking so low that he'll deliver blackmail photos for the money that would allow him to depart. Indeed, at film's end Jack throws the photos into the river, his integrity intact. He then walks through the slum streets, waving at and chatting with everyone he passes. Unreal life goes on in Singapore and he's resigned to losing himself in it once more. Just getting by will continue to be his stock-in-trade.

▶ BEST ACTRESS

WINNER:
Sally Field *(Norma Rae)*
Other Nominees: Jill Clayburgh *(Starting Over)*, Jane Fonda *(The China Syndrome)*, Marsha Mason *(Chapter Two)*, Bette Midler *(The Rose)*

▼

THE BEST CHOICE:
Sally Field *(Norma Rae)*
Award-Worthy Runners-Up: Jill Clayburgh *(Starting Over)*, Jane Fonda *(The China Syndrome)*, Diane Keaton *(Manhattan)*, Bette Midler *(The Rose)*

For the sixth time in the seventies I agree with the Academy's choice for Best Actress: Sally Field in *Norma Rae,* for playing a Southern textile worker who helps organize a union. Most of the earlier winners played women who were distinguished by excessive self-interest: Glenda Jackson in *Women in Love,* Jane Fonda in *Klute,* Liza Minnelli in *Cabaret,* Louise Fletcher in *One Flew Over the Cuckoo's Nest,* and Faye Dunaway in *Network.* But Field's victory affirmed that the trend was over. Following *Annie Hall*'s Diane Keaton and *Coming Home*'s Jane Fonda, she was the third of six consecutive winners who played completely sympathetic women, and the second straight winner to play a woman who experiences personal growth while working to benefit others (the typical Fonda role).

Directed by political liberal Martin Ritt *(The Molly McGuires, The Front)* and scripted by Irving Ravetch and Harriet Frank, Jr., this true story is set in a Southern Baptist town in which almost everyone, including Norma Rae and her parents, works in the O. P. Henley Textile Mill. Thirty-one-year-old Norma Rae has a young daughter from a husband who was killed in a bar fight and a younger son from one of her meaningless lovers over the years. She's frustrated by the low salaries and working conditions at the mill, and is vocal with her complaints. She decides to help Reuben (Ron Leibman), an organizer from New York, build up support for a union at the mill. He is the first Jew she has ever met. They work tirelessly, becoming close friends. She becomes more determined to help him after her father dies on the job, she is harassed by management, and her minister turns her out of the church rather than have black workers attend an organizational meeting there. She stubbornly refuses to buckle under. Her new husband, Sonny (Beau Bridges), complains about her devoting all her time to organizing and being with Reuben, but when she refuses to quit in order to do the housework, he gives in, taking over those chores. Their love becomes stronger. Management spreads rumors about Norma Rae's promiscuity. When she copies the words from an illegal memo stating that blacks will be taking over whites' jobs if a union is voted in, they have her arrested. But before she is taken away, she stands on a table in the factory and above her head holds a sign that says UNION. The other workers shut off their machines. In a close vote the workers elect to become part of the Textile Workers' Union of America. Reuben and Norma Rae are delighted, though saddened because the relationship that meant so much to both of them must end. They shake hands and he drives back to New York.

"I'm not perfect," Norma Rae tells her children. "I've made mistakes." But she's about the closest to perfect any woman has been on the screen since Ingrid Bergman's nun in *The Bells of St. Mary's.* That's why the two men so marvel at her: Reuben says, "If the situation ever called for a smart, loud, profane, sloppy, hardworking woman, I'd pick you every time, kid"; and after she refuses to give in to his demands to quit organizing and devote more time to him and the housework, the impressed Sonny still expresses his lifetime devotion to her.

Sally Field is terribly upset and embarrassed after the factory management has her arrested in Martin Ritt's *Norma Rae*.

That's why her well-behaved children listen to and respect her. That's why the male management at the mill becomes so frightened of her, after their attempts at manipulating her fail, that they harass and have her arrested. That's why when she climbs on the table at the mill and defiantly raises the union sign, all her coworkers—male and female, black and white—shut off their machines: for her, and not out of peer pressure. Here's a woman who has little education, who has a bad reputation, and who has never been kind to herself. Yet she says, "One of these days I will get myself all together," and proceeds to pick herself up. And making good use of her heart, guts, hard head, and big mouth, accomplishes so much that she deserves all the admiration she receives. What's most commendable is that she isn't interested just in improving her own life—she quits the high-paying work-checker position management gives her as a way of driving a wedge between herself and her coworkers. She wants to improve the lot of all mill workers, which will make her own job more respectable. "You know, cotton mill workers are known as trash to some," she laments to Reuben. "I know the union's the only way we're going to get our own voice, make ourselves any better. I guess that's why I push." Her motives are pure: "I believe in standing up for what is right."

Field does an extraordinary job as this woman who displays remarkable courage and tenacity. It's fun seeing this small-framed woman with a teenager's face stand up to intimidating men, ignoring their threats, shouting at them, issuing threats of her own, making them think she's too big for her britches. Naturally, Norma Rae appealed to feminists, but the reason the character didn't alienate the mass audience—in fact, everyone cheered her—was that the wholesome Field was in the part. She was the perfect choice to play a woman so trusted by her neighbors and fellow workers that they would listen to her talk about something as radical as a union, and be swayed to her way of thinking.

Field touches every scene with honest emotions. Norma Rae admits she has a big mouth, with which she always speaks the truth, but we can tell everything going on in her mind just by looking at her expressive eyes, open mouth, and open-book face. Field conveys Norma Rae's depth of emotions—her love for Sonny, her kids, her father and mother, and on a different, never fully explored level, for Reuben. Field has several wonderful scenes: hearing Johnny Cash on the jukebox, she recalls for Sonny and Reuben the night her first husband was killed; Norma Rae answers Sonny's proposal with "Kiss me—if that's all right, then everything else will be"; when the minister who refuses to allow her to use the church for an integrated union meeting tells her, "We're going to miss your voice in the choir, Norma," she responds, "You're going to hear it raised someplace else"; Norma Rae answers Sonny's fit with a bigger fit of her own; in a sexy scene Norma Rae and Reuben skinny-dip in a river, never touching each other; Norma Rae and Reuben, at a lunch counter, talk about her latest temper tantrum; Norma Rae tells her children all about herself; Norma Rae raises the union sign; Norma Rae and Reuben bid farewell, telling each other they were special in each other's lives. Ritt wisely used no cuts (and no music) in certain scenes to allow Field freedom to let emotions develop as she speaks Norma Rae's words. This is why the lunch-counter chat and her scene with the children are so effective.

Field had not yet lived down being the star of television's *Gidget* and *The Flying Nun*—although she was surprisingly good in those parts. She had deservedly won an Emmy for a powerhouse performance as a multiple personality on the TV movie *Sybil*, but her film roles had been trivial. Her star-making performance in *Norma Rae* was a revelation.

1980

▶ BEST PICTURE

WINNER:
Ordinary People (Paramount; Robert Redford)
Other Nominees: *Coal Miner's Daughter, The Elephant Man, Raging Bull, Tess*

▼

THE BEST CHOICE:
Raging Bull (United Artists; Martin Scorsese)
Award-Worthy Runners-Up: *The Empire Strikes Back* (Irvin Kershner), *The Long Riders* (Walter Hill), *Ordinary People* (Robert Redford), *Tess* (Roman Polanski)

Ordinary People received much praise from critics and moviegoers when it was released in 1980. It then won Academy Awards for Best Picture, Robert Redford's direction (his debut), Timothy Hutton's supporting-actor performance (although he was the star), and Alvin Sargent's adaptation of Judith Guest's prize-winning first novel about the deterioration of a middle-class family due to Hutton's brother's death and the inability of mother Mary Tyler Moore to love anyone else. Its reputation has since diminished, so that it's now thought of as a mainstream family drama. Meanwhile the reputation of one of the nominated films it defeated, *Raging Bull,* Martin Scorsese's violent biography of former middleweight boxing champion Jake La Motta (Robert De Niro), has grown to almost legendary proportions. An *American Film* poll of critics rated it as the best film of the eighties. I am not among those who think it a great film, although I acknowledge there are great things about it. I actually prefer the *now* underrated *Ordinary People*—which dealt with difficult "mother-love" themes not handled in other films—and my other "Award-Worthy" Runners-Up. However, so solid is *Raging Bull*'s popularity among the better critics and most astute film cultists that it surely deserves the Alternate Oscar for 1980.

Raging Bull begins in 1964, when a middle-aged and very heavy La Motta (De Niro put on an enormous amount of weight for the role) stands in his dressing room rehearsing a nightclub act. We then flash back to 1941, when the trim, undefeated middleweight contender knocks out his opponent but loses on a decision because the count came after the final bell. He is already a loser. During the course of the movie, scenes switch back and forth between La Motta in his apartments/hotel rooms, nightclubs, and the ring, with an occasional municipal pool, boxing gym, jail cell, and public garage providing slight variety. The matches themselves are shown briefly, and then only moments that are extremely brutal. Highlights include his championship win over

Marcel Cerdan, his savage beating of Tony Ginero (after second wife Vickie referred to him as "good-looking"), his fixed-fight loss to Billy Fox, and several bouts with Sugar Ray Robinson, only one of which he won. After breaking off from his first wife (she just disappears from the movie), he has only two significant relationships, that with Vickie (Cathy Moriarty), who loves him enough to put up with his possessiveness and abuse for many years, and with his smarter brother and manager, Joey (Joe

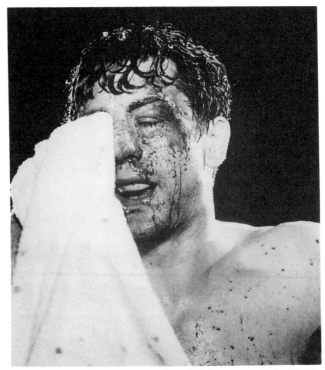

Robert De Niro in one of many brutal fight sequences in Martin Scorsese's *Raging Bull.*

Pesci). He drives them both out of his life with violence and jealousy against any man, including Joey, who comes near Vickie. Conversations mostly deal with food, boxing, La Motta's weight, La Motta's jealousy, or, most often, nothing. After his retirement from the ring he operates a nightclub in Miami but is arrested for fixing up an underage girl with male clients. Then he works as a comic-emcee at a New York strip joint. He attempts a reconciliation with a still-resentful Joey. He ends up taking gigs in which he does recitations of everyone from Shakespeare to Rod Serling to Budd Schulberg.

De Niro and Pesci are exceptional, employing a dialogue pattern that confirms Jake and Joey have been close since childhood. Joey is volatile and argumentative, but is slightly tamer than his cuckoo gangster in Scorsese's *GoodFellas*. Cool blond Moriarty is also impressive in her debut. It was a difficult part because almost all of Vickie's reactions are dependent on the mood of her loving, but controlling, brutal husband; likewise, the actress had to hold back and respond to each of De Niro's particular deliveries, many of them improvised. Equal to the acting is Michael Chapman's gorgeous black-and-white, full-screen cinematography. His shots of old New York and Miami hauntingly capture the *feel* of the past. Even better are his sharply focused, surreal, almost hallucinatory shots of La Motta's fights. At times he'll employ slow motion, as when La Motta eyes his opponent across the ring, and suddenly you feel you're watching one of those nature films in which a fierce tiger, also shot in slow motion, eyes its prey. The innovative editing of the fight sequences helped win Thelma Schoonmaker the picture's one technical Oscar.

As always, Scorsese's direction is inventive and forceful—you feel and hear *every* blow in and out of the ring. And his direction of his actors is superb, as all his characters come across as natural and real. But whereas *Ordinary People* gets into the minds of its characters, *Raging Bull* stays at arm's length from its protagonist, Jake La Motta. We can only watch La Motta, without ever being able to figure out what makes him tick. We frustrated viewers—again, I am not an admirer of *Raging Bull*—must respond as passively to this wife abuser as to Michael Rooker's unmotivated woman-killer in *Henry: Portrait of a Serial Killer*. It becomes unpleasant. Scorsese and Schrader don't attempt to justify his actions. No matter that he is tortured by inner demons and self-hatred. He is a mean man who can perfectly express his meanness in the ring. Even when he's champion, he's a bum. If De Niro weren't playing him, we might follow Moriarty to the exit.

▶ BEST ACTOR

WINNER:
Robert De Niro *(Raging Bull)*
Other Nominees: Robert Duvall *(The Great Santini)*, John Hurt *(The Elephant Man)*, Jack Lemmon *(Tribute)*, Peter O'Toole *(The Stunt Man)*

THE BEST CHOICE:
Robert De Niro *(Raging Bull)*
Award-Worthy Runners-Up: Bob Hoskins *(The Long Good Friday)*, Peter O'Toole *(The Stunt Man)*

Bob Hoskins gave my favorite performance by an actor in 1980, as a ferocious Edward G. Robinson–like gangster in *The Long Good Friday*. But Hoskins was an unknown then and the English film wasn't widely seen in America, so his failure to be nominated for Best Actor wasn't surprising. Anyway, I wouldn't have given Hoskins the award over Robert De Niro, for his portrayal of boxer Jake La Motta in *Raging Bull*. Hoskins was great playing a character with tremendous personality, while De Niro was great playing a character who, despite having stone hands and jaw, has no personality. De Niro had a tougher task.

The film begins in 1964, with a heavy, middle-aged La Motta practicing his nightclub act. We then go back to the early forties when he was a young, undefeated middle-weight contender. He takes pride in the fact that he can't be hurt, that no one can knock him down. When he's not fighting in the ring, he squabbles with his wife in his small New York apartment. Joey, his smaller brother and

Robert De Niro, here with Cathy Moriarty, put on much weight to play Jake La Motta after he retired from the ring in *Raging Bull*.

manager, introduces him to a pretty blonde, Vickie (Cathy Moriarty), who becomes Jake's second wife. Jake hands Sugar Ray Robinson his first loss, but he still can't get a title shot unless he does a favor for a mobster. He throws a fight to Billy Fox. He cries in his dressing room. He is suspended. However, in 1949 he fights Marcel Cerdan for the crown and emerges victorious. His home-life is rocky, as he is jealous of any man who comes near Vickie. He often slaps her. He even suspects Joey of cheating with Vickie and beats him. Insulted, Joey withdraws from Jake's life, leaving him with no friends. He loses his crown but continues fighting. Even when battered he refuses to go down. After retiring, Jake opens a nightclub in Miami. Vickie leaves him. He is thrown in jail for having set up an underaged girl with one of his customers. In jail he tearfully smashes his head against the wall. He becomes a strip-joint comic in New York. He tries to patch things up with Joey, but Joey still harbors a grudge. Jake does recitations at the Barbizon Plaza.

Once again, director Martin Scorsese and De Niro have collaborated on a film about an unlikable character, and the going gets rough. La Motta comes across as just another of Scorsese's inarticulate, incorrigible, misogynistic, violent, self-destructive Italian punks. He seems to have no pride, except that he cries after throwing a fight and after winning the title. And, yes, he likes proving he can take a punch, whether thrown by Sugar Ray Robinson in the ring ("You never got me down, Ray!") or Joey in the kitchen ("Do me a favor—I want you to hit me in the face"). What La Motta likes to do—and he does it sometimes instead of sex—is beat up people, in the ring and at home. He expresses himself with his fists. All the conversations that scriptwriter Paul Schrader, Scorsese, and the improvising De Niro give him are repetitive and circular, nonsensical, and empty. All he does is eat, argue with Joey and Vickie, and fight. Because we can detect no motivation for his jealous tantrums and abusiveness, or reasons why he is such a creep, we can't interact with the character, just watch him at a distance.

That we keep watching is because De Niro is so powerful that we are paralyzed in our seats. He is riveting, whether stalking his opponent in the squared circle or his wife in his house, whether throwing and receiving painful blows or having temper tantrums, whether delivering awful monologues or having tearful breakdowns those few times he pays attention to what he has accomplished or how he has failed. La Motta is such a stupid bastard that we get fed up with him long before he retires and puts on a lot of weight. But the performance by De Niro, who assured himself of an Oscar by adding many extra pounds for these later scenes, is fascinating. What's amazing is that while De Niro is trapped in a character who barely changes over the years, he still gives a performance that is excitingly unpredictable.

▶ BEST ACTRESS

WINNER:
Sissy Spacek (Coal Miner's Daughter)
Other Nominees: Ellen Burstyn (Resurrection), Goldie Hawn (Private Benjamin), Mary Tyler Moore (Ordinary People), Gena Rowlands (Gloria)

THE BEST CHOICE:
Ellen Burstyn (Resurrection)
Award-Worthy Runners-Up: Judy Davis (My Brilliant Career), Shelley Duvall (The Shining), Jodie Foster (Foxes), Goldie Hawn (Private Benjamin), Helen Mirren (The Long Good Friday), Gena Rowlands (Gloria), Sissy Spacek (Coal Miner's Daughter)

Robert De Niro wasn't the only one who put on extra pounds for a biographical film in 1980. Playing country music queen Loretta Lynn in *Coal Miner's Daughter,* Sissy Spacek gained weight to be Lynn in her thirties and even lost weight to play her in her teens. Whereas De Niro learned to box like Jake La Motta, Spacek learned to sing like Lynn. And to talk like her. And to be like her. She even looked like her! Indeed, Spacek was the best choice imaginable to play Lynn—few stars in movie bios have been as convincing. She is truly marvelous; and considering that she hadn't won an Oscar yet (a case could have been made for either *Carrie* or *Three Women*), her selection by the Academy was more than justified.

However, taking into consideration that Spacek is receiving my Alternate Oscars for 1976 and 1981, I'd like to give the 1980 award to Ellen Burstyn in *Resurrection.* She gave a truly haunting performance that was the equal of Spacek's, yet few people saw it. Regardless of awards Spacek's movie was already a hit at the box office. An Oscar would have given Burstyn and Daniel Petrie's sleeper much deserved attention.

At the beginning of the film Burstyn's Edna McCauley is happily married to a California factory worker. Their new car plunges down a mountain slope, causing his death. She experiences death but is revived, her legs paralyzed. Her unemotional widower father (Roberts Blossom) takes her home to Kansas. She is happy to be reunited with her grandmother (Eva Le Gallienne) and other relatives. At a picnic a little girl starts to bleed. Edna puts her hands on the girl and the bleeding stops. Her

In the deeply moving final scene of *Resurrection*, white-haired recluse Ellen Burstyn gives a healing hug to a boy who, until this moment, had been dying of cancer.

grandmother notices that Edna's hands are hot. Later Edna rubs her hands on her own legs. She also does exercises. She learns to walk again. People with ailments and diseases come to Edna. She cures about seventy percent of the people with her touch. She says she cures in the name of love, refusing to say that Christ works through her. One man accuses her of doing the devil's work. She saves his ne'er-do-well son, Cal (Sam Shepard), who was knifed in a fight. She and Cal have an affair. He tells her to include Christ in her work, but she doesn't feel comfortable doing so. Reading the Bible constantly, Cal becomes convinced that she is evil. He tries to kill her, but only grazes her shoulder with a bullet. Edna goes away and disappears. Years later, she is working in an out-of-the-way roadside gas station, which she took over from the elderly owner (Richard Farnsworth) she met on her way to Kansas. A couple with a dying child pass through. She hugs the boy, without letting any of them know that she is healing him.

Burstyn wanted to make this film because of the expe-rience she'd had with a healer who helped cure her son. It was meant to be a spiritual film about the power of goodness and love, but except for an ill-advised run in the Bible Belt, it was promoted by Universal as a spooky movie about a woman with strange powers. (Actually, Universal's version *reads* better.) Burstyn had to get involved in the promotion herself. This likely is the reason she was even considered when the Academy chose its nominees. But the picture never got a fair shake.

The film is directed (by Daniel Petrie) and written (by Lewis John Carlino) in a nonexploitive manner and Bur-styn exhibits none of the hysteria that distinguishes most movie healers. She comes across as a smart, witty, kind, but unexceptional woman. Healing is the only thing she does that is unusual. When she heals, Edna is calm, tender, and compassionate, feeling the pain of those who need her help. And at times she is funny, having her own set of "death" jokes for the crowd that watches her. What makes her special is her humility. She praises those she heals, telling one woman, "Oh, you're just wonderful," and she always thanks them afterward. She wants no praise or thanks for herself and offers none to Christ, although she doesn't discount His presence. The film's theme is expressed by her grandmother, who says there wouldn't be so much "bother" in the world if people loved each other as much as they love God. Edna heals, not because she hears voices, but because she loves the people who come to her.

Where did Edna's tremendous capacity for love come from? She apparently stored it up as a child, while growing up in her father's loveless home. In fact, Edna's one excessively emotional moment—which is powerfully played by Burstyn—comes when her father calls her trash and kicks her out. Her response: "I'll go and I don't ever want to see you again either. You're a hard, stupid old man without an ounce of love or understanding anywhere and I am sick to death of trying to get you to love me."

Resurrection has one of my favorite movie endings. Edna, now with wild white hair, becomes fast friends with the sweet little boy who is dying of cancer. When he is about to leave with his parents, she gives him a puppy, and asks for a hug in return. She bends down and gives him a long embrace, with her hands firmly touching his back. We look at Burstyn's face and feel the goodness moving through Edna into his small sick body. We know that she is secretly healing him—and we cry because Edna isn't telling the boy or his parents that she is responsible for their upcoming happiness. When the boy instinctively says thank-you she responds truthfully, "Thank *you*."

1981

▶ BEST PICTURE

WINNER:
Chariots of Fire (Ladd Company/Warner Bros.; Hugh Hudson)
Other Nominees: *Atlantic City, On Golden Pond, Raiders of the Lost Ark, Reds*

▼

THE BEST CHOICE:
Reds (Paramount; Warren Beatty)
Award-Worthy Runners-Up: *Atlantic City* (Louis Malle), *Cutter's Way* (Ivan Passer), *Raiders of the Lost Ark* (Steven Spielberg)

n 1981 the British dark horse *Chariots of Fire,* a slow-moving film about running, won the race for Best Picture as three powerhouse American films—Mark Rydell's *On Golden Pond,* director Steven Spielberg and executive producer George Lucas's *Raiders of the Lost Ark,* and Warren Beatty's *Reds*—canceled each other out in the balloting. Directed by Hugh Hudson and produced by David Puttnam, it received mostly excellent reviews and had numerous admirers, but rarely had a Best Picture winner been detested by so many. Those who protested its victory called it "boring" and rated it as bad *Masterpiece Theatre.* At the time I was annoyed that this "true story" about two British runners who find Gold at the 1924 Paris Olympics—Jewish Harold Abrahams (Ben Cross) and Scottish missionary Eric Liddell (Ian Charleson)—distorted the facts. However, I was impressed by the leads (and supporting actors Ian Holm and John Gielgud), admired its noble themes (having to do with courage and integrity in face of bigotry), and like most everyone, before the parodies began, felt a surge of emotion as a parade of proud athletes glided across the screen to Vangelis's myth-making, Oscar-winning score. Vangelis's music would have given any 1981 film heroic stature, from *Heaven's Gate* to *My Dinner with Andre,* and that's what I think put *Chariots of Fire* over the top. Take away the music and the picture would have seemed minor, completely dwarfed by the likes of *Raiders of the Lost Ark* and *Reds,* two epics that more than matched their filmmakers' extremely lofty ambitions.

Raiders of the Lost Ark, introducing Harrison Ford's indomitable action hero, Indiana Jones, is much better than the old-time serials it salutes, but rather than diminishing those films, it recaptures the feeling of excitement and awe they originally held for kids. It ranks with *The Adventures of Robin Hood* as the most enjoyable and best-made action-adventure film and is certainly worthy of the Best Picture Oscar. But since it didn't need the award for financial success and lasting popularity, I'd prefer giving it to *Reds.* Beatty won a Best Director Oscar

over Hudson and Spielberg (and Rydell and Louis Malle), Maureen Stapleton was the Supporting Actress winner (for her argumentative but caring Emma Goldman), and Vittorio Storaro won for Cinematography, but a Best Picture Oscar might today sway more Americans into watching this 196-minute film with a communist as its hero. (Tellingly, when Irwin Winkler reworked Abraham Polonsky's script for the 1991 blacklist film *Guilty by Suspicion,* he changed Robert De Niro's hero from a communist to a political innocent.)

Reds was Beatty's pet project, an expensive and, because of its title and leftist sentiment, potentially disastrous epic that he produced, directed, scripted with Trevor Griffiths, and starred in as John Reed, American radical journalist-theoretician-organizer. Reed's firsthand account of the October Revolution, *Ten Days That Shook the World,* earned him a propaganda job with the Comintern and burial inside the Kremlin. *Reds* has some editing problems, but the acting by Beatty, Diane Keaton (as Reed's assertive wife, Louise Bryant), Stapleton, and Jack Nicholson (as a bitter Eugene O'Neill) is superb. Leftist intellectuals are treated fairly for a change (they're witty, tender, and humanistic), the dialogue is consistently sharp and intelligent, Storaro's cinematography is brilliant, the music by Stephen Sondheim and Dave Grusin is evocative, and the direction by Beatty is full of passion.

The film begins in 1915, when Reed first meets free-spirit Bryant, a married aspiring writer, in Portland, Oregon. It takes us through their life together in Greenwich Village (where she comes at his request after she breaks up with her husband) and Provincetown—writing, acting, arguing, loving each other—her affair with O'Neill (who is shattered when she returns to Reed) during one of Reed's many political sojourns, and their marriage, separation, and reconciliation while together in Russia; then their separation when he returns to Russia, and his death (due to kidney failure and tuberculosis) in Moscow in 1920, with her at his side. Their romance isn't merely

Warren Beatty's John Reed and Diane Keaton's Louise Bryant interview soldiers on the Russian border in the Beatty-directed romantic-political epic, *Reds*.   (Photo credit: Dan Weaks)

played against a political backdrop but is fueled by their involvement (he is obsessed, she is a curious reporter) in the politics of the day. The picture conveys the excitement one feels (which often leads to sex) when involved in a political movement that seems to be affecting the world for the better, and the crushing disillusionment one feels when others derail or coopt the movement: the American Socialist party splits apart; the bureaucrats who take over Russia forget the ideas and ideals that led to the October Revolution. Watching Reed speak at rallies and organize workers, and Reed and Bryant race around the world in search of significant political stories, one feels swept up in history. When Reed and Bryant march with the Russians through the streets as they celebrate the October Revolution and attend mass rallies, we share their excitement.

But it's equally exciting to watch the romance between Reed and Bryant evolve, their attempts to give stability to their marriage in an unstable world. Beatty has a soft spot for Reed, and plays him as a highly intelligent, idealistic, well-meaning, quirky, slightly foolish, sweet man. He is shy and hesitant and is slightly overwhelmed by Bryant's forceful personality, yet when it comes to politics, he'll enthusiastically talk a blue streak, never doubting the correctness of his own beliefs. Bryant worries that he is more dedicated to leftist politics than to her, yet he doesn't forget to bring her white lilies when he comes home, is supportive of her work and respectful of her opinions of his work, and, come crunch time, proves his devotion. That love and politics are of equal value to Reed is apparent when he writes Louise a love poem on the back of an IWW leaflet, and when he tells the Russian Zinoviev (played by the late Polish writer Jerzy Kosinski) that he'd prefer returning home to his family than being a propagandist for the Russian government.

Keaton's Louise Bryant is a dynamic woman who trea-

sures her independence. She worries that it is threatened by her relationship to Reed and her deep love for him. In fact, she has a hard time accepting the degree of independence the feminist Reed allows her. He tolerates her having slept with O'Neill, but she walks out when he tells her that he slept around also (perhaps he is lying because he's so hurt about O'Neill). She spends the film trying to find a comfortable niche for herself, both among the leftist intelligentsia and in her marriage to a man whose work is more significant than her own. Bryant delivers almost every line to Reed as if she were challenging him, prodding him, trying to initiate an argument. But he's sensitive enough to realize that she's just insecure, and he usually won't fight with her. Instead, he loves her and wins her over. She always worries she is becoming "a boring, clinging little wife," yet when he is in trouble, she relinquishes her life in America to sneak out of the country and undertake an arduous journey to be with him in Russia—shades of independent Marlene Dietrich following Foreign Legionnaire Gary Cooper into the desert in *Morocco*. Then she nurses him on his deathbed. Her brave actions are a sign of strength and a commitment to her love for Reed, and win her the hard-earned respect of Emma Goldman ("I underestimated you").

Beatty and Keaton are both outstanding, particularly in their scenes together. It's not surprising they were off-screen lovers at the time. They have several terrific argument scenes that are so much more convincing than the stagy battle between Keaton and Al Pacino in *The Godfather II*. I like the way politics enters the arguments, as when Reed tells Bryant that if she wants her writing to be taken more seriously, she will have to write about more serious political subjects; and when Bryant mocks him for thinking America is headed for a revolution and insisting (this time *he* takes himself too seriously) it's essential for *him* to go to Russia and get recognition for the newly formed Communist Labor party of America. "You're not a politician, you're a writer," she reminds him. And just as he was correct about her, she knows him as well. When Zinoviev edits his propaganda speeches, Reed chooses writing over politics: "Nobody rewrites what I write."

Reed and Bryant were meant to be together, especially after all they go through together during a turbulent era ("What a time it was," says Reed). That's why we're so happy when they reunite at the Moscow depot, after his imprisonment in Finland and propaganda mission to the Middle East, and her impossible journey. It is an extremely moving scene, with the tearful Bryant (Keaton at her most endearing) walking toward the worn-out (dying) Reed, oblivious of the bystanders she brushes against, and hugging him as he says, "Don't leave me. Please don't leave me." This is one of my favorite tear-jerker scenes in the cinema. It is only one of several warm, intimate, extremely emotional scenes that one wouldn't expect to find in a picture entitled *Reds*.

▶ BEST ACTOR

WINNER:
Henry Fonda *(On Golden Pond)*
Other Nominees: Warren Beatty *(Reds)*, Burt Lancaster *(Atlantic City)*, Dudley Moore *(Arthur)*, Paul Newman *(Absence of Malice)*
▼

THE BEST CHOICE:
John Heard *(Cutter's Way)*
Award-Worthy Runners-Up: Warren Beatty *(Reds)*, Albert Brooks *(Modern Romance)*, Henry Fonda *(On Golden Pond)*, Harrison Ford *(Raiders of the Lost Ark)*, Burt Lancaster *(Atlantic City)*, Steve Martin *(Pennies from Heaven)*, Donald Sutherland *(Eye of the Needle)*, Treat Williams *(Prince of the City)*

After forty-five years as a leading man Henry Fonda finally received a long-overdue Best Actor Oscar, for Mark Rydell's 1981 surprise hit, *On Golden Pond.* Although the film itself is sappy and manipulative (I liked it anyway), Fonda was superb as usual, playing an irascible old man who keeps his love and warmth well hidden, especially from his grown daughter. It also was special to see him finally play opposite Katharine Hepburn (they'd never even met!) and to appear in his only film with his daughter, Jane. But it was generally conceded that Fonda's award was not specifically for this role but for all his great performances in a long and remarkable, though Oscarless, career. This career-achievement award came, appropriately, soon before Fonda's death. Because Fonda was my choice for an Alternate Oscar for his Tom Joad in 1940's *The Grapes of Wrath,* there is no need now to go along with the Academy and give him an award to compensate for earlier neglect, especially since there was an unusually large number of terrific performances by actors in more interesting roles. My selection as Best Actor is John Heard. He wasn't nominated for *Cutter's Way* (its original title was *Cutter and Bone*), and it's likely that the few Academy voters who saw this sleeper didn't even consider nominating him. It was hard enough to put up with Fonda's constantly sniping character in *On Golden Pond,* but Heard's antihero in Ivan Passer's offbeat, splendidly acted *Cutter's Way* really tests one's tolerance.

Heard's Alexander Cutter is an angry Vietnam vet who detests the fat cats who stayed home while he went to fight a meaningless war and lost an eye, arm, and leg. He also resents his best friend, Richard Bone (top-billed Jeff Bridges), who had avoided the war, just as he has always avoided all possible danger and commitment. Even now Bone is an overaged Santa Barbara beach bum who lives on a yacht and makes his money sleeping with older women. Bone puts up with Cutter, accompanying him on his nightly drinking sprees, when he insults everyone. Meanwhile, Cutter's neglected, depressed wife, Mo (Lisa Eichhorn), stays home and drinks. One night, Bone witnesses a man dump the murdered body of a female hitchhiker into a garbage bin. He doesn't think he could recognize the killer, but when arrogant oil tycoon J. J. Cord (Stephen Elliott) rides by in a parade, Bone auto-

matically tells Cutter, "That's him!" He later retracts his statement, but Cutter, who hates men like Cord, won't let the matter drop. Enlisting the help of the dead girl's sister (Ann Dusenberry), he tries to convince Bone to help trap Cord. They send a blackmail note to Cord, believing his response will indicate his guilt or innocence. Furious at his recklessness, Mo kicks out Cutter. She sleeps with Bone, who, characteristically, won't stay the night. She is killed when the house is bombed. Cutter decides to kill Cord. Surprisingly, Bone goes with him to Cord's house. Bone is captured by Cord's security guards. Cutter eludes the guards by riding Cord's horse directly into his house. He comes upon Cord speaking to Bone. Mortally wounded, Cutter hasn't the strength to fire the gun he points at Cord, who won't deny he was the killer. Finally making a commitment, Bone pulls the trigger for him.

In the late seventies and early eighties there was no one better than John Heard at playing young misfits, be it hipster icon Jack Kerouac in *Heart Beat,* or sixties survivors in *Between the Lines, Head Over Heals/Chilly Scenes of Winter,* and *Cutter's Way,* three major cult films of the Woodstock generation. He played his real characters with intelligence, fury, and the correct dose of past-

Longtime friends Jeff Bridges and Arthur Rosenberg are the only ones who can still tolerate John Heard in *Cutter's Way.*

their-eras confusion. They feel frustration because while they remain young the world is aging around them and changing in ways antithetical to what they had striven for. Yet even his dropouts hold on to their values. They are being pushed into obsolescence but want to make a last stand. Heard's Cutter, a brilliantly conceived and played character, talks nonstop in a raspy, abrasive voice, philosophizing, complaining, and cursing, agitating, offending, and embarrassing everyone around him—especially those closest to him. He has worse manners than the one-legged, one-armed, one-eyed pirates he resembles. He drinks far too much, dresses sloppily and is ill-groomed and hostile, has suicidal tendencies, is full of self-pity, and puts himself on public display. He always reminds everyone that he's crippled. So irritating is this cripple that you'll likely want to trip him. Heard plays someone who thrives on martyrdom but, interestingly,

he makes Cutter's personality so repellent (especially in the way he treats Mo) that pity is the last thing viewers will want to give him. It took guts for Heard to play such a character and have to win audience sympathy for the film to succeed. It is only when we think long and hard, and watch Cutter fearlessly gallop to his death through enemy forces, to give some meaning to Mo's death, that we realize that Cutter really is a martyr. In a world with few heroes Cutter proves to be the rarity. He wasn't bluffing: his final action backs up all his angry words and seemingly empty threats. We now admire his romanticism (he has spoken of the Three Musketeers and Babe Ruth) in an age when sixties optimism has been crushed; his willingness to sacrifice himself once again (this time for a just cause); and for getting Bone finally to accept moral responsibility and take the dying Cutter's lead— "Cutter's Way."

▶ BEST ACTRESS

WINNER:
Katharine Hepburn *(On Golden Pond)*
Other Nominees: Diane Keaton *(Reds)*, Marsha Mason *(Only When I Laugh)*, Susan Sarandon *(Atlantic City)*, Meryl Streep *(The French Lieutenant's Woman)*

▼

THE BEST CHOICE:
Sissy Spacek *(Raggedy Man)*
Award-Worthy Runners-Up: Diane Keaton *(Reds)*, Margot Kidder *(Heartaches)*, Susan Sarandon *(Atlantic City)*, Meryl Streep *(The French Lieutenant's Woman)*

Katharine Hepburn won her fourth and final Best Actress Oscar playing the understanding wife of crotchety Henry Fonda in *On Golden Pond*. The Academy voters apparently thought it fitting that Fonda and Hepburn both win for their only film together. Since I'm taking away Fonda's Oscar, I think it fitting that I take away Hepburn's. She gave an excellent performance but there really wasn't much she could do to upgrade one of her least interesting women. Of the nominated actresses Diane Keaton was easily my favorite for playing Louise Bryant, opposite Warren Beatty's John Reed, in *Reds*. But there was one performance I preferred. It was by Sissy Spacek. I took away Spacek's Oscar in 1980, despite a standout portrayal of Loretta Lynn in *Coal Miner's Daughter,* knowing I'd give her an Alternate Oscar in 1981 to call attention to a performance of equal merit in *Raggedy Man*.

Gregory, Texas. 1944. Spacek is Nita Longley, a divorced mother of two young boys, Harry (Henry Thomas) and Henry (Carey Hollis, Jr.). She works as the town's lone telephone operator. The switchboard is located in her house, so she is always confined inside, while her boys run free. They could use a father. Nita doesn't know what happened to her unfaithful ex-husband after he joined the army. She doesn't recognize the disfigured raggedy man, Bailey (Sam Shepard), who protectively

watches her house from afar. Being an operator is depressing because she hears all the bad news from the war. Also, she doesn't make enough money to support her kids. She wants a secretarial job with regular hours. But her boss, Mr. Rigby (R. G. Armstrong), insists she's frozen in her job because of new laws resulting from the war. Lowlife brothers Calvin and Arnold (William Sanderson, Tracey Walter) ask Nita for a date. She refuses, saying she is tied to her work. Teddy (Eric Roberts), a kindly young sailor on leave, passes through town, stopping at Nita's house to use the phone. They swiftly become friends. The boys adore him too. He stays a few days, setting off the town gossips. Nita and Teddy become lovers. Too troubled by her inability to control her children, she sends him away, hoping they will meet up again. Upset that Nita let Teddy stay with her, Calvin and Arnold enter Nita's house late at night and try to rape her. She is rescued by Bailey, who kills both men and dies himself. She recognizes Bailey as her former husband. Having found out that Rigby lied about her job being frozen, Nita packs up her belongings and kids and goes to find secretarial work in San Antonio. On the bus she and the kids realize that the boys' father loved them more than anyone else could love his family. It makes them proud.

Sissy Spacek hugs her two young sons in *Raggedy Man*.

After Spacek's success in *Coal Miner's Daughter* she had enough clout to get financing for a low-budget film that would star her and mark the directorial debut of her husband, former set designer Jack Fisk. The unfortunate, horror-movie-like climax was responsible for most of the negative reviews that precipitated the film's dismal box-office showing. Which is a shame, because until that point it's the most lyrical and romantic of films, with an authentic small-town Texas ambience, smart dialogue, provocative characters, evocative sets and cinematography, and terrific, quite unusual interaction between Nita and Teddy, Nita and Mr. Rigby, Nita and her boys,

Teddy and the boys, and Nita and the boys with villains Calvin and Arnold. I think Nita is one of Spacek's most mature, capable, and appealing characters. She reveals exciting parts of herself that had been hidden in earlier films. It's obvious that the man directing her scenes knows her very well and loves her very much. He often keeps her in extreme close-up, and there are many moments when she isn't just pretty but ravishing. Fisk makes us fall for Nita by having her do simple things that reveal so much: we watch her perform like a whiz at the switchboard; run through her house and climb on her bed to pose with a dress she'll wear for Teddy; dance seductively with Teddy, spinning out of his arms to turn off the switchboard; dance alone with her broom to the Andrews Sisters' "Rum and Coca-Cola"; excitedly yet carefully and sensually put her hand into the sheer rayon stockings Teddy has given her; touch up her hair just to join Teddy and the boys for a few seconds of kite flying only about twenty feet away; throw her own food outside after she angrily did the same to her discourteous children's; and lovingly and protectively look in on her sleeping children, forgetting all about their recent rudeness toward her. Fisk gave Spacek the freedom to create a character through nuance rather than speech. But Nita speaks up, as when she cuts down the gossips with a curt "It's nobody's business what I do"; erupts when Mr. Rigby implies that she, an operator, doesn't know about the war; stands up to her tough boss for the benefit of her children's future; and has warm conversations with Teddy.

Spacek obviously enjoyed playing a mother, because she displays genuine affection and concern for the two boys in all their scenes together. I also like Spacek's scenes with Roberts, who should have gotten a Supporting Actor nomination. The affair between Nita and Teddy is quite tasteful. Screenwriter William D. Wittliff wisely didn't allow them to sleep together until it's clear why they are attracted to each other and how they fill each other's current needs. They don't care if they scandalize the town, but they make sure what they do doesn't go against their own high moral standards. Spacek has played so many unattached females that she's rarely thought of as a romantic lead. But Nita and Teddy, with Spacek and Roberts in the parts, are definitely among the most likable movie lovers in memory.

1982

▶ BEST PICTURE

WINNER:
Gandhi (Indo-British Films/Columbia; Richard Attenborough)
Other Nominees: *E.T.—The Extra-Terrestrial, Missing, Tootsie, The Verdict*

▼

THE BEST CHOICE:
E.T.—The Extra-Terrestrial (Universal; Steven Spielberg)
Award-Worthy Runners-Up: *Blade Runner* (Ridley Scott), *Gandhi* (Richard Attenborough), *Moonlighting* (Jerzy Skolimowski), *Tootsie* (Sydney Pollack)

Mahatma Gandhi would have been humbled by Richard Attenborough's worshipful epic of his life, but movie-goers, critics, and Academy members greatly admired this sweeping, beautifully shot, skillfully acted (Ben Kingsley won an Oscar) biography of the Indian who believed social change can best be achieved by nonviolent, provocational resistance. They also appreciated that Attenborough, who won the Oscar for Best Director, spent twenty tough years trying to get financing for his dream film. His admiration for his subject is apparent in every frame. In fact, the picture's major problem is that Attenborough's Gandhi is too much of a saint. Afraid to challenge his audience, Attenborough ignored Gandhi's most controversial political stands. Some detractors think that was enough reason for *Gandhi* not to have won the Best Picture Oscar over four formidable nominees. I think a more valid reason was the sheer quality of Steven Spielberg's enchanting *E.T.—The Extra-Terrestrial.* But the Academy that fourteen years before had mistakenly rejected the coldest of science fiction films, Stanley Kubrick's *2001: A Space Odyssey,* now did the same to the warmest of science fiction films. *E.T.,* the L.A. film critics' Best Picture choice, won Oscars only for John Williams's Original Score (which Spielberg uses effectively to keep us in suspense, raise and lower our spirits, and manipulate us into tears), Visual Effects (by Carlo Rambaldi, Dennis Murren, and Kenneth F. Smith), and Sound Effects Editing (by Charles L. Campbell and Ben Burtt).

Spielberg would have had trouble finding a hero who was more peaceful than the pacifist Indian in a loincloth. So he invented one, a sweet alien from outer space, who quickly emerged as the only figure in 1982 who would have beaten Gandhi in an international popularity contest. At very least E.T. deserved a Best Supporting Actor nomination. At the beginning of the picture, which was written by Melissa Mathison (co-writer of *The Black Stallion*), E.T. and other aliens are collecting plants in a wooded area near suburbs in southern California. When

scientists converge on the area, the spaceship leaves without him. He is befriended by a nice, resourceful, lonely ten-year-old, Elliott (Henry Thomas), who brings him into his room. *Elliot*T and E.T. immediately form a strong bond, whereby the boy can sense what his new friend feels. E.T. also becomes a special friend to Elliott's

The beloved title creature of Steven Spielberg's *E.T.—The Extra-Terrestrial,* the all-time box-office champion. (Copyright by Universal Pictures, a Division of Universal City Studios, Inc. Courtesy of MCA Publishing Rights, a Division of MCA, Inc.)

older brother (Robert MacNaughton) and younger sister (Drew Barrymore). He learns how to talk and conveys that he longs for home. The kids help him send a message to the ship ("Phone Home!"). Meanwhile, their recently divorced mother (Dee Wallace) is too unhappy and distracted to realize that there is something weird going on. The kids and E.T. become increasingly attached to each other but the fragile alien becomes seriously homesick. Government scientists charge into the house and do tests on the ill alien. They think he dies, but Elliott's tears bring him back. Elliott and his brother and some neighborhood kids help E.T. escape the police and scientists and reach the wooded area as the spaceship returns. E.T. says goodbye to his three friends and hugs Elliott. E.T. wants Elliott to come with him. The teary Elliott wants E.T. to stay. E.T. goes home alone.

Spielberg expected *E.T.* to be a small picture, but it hit a universal nerve—E.T. could be seen as a myth figure—and went on to become the highest grossing picture of all time, passing *Star Wars*. It was a picture made for kids, but it had elements to which adults responded more strongly. Sourpusses begrudged Spielberg his success and accused him of just trying to push all the right buttons, but far from thinking him calculated, I believe he made all the right choices instinctively. *E.T.* has excitement, a great deal of quirky wit and slapstick, charm, magical special effects, appealing kids whose dialogue is kidlike, and a wonderful alien with undeniable appeal. It's significant that Spielberg conceived his story when he himself was lonely. Because the visitor who becomes pal

to this boy who misses his father is much like Robert Louis Stevenson's "imaginary playmate"—I've long thought that E.T. is the ideal friend for all kids (especially those without two parents) who wish their stuffed animals would hug them back. For adults he'd make a good visiting relative or loyal "drinking" buddy who'd patiently listen to all problems.

E.T. is a twist on *The Wizard of Oz,* from which it borrows images. This time three youngsters help an adult return to his own world (like Dorothy, E.T. believes there is no place like home). In truth, the film has far more sympathy for and understanding of children than the 1939 classic. Whereas Judy Garland's Dorothy is supposed to grow up because of her experiences, Spielberg's kids—though they've seen the corrupt world in action—are not required by the filmmaker to grow up at all! It is because they are young and innocent that they don't fear E.T. but befriend him, when adults are hostile. And only these youngsters could help E.T. elude dangerous adults and help him escape at the end. Peter Coyote's scientist tells Elliott that he's been dreaming of meeting an alien since he was Elliott's age. But his motives have changed: boys want to play with aliens, adults want to experiment on them. *E.T.* celebrates children.

E.T.'s costar, Henry Thomas, is the too-often-forgotten reason why the film is so popular. He's so appealing in a difficult part that, like the scientist, we easily accept his Elliott as our surrogate. We allow him—and only him—to fulfill our dream of meeting the perfect alien.

▶ BEST ACTOR

WINNER:
Ben Kingsley *(Gandhi)*
Other Nominees: Dustin Hoffman *(Tootsie)*, Jack Lemmon *(Missing)*, Paul Newman *(The Verdict)*, Peter O'Toole *(My Favorite Year)*

▼

THE BEST CHOICE:
Dustin Hoffman *(Tootsie)*
Award-Worthy Runners-Up: Albert Finney *(Shoot the Moon)*, Jeremy Irons *(Moonlighting)*, Ben Kingsley *(Gandhi)*, Paul Newman *(The Verdict)*

In 1982 the Academy voters chose a man in a loincloth over a man in a dress. Their selection of Ben Kingsley as *Gandhi* over Dustin Hoffman as *Tootsie* probably had less to do with the actors' unusual attire than that Kingsley appeared in a drama playing one of history's great men while the runner-up starred in a fictional New York–set comedy. The Academy chose *Gandhi* as Best Picture over *Tootsie* because it believed Richard Attenborough's epic was a more significant film, and apparently they considered Kingsley's performance more significant than Hoffman's. Besides, it had awarded Hoffman an Oscar only three years before for *Kramer vs. Kramer*. *Gandhi* was the first major role for the Anglo-Indian Kingsley and

because he was an unknown who looked like Gandhi it made his performance particularly persuasive. At the time I also thought he deserved the Oscar. Since then Kingsley has become familiar in other roles, so when I see him as Gandhi I no longer sense that aura. Now I can detect the *acting*. He's still impressive, but now that we don't completely identify him with Gandhi we have less patience for his saying every line as if it were both simple and profound. I'd much rather listen to Hoffman's straight-from-the-lip Tootsie.

Hoffman is Michael Dorsey, a talented and dedicated New York actor. His agent, George (played by *Tootsie*'s director, Sydney Pollack), informs him that he's too diffi-

Dustin Hoffman's Michael Dorsey is made up as soap actress Dorothy Michaels and is ready to put her three cents' worth into a discussion of a scene between Dabney Coleman's director Ron Carlysle and George Gaynes's actor John Van Horn in *Tootsie*.

cult to be employable. He needs money to produce and star in a play *(Return to Love Canal)* written by his apartment mate, Jeff (Bill Murray). So he disguises himself as a woman, Dorothy Michaels, and wins a part in a daytime soap opera. Dorothy seems to have a life of her own; and improvising on the set, she turns her character into a staunch advocate of women's rights. She becomes a cult phenomenon across America, inspiration for women who need to assert themselves in relations with men. The other female characters become stronger, as do the actresses who play them. Dorothy becomes best friends and role model to Julie (Jessica Lange won a Best Supporting Actress Oscar), a sweet actress on the show who is dating the sexist director Ron (Dabney Coleman). Michael loves Julie, but can't reveal his identity to her. He also can't tell his actress friend Sandy (Teri Garr) that he's the one who won the part she'd wanted on the soap. Meanwhile, Julie's father (Charles Durning) falls for Dorothy and proposes to her. When Julie breaks off with Ron, Dorothy tries to kiss her—Julie thinks her a lesbian and sends her away because she can't return that kind of love to her. Michael thinks the world of Dorothy, but he realizes he can't carry on the deception. On a live broadcast Dorothy reveals herself to be a man, who says he was as proud as his dead sister was to have been a woman. The furious Julie slugs Michael in the stomach and makes it clear their relationship is over. After much time passes, they will be reconciled. Julie says that she misses Dorothy. Michael says that he still has Dorothy in him and that he'll treat Julie with the same sensitivity Dorothy did. Only, he wants to try it without a dress from now on.

Hoffman first thought of doing *Tootsie* when he was finishing *Kramer vs. Kramer,* in which he becomes both father and mother to his son. As he told *American Film* interviewer Mitch Tuchman, "I was very excited about a new feeling—what makes a man, what makes a woman, what is gender. I had a lot of conversations with [screenwriter] Murray Schisgal, over what masculinity is, what femininity is, the difference between homosexuality and femininity in men. Suddenly he asked me this question: 'What kind of woman would you be if you were a woman?' . . . So we started to experiment. . . . After a year, when the day came when I looked and sounded like a woman, I made a crucial decision: I'm not going to try to do a character; I'm just going to be myself behind this and see what happens."

In one of his few outright comedies Hoffman is a delight playing two characters who justifiably get separate listings in the final credits. He is equally funny as Michael trying on women's dresses—"I don't have the right shoes for it, I hate the way the horizontal lines makes me look too hippy, and it cuts me across the bust"—and Dorothy taking care of Julie's baby or warding off the advances of men. One of the funniest scenes has Dorothy's character hitting over the head a lecherous actor (George Gaynes) nicknamed "the tongue," rather than kissing him as the script dictated. The viewer thinks, as he watches the scene, that *Tootsie*'s writers, Murray Schisgal, Larry Gelbart, Hoffman, and (uncredited) Elaine May thought this bit up so Hoffman wouldn't actually have to kiss a man on screen—but the aged actor is so impressed by Dorothy's improvisation that once the studio camera is off he kisses her anyway, right on the mouth. Hoffman's shocked, shriveled-mouth expression is a gem. Hoffman has many other hilarious moments—as Michael he has terrific scenes with the deadpanning Murray, hysterical-neurotic Garr, and crazed Pollack (their Russian Tea Room scene is a classic)—as well as some surprisingly sweet, serious moments with Jessica Lange. It's good that Michael wasn't made into the biggest sexist pig around, because we see that even the average man must change. We're glad that until Michael is able to change, Dorothy is around when Julie needs a friend.

Supposedly Hoffman used his mother—who called him "Tootsie" as a child—as a model for Dorothy, but obviously most of her character came from inside. There's little doubt that Hoffman is as proud playing Dorothy as Michael is being her. And like Michael, who is in search of a new identity, Hoffman lets Dorothy free a suppressed part of his personality, helping give himself a clearer identity. When Michael frees his female side, he becomes smarter (he says this), gentler, more sensitive, and less inclined to blame others for his failures. I like it that Michael doesn't base Dorothy on females he knows, but allows her a life of her own, influenced by his knowledge of chauvinistic men and their power games and infidelities. Dorothy untraumatically raises his sexual consciousness. He becomes an optimistic, confident person. "Dorothy was able to accept the way she looked," Hoffman told Tuchman. "I couldn't. She was able to have a tremendous amount of self-respect and I guess for that reason, it was hard to lose her [and move on to other characters]." On the other hand Michael is wise enough to keep Dorothy as part of his personality—otherwise he wouldn't be a worthy friend and lover for Julie.

▶ BEST ACTRESS

WINNER:
Meryl Streep *(Sophie's Choice)*
Other Nominees: Julie Andrews *(Victor/Victoria)*, Jessica Lange *(Frances)*, Sissy Spacek *(Missing)*, Debra Winger *(An Officer and a Gentleman)*

▼

THE BEST CHOICE:
Jessica Lange *(Frances)*
Award-Worthy Runners-Up: Julie Andrews *(Victor/Victoria)*, Diane Keaton *(Shoot the Moon)*, Sissy Spacek *(Missing)*, Debra Winger *(An Officer and a Gentleman)*

Like everyone else, the Academy members were in awe of Meryl Streep's dramatic skills, including her ability to do accents. So they eagerly gave her the Oscar for her guilt-ridden Polish-Catholic concentration camp survivor in Alan J. Pakula's film of William Styron's *Sophie's Choice.* Streep has some powerful moments when one can't help being stunned by her talent, but I think the Academy wrongly rewarded that talent rather than her performance. As in other early, humorless Streep films, her portrayal is too calculated and mannered, as if she was far more interested in the role as a vehicle for an actress than in the *woman* she is playing. She might well have watched Jessica Lange, who, as the ill-fated actress Frances Farmer in *Frances,* invested herself in the woman rather than the part. Lange won the Academy Award for Best Supporting Actress for *Tootsie,* but it was a consolation prize for having given such an impressive performance in *Frances* and still losing to Streep as Best Actress. If the Academy had correctly selected her Best Actress for *Frances,* then Lange's *Tootsie* costar Teri Garr could have won the Supporting Actress Oscar she deserved more than Lange (who actually was a leading lady in *Tootsie*).

Directed by former editor Graeme Clifford and scripted by Eric Bergren, Christopher DeVore, and Nicholas Kazan, *Frances* begins when Frances Farmer is a high-school student in Seattle. She wins an essay contest for a piece about God being dead, but her mother, Lillian (Kim Stanley), is the only one in town who appreciates her effort. The domineering, slightly loony Lillian has always taught her daughter to speak her mind. In time Frances becomes an actress. She wants to work in serious stage productions in New York but signs a contract with Paramount. She doesn't like her own work and detests the efforts of the studio executives to make her toe the line. But Lillian eats up her daughter's fame and couldn't be happier. Frances's marriage to an unsuccessful actor breaks up after she sleeps with a longtime acquaintance, reporter Harry York (Sam Shepard), her one loyal friend. The unhappy Frances walks out on Paramount and goes to New York to work in Harold Clurman's leftist Group Theatre. She falls in love with playwright Clifford Odets. But Paramount puts pressure on Clurman and Odets, who, needing financing, push out Frances. Odets returns

Jessica Lange was voted Best Supporting Actress for *Tootsie*, but she was much more dynamic as the lead in *Frances*, as embattled actress Frances Farmer.

to his wife. Shattered, Frances returns to Hollywood. There she is hounded by gossip columnists and punished by Paramount with embarrassing roles. She drinks heavily and takes pills. She has a run-in with a cop, and after slapping an insulting studio hairdresser, she is thrown in jail for six months. She refuses to behave and continues with tantrums and violent behavior. She is placed in a mental hospital. She undergoes therapy from an authoritarian psychiatrist and is given shock treatments. Harry helps her escape. She goes back to live with Lillian, and is placed under her care. When Frances refuses to go back to Hollywood, Lillian goes berserk, initiating a violent reaction from Frances. Lillian has her daughter committed to the asylum. There she suffers a hellish existence and is finally given a lobotomy. After her release she is tame and speaks of God.

Frances is a sloppy, jumbled film that is populated by vicious caricatures of men in authority and women with power, but Lange's gutsy, realistic performance emerges unscathed. That she was let down by those who made the picture seems ironic considering that the movie is about betrayal. Fighting for her identity and sanity,

Frances refuses to be "what you want to make me—dull, average, normal." She endures humiliation, harassment, confinement, physical pain, mental anguish, and the destruction of her body and mind in order to maintain her identity. Meanwhile all those around her who are frightened by such hostile independence turn against her, including a mother who once inspired her to be true to herself. She suffers so much that we viewers want her to cool it so she'll have time to recover from the latest violation on her life. But she never lets up, never backs down from an argument or physical confrontation, never lets anyone have the satisfaction of controlling her. We don't know whether to agree with her own assessment that she isn't insane, but if she is, we blame others for her condition and wish that somebody would help her. She is well aware that those who pretend to want to cure her "madness" are actually trying to break her will.

Lange immediately sought her comedic role in *Tootsie* to disengage herself from the devastatingly emotional experience she had playing Frances Farmer. She says she was a wreck after *Frances,* which is understandable considering all the wear and tear, all the crying, screaming, and fighting she goes through in the film. Rarely has an actress put so much of herself into a character, and considering that Frances is constantly battered and finally destroyed, Lange was unable to experience any joyful release.

In her teenage scenes Lange's performance is reserved. We usually can tell what Frances is thinking simply by the way she cocks her head, moves her eyes to the side, and smiles knowingly, her lips tightly together and moving in small circles. At this time, Frances is suspicious about the world and knows that she's basically on her own, but is quite optimistic. Her romanticism will be crushed in Hollywood and again in New York. From then on she has no direction in life, no trust in anyone but Harry, no one but her self-destructive self to protect her. In Lange's voice we find Farmer's strength and her hurt, her defiance and her suspicion that whoever she's talking to will turn against her. In her screaming and physical tantrums (against the cop, hairdresser, and her mother), we recognize the fury and desperation. What is most sad and most admirable about Lange's Farmer is that although she is worn out, wounded without the possibility of healing, and helpless, she carries on the fight . . . alone. She knows her situation is hopeless, but rather than admit that to her enemies, she accedes to more of their abuse. When Farmer has her lobotomy and we look at Lange's glazed eyes and battered face, we realize why this film has been so uncomfortable an experience: Lange's deep immersion in the role of the long-suffering, brutalized Farmer has made us feel as sorry for her as for the woman she plays.

1983

▶ BEST PICTURE

WINNER:
Terms of Endearment (Paramount; James L. Brooks)
Other Nominees: *The Big Chill, The Dresser, The Right Stuff, Tender Mercies*

THE BEST CHOICE:
The Right Stuff (Ladd Company/Warner Bros.; Philip Kaufman)
Award-Worthy Runners-Up: *Local Hero* (Bill Forsythe), *Man of Flowers* (Paul Cox), *Terms of Endearment* (James L. Brooks)

The Right Stuff, director-screenwriter Philip Kaufman's epic adaptation of Tom Wolfe's best-seller about test pilot Chuck Yeager (Sam Shepard) and America's seven Mercury astronauts, was expected to be the picture of the year and possibly propel John Glenn to a 1984 Democratic presidential nomination. But it was a box-office failure and the picture of the year turned out to be James L. Brooks's *Terms of Endearment,* a seriocomedy about

the thirty-year relationship between an infuriatingly resolute widow (Shirley MacLaine) and her equally indomitable daughter (Debra Winger), ending with the daughter's death from cancer. *The Right Stuff* could have used "glamour" Oscars to help it at the box office, but won only for Best Sound, Best Sound Effects Editing, Best Original Score (Bill Conti), and Best Editing. *Terms of Endearment* won Oscars for Best Picture, Best Actress

The seven Mercury astronauts happily pose for photographers, realizing they can use the media to their own advantage in squabbles with the government in Philip Kaufman's *The Right Stuff.*

(MacLaine), Best Supporting Actor (Jack Nicholson revived his career as the onetime astronaut who wins MacLaine's heart), Best Director, and Best Adapted Screenplay (Brooks), for which Kaufman wasn't even nominated. *The Right Stuff* has since gone on to become a cult favorite of critics and moviegoers over thirty, while the reputation of *Terms of Endearment* has gone downhill—it is often spoken of as just an elaborate TV movie. I am a big fan of *Terms of Endearment.* The acting by the three leads is wonderful and the relationships between MacLaine and Winger and MacLaine and Nicholson aren't reminiscent of any others in film (or television!); it earns tears and laughter; and it has a terrific theme: in a crisis, especially a life-and-death situation, even irresponsible people will come through for those they love. That I choose *The Right Stuff* over *Terms of Endearment* as 1983's Best Picture is no slight of Brooks's film. *The Right Stuff* is, I believe, a legitimate candidate for the best American film of the eighties.

Kaufman successfully conveys Wolfe's notion that Yeager and other early test pilots, and the early astronauts ("astronaut pilots," they call themselves) who followed, belong to American mythology as surely as the early Western pioneer-heroes who tamed the frontier. The early scenes are, in fact, set in the West (of the late forties and early fifties), in California, with much conversation taking place in a bar and Yeager and his wife (Barbara Hershey at her most appealing) riding horses. Much of this is shot like a John Ford Western, with rugged archetypes—Shepard has much charisma and authenticity—set against the landscape and sky. Like the typical movie "Westerner," these test pilots are rooted in a pure, less civilized time, and realize that *progress* will make them

anachronistic, if not obsolete. Kaufman admires Ford, and it's likely that his script was partly inspired by *The Man Who Shot Liberty Valance.* In the Ford film John Wayne secretly killed villain Liberty Valance, making it possible for the more respectable James Stewart (who the public thinks did the killing) to achieve fame and glory, while Wayne withdraws into anonymity (remembered only by Stewart and wife Vera Miles). In the Kaufman film Yeager, a true hero whose breakthroughs as a test pilot made the space program possible, withdraws into anonymity while immediate fame goes to the better educated, more image-conscious men who become astronauts without having done any pioneering.

At the film's beginning Yeager is the only hero. He and the other test pilots—real men to be sure—mock the astronauts because they haven't the purity of purpose that they consider essential to pioneers. And Yeager himself doesn't want to join them in a space program that an inept, confused government exploits as a public relations sideshow. Initially, the seven Mercury Program astronauts—John Glenn, (Ed Harris), Alan Shepard (Scott Glenn), Gordon Cooper (Dennis Quaid), Gus Grissom (Fred Ward), Deke Slayton (Scott Paulin), Scott Carpenter (Charles Frank), and Wally Schirra (Lance Henrickson)—are self-serving, glory-hungry, competitive men, who don't justify respect. They let themselves (and their wives) be manipulated by the government into media superstars, shills for the space program, and phony symbols of American patriotism. They are bought off by high salaries, fame, and, in some cases, the opportunity to meet "groupies."

But the men change when, their pride as pilots aroused, they insist on some measure of control over their missions. Not content to be mere human versions of the chimpanzees the government sends into space, they band together and, in spite of corruptive pressures from the government, come to represent the best in American ideals. They become worthy of Kaufman's tribute once they mature, and become the true heroes and pioneers in a program only they seem to know the value of—they know the meaning of patriotism, and it's not what the government is dishing out. And they win Yeager's hard-earned admiration. When he hears others still laughing at the astronauts, despite their accomplishments, he silences them: "It takes a special kind of man to volunteer for a suicide mission, especially when it's on TV." The entire government turns against Grissom when there's a hitch in his mission, but all we're interested in is Yeager's approval: "Old Gus, he did all right." Yeager realizes that these men also have "the right stuff."

Each of the astronauts also achieves the respect of his six confreres, something that would have meant little to any of them at the beginning. Even the cocky Cooper gets so carried away singing the praises of the other men and of one other pilot he remembers (certainly Yeager) that his bragging about his own skills now seems hollow. In a moving scene in which the astronauts are guests of honor at a mammoth tribute, instead of watching Sally Rand they gaze at each other with knowing smiles, telling each other that no one in the entire world knows what they've been through as individuals and as a team. (The film also makes the point that wives of astronauts are another, equally brave, select group.)

The Right Stuff has standout performances from Shepard, Hershey, Harris, Ward, Quaid, Glenn, Pamela Reed (as Trudy Cooper), Veronica Cartwright (whose Betty Grissom thinks the military has not adequately rewarded Gus and her for years of sacrificial service), and Kim Stanley (as former aviatrix Pancho Barnes). These performers obviously share Kaufman's love for their characters, flaws and all.

Some of the film's absurd (though fact-based) humor and satire falls flat, and the scatalogical humor becomes tiresome, but the picture has remarkable scope; dazzling

photography by Caleb Deschanel; incredible, nail-biting, and often almost spiritual flying sequences in jets and rockets; romance (I love the scene in which Glenn converses patiently with his stuttering wife, whom he's loved since they were ten); sex (even with clothes on Hershey and Sam Shepard are exciting); and wit. Better than any other film *The Right Stuff* illuminates the difference between what is heroic and what the public is manipulated into believing is heroic. Watching this movie that celebrates *true* American heroes who no longer care if they're considered heroes, it's hard not to feel great emotion (tears will fill your eyes), tremendous pride that our country can produce such men, and even a huge rush of American spirit.

▶ BEST ACTOR

WINNER:

Robert Duvall *(Tender Mercies)*

Other Nominees: Michael Caine *(Educating Rita)*, Tom Conti *(Reuben, Reuben)*, Tom Courtenay *(The Dresser)*, Albert Finney *(The Dresser)*

▼

THE BEST CHOICE:

Michael Caine *(Educating Rita)*

Award-Worthy Runners-Up: Tom Conti *(Reuben, Reuben)*, Jeremy Irons *(Betrayal)*, Norman Kaye *(Man of Flowers)*, Anthony Perkins *(Psycho II)*, Charles Martin Smith *(Never Cry Wolf)*

Defeating four British nominees, Robert Duvall was voted Best Actor of 1983 for playing a distinctly American part in *Tender Mercies,* which ironically was directed by Australian Bruce Beresford. In one of his rare leads Duvall was an alcoholic, divorced country music singer who finds a new, sober, and more peaceful life with a young widow (Tess Harper) and her son at a motel–gas station. He was a popular choice, but I found his restrained portrayal extremely irritating—in fact the entire cast, but for the refreshingly hysterical Betty Buckley, gives subdued, emotions-in-check, phony "honest" performances. You just wish the whole lot of them would start tickling each other.

Michael Caine would win a Supporting Actor Oscar for Woody Allen's 1986 ensemble piece, *Hannah and Her Sisters.* Even if that award wasn't meant to acknowledge his lengthy Oscarless career, I think it inappropriate that he'd win for a supporting role when he'd always been a terrific leading man. Surely, the Academy members realized that Caine might never again have a shot at a Best Actor Oscar, so they didn't want him to end up empty-handed. There would have been no need for such considerations if they'd given him a Best Actor Oscar for one of his earlier performances. For which role? I would choose his alcoholic and divorced (yes, him too) literature professor in *Educating Rita,* opposite Julie Walters.

Walters had starred in the play, which also was written

by Willy Russell and directed by Lewis Gilbert. She's "Rita," actually Susan, a married, working-class hairdresser who is determined to better herself through a knowledge of literature. She attends an "open university" and is assigned Caine's Frank Bryant as a tutor. A self-pitying, usually soused, failed poet, he is energized and stimulated by his new pupil, who has an unaffected approach to great literature. He enjoys watching her become knowledgeable but feels uncomfortable when she starts writing standard literary criticism. Rita's husband leaves her because she doesn't want to have a baby until she's ready. Frank's girlfriend leaves him. Rita goes away to study for the summer, and returns as a literature scholar. There is little more Frank can teach her, which upsets him. He also thinks she has changed and misses the honesty she conveyed before she became sophisticated. She resents his being jealous that his pupil now knows as much as he does, and she stays away from him. He starts drinking again and gets into trouble with the administration. She passes her major exam. She thanks Frank for his help and lets him know that she hasn't severed ties to the person who first entered his office. She thanks him for what he has given her—in return she gives him a haircut. Frank leaves for Australia, after asking Rita to go with him. She sees him off at the airport. He has stopped drinking because of her. They are proud and appreciative of each other. They hug goodbye.

In the best way possible, former hairdresser Julie Walters pays back her mentor, Michael Caine, for how he changed her for the better in *Educating Rita.*

Educating Rita was a showcase for Julie Walters, and she gives a dynamic performance, full of grit and wit. But Caine matches her every step of the way. As Rita changes in dramatic ways, we notice subtle changes in Frank. As his drinking drops off, he again looks out his window with clear eyes at the pretty world outside, starts to care again about teaching, is excited again about literature, smiles, has energy, looks trimmer (Caine put on weight for the role), and likes himself again. When Rita leaves his sphere of influence, getting stimulation and experi-

ences elsewhere, he is crushed, reacting with spite and martyrdom. He orders her to go away. Obsolete again, he returns to booze. His attitude becomes obnoxious, but Caine makes it evident that Frank is feeling emotions that he hasn't experienced for years. So while he tries to destroy himself—if the drinking doesn't wreck him physically, it will at very least cause him to lose his position— he also looks deeply inside himself and unexpectedly finds good qualities, the result of his relationship with Rita. Before, he selfishly hadn't wanted her to take the big exam—validation that she no longer needs him—but when he peeks inside the examination room he smiles at her presence there. He does want her to move ahead in her life, which is how a good teacher should feel. She will inspire him to move ahead in his own life.

As Frank Bryant, tutor of someone who had a background much like Caine's own, he got the opportunity to be intelligent, tender, funny, bitter, self-pitying, and insecure. "Caine gives a master film performance," wrote Pauline Kael, perceptively adding, "You can see the professor's impotence in his pink-rimmed, blurry eyes; he's crumbling from within. Caine lets nothing get between you and the character. You don't observe his acting; you just experience the character's emotions. You feel his smirking terror." After Rita's transformation from honest woman to pretentious sophisticate, Frank alludes to Mary Shelley's creation of a monster. Significantly, while he begrudges himself for having altered Rita, he is the one who is acting like a monster. You really do feel his "smirking terror" as he gazes at this woman who has outgrown him and wants her freedom. What's really scary, for many of us men anyway, is that we can identify with Caine's abandoned mentor at this moment.

▶ BEST ACTRESS

WINNER:
Shirley MacLaine *(Terms of Endearment)*
Other Nominees: Jane Alexander *(Testament),* Meryl Streep *(Silkwood),* Julie Walters *(Educating Rita),* Debra Winger *(Terms of Endearment)*

▼

THE BEST CHOICE:
Shirley MacLaine *(Terms of Endearment)*
Award-Worthy Runners-Up: Jane Alexander *(Testament),* Rosanna Arquette *(Baby, It's You),* Bonnie Bedelia *(Heart Like a Wheel),* Barbara Hershey *(The Entity),* Meryl Streep *(Silkwood),* Barbra Streisand *(Yentl),* Julie Walters *(Educating Rita),* Debra Winger *(Terms of Endearment)*

The year 1983 was remarkable for leading ladies. The five nominees all gave exceptional performances, as did the unnominated Rosanna Arquette, Bonnie Bedelia, and Barbara Hershey (terrific in the mediocre *The Entity*)— nonstars who appeared in out-of-the-mainstream pictures—and Barbra Streisand, whom the Academy unfairly scorned, not only for having starred in the ambitious *Yentl,* but also for having had the audacity to direct,

produce, and cowrite it. Cases could be made why each of these actresses—and maybe *Cross Creek*'s Mary Steenburgen and *Betrayal*'s Patricia Hodge—deserves the Oscar. But none would be stronger than for Shirley MacLaine in director-writer James Brooks's tragicomic *Terms of Endearment,* from Larry McMurtry's novel. Surely the Academy was itching to give her an Oscar to honor her twenty-five years in movies, but as it turned out, she gave the performance of her career, definitely worthy of an Oscar.

Terms of Endearment is about the combative yet loving and mutually dependent relationship between Aurora Greenway and her daughter, Debra Winger's Emma, ending with the thirty-year-old Emma's painful death from cancer. The film begins with the recently-married Aurora climbing into Emma's crib to poke her too-quiet baby. She wants to make sure Emma's only sleeping—the annoyed, frightened wails bring Aurora relief. So starts a relationship that is characterized by Aurora's willingness to continuously disrupt Emma's life "for her own good." The overbearing, opinionated, tactless Aurora will never spare her daughter harsh criticism to shield Emma's feelings. Nor will she compromise her conservative principles just to make her daughter feel good (so she rarely makes her feel good). Surrounded by sexless suitors, she tries to make everything prim and proper, but Emma stubbornly clings to her wilder ways. She even marries Flap (Jeff Daniels) although her mother thinks him irresponsible. Eventually Emma and Flap leave Texas for Iowa, where he teaches. They raise three children. Aurora and Emma speak daily on the telephone. Living apart, these two different women become close friends, seeking out each other's advice and support and sharing confidences about affairs like giddy schoolgirls. Aurora takes pride in telling her delighted daughter that she's having her first affair in fifteen years, with former astronaut Garrett Breedlove (Jack Nicholson). It is Garrett's love that softens Aurora and sweetens her. Like her daughter Aurora now acts irrationally and spontaneously in love and life. But Garrett doesn't want to be tied down and breaks up with Aurora. Aurora is humiliated and lonely. Then Emma learns she has a fatal disease. Aurora devotes all her time to taking care of her daughter. Garrett unexpectedly returns, giving Aurora needed support. They will take care of Emma's kids after her death, because Flap is incapable of doing so. Aurora will be a better mother this time around—and she'll have Garrett's help.

Hoping to get an Oscar, MacLaine turned down roles for almost two years while waiting for Brooks to get studio backing for *Terms of Endearment.* Her decision paid off. Brooks approached other middle-aged actresses to play Aurora but gave the part to MacLaine because she was the only one who responded to the comic elements in the script. She based her character on the outrageously opinionated Martha Mitchell, wife of Nixon's crooked attorney general, John Mitchell. Martha spent much of a typical day gabbing to reporters over the phone. MacLaine doesn't treat her character with condescension, because she recognizes Aurora's extraordinary qualities. Instead she makes sure we know that Aurora recognizes her own peculiarities and foibles; there is self-mockery evident in Aurora's every expression—she knows when she is being foolish or pretentious. Aurora responds so well to Garrett because he thinks her snooty attitude is as funny as she knows it is. Being around him it's not only okay to make a fool of herself—what a mess she is

when she climbs out of his sports car—there's no way she can avoid it. It's truly delightful watching MacLaine's Aurora go belly-to-potbelly with Nicholson's Garrett, who reluctantly comes to realize that he's no longer a young Lothario. At this point in their lives—in a crisis situation—they peak as human beings, admit they love and need each other, and will be the best parents imaginable for Emma and Flap's neglected kids.

It's also exciting watching MacLaine play scenes with Winger. There was supposedly much strife on the set between the two actresses, yet on the screen they seem to appreciate each other's talents and the love between mother and daughter comes through despite *their* great differences. The friction between the stars seems to benefit their scenes together. MacLaine, a major star in the sixties, and Winger, a major star in the eighties, are among the best at expressing vulnerability under tough exteriors, and they each brought that skill into play in *Terms of Endearment.* But in this film MacLaine—perhaps taking a cue from Winger's characters—didn't play the total victim she had done in the past. When she is hurt and cries, she fights back rather than crumbling. MacLaine's Mrs. Greenway is tough. On her first date with Garrett she takes out a shawl after he warns her about her hair blowing in his car, saying, "Grown women are prepared for life's emergencies." She had no idea of the magnitude of the upcoming emergencies in her life—but she *is* prepared.

MacLaine has many memorable moments in the movie. When Emma announces her first pregnancy, Aurora is hysterical: "Why should I be happy about being a grandmother?" When Emma leaves for Iowa, Aurora can't hold back tears and her embrace is so tight that Emma comments, "That's the first time I stopped hugging first—I like that." When she plays Queen Bee to her suitors, she tells one, "Don't worship me until I've earned it." When

While daughter Debra Winger gets the hugs and attention, Shirley MacLaine contemplates the sad ironies of life in *Terms of Endearment.*

Garrett and Aurora kiss while drenched in water, she almost breaks his hand after he puts it on her breast (the film's funniest moment). I love her phone call to Garrett in which she invites him to see a painting in her bedroom, which both know is an invitation to bed. She is extremely nervous while he makes his decision. When Garrett begins his seduction by calling her baby, she pulls away, feigning insult, saying, "Who do you think you're talking to like that? Don't you realize I'm a grandmother?"—only to then grab his face, plant a wild kiss on his lips, and clutch him madly (a great moment!). I like it when she lies with him in bed, smiling broadly while enjoyably but dutifully listening to his ramblings about his astronaut days. I also like it when she tells off a doctor for being stingy with information about Emma's illness and when she runs through the hospital corridors insisting in the loudest of voices that Emma be given her painkiller on time: "Give my daughter the shot!" When Emma's oldest son says something nasty about his dying

mother, Aurora slaps him and then, while hugging the crying boy, says, "I'm sorry, but I just can't have you criticizing your mother around me"—this coming from the woman who had always been Emma's worst critic.

My favorite moment is when Garrett comes back to Aurora in her time of need. When she sees him, she is tired and haggard, and her dry lips part slightly in thankful surprise. She walks to him and they embrace with true affection. She says, "Who would have expected you to be a nice guy." Later she drops him at the airport, and tells him she loves him. They walk away from each other, but she calls him back, asking for a reaction to what she has just said. With that wide Nicholson grin Garrett says he'll give her his stock answer: "I love you, too, kid." And he kisses her. In her selfless care for the dying Emma and her grandchildren, Aurora hasn't done anything to warrant being worshiped (even by her suitors), but she certainly has earned everyone's love.

▶ BEST PICTURE

WINNER:
Amadeus (Orion; Milos Forman)
Other Nominees: *The Killing Fields, A Passage to India, Places in the Heart, A Soldier's Story*

▼

THE BEST CHOICE:
The Killing Fields (Goldcrest/International Film Investors/Warner Bros.; Roland Joffé)
Award-Worthy Runner-Up: *This Is Spinal Tap* (Rob Reiner)

The Academy assured itself of a "prestige" Best Picture winner when it nominated only high-minded, high-brow adult pictures, all of which in some way dealt with discrimination. You wouldn't find *The Terminator, The Brother from Another Planet, This Is Spinal Tap, Romancing the Stone, Stranger Than Paradise, Ghostbusters, Purple Rain, Splash, The Karate Kid,* or *Beverly Hills Cop* among these nominees, although a few of them were better choices. In the final balloting Milos Forman's *Amadeus* beat cofavorite *A Passage to India,* an epic presentation of E. M. Forster's novel that was David Lean's first film in fourteen years. Adapted by Peter Shaffer from his 1979 fictional play, *Amadeus* is about the obsessive jealousy felt by eighteenth-century Italian hack court composer Antonio Salieri (little known F. Murray Abraham won an Oscar), for the crude Wolfgang Amadeus

Mozart (Tom Hulce), and his attempt to ruin the young genius's career. The acting is splendid and it's the rare film that shows an artistic genius in the act of creating. But since none of the various characters changes at all from the first time we see him, most scenes are merely repetitions of earlier ones. The dialogue and situations are embarrassingly trite and anachronistic (they would fit fifties TV comedies) and the film's major theme, the sad discrepancy between the rich Salieri's *popular* music and the starving Mozart's much better *unpopular* music, was surely inspired by what goes on today when adventurous musicians make less money than less talented but more commercial performers.

Almost everybody who saw *The Killing Fields* in 1984 was greatly affected. But for some reason it never had the strong backing for Best Picture that would carry the

In Cambodia in 1973 Haing S. Ngor's Dith Pran serves as interpreter for Sam Waterston's reporter Sydney Schanberg in *The Killing Fields*.

equally controversial but American-made *Platoon* to an Oscar in 1986. Perhaps it was because it was British, and Americans resented having Brits raise their political consciousness—no matter that it wouldn't have been made by Americans. Or perhaps they didn't want to give producer David Puttnam another Oscar so soon after *Chariots of Fire,* a choice that still rankled many. Surely, this wasn't the film Hollywood's old guard screened for guests at lavish dinner parties, so it's likely that many voters never saw what they feared was a brutal, anti-American film (which it is only to a small extent). That's too bad, because *The Killing Fields* is, despite flaws, a remarkable achievement that stands far above the other nominees. Still enlightening about what transpired in Cambodia in the 1970s—and helping us understand what has happened there since—it has more than withstood the passage of time.

This true story begins in 1973. *New York Times* foreign correspondent Sydney Schanberg (Sam Waterston) is covering America's secret bombing campaign in Cambodia. Cambodian Dith Pran (Dr. Haing S. Ngor) is his assistant and interpreter, whom Schanberg takes for granted. When the communist Khmer Rouge take control of the country, Pran sends his family to America with all the fleeing foreigners, but at Schanberg's urging remains behind with him to help cover the story. As the Khmer Rouge, consisting of many gun-happy teenagers, march into Phnom Penh, Schanberg realizes that everyone there is in danger, particularly Pran. Pran's pleading saves Schanberg and other English-speaking reporters from execution by a patrol. Finally Schanberg realizes what a remarkable person Pran is and what a dear friend he has been. But when Schanberg and other foreign journalists are sent back home, he can't take Pran with him. Schanberg looks after Pran's family in America and writes hundreds of letters to try to locate Pran. He feels tremendous guilt for having persuaded Pran to stay with him just so he could attempt to win journalism awards. Mean-while Pran remains in Cambodia, where three million people (including all intellectuals) are massacred and dumped in the muddy "killing fields." He slaves in the mud for countless hours each day at a "reeducation" camp, pretending to have no education, no memory, no mind. He nearly starves, he is almost killed by guards. He escapes the camp, and eventually escapes the country, just when the South Vietnamese drive out the Khmer Rouge. In 1979 Schanberg and Pran reunite at a refugee camp. They embrace.

An ambitious work, *The Killing Fields* is both a fascinating human drama and a riveting, eye-opening account of a unique and tragic historical event. It's no "buddy" picture but the deeply moving story of two seemingly different men from completely different cultures who, just when they finally learn to respect and love each other on equal terms, are pulled apart by historical forces . . . only to be, impossibly, reunited years later (as we hear John Lennon's "Imagine"). It's also a vivid depiction of America's secret war in Cambodia and its terrifying aftermath. While it's not very political—you'll have to supply your own background for the Khmer Rouge—it does make the brave statement that the bloodbath in Cambodia was the result of $14 billion worth of U.S. bombings, which dislocated the society. Moreover, its unforgettable scenes at the "reeducation" camp—where people "disappear," history is erased (it is Year Zero), and kids are indoctrinated to turn against their parents—should refute all those who contend Orwell was too pessimistic and that things didn't turn out as badly as he'd expected.

First-time director Roland Joffé and cinematographer Chris Menges (who won a deserved Oscar) had background in documentaries, and you always get the sense that what you're watching is authentic. It's hard to believe that scenes were staged and that filming took place in Thailand. It's hard to believe that we aren't witnessing the Americans back out of Phnom Penh, minutes before Khmer Rouge soldiers roll in on tanks, with celebrating little kids riding on top with the teenage soldiers. There is always a sense of urgency, a sense of confusion and panic. When Cambodian soldiers execute rebels and demand that witnesses Schanberg and Pran leave or else, we want our heroes to get the hell out of there. When a gun-happy Khmer Rouge patrol starts executing prisoners and hold Schanberg and others ready for slaughter, we really hope Pran can convince the young leader to let them go, because we do fear for them. We feel we know exactly what it's like for foreign reporters to cover a war, without protection. Any time Schanberg and/or Pran arrive at a location, we sense that something has happened there already, as there is dust and smoke from explosions (Menges does a great job with lighting), debris and bodies scattered about, and chaos. That Joffé and Menges didn't sensationalize what is on screen also makes it all seem real. We wouldn't expect anyone to make up a quick bit where there is an explosion and an American-made Coke machine goes flying by a crying, motherless baby and an injured water buffalo. It's so weird it has to be real, right?

What also lends authenticity to *The Killing Fields* is the casting of the two leads. Waterston's Schanberg is quite convincing. He isn't the typical movie hero but, before Pran saves his life, an arrogant, self-serving SOB (which all great journalists must be, according to this film). We admire the aggressive way he pursues a story, even when danger lurks—we *believe* a story means that much to him—but don't like his patronizing attitude toward Pran and disinterest in other Cambodians as individuals. In a typical movie we'd see everything through the white journalist's eyes, and since this film was based on a Schanberg story in *The New York Times,* we could expect that here. But we leave Schanberg and stick with Pran through his painful years in Cambodia under the Khmer Rouge. This is tantamount to having made Tonto rather than the Lone Ranger the hero of that old Western

series—it would never have been done! Schanberg may be the protagonist of this film, but it is a celebration of Pran, a man of amazing selflessness, courage, and indomitable spirit. So Pran is given considerable screen time. Haing S. Ngor gives true credibility to this role because he was a nonactor whose flight from Cambodia much paralleled his character's—only, it was sadder in that his real family starved to death. When you watch Ngor, you know he feels the suffering of his character and the tragedy that has befallen his country. He won the Best Supporting Actor Oscar for his sensitive, dignified performance. Of course, it was no consolation for what he went through. But he hoped the award, like the film itself, would call attention to the fact that the suffering in Cambodia had not ended.

▶ BEST ACTOR

WINNER:
F. Murray Abraham *(Amadeus)*
Other Nominees: Jeff Bridges *(Starman)*, Albert Finney *(Under the Volcano)*, Tom Hulce *(Amadeus)*, Sam Waterston *(The Killing Fields)*

▼ ───

THE BEST CHOICE:
Albert Finney *(Under the Volcano)*
Award-Worthy Runners-Up: F. Murray Abraham *(Amadeus)*, Victor Banerjee *(A Passage to India)*, Tom Hanks *(Splash)*, Joe Morton *(The Brother from Another Planet)*

The race for 1984's Best Actor was considered wide open when the New York Film Critics chose Steve Martin for *All of Me,* the National Board of Review selected Victor Banerjee for *A Passage to India,* and *Amadeus*'s F. Murray Abraham and *Under the Volcano*'s Albert Finney were voted cowinners by the L.A. Film Critics. When neither Martin nor Banerjee was nominated for an Oscar, Abraham and Finney seemed to have the inside track. Abraham, who had the benefit of being in a critical and box-office success, beat out his famous British opponent, becoming the least known Best Actor in history, and the first of Arab descent. His performance as mediocre court composer Antonio Salieri, who jealously ruins the career of genius Wolfgang Amadeus Mozart (Tom Hulce), is certainly the best thing about that picture—his villain is chilling, a monster not unlike petty and territorial people with power whom we have all known. However, it just doesn't compare with Finney's brilliant portrayal of a drunk down Mexico way in John Huston's compelling box-office flop of Malcolm Lowry's supposedly unfilmable cult novel.

Twenty-eight-year-old Guy Gallo's first screenplay streamlined Lowry's convoluted 1947 novel so that it becomes almost exclusively a character study. It is set over two days in November 1938, in Cuernavaca and a neighboring town. Finney is Geoffrey Fermin, a perpetu-

ally drunk former British vice consul. He is still shattered by the departure of his wife, Yvonne (Jacqueline Bisset's best performance), who went to New York to resume her acting career a year ago. He carries around her unopened letters, afraid of what she has written him. He prays for her return. The next day, she returns, as she said she'd do in her letters, willing to resume their marriage although she doesn't expect him to sober up. He tries to make love to her but is impotent. Geoffrey, Yvonne, and his half-brother Hugh (Anthony Andrews) take a bus ride to a nearby town. Although he has several tantrums and drinks whenever he has the chance, Geoffrey is in a fairly cheery mood. He lets Yvonne and Hugh go off to enjoy themselves together. Later Yvonne suggests that she and Geoffrey move away and start a new life together. Geoffrey is quite enthusiastic fantasizing about their future life, but to be mean he says that they'll invite Hugh so she can sleep with him. He then further insults Yvonne by telling her she wasn't a good wife because she never provided him with children. Chugging down liquor, he walks up a hill and drinks in a bar-whorehouse. He finally reads Yvonne's letters and is touched by her love for and commitment to him. A whore pulls him into a back room for sex. When Yvonne and Hugh come looking for Geoffrey and find out what he is doing, Yvonne flees, with Hugh following. Drunk Geoffrey is bullied by the owner

Wearing dark glasses to protect his bloodshot eyes from the sun, Albert Finney's Geoffrey Fermin attempts reconciliation with Jacqueline Bisset's Yvonne in John Huston's adaptation of Malcolm Lowry's novel, *Under the Volcano*.

and several undesirables who demand money and then take Yvonne's letters. He draws a saber he finds on a nearby table and demands the return of the letters. He fearlessly insults the men who took them. They shoot and kill him. Yvonne hears the shots and runs up the hill. She is struck and killed by a frightened horse, which broke free upon hearing the shots. Hugh kisses her on the mouth.

While filming was going on in Mexico, Huston told Pete Hamill that "this fellow Finney is giving one of the finest performances I've ever seen. I thought he would be good; but I never dreamed that he would be as good as he is. Or that *anybody* would be as good as he is." Seeing the completed film, we realize that Huston's assessment was correct. Once considered Olivier's successor on the English stage, Finney has had a marvelous screen career, with memorable performances in such films as *Saturday Night and Sunday Morning, Tom Jones, Two for the Road, Charlie Bubbles, Gumshoe,* and *Shoot the Moon,* but this is far and away his most powerful characterization. It's impossible not to be jolted by Finney, particularly when his consul prays for Yvonne's return; turns his head repeatedly upon her return before realizing she's not a hallucination; unfairly tells off Yvonne in their final scene together; unleashes a tirade against the armed bullies who stole Yvonne's love letters; and when in many other scenes he experiences delirium tremens. He acts with every muscle in his face, his eyes, his teeth, his body, his voice. I love how he walks, how he stumbles about, how he leans over to pet a stray dog, how he folds his arms over his chest, how he talks loudly and excessively, how he tries to control his shaking with

immediate imbibing, meeting his bottle or glass halfway. He is fierce, intense, loud, ironic, pathetic, obnoxious, tragic. He is always drunk, and always interesting.

In general I tire quickly of screen drunks, but Finney's Consul is riveting. Hamill: "When he is supposed to be drunk, he is drunk; not the comic drunk, not the grotesque, exaggerated drunk of so many bad performers. Finney as the Consul plays an intelligent man, a man of language and smothered passions, who has moved past the point where the world is clear, yet remains capable of sudden explosions of clarity. It's in the way he stands, in the looseness of his features that suddenly snap into tension. It's in his great angers, breaking out of the emotional ice jam that the Consul made of his life."

Finney's Consul consistently disappoints us, repeatedly pushes away his opportunities for salvation, yet we admire him, detecting greatness. We can understand why the beautiful Yvonne would return to him, why her love for him does not diminish. We know the depth of his feelings. We recognize the self-hatred he feels for having spoiled everything, his tenderness that he can now display only to that stray dog, and his undying love for Yvonne, for whose return he actually prays in front of a shrine. That's why we're not surprised—though we are impressed—when he dies unlike a coward, standing up to the bullies with a saber and vicious words, demanding Yvonne's love letters. After being shot several times and falling to the ground, his last words are "Christ, what a dingy way to die," but we think he dies admirably—much more gallantly than Humphrey Bogart does under similar circumstances in Huston's *The Treasure of the Sierra Madre.* And he dies in character.

► BEST ACTRESS

WINNER:
Sally Field *(Places in the Heart)*
Other Nominees: Judy Davis *(A Passage to India),* Jessica Lange *(Country),* Vanessa Redgrave *(The Bostonians),* Sissy Spacek *(The River)*

▼

THE BEST CHOICE:
Kathleen Turner *(Romancing the Stone)*
Award-Worthy Runners-Up: Judy Davis *(A Passage to India),* Sally Field *(Places in the Heart),* Daryl Hannah *(Splash),* Molly Ringwald *(Sixteen Candles),* Kathleen Turner *(Crimes of Passion),* Lesley Ann Warren *(Choose Me)*

After winning her second Best Actress Oscar for Robert Benton's Depression-era drama *Places in the Heart,* the deliriously happy Sally Field semifoolishly told all of us that "I can't deny the fact you like me—right now you *like* me." Well, we would have liked Field just as much if she hadn't won for her moving performance as a brave small-town Texas widow who saves her farm by bringing the cotton crop in with the help of her unusual friends. But in 1984 I preferred Kathleen Turner. In Ken Russell's *Crimes of Passion* she had some of her finest and most daring screen moments as a woman who is wild prostitute China Blue by night and a prim, man-fearing clothing designer by day. But that picture goes haywire—turning into an awful *Psycho* derivation (complete with a crazed Anthony Perkins)—before Turner can fully explore her character. Fortunately, Turner gave another fully developed Oscar-caliber performance this year, as a nice woman, in Robert Zemeckis's extremely enjoyable *Romancing the Stone.* This picture made a lot of money, but in a year in which all the Actress nominees were in dramas, the Academy didn't consider the star of this funny romantic-adventure, despite her having given us the year's most captivating female character.

Turner is Joan Wilder, a famous romance novelist who never experiences love of her own. Still she dreams of men similar to the heroes of her books. The usually unassertive Joan flies from New York to Colombia because her sister is in trouble. In her possession is a treasure map that her sister's husband mailed to her before he was murdered. Now her sister's kidnappers, Ralph and Ira (Danny DeVito and Zack Norman) want the map in exchange for her sister. A villainous stranger directs her to the wrong bus and she winds up in the country. After the bus crashes, he tries to kill her for the map. But another stranger happens along. Jack T. Colten (Michael Douglas) chases away the villain with his gun. Joan pays him to take her to a town. They have many adventures in the jungle, repeatedly escaping from the villain and his military forces. Joan falls for Jack and learns to trust him. They make love. She decides to find the treasure with him, hoping that he'll be able to buy the boat he always wanted so they can sail around the world together. They use the treasure map and find an enormous jewel. Ralph tries to take it from them, but

when the villain and his troops turn up, Joan and Jack get away. But the two of them split up, with the jewel in Jack's possession. She worries that he'll not keep their rendezvous. Joan delivers the map to Ira, who frees her sister. But the villain appears with Jack as his prisoner. Jack did try to keep the rendezvous. When the villain threatens to feed Joan's hand to an alligator, Jack kicks the jewel to him. He catches it and the alligator bites off his hand and swallows the jewel. There is a wild melee, in which the stranger tries to kill Joan but is devoured by alligators. Joan is upset when Jack takes off. She's back in New York and lonely when Jack appears outside her apartment on

Kathleen Turner finds herself lost in the Colombian jungles in Robert Zemeckis's *Romancing the Stone.*

his new boat—he caught up with the alligator. They will sail around the world.

Turner had been so convincing as the femme fatale in her 1981 debut film, *Body Heat,* that her charming dazzling portrayal of the completely likable Joan Wilder was a wonderful surprise. We root for Joan as we do for few heroines in adventure films, and enjoy watching her transition from a timid easy-touch in New York to a brave and capable, yet still sweet and sentimental, heroine in the real jungle: Wilder in the wilderness. With eyes wide in almost every shot she expresses the excitement of being involved in a great adventure and of falling in love—"You're the best time I've ever had," she tells Jack. Unlike Matty Walker in *Body Heat* Joan makes no effort to be sexy. But with Turner's sensual, throaty voice, those excited eyes, bare-legged poses that are befitting her novel's heroines, and, as Turner said, "no rules for herself," she is quite sexy. She may think of herself as prim and proper but the whole time we sense that she is ready for love, that every inch of her body will respond to the right man's touch. Jack responds to that part of her he knows is emerging. That she doesn't back away from him—and in fact is open and honest with her feelings toward him—spurs him on. Turner told *Prevue* magazine, "I enjoy playing characters who lead dual lives—presenting an alternate version of themselves to others. I also like vulnerable women who display their emotions without a protective mask."

As usual, Turner puts a full effort into her performance, getting into her character and giving her personality. While she and screenwriter Diane Thomas created a woman who will be alluring to men, I think that their primary goal was to make Joan appeal to women, which Matty Walker certainly does not. I think they wanted women viewers, especially single and lonely women, to identify with Joan's "hopeful romantic." In the early scenes they set up a character who cries about the romance in her own books; walks around her apartment in sloppy attire, talking to herself and her cat Romeo; and is such an easy touch that she is almost talked into buying a toy monkey by a sidewalk huckster. She is funny, smart, and pretty, yet can't see ever having the opportunity to meet the right man. Suddenly she is forced to take a chance and experience adventure, although she confides to her friend that she fears she's not up to it. And she comes through, proving herself to be a brave woman and a desirable, passionate lover (who has sex without guilt). I think she is meant to be inspiration for every woman viewer who needs a nudge to pursue her exciting dreams.

1985

▶ BEST PICTURE

WINNER:
Out of Africa (Universal; Sydney Pollack)
Other Nominees: *The Color Purple, Kiss of the Spider Woman, Prizzi's Honor, Witness*

▼

THE BEST CHOICE:
Brazil (Embassy International/Universal; Terry Gilliam)
Award-Worthy Runners-Up: *Insignificance* (Nicolas Roeg), *Out of Africa* (Sydney Pollack), *Prizzi's Honor* (John Huston), *Silverado* (Lawrence Kasden)

In selecting 1985's Best Picture the Academy again played it safe. It nominated four pictures that might better have been approached by the various filmmakers as strictly art-house projects but were instead written, cast, and/or directed to assure mainstream appeal. The exception, *Prizzi's Honor,* was made with more integrity. I am fond of the Academy's winner, Sydney Pollack's *Out of Africa,* an elegant epic in which Meryl Streep gives a strong, earnest performance as aristocratic Danish author Isak Dinesen. However, my choice for Best Picture is among those missing from the Academy's select circle: *Brazil,* an amazingly ambitious and inventive futuristic epic directed by Monty Python's American alumnus, Terry Gilliam.

Universal—actually Sid Sheinberg, president of parent company MCA—threatened to shelve the picture because Gilliam refused to trim it to below 131 minutes (Universal's *Out of Africa* runs 153 minutes, average time for Best Picture winners of the period) and to alter its gloomy ending. Gilliam even resorted to taking an ad in

In his dreams Jonathan Pryce is a great winged warrior in Terry Gilliam's imaginative political fantasy, *Brazil*.

Variety to ask for support to rescue his film. It was rescued unexpectedly when it was given prizes by the Los Angeles Film Critics for Best Picture, Best Director, and Best Screenplay (by Gilliam, Tom Stoppard, and Chuck McKeown). Then Sheinberg felt pressured to release the picture as is. At this point releasing Gilliam's heralded version seemed to make the most sense: then it would have a shot at Academy recognition, which would give it a chance to recoup its high cost. Yet Sheinberg didn't want to promote *Brazil* at the expense of his *Out of Africa* and of his own reputation for good taste. In any case, the Academy wasn't about to endorse a futuristic science fiction polemic, especially one made by someone Universal was labeling a troublemaker. Unjustly, *Brazil* was nominated only for Original Screenplay (won by *Witness*), and Art Direction (one of *Out of Africa*'s six Oscars). Without Oscars or nominations the best *Brazil* could achieve was cult status.

We're "somewhere in the twentieth century," in a totalitarian, form-obsessed state that is experiencing its thirteenth year of terrorist bombings. Sam Lowrey (Jonathan Pryce) leads a complacent life as a low-level bureaucrat working in the Records Division of the Ministry of Information. Meek and dull in real life, he daydreams about rescuing a beautiful blond princess. A typing error results in the arrest of an innocent man, Buttle, who is tortured to death in place of the terrorist, Harry Tuttle (cigar-chomping Robert De Niro). Lowrey unsuccessfully attempts to give the widow a check for compensation. He discovers that Mrs. Buttle's neighbor, Jill Layton (Kim Greist), is the spitting image of the woman in his dreams. Using his mother's influence (Katherine Helmond), he takes a promotion to Information Retrieval to learn about Jill. He discovers that she is in danger of being arrested for protesting Mr. Buttle's death. He tries to protect her, but she thinks he's screwy after he forces her to drive through a government roadblock. Eventually, she learns to trust him. They make love. They are both arrested. Sam's friend Jack (Michael Palin), who also works for the government, begins to torture him to death. Suddenly

Jack is killed by Harry, who whisks Sam to safety, and Sam and Jill escape. But Sam is just dreaming of his rescue. He is permanently dreaming, his mind's escape from Jack's torture.

"Walter Mitty Meets Franz Kafka" is how Gilliam termed his thematically daring, surrealistic vision of a dystopian future, the nightmarish experience of a passive dreamer who learns first-hand about the terrifying mechanics of totalitarianism. Lewis Carroll was certainly an equal inspiration. Sam's real world is full of Mad Hatterish characters, and the conversations and events that transpire in his waking world are as illogical as those of his dreams. Sample dialogue:

Sam: Say hello to Allison and the twins.
Jack: Triplets.
Sam: Triplets? God, how time flies.

The fourth influence was, of course, George Orwell. For those who debate whether World War II Britain or postwar Russia was Orwell's model for Oceania, Gilliam offers what appears to be a post–World War II Britain that is a Russian satellite. Bumbling Britishers badly perform (often apologetically) the strong-arm tactics we associate with Russian agents and police. Whereas we picture the post–World War II Russian bureaucracy as being efficient, the one Gilliam presents is similar to those we've experienced ourselves. Nothing in this world works, including elevators, gadgets, heating systems, and people with jobs: "An empty desk is an efficient desk," Sam's new boss insists. It's all so silly—including the ill-conceived police raids, prisoners with bags over their heads, and torturer Jack wearing a baby mask—that it's almost inconceivable that this totalitarian regime can be deadly. But it is; seriously so. As in *1984* the hero and heroine are arrested while making love and he is subjected to torture. But what happens to Sam in *Brazil*'s controversial ending is much happier than what happens to Winston Smith. At least this totalitarian regime can't control a man's dreams: "We've lost him," acknowledges the dejected Jack.

Many viewers and critics were unimpressed by Gilliam's black comedy, but I think it's a near masterpiece. Yes, the story bogs down in spots—Sheinberg was right, it's too long—but *every* shot is imaginative, bizarre, and fascinating. The design-oriented Gilliam (who did the animation for Python) presents a weird-looking, retrofitted, anachronistic world where clothes and buildings are of an earlier era and props are either old or came from several decades back and have become part of some *new* type of assembled gadgets (i.e., a screen and nonelectric typewriter are this new world's computers). Vehicles are either too small (Sam's government car) or too big (Jill's truck). Particularly strange are the elaborate office and apartment sets, with long corridors and stairwells, and with such clutter as poles, heating ducts, twisted wiring, filing cabinets, black-and-white TV screens showing movies from the thirties and forties, manual typewriters, and all kinds of thingamajigs. It's as if everything ever patented has been put to use, mostly by the government. Everywhere we look in the frame, something interesting catches our eye. And always the full image on the screen—there is considerable movement within the huge sets—is impressive; sometimes it is stunning.

The film's images, characters, and themes will recall such movies as *Potemkin, Blade Runner, Slaughterhouse-Five, Little Murders, Casablanca,* and *Dr. Strangelove,* which all have at least minor political subtexts. *Brazil's* happy title tune (Ary Baroso's thirties song) that plays at the end in insane Sam's closeted mind recalls Stanley Kubrick's ironic use of "We'll Meet Again" as the world is destroyed in *Dr. Strangelove,* as well as escapist musicals

of the Depression. Perhaps the most unusual aspect of this odd film is that Gilliam makes the bureaucracy so despicable and the rich public (Sam's mother spends her time getting face-lifts) so obnoxious that we're actually willing to accept as a savior a character who is referred to as a *terrorist* (De Niro's Tuttle is never called a revolutionary). It wouldn't be surprising to learn that this played a part in the Academy's refusal to nominate *Brazil* for Best Picture.

▶ BEST ACTOR

WINNER:

William Hurt *(Kiss of the Spider Woman)*
Other Nominees: Harrison Ford *(Witness),* James Garner *(Murphy's Romance),* Jack Nicholson *(Prizzi's Honor),* Jon Voight *(Runaway Train)*

▼

THE BEST CHOICE:

Jack Nicholson *(Prizzi's Honor)*
Award-Worthy Runners-Up: Albert Brooks *(Lost in America),* Harrison Ford *(Witness),* Michael J. Fox *(Back to the Future),* Sean Penn *(The Falcon and the Snowman)*

The Academy voters tried to show that they were more interested in performances by actors than in the types of characters they played when they gave its 1985 Best Actor Oscar to William Hurt for Hector Babenco's *Kiss of the Spider Woman.* Hurt played a feminine homosexual who is confined in an Argentine prison on a child-molestation charge. I think the voters might have held back their votes if Hurt's character hadn't been toned down from Manuel Puig's book. So that mainstream audiences would be able to sympathize with him, he doesn't explain the circumstances of his crime or vent his deepest, angriest thoughts about what it means to be gay in this particular society. Hurt is an exceptional, intelligent, chance-taking actor. He certainly makes an impression, but after a while you realize he's using flamboyance to mask a thinly written character. Also, he never lets us forget that he's just playing a part, preventing us from finding truths in the unusual person he's portraying. My choice for Best Actor is Jack Nicholson, whom I also picked in 1970 for *Five Easy Pieces* and in 1975 for *One Flew Over the Cuckoo's Nest.* Nicholson regained his star status as the result of his Best Supporting Actor performance in 1983's *Terms of Endearment,* paving the way for a starring role in John Huston's seriocomic *Prizzi's Honor,* which was adapted by Richard Condon and Janet Roach from Condon's novel. His oddball Brooklyn gangster is one of his finest characterizations.

Nicholson's Charley Partanna is godson of Don Corrado Prizzi (William Hickey), the head of the Prizzi crime family. Since he was very young, he has believed that family comes first. He carries out the family's most difficult, important crimes, yet off the job he's a somewhat

dopey fellow who worries about his love life. At a wedding he spots guest Irene Walker (Kathleen Turner) and immediately falls in love. But she lives in California. He flies to Los Angeles and on their first date they agree to marry. Charley assassinates a man who stole some Prizzi money and discovers that Irene was his wife. She swears she had no part in her husband's crimes, including a rubout and the stealing of Prizzi money. He catches her in these lies and finds out that she is a hit woman. Still, they marry. Charley is assigned a kidnapping. Irene volunteers to participate and devises the plan. But during the getaway she kills a police captain's wife. The police

On their first date Jack Nicholson confesses his love for Kathleen Turner in John Huston's *Prizzi's Honor.*

demand that the Prizzis deliver a fall guy. Turner, the Polish outsider, is the natural choice. Meanwhile Maerose Prizzi (Anjelica Huston won a Supporting Actress Oscar), Charley's vengeful former lover, also puts pressure on the Prizzi family to get rid of Turner. She tells her father that Charley forced himself on her. Her father hires an assassin to rub out Charley: Irene. He doesn't know she is married to Charley. Charley suspects he's being set up. Irene confesses that she was hired to do him in. Charley tries to smooth things over between the outsider Irene and his godfather, who insists he kill Irene because she stole Prizzi money. Irene suspects Charley has turned on her. That night, she loads a gun to kill him and he prepares to throw a knife at her.

Nicholson spent a lot of time hanging out in Brooklyn numbers joints, learning gangsterese and gangster style, to prepare for Charley Partanna, a characterization different from all others in his career. With his top lip hanging stupidly over his teeth, confused eyes, an expression out of *Mad,* and the mumbling voice of a punch-drunk fighter, he seems to be attempting a Humphrey Bogart caricature or spoofing Robert Sacchi, the "Man with Bogart's Face," whom he sounds like. Not once does he revert to his sly-eyed, grinning expression. He has no taste in clothes, has no class, is pretty stupid: when art deco is mentioned, he asks, "Art who?" His most frequent words are *yeah, Christ,* and *Jesus,* as in "Jesus, what a

beautiful song." He's such a dumb shmoe that he throws us off guard. We feel sorry for him for having a deceitful wife, whom he keeps forgiving. And we think him benevolent even when committing crimes, his one talent.

Here's a sweet fellow who's always giving presents to anyone who does him a favor, who cooks for his father, who gives his heart to Turner. He falls in love with Turner at first sight, thanks the heavens when she agrees to have lunch with him, and proposes on their first date: "Nobody in my whole life has affected me anything like the way you make me feel. I love you. That's it. That's everything. I love you." He's such a romantic that he'll never forget *anything* about that lunch, forgives all her lies to him—"I can't kill you the way I feel about you; I look at you and see what I want to see"—reads about love so he can get a better understanding of his feelings for her; reluctantly agrees to risk being the laughingstock of Brooklyn by letting his wife help with the kidnapping ("I didn't get married so my wife could go on working"); and *almost* goes against the family by refusing to kill her. What a considerate lover! We had little faith in Irene from the beginning, but Charley always seemed too decent to turn on her, even for Prizzi's honor. What finally happens between Nicholson and Turner proves they really are meant for each other, that they play by the same rules. Charley isn't such a nice guy after all.

▶ BEST ACTRESS

WINNER:
Geraldine Page *(The Trip to Bountiful)*
Other Nominees: Anne Bancroft *(Agnes of God),* Whoopi Goldberg *(The Color Purple),* Jessica Lange *(Sweet Dreams),* Meryl Streep *(Out of Africa)*

▼

THE BEST CHOICE:
Theresa Russell *(Insignificance)*
Award-Worthy Runners-Up: Rosanna Arquette *(Desperately Seeking Susan),* Laura Dern *(Smooth Talk),* Mia Farrow *(The Purple Rose of Cairo),* Whoopi Goldberg *(The Color Purple),* Geraldine Page *(The Trip to Bountiful),* Miranda Richardson *(Dance with a Stranger),* Meryl Streep *(Out of Africa),* Kathleen Turner *(Prizzi's Honor)*

It's not easy to beat a legend. But it's easy to lose to one. In 1985 Anne Bancroft, Whoopi Goldberg, Jessica Lange, and Meryl Streep probably would have resented losing to one another, but they seemed almost relieved when the fifth nominee, Geraldine Page, was named Best Actress. Who could have argued about victory for Page, a genuine legend who capped a thirty-five-year movie career with an impeccable performance in *The Trip to Bountiful,* as an unappreciated, lonely woman who has the urge to visit her small hometown one more time. The Academy made a safe choice, a career-tribute award for the gifted, popular actress of film and theater (she was one of the original "Method" actresses), who had already been nominated seven times for Best Actress and

Best Supporting Actress without winning. I always felt Page was a stage actress just visiting the cinema—in fact, her two greatest film successes, *Sweet Bird of Youth* and *Summer and Smoke,* had been her greatest stage roles. Nonetheless, in most years I would have gone along with a career-tribute Oscar for this fine actress or even an Oscar to honor her touching performance in *The Trip to Bountiful.* However, in 1985 there were several performances by actresses that were at least equal to Page's and more cinematic. I think the performance of the year was by Theresa Russell in her husband Nicolas Roeg's beguiling *Insignificance.*

Adapted by Terry Johnson from his 1982 London play, this apocalyptic comedy takes place in New York during

Theresa Russell's Actress explains the Theory of Relativity to Michael Emil's Scientist in Nicolas Roeg's *Insignificance.*

one night and morning in 1954. Russell is The Actress (who is meant to be Marilyn Monroe). After suffering through four hours of having her skirt blown into the air while standing over a grate as her director tried to get the perfect shot, she goes to a hotel to visit one of her idols, The Scientist (Michael Emil is delightful as "Albert Einstein"). The aged German Jew is in town to speak before a peace conference, but a right-wing Senator (Tony Curtis as "Joe McCarthy") threatens to destroy his life's work (about finding the shape of the universe) if he doesn't instead speak in favor of nuclear testing in front of the Atomic Energy Commission. The Scientist doesn't know the sex symbol whom all America, including the Senator, is crazy about. But she quickly wins him over. She impresses him with her intelligence, explaining the Theory of Relativity to him. Meanwhile she flashes back on how she used her sexuality to get farther in her career and to lasso her husband. But now she is thrilled to be having a conversation with an intellectual. Not that she wouldn't also sleep with him if her stupid husband, a famous onetime Ballplayer (Gary Busey as "Joe Di-Maggio"), didn't turn up, insisting she come back to him. He tells the Scientist that her insides are torn up and she probably can't ever have the baby they want. The Actress and the Ballplayer reconcile and she informs him she is pregnant. She is alone in the Scientist's room the next morning when the Senator shows up. He assumes she is just a look-alike for the famous Actress he worships. When he threatens to destroy the Scientist's papers, she offers her body to stop him. He slugs her in the stomach. Left alone, she suffers a miscarriage. Without telling the Ballplayer this, she tearfully sends him away. While looking at the Actress, the Scientist sees the world being destroyed by a nuclear bomb and her burning to death. But he just imagined this. The Actress cheerfully tells him bye and goes off to resume her career.

Playboy correctly called Theresa Russell "the thinking man's sex symbol." This shapely, long-haired blond with mysterious green eyes, a sensual smile, and catlike features earned that reputation playing passionate, neurotic women who exhibit unbridled sexuality and are seductive predators. She's a terrific, daring actress, but oddly is only at ease when she can incorporate sex into her performance. Nicolas Roeg always provided his girl-friend-wife roles that would allow her to do just that. She'd already been in his *Bad Timing: A Sensual Obsession* and *Eureka.* Of her part in *Insignificance* she told Jeffrey Ressner, "I could identify with the Marilyn character's using men to get what she wanted and furthering herself by using her sexuality. She was not nearly as much of a victim as people think she was. She really wanted to be a star, and that was her driving thing. On one side she was confused and she did need support, but on the other hand, all she wanted was stardom and being loved by everyone."

Like other Russell characters The Actress/Marilyn Monroe uses sex and a cheery attitude to cover up her sadness, pain, disappointment. When we first see her, leaving her humiliating shoot and her husband, she seems harried, worn out, depressed, even a bit scared. But when The Scientist first sees her, a few minutes later, she has gotten her "act" together and is completely upbeat and sexual. Her plan is to seduce this genius with her mind (and a few uninhibited body movements)—it's fitting because tonight she prefers his intellect to the brawn of her stupid husband. She turns him on with her exciting crawling-on-the-floor, prop-filled, brainy demonstration of the Theory of Relativity, but snaps back to reality with the sudden appearance of the Ballplayer. And the sad Marilyn we saw in the first scene returns for the rest of the film. *Insignificance* attacks America (represented by the Senator) for persecuting, victimizing, and exploiting its celebrities. Russell's Actress is presented as the ultimate (bleeding) victim—though not a victim until she became a star—punched at home by her husband and in this hotel room by a U.S. government official.

Russell creates an endearing character, exhibiting the sweetness, intelligence, vulnerability, hurt, and crushed romanticism that we associate with Monroe. Like Monroe's own characters Russell's Monroe excites us sexually, whether crawling around on the floor during her remarkable scientific demonstration (the film's highlight), or walking around with a sheet held against her nude body. And she also makes us laugh: Trying to get the working Scientist into the sack, she tells him: "You're calculating the shape of space, right? And when you finish you'll have expressed the precise nature of the physical universe. So do it tomorrow. It'll be here, I won't." And like Monroe, Russell makes us feel her character's mental anguish and physical pain. When she self-destructively marks her mirror image with smeared lipstick, when she writhes in pain after the Senator's punch has initiated a bloody miscarriage, and when she tearfully tells her husband that she doesn't want to be with him anymore, we tremble with her. It's amazing that Russell is able to shake us so, emotionally, when just a few minutes before she was making us laugh and turning us on. But that's the kind of talent Russell reveals in her finest performance.

▶ BEST PICTURE

WINNER:

Platoon (Hemdale/Orion; Oliver Stone)
Other Nominees: *Children of a Lesser God, Hannah and Her Sisters, The Mission, A Room with a View*

▼

THE BEST CHOICE:

Platoon (Hemdale/Orion; Oliver Stone)
Award-Worthy Runners-Up: *A Room with a View* (James Ivory), *'Round Midnight* (Bertrand Tavernier), *Salvador* (Oliver Stone), *Sid and Nancy* (Alex Cox)

Oliver Stone scripted *Platoon* in 1976, which is when he has always thought it should have been made. But at the time Hollywood figured no one was ready for a film about the Vietnam War. In 1978 a spate of Vietnam films were produced—the Best Picture–winning *The Deer Hunter, Coming Home, The Boys in Company C, Go Tell the Spartans*—but no studio was interested in financing *Platoon,* since Stone was an unknown at the time. After 1978 there was a renewed reluctance to make Vietnam films. Interestingly, books on the subject flourished after the dedication of the Vietnam War Memorial in Washington, in November 1982, which seemed to disprove the studio's contention that America—and vets—hadn't healed enough to deal with the war. Yet Stone, who had by the mid-seventies amassed an impressive track record—he wrote the scripts for *Conan the Barbarian, Scarface,* and the Oscar-winning *Midnight Express,* and directed *The Hand,* a creepy but erratic Michael Caine horror flick, and the leftist *Salvador*—still couldn't get any studio to bite on his project. Finally, England's tiny Hemdale gave him a modest $6.5 million and sent him to the Philippines, figuring it couldn't do any worse with *Platoon* than it had with the box-office dud *Salvador* (a better film if not for some ragged sections).

A surprise box-office smash, critics' favorite, and the winner of Oscars for best picture, director, editing, and sound, *Platoon* turned out to be the Vietnam War film that everybody had waited for, and many needed. It depicted the war experience that many vets remembered but couldn't explain to those they had returned to; and it vindicated those who had protested the war on the grounds that it couldn't be won, was so poorly conducted that our young soldiers were consistently being slaughtered on pointless missions ("Hell is the impossibility of reason"), and was turning our frightened young men into racist, amoral monsters who raped and murdered without being punished.

There were many who accused the film of being inaccurate or one-sided, but the fact that Stone was a Vietnam vet gave his picture the verisimilitude lacking in other films about this war. The model for the movie's hero, Chris Taylor (Charlie Sheen), Stone dropped out of Yale in 1965, enlisted, and volunteered for duty in Vietnam, where he'd once taught English. He served in the 25th Infantry, near the Cambodian border, a middle-class intellectual among the poor, barely educated, anonymous, and expendable whites and blacks who were snapped up in the draft or volunteered because they had no other job opportunities. Like Taylor, Stone was wounded twice and decorated, experienced tremendous fear and confusion, did reprehensible things, witnessed even worse atrocities being committed by his platoon mates, prevented the rapes of two Vietnamese females by our soldiers, took drugs, was so stoned that he fought wildly and bravely in battle, made a miraculous toss of a grenade into an enemy nest (which would have resulted in several GI deaths if he'd missed), learned that survival took precedence over morality, and emerged from Vietnam heavily into drugs and completely disillusioned about a war he'd once thought was justified. The innocent young man had been corrupted.

"Vietnam As It Really Was" is how the film was described on the cover of *Time.* The Vietnam that Chris Taylor finds when he joins the Bravo Company's 25th Infantry in September 1967 is not what he expected. As the soldiers march through the thick jungles—"like ghosts on the landscape"—they are plagued by mosquitoes, hungry ants (of various colors and appetites), leeches, snakes, mines. They are always fatigued, sick, filthy (Stone kept extra dirt on hand), wet, disoriented. (Stone and the actors go through two weeks of arduous "boot camp" with Vietnam vet Dale Dye, who has a bit part in the film.) Their discomfort only temporarily eases their overwhelming fear of the unseen enemy in the darkness. In battle there are flashing lights and constant loud noises: gunfire, bombs, planes, choppers, and the

Newly arrived in Vietnam, young soldier Charlie Sheen (L) must choose to follow either the evil, scar-faced Tom Berenger or the good Willem Dafoe in Oliver Stone's *Platoon*.

all-too-familiar call, "Medic!" Injuries greatly hurt the body and shock the mind; death is extremely painful. Frightened men, stoned men, and psychotics (such as Kevin Dillon's "Bunny") have just as much a chance of being effective in battle as brave men. In this unheroic war only a few acts amount to true heroism; in Stone's view the heroes are not those who kill the most enemies but those who stand up to their wrongheaded fellow soldiers. Because there are no rules in the jungle, confused soldiers must reach deep into themselves to determine right from wrong—so war, according to Stone, becomes almost spiritual. The members of this platoon, commanded by an ineffectual, inexperienced young lieutenant, side with either Willem Dafoe's messianic sergeant Elias or Tom Berenger's brutal, inhuman, scar-faced sergeant Barnes, the embodiments of "good" and "evil." Taylor acknowledges that the two men fight for his soul. Barnes shoots Elias, the only one who has stood up to him; Chris shoots Barnes, exorcising the evil in himself. It's little wonder that one critic said this film has more symbolism than an Italian film festival.

I remember that when *Platoon* came out, people had the same apprehension about seeing it as they would a gruesome horror film. There are numerous chilling moments in the picture—the awakening Taylor first seeing the approaching enemy in the darkness; soldiers being blown up; an officer losing contact with a scared, endangered soldier on a walkie-talkie and then hearing Vietnamese; Elias sneaking through a Vietnamese bunker complex; the amazingly filmed, helter-skelter final battle. But the reason we were wary of the picture was the sequence in which Taylor's platoon—which is vengeance bent after the deaths of two men—enters a farming village, bullies the North Vietnamese peasants living there, shoots their animals, brutally kills innocent people, threatens to kill children, attempts rape, and torches all the houses. Everyone had heard of My Lai, of course— and those in the antiwar movement knew of widespread criminal activities by our GIs (as revealed by returning vets in the documentary *The Winter Soldier*)—but it was still completely unnerving to see our soldiers portrayed as degenerates in a Hollywood picture. What is so terrifying about this scene is that from it we can deduce (as Stone wants us to) that such horrifying acts by our troops were not uncommon during this war. After all, *this* platoon has only a few bad apples. Sadly, Taylor and the other soldiers who participate in, or don't try to stop, the atrocities are typical, familiar American boys, changed by war and given free rein to reveal their dark sides. As Taylor/Stone surmises, "I think now, looking back, we did not fight the enemy. We fought ourselves and the enemy was us."

Platoon remains powerful, the definitive Vietnam War film. The dialogue ("The only way you get some pussy, man, is if the bitch dies and wills it to you; and then— maybe") would get a blush from Jack Nicholson in *The Last Detail*. The village scene is still gut wrenching. The battle scenes are still harrowing. *Platoon* would still work as an antirecruitment film, for as critic Ralph Novak wrote back in 1986, "No sane person should want to get any closer to war than this film."

► BEST ACTOR

WINNER:
Paul Newman *(The Color of Money)*
Other Nominees: Dexter Gordon *('Round Midnight)*, Bob Hoskins *(Mona Lisa)*, William Hurt *(Children of a Lesser God)*, James Woods *(Salvador)*

▼

THE BEST CHOICE:
James Woods *(Salvador)*
Award-Worthy Runners-Up: Harrison Ford *(The Mosquito Coast)*, Dexter Gordon *('Round Midnight)*, Bob Hoskins *(Mona Lisa)*, Gary Oldman *(Sid and Nancy)*

In 1986 cult favorite James Woods unexpectedly received a Best Actor nomination for playing photojournalist Richard Boyle in writer-director Oliver Stone's semifactual *Salvador.* Few Academy voters had seen the picture when it was released, but when Stone's *Platoon* became the film of the year, they got hold of the videotape. Even those who were turned off by the leftist, anti-American politics of the film and by Woods's repellent character were blown away by his performance. However, in this year, not Woods or any of the other nominees had a chance to beat Paul Newman for the Oscar. After six failed nominations no one could tolerate another loss for Newman, so he was a lock for Martin Scorsese's *The Color of Money*, a sequel to *The Hustler*. Again Newman played "Fast" Eddie Felson, the role that should have won him the Oscar a quarter of a century before. He was never better with dialogue than in *The Color of Money*—it's exciting *listening* to him—but the older Eddie is not as interesting as he once was, often taking the backseat to Tom Cruise's young hustler. In fact, it's difficult to remember Newman's performance. Not so with Woods in *Salvador*—he is unforgettable.

Boyle can no longer pay his rent, borrow any more money, or get journalism assignments from the Pacific News Service, so his wife takes the baby and goes back to Italy, tired of his drinking and his unpaid debts. Boyle figures he can find story material in El Salvador, where in 1980–81 the government, troops, and death squads are trying to put down guerrillas with the help of the United States. He convinces his deejay friend, Doctor Rock (James Belushi), to drive down with him, promising him a paradise of inexpensive sex, drugs, and liquor. They find that, but also tremendous misery among the peasantry. Death squads have killed or taken away thousands of suspected dissidents and no one is safe. The guerrillas have taken to the hills. As usual, Boyle borrows money to get by and scrounges for assignments. Government officials, U.S. representatives, most of the press corps, and even those on the left detest Boyle because he is such a nuisance and fuckup. But photographer John Cassady (John Savage) lets him tag along in the countryside, where they find thousands of people killed by the death squads. Boyle had been in El Salvador once before and resumes a relationship with the beautiful Maria

(Elpedia Carrillo). He promises to reform for her sake. Her young brother is arrested and tortured to death, perhaps because of his association with Boyle. Tensions get worse when Archbishop Romero is assassinated for speaking out against government suppression. Nuns are raped and killed by death squad members, resulting in an end to American financial and military aid. The rebels use violence to take control of much of the country, prompting the U.S. ambassador (Michael Murphy) to seek and receive U.S. military aid to the endangered government. After being nearly beaten to death at the border, Boyle sneaks Maria and her two kids out of the country. However, she is taken off a bus by immigration officials before they can cross into the United States. He worries what will happen to her back in her troubled country.

No one is better at playing hustling, live-wire, sleazeball opportunists than James Woods, and he found his ideal role as Richard Boyle. "I'm a fucking weasel," he tells Maria, "there's no doubt about it." He drinks and whores; takes drugs and smokes like a furnace; borrows

James Woods and John Savage photograph bodies of civilians that secretly have been dumped in the wilderness by soldiers in Oliver Stone's *Salvador.*

money he'll never pay back; lies, brags, cons, annoys, gets in everyone's face (sometimes burping); wears hideous clothes, and cheap, gaudy watches with which to bribe everyone; coaxes Rock to San Salvador by saying, "Where else can you get a virgin to sit on your face for seven dollars?" and "You're going to be in pig heaven"; reacts to a burning corpse in the road with the words "Relax, man, it's just some guy"; responds to "You look like shit," with *"Gracias."* Yet, Oliver Stone told Pat McGilligan for *Film Comment,* "Richard is much worse than Jimmy. . . . Jimmy didn't want to play him as raggedy and as scummy as Richard really is. Jimmy wanted to make the story more heroic, whereas I wanted to push it in an antiheroic direction. Jimmy feels he made Richard more attractive to a larger group of people, although some people would say, 'That's attractive?' Let's say he made him more accessible."

"I hate the guy I played," Woods told Eve Babitz of *American Film,* "I think he's a total asshole. I don't [actually] hate him; I'm indifferent to him—the kind of guy who is a drunken, boring, disgusting fool who's always gypping people with money and lying and bull-shitting and all the wonderful things that compulsive/obsessives do—but I loved the story. And I found a way of turning that character into a fictional amalgam of what he is and what I hoped he could be in his life, which caused untold amounts of 'violence' between me and Oliver Stone. . . ." As Woods told *Time:* "Working with Stone was like being caught in a Cuisinart with a madman. And he felt the same about me. It was two Tasmanian devils wrestling under a blanket."

Although Stone and Woods argued about the direction the character would take—Woods began to see Boyle as a "mad poet"—it seems likely that Woods agreed with Stone's overall concept: "I was interested in the character of Boyle as this sort of renegade journalist, a selfish rascal who, through his exposure to the country, becomes more unselfish, and who, through his love for the woman, starts to become something he wasn't in the

beginning. It's a transformation . . . a liberation." We always admire Boyle's guts—he'll confront anyone, he'll yell his head off even when in great danger—but as the film progresses we also learn to admire his feelings. He does have a conscience, he does love some of the troubled people, he does care and put himself in jeopardy on their behalf—he even cares about the integrity of his job as photojournalist, making sure his dead friends' photos get published. We admire his standing up to Reagan's right-wing representatives, stating the U.S. should stop thinking every insurgent is a communist and stay out of what is a civil war. He expresses Stone and Boyle's view of the political situation in El Salvador.

Although Stone and Woods argued, the director still trusted his actor enough to let him improvise throughout the film, even keeping in much that differed from his original concept. That line about being a fucking weasel was improvised by Woods, who had just been called that himself by his angry director. Woods's most famous scene—his hilarious yet poignant confession after thirty years out of the church—was improvised, and expressed Woods's own vision of his character: "I've done a lot of, you know, carnal sins, and drunk a lot of alcohol, and done some drugs. I've kind of weaseled around a lot in my life, trying to get the edge all the time. But basically, I would say I'm a good-hearted person. I haven't really done anything malicious in my life. I haven't done anything really great in my life either. I've tried to do some things, tried to find some truths. And I do love this woman. . . ." He tells the priest that he's willing to change for her, asking if it's okay if he still drinks a little and has a few hits on joints. . . . Told to say a few Hail Marys, he says if he'd known that would be the extent of his punishment, he'd have come to confession much earlier. It's a great bit of acting, and the only time Woods allows himself to be calm in the picture. We now know for sure that while Boyle is still a fuckup, he's at least a well-meaning one. Maria could do worse for a lover and we could do worse for a hero.

▶ BEST ACTRESS

WINNER:
Marlee Matlin *(Children of a Lesser God)*
Other Nominees: Jane Fonda *(The Morning After),* Sissy Spacek *(Crimes of the Heart),* Kathleen Turner *(Peggy Sue Got Married),* Sigourney Weaver *(Aliens)*

▼

THE BEST CHOICE:
Melanie Griffith *(Something Wild)*
Award-Worthy Runners-Up: Jane Fonda *(The Morning After),* Chloe Webb *(Sid and Nancy)*

If the Academy could vote a Best Actress Oscar for Jane Wyman, who can hear and speak, for playing a strong-willed deaf-mute in 1948's *Johnny Belinda,* then there was no reason it couldn't vote Marlee Matlin, who can't

hear, an Oscar for playing a strong-willed woman who is deaf yet (finally) speaks in the sentimental *Children of a Lesser God.* As a deaf teacher who has a troublesome affair with a teacher who can hear (played by Matlin's then lover, William Hurt) the twenty-one-year-old Matlin gave a much better, fuller performance than Wyman, who was too low key and spent most of her screen time trying out sweet expressions for the camera. Matlin proved to be an appealing actress, with talent, beauty, that winning combination of strength and vulnerability, and the ability to convey emotion. She is more attentive than other actresses and more contemplative—she actually seems to be "listening." I like Matlin, here and on her later TV lawyer series *Reasonable Doubts.* Yet—and I may be swayed by my dislike of the film—I don't see anything truly exceptional about her portrayal, other than that she was an actress who although deaf managed to do a fine job as a lead in a major film. (Now we take Matlin's acting skills for granted.) Like everyone else I was glad that the sentimental vote carried the underdog Matlin to an Oscar victory over four well-known, formidable nominees. However, if I were choosing 1986's Best Actress on performance alone, I'd pick another underdog, the un-nominated Melanie Griffith for *Something Wild,* giving her a slight edge over the unnominated and unknown Chloe Webb, who was terrific in *Sid and Nancy.*

Jonathan Demme's quirky comedy-drama, *Something Wild,* begins in New York. Charlie Driggs (Jeff Daniels) is on his lunch break, daring to leave without paying the check, when he is picked up by Griffith's Lulu, a wild young woman who wears a Louise Brooks wig and wild bracelets. She drives him to a New Jersey motel, handcuffs him to a bed, and makes mad, passionate love to him. She steals money from a liquor store. They go to a restaurant and she sticks him with the check, knowing he used all his cash on the room. He makes a mad dash to her car for the getaway. Although he shows her a picture of his wife and kids, he admits he is attracted to her and excited by her unpredictability, and accompanies her to Pennsylvania to meet her mother. She says her real name is Audrey. She tells her mother that she and Charlie are married and live in Long Island. With her hair now blond, she takes him to her tenth high school reunion. There, Charlie is unnerved to meet up with a coworker. Audrey introduces herself to him as Charlie's lover. His coworker is impressed. Also at the reunion is the tough Ray (Ray Liotta), whom Audrey isn't happy to see. The coworker tells Ray what in fact is true, that Charlie's wife took the kids and ran off with the family dentist. Ray takes Charlie and the reluctant Audrey for a ride. He robs a store and breaks Charlie's nose, then takes Charlie and Audrey to a motel. Ray is Audrey's husband, who has just gotten out of jail. She wants nothing more to do with him, but she hasn't much choice now. She becomes angry when she learns Charlie lied about still having a wife. She convinces Ray to let him go free. But Charlie follows Ray and Audrey south. He then runs off with her, leaving the broke Ray in a diner with an unpaid check and police in a nearby booth. But Ray follows them to Charlie's Long Island house. And there is violence.

Playing erotic Holly Body in Brian De Palma's *Body Double* had been the big break for Griffith, the young-looking, baby-voiced daughter of Tippi Hedren. It

Melanie Griffith is about to stick the penniless Jeff Daniels with the check, but she'll have a car with its motor running waiting outside the door in Jonathan Demme's *Something Wild.*

brought her back into the mainstream, where she hadn't been since 1975, when promiscuous teen roles in *Night Moves* and *Smile* made her future look bright. However, her Lulu/Audrey in Demme's *Something Wild* is the picture that legitimized Griffith as lead actress, paving the way for her most popular role, *Working Girl.* Oddly, this was the first time that she didn't have to test for a part—Demme called her. "Jonathan gave me a lot of room with the character," she told Guy Trebay of *Premiere.* "He let me make up Lulu's look. The black [Louise Brooks] wig wasn't in the script at all. The armloads of bracelets. The handcuffs. That was all mine." As Trebay notes, "Even those who found fault with the film were won over by Griffith's handcuff-toting heroine. As Lulu/Audrey, a randy, self-invented seductress, full of quirky stage business, Griffith was inspired."

Griffith is exciting in the early scenes when she seduces Daniels and takes him to the motel. Other actresses might have had difficulty with these uninhibited scenes of wild drinking and kinky sex, but Griffith was at ease. She had always emphasized sex and aberrant behavior in her roles. What's interesting is that these are the only sexual scenes in the film—except for a little smooching in Audrey's Pennsylvania bedroom. From then on Griffith impresses us solely with her acting, creating a captivating, multifaceted character with all kinds of emotions. As Mike Nichols would say, "You can see right into her feelings." So in control in the early scenes, Audrey turns out to be extremely vulnerable—although she is neither docile nor accommodating to Ray. Her voice quivers with affection for Charlie, hatred for Ray. She gives the impression that she has been badly hurt in the past—in every way possible—and to wipe out memories of her sadness she tries to bring happiness to nice people, like Charlie (giving him excitement) and her mother (presenting her with a nice son-in-law). She takes comfort from nice people and tries to pay them back by bringing them unexpected joy, breaking all rules to do her good deeds. But she fears that all this happiness is short lived. When Ray returns to her life, we see that she hasn't fully recovered from her past torment. Her sad look makes us think she is screaming and crying on the inside. She pretty much accepts that misery has reentered her life, because it has been there almost the entire time.

Pauline Kael, in *The New Yorker,* wrote about the strong impression Griffith makes in the film: "Melanie Griffith's dark Lulu turns into blond, fresh-faced Audrey, who suggests Kim Novak and, a bit later, Ginger Rogers, but Griffith's tarty, funky humor is hers alone. She has the damnedest voice; it sounds frazzled and banal—a basic mid-American-girl voice—but she gets infinite variations into its flatness. She can make it lyrically flat. That voice keeps you purring with contentment. It can be as blandly American as Jean Seberg's voice when she spoke French, and Griffith has a bland American prettiness too. But her delicate head is perched on an intimidatingly strong neck, and she never seems innocent. (Has anybody ever looked better in smeared lipstick?) Her role ranges from confident kook to girl with misgivings to terrified woman, and I thought her amazingly believable—even in the first section when that dark hair looks as if it could stand up without her." Most critics didn't write about Griffith's immense talent and special appeal until *Working Girl.* Kael was one of the few who recognized that Griffith had already found the perfect showcase in *Something Wild.*

▶ BEST PICTURE

WINNER:
The Last Emperor (Hemdale/Columbia; Bernardo Bertolucci)
Other Nominees: *Broadcast News, Fatal Attraction, Hope and Glory, Moonstruck*

▼

THE BEST CHOICE:
Empire of the Sun (Warner Bros.; Steven Spielberg)
Award-Worthy Runner-Up: *House of Games* (David Mamet)

It is as impressive as *Jaws, Close Encounters of the Third Kind, Raiders of the Lost Ark,* and *E.T.,* but many moviegoers forget Steven Spielberg even made *Empire of the Sun,* which grossed even less than his certified disaster, *1941.* Its lack of recognition resulted in part from its having a non-Spielbergian story that didn't appeal to his action-adventure fans; a premise—a British boy's unusual perception of the Second World War going on around him—that was similar to, if less amusing than, that of John Boorman's Best Picture–nominated *Hope and Glory;* and a title that got confused with sometime partner George Lucas's *The Empire Strikes Back* and Bernardo Bertolucci's *The Last Emperor,* 1987's Best Picture winner. Bertolucci's film, which also was shot in China—including the Forbidden City—was a monumental achievement, with incredible visuals. But while it tells the amazing story of Pu Yi, who became a powerless emperor in 1908 at the age of three and ended up as an anonymous Peking gardener when the communists came to power, it is strangely uninvolving. On the other hand, while at times you can't fully comprehend what is going on in the mind of the troubled and confused little boy in *Empire of the Sun,* you never stop trying . . . and you never stop caring.

The protagonist of Spielberg's $35 million epic, which Tom Stoppard adapted from J. G. Ballard's autobiographical novel, is Jim Graham (Christian Bale), who ages from nine to twelve during the course of the story. Jim, a brilliant, precocious boy with a fascination for Japanese airplanes, lives with his rich British parents in the suburbs of Shanghai, where he was born. It is 1941 and the Japanese have invaded China, prompting the fifteen thousand British to attempt flight from the country. Jim is separated from his parents during chaos in the crowded streets. After spending many days awaiting their return home, he ventures through the city and falls in with Basie

Christian Bale's Jim Graham should be frightened, but his mind is so confused after time in a prison camp that he thrills to the attack of American P-51's on the adjoining Japanese air base in Steven Spielberg's *Empire of the Sun.*

(John Malkovich), an American "operator." They wind up in a Japanese internment camp, where Jim uses what he learns from Basie, top dog in the American adult quarters, to become a first-rate hustler and scavenger. If any adult or child wants food or cigarettes or anything, he comes to Jim. Jim is fascinated by the Japanese planes and pilots on the airfield the prisoners built. When the field is attacked by Americans, he becomes so excited by the activity in the air that he stands in the open, crazily shouting praise at the warring planes. When he comes to his senses, he cries that he doesn't know what his parents look like anymore. With the war drawing to an end, the freed prisoners begin a mass exodus. Many die of hunger. Jim returns to the camp. Basie and other scavengers turn up. When they kill a young Japanese flier Jim has befriended, he turns against Basie. American soldiers arrive and the confused boy *surrenders* to them. His parents discover him at a children's camp. He comes out of his near trance and hugs them.

Empire of the Sun received six Oscar nominations, including ones for Al Daviau's exquisite cinematography and John Williams's splendid score. But that the nominations all came in technical categories was reflective of the general disinterest in the film among the Hollywood elite, moviegoers throughout the country, and critics. The picture received mixed reviews, with the most negative pieces coming from those who thought the film wasn't faithful to the book, particularly in dealing with the unique bond between Jim and Basie. However, there were some major critics who had tremendous regard for the film. Andrew Sarris, not a Spielberg fan in the past, thought it might be the year's best picture; and Vincent Canby asserted it was "a grand adventure movie" and "the best film ever made about childhood by a director born and bred in this country."

I acknowledge that the second half of the picture is flawed—there seem to be gaps in the story line (were scenes shot and then discarded?), some of the story seems muddled, the relationships between Jim and various camp residents aren't fully developed. Yet both Spielberg's wondrous images and the human drama have an immense affect on me. Some of those visuals (and I'm including Spielberg's staging) are awesome, some are bizarre, some are haunting, some are surreal, many are like nothing else in movies. Significantly, Spielberg gets as much emotion into simple visuals—lonely Jim races his bike through his deserted house, camp inmate Mrs. Victor unpacks Jim's suitcase to signify that she wants him to move back with her and her husband (she had sent him to the men's dormitory)—as he does with ones featuring hundreds of extras and much action. It is a spectacular sequence when Jim is separated from his mother while an enormous, frightened crowd bulldozes through the streets, Japanese troops march on their heels, and Chinese snipers fire on the intruders from rooftops. Oddly, Spielberg manages to fill you with emotion (just as John Ford could) with beautifully composed shots of Jim saluting Japanese pilots and, in one tearful moment, honoring them with a song. "What's interesting about *Empire of the Sun*," Spielberg said, "is that Jim is in control. He aspires to be in control in such a maniacal way that he aligns with the winning side, no matter which it is. I have said that *Empire of the Sun* is the story of a boy in search of heroes. And you have to be in control to do that. *Empire* sort of goes against the grain of how I usually define the protagonist. . . . For me, it's [typically] someone who is no longer in control of his life, who loses control and then has to somehow regain it."

We don't identify with Jim as we do with, say, Oliver Twist, although Jim relates to Basie (one of his "heroes") as Oliver does to Fagin. He isn't an innocent waif abandoned in a merciless world. Because he's a kid, we sympathize with him, but he's not really a sweet kid. He deserves the slap the young Chinese woman gives him once she is no longer his parents' servant. He is arrogant and self-absorbed, a self-proclaimed atheist (it's his smugness about this that's annoying), a fan of the Japanese military, a boy who can easily be corrupted into greedy behavior by Basie. We watch him at a distance, as we do the equally troubled Antoine Doinel in François Truffaut's *400 Blows*—whom he recalls clearly when he wolfs down milk he finds, just as the hungry Antoine does with milk he steals. We admire his ingenuity, his courage, and his resilience, and we detect an altruistic streak (he gets food for those who need it, without expecting payment). Yet we don't want to be him or even befriend him because we realize that while some of his war experiences may seem fun to him, they are corrupting him and taking a terrible toll on his mind. Sure enough, at the end he is traumatized. Only parental love could repair either Jim or Antoine Doinel. Antoine doesn't receive it at the end of Truffaut's autobiographical film, but it is there for Jim, when his loving parents track him down.

Spielberg told *The New York Times* that while *Empire of the Sun* was one of his most difficult movies to make, it was also one of his most efficient. That's because young Christian Bale, who is in every scene, was always at his best on the first take. Supposedly his remarkable performance—the best by a boy actor within memory—had less to do with his conception of the role than his ability to duplicate how Spielberg personally acted out every scene for him. As Vincent Canby noted, "This doesn't underrate the child's contribution, including his intelligence, wit, looks, and natural mannerisms, but it does explain why a handful of directors consistently obtain better, richer performances from children than do other directors." That Spielberg could get Bale to skillfully play such a complex, physically and mentally exacting part with complete abandon—which is the only effective way Jim could be played—demonstrates that he had earned the boy's complete trust. For that alone Spielberg should have received a Best Director nomination. But since he produced many other marvels in the film, his neglected masterpiece deserved the statue for 1987's Best Picture. As Spielberg himself admitted, they won't be making pictures like this anymore.

▶ BEST ACTOR

WINNER:
Michael Douglas *(Wall Street)*
Other Nominees: William Hurt *(Broadcast News)*, Marcello Mastroianni *(Dark Eyes)*, Jack Nicholson *(Ironweed)*, Robin Williams *(Good Morning, Vietnam)*

▼

THE BEST CHOICE:
Joe Mantegna *(House of Games)*
Award-Worthy Runners-Up: Christian Bale *(Empire of the Sun)*, Nicholas Cage *(Raising Arizona)*, Danny DeVito *(Tin Men)*, Michael Douglas *(Wall Street)*, Jack Nicholson *(Ironweed)*, Terry O'Quinn *(The Stepfather)*, Lou Diamond Phillips *(La Bamba)*, Donald Sutherland *(Wolf at the Door)*

Twelve years after he won the Academy Award as the producer of 1975's Best Picture winner, *One Flew Over the Cuckoo's Nest,* Michael Douglas won again, unexpectedly, for Best Actor. His father, Kirk Douglas, was a better actor than Michael, but didn't win an Oscar in a lengthy career that produced many terrific performances. But Kirk was proud of his son's portrayal of ruthless corporate raider Gordon Gekko, who corrupts Charlie Sheen in Oliver Stone's *Wall Street,* for his son had done a great job as the type of manipulative heel Kirk would have loved to play in his prime. Among the nominees who had a shot at the Oscar—Marcello Mastroianni was nominated merely for show, the Academy's periodic token nod to all foreign actors—I rank only *Ironweed's* Jack Nicholson more deserving than Douglas. But considering Nicholson won his Best Actor Oscar for Douglas's film in 1975, it seems fair that he allow Douglas his one opportunity at the acting award. However: there were several unnominated actors who I think gave stronger performances than Douglas, and who deserve equal consideration. These include Danny DeVito in Barry Levinson's *Tin Men,* child actor Christian Bale in Steven Spielberg's *Empire of the Sun,* and Joe Mantegna in David Mamet's *House of Games.* The extremely talented, Chicago-born Mantegna had won a Best Dramatic Actor Tony for Mamet's *Glengarry Glen Ross,* and when Mamet directed his first film he wanted this unorthodox leading man to play his unorthodox male antagonist. Mantegna's portrayal of a slick and shrewd, philosophical con man in Mamet's tricky melodrama was one of the most exciting and original performances of the eighties, and the best of 1987.

Lindsay Crouse, Mamet's wife, is Margaret Ford, a successful psychoanalyst and best-selling author of books having to do with compulsive behavior. When Billy, a young male patient, threatens suicide because he owes $25,000 to a gambler, Mike (Mantegna), she takes away his gun and goes to the seedy part of town to confront Mike. She is attracted and fascinated by this compelling con man, and can tell that he's not the type to commit violence. He says he'll forget Billy's debt, if she'll help him out in a scheme involving a poker game. She does so, but just before she is taken for $6,000 to pay for Mike's losses to a gun-packing opponent, she realizes that the gun is fake and that Mike and the other guy are conning her. Rather than holding a grudge, she asks Mike to tell her about all the cons he does—supposedly for a new book. She watches him work and becomes increasingly intrigued. She makes love to him in a hotel room they sneak into. He gives her opportunities to break rules, and this excites her. He says she is a criminal at heart. She insists on participating in his next scheme, in which he and an accomplice fleece a stranger. But she discovers the stranger is an undercover cop. There is a struggle and she kills him. Margaret steals a car so they can escape the hotel, but Mike's accomplice leaves be-

Con man Joseph Mantegna fascinates psychoanalyst Lindsay Crouse, who is falling into his trap, in David Mamet's *House of Games.*

hind the $80,000 they have borrowed from the mob. She gives them the money so they won't be killed. They abandon the stolen car and separate. The next day, Margaret sees Billy driving that car. She goes to a bar at which Mike hangs out and sees him dividing her money among his partners, including the man she supposedly shot, and mocking her. She had been set up by Billy at the beginning. Mike goes to the airport to fly to Las Vegas. Margaret meets him there, pretending she is being followed. He realizes she is onto him. He is remorseless. She kills him with Billy's untraceable gun. She goes out to lunch, taking delight in stealing a lighter from the woman at the next table.

Mike serves as a corruptive influence on Margaret, a counter to her good angel, her psychologist mentor, played by Lilia Skala. He makes her want to commit crimes and then provides her with the opportunities; meanwhile, Margaret's elderly friend instructs her to forgive all her bad thoughts. On the one hand Mike is lucky that Margaret takes the aged doctor's careless advice, because it allows Margaret to give in to the amoral thrills Mike offers her and thus become his pigeon—she can never go to the police without incriminating herself. On the other hand, Mike is unlucky because this advice frees Margaret to kill him without guilt. Not knowing he wasn't the only one influencing Margaret, he underestimated her criminal potential—a big mistake for this cocky con man.

Mantegna gives a perfect portrayal of an expert con artist. He keeps us completely off balance, so that we never know whether Mike is to be trusted—which is the way Mike would want it himself. Mantegna isn't matinee-idol handsome, but with his intense eyes, thick black eyebrows and hair, overwhelming confidence, and strong presence, Mike comes across as mysteriously attractive. Margaret melts under his seductive gaze. She lets him

take control, in an exciting rather than frightening way. Like Margaret we are impressed by his cool, his wit, his refusal to bilk people who can't afford it, his adament philosophy about life and work, his calm when in the hotel room—"I'm going to wash up. Then let's get out of this guy's room." He dresses slickly but there seems to be a common man under the attire, like some guy you'd meet at the ballpark: confronted by his unfriendly poker opponent, he responds, "Where am I from? I'm from the United States of Kiss My Ass." Mike speaks in such a clear, unruffled, honest manner—he even admits to Margaret that "I'm a con man. That's what I am: a criminal"—that we tend to believe whatever he says. He seems so self-assured that one would think he has no reason to lie. But for someone so cocky he has suspicious moments of vulnerability—when he loses money at cards, when he loses the Mafia money—and these throw us off guard, just as they do Margaret, whose instincts tell her to bail him out of trouble. He also seems too classy to treat Margaret like dirt, like a frat boy who uses a girl and then moves on, but: "Golly, Margaret, well, that's just what happened, isn't it? . . . You say I acted atrociously. Yes, I did. I do it for a living." No conscience, no remorse. His frat-boy kiss-off, "But we've had fun, you must say that," proves that he is the lowest of the low.

Mike seems to have been written specifically for Mantegna. He can deliver Mamet's seemingly awkward lines and give them force, humor, irony. Mike is the head of his gang, a man who must repeatedly give intricate instructions, so even when speaking to Margaret he always uses precise diction and extra words to make sure that what he's saying has clarity. When there is confusion, he explains things further. Before he says something, he always wants to make sure that he has the attention of his listener, so he begins sentences with "Listen to what I'm going to tell you"; "Listen to me"; "What's going to happen is this"; "I say this: I say that . . ." He repeats questions asked of him, he repeats words he has just said himself, breaks long sentences into two or three short ones: "You see—the thing of it is: you just said *my* knife. *My* knife. You said you took *my* knife." Awkward in the mouth of another actor, such phrasing, as delivered by Mantegna, has surprising intensity. I also like the way Mantegna puts subtle emphasis on words so we know that Mike uses them strictly for sarcastic effect, like *miffed* or *naughty* or *golly.* And I love it when the wide-eyed but calm and creepy Mantegna delivers his weirdest line—actually *two* lines—after discovering Margaret is onto him: "Oh, you're a bad pony. And I'm not going to bet on you."

Mantegna is riveting the entire film, but he saves his best for last. What a death scene! It comes complete with the bleeding, twisted man insulting Margaret between the shots that smash into him, spitting at her, defiantly refusing her demand that he beg for his life, and a great final line: "Thank you, sir. Can I have another?" Of course, because it's Mike talking, it's a great final *two* lines.

▶ BEST ACTRESS

Cher *(Moonstruck)*
Other Nominees: Glenn Close *(Fatal Attraction)*, Holly Hunter *(Broadcast News)*, Sally Kirkland *(Anna)*, Meryl Streep *(Ironweed)*

▼

THE BEST CHOICE:
Meryl Streep *(Ironweed)*
Award-Worthy Runners-Up: Glenn Close *(Fatal Attraction)*, Lindsay Crouse *(House of Games)*, Holly Hunter *(Broadcast News)*, Holly Hunter *(Raising Arizona)*, Anjelica Huston *(The Dead)*, Sally Kirkland *(Anna)*, Christine Lahti *(Housekeeping)*, Emily Lloyd *(Wish You Were Here)*

Meryl Streep generously bestowed praise for costar Cher when they played housemates in 1983's *Silkwood.* An endorsement from our foremost movie actress surely did much to build the confidence of the much-publicized singer-entertainer, who was trying to make the transition to movies and prove herself more than a gossip-magazine headline. Afterward she gave a strong lead performance in Peter Bogdanovich's *Mask,* as the fiery, unconventional mother of a disfigured boy, but her hopes for an Oscar nomination weren't realized, perhaps because the Academy believed her much-reported battles with her director were most unbecoming of a true movie star. But in 1987 Cher was legitimized in the industry when she was elected Best Actress for playing an Italian woman who finds romance in *Moonstruck,* becoming the first star

with one name to be so honored. Since everyone was used to seeing Cher in the press, they didn't resent the massive publicity campaign surrounding her nomination. Anyway, the picture was popular, Cher's performance was well received, and she represented someone who had come up from the ranks (we remembered her breaking in with Sonny on *Shindig*) to succeed on a major level. There might have been a revolution if she'd lost in 1987. Today her selection seems to have been a flight of fancy. She did give a fine, funny performance in *Moonstruck*—even if her accent comes and goes—but there were many super performances that year that better stand the test of time. My choice is Cher's onetime costar, Meryl Streep, for Hector Babenco's film of William Kennedy's *Ironweed.* I have bypassed Streep's earlier, her-

Once a well-known singer, homeless Meryl Streep has a moment of happiness when boyfriend Jack Nicholson returns her briefly to the spotlight in *Ironweed,* from William Kennedy's Pulitzer Prize–winning novel.

alded performances—including her Oscar winner in *Sophie's Choice*—for one that is relatively obscure despite the nomination. (More attention also should be given to Streep in 1988's *A Cry in the Dark.*) Of all Streep's standout characterizations none has been better than her portrayal of a dying but still combative derelict.

The setting is Albany in 1938. Streep plays Helen, longtime companion to Jack Nicholson's Francis Phelan. She was once a successful singer and pianist. Francis has been on the rough streets for more than twenty years, having abandoned his wife (Carroll Baker) after he accidentally dropped their baby, breaking his neck. He is tormented by his past, but in the present finds comfort in Helen's companionship, although she is so ornery that no one else can put up with her contentious manner. She doesn't tell him that she is suffering extraordinary pain in her stomach and side, vomits, and can no longer eat. Helen and Francis wander about the freezing streets, spending time at a bar, visiting friends—where Francis gets a sandwich and Helen gets into a squabble—looking for shelter. The next day Francis goes to make peace with his wife, grown son, and daughter. Meanwhile, Helen wanders around alone, playing a piano in a music store, trying to sleep in a library, griping about how her mother and brother betrayed her sometime in the past, having fits on the street, and praying in church, where she finds some money. She checks into a nice room, lays all her nice belongings out, and washes her body. She falls from the pain in her side. When Francis comes to the room, he finds her dead on the floor. He promises her that he'll someday get her a gravestone. Francis takes a train out of town.

Her blond hair stuck under a red hat, her teeth in need of repair, her short-stepped but aggressive walk marred by an almost imperceptible hitch, her shaky hands holding her coat against her cold body, her pretty face distorted into a hollow death-mask by years of anguish, her twisted mouth prepared to spew loud, angry words, her mind wandering, Streep is completely convincing as a woman who has toiled on the streets for years. She has been tough enough and gutsy enough to survive, but she fears her days are numbered: "I believe you die when you can't stand it anymore—you take as much as you can and then you die." She has no real regrets: "What if I did

drink too much wine—whose business is that anyway? . . . Who knows how much I didn't drink?" All she wants is a gravestone when her time has come—and Francis loves her enough at least to promise to get her one.

Janet Maslin writes: "Meryl Streep, as ever, is uncanny. Miss Streep uses the role of Helen as an opportunity to deliver a stunning impersonation of a darty-eyed, fast-talking woman of the streets, an angry, obdurate woman with great memories and no future. There isn't much more to the film's Helen than this, and indeed the character may go no deeper, but she's a marvel all the same. Behind the runny, red-rimmed eyes, the nervous chatter, and haunted expression, Miss Streep is even more utterly changed than [Nicholson as Francis], and she even sings well."

As Maslin points out, one of Streep's finest moments is when Helen sings "He's Me Pal" to a barroom full of disinterested patrons, imagining herself once again regaling an audience comprised of the cream of society. It's very moving when she comes back to the real world and real audience and shows disappointment—only for a second, because she refuses to indulge in self-pity. Streep has other powerful, deeply affecting moments, such as her prayer as she kneels in church: "I'm not a drunk and I'm not a whore, and I never let a man use me for money. . . . I never ever betrayed anybody and that's what counts." I love her thankful expression when her prayer is answered with the discovery of much-needed money. Other memorable scenes include her fit in the library and then on the street—she screams at passersby—upon remembering what her family did to her; her giving a hand-job to an ugly old drunk she shares an abandoned car with for the freezing night so that he won't maul her aching body—she is used to such tribulations; her taking care of herself in the hotel room.

But what I remember most are Francis and Helen walking through the streets, arguing some, but expressing love and need for each other. It's incredibly moving when he warms her with his coat and when she holds him tightly—when monied people wouldn't touch either with a ten-foot pole. In such moments we understand the immense loneliness that such people suffer, and how fortunate Helen has been to have spent her last years with Francis.

▶ BEST PICTURE

WINNER:
Rain Man (United Artists; Barry Levinson)
Other Nominees: *The Accidental Tourist, Dangerous Liaisons, Mississippi Burning, Working Girl*

▼

THE BEST CHOICE:
A World Apart (Working Title/Atlantic Entertainment Group; Chris Menges)
Award-Worthy Runner-Up: *Dangerous Liaisons* (Stephen Frears)

During the year and a half *Rain Man* was in development, several directors and writers came and went, but Dustin Hoffman remained firmly committed to the project, believing he'd be remembered equally for his role of an autistic savant as for his Ratso Rizzo in *Midnight Cowboy*. Finally Barry Levinson (*Diner, Tin Men*) took over as director and, working from a Ron Bass script, brought in the "unfilmable" project under budget and ahead of schedule. *Rain Man,* Hoffman, and Levinson won Oscars. *Rain Man* is about a young hustler (Tom Cruise) who wants to finagle his father's inheritance from the institutionalized, autistic older brother he's just learned he has. But during their time on the road together he comes to admire and love him. The picture has flaws—goes in hokey directions—but it also has humor, sweetness, and captivating performances by Hoffman and Cruise, whose combined appeal made this picture an unexpected hit with all age groups.

My choice for Best Picture of 1988 also deals with two family members of different ages who have a crumbling wall between them. Only, the relationship is that of a politically committed mother and neglected teenage daughter in the South Africa–set *A World Apart;* and their growing understanding of each other—the human drama—serves only as our key to a larger, equally important *political* story dealing with the girl's coming to understand the not-so-innocent "world" around her. *A World Apart* made more than forty critics' Top Ten lists and was a Special Grand Jury Prize winner at the Cannes festival (where Barbara Hershey was voted Best Actress), yet it wasn't even nominated by the Academy. It remains surprisingly neglected.

It's 1963. Molly (Jodhi May), a thirteen-year-old Caucasian girl, lives with her mother and father, Diana (Barbara Hershey) and Gus Roth (Jeroen Krabbé), two younger sisters, grandmother, and black servant, Elsie (Linda Mvusi), in a lovely home in suburban Johannesburg. She attends a fine all-white girls' school and is entrenched in middle-class life. But her values are different from those of most of her schoolmates—and most adult Afrikaners—because in her house, blacks have always been treated like equals. Diana even throws racially mixed parties. Diana and Gus are antiapartheid activists. He flees the country to avoid arrest. Diana continues to work for a radical journal. Molly resents that Diana has little time for her, and she often must turn to Elsie for affection. Diana won't even explain her own work or why Gus fled. After continued harassment from the police Diana is thrown into jail, the first white woman incarcerated under the new ninety-day detention act. Molly's world crumbles. Already harassed in school because of her leftist father, Molly loses even her best, most loyal friend. She goes with Elsie to the black ghetto, and takes comfort in the friendship she finds there from Elsie's family. She witnesses police rampaging through a church to arrest Elsie's activist brother, Solomon (Albee Lesotho). He will be tortured to death. After a second ninety-day detention the ill Diana is sent home, under house arrest. Police

Barbara Hershey and daughter Jodhi May march together with black South Africans at the funeral of a black friend who was murdered while in police detention in *A World Apart.*

harassment continues. Molly insists that Diana pay more attention to her. Diana expresses her love for her daughter, but makes it clear that her political work must continue even though it will mean she can't be the mother Molly wants. Diana, despite being under house arrest, accompanies Molly to Solomon's funeral. Together, they will be part of the continuing struggle for freedom. Heavily armed troops arrive. Passive no more, blacks confront them with rocks.

A World Apart is a semiautobiographical work by Shawn Slovo. Her father, Joe Slovo, headed the outlawed South African Communist party, and was the only white member of the executive body of the African National Congress. Her mother, Ruth First, was editor of several antiapartheid journals, and was the first white woman incarcerated under South Africa's infamous 1963 ninety-day detention law. First was assassinated by a letter bomb in 1982 and Slovo decided to write a script (for a course at Britain's National Film School) to deal with her suffering after her mother's death. As she told Marybeth Kerrigan in *American Film,* "We didn't have a very good relationship, my mother and I. It was very volatile. . . . Then suddenly she wasn't there anymore, but the feelings were. Writing was a way of working out those feelings." As Kerrigan points out, it was ironic that Slovo's working relationship with Hershey resurrected some of those mother-daughter tensions: "Barbara thought it was her film, but it's really about how the child copes with the political choices her parents have made. It's much more the child's story."

This is a wrenching but still uplifting story ("uplifting" in that Molly develops a political consciousness and at least earns the attention of her mother), as seen through the eyes of the child who must grow up before she's ready. From playing with Hula-Hoops and doing the twist on the manicured front lawn, she ends up attending the funeral of a tortured black activist in the poor black district, with armed white troops arriving to break up the gathering. As I see it, this is a film about how Molly, at great sacrifice, comes to understand (though not fully condone) Diana's deep commitment to politics. She doesn't achieve that understanding from speaking to her mother—Diana instills good values but never fully explains anything to her. She learns from observing Diana: at work, greeting black activists (with more warmth than she gives her daughter), and being harassed by police. And she learns from seeing what happens to Diana as the result of her political activism; to herself in school because she is Diana and Gus's daughter; and to the blacks she visits in their shantytown. She's still a kid with a kid's vocabulary—she charges the police who spy on her home, but all she can think to say is "Go away and leave us alone!"—nevertheless, *after* her experiences, she can raise her fist and chant *"Amandla! Awethu!"* (Power! Is ours!) in sincere solidarity with the antiapartheid movement. She doesn't attend Solomon's funeral just to be with her mother, but because he was her friend too. She stands with Diana, but not to show she's joining her mother; she shows Diana that she, too, is joining the

surrounding blacks in the movement. She begrudgingly accepts that Diana will never be the mother she needs—as they agree, "It's unfair"—in exchange for her mother's agreeing to never shut the office door on her again, especially when the behind-doors subject is the politics that is so affecting the young girl's life.

In his debut as director, Chris Menges (the British cinematographer of *The Killing Fields, The Mission,* and other films) gets strong and quite lovely performances from Hershey and May. The roles are difficult because within their relationship, both are imperfect, insensitive, and uncommunicative. As actresses they must play scenes together in which there is no rhythm to the dialogues, since Diana and Molly don't really have conversations. And they must play characters who never fully get our sympathy except when they are away from each other and being slapped around by the outside world. With hair combed back, shoulders stiff, a fixed expression, and British South African accent, Hershey plays a woman who, one can surmise, sacrificed her glamour, warmth, humor, and much of her humanity (such as her ability to be a "good" mother) in her quest for human rights. Jodhi May, whose eyes penetrate and whose smile goes straight to your heart, is even better. Not once does she seem to be acting.

Menges, an ex–documentary cameraman whose cinematography gave a documentary look to *The Killing Fields,* worked with his own cameraman, Peter Biziou, to accomplish the same in *A World Apart.* One recalls Haskell Wexler's *Medium Cool,* in which the actors mingle with real demonstrators, because you feel as if those people around Hershey and May don't realize that they're being filmed for a movie. And often, you're not even sure about May. That's how authentic everything is. Scenes in the street and in the black neighborhood are particularly realistic, because of the style of camerawork and the sense that life goes on here exactly like this when that camera isn't around. (Filming actually took place in Zimbabwe.) Menges, producer Sarah Radcliffe, and Slovo made the wise decision not to sensationalize anything, which contributes to our belief that what is taking place is real. We aren't even shown Solomon being tortured. Instead we are shown single events that by themselves are, in movie terms, mild: a black is run over in the street and the white mother of Molly's friend won't drive him to a hospital and get involved; at night, police with dogs enter Diana's newspaper office; police charge into Diana's integrated party; Diana is arrested without there being charges leveled against her; Diana is slapped by an officer; Diana is deprived of books while in jail; a few minutes after her release Diana is arrested again; police charge into a black church and arrest Solomon; the father of Molly's best friend chases Molly away from his house; police continue to raid Diana's house. These single events add up. So when at the end, armed troops arrive at Solomon's funeral to break up the peaceful assembly, audiences moan, loudly saying exactly what the blacks on screen are thinking: "Enough!"

▶ BEST ACTOR

WINNER:
Dustin Hoffman *(Rain Man)*
Other Nominees: Tom Hanks *(Big)*, Gene Hackman *(Mississippi Burning)*, Edward James Olmos *(Stand and Deliver)*, Max von Sydow *(Pelle the Conqueror)*

▼
___

THE BEST CHOICE:
Tom Hulce *(Dominick and Eugene)*
Award-Worthy Runners-Up: Kevin Costner *(Bull Durham)*, Tom Cruise *(Rain Man)*, Tom Hanks *(Big)*, Dustin Hoffman *(Rain Man)*, William Hurt *(The Accidental Tourist)*, Jeremy Irons *(Dead Ringers)*, John Malkovich *(Dangerous Liaisons)*

In *Rain Man* the once self-interested Tom Cruise is determined to take care of his autistic older brother, Dustin Hoffman, whom he has just gotten to know. In *Dominick and Eugene,* after growing up together, Ray Liotta decides it's time to let his brain-damaged older (by twelve minutes) brother, Tom Hulce, live on his own while he pursues his own career. Both films were well-made, heartfelt, touching, occasionally cloying human dramas about love between adult brothers. Barry Levinson's *Rain Man* was an enormous financial success, due in great part to the box-office magnetism of its two famous stars, and won Oscars for Best Picture, Best Director, and Best Actor. Meanwhile, Robert M. Young's sleeper received modest distribution, in part because it featured leads without box-office clout, and was shut out in the Oscar race. Hoffman was so highly praised for his performance in *Rain Man* that no one seemed to notice that Cruise was even better in the same film, an emotional whirlwind. So it's not surprising that no one thought to compare Hoffman with Hulce, who played another character with a brain disorder. If the two films were screened back-to-back, I think Hulce's performance would touch more viewers.

The sweet, sensitive, trusting Dominick, or Nicky, shares a small Pittsburgh apartment with his twin brother, Eugene. Although brain damaged—"I'm slow, not stupid!"—he has put Eugene through medical school by working on a garbage truck. Their mother died during childbirth and their father "went away," so they have always been together and are extremely close. Eugene has always protected Nicky from anyone who tries to take advantage of him. Nicky doesn't remember the time before he hurt his head; Eugene has always told him that he fell down. Eugene is accepted to do his residency at Stanford, but he worries about leaving Nicky alone, especially after Nicky's dog is killed. Eugene dates Jennifer (a fine performance by Jamie Lee Curtis), whom he tutors. Nicky's working buddy, Larry, convinces Nicky that Eugene is throwing him over for Jennifer. Nicky likes Jennifer but becomes jealous, leading to arguments with Eugene. Nicky is terrified by Eugene's anger—anyone getting mad frightens him. Nicky is friends with Mike, a young boy on his route. The boy's mean father (David Strathairn) often beats the boy, but that fact doesn't dawn

on Nicky until one day, while picking up garbage at his house, he sees the father throw the boy down the stairs. He becomes terrified. After the boy dies, the father threatens to kill Nicky if he squeals. While the father and his wife are talking in their house, Nicky runs off with their baby. The police surround him in a vacant building; Eugene goes in to talk to him. Nicky now remembers that it was their father who hurt him—and indeed Eugene admits that their father repeatedly hit Nicky on the head when the boy tried to protect Eugene from a beating. This damaged Nicky's brain. Eugene promises Nicky that the baby will be safe, so Nicky gives up. The father tries to shoot Nicky, but Eugene and the police stop him. Nicky tells the police what happened to Mike, and the father is arrested. Nicky is something of a hero, respected by his workmates. He assures his brother that he will be fine while Eugene is away in California.

In *Rain Man* Dustin Hoffman had the advantage of being able to act any way he wanted because most of us were unfamiliar with how autistic men behave. So Hoffman could do no wrong. On the other hand, Hulce played someone we might mingle with in society, whom

Loving brothers Tom Hulce (R) and Ray Liotta walk their dog in *Dominick and Eugene.*
(Photo Credit: Brian McLaughlin)

we might categorize as retarded and then foolishly dismiss. His goal was to individualize Nicky. Where Hoffman tried to get a type right, Hulce created a character. And what a sweet character Nicky is. The nicest guy in the world. At night he prays, "Help me to be on time so I don't lose my job, and don't let anybody hurt anybody." In church he looks at the crucified Jesus and states, "If I was God, I wouldn't let that happen to my boy." He worries about the reasons anyone would get mad, even the Incredible Hulk, one of his idols (Hulce beefed up for this role). And he does good deeds for everyone, even protecting a baby he has never seen before from an abusive father.

He plays with his dog, reads comics, sees science fiction movies, watches television with an elderly neighbor (who thinks he's "God's boy"), is a regular at the local pizza joint, wants to go to Wrestlemania, always tells his brother he loves him, talks enthusiastically about all kinds of topics others might consider trivial, smiles a lot, speaks his mind—even making throwing up the topic of dinner conversations. He's a good worker, a good friend, a terrific brother (he takes pride in helping Eugene become a doctor), and a good Christian. Director Young said to Marlaine Glicksman, "Nicky is a beautiful character, but he's been damaged, and has lost part of his conceptual abilities. And people like that have been [pre]judged [as inferior] because the conceptual part of the brain is thought of as the higher part of the brain. In so-called primitive societies they value much more the intuitive, nonconceptual approach, a ritual approach, sensate. . . . Nicky [is like] a primitive. . . . Nicky is very direct in his love and his needs. His way of experiencing is very direct, while a lot of us get so conceptual, we miss the poetic, concrete, sensate part of living."

By film's end we think of Nicky not as retarded, but as quirky. And brave. And remarkable. As we watch and listen, we realize that he has the right take on the world. We realize that every life he touches improves. It's little wonder that Hulce has such joy playing this part, showing us all sides to Nicky's fascinating personality—including his flaws. It's a completely fascinating performance, with particular care given to body movements and facial expressions, some of which you won't forget. Hulce has many fine moments, including his dance with Larry's friend Mrs. Vincent, in which his body suddenly becomes graceful and he experiences new freedom; his cheery shower with Eugene, in which he laughs while his brother washes his hair; his argument with Eugene, during which he becomes frightened by Eugene's fury. All Hulce's scenes with Ray Liotta are beautifully, tenderly played by both actors. Hulce received an Oscar nomination as the title character in *Amadeus,* but I think he was much better (and much different) in *Dominick and Eugene.* In fact, one wouldn't think from the earlier film that he could deliver a performance of this quality. Unfortunately, few people noticed and Hulce's once-promising career has continued to flounder.

▶ BEST ACTRESS

WINNER:
Jodie Foster *(The Accused)*
Other Nominees: Glenn Close *(Dangerous Liaisons),* Melanie Griffith *(Working Girl),* Meryl Streep *(A Cry in the Dark),* Sigourney Weaver *(Gorillas in the Mist)*

▼

THE BEST CHOICE:
Jodie Foster *(The Accused)*
Award-Worthy Runners-Up: Glenn Close *(Dangerous Liaisons),* Melanie Griffith *(Working Girl),* Gena Rowlands *(Another Woman),* Susan Sarandon *(Bull Durham),* Meryl Streep *(A Cry in the Dark),* Sigourney Weaver *(Gorillas in the Mist)*

"Cruelty may be very cultural and very human—but it's unacceptable." These strong, heartfelt words highlighted Jodie Foster's acceptance speech for having won 1988's Best Actress Oscar for *The Accused,* a film she made to express those precise sentiments. It was somewhat of a surprise that Foster would win for Jonathan Kaplan's low-budget, Canada-filmed feminist project, playing a young woman who is gang-raped in a tavern while men cheer on her attackers. (The film was based on the 1983 sexual assault case in New Bedford, Massachusetts.) Foster was a well-respected actress whom we'd watched grow up, but most of her films, particularly those she had made since graduating from Yale, had been distinctly non-Hollywood—*The Accused,* despite its subject matter, was one of the few that was even remotely commercial. Foster's chances for victory seemed particularly slim because her competition was extremely strong, with Melanie Griffith and Glenn Close apparently having the inside track. It didn't seem to favor her that in 1988 Foster was only one of several actresses (including nominees) who played women who fight for their integrity and dignity in a male-run world. However, it turned out that viewers greatly responded to her performance as a flawed character (who needed this sensitive actress to express her feelings properly and put us firmly on her side). When Foster's name was announced Academy Award night, it suddenly made perfect sense that she should win.

Foster plays Sarah Tobias, a poorly educated waitress who lives in a trailer with her drug-dealer boyfriend. One night, after a fight with him, she puts on a sexy outfit and goes drinking at a tavern, The Mill. Later that night she flees the tavern, while a bystander, a scared college student, Ken (Bernie Coulson), anonymously reports her rape. Kelly McGillis's sleek attorney Katheryn Murphy sees the bodily damage that has been done to Sarah and agrees to charge three men with rape. But because of Sarah's bad reputation, and because Sarah was stoned on the night in question and was kissing her first attacker, Katheryn plea-bargains, sending the men to jail for only a brief term on a nonsexual "reckless endangerment" charge. Sarah feels betrayed by Katheryn for having made this deal without her permission; she had been badly harmed and humiliated both by the attackers and by those who had egged them on. She is insulted that Katheryn wouldn't think her a worthy witness—as if only a certain type of woman can hope to win a rape case. Depressed, she kicks out her unsupportive boyfriend. When one of the men who cheered her rape at The Mill harasses her, she drives her car into his pickup, wrecking both vehicles and ending up in the hospital. Katheryn realizes she has done wrong and convinces Sarah to help her prosecute three other men who encouraged the rape. The charge will be "criminal solicitation," and if they are convicted the rapists will have to serve full five-year terms instead of getting out in nine months. Katheryn tracks down the anonymous caller—a friend of one of the rapists—and his testimony, along with Sarah's, convinces the jury to convict the men. Sarah and Katheryn look at each other with appreciation.

As a teenager and even before, Foster's characters were worldly beyond their years, sexually aware even if not experienced, and led the sort of unstable, unsafe lives that were better suited to older females. Her "allure," wrote Linda R. Miller, "was a hybrid of child and adult." Foster did sexually attract older male viewers, including John Hinckley, who—tantalized by her child prostitute in 1976's *Taxi Driver*—stalked her at Yale and shot Ronald Reagan in her honor in 1981. When she returned to movies after graduation, it was expected that Foster would take roles that wouldn't cause any association to Hinckley. However, in 1988 one of her characters was threatened with rape by an admirer in *Five Corners,* and another was raped by three men in *The Accused.* Always willing to take risks, Foster explained that she was drawn to play heroines who overcome victimization. One of the reasons she got the part was that of the tested actresses, she was the only one who had no hesitancy about doing the rape sequence. She found that her gyrating, exhibitionistic solo dance in the bar prior to the rape was much more difficult.

In the first scenes Foster's battered Sarah is *hoarse*. In Tom Topor's script her near loss of voice serves as a metaphor for all raped women with bad reputations who

Furious Jodie Foster hurts herself while ramming her car into the truck of a man who encouraged her rape in *The Accused*.

can't receive justice because what they say will not be listened to. As the opposition lawyer tells the jury, "Her sworn testimony is nothing, and you must treat it as nothing." Sarah lashes into Katheryn for offering a plea bargain rather than letting her testify against her rapists: "I wouldn't make a good witness, right? I'm too fragile. My past is too questionable. I'm a drunk. I'm a pothead, a drug addict, I'm just a slut who got bounced around a little bit in a bar, right? So I didn't get raped, huh? I never got raped. . . ." Her voice is no longer hoarse by this time, but Sarah realizes that still no one listens. Not Katheryn, not Sarah's boyfriend, not even Sarah's mother—who can't tell by Sarah's shaky voice that she needs to come home for a visit. The film is about how Sarah and Katheryn work together to make sure that what Sarah says has meaning.

At first Katheryn, who represents us, is reluctant to side with Sarah. A part of her thinks Sarah was asking for what happened to her by drinking, smoking pot, and arriving at The Mill in provocative dress. Then, as Sarah admits, she flirted with, danced with, and kissed the young guy who shortly afterward raped her. Katheryn changes her mind when Sarah opens up to her; Foster (watch her eyes and listen to her voice this entire film!) is shattering as her character tells the slightly older, more mature, and more successful woman, "You don't understand how I feel. I'm standing there with my pants down and my crotch hanging out for the world to see and three guys are sticking it to me and a bunch of other guys are yelling and clapping and you're standing there telling me that [your plea bargain] is the best you can do. If that's the best you can do, then your best sucks. Well, I don't know what you got for selling me out, but I sure as shit hope it's worth it." We are also convinced at this point, but when the rape sequence is shown near the end of the film, we are tested. Foster intentionally alienates us with her attitude and sluttish behavior as Sarah. We are allowed to see that the young men in the back room of the tavern are picking up wrong signals from Sarah as she acts like a tramp. But when Foster resists and says *No,* Kaplan hopes we immediately want the men to stop, to let her go. Because she doesn't approve of her treatment, the image is not erotic at all, but ugly: Her face and mouth covered by hands, her hands held down, her eyes

terrified, her body on a pinball machine with the men on top of her doing the same hip actions they'd do while playing pinball. We can see why she later is determined to take on these rapists and those who rooted them on—after this ordeal she wants to prove she is a human being who must be respected. In court, in another great Foster scene, Sarah will put everything on the line and subject herself to further humiliation, just to show that whatever she says has significance, especially the word *No.*

1989

► BEST PICTURE

WINNER:
Driving Miss Daisy (Bruce Beresford)
Other Nominees: *Born on the Fourth of July, Dead Poets Society, Field of Dreams, My Left Foot*

▼

THE BEST CHOICE:
Henry V (Renaissance/BBC/Curzon; Kenneth Branagh)
Award-Worthy Runners-Up: *Do the Right Thing* (Spike Lee), *True Love* (Nancy Savoca)

Spike Lee's Brooklyn-set *Do the Right Thing* dealt with familiar themes of the African-American director-writer-actor, including: racial tension; individual blacks establishing their own identities and finding their own sources of pride; friction between these seemingly different blacks and their unity when they experience a common problem; doing the right, responsible thing. Presenter Kim Basinger made a fool of herself Oscar night by chastising Academy members for not having nominated Lee's film for Best Picture. No doubt it was bypassed because it was considered too controversial when, ironically, the film's interesting resolution is anything but. How it must have galled Lee that the Best Picture winner was Bruce Beresford's *Driving Miss Daisy,* from Alfred Uhry's play about the evolving friendship between a black chauffeur and a difficult Southern woman, because that film was cheered for avoiding controversy. In fact, it seemed to want us to be nostalgic for the South as it was before blacks began fighting for equal rights. I also didn't like it that the film/play emphasized the life of the woman, when the chauffeur was a much more interesting character. Certainly Lee's film deserved the Oscar more than Beresford's.

But while arguments about the two American films were being waged, all but forgotten was director-star Kenneth Branagh's brilliant British production of Shake-

speare's *Henry V.* It was a film that everyone was awed by and raved about, yet when nominations were made it was bypassed for the likes of *Dead Poets Society, Field of Dreams,* and *Driving Miss Daisy.* This was a remarkable achievement, especially for a first-time director.

When he made *Henry V,* Kenneth Branagh was twenty-eight the age of his character (Olivier was over forty when he directed and starred in his 1945 film version). Although unknown in America, Branagh was already being hailed as the "new Olivier" in Great Britain. In 1984, at twenty-four, he'd made a major impression as the youngest actor ever to play Henry V for the Royal Shakespeare Company. Next, he starred in the British television miniseries *Fortunes of War,* formed his own repertory group—the very successful Renaissance Theater Company—penned two plays and an autobiography, *Beginnings,* and starred in two movies, *High Season* and *A Month in the Country.* Then, with a small budget of $7.5 million, the commitment of some of England's greatest actors (including Paul Scofield, Derek Jacobi, Brian Blessed, Alec McCowen, Robert Stephens, and Ian Holm), and a seven-week shooting schedule (less than a third of the time Olivier took), he embarked on his ambitious rendering of *Henry V.*

Of course, Shakespeare rarely translates to movies, so Branagh's primary goal was to make the Bard more

As tender in love as he is furious in battle, Kenneth Branagh's brash king quickly wins the heart of the daughter of the French king, played by Emma Thompson, in *Henry V.*

accessible. Although he didn't change any of the language, he and his sterling cast deliver their lines in a natural way, as if in heated discussion. Olivier's version was more poetic, but in Branagh's film the words are much more potent. That's because every line is delivered by the characters with the intention of having an impact on the characters spoken to—no words are wasted by these people whose lives are put in turmoil by Henry's ascent to the throne and his decision to conquer France. Wisely, Branagh forgets his theater roots and films his characters in extreme close-ups to make us concentrate on what they say, especially when the language is difficult to understand, and "to help make them more human beings instead of some anonymous army." And Branagh tried to make his story and his character more contemporary by eschewing the heroism of Olivier and exploring the manner in which the fallible Henry copes with the demands of being a king. As in Shakespeare, Henry matures while on the job. We first see Henry *after* watching the men in court bow to him as he passes—then the youthful, nonmuscular Kenneth Branagh slumps into his throne and we are not impressed. As Branagh intended it, this Henry starts out as just one of the guys. But soon he'll break from old pals Falstaff and Bardolph, challenge the French, and persuade his men to follow him into battle despite five-to-one odds, for glory, for England, for God, for their king.

Olivier's Henry was decisive and gallant. That's because his film was made during World War II and was propaganda. His Henry was meant to serve as a symbol of unflinching British leadership, forever exhorting Brits to go "into the breach" to fight evil enemies. On the other hand, Branagh's Henry is someone who learns to be a great leader, overcoming the loneliness of his lofty position and grave self-doubts. The battles the British win at Harfleur and Agincourt are fought by brave men under a courageous, determined leader. However, the fighting is anything but heroic and the end result is tragic despite Henry's claim of victory—indeed, this can be seen as an *anti*war film.

Henry V is beautifully photographed and has many striking images—including many surrounding the Battle of Agincourt. Unforgettable is the long, wordless scene in which Henry carries a dead boy past all the carnage. But it is the marvelous acting that carries the day—especially by Branagh. "He doesn't look like a Shakespearean matinee idol," wrote Richard Corliss in *Time,* "this thin-lipped Irishman with puddingy skin and a huge head piked like a pumpkin on his stocky frame. He lacks conventional star magnetism: the athletic abandon, the flaming sexuality, the audacity of interpretation that risks derision to achieve greatness. . . . In short, Branagh seems as remote from Laurence Olivier as, say, Sandra Bernhard is from Sarah Bernhardt."

But Branagh is marvelous, whether expressing outrage about the French king's insulting gift of tennis balls to facilitate him on his ascension to the throne (proving to the French courier and his own advisors that he has *balls*); giving his men the best pep talks this side of Knute Rockne; or proposing to the lovely daughter of the French king (Branagh would marry leading lady Emma Thompson), with love, humility, and broken French that amuses them both. With a soft yet powerful, beautifully resonant voice, Branagh delivers every line with great thought and deep conviction. He has wit, he has fire. He gives a straightforward, nonegocentric performance meant to impress upon us viewers that he's just a working-stiff actor and not some elitist Shakespearean operating on a level far over our heads. But we recognize his great talent. Just as his Henry V can no longer pass as a common man, Branagh can no longer pass as a common actor.

▶ BEST ACTOR

WINNER:
Daniel Day Lewis (My Left Foot)
Other Nominees: Kenneth Branagh (Henry V), Tom Cruise (Born on the Fourth of July), Morgan Freeman (Driving Miss Daisy), Robin Williams (Dead Poets Society)

▼

THE BEST CHOICE:
Daniel Day Lewis (My Left Foot)
Award-Worthy Runners-Up: Kenneth Branagh (Henry V), Tom Cruise (Born on the Fourth of July), John Cusack (Say Anything), Matt Dillon (Drugstore Cowboy), James Woods (True Believer)

Until 1989 it was unprecedented for an actor with only cult credentials to be selected Best Actor by the Academy. But Daniel Day Lewis, whose previous leads were in the nonmainstream My Beautiful Laundrette, A Room with a View, The Unbearable Lightness of Being, and Stars and Bars, won an unexpected and much-deserved Oscar for My Left Foot, playing rambunctious Irish artist-memoirist Christy Brown, a victim of cerebral palsy. The intense young British actor didn't expect this unsentimental bio to be anything more than a cult item either. In fact, Day Lewis (whose name isn't hyphenated in the film's credits) worried whether the film would ever get made, much less released, when he agreed to do it for first-time producer Noel Pearson, and first-time cowriter-director Jim Sheridan, both of whom came from the theater. "We thought it could become a film no one would want to see," he told Annette Insdorf. "We never really knew how far we could go without alienating the audience. . . . [Jim Sheridan] and I fueled each other's inclination to take things further and further. We didn't know whether the relentless physical disturbance could be contained within the frame of the film. We never really found out, but got to the point where we didn't care." Rather than being turned off by Day Lewis and Sheridan's unsanitized, unsentimental approach to Brown, critics and viewers responded positively, and with strong emotion. The picture became a surprise box-office hit and Day Lewis became a surprise award winner.

The film begins with the bearded, wheelchair-bound Christy appearing as an honored guest at a charity benefit. While waiting for his introduction, he is attended by a nurse, Mary (Ruth McCabe), with whom he flirts. She reads his autobiography, which he typed with his left foot. Christy grew up in a tough Dublin working-class neighborhood, one of thirteen surviving children (there were twenty-two pregnancies) of his strong, kind mother (Best Supporting Actress Brenda Fricker) and proud, authoritarian father (Ray McAnally). He had a special bond with his mother—once he saved her life—who was the only one who could fully understand his hampered speech, and the first to see he had intelligence. One day Christy used a piece of chalk that he wedged between toes on his left foot to write the word MOTHER on the floor. His father carried him to the local tavern and introduced him: "This is Christy Brown. My son. Genius." All the Browns stuck by Christy and he thrived because of their attention and because of their sacrifice on his behalf—finally he got a wheelchair, replacing the cart in which he'd always been rolled around. Christy took up painting with his left foot and showed remarkable talent. When he was an adult, Dr. Eileen Cole (Fiona Shaw) gave him physical therapy and encouraged his artistic and intellectual pursuits. He was able to get his own art exhibition. Unfortunately, he fell in love with Eileen and was heartbroken that she loved another. But he came to this benefit at her request, along with his mother (his father had died) and other family members. On the inside of his book he now writes to Mary, Be with me. She thinks it over and decides to accept his invitation. They will marry.

In preparation for playing Christy Brown, Day Lewis spent eight weeks at Dublin's Sandymount clinic for the disabled and worked with an Irish painter, Gene Lambert, who had been disabled in an automobile accident. He was inspired to write and paint because of the role—some of the artwork in the film is Day Lewis's—and learned to write with his left foot, not the easiest of tasks.

Daniel Day Lewis's Christy Brown, who has the most powerful and adept foot around, is the ideal choice to make a free kick in soccer in My Left Foot.

Throughout the making of the film Day Lewis stayed in character, sitting twisted in a wheelchair, jerking his head from side to side and up and down, and speaking out of the side of his mouth. Cast and crew had to attend to his needs. Of course, all the dedication paid off, with a spellbinding portrayal. It probably helped that Christy Brown wasn't a benign sort, but heavy-drinking and strongly egotistical, because Day Lewis takes the discomfort to which he subjects his body, à la Lon Chaney, and during his performance allows it surface as Christy's rage. His Christy not only has tantrums—responding to Eileen's engagement, he smashes his head against a restaurant table and yanks the table cloth with his teeth—but his glare could send one to the hospital.

Despite Day Lewis's being seated for most of the film, this is a physical performance. His Christy always seems to be trying to burst out of his skin, not just leap up from his confining wheelchair. He doesn't relax for a minute. Christy's major problem is that he desperately wants to communicate like other people, but can't because of

obvious obstacles. This inability to communicate is common to other Day Lewis characters. "I am much more touched by people who have difficulties with [communication]," Day Lewis told Hilary De Vries for *Rolling Stone*. "To varying degrees we're all incapable of communicating. It's the thing that causes us the most distress, which forces us to confront our isolation, our aloneness, and that's inescapable. It's something we shouldn't have to be fearful of, something we should understand as inevitable. And the less able we are to communicate in a conventional way, the more aware we are of that isolation. In my nightmares I occupy that same dimension."

Christy Brown found unconventional ways to get his ideas across—the most peculiar and most effective way being to use his left foot, which has amazing strength (how he can kick a soccer ball!)—but he can turn out the most tender of words: "[Mary,] be with me." And Day Lewis found that his unconventional way to communicate was through acting and getting deep inside such expressive and fascinating characters as Christy Brown.

▶ BEST ACTRESS

WINNER:
Jessica Tandy *(Driving Miss Daisy)*
Other Nominees: Isabelle Adjani *(Camille Claudel)*, Pauline Collins *(Shirley Valentine)*, Jessica Lange *(The Music Box)*, Michelle Pfeiffer *(The Fabulous Baker Boys)*

▼

THE BEST CHOICE:
Jennifer Jason Leigh *(Heart of Midnight)*
Award-Worthy Runners-Up: Isabelle Adjani *(Camille Claudel)*, Andie MacDowell *(sex, lies, and videotape)*, Winona Ryder *(Heathers)*, Annabella Sciorra *(True Love)*

Jessica Tandy is a wonderful actress and nice woman, so it would seem pretty cruel to protest her winning an Oscar at the age of eighty after all the joy she has given during her long career. But if the Best Actress Oscar she received for playing the set-in-her-ways Southern woman in *Driving Miss Daisy* was meant to be a career award, I do protest it on the grounds of her having neglected the cinema for the theater during most of her career. She gave terrific performances when she appeared in films, but those were only sporadic occasions—not enough to deserve a tribute. If she received the statue strictly for her appearance in *Daisy*, I—acknowledging my dislike for the picture—again protest. Perhaps it's the script or Alfred Uhry's play that is to blame, but Tandy doesn't convince me that the emphasis of the film should be on her character's life rather than the fuller, more interesting life of her black driver, played by Morgan Freeman. I much prefer giving the Oscar to one of several offbeat young actresses who created exciting characters that we wanted to learn more about—as opposed to wanting to learn more about the men in their lives instead. Isabelle Adjani's obsessive performance in *Camille Claudel*, An-

die MacDowell's daringly revealing performance in *sex, lies, and videotape*, Winona Ryder's breathless performance in *Heathers*, and especially newcomer Annabella Sciorra's natural performance in the sleeper *True Love*, were all deserving of an Alternate Oscar. But my choice is Jennifer Jason Leigh, who gave one of her several quirky, interestingly conceived and acted performances of the era, in probably her least-seen film, *Heart of Midnight*, written and directed by Matthew Chapman.

Leigh is Carol. Ever since she was a child, she has hated to be touched, although she doesn't know why. She has had several breakdowns and a history of disturbed, hysterical behavior. She sees that her one chance for recovery is to move away from her mother and into a deserted club, Midnight, which her uncle Fletch willed to her. She discovers that it formerly had been a sin palace and that the multiroom living quarters above had been used for sadistic activities, all recorded on tape. While workers renovate the club below to turn it into a legitimate club, Carol lives above. While suspecting that someone else is present, living behind the walls, she worries that she is imagining the sounds and clues. Three

Jennifer Jason Leigh tries to avoid another mental breakdown in *Heart of Midnight.*

young street punks break into the club and two molest her. She escapes with the third one's help. Police don't believe her story because of her history. A handsome man Peter Coyote turns up, who Carol assumes is Sergeant Sharpe, investigating the crime. He befriends her and tells her to trust him. But it turns out that he is an impostor. He is really Larry, who is just out of prison—he hated his former partner, Carol's uncle Fletch. Unknown to all but ourselves, Sharpe was murdered when he came to speak to Carol at the club. Carol's world is falling apart. She trusts no one. Then she discovers a secret passageway behind the walls. Carol is chained by the intruder, a young, demented female who is made up to look like a male; she is Sonny (Gale Mayron), Larry's sister. Sonny claims she was Fletch's (forced) lover and accomplice in crime. She says Fletch also molested Carol as a child, the reason she can't stand to be touched. Trying to carry on as Fletch would want her to, Sonny tries to kill Carol. Larry rescues Carol, but is wounded himself. Sonny and Carol embrace, bonded by their victimization at the hands of Uncle Fletch. Sonny shoots herself, but before she can also shoot Carol, police finish her off. Carol and Larry soon dance in her new nightclub.

"The classic Leigh film," wrote Philip Weiss in *Rolling Stone,* "possesses all the trappings of a B movie, stays in the theaters for only a few weeks, and is memorable mostly for a mesmerizing performance by Jennifer Jason Leigh." Such is the case of *Heart of Midnight,* a silly low-budget variation on *Repulsion* (in which Catherine De-

neuve played Carol). In terms of merit, it didn't deserve more than the minor distribution it received; yet it contains a jolting performance by one of this era's most fascinating, offbeat, and daring young actresses. Leigh is a tiny, innocent-looking blonde who repeatedly finds herself in films with strong, often perverse sexual content, usually playing exploited or victimized women, including rape victims and prostitutes (in *The Men's Club, Last Exit to Brooklyn, Miami Blues*). Most of these women have guts, resilience, unusual wit, and other admirable qualities but, not knowing how to accept love, dislike themselves and are self-destructive. "What's drawn me to these women," Leigh told Gavin Smith, "is their neuroses or abandon, or how complicated, inhibited, or uninhibited they are, or how graphic and terrible their lives are."

Known for doing extensive research before playing parts, including writing up back histories, Leigh prepared for *Heart of Midnight* by meeting with women who had been abused as children, speaking with psychologists, and attending crisis clinics. "*Heart of Midnight* is a character study into madness," she told Robert Seidenberg of *Premiere,* "[about] someone who doesn't like herself and doesn't know why. And through the course of the film she finds out and decides it's easier to be mad than to exist with this knowledge."

Although the picture doesn't jell as a whole, it does provide Leigh with her greatest showcase, away from the male-dominated and ensemble films in which she usually plays (and steals). Putting her research to work, she creates a beguiling character. Every time she looks in the mirror (these are great moments), she reveals through expressions or words her dislike for herself, even her looks: "U-g-l-y, you ain't got no alibi. You're ugly. Uh-huh. Ugly." She says, "I don't want to look like this." Also she thinks she's going mad and that her world is crumbling: "My life's a joke." Yet she still tries to take control of her life, to make her own decisions about her future. As she tells her mother when she leaves home for life at Midnight, "If I go down there and I can't make this work, if I have another breakdown and I'm forced to come back here, then I'll probably never recover. Yes, it's a terrible risk . . . and I'm taking it."

Leigh doesn't play her character as an intense woman—Carol's not as mad as she suspects—but she plays her as someone who's definitely strange. And not only because she carries on conversations with herself (especially in the mirror) and imagined guests, or that she races her bike through the narrow halls, or that she sings along to Ethel Waters, a most unusual musical choice. Leigh's eyes and head movements are always slightly askew; even her way of walking is different, because for some reason she wears a cast over one foot. She keeps withdrawing, partly from fear of physical harm, partly from fear of mental anguish ("Don't try to psychoanalyze me," she angrily tells Sharpe/Larry). Yet she keeps forcing herself to return and face her problems head-on: staying by herself the night she is attacked; walking determinedly back into her dangerous club when she knows there is someone else inside; and shuffling along the halls with legs spread, pointing her pistol downward, hitting it aggressively against the floor. "Do you hear that, you little shit? It's the sound of my gun pointed at your head." She's not so timid.

Nothing Leigh does in this film is predictable, yet everything is logical in the context of the character. She has many great moments. I think the scene that affects me most is the attack on her by the two intruders, which is nearly as jarring as the rape of Jodie Foster in *The Accused.* And it's not a gratuitous moment, as some might complain. Carol doesn't resist at all, but just allows them to do what they want with her body. We wonder why she doesn't fight back as women are supposed to do in

modern-day movies. But then we look at Leigh's face and see the little girl who blanked out all her feelings years before when her uncle did similar things to her (we figure out about the uncle before Carol does). At this moment we understand the depth of Carol's pain. And we sense Leigh's great compassion for her victimized character. As in other Leigh films, we can tell that the actress would like to help her character escape her horrors, but lets her character's sad life play itself out. At the end there is never full happiness for a Leigh character, but Carol at least experiences temporary peace and comfort.

1990

▶ BEST PICTURE

WINNER:
Dances with Wolves (Orion; Kevin Costner)
Other Nominees: *Awakenings, Ghost, The Godfather, Part III, GoodFellas*

▼

THE BEST CHOICE:
Miller's Crossing (Circle Films/20th Century Fox; Joel Coen)
Award-Worthy Runners-Up: None

The new decade began with a disappointingly unimpressive year for movies. The nominations were a sorry lot, with only director-star Kevin Costner's epic Western, *Dances with Wolves,* and Martin Scorsese's gangster picture, *GoodFellas,* deserving of being on such a list (though they are not on my list). *Awakenings* starts out fine, but fades once Robert De Niro's patient becomes more important than Robin Williams's doctor. The critics overwhelmingly preferred *GoodFellas,* based on Nicholas Pileggi's *Wiseguy,* an unheroic fact-based novel about Henry Hill's life in crime. But the public and the Academy voters sided with *Dances with Wolves,* about an idealistic Union soldier who takes up with the Sioux in the 1860s. Everyone had to admire Costner for having risked much money and his reputation to get across his personal, deeply-felt vision about the nobility of the American Indian and their mistreatment by U.S. soldiers and government. He chanced making a movie about a hero who is, as its screenwriter-novelist Michael Blake points out, "a traitor," and to work in a supposedly dead genre (part of its popularity can be attributed to the fact that Western-hating viewers didn't recognize it as a Western). It was helmed with assurance by its first-time director, smoothly

acted, and beautifully photographed. While its ending is a copout—the disappointed soldier and his white wife actually will be better off because the Indians left them behind—the picture is a success; in recent years few films have been made with such passion for their subject. In a near Oscar sweep it became the first Western since *Cimarron* in 1930–31 to win the Academy Award (and Costner won as Best Director). If the year had had no great films, I'd go along with the Academy's choice. However, there was one neglected near-masterpiece, the wacko gangster film, *Miller's Crossing,* written by producer Ethan Coen and directed by his brother Joel Coen.

The setting is an unnamed eastern city during Prohibition. The town is run by the aging Irishman Leo (Albert Finney), whose chief advisor is the intelligent, nonviolent Tommy (Gabriel Byrne), the only man he trusts. Leo controls the mayor and the chief of police. However, the Italian Johnny Caspar (John Polito), whose chief henchman is the brutal Eddie Dane (J. E. Freeman), is becoming a threat to Leo's supremacy. Caspar tells Leo that he wants Bernie Bernbaum killed because Bernie has been selling information about fixed fights to gamblers, cutting into Caspar's profits. But Leo refuses to allow this because

Gabriel Byrne calms Jon Polito in the grisliest scene in Joel and Ethan Coen's *Miller's Crossing*.
(Photo credit: Patti Perret)

Bernie is the brother of his tough mistress, Verna (Marcia Gay Harden). Tommy tells Leo to allow the unlikable Bernie's murder because Verna isn't worth his going to war with Caspar. Fearing Leo's life is in danger, Tommy confesses to him that he also has been sleeping with Verna. Leo beats him up and kicks him out of his organization. Caspar becomes the major power in town, taking control of the mayor and chief of police. Much to Dane's chagrin he recruits Tommy into his operation. Tommy must prove his loyalty by killing Bernie in the wilderness, at Miller's Crossing. He allows the pleading Bernie to live, on the condition that he doesn't let anyone know he's still alive. Dane doesn't believe Tommy killed Bernie, so he takes him back to Miller's Crossing to find the body. A body is there, with its face shot in. Bernie murdered Dane's male lover, Mink—but Dane can't recognize the corpse. Bernie tries to blackmail Tommy, saying he'll come out into the open unless Tommy kills Caspar. Tommy convinces Caspar that Dane and Mink (who he says is still alive) are secretly selling information about fixed fights. Before Dane can kill Tommy, Caspar brutally kills Dane. Tommy maneuvers Caspar to rendezvous with Mink, only Caspar finds Bernie there instead. Bernie kills him. Tommy tells Bernie that they'll blame the murder on Dane. He takes Bernie's gun to supposedly hide the evidence, but then reveals Dane is dead. Without reason he points his gun at Bernie. Bernie again pleads for his life, thinking Tommy hasn't got what it takes to kill anyone. Tommy blasts him between the eyes. Only Tommy and Leo are left alive. Leo will marry Verna. Tommy won't accept Leo's offer to work for him again.

As with the Coens' *Blood Simple, Raising Arizona,* and *Barton Fink, Miller's Crossing* has a fascinating array of weird characters, visual daring, a convoluted plot, and bizarre humor that is often hidden underneath ferocious violence. Like those other films it breaks rules in exciting ways. Everything about this film is unorthodox: the characters, the gangsterese, the particular voices and deliveries of the characters, the choreography of violent scenes (awesome), the music, and the camera angles and the placement of characters within the frame. We seem to be in an alternate universe, where everything and everyone is off kilter. Other than a Leo Gorcey, who would say things like "What are you chewing over?"; "The last time we jawed, you gave me the high hat"; "Take your flunky and dangle"; and "I'll see where the twist flops"? (Only Tommy talks straight.) Other than in early Dashiell Hammett novels (which certainly influenced this picture), where else could our reckless (and self-destructive) hero be brutally beaten no fewer than five times—even Verna slugs him—be kicked in the face twice and knocked down a flight of stairs, and still come away with only a bloody lip? The story of a man who pits two families against each other so that all the bad guys on both sides are killed off was filmed before, but only as a Japanese (ex-)samurai film, Akira Kurowsawa's *Yojimbo,* and an Italian western, Sergio Leone's *A Fistful of Dollars.* Like those two films *Miller's Crossing* is, in addition to being a fascinating gangster film and tale of loyalty and betrayal, a delirious put-on.

The Coens get splendid performances from Finney, Byrne, Polito, Turturro, and a number of other players. (I don't mean to slight Harden, but except when she's punching Tommy, this muscular picture works best when the frame is populated by forceful masculine presences.) In addition to being in bloody action scenes they each have wonderful monologues. I love the early scene when Polito's Caspar complains to Leo about the diminishing *ethics* found in the crime arena, saying "If you can't trust a fix, what can you trust?" After Polito grabs our attention, Finney does him one better, as Leo (who sits at an odd angle) tells Polito in no uncertain terms that he will not allow Bernie to be killed. This is one of Finney's finest screen characterizations. Turturro steals the screen every time he appears as his Jewish, homosexual sleazeball—he deserved to be the year's Best Supporting Actor. His great moment comes out at Miller's Crossing, when he drops to his knees in front of the armed Tommy and cries for his life, repeatedly saying, "I'm praying to you. Look in your heart!"

This scene is one of the film's many highlights and, like every other great sequence, it is lensed, staged, and acted in a completely original manner. Two other scenes—in these violence *is* unleashed—will definitely stick in the memory. One is the vicious scene in which the temperamental Caspar prevents Dane from strangling Tommy by bashing in Dane's face and shooting him in the back of the head—meanwhile a hefty male boxer, who is also in the room, screams in horror. My favorite scene has Finney thwarting a murder attempt by two of Caspar's goons who enter his second-story bedroom. He calmly puts down his cigar, grabs a gun, dives under his bed, shoots one hood in the foot and then in the head

after he falls, hops out his window and rolls down his roof and to the ground, turns and machine-guns the other hood who stands at the bedroom window of the burning house, exchanges fire-belching gunfire with more hoods in a moving car, continues firing at the car as he follows it down the street while on foot and in his robe, triumphantly watches the car explode, and puts another cigar in his mouth. This incredibly choreographed scene is played out while Frank Patterson's stirring rendition of "Danny Boy" blends with the gunshots on the soundtrack.

The film's one uncertain scene is the ending. Tommy arrives late at Bernie's funeral, which is attended only by Leo and Verna. Leo tells Tommy he forgives him for having slept with Verna, but Tommy doesn't want absolution. He also refuses to work again for Leo. It's really hard to figure out what the Coens intend here. My own guess is that Tommy isn't refusing Leo's offer because he wants to distance himself from crime again. I think he now thinks himself unworthy to work for Leo, who, with Caspar dead and Tommy corrupted, is the one ethical criminal left in town.

▶ BEST ACTOR

WINNER:
Jeremy Irons *(Reversal of Fortune)*
Other Nominees: Kevin Costner *(Dances with Wolves)*, Robert De Niro *(Awakenings)*, Gerard Depardieu *(Cyrano de Bergerac)*, Richard Harris *(The Field)*

▼

THE BEST CHOICE:
Gary Oldman *(State of Grace)*
Award-Worthy Runners-Up: Michael Caine *(A Shock to the System)*, Michael Gambon *(The Cook, the Thief, His Wife & Her Lover)*, Richard Gere *(Internal Affairs)*, Jeremy Irons *(Reversal of Fortune)*, Paul Newman *(Mr. and Mrs. Bridge)*, Robin Williams *(Awakenings)*

Kevin Costner had a marvelous night at the Oscars, taking home a ton of awards for his *Dances with Wolves,* including ones for Best Director and Best Picture. So he didn't really mind losing in the Acting category. Robert De Niro was expected to win his first award in eleven years as a patient who is temporarily brought out of a deep sleep in *Awakenings,* although the unnominated Robin Williams was more impressive as his kindly doctor. But De Niro was upset by British actor Jeremy Irons, who played Claus von Bulow in *Reversal of Fortune.* I was tempted to give this brilliant actor an Alternate Oscar for earlier appearances in *Moonlighting, Betrayal,* and *Dead Ringers* (on awards night he thanked that film's director, David Cronenberg, for helping him through his best and most difficult role: perverse twin brothers). So it would have been easy to go along with the Academy's choice in 1990. However, while I think Irons did a fine job as Von Bulow, the voice he came up with sounds exactly like Boris Karloff—which takes away from my appreciation of his performance. (Costar Ron Silver seemed to be doing Groucho Marx.) But even if Irons hadn't sounded like the British bogeyman, I would have given my Alternate Oscar to Gary Oldman. His dynamic performance in Phil Janou's little-seen *State of Grace* was that film's saving grace.

Top-billed Sean Penn (good as Terry Noonan) returns to New York's Hell's Kitchen after having left mysteriously a few years before. His onetime best friend, third-billed Oldman (as Jackie Flannery) is thrilled to see him and immediately tells his older brother, Ed Harris (as Frankie Flannery), to let him into his gang. Penn helps Oldman set fire to abandoned buildings, make collections, and do other rotten business. Oldman never would suspect that Penn is an undercover cop who is trying to sabotage a plan by Harris to link his Irish gang to that of an Italian mobster. The always drinking, volatile Oldman becomes crazed when John C. Reilly (as Stevie), a good friend of his and Penn's, gets his throat slashed. He assumes the Italians did it because Reilly owed money, but Penn learns that Harris did the rubout as a favor to the Italians. The depressed, angry Oldman murders three top men in the Italian gang. Harris, who has moved from Hell's Kitchen to a fancy home in New Jersey, had wanted to impress the Italians with his smooth operation. So he agrees to kill Oldman. Penn witnesses the killing. On St. Patrick's Day he charges into a bar frequented by Harris and kills him and all his gang.

A onetime British working-class kid, Oldman quickly established himself as one of the cinema's most original, exciting actors. Specializing in reckless, dangerous, or endangered characters, he has shown the courage to go the limits and express his own inner turmoil on the screen. He was stunning in two real-life roles: in *Sid and Nancy* he was punk-rock singer Sid Vicious, a heroin addict who killed his girlfriend and took his own life; in *Prick Up Your Ears* he was playwright Joe Orton, who was murdered by his jealous male lover. Oldman didn't see many connections between these two characters and the fictional Jackie Flannery, only that they are all angry outlaws and outsiders.

Oldman is riveting as his Irish street punk. He has wild, greasy, unwashed hair that is combed to each side but falls over his baby face. He wears dark pants, a leather jacket, an open vest, and a T-shirt for days at a time. He is extremely hyper and edgy (particularly before a hit), always moving about demonstratively. He often uses violence to get rid of his energy and venom. He smokes constantly, drinks any time he sits, is sweaty and dirty, and talks and laughs incessantly, often complaining about the changing neighborhood (actually his anger at those who are moving in hides his anger at those who have moved out, including his brother and sister). He is proud of his dirty work—partly because he does it for his older brother—and, again, he uses strong-arm tactics to free his anger. He is capable of great violence, using his feet, teeth, forehead, and anything he can lay his hands on. He has a sentimental side, but when he's in a bad mood, he'll beat or shoot any outsider who gets in his way or on his nerves. In one scene he mercilessly beats and kicks a guy who was just talking to his girlfriend; in another he shoots three Italian gangsters who invited him to their table for a drink, punctuating his work with: "Fuck it."

Jackie's savage violence and heavy drinking make him extremely frightening, yet we somehow feel sympathy for him. He's like a trusting family dog who doesn't know any better than to viciously attack visitors and neighbors. He's sensitive and has admirable loyalty to Frankie, his sister (Robin Wright), Terry, and Stevie, and their affection means everything to him because he doesn't have much self-esteem. We blame Frankie for what Jackie has become. We feel bad that he must drink so heavily because "I can't remember shit—that's the way I like it." And that his world seems to be falling apart with the death of Stevie and the new friction between himself and Frankie: "I gotta get outta here—I feel like I'm on Mars. I feel surrounded." We feel for him when he breaks down in church.

As Oldman told Robert Seidenberg for *American Film,*

Gary Oldman is the terror of Hell's Kitchen in *State of Grace.*

the key to playing Jackie was to "either consciously or subconsciously [find] something that I can like about the character. And I found Jackie to be, in many respects, an innocent. There's a lot of lovely things about Jackie. To some extent I found him rather charming and rather sweet and rather a tortured spirit. But nothing a big cuddle and a lot of love wouldn't cure. Whatever he does, I, as the actor, can forgive him. Whether you, as the audience, forgive him or have compassion or empathy for him, that's for us to find out." We can understand why Terry likes Jackie so much—he recognizes Jackie's sweetness and depth of feelings. And when we see Oldman's hurt, confused, disappointed expression when Frankie pulls a gun on Jackie, and then see him fall into a bloody heap, we forgive Jackie everything.

▶ BEST ACTRESS

WINNER:
Kathy Bates *(Misery)*
Other Nominees: Anjelica Huston *(The Grifters)*, Julia Roberts *(Pretty Woman)*, Meryl Streep *(Postcards from the Edge)*, Joanne Woodward *(Mr. and Mrs. Bridge)*

▼

THE BEST CHOICE:
Mia Farrow *(Alice)*
Award-Worthy Runners-Up: Julia Roberts *(Pretty Woman)*, Meryl Streep *(Postcards from the Edge)*, Joanne Woodward *(Mr. and Mrs. Bridge)*

Early on it seemed like Julia Roberts would be carried to an Oscar by a unified popular and critical wave for

playing a too-happy L.A. hooker in the summer blockbuster, *Pretty Woman.* She adorned magazine covers and even out-of-the-mainstream critics rhapsodized about the young star, though most weren't so kind to the film. Yet when Roberts received an Oscar nomination, all her champions vanished and all one could hear were attacks on the Academy's foolish choice. It was now held against her that she'd been in a highly commercial comedy. Word in Hollywood was that the race was between Anjelica Huston for her hard-boiled performance in Stephen Frears's *The Grifters* and Joanne Woodward for the ultra-civil comedy-drama *Mr. and Mrs. Bridge*, opposite Paul Newman. It would be Woodward's first Oscar in twenty-three years. However, everybody seemed to be raving about dark horse Kathy Bates for Rob Reiner's *Misery*, which William Goldman adapted from Stephen King's novel about a deranged fan who imprisons her novelist idol (James Caan). And sure enough, movie newcomer Bates—known best for her stage performance in *'Night Mother*—won for her loony bird. I was happy for her because she had toiled so long in the theater without achieving fame, and she gave a sweet acceptance speech. But I found her performance erratic, her character more annoying than interesting, her celebrated mood swings unconvincing. Also her character was familiar to horror movie fans.

My choice for 1990's Best Actress is Mia Farrow, who gives a radiant performance as the title character in Woody Allen's *Alice*. The Academy had ignored Farrow in the past, although she had been consistently terrific in Allen's previous New York movies, and again it failed to give her so much as a nomination. Because this unusual film failed to reach a large audience after even many East Coast critics, Woody's biggest supporters, unfairly dismissed it, nobody protested the slight. So Farrow's best performance to date has never received due recognition.

Fifteen years ago Alice gave up her fashion career to marry the wealthy Douglas (William Hurt). Now they live in a fancy East Side apartment, with their two kids and several servants. She spends her time shopping, having beauty treatments, and being a good wife to Douglas. Raised a Catholic—her idol is Mother Teresa—she feels guilty just for being madly attracted to a sax player, Joe (Joe Mantegna), a single father whose kids attend her kids' school. She is too shy to talk to him. Having a painful back, she goes to Dr. Yang (Keye Luke), a weird acupuncturist-herbalist, who realizes that her problem is caused by her attraction to Joe. He gives her a special herb. The next day she uninhibitedly flirts with Joe and they make a date. But later she feels too guilty and scared to keep it. She takes more of Yang's potions. One makes her invisible: she watches Joe make love to his ex-wife (Judy Davis). Another allows her to be with the ghost of her first love, Eddie (Alec Baldwin), of whom Joe reminds her. After several false starts and near break-offs, Alice and Joe consummate their love. When invisible, Alice goes to Douglas's office and catches him making love to a coworker. He has been unfaithful for years. She breaks up with him. She goes to Joe, but he sadly tells her that he is returning to his ex-wife. Yang gives Alice a potion that will make any man love her completely. She can choose between Douglas and Joe. She chooses neither. She goes to Calcutta to work with Mother Teresa. With better values she returns to New York and happily brings up her kids alone.

In most of her Woody Allen films Farrow's character seeks and sometimes finds happiness. Her women are either on the search for a better life from the outset or, as in the case of Alice Tate, learn they have had only an illusion of happiness. In *Alice*, as in *Broadway Danny Rose, The Purple Rose of Cairo,* and *Hannah and Her Sisters,* the man Farrow is with is unworthy of her. (At the end of *Crimes and Misdemeanors* she foolishly chooses an unworthy man.) As in *Danny Rose* and *Purple Rose,* it takes the attention of another, more considerate man, Joe, to improve Alice's self-esteem and make her realize that she isn't getting the respect or kindness at home that she deserves. Once the lover has served as catalyst, she takes the road to self-discovery by herself, and likes what she finds. With her physical fragility, fawn eyes, and sweet nature, Farrow is one of our most vulnerable actresses. And since Allen photographed this woman he loved in a way to make us fall in love with her, too, we can't help but root for her women in crisis. We root particularly hard for the confused, guilt-ridden Alice, whose world crumbles around her. As is not the case in *The Purple Rose of Cairo,* which has correctly been called a serious version of *Alice,* Farrow's heroine is able to escape the ruins of her life and reconstruct a better world for herself.

For much of the film Farrow's Alice is mousy, afraid to break her routine, guilt ridden for merely thinking of another man, and neurotic to the point where she has developed a chronic backache. She reminds me of Woody Allen's early neurotics and hypochondriacs. She even has an Allen-like nervous edge to her voice, and asks questions as if she fears the world has changed drastically

Mia Farrow on a shopping spree in *Alice*.

while she was asleep. Nobody but her sister and kids are exactly who she has believed they were. And Alice herself is a much different person than she thought she was. Having an affair would have been unthinkable in the abstract, but Joe is a real person and she is the one who initiates it and pushes it to its limits. She's nervous as hell when he makes love to her—she can't stop talking about Mother Teresa—but she doesn't think of backing out.

Kathy Bates was praised for her mood swings in *Misery*, but Farrow matches her in *Alice*. We often take Farrow's talent for granted, but in Alice we see how versatile she is, because Alice changes before our eyes while Allen patiently directs his camera at her. Probably the film's highlight is when the shy Alice, who has just taken a potion, suddenly turns to Joe, whom she has never spoken to before, and tells him he has "fire" in his eyes. Then she completely excites him with her brazen flirta-tion, using sexual innuendo and jazz lingo that she's never said in her life. Her sophisticated delivery and naughty-eyed expression are like nothing we've seen Farrow do before. A few days later, Alice is a nervous wreck when she visits Yang and, in another one-take scene, switches from crazed to calm as she smokes opium—the change is subtle but the humor great. So is the talent. Farrow also has excellent scenes in which she tells off Joe for wanting an affair (actually she's mad at herself); she dashes around the apartment dressing for her rendezvous with Joe; she is patronized by a former friend (Cybill Shepherd) who has made it big in televi-sion; she and Joe talk at the circus (male viewers will want her for a date), and she visits Dr. Yang. Farrow is on the screen the entire time, except when Alice is invisible, and she is never less than enchanting.

1991

▶ BEST PICTURE

WINNER:
The Silence of the Lambs (Orion; Jonathan Demme)
Other Nominees: *Beauty and the Beast, Bugsy, JFK, The Prince of Tides*

▼

THE BEST CHOICE:
An Angel at My Table (Hibiscus/New Zealand Film Commission/FineLine; Jane Campion)
Award-Worthy Runner-Up: *JFK* (Oliver Stone)

If you listened to the confounded Hollywood pundits prior to the Oscar telecast in March of 1992, you would have thought that none of the five nominees had a chance to be voted 1991's Best Picture. (My hunch is that word of mouth would have propelled the very likable *Fried Green Tomatoes* to an Oscar if it had been given legiti-macy by being nominated.) Not even *The Silence of the Lambs* was considered a strong bet for an Oscar, although it had racked up awards elsewhere. Supposedly it would lose because of its sordid subject matter, New York-director Jonathan Demme's outsider status, and its too-early February release. However, in a movie year so weak that the Academy nominated five pictures it wasn't overly fond of, *The Silence of the Lambs* swept the awards, taking not only the Best Picture Oscar but also Best Director, Best Actor, Best Actress, and Best Screenplay. The reality was that Academy voters were much more tolerant of its perverse characters and serial killing theme than they had been in the days of *Psycho*—television had made such things mainstream. Voters were swayed by the criti-cal acclaim; assumed that Demme and his respected stars, Anthony Hopkins and Jodie Foster, wouldn't be associ-ated with a film without artistic merit; felt sympathy for the film's bankrupt distributor, Orion, the one studio with integrity; and, significantly, were able to see the film just prior to the election because of its very successful video and cable-TV releases.

I was glad that a "horror" film finally won as Best Picture and that good-guy Jonathan Demme won as Best Director. But like many who read Thomas Harris's terri-fying thriller before seeing the film, I was disappointed. A film would have to be twice as long to do the novel justice. In the rush, all the action and events are terribly compressed and the psychological complexity, the bond between the female characters, the orphaned daughter–surrogate father themes, the mystery elements, plot twists, quirky characters, and much suspense were lost. So powerful are the direction (Demme used many extreme close-ups) and lead performances and so harrowing are certain images that the picture's shallowness isn't apparent until later when you can't really unravel themes or satisfactorily dissect characters.

While undeniably enjoyable, Disney's *Beauty and the Beast,* the first animated cartoon nominated for Best Picture, needed a couple more good songs to reach the level of *Show White and the Seven Dwarfs* and *Pinocchio; Bugsy* needed more excitement and a reason to have been filmed in the first place; and *The Prince of Tides* could have done without the embarrassing romance montage. Of the nominated pictures, I think only Oliver Stone's controversial *JFK* seems worthy of being Best Picture. Yes, it's a flawed film—weren't there any witnesses on the mall who disagree with Stone?—but it's dazzlingly constructed, photographed, and edited. Even if you disagree with Stone that every louse connected to the government and military conspired to kill Kennedy, you have to admire a filmmaker who so aptly conveys what he himself believes (surprisingly, Stone convincingly defended his much ridiculed "facts" and speculation before all comers, including the nation's press corps). Terrific agitprop, *JFK* angered a lot of people even before it was released and ultimately forced politicians to call for the opening of secret government and military files on the Kennedy assassination, reason enough to warrant the film's commendation. Of course, I doubt if I'd be so supportive of a well-made right-wing film that tried to prove there was no conspiracy.

Four of the five nominees were box-office blockbusters. Only *Bugsy,* in which Warren Beatty made a folk hero out of gangster Bugsy Siegal, would have benefited substantially from a Best Picture Oscar. But I'd rather give the award to a better biography of a more respectable figure, celebrated New Zealand author Janet Frame. It's safe to say that not one person in Hollywood even considered nominating this offbeat picture. Since it wasn't as fiercely championed by American critics as her debut film, *Sweetie,* New Zealand director Jane Campion's elegant *An Angel at My Table* fell by the wayside.

Financed jointly by New Zealand and Australian television networks, Frame's three-volume autobiography was intended to be a three-part television miniseries. The three-hour picture begins when Frame is a young girl (child actress Alexia Keogh will etch herself in your memory) growing up in the South Island of New Zealand. Janet, her three sisters, epileptic brother, well-meaning but temperamental father, and distracted mother lived together in a cramped house. She is close to her sisters but is too shy and plain—she has a chubby, clownish face and body and a jungle of unmanageable red hair—to make friends in school. She constantly feels out of place and humiliated in the presence of the other children and teachers. Her father makes her break off her friendship with a neighbor girl. Janet finds solace in writing. An older sister drowns. As a teenager (Karen Fergusson), Janet continues to experience loneliness. But she excels in writing courses. Time passes and Janet (a fine, controlled performance by Kerry Fox) goes off to college

In the opening of *An Angel at My Table* (top), young Janet wanders into the sunshine and then turns and runs for seclusion. As an adult (bottom), Janet (Kerry Fox) again exits from the sunshine when she enters an asylum.

and lives with an aunt, who kicks her out for eating her candies. Another sister drowns. Janet's teeth rot. She continues to write and has pieces published. But she is still withdrawn. She panics while teaching children and runs away in tears. Those she trusts urge her to enter a hospital. Diagnosed as a schizophrenic, she spends eight years in an asylum and is given over two hundred shock treatments. She is due for a leukotomy when the superintendent decides it's not necessary upon learning she recently has had a book of stories published. Out of the asylum, she accepts eccentric writer Frank Sargeson's invitation to stay on his property and write a book, which is accepted for publication. She goes to London and Ibiza to experience life and has her first love affair, with an American on vacation. She is sad when he returns home. She voluntarily enters another asylum where she learns that she had been misdiagnosed as a schizophrenic (her therapist tells her that it's perfectly okay for her not to mix with other people if she doesn't want to). Her writing becomes increasingly heralded. She returns to New Zealand and lives behind the house of her surviving sister. Otherwise she is alone, content to write.

Jane Campion's debut film as writer-director, the Australian *Sweetie,* was an audaciously scripted and filmed David Lynch–like black comedy about two oddball sisters. Again Campion makes an alternately harsh and tender film about an outcast who is the product of a dysfunctional family. There are again quirky characters and bizarre (this time *true*) plot elements in *An Angel at My Table*—scripted by Laura Jones and (uncredited) Campion. But Campion was careful not to call attention to herself and away from her subject by resorting to extreme stylistic impositions. Instead she masterfully concentrates on her frame. Inside, she recreates Frame's cluttered, askew, unfriendly world. Although presented in detached, low-key style—perhaps this is how Campion thinks the shy writer would have filmed her own work— the film has tremendous impact because one senses Campion feels a bond with Frame both as an artist and a woman who has struggled to find a way to communicate. The perceptive director is determined to correctly tell this story of a woman who was able to emerge from a horribly painful life by turning to writing. Amy Taubin wrote in the *Village Voice:* "Campion manages to dramatize the internal development of a woman writer's consciousness in terms of her experience of the physical world. Exquisitely accurate in its depiction of female desire—and the terrifying attempts of the medical establishment to regulate it—it's a film only a woman could have made."

A definite female sensibility is evident throughout the film (which was directed, produced, written, and edited by women). While a male director might have exploited the more sensational aspects of Frame's story, specifically her hellish years in the asylum, Campion instead chooses to emphasize the confused, traumatized Janet dealing with her first menstrual periods; the liberating nature of her first love affair (I love how she swims nude for her gazing lover, sensually and gracefully turning over in the water in a manner that excites him); the slight pride this humble woman has when, upon her return home, male reporters scurry up a steep hill in order to interview and photograph her; the way Janet's anxiety disappears as soon as she sits with her user-friendly manual typewriter. Whereas a male director might have been uncomfortable with such a passive, unsure, heroine—Kerry Fox may remind some of Melanie Mayron—Campion is in tune with this gentle woman who finds her romance in music, poetry, and literature and is sympathetic with her comforting withdrawal into a less forbidding world of creativity. We sense the kick she has directing the therapist who tells Janet: "If anyone tells you to get out and mix and you don't want to—don't!" And it's important to Campion that once Janet becomes somewhat famous, her inability to communicate in social situations doesn't disappear. Her shyness is not a bad trait.

Yet while the film does have a feminine/feminist perspective, its sympathies lie with artists of both genders, for by the nature of their occupations, they all experience loneliness and isolation. Of course, Hollywood studios wouldn't bother to finance movies about such themes as loneliness and isolation. American filmmakers make movies about outcasts and underdogs, but don't really have as strong an attachment for them as Campion has for Frame. Artists by nature should be outsiders and idealists, but Hollywood is comprised of now-successful insiders who are no longer connected to the struggling artists they once were. That's why you'll never see a film like *An Angel at My Table*—which celebrates the outsider, loner artist—coming off the American assembly line.

▶ BEST ACTOR

WINNER:
Anthony Hopkins *(The Silence of the Lambs)*
Other Nominees: Warren Beatty *(Bugsy)*, Robert De Niro *(Cape Fear)*, Nick Nolte *(The Prince of Tides)*, Robin Williams *(The Fisher King)*

▼

THE BEST CHOICE:
Wesley Snipes *(New Jack City)*
Award-Worthy Runners-Up: Anthony Hopkins *(The Silence of the Lambs)*, Nick Nolte *(The Prince of Tides)*, River Phoenix *(My Own Private Idaho)*

Nick Nolte was the favorite for Best Actor of 1991 for his stirring portrayal of a football coach with a tragic past and unsettled future in *The Prince of Tides.* Sensitive, witty, intelligent, forceful, and romantic, Nolte gave his finest performance since his football player in *North Dallas Forty.* Besides, a vote for him was regarded as compensation from the Academy for having failed to nominate Barbra Streisand in the Best Director category.

Nolte's chief competitor was Anthony Hopkins for his chilling portrait of a deranged, cannibalistic psychiatrist in *The Silence of the Lambs.* Since his screen time was limited, Hopkins gambled by insisting Orion promote him as Best Actor rather than push him into the Supporting Actor race, a competition he would have won easily. He followed the lead of another star from England, Australian-born Peter Finch, who spurned a Supporting

Actor nomination for 1976's *Network*. Like Finch (who died while promoting his Best Actor nomination), Hopkins won the Best Actor Oscar. That he received a wildly enthusiastic standing ovation from the Oscar-night audience—somewhat surprising since he had earned little more than minor respect during his twenty-four-year film career—indicated that his election was a runaway. Nolte apparently had no chance against the man who brought Dr. Hannibal Lecter to the screen. Hopkins's "Hannibal the Cannibal" had become an instant folk hero in Hollywood, the subject of jokes by Johnny Carson and everyone else, the hottest figure in town since Macaulay Culkin stayed *Home Alone* in 1990. This fine, versatile actor who had been expected to become the English theater's successor to Richard Burton had won the award that had cruelly eluded Burton.

Hopkins's monstrous yet erudite, unblinking psychopath is a cross between an intellectual pervert, a haughty elocution teacher, a sadistic gym teacher/Boy Scout leader, and the man you'd least like to have dinner with. It's depraved enough that he feasts on body parts of his murder victims, but he also derives pleasure from raping the mind of young, pretty, and vulnerable FBI trainee Clarice Starling (Jodie Foster). Yet while he is vicious to everyone else because he feels the pathetic, gone-to-hell world deserves such scornful activity, he is vile to Clarice for the specific, not unkind purpose of liberating her from her inner demons. In creating one of the horror genre's more diabolical fiends, Hopkins gave a splendid, ferocious performance—which director Jonathan Demme enhanced by shooting him often in magnified close-up at spooky angles. If Hopkins's performance seems at all imperfect, it is only because the character is of one note.

As unforgettable as Hopkins is in *The Silence of the Lambs,* Wesley Snipes's performance as another type of villain in Mario Van Peebles hip street film *New Jack City* gives him a run for his money. Snipes got more attention in 1991 for a less impressive performance in Spike Lee's controversial *Jungle Fever,* in which he and Annabella Sciorra broke down movie barriers by having an interracial affair. That film was stolen by Samuel L. Jackson, who played Snipes's addict brother. Since Jackson didn't receive a Supporting Actor nomination from the Academy for playing a junkie—years before the Academy ignored Morgan Freeman's marvelous turn as a sadistic pimp in 1987's *Street Smart*—it stands to reason that the Academy wouldn't consider nominating Snipes for playing another movie stereotype, a drug-dealing ganglord, even if he (like Jackson and Freeman) gave a new spin to the part. That *New Jack City* was easy to categorize as just another violent blaxploitation film—I think it is somewhat better than that—it was permissible for Academy voters to ignore Snipes's great performance. But I won't: I am selecting him as the first black actor to win an Alternate Oscar.

Snipes's Nino Brown used to be a basketball teammate of Gee Money (Allen Payne), but in 1986 these best friends are serious drug-runners in New York's black

Wesley Snipes's Nino Brown threatens his best friend Gee Money (Allen Payne) in *New Jack City*. He is about to do much worse to the seated Kareem (Christopher Williams).

ghetto. When Scott (rapper Ice-T) informs Nino about crack, Nino figures out how to build an empire on this addictive new drug. Their murderous gang takes over a city project and turns it into a fortress where crack is both manufactured and sold. Relying equally on a security force and computers, Nino's operation grows into a one-million-dollar-a-week business. The ghetto is strewn with new addicts and dead bodies. Yet many of the poor people and kids in the ghetto consider Nino a hero for providing jobs and Thanksgiving turkeys and for standing up to the law. The black "Cash Money Brothers" vie with Italian ganglords for control of the ghetto. Meanwhile, policeman Stone (played by director Mario Van Peebles) forms a task force to gather evidence that will put Nino in jail. It is comprised of two suicidal undercover cops, Scott and Nick (Judd Nelson as the only white major character). With the help of an ex-druggie, Pookie (Chris Rock), they infiltrate Nino's operation. Pookie is killed. Nino flees the city project but continues to have power. His friendship with Gee Money is strained because he has taken his girlfriend and has become dictatorial. With Gee Money's help, Scott befriends Nino. He tapes Nino making an illegal transaction. Nino flees. He kills Gee Money. Scott arrests Nino and almost beats him to death for having killed his mother years before. Nino is tried, but much to the anger of Scott and Nick, gets only a short sentence when he gives evidence against the money-man behind the organization. Nino gloats as he leaves the courtroom, but is gunned down by an elderly man who is tired of his destruction of ghetto children.

While many critics would disagree, I think *New Jack City* delivers a sincere anti-drug message, putting equal blame for the drug infestation of the black ghetto on the government and the black gangsters who take advantage of the system, and informing kids why they shouldn't worship even the hippest and bravest of the druglords. Snipes gives an intelligently conceived portrait of a character who could very easily have slipped into stereotype. Using equal parts humor, nonchalance, street smarts, and intelligence, Snipes makes Nino a familiar figure, an amiable guy you might meet at the playground or hanging out in the neighborhood. He isn't far removed from the people around him. Indeed, at first he prides himself as one of the few from the ghetto who has figured out a way, any way, to beat the system that has destroyed the black world. He would like to think that his criminal work is a political act—"You've got to rob to get rich in the Reagan era!"—and fancies himself as a Robin Hood when he puts a pittance of his vast earnings back into the community—sponsoring kids' basketball games, giving turkeys to the poor, even providing jobs in the drug business. He is a godfather whose congeniality and charisma cover up the fact that he has become a megolo-maniac—"The world is mine! All mine!"—who no longer cares for the little people around him, a monster of incredible proportions.

So it is that Snipes methodically does away with the nicer elements of Nino's personality. True, in a well-acted scene he sheds real tears when he and Gee Money hug on a rooftop and reaffirm their friendship, but he immediately shoots his lifelong buddy in the head. His tour-de-force scene comes earlier, right after Nino loses his drug building to the police and a fortune in drugs. He

confronts his frightened underlings about their mishandling of the situation (specifically, letting Pookie into the building with a video camera). As they uneasily sit at a long table, he paces behind them, at one time jump-roping over the long dog-chain he carries. He terrorizes everybody. To punctuate his anger he puts a blade through the hand of one surprised bad guy, explaining, "I never liked you anyway, pretty motherfucker!" In a similar scene, Robert De Niro's Al Capone in *The Untouchables*—remember what he angrily did to that annoying gangster's head?—had nothing over Snipes's Nino Brown.

Whereas Anthony Hopkins's Hannibal Lecter chooses his victims one at a time because he only has so large an appetite, Snipes's druglord, Nino Brown, practices genocide in order to quench his constant hunger for money and power. Whereas Hannibal commits his crimes because he is a lunatic, Nino commits his misdeeds with a clear, shrewd mind, thereby proving that you aren't necessarily criminally insane if you don't have a conscience. Hannibal fascinates viewers. Nino infuriates them. We're actually glad that Hopkins's Hannibal Lecter escapes death at the end of *The Silence of the Lambs*. We wouldn't accept such a lenient end for Snipes's Nino Brown.

► BEST ACTRESS

WINNER:
Jodie Foster *(The Silence of the Lambs)*
Other Nominees: Geena Davis *(Thelma & Louise)*, Laura Dern *(Rambling Rose)*, Bette Midler *(For the Boys)*, Susan Sarandon *(Thelma & Louise)*

THE BEST CHOICE:
Lili Taylor *(Dogfight)*
Award-Worthy Runners-Up: Geena Davis *(Thelma & Louise)*, Jodie Foster *(The Silence of the Lambs)*, Kerry Fox *(An Angel at My Table)*, Mary Stuart Masterson *(Fried Green Tomatoes)*, Mimi Rogers *(The Rapture)*, Susan Sarandon *(Thelma & Louise)*, Alison Steadman *(Life Is Sweet)*

We longtime Jodie Foster enthusiasts who watched the wondrous young actress grow up onscreen in offbeat roles in such cult films as *Taxi Driver, Bugsy Malone,* and *The Little Girl Who Lives Down the Lane,* and then move even farther out of the mainstream in *Carny, Foxes, The Hotel New Hampshire, Siesta, Five Corners,* and *Stealing Home,* always assumed the Academy would never think her the proper type to be honored with a Best Actress award. It was great but somewhat disconcerting when she won in 1989, after she starred in what she believed was another offbeat project, *The Accused,* and it became a surprise commercial hit. But even more jolting: who would have thought Foster would be so embraced in Hollywood that she would beat Meryl Streep to two Best Actress awards? Or that she would join Luise Rainer

(1936's *The Great Ziegfeld,* 1937's *The Good Earth*) and Katharine Hepburn (1967's *Guess Who's Coming to Dinner,* 1968's *The Lion in Winter*) as the only actresses to win Oscars for consecutive performances?

Foster followed up her star-making performance as a rape victim who demands justice in *The Accused* with her portrayal of FBI trainee Clarice Starling, who tracks down a perverse serial killer in *The Silence of the Lambs.* She took the part after director Jonathan Demme's first choice, Michelle Pfeiffer, rejected it because she found the picture's subject matter too painful. Foster probably did a better job than Pfeiffer or any other lead actress could have done, for it is not that strong a part as written; there is little for an actress to work with. Foster makes it seem like a great part, delivering an assured, cerebral

Lili Taylor's Rose wins the heart of River Phoenix's marine Eddie Birdlace in *Dogfight*.

performance. She is very subtle, relying a little on a lower-class West Virginia accent, and a great deal on eye movements (which are emphasized because in this film her hair is jet black), and slight, nervous smiles that reveal so much about her fears, vulnerability, and even thoughts of deception. Foster is impeccable, more than holding her own in intense scenes with Anthony Hopkins as genius psychopath Hannibal Lecter. If I don't like Foster—the cinema's finest natural actress—as much here as in other parts, it is only because her performance seems much more calculated. (I admit that she may come across this way because Clarice herself must be ever vigilant about not wavering from her own "performances" before her surrogate fathers, Hopkins's Hannibal and Scott Glenn's FBI agent.)

Foster's brave, shrewd, daringly honest Clarice is certainly a better role model than Susan Sarandon and Geena Davis's well-acted outlaw pals in the popular *Thelma & Louise.* Feminist screenwriter Callie Khourie, whose screenplay won an Oscar, was, when speaking before the Academy and pro-choice demonstrators in Washington, presumptuous enough to believe all feminists embraced her violent, power-claiming heroines. But I think many would opt for the friends played by Mary Stuart Masterson and Mary Louise Parker in *Fried Green Tomatoes,* who are equally supportive and more loving (in not that dissimilar a situation), and far less reckless and self-destructive.

In a terrible year for movies but an exceptional one for lead actresses, my favorite female performances were unnominated ones: Masterson in *Fried Green Tomatoes;* Mimi Rogers as a nympho-turned-Jesus-freak in Michael Tolkin's daringly blasphemous God-exists-but-isn't-worthy-of-our-devotion work, *The Rapture;* and, best of all, Lili Taylor in the sorrowfully neglected romance, *Dogfight.*

In 1963, a young marine, Eddie Birdlace (River Phoenix), and his three equally rowdy buddies have a leave in San Francisco before going off to Vietnam. They play one of their usual games: whoever can pick up the ugliest date—a woman you wouldn't want to be seen with at a dogfight—wins money in a pool. After several failures, Eddie sweet-talks Rose (Taylor), a chubby, plain-looking young waitress, into coming to the "party." She tells him she wants to be a folksinger and join the Peace Corps, to make a difference. Before they reach their destination, Eddie tries to convince her to go elsewhere because he realizes she is too nice to be taken advantage of. But she wants to go to the party. One of his friends wins the pool in an underhanded manner. Rose finds out about the "dogfight." She slaps and tells off Eddie. Later Eddie goes to her home and apologizes. They spend an eventful night together, opening up to each other and becoming close. Eddie even tones down his cussing at her insistence. Finally, they tenderly make love. In the morning, he leaves. He throws out her address. The times become turbulent in America and in Vietnam. They meet again.

A talented young actress with an unusual combination of spunk, sharp wit, and charm, Lili Taylor is, unfortunately, still an unknown. She gave a spirited performance as one of the three waitress-girlfriends in *Mystic Pizza,* but of course that's the film in which Julia Roberts was discovered. And Nancy Savoca's little charmer, *Dogfight,* was a picture everyone "meant to see" but let slip away. Savoca, one of America's most exciting and original directors, helped inspire Annabella Sciorra and Ron Eldard (as an engaged, battling young Italian-American couple) to portray *real,* endearingly flawed characters in her wonderful debut film, *True Love.* She also proved herself to be one of America's few directors who makes films about characters, male and female, for whom she has true affection. In *Dogfight,* which was written by ex-Marine Bob Comfort, Savoca again roots for her young lovers as they fumble through their lives and struggle to make a rocky relationship work. My guess is that Savoca made sure her two young leads felt much warmth for the characters they played. If Taylor's Rose comes across as almost perfect, it's because the actress brought out that in her. Taylor put on twenty pounds and some unflattering clothes and makeup to play Rose, and then spends the entire film showing us, and Eddie, what an attractive young woman Rose is. When Eddie ultimately says she looks beautiful as she climbs into bed with him, we realize that he is telling the truth. Phoenix's Eddie was just lucky to have stumbled on a near-perfect girl, a "rose," on his way to a dogfight.

When I first saw this movie, I felt extremely sad when I saw the early scene in which Lili excitedly prepares for her date with Birdlace. I was preparing for what I assumed would be devastating humiliation for her. But once Rose discovers the reason for Eddie's instant interest in her, she doesn't slink to the floor and allow her ego to evaporate. She comes out swinging, literally, repeatedly slapping Eddie for his detestable behavior. She's sweet but she's also a fighter for what is right. She is very sad when she returns to her room but she is not destroyed. She doesn't look into a mirror and whimper about being an ugly duckling. Whereas another actress might have played Rose as a wallflower, as Sissy Spacek did the shy girl in *Carrie,* Taylor won't allow Rose to be a victim. Rose's optimism about the world in general extends to herself. She isn't overly confident, but she realizes she has much to offer. Unsure but not afraid to take chances, she sings for Eddie; not worried about opening up to a marine who has probably had countless lovers, she invites him to her room for her first sexual experience. She sees the worth in herself, just as she sees it in Eddie. He is worthy of being her first lover; and she knows, as he fully comprehends years later, that she is more than worthy of being his lover.

Taylor is so winning throughout that it's hard to pick out her finest moments. I love when she performs for Eddie, amateurishly plinking on a piano and singing too softly, but with such passion and sincerity that he is deeply affected. And when, in a scene from the sixties I really identified with, she excitedly tells him about the folk singers whose pictures are on her walls and then plays him her favorite (Joan Baez). And when she exhibits a content, mature, and extremely pretty look as she kisses Birdlace goodbye on the morning after their lovemaking. Her final moment in the film is also very moving. You feel for Rose and the actress who so appreciates her. Long after I saw *Dogfight,* I found myself thinking of both Lili Taylor's lovely character and her lovely performance.

Index